ISBN 978-1-330-44618-8
PIBN 10063385

This book is a reproduction of an important historical work. Forgotten Books uses
state-of-the-art technology to digitally reconstruct the work, preserving the original format
whilst repairing imperfections present in the aged copy. In rare cases, an imperfection in
the original, such as a blemish or missing page, may be replicated in our edition. We do,
however, repair the vast majority of imperfections successfully; any imperfections that
remain are intentionally left to preserve the state of such historical works.

English
Français
Deutsche
Italiano
Español
Português

www.forgottenbooks.com

Mythology Photography **Fiction**
Fishing Christianity **Art** Cooking
Essays Buddhism Freemasonry
Medicine **Biology** Music **Ancient
Egypt** Evolution Carpentry Physics
Dance Geology **Mathematics** Fitness
Shakespeare **Folklore** Yoga Marketing
Confidence Immortality Biographies
Poetry **Psychology** Witchcraft
Electronics Chemistry History **Law**
Accounting **Philosophy** Anthropology
Alchemy Drama Quantum Mechanics
Atheism Sexual Health **Ancient History**
Entrepreneurship Languages Sport
Paleontology Needlework Islam
Metaphysics Investment Archaeology
Parenting Statistics Criminology
Motivational

Psychological Revie
ih

EDITED BY

J. MARK BALDWIN
PRINCETON UNIVERSITY

AND

J. MCKEEN CATTELL
COLUMBIA UNIVERSITY

WITH THE CO-OPERATION OF

FRED BINET, ÉCOLE DES HAUTES-ÉTUDES, PARIS; JOHN DEWEY, UNIVERSITY CHICAGO; H. H. DONALDSON, UNIVERSITY OF CHICAGO; G. S. FULLERTON, UNIVERSITY OF PENNSYLVANIA; JOSEPH JASTROW, UNIVERSITY OF WISCONSIN; G. T. LADD, YALE UNIVERSITY; HUGO MÜNSTERBERG, HARVARD UNIVERSITY; M. ALLEN STARR, COLLEGE OF PHYSICIANS AND SURGEONS, NEW YORK; CARL STUMPF, UNIVERSITY, BERLIN; JAMES SULLY, UNIVERSITY COLLEGE, LONDON.

Volume IV.   1897.

PUBLISHED BI-MONTHLY BY

THE MACMILLAN COMPANY,

41 N. QUEEN ST., LANCASTER, PA.

66 FIFTH AVENUE, NEW YORK; AND LONDON.

PRESS OF
THE NEW ERA PRINTING COMPANY,
LANCASTER, PA.

CONTENTS OF VOLUME IV.

ALPHABETICAL INDICES OF NAMES AND SUBJECTS WILL BE FOUND AT THE END OF THE VOLUME.

ARTICLES.

DISCUSSION AND REPORTS.

PSYCHOLOGICAL LITERATURE.

CONTENTS.

Article of BRYAN AND NOBLE.

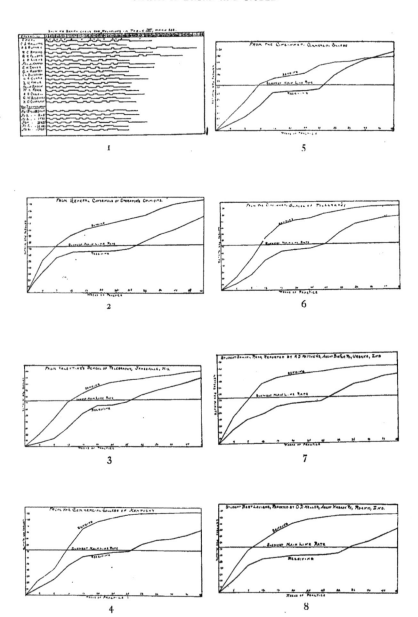

VOL. IV. NO. 1.   JANUARY, 1897.

THE PSYCHOLOGICAL REVIEW.

THE 'KNOWER' IN PSYCHOLOGY.[1]

BY PROFESSOR G. S. FULLERTON,

University of Pennsylvania.

Gentlemen: In the presidential address which I have the
honor to read to-day before your Association, I have taken up
a psychological problem which seems to me of importance both
to psychology and to epistemology, and one which has not, I
think, in the general advance of the science of psychology, been
treated with the same clearness, or had applied to it the same
scientific method, that has led to such good results elsewhere.
I allude to the problem of the self or 'knower' as contrasted
with those problems arising in the consideration of 'things
known,' whether phenomena or 'external' things. I am not
here directly concerned with the question of the so-called 'empirical' self, that psychical complex which has been analyzed
and discussed much as one analyses and discusses any other
mental content. It may, it is true, be difficult to enumerate the
elements of which this is composed, but the attitude of the
psychologist toward it is sufficiently definite, and the only mystery that the subject presents is the mystery of incomplete knowledge. In discussing it the psychologist at least means something. He applies the scientific method, aiming at and hoping
for clear and exact results. The self with which I am concerned
is the knower, that indefinite something to which attaches, not
merely the mystery of incomplete knowledge, but also, as I cannot but believe, the mystery of misconception; it is that elusive

---

[1] President's address before the American Psychological Association, Boston Meeting, December 30, 1896.

entity so generally cherished by philosopher and psychologist, which hides itself in clouds and darkness, and whose incomprehensible attributes are accepted without protest by a faith which rests upon tradition and custom.

My statement that I am concerned with the self as knower and not directly with the empirical self commonly said to be 'known' needs a word of explanation, and this I may insert here, though I think my meaning will be made sufficiently clear during the course of my address. I am interested in the question of what *knowledge* means in psychology, and I discuss the self as the accepted subject of the act of knowing. Of course, any light which may be cast on the nature of knowledge will help to make clear what is meant by speaking of anything as 'known,' and will help us to a better comprehension of the 'empirical' self in so far as it is a something known. Moreover, since the self as knower and the self as known have been and are generally very loosely distinguished from one another and even declared identical, it will be impossible for me to confine myself strictly to the self as knower. I must take the self as I find it, vague, ambiguous, inconsistent, and must simply try to come to some conclusion about its 'knowing' function.

So much for my aim. I shall try to remain so far as possible on psychological ground in my discussion, although the matter is, as I have said, also of interest to the epistemologist. One approaches such a theme, in the presence of this critical audience, with a certain reverent hesitation, and would gladly pour out a libation, praying, as did Plotinus, for the gift of correct discernment.

In a paper which I read three years ago before this Association I tried to make clear the nature of the work done by the psychologist, and to set forth the assumptions upon which he must proceed and the method he must employ. I maintained that he must assume the existence of an external physical world, and the existence of certain copies or representatives of it intimately related to particular bodily organisms. These transcripts of the external world, as I expressed it in a later paper, supplemented by certain elements not supposed to have their prototypes without (feelings of pleasure and pain etc.,) are, for the psychologist, minds. He must by applying the method of introspection, observation and experiment, strive to obtain a knowledge of such minds and reduce their phenomena to laws. He must conceive each mind or consciousness as shut up to its own representations of things and dependent upon messages conveyed to it from without. Ideas are to him, like images in a mirror, numerically distinct from the things which they represent and of which they give information. I further indicated that *knowledge* must, to the psychologist, be a mental state of some kind, a complex in consciousness, and it follows that it must be studied by the usual psychological method. I maintained, finally, that psychology as natural science should resolutely confine itself to mental phenomena, and eschew all such metaphysical entitles as ' substrata,' ' unit-beings,' or ' transcendental selves.' I added that whether one conceive of conscious states as ' parallel ' to brain states, or conceive of them as belonging with these latter to the one series of causes, and determining physical movements, in either case one may study them from the natural science point of view. They are in any case phenomena which may be analyzed and described, and the relations of which to other phenomena may be determined by accepted scientific methods.[1]

A mind is, therefore, to the psychologist, a little world in itself, cut off from others, and ' knowing ' them only through their representatives in it. It is, moreover, a very complex world, and the phenomena it presents are by no means easy to analyze and classify. Some things in it seem to stand out clearly ; some remain after our best efforts dim and vague. It is quite conceivable that some things supposed to live and move and have a real being in this world are mere chimæras, having no existence at all except in the imagination, where they lead a dubious existence rather as symbols of the unknown than

[1] In the earlier of the two papers alluded to I point out the inconsistency of the psychologist's position. To cut off minds from things, giving them mere copies or representatives, and then to use the method of observation and experiment, as though the observer were directly conscious of his own ideas and at the same time of his own and other men's bodies, is, of course, flatly self-contradictory. The psychologist has, however, the right to use a convenient fiction, and it need not bring him to grief as long as he remains upon psychological ground.

as concrete intelligible representations. It is not difficult, in the obscurity which still covers much of our mental life, to confound one thing with another, to create a phantom, or to seek diligently for the solution of a problem which need never have been raised.

Certain problems the psychologist may, as I have said, set aside at the outset. All metaphysical entities supposed to be beyond consciousness, and to 'underlie' phenomena, he may simply disregard. He is, to restate my former description of his task in perhaps a broader way, concerned with the contents of consciousness, mental phenomena and their interrelations, and whatever else (if there be anything else) sufficiently resembles mental phenomena to be found in a consciousness. He is also concerned with the relations of mental phenomena to the material world, a something which can be observed and experimented upon. His method is scientific and has already been applied with satisfactory results to some of the phenomena in consciousness. It should be, I think, his duty to strive to apply the same method to everything in this realm. If some things in consciousness need to be further studied from another point of view, and by another method, he may safely leave this task to another workman. Still, even if he remain on his own ground, and regard as the proper object of his studies the contents of consciousness and the physical conditions or accompaniments of this or that psychical fact, it is nevertheless possible that he may fall into some such difficulties or perplexities as are indicated in the preceding paragraph. One need not have a very broad acquaintance with psychological doctrines to see that the task of the psychologist is by no means an easy one, and that warring opinions concerning psychical phenomena may be held with great obstinacy and strong conviction.

Of course, when a writer does not accept and hold to the standpoint of the psychologist as I have defined it, there are still other errors into which he may fall. He may wander into the realm of the metaphysician and return with a self which is not the self of consciousness, the psychologist's self at all. He may confuse this with the psychologist's self, and keep talking about two things while he supposes himself to be discussing only one. He may transport the self into a world in which reasonable explanations of things, couched in intelligible language, will be sought for in vain. He may make of 'knowledge' a something not in consciousness, and yet not out of consciousness; a thing inconsistent, inscrutable, and, I believe, unpsychological. That many writers have been, and that many are, guilty of these things ' *et enormia alia*,' it needs little knowledge of the history of speculative thought to reveal. It is because I am compelled to refer to the works of such writers that I have promised only to *try* to keep upon psychological grounds.

But to come to the particular point which I wish to discuss to-day, the psychological problem of the knower and the known. The plain man, who has not gotten beyond the psychology of common life, has always distinguished in some vague way between himself as knower or doer and the objects which he knows or acts upon. The distinction has become crystallized in language and appears to have past current everywhere and at all times. And in the History of Philosophy we find drawn, with more or less clearness, almost from the beginning, the distinction between that which knows, the mind, soul or reason, and the thing known, which may be either an external thing or a psychical state. I do not propose to weary you with an exhaustive examination of the opinions of philosophers, ancient and modern, but a glance at some of them will, I think, prove helpful in the discussion of our problem.

It is difficult to select from such a cloud of witnesses, but I may mention, in passing, among the ancients, Anaxagoras, Democritus, Plato, Aristotle, the Stoics, the Epicureans and the Skeptics, in all of whom the distinction is sufficiently emphasized. Thales doubtless distinguished in an unanalytic way between himself and the object of his knowledge, but in what little we know of his doctrine his ideas upon this subject do not come to the surface. Perhaps the problem of knowledge had not presented itself to him as a problem. With the growth of reflective thought it comes more and more into view, and the knower grows, I can hardly say more definite, but at least more definitely an object of discussion. This it is with Plato and Aristotle, whose distinction between reason and the lower psych-

ical functions has moreover a flavor of the modern distinction
between the rational and the empirical self. In Plotinus the
soul, or subject of knowledge, has definitely put on the incomprehensible aspect with which later speculation so constantly
clothed it. It is not in space; or, rather, it is in space in an
unintelligible and inconsistent way; it is all in the whole, and
yet all in every part of the body. It is divided because it is in
all parts of its body, and undivided because it is in its entirety
in every part. With Augustine, who set his stamp so authori-
tatively upon the thinking of the centuries which succeeded his
own, it behaves no better, being still all in the whole and all in
every part of the body. It knows itself and what is not itself.
Its properties are not related to it as material qualities are to
material substance; they share in its substantiality, although it
has them, and must not be regarded as *being* them. To make
this confusion, if possible, worse, Cassiodorus maintains that
the soul, which knows things spiritual and material, is, as a
whole, in each of its own parts.

Into the tangles of the Scholastic Philosophy I shall not attempt to enter. Suffice it to say we find everywhere a knower
and a known, and this knower, which knows both itself and
what is not itself, and may even know itself more certainly
than it knows external objects, remains throughout a mystery
and a perplexity.

In the Modern Philosophy some of the subtleties of scholastic
thought disappear, but, until we come to Hume, the problem remains, I think, much what it was before. With Bacon, Hobbes
and Descartes the mind is still the knower, and an ill-defined
and shadowy knower. With Descartes it knows itself better
than it knows external things. Spinoza's position is an odd and
very interesting one. The mind is the idea of the body, or that
mode in the attribute thought, which corresponds to the body,
a parallel mode in the attribute extension. The mind is composed of ideas, and may be called the knowledge of the body.
But there is also such a thing as the idea or knowledge of the
mind, and this is related to the mind just as the mind is related
to the body. Spinoza finds it impossible, it is true, to keep the
idea of the mind apart from the mind itself, since they are both

modes in the one attribute and thus melt into one. His doctrine is not consistent, but its purpose is clear. It appears to him that knowledge demands a knower and a known, and he cannot conceive the knower as playing the part of both. He therefore explains the mind's knowledge of itself by splitting it into a fictitious quality, which fades again into unity.[1] It is interesting to note that to Spinoza the mind is composed of ideas; it is not a something distinct from them and behind them. In Locke there appears again the ambiguous double self, the noumenal and the phenomenal. It is the latter which is directly perceived; the former remains ' an uncertain supposition of we know not what.' Berkeley, the Idealist, basing himself upon Locke's conclusions, classifies the objects of human knowledge as ideas of sense, ideas of memory and imagination, the passions and operations of the mind, and the self that perceives all these. Those who are familiar with the ' Principles ' will remember that even Berkeley's clear and graceful sentences leave the reader's mind in a hopeless confusion regarding this last object and the nature of its relation to its own ideas.

In his general demolition of the noumenal and the tradition, Hume cast out everything except what we may now call the empirical self, the self as a complex of mental phenomena. He uses the word, to be sure, as it has since been used by others, to cover our whole mental life, and as equivalent to the word mind. He regards the mind as "but a bundle or collection of different perceptions which succeed each other with inconceivable rapidity, and are in a perpetual flux and movement." Spinoza had, as a psychologist, gone nearly as far, but his mediæval realistic metaphysic, and his desire to have in all cases a knower distinct from the thing known, obscured the force of his teachings. Hume himself, who has written on this as on all subjects with acuteness and admirable lucidity, occupies himself chiefly with destructive criticism, and furnishes no answers to the many objections and inquiries which naturally suggest themselves, and which did suggest themselves to his successors in philosophy. He has, however, done much in clearing the ground for a profit-

---

[1] See my volume, ' The Philosophy of Spinoza;' Note on the Mind and its Knowledge. 2d ed., N. Y. 1894, pp. 317-324.

able discussion of the question. His writings performed, moreover, the signal service of stimulating to a new course of thought
Immanuel Kant, the Sage of Königsberg.

We owe it to Kant, that keen, systematic and inconsistent
thinker, that the terms phenomenon and noumenon have become
household words. This is no small gain. If a man loosely
talks about the self as knowing or doing something, and we
ask him whether he refers to the noumenal or to the phenomenal
self, only to receive the answer that he does not know, we have
now the right to refuse him respectful attention. He does not
know what he means to say himself, and it is not likely that his
words can profit others. Kant, in the *Critique of Pure Reason*, condemns the noumenon to outer darkness, and shuts up
psychology to the world of experience, the phenomenal world.
He is not, however, content with Hume's ‘bundle’ of perceptions, but distinguishes between the multiplicity of psychical
elements forming the content of consciousness and a something
—not a noumenon, but a something in consciousness—an
activity, or whatever one may choose to call it, which makes
possible the combination of this multiplicity into the unity of a
single consciousness. On this depends the consciousness ‘I
think’ which accompanies all my ideas. The empirical self, as
a complex of psychical elements, is to be distinguished from
this rational self. This doctrine has had and still has so deep
an influence, that it is especially worthy of note in any historical
study of the self as knower.

Let me now turn to the treatment of this problem by modern
psychologists. The necessary limits of such a paper as this of
course preclude anything like an exhaustive treatment of the subject, and I must content myself with an examination of the doctrines of but a few writers. I shall, however, try to select those
which seem to me fairly representative of the thought of our time.
We do not, I think, find among them much that is distinctly
new, though we find, as might be expected, modifications of
the views to which I have already referred.

Perhaps I should begin with the descendants of Kant (the
line of descent runs through Hegel), a rather numerous and aggressive body, who take their psychology seriously, and are apt

to keep one eye on their metaphysics or theology while discussing psychological problems. As a protagonist of these I may take Professor T. H. Green. Mr. Green repudiated the Kantian noumenon and avowedly confined human knowledge to the field of experience, but he did not approve a Humian experience consisting of a bundle of percepts. He found it necessary to assume in experience a principle of synthetic unity; a principle not to be confounded with any of the elements making up the experience, nor subject to their conditions; a principle which, in some fashion, knits together the manifold of sense into an organic unity. " Thus," he writes,[1] " in order that successive feelings may be related objects of experience, even objects related in the way of succession, there must be in consciousness an agent which distinguishes itself from the feelings, uniting them in their severalty, making them equally present in their succession. And so far from this agent being reducible to, or derivable from a succession of feelings, it is the condition of there being such a succession; the condition of the existence of that relation between feelings, as also of those other relations which are not indeed relations between feelings, but which, if they are matter of experience, must have their being in consciousness. If there is such a thing as a connected experience of related objects, there must be operative in consciousness a unifying principle, which not only presents related objects to itself, but at once renders them objects and unites them in relation to each other by this act of presentation; and which is single throughout the experience."

According to this passage, the knowing or distinguishing agent is conscious and self-conscious, is in consciousness, makes a consciousness possible by uniting different elements, and is single throughout the experience. We find elsewhere that this principle is not *in* consciousness but *is* consciousness, and that everything that exists is in it; that it is intelligence; that it is a subject or agent which desires in all the desires of a man and thinks in all his thoughts. Notwithstanding that it is all this, it has, nevertheless, no existence except in the activity which constitutes related phenomena; and it is, in the words of

[1] *Prolegemena to Ethics*, § 32.

the author[1] 'neither in time nor space, immaterial and immovable, eternally one with itself.'

The mere statement of the attributes of Mr. Green's spiritual
principle would seem to be sufficient to condemn it. A faith
robust enough to remove mountains might well shy at the task
of believing that the single subject or agent which desires in all
the desires of a man and thinks in all his thoughts, which is
conscious and self-conscious, is still only an activity without existence except as it constitutes the objects of experience, and
which, though it does not exist in time, is equally present to all
stages of a change in conscious experience. Think of it! the
activity which constituted my thought of yesterday did not exist yesterday, when my thought did; and the activity which
constitutes my thought of to-day does not exist to-day, while
my thought does! Both activities are one, for the activity
which constitutes objects is 'eternally one with itself.' What
can this mean? If the phrase is to be significant at all, must
it not mean that the activity in question is 'always' the same
activity? and does not 'always' mean 'at all times?' And
what, in Heaven's name, is an 'immovable' activity? Moreover, is it fair to a genuine activity, however abnormal, to call
it a principle or subject or agent?

But even supposing it possible for an activity to be all that
Mr. Green asks it to be, even to be timelessly present at all
times, how are we to conceive of such a thing uniting the elements of any possible experience? Shall we merely assume
that it has a vague and inscrutable uniting virtue, as opium was
once assumed to have a dormitive virtue? Mr. Green gives no
hint of the method by which this activity obtains its result. He
does not seek light on this point by a direct reference to experience, for he does not even obtain his activity by direct introspection; he obtains it as the result of a labored process which
strives to demonstrate that it must be assumed or experience
will be seen to be impossible.

I have read Mr. Green's book with a great deal of care, and
have tried to read it sympathetically. Of course, those who
sympathize with his doctrine will be inclined to think that, as

[1] § 54.

regards the latter point, I have met with indifferent success. I must confess that the book appears to me to be valuable to the psychologist chiefly as a warning. I have not found Mr. Green's utterances, in one sense of the word, incomprehensible. His doctrine is not fundamentally new. He has taken the Kantian unity of apperception, made of it an hypostatized activity, tried to keep it free of space and time relations, and used it as an explanation of the unity of experience, or as I should prefer to say, of consciousness. He has given us the same inconsistent *totum in toto* thing that we find in Plotinus and St. Augustine. He is, however, a Post-Kantian, and he has included this thing in ' experience.'

It would, of course, be unfair to judge of all Neo-Kantians or Neo-Hegelians on the basis of the utterances of even so prominent a member of the school as Mr. Green. Nevertheless, the way of thinking which characterizes the school seems to me much the same in all, and this is a way upon which, I believe, psychology as science should be careful not to enter. It has led our colleague, Professor Dewey, who can write so clearly when he forgets to what school he belongs, to express himself regarding the intuition of self as follows:[1] " We are concerned here especially with what is called self-consciousness, or the knowledge of the self as a universal permanent activity. We must, however, very carefully avoid supposing that self-consciousness is a new and particular kind of knowledge. The self which is the object of intuition is not an object existing ready made, and needing only to have consciousness turn to it, as towards other objects, to be known like them as a separate object. The recognition of self is only the perception of what is involved in every act of knowledge. The self which is known is, as we saw in our study of apperception and retention, the *whole* body of knowledge as returned to and organized into the mind knowing. The self which is known is, in short, the ideal side of that mode of intuition of which we just spoke ;[2] it is their meaning in its unity. It is, also, a more complete stage of intuition, for, while in the final stage of intuition of

[1] *Psychology*, 3d ed. p. 242.
[2] *I. e.*, Intuition of the World or Nature.

nature we perceive it as a whole of interdependent relations, or
as self-related, we have yet to recognize that we leave out of
account the intelligence from which these relations proceed.
In short, its true existence is in its relation to mind; and in
self-consciousness we advance to the perception of mind.''

The self as here described is a universal, permanent activity;
it is only what is involved in every act of knowledge, and yet is
the *whole* body of knowledge; as returned to and organized into
the mind knowing—in other words, into the activity involved in
every act of knowledge. Moreover, although it is the whole
body of knowledge as thus organized and returned, it is the
source of the relations obtaining between the objects making up
the world of knowledge. Can any one form a clear notion of
such a self? Professor Dewey gives the reader little assistance
in making plain to himself how the whole body of knowledge
can be returned to and organized into a universal, permanent
activity; and he leaves unsolved the problem of how an organized whole consisting of things in relation can itself be the source
of relations which make it what it is. Surely this is not sense or
science. It is not in place in a modern work on psychology.
Taken literally the phrases quoted do not convey any meaning;
and taken loosely and figuratively they express, I think, quite
as much error as truth. The error here is the error of Green;
but the language of the extract is more distinctly the phraseology
of a school, and further removed from the plain diction of common life and science. This is, I think, an aggravating circumstance.

Another of our colleagues, Professor Baldwin, has placed
himself beside Green and Dewey, and, in so far, has abandoned
the standpoint of scientific psychology. In his volume on Feeling and Will, he does not often, I think, stray far from the path
of empirical psychology, though there is sometimes an indefi-
niteness of expression which leaves me rather in the dark as to
his true meaning. The following, however, is unmistakable:[1]
"We may well notice that neither the manifoldness nor the
unity of feeling could be apprehended as such in the absence of
a circumscribing consciousness which, through its own unity,

[1] N. Y., 1894, p. 79.

takes it to be what it is. Suppose we admit that at the beginnings of life the inner state is simply an undifferentiated continuity of sensation; what is it that *feels* or *knows* the subsequent differentiation of parts of this continuity? It cannot be the unity of the continuity itself, for that is now destroyed; it cannot be the differentiated sensations themselves, for there are many. It can only be a unitary subjectivity additional to the unity of the sensory content, *i. e.*, the form of synthetic activity which reduces the many to one in each and all of the stages of mental growth. The relations of ideas as units must be taken up into the unit idea of relation, to express what modern psychology means by apperception."

In the same category with the above we must put Professors Höffding and Murray, and, I fear, also John Stuart Mill. Mill's chapter on the Psychological Theory of Matter as applied to Mind[1] regards consciousness as a 'string of feelings,' and holds it to be an ultimate and incomprehensible fact that a string of feelings can be conscious of itself as a string. In the appendix to the chapter, printed in the later editions of his work, he admits the existence of an inexplicable tie or law, which is a reality, and connects the feelings with each other. The Neo-Kantian will recognize in this the self for which he enters the lists, though he may disapprove of Mill's forms of expression. I am even tempted to include in the list our colleague, Professor James—at least Professor James in one of his moods, for, although he characterizes the phrase 'united by a spiritual principle' as absurd and empty, yet in the same paper he maintains[2] that "union in consciousness must be made by something, must be brought about; and to have perceived this truth is the great merit of the anti-associationist psychologists." As, however, he also maintains that if there were a 'soul' it might serve as an explanation of this union, possibly it would be as just to class him with those who hold to a noumenal self. Perhaps it would be best not to class him at all, as he appears so undecided as to what he wants. It is clear, however, that he wants *something* to do the knowing.

[1] Examination of Sir William Hamilton's Philosophy.
[2] 'The Knowing of Things together,' PSYCHOLOGICAL REVIEW, March, 1895.

I do not think that the substratum soul in its bald and un-compromising aspect, the Lockian 'I know not what,' the Kantian noumenon clearly recognized to be noumenal, plays an important part in the psychological thinking of our time. Still, it is possible to modify or dilute this entity and hold to it in a certain indefinite and inconsistent way. I think this is done by our colleague, Professor Ladd, whose valuable writings are justly attracting no small attention among our contemporaries.

I find in Professor Ladd's last two books many signs of a development in what I must consider the right direction. He is evidently gravitating, although with reluctance, toward psychology as science. His utterances may be collected under two heads according as they reveal the position in which he has heretofore been intrenched, or as they indicate the goal toward which he is moving. Let us glance at a few passages, begin-ning with some of those which fall under the former head.

We are told by Professor Ladd that the final aim of psychol-ogy is 'to understand the nature and development, in its rela-tions to other beings, of that unique kind of being which we call the Soul or Mind.'[1] Our author complains that the larger num-ber of those who cultivate psychology as an empirical science habitually regard consciousness, and the phenomena of con-sciousness, merely ' content-wise.' They overlook or deny the fact that all consciousness and every phenomenon of conscious-ness, makes the demand to be considered as a form of function-ing, and not as mere differentiation of content. All psychic energy is self-activity; it appears in consciousness as the ener-gizing, the conation, the striving, of the same being which comes to look upon itself as attracted to discriminate between this sen-sation and that, or compelled to feel some bodily pain, or solic-ited to consider some pleasant thought. Thus all psychic life manifests itself to the subject of that life as being, in one of its fundamental aspects, its own spontaneous activity.[2] Again: knowing is distinguished from mere imagining, remembering or thinking, in that it involves belief in reality ; and psychological

---

[1] *Philosophy of Mind*, N. Y., 1895, p. 64.

[2] *Philosophy of Mind*, pp. 85-88. *Psychology, Descriptive and Explana-tory*, N. Y., 1895, p. 215.

analysis shows that knowledge is impossible without this rational, metaphysical belief, or metaphysical faith.[1] "The psychological analysis of any state of so-called knowledge," says Professor Ladd,[2] "of any of those psychoses properly described by the affirmation 'I know,' shows that all knowledge implicates reality, envisaged, inferred, believed in—we do not now stop to inquire into the manner of implication. Especially is this true of every act of so called *self*-knowledge; for the psychologist is simply ignoring what everybody means by the word, unless he understands the reality of the self-knowing and the self-known, the one self, to be involved as an immediate datum of experience."

From the above so much at least is clear: Professor Ladd believes in a unique kind of being called Soul or Mind, and regards all psychic life, every form of consciousness, as the energizing or striving of this being, holding, further, that all this is manifested to this being as its own spontaneous activity. Moreover this being knows itself, and knows itself as a reality. But whether this reality which knows itself and is the subject of all conscious states is itself in consciousness or not remains rather unclear. The statement that knowledge 'involves belief in reality' would certainly, if words are to be taken in their usual senses, indicate that the reality is not immediately given in experience; and the further statement that knowledge 'implicates reality, envisaged, inferred, believed in,' is vagueness itself, and gives little help in clearing up the matter. It is to be regretted that Professor Ladd did not stop at this point to inquire 'as to the manner of the implication,' for he has not made it clear anywhere else. The latter part of the last extract, which makes the reality of the self an immediate datum of experience, should, perhaps, settle the question; for where the reality of a thing is, there it seems reasonable to expect to find the thing also. Yet, on the other hand, it is maintained that to describe self-consciousness, as a *mere* state or *mere* activity of a definite kind, is imperfectly to describe it, and that 'self-knowledge, although it comes as the result of a development, implies a knowing being that knows itself, in an actual indubitable

---

[1] *Philosophy of Mind*, p. 100. *Psychology*, p. 513.
[2] *Philosophy of Mind*, p. 63; *cf. Psychology*, pp. 511–517.

experience, really to be."[1] It appears, thus, that we are not to regard the self as either content of consciousness or activity; so that the empirics complained of above for overlooking the aspect of consciousness which makes it a 'form of functioning' would still be in the wrong even if they included this in their treatment of it. They would have accepted, it is true, every aspect and element of consciousness, but would have left out the real being, which knows itself in an act of metaphysical faith really to be. This speaks for something very like a noumenon; and one begins to feel decidedly that one must accept this as Professor Ladd's doctrine when one remembers that in the same chapter with the sentence above quoted he denies knowledge of mere phenomena to be knowledge at all, and maintains that the word phenomenon has absolutely no meaning except as implying some particular being *of* which, and some being *to* which, the phenomenon is. Professor Ladd prefers, it is true, the expression 'real existence' to 'noumenon,' but that is a mere detail. I conclude, then, that our colleague holds to a noumenal self of some sort, which is responsible for the phenomena of consciousness; and yet, turning at this juncture to the end of the chapter, I am again thrown into confusion by the author's summary of the discussion from which I have taken the above sentiments. I there[2] find that "the peculiar, the only intelligible and indubitable reality which belongs to Mind is its being for itself, by actual functioning of self-consciousness, of recognitive memory, and of thought. Its real being is just this 'for-self-being' (Für-sich-seyn). Every mind, by living processes, perpetually constitutes its own being, and knows itself as being real. To be self-conscious, to remember that we were self-conscious, and to think of the self as having, actually or possibly, been self-conscious—this is really to be, as minds are. And no other being is real mental being." This extract, which the author presents as the sum of the whole matter, seems unequivocally to make of the self nothing more than an activity of consciousness, and, whatever that may be, a self-constitutive activity. It smacks strongly of Neo-Kantism.

[1] *Philos. of Mind*, p. 127.
[2] *Philos. of Mind*, p. 147; *cf. Psychol.* p. 638.

But what now becomes of that object known, which is not merely an object 'for the knowing process'?[1]

Although it is difficult to gain from Professor Ladd's writings any clear idea of what the active subject of mental phenomena really is, one may at least guess from certain passages what he is anxious that it should not be. "This active agent," he remarks,[2] "actually here and now active and knowing itself as active, is indeed no transcendental being, up aloft in the heavens of metaphysics; but then neither is it submerged beneath the slime, or covered with the thin varnish, of purely empirical psychology." It holds, as it seems, a middle course, and combines the properties of a noumenon, a Neo-Kantian self-constitutive activity and an empirical psychosis.

The last mentioned aspect of Professor Ladd's self or agent, and the one which fixes the goal toward which, as it seems to me, he is moving, comes out very clearly in his work on Descriptive and Explanatory Psychology. We there find that knowledge or cognition is only studied by scientific psychology as a complex psychosis;[3] that human mental life does not begin with knowledge; that it not only grows *in* knowledge, when knowledge is once attained, but it grows *into* knowledge only when certain conditions are fulfilled.[4] The truth that all knowledge implies a development has not, we are told, been hitherto sufficiently emphasized by psychologists, for "at first and for a considerable but indefinite time after birth the child has no such development of any faculty as to make knowledge possible. To it there is no 'Thing' known; to it there is no self as an object of knowledge. This is, however, far from affirming that the child has no states of consciousness whatever—no sensations, no mental images, no feelings, no conation and motor consciousness. Even a considerable development of discriminating consciousness, as the inseparable accompaniment and indispensable condition of all mental development, may take place before the first act, or process, worthy to be called knowledge is reached."[5] It is insisted

---

[1] *Philos. of Mind*, p. 100. *Psychol.* p. 513.
[2] *Philos. of Mind*, p. 106.
[3] *Psychology*, N. Y., 1895, p. 508.
[4] P. 509.
[5] P. 510.

that " all objects of knowledge, psychologically considered, are alike to be regarded as states of consciousness; all states of consciousness are time processes in the on-flowing stream of consciousness. This is as true of the things perceived by the senses as it is of the self known in self-consciousness."[1] Again: " In the earlier stages of mental life no psychoses can be discovered which are worthy to be called a knowing of self."[2] The gradual development of the psychosis called a knowledge of self, Professor Ladd traces at length, and concludes thus: " Finally, it is by complex synthesis of judgments, based on manifold experiences converging to one conception—the resultant of many acts of memory, imagination, reasoning and naming—that the knowledge of the Self as a Unitary Being is attained." Only at this stage is self-consciousness in its highest sense possible; but in this stage " in one and the same act the mind makes itself the object of its self-knowledge, and believes in the real being of that which it creates as its own object."[3]

Surely all this is plain and unvarnished empirical psychology, with only a few traces of the old-fashioned rationalistic doctrine. It is psychology as science. But it is very hard to fit it to what has preceded. We find here that in the earlier stages of consciousness there is no self as known. It, of course, follows that during these stages there also exists no self as knowing, no agent, no reality; for is it not true that consciousness regarded as objectively discriminated, and consciousness regarded as discriminating activity, are only two sides of one and the same consciousness?[4] and are not the self-knowing and the self-known the one self?[5] and does not the existence of this one self depend upon its actual functioning as self-consciousness? " To be self-conscious, to remember that we were self-conscious, and to think of the self as having, actually or possibly, been self-conscious—this is really to be, as minds are."[6] There are then sufficiently complex consciousnesses containing sensations,

[1] P. 519.
[2] P. 523.
[3] Pp. 531, 532.
[4] *Philos of Mind*, p. 89; *Psychol.* p. 291.
[5] *Philos. of Mind*, p. 63; cf. *Psychol.* p. 532.
[6] *Philos. of Mind*, p. 147; cf. *Psychol.* p. 638.

images, feelings, motor impulses, and even a considerable development of discrimination, which are not the manifestation of any reality, or the states of any being. As yet there is no mind or self of which they may be the manifestation. Here are activities without any 'thing' that is active. Here are phenomena without any reality *of* which and *to* which they are the phenomena. We must then abandon the position that all psychic energy is the activity of the self, for the self must be begotten or beget itself before it can act; and we must also reconsider the statement that the word phenomena has no meaning except as implying some particular being *of* which, and some being *to* which, the phenomenon is.

The two elements in Professor Ladd's doctrine cannot, I think, by any possibility, be made to harmonize. It is war to the death; and I believe the careful reader of the earlier and later works of our colleague will see that the issue of the conflict is scarcely a matter of doubt. Professor Ladd's soul as 'envisaged reality' is gradually slipping away from him. I should not be surprised to see him in some later work apostrophizing it after the manner of Hadrian:

"Animula vagula, blandula,
Hospes comesque corporis,
Quae nunc abibis in loca?"

Let us hope that, when it does take its departure, it may find some abode with an atmosphere less rarified than the heaven of the transcendentalists, and let us also hope that it may escape a damp and unpleasant interment in so-called empirical 'slime.'

I have dwelt at length upon Professor Ladd's doctrine both because of our own interest in his work and because it has seemed to me profitable to show into what perplexities even a learned and really scholarly man is in danger of falling, when he wanders from the narrow way of scientific psychological method, and takes to what Diogenes Laertius calls a noble line in Philosophy, dealing with the incomprehensible. It remains for me to say a word concerning those whom I may call the successors of Hume. I think we will all admit that Hume wrote rather crudely concerning the self, and that his 'bundle' of perceptions is by no means able to take its place without modification in a modern psychological treatise.   I do not mean, therefore, in speaking of the successors of Hume, to indicate that those referred to write in the same crude fashion.   I only mean to indicate that they have abandoned the traditional self of the History of Philosophy, and have not replaced it by an hypostatized unitary activity in consciousness or in ' experience,' but regard it as the whole task of the psychologist to study the ' content' of consciousness in a broad and reasonable sense of the word content.   In this class I place Professor Wundt, as he appears in his later writings;[1] Professor Külpe, who states and maintains more unequivocally than Wundt, Wundt's later psychological doctrine;[2] Professor Ziehen, who almost succeeds in leaving out of his clear little book on Physiological Psychology, all non-psychological reference ; and Professor Titchener, who holds that there is no psychological evidence of a mind which lies behind mental processes, and no psychological evidence of a mental ' activity' above or behind the stream of conscious processes.[3]   It is interesting to note that these men have approached psychology from the physiological and experimental side ; and one is tempted to think that the novelty of their task and the conditions under which they have been compelled to approach it, have somewhat loosened for them the bonds of tradition, and have enabled them to place themselves more completely on the ground proper to psychology as science than it has been possible for a goodly number of their co-workers to do.[4]

It is unnecessary for me to say that I regard their position as the right one, though I should not like to be understood as ap-

---

[1] Grundzüge, Leipzig, 1893. *Human and Animal Psychology.* London, 1894.
[2] Grundriss, Leipzig, 1893.
[3] *Outline of Psychol.*, N. Y., 1896; p. 341.
[4] It is proper for me to state that none of these writers have appeared to me to fully appreciate the significance of their own position for the psychological doctrine of ' knowledge.' A commentator always treads upon uncertain ground, but I am inclined to believe that their scientific attitude in treating of the self has really been brought about by the causes to which I have alluded. They have wished to avoid metaphysics and hold to clear psychological concepts. This does not necessarily imply that they have seen the total value of these concepts either for Psychology or Epistemology. I suppose all the writers I have mentioned would give a goodly share of the credit for bringing before the public the doctrine I am discussing to Wundt, although he has not been the most happy in giving its expression.

proving all the details of their treatment of psychological problems. The study of the content of consciousness and of the
relations of mental phenomena to the physical world seem to
me the proper task of the psychologist as psychologist. And
by the words ' content of consciousness,' I do not mean content
in the Kantian sense, a something contrasted with ' form ;' I
mean all that is to be found in consciousness, including relations,
changes and activities. But relations, changes and activities
should be treated in a scientific and intelligible way. If I have
a perception of three black dots on a white surface, so related
to one another that lines joining them would form an equilateral
triangle, surely the relations of the dots are as much a part of
my perception as the color of the dots ; and, if I see again
on the following day three similar dots similarly related, I am
surely not justified in declaring the relations perceived on the
two occasions, to be identical in any sense in which the dots are
not. If, further, I describe the formation of any psychosis in
consciousness to-day as the manifestation of an activity, and the
formation of a like psychosis in consciousness to-morrow, as
also the manifestation of an activity, surely the two activities
should be as carefully distinguished as the psychoses themselves, and each relegated to the particular time at which it manifested itself. The word ' activity ' is not a word to conjure
with ; and when speech ceases to be intelligible, silence is golden.
There is nothing in the view of the task of the psychologist which
I am advocating, to make him overlook or slight any phenomenon or aspect of consciousness. He is not compelled to regard
our mental life as composed of unrelated elements, or to look
upon it as passive or mechanical. He need not betake himself
to unusual or misleading expressions such as the ' self-com-
pounding ' or ' agglomeration ' of ideas. He has the same right
others have to take language as he finds it, and to do his best
with it, striving only to be clear and exact and to avoid being
misunderstood. He must recognize that when men say ' I think,'
' I believe,' ' I know,' ' I feel,' ' I will,' ' I remember,' ' I am
self-conscious,' these words indicate the presence in consciousness of complex psychoses, which it is his duty to analyze to the
best of his ability. His task is not an easy one ; and even if he

follow loyally a good method, confining himself resolutely to the field that I have indicated, he may for a long time to come expect to find in it much that cannot be so brought into the light as to make him confident that he has completely analyzed and described it. Notwithstanding all this, he may take comfort in the thought that his method is the true one. Even if the goal be far distant, it is something to be on the right road.

I have no doubt that many will object that this simply abandons the psychological problem of the knower and his knowledge, and does not solve it. They will insist: How can there, after all, be a consciousness, unless something unifies it? can one psychosis know another? or ' a string of feelings' know itself as a string? Where in all this is the knowing? I answer, the psychological problem is indeed abandoned, for it is only through a misconception that such a psychological problem exists at all. How the traditional knowing self came into being and became a perennial stone of stumbling to the speculative mind, it is not, I think, difficult to conjecture; and a brief exposition of what I believe to be the genesis of this self will be the best justification of my statement that the problem has no right to demand a solution.

It is generally accepted among psychologists that, at an early stage of the mind's development, the chief constituent of the notion of the self, and perhaps the only one that stands out with sufficient clearness to occupy the attention, is the idea of the body. When the child says ' I see,' ' I hear,' ' I feel,' he is not thinking of the self of the philosophers, but is recognizing the fact that, given his body in such and such a relation to other objects, he has certain experiences. His body stands over against other objects and is distinguished from them. It sees with its eyes, hears with its ears, feels with its hands. It not only sees, hears, and feels other objects, but also sees, hears and feels itself. It perceives not merely that it is acted upon, but also that it acts upon other things, bringing about changes in them. It is the constant factor in experience, while the objects with which it occupies itself succeed one another in a more or less rapid succession. Moreover, it is an interesting object, with which are bound up in a peculiar manner the pains and pleasures of the individual. No wonder it becomes the centre of the little world in which it has its being, a world concrete, unreflective, external, if I may be permitted to use this relative word when the correlative can not as yet be regarded as having made its way into the light of clear consciousness—at least a world objective and material in the sense that what comes later to be recognized as objective and material almost wholly constitutes it. And from the crude materialism of the infant mind to the crude animism of the savage the step is but a short one. That duplicate of the body, which in dreams walks abroad, sees and is seen, and acts as the body acts, has simply taken the place of the body as knower and doer, and its knowing and doing obtain their significance in the same experience. The thought of the child is duplicated in the new world opened up by the beginnings of reflection.

Now, I believe that the student of the History of Philosophy who is able to read between the lines can see in the highly abstract and inconsistent '*totum in toto*' soul of Scholasticism, and in the 'transcendental unity of apperception' of Kant, a something that has grown by a process of refinement from these rude beginnings. These nebulous entities do not make their appearance upon the stage unheralded. We find early in the history of thought a material soul which knows things by contact with the effluxes thrown off from material objects. It is an object among other objects, as is the body, and the nature of its knowing is clearly analogous to that of the body's. We have, later, a soul in part fettered to the body, and, as it were, semi-material. We have, finally, a soul abstract and unmeaning, a shade, a survival from a more concrete and unreflective past. It is worthy of note that with this development the soul and its method of knowing become more and more unintelligible. How the soul as noumenon or as super-temporal activity can know anything or do anything, no man can pretend to understand. The reason is not far to seek. In the successive transmutations through which it has passed, almost all reference to the primary experience out of which the notion of a soul or self as knower and doer took its rise has been lost. Were such reference completely lost, it would go hard with the hypostatized abstractions of the Noumenalist and the Neo-Kantian. As it is, they hold their own because men really do find in their experience something which seems to speak for them in a certain vague and inarticulate way. They can form no conception of the method by which a noumenon or a Neo-Kantian self-activity can account for their experiences, but they prefer these to nothing at all; for must there not be a knower? do *they* not really *know?* Their position is one quite easy to understand. It is not exclusively to the childhood of the individual or of the race that we need go to find the body an important element in the self-idea. The developed man has much the same experience as the child, and instinctively interprets it in the same way, although reflection has furnished him with the means of correcting this instinctive interpretation. Even the psychologist who writes clearly and systematically concerning the empirical self, which he recognizes as nothing more than a complex in consciousness, may retain as a troublesome and inexplicable entity a second self, the knowing self contrasted with the self known —identical with it, and yet distinguished from it; the same, and yet not the same. Here he may revel, as those who have preceded him have reveled, in self-contradictions and unintelligible discourse. He may apply to the self the unhappy title of ' subject-object' and endeavor to separate a thing from itself, positing a relation between the two, when there are not two but one to be related. It requires but a moment of unprejudiced reflection, it seems to me, to see that all this is absurd and unmeaning. The only question of real interest is: How have men come to speak in this way? The answer I have indicated above. When one whose chief idea of the self is the body[1] speaks of perceiving himself among other objects, he has reference to an experience which he and others constantly have; and he has used a certain expression to call attention to that experience. His thought may not be clear and analytic. His statement, if the words be taken quite literally, is meaningless. Still, he means something by it, and it is the duty of the psy-

[1] Of course, I have no intention of taking here any position regarding the body as a material, external thing. Any one who pleases may substitute for the word such expressions as ' experience of the body,' ' relatively permanent organic feelings,' etc.

chologist to show him what he means. It is not his duty to turn an inconsistency of expression into an inconsistency of thought, and find in his words what, in their proper interpretation, they do not contain. Our Noumenalist, or our Neo-Kantian, thus bases himself upon an experience, even though he misinterprets it. He draws from experience the impulse to carry over into a region in which it has no right to exist the notion of a bodily self. He refines it, he purifies it of all that is earthly and concrete, starves it to a shadow of its former self, and yet expects of it its former tale of bricks—knowing and doing.

This I cannot but regard as delusion; as a misinterpretation of our common experience. This path let the psychologist avoid. To him knowledge is a psychosis to be analyzed; so is self-knowledge. The unity of consciousness he may accept as he finds it, striving to make clear to himself what he means by 'unity' in general, and by the unity of consciousness in particular. To attempt to explain the ultimate nature of consciousness by the assumption of hypothetical entities not to be found in consciousness, or by ascribing inconceivable virtues to hypostatized activities, seems to me an unprofitable task.[1]

My address is already longer than I intended to make it, and yet I feel with regret that I have not been able to speak on some of the points upon which I have touched, as clearly and fully as I could have wished. Nevertheless, I must beg your indulgence in allowing me to mention very briefly one point more. Psychologists are men, and may be assumed to share the hopes and fears common to men of their degree of intelligence. It is quite possible that some among us have already mentally characterized my position by applying to it the damnatory phrase

---

[1] In spite of the fact that I heartily dislike seeing a discussion encumbered with foot-notes, I must add one more. I have said at the outset that I would try to confine myself to psychological ground. I have, hence, raised none of the epistemological questions which are suggested by the one question I have been discussing. I have not criticized from the standpoint of epistemology the psychological standpoint, nor asked how one may *know* that there is an external world. I have not asked what it means for two men to know the same thing, or how one consciousness can be known to be outside of another. I have simply discussed the general problem of knowledge and of the knower in psychology, and I have stated the problem in its simplest form. Until some satisfactory solution is given to the problem as thus stated, it seems to me to be futile to attempt the solution of more intricate problems of the same nature.

'psychology without a soul,' and have felt that what I have said militates against the existence of the soul after death. My discussion has, however, left this question just where it was before. It was pointed out by Mill long ago, that if it is possible for a 'string of feelings' to have a continued existence in this life, there can be no *a priori* objection to its having such an existence in another. Even so I would say, if a consciousness can here develop during a period of years, and retain that identity which it is the duty of the psychologist to analyze and describe, there is nothing in a man's repudiation of noumena or supertemporal activities to prevent him from believing that his conscious life may continue indefinitely. My reference to this matter may be a little out of place, for we are here to-day as psychologists, and have before us a definite and limited field of labor. Still, it is hard for men to approach scientific questions without asking what is their bearing upon theological or religious convictions. Perhaps it is right that such questionings should arise. I have added this paragraph in the hope that what I have said may not meet with a prejudice arising out of a mere misunderstanding, and be condemned through the application of a question-begging phrase.

STUDIES IN THE PHYSIOLOGY AND PSYCHOLOGY OF THE TELEGRAPHIC LANGUAGE.

BY PROFESSOR WILLIAM LOWE BRYAN AND MR. NOBLE HARTER.[1]

Indiana University.

In March, 1893, Mr. Harter began at the Psychological Laboratory of the Indiana University a study of certain problems connected with the acquisition of the telegraphic language. Eleven months were spent at and away from the University in a preliminary study of these problems, in the light of his own experience, and by diligent, personal cross-examination of thirty-seven operators, employed by the Wabash Railway Company and by the Western Union Telegraph Company. Of these, seven were recognized as experts, twenty-two as men of average experience and ability, while eight had barely enough skill to hold their places. Twenty-eight of the number had been personally known to H. from two to sixteen years. Throughout these and the subsequent investigations, the members of the telegraphic fraternity showed the most cordial interest and readiness to help.

In March, 1894, H. began at the University Laboratory, an experimental study of individual differences in telegraphic writing. The experimental part of this study continued until August, 1894, and the study of the results until June, 1895. A review of certain phases of the results was made in January, 1896. During the winter of 1895–96 he was engaged with the study of the curve of improvement in sending and receiving.

II. THE PRELIMINARY STUDY.

The first year's work was in the nature of an exploring expedition in search of the problems which would repay fuller in-

---

[1] N. H., a graduate student of Psychology at Indiana University, was for many years a railroad telegrapher, and is an expert in that branch of telegraphy. The experiments were made under Professor Bryan's direction.

vestigation. It seems best, on the whole, to give a somewhat gossipy, through brief account of this exploration. The method of exploration consisted in cross-examining the operators with questions which, on the one hand, seemed to have psychological or physiological significance, and which, on the other hand, in the light of H's personal experience, gave promise of answers.[1]

The student learns to distinguish most of the letters of the telegraphic alphabet in a few hours or days at most; but after distinguishing them clearly at one time, he generally finds himself confused by the back stroke, and must re-learn the letters many times before this difficulty is overcome. The back stroke is the stroke of the armature against the adjusting screw above it. Those letters composed of simple dots or dashes are mastered first, then those composed of dots and spaces, and lastly those most complex, as, J (— . — .), X (. — . .) Q (. . — .).

As the characters composed of four, five and six dots, are made more rapidly than the learner is able to count, much practice is necessary before he can recognize surely the number of dots in such groups. When a considerable degree of speed in receiving is reached, the space between the letters of a word becomes so small that one ceases to recognize it consciously, the letters seem to blend together, and the word is recognized as a sound whole. Thus, expert operators read *words* from their instruments; and, as will be seen later, these group themselves into larger wholes, so that the sentence becomes the conscious unit, much as in the reading of printed matter. Of course, the short and frequently recurring words are the first ones to have their parts melt together. A learner is thus very soon able to distinguish such words as, 'the,' 'is,' 'and,' etc., when written swiftly on the main line in their proper connection, while he cannot understand even a single letter in other words. This observation shows that a given group of sounds, for example those making the letter H, may be apperceived in one instant because occurring within a larger known group, and then not apperceived a moment later because occurring as part of an unknown group.

---

[1] To save circumlocutions, technical words in common use among telegraph operators and whose meaning is plain, will be used in this article.

There are distinct specialties in telegraphy, so that while an operator may be competent in one department he would be a failure in another department requiring no greater speed, until he had acquired the vocabulary of that department. Thus, a commercial operator would be 'lost' in a yard office, or the train dispatcher in taking markets. It is the opinion of experienced operators that while there are many exceptional cases of quickness and slowness in learning,[1] it requires from two to two and a half years to become an expert operator. Through lack of energy to practice, except when compelled by the nature of their work, few operators reach their maximum, while many have little more than the skill actually required in their daily work. To gain expertness, work increasing in difficulty must be faithfully done. For a fuller discussion of this point see below, part IV.

The effect of sending a long strange word swiftly is to cause the receiver to make an error or break—that is, to ask for a repetition of the word. Many operators are very sensitive on the subject of breaking, and some do not hesitate to supply the most probable word and thus avoid what they consider a humiliation. Sometimes an obnoxiously smart young operator is allured through his pride against breaking, into a trap, whose psychology is significant. The date and address of a message are sent at a rapid rate, followed by the period which separates the address from the body of a message. The letters of the alphabet in order are then plainly but rapidly sent to him. The receiver expects a message. In the first few letters he recognizes no word group. He hopes to see the connection a little farther on. He is finally compelled to break. It is sometimes possible to repeat this trick several times without the victim discovering it. In this case evidently the strenuous effort of attention to recognize word groups has prevented the recognition of a most familiar group, namely, the alphabet in order.

Another interesting apperceptive illusion, to which even ex-

[1] A story is told of an Indiana operator, who, after three months' practice, was able to receive Garfield's Inaugural Address. Stories of this sort must be taken with a grain of salt. The more of telegraphy you know, the more salt it takes.

pert operators are subject, arises in the following way : The adjustment of the armature of the sounder is controlled by set screws so that the down stroke and up stroke may be differentiated. The down strokes, of course, correspond to the dots and dashes of the Morse code. Whether a dot or dash is intended, is determined by the length of time between the down stroke and the following back stroke. It is evidently essential that the down stroke and the back stroke should he clearly distinguishable. Making this distinction is one of the greatest difficulties in learning telegraphy. The student may learn to recognize several of the simple dotted letters in a few minutes; yet after an hour, when *e*, a single dot, is made, he interprets the two sounds which he hears as *i*, which is two dots. Learners seek to assist the ear by watching the teacher's hand or the armature of the sounder. This device must, of course, be prohibited, and the learner required to depend on the ear alone. Several instances have been observed in which expert operators have made the same sort of error when listening to strange instruments in which the down stroke and back stroke were not very clearly different. In such cases the experts were unable to understand even a single letter. By a sort of inversion of attention the back strokes are heard as down strokes, and *vice versa.*

The rate of receiving varies greatly. On train wires, about twenty to twenty-five words, of four letters each, per minute, may be taken as the ordinary rate of communication. Among lower grade operators the ability to send is greater than the ability to receive, but with experts the reverse is generally true. The highest sending record, so far as known, is forty-nine words per minute. When the type-writer is used the ability of the receiver exceeds that of the sender. Words in cipher cannot be received so rapidly or so accurately as ordinary language. The telegraph companies recognize this fact by charging very high rates for combinations of letters forming other than ordinary English words. Errors in the transmission of messages are comparatively few, and it is the common feeling of telegraphers that they could testify more surely in Court concerning what they have heard on the line than concerning what they have heard from personal interview, or as to the accuracy of a message which they have copied from a sounder than as to one which they have copied from dictation.

External disturbances have a very great effect upon inexperienced operators, but affect the experienced operator very little. 'It is not uncommon to see an operator doing a large amount of important work in a small room where half a dozen sets of instruments are working, trainmen running in and out, talking excitedly and asking questions, engines moving by the window and trucks running noisily by on the platform. Yet the operator works ahead, calmly and rapidly, and even briefly answers questions addressed to him. Where a number of sounders work close together, pieces of tin, brass or the like may be attached so as to give each a distinguishable tone. Many men can receive from an instrument adjusted low in the presence of others sounding much louder. The ability to do this, however, is much lessened by lack of practice. Dispatcher C. was a copyer for several years in an office where he worked with several instruments close together. After he had been promoted two years to a dispatcher's desk, where but one instrument was used, he lost the ability to do the work he had formerly done, being confused by the working of the other instruments.

Subjective disturbances, as fear, anger, excitement, etc., have little effect on expert men other than to make them more fluent in the use of the telegraphic language. Operators are keenly alive to the presence of those with whom they communicate, so that they do not feel alone, although no one is physically present. This feeling causes young operators to suffer keenly from stage fright, especially when making their debut. The first work generally consists in reporting a train to a dispatcher. The debutant is very anxious to do so, and practices hard so as to do it well, but almost invariably does it in such a manner as to attract the attention of all the operators on the line. It is not unusual to see a beginner sweating profusely in a cold room from the exertion of taking an easy ten-word message. A similar fact appears in the difficulty which the young operator has to keep up a conversation. He writes very slowly, and yet he cannot think of enough things to say.   The organizing imagination seems paralyzed by the presence of his audience. In one who is not an expert the emotions of fear, of anger and even of joy, generally paralyze invention, so that only spasmodic or meaningless sound groups can be made, and every one recognizes that the man is ' rattled.'   The ability to receive is also often so affected that he is unable to recognize anything.   This is particularly true in the case of fear.

The telegraphic language becomes so thoroughly assimilated that thinking apparently resolves itself into the telegraphic short hand used in conversation.   This telegraphic short hand is an abbreviated code in which the vowels and many consonants are thrown out.   One thinks in telegraphic terms.   An odd expression or an unusual message attracts the operator's attention, while he is directly engaged with some other work.   Operators who work at night depend on their office call to waken them.   The sensation is that of hearing one's name repeated softly over and over.   When the operator is worn out by loss of sleep or physical fatigue he is, of course, more difficult to awaken.   At such times the sender writes the office call very distinctly and makes unusually long spaces.   This seems to add emphasis to the call. The anger flutter, a whir made by rapid alternate strokes of the first and second finger, is also employed with good effect to awaken sleeping telegraphers.

How thoroughly the telegraphic language is mastered in some cases is illustrated by the fact that expert operators ' copy behind' three or four words; sometimes ten or twenty words; that is, the receiving operator allows the sender to write a number of words before he begins to copy.   It is then possible for him to get something of the sense of the sentence in advance. The operator is thus able, not only to punctuate and capitalize, but also to keep run of the grammatical structure.   Yet, while he would detect an error, or notice that a word was not appropriate in the connection used, and be able to suggest to the sender what the word should be, the language of the message as a whole may have little or no meaning to him.   Several cases illustrating this fact have been observed.   The most notable case was given by Chief S.   A message for the superintendent was received by a very skillful operator. Any one might have seen from its contents that it required immediate delivery and action. Some word in the message had been so written that it was misread and missent by the sending operator. The receiving operator saw that this word did not make sense, and suggested to the sender that it might be another word similar in appearance. The sender decided that this was true and the message was corrected accordingly. The receiving operator placed the message upon the superintendent's hook, where it was found by a clerk too late for the action required. The receiver could not believe that he had received such a message until his copy was shown him. The details described were then recalled. The railway companies recognize this tendency to automatism by requiring dispatchers not to send out train orders until they have been assured by the operator to whom the orders are sent that he has displayed the proper signals.

The most striking example of complete mastery of the telegraphic language is seen in the daily work of a train dispatcher on a trunk line. Except when there is a very unusual amount of traffic, the dispatcher records the movements of trains as reported on a train sheet, figures on a special meeting point for trains, sends out the order, and as it is repeated by one office, copies it in the order book, checks it again as the next office repeats it, acknowledges its correctness and gives his official sanction; but while this very important work is being done, he figures on other meeting points in which the weather, length of side tracks, size and heaviness of trains, grades and probable delays are items. By the time the first order is completed, he has decided on the next line of action, and so it goes on for the eight hours he is on duty.

When not influenced by nervous diseases, practice enables nearly all to make groups of four, five or six dots with great rapidity. For the accuracy with which this is done see below part IV. Measurements made with the chronograph showed this rate to be as high as twelve dots per second. Letters forming words are written much more rapidly and with greater precision than letters taken at random. The same is true of words in connected discourse as compared with words in random order.

The effect of emotion upon sending is to give greater facility of expression to expert men, while beginners are in a greater or less degree paralyzed. The syllable 'ha' repeated, indicates laughter and is frequently used without any other external sign even when the operator's risibles are considerably excited. The uninitiated spectator might not suspect that the conversation was humorous. On the other hand, the anger flutter described above is invariably accompanied by a strong facial expression of passion.

Tests were made to ascertain the average rate of sending. The best results were obtained from two one-minute trials of dispatcher K. At the first trial he wrote thirty-nine words of a hundred and eighty-six letters, making four hundred and sixteen impacts upon the key. At the second trial he wrote forty-two words of a hundred and ninety-two letters, or four hundred and twenty-nine impacts. This shows a speed of seven and two-tenths movements per second. If the words in the Cincinnati contest, where the winner wrote forty-nine words per minute, averaged as many impacts per word as in the above cases, the rate would be eight and one-tenth impacts per second. Comparison of these results with the maximum rate of voluntary movement as determined by Von Kries,[1] Dressler[2] and Bryan[3] must, of course, take into account the important differences between the conditions in the tests made.

Every operator develops a distinctive style of sending so that he can be recognized readily by those who work with him constantly. (See III. below.) Mr. S., a dispatcher of much experience, works daily with forty or fifty men and states that, after hearing four or five words, he can readily recognize the sender, or be sure that he is not one of his men. Where two or more operators work in the same office they sometimes change before the appointed time, or work for each other without permission. When a train is reported, however, in such cases, the dispatcher often asks where the other operator is. Operators who feel secure in the seclusion of their offices have

[1] Du Bois Reymond, *Archiv f. Physiologie*, 1886. Suppl. I.
[2] *Am. Jour. Psychol.*, IV., p. 514.
[3] *Am. Jour. Psychol.*, V., p. 1.

sometimes been detected in making improper and impertinent remarks on the line, by their style of sending. Two instances were noted where men were discharged for offenses detected in this manner. Young operators have a peculiar way of grouping the letters of words, which gives the impression of some one walking unsteadily as when partially intoxicated. Many dispatchers claim that they can generally recognize a woman by her style of sending.

The best time to learn telegraphy is doubtless before the age of eighteen. The most expert operators have learned as a rule, when quite young. It is very difficult and often impossible to become even a passable operator, when the start is made after thirty. While extreme age weakens and limits the power of the operator, the maximum skill seems to be retained up to the age of sixty-five. This point, however, demands special investigation. Severe headaches and other painful diseases interfere with the work of the operator. Mr. S., now a train master, regards the use of tobacco as hurtful to operators. Mr. W. a Western Union Superintendent thinks tobacco invariably injurious to his men. Many operators do not consider a moderate use of tobacco as detrimental. All agree, however, that intoxicants make a man not only unreliable, but dangerous. To be found in a saloon means discharge on many railroads. The work of telegraphers is much affected by nervous diseases. Writers' cramp frequently disables the sending arm, and causes the retirement of the operator, unless he learns to send with the other arm, a difficult matter with most men so afflicted. Sometimes rest and treatment relieve this difficulty, at least temporarily. Mr. Y. had suffered from a nervous affection which made it difficult for him to stop when making four or five successive dots. He would make ten or twelve dots in writing letters composed of these groups.

III. INDIVIDUAL DIFFERENCES IN TELEGRAPHIC WRITING.

The telegraphic language is singularly well adapted to the experimental study of many problems in physiology, phychology and even philology. Indeed, if one were required to invent a generation-long experiment for the exact study of certain phases of language, one could scarcely hope to find a better; for, on the one hand, no other language used by man can be so completely translated into exactly measurable symbols; while, on the other hand, the manifold personal differences in the operators are shown by investigation to be represented in those symbols. As illustration and proof of these assertions, the following study of individual differences in telegraphic writing is offered.

Apparatus.—The DuPrez signal was adjusted to write upon the Marey drum, being carried transversely by the automatic carriage which Verdin supplies with the Marey drum. The Marey chronograph in circuit with the Kroneker Interrupter gave the time control.

The experiment.—The sentence, " Ship 364 wagons via Erie quick," was written by each subject about a dozen times in succession. This sentence was chosen because it contains almost every sort of difficulty which the telegraphic language presents: 'Ship' is composed of groups of three, four, two and five dots. Each of the figures 3, 6, 4 is somewhat difficult, especially the 6, which is composed of six dots. 'Wagons' contains two letters which have two dashes in succession. 'Via' is a simple word presenting no special difficulty. 'Erie' is by far the hardest word in the sentence. By a little change in the time relations, one would get oye, erc, sic, eeye. Such words are usually written with extra care and with longer spaces. The word 'quick' has several dashes, of which the last one is likely to be longer than the others, since it closes the word and the sentence. The sentence as a whole is as follows: S (...), h (....), i (..) p (.....), 3 (...—.), 6 (......), 4 (....—), w (.——), a (.—), g (——.), o (..), n (—.), s (...), v (...—), i (..), a (.—), E (.), r (. ..), i (..), e (.), q (..—.), u (..—), i (..), c (.. .), k (—.—).

The subjects.—By connecting the Du Prez signal with the main lines of the Western Union Telegraph Company and of the Monon Railroad Company, about sixty operators were tested. It was found that it would require several years of continuous work to investigate all of these records by the method decided upon. Accordingly sixteen of the number were selected, some of them being expert, some ordinary and some poor operators. Following is a brief characterization of the men, grouped somewhat in the order of their ability as telegraphers, beginning with the less expert. A. B. Guthrie, student I. U., age 21, 5 months' experience as student in a telegraph office; C. G. Mallotte, student I. U., age 22, 2 years' experience as student in an office, 3 months in charge of a small office; Prof. G. E. Fellows, department of European history, I. U., age 43, 5 years' experience in charge of railroad office about 13 years ago; R. C. Brooks, student I. U., age 21, 3 years' experience in charge of an office; L. A. Clark, agent Monon, Crawfordsville, Ind., age 40, experience 17 years; C. L. Buchanan, agent Monon, Ellettsville, age 57, experience 25 years; G. W. Dyer, agent Monon, Bainbridge, Ind., age 60, experience 33 years; Geo. H. Godfrey, Manager W. U., New Albany, Ind., age 55, experience 31 years; Mrs. Z. M. Apple, Manager W. U., French Lick Springs, Ind., age 24, experience 5 years; Miss Nellie Green, operator Monon, Louisville, Ky., age 24, experience 5 years; A. B. Evans, Manager W. U., Bloomington, Ind., age 27, experience 10 years; Noble Harter, graduate student of Psychology, Indiana University, age 37, experience 21 years; C. W. Goodman, dispatcher, Monon, age 32, experience 15 years; H. O: Chapman, dispatcher, Monon, age 27, experience 10 years; W. H. Fogg, dispatcher, Monon, age 26, experience 10 years; E. B. Cassell, chief dispatcher, Monon, age 36, experience 18 years.

Measurement of Results.—Each character in the tracings obtained was measured. There are one hundred and forty-nine characters to be measured if the sentence is written without error; but, as in many cases, too many characters were made, the actual number to be measured was considerably greater. Eight repetitions of the message by each of the sixteen subjects were measured, so that the total number of measurements made was about twenty thousand, and required several months. The measurements were made to the nearest half millimetre. The rate of the drum was so adjusted that forty-seven mm. correspond to one second of time. Most of the errors must then evidently be less than five thousandths of a second, and an error of ½ mm. would be about one hundredth of a second. Higher accuracy could have been obtained easily, and was obtained in individual cases by increasing the rate of the drum and so lengthening the lines to be measured. But upon careful consideration, the degrees of accuracy given was proved to be sufficient for the experiment proposed.

Methods of Treating Results.—Several methods of treating the results were employed for the purpose of bringing out different points.

First Treatment.—The theoretical Morse alphabet is composed of the following elements: A, the dot, one unit of time; B, the dash, three units of time; C, the short space between the parts of a letter, one unit of time; D, the long space, in spaced letter, two units of time; E, the space between letters, three units of time; F, the space between words, six units of time. This is the ideal scheme which each operator has tried to learn. Now it is possible to compare the actual writing of each individual with this ideal scheme by taking the actual length of his dot as a unit and by then computing the actual ratios of the other elements to this unit. This computation was made for each individual. The average length of dot, dash, etc., being used. The results are given in Table I.

It was found by a study of the individual results that the several values of a given character are not accidental variations from their average value, but that there are constant differences between the times required for the same character in different parts of the sentence or even of the same word. These facts, which affect the value of Table I., will be considered further on. The table proves its value in spite of this or any other defect, however, by the fact that it affords a means of identifying any one of the individuals represented in it. If a single one of the sentences written by one of the subjects be treated by the method employed in constructing the table, a comparison of the several ratios obtained and their sum with the values given in Table I., will in every case show a correspondence so much more exact with one of the sixteen than with any of the others, that the identification will be beyond question.

TABLE I.

NAME.	A	B	C	D	E	F	TOTAL.
IDEAL CODE	1.00	3.00	1.00	2.00	3.00	6.00	16.00
C. G. MALLOTTE	1.00	1.95	1.13	1.55	1.76	2.09	9.48
A. B. GUTHRIE	1.00	4.66	2.33	3.51	5.80	7.44	24.74
R. C. BROOKS.	1.00	3.02	1.18	2.41	2.88	4.05	14.54
G. E. FELLOWS.	1.00	3.47	1.24	3.09	5.32	6.76	20.88
A. B. EVANS	1.00	2.30	.89	1.98	2.10	2.65	10.92
NOBLE HARTER	1.00	2.83	.95	2.31	3.08	6.44	16.61
G. W. DYER	1.00	2.85	1.09	2.20	2.93	5.37	15.44
G. H. GODFREY.	1.00	2.27	.76	1.77	2.02	4.15	11.97
C. L. BUCHANAN	1.00	2.64	1.02	1.86	2.50	4.68	13.70
L. A. CLARK	1.00	2.38	.70	2.31	2.95	4.91	14.25
Z. M. APPLE	1.00	2.45	.94	1.77	2.45	3.58	12.19
NELLIE GREEN	1.00	2.49	.85	1.81	1.92	2.87	10.94
W. H. FOGG	1.00	2.98	1.08	2.40	2.71	3.00	13.17
E. B. CASSELL	1.00	2.61	1.06	2.23	3.01	4.12	13.92
C. W. GOODMAN	1.00	2.32	.87	2.13	2.42	3.14	11.88
H. O. CHAPMAN.	1.00	2.50	.94	1.97	2.87	3.36	12.71

In order to obtain average values which should represent more homogeneous values and also to show characteristic individual differences in a single short and easy word, the results for the word 'via' were treated in the following way. As above, each man's average dot for the six dots in the word was taken as the unit, and the length of each character was computed as a per cent. of that unit. The ideal scale is given for comparison, also, the variation of this average dot from the typical dot, *i. e.*, the average of all the dots in the sentence.

In order to prove the identifying value of this table, two tests were made: A friend selected single records from three of the operators. Computations of these records by the same method as that used in making the table gave results which could be unmistakably identified. Then, records of three others were measured from the original tracings and the results

TABLE II.

Name.	A•	C	A•	C	A•	C	B̄	E	A•	C	A•	E	A•	C	B̄	F	Total.	Dot or Unit.	Typical Dot.	Var.
C. G. Mallotte	1.07	1.11	.93	1.22	1.22	1.22	2.51	1.47	.93	1.00	.93	1.97	.89	1.07	2.29	2.36	22.19	2.79	3.05	.26
A. B. Guthrie	1.19	2.10	1.10	1.95	.71	2.24	4.86	4.00	.81	1.76	2.24	4.67	.95	1.86	4.33	6.14	40.91	2.10	1.92	.18
R. C. Brooks	.85	1.32	1.06	1.28	1.32	1.36	2.60	2.13	.85	1.19	1.06	3.67	.85	1.02	4.04	5.06	29.06	2.35	2.45	.10
G. E. Fellows	1.07	1.23	1.00	1.29	.89	.87	3.99	6.32	1.07	1.26	1.03	5.16	.96	1.12	3.52	6.49	37.29	3.02	2.97	.05
A. B. Evans	.95	.86	.90	.72	.90	.99	2.52	1.44	1.12	1.04	1.22	2.25	.90	.95	3.11	2.93	22.80	2.22	2.39	.17
Noble Harter	.76	1.03	1.21	1.03	1.35	1.10	3.11	2.59	.83	1.03	1.10	2.48	.76	1.00	3.42	6.69	29.53	2.90	3.12	.22
G. W. Dyer	.91	1.16	1.19	1.03	1.23	1.03	2.81	2.08	.91	1.30	1.04	2.80	.68	1.01	3.43	6.54	29.15	3.07	3.28	.21
G. H. Godfrey	.92	.95	.95	.95	1.10	.83	2.38	1.10	.89	.86	1.19	2.09	.92	.74	2.69	4.09	22.65	3.35	3.72	.37
C. L. Buchanan	.96	.99	1.21	1.02	1.11	1.21	2.82	.96	1.05	1.08	1.08	1.48	.59	1.11	4.37	4.31	25.35	3.23	3.44	.21
L. A. Clark	.91	.59	1.13	1.06	1.00	.85	2.70	1.91	.94	.75	1.03	2.22	.97	.68	3.82	7.21	27.77	3.19	3.43	.24
Z. M. Apple	1.00	.86	1.04	1.07	1.10	1.21	2.94	1.38	.93	.76	1.04	2.01	.86	.93	3.18	3.25	23.56	2.89	3.06	.17
Nellie Green	1.03	.81	1.03	.96	.92	.96	2.57	.96	.85	.88	.99	2.12	.81	.85	2.94	4.08	22.76	2.72	2.69	.03
W. H. Fogg	.66	1.13	1.17	1.13	1.17	1.17	2.72	1.83	.89	1.17	1.32	2.22	.78	1.05	3.66	3.15	25.22	2.57	2.69	.12
E. B. Cassell	.92	1.10	1.10	1.03	.96	1.07	2.54	2.35	.88	1.07	1.10	2.09	1.03	.92	3.31	5.22	26.69	2.72	2.76	.04
C. W. Goodman	.92	.62	1.10	.92	1.03	.92	2.46	1.69	.82	1.10	1.10	2.28	1.03	.88	2.64	3.71	23.22	2.72	2.78	.06
H. O. Chapman	1.05	.98	1.12	1.05	1.22	.98	2.44	1.74	.77	.94	1.05	2.44	.80	.84	2.86	4.18	24.46	2.87	3.02	.15
Ideal	1.00	1.00	1.00	1.00	1.00	1.00	3.00	3.00	1.00	1.00	1.00	3.00	1.00	1.00	3.00	6.00	29.00	Av. 2.80	Av. 2.92	.12

TABLE III.

No.	A .	C	A .	C	A .	C	B |	E	A .	C	A .	E	A .	C	B |	F	T'T'L.	Av. DOT.	IDENTIFIED AS
1 (a)	.51	1.15	1.15	1.15	1.15	1.15	2.70	1.74	.97	1.15	1.35	2.30	.77	.97	3.67	3.09	24.97	2.59	W. H. F.
1 (b)	.66	1.13	1.17	1.13	1.17	1.17	2.72	1.83	.89	1.17	1.32	2.22	.78	1.05	3.66	3.15	25.22	2.57	
2 (a)	.93	.93	1.23	1.08	1.08	1.23	2.82	.93	1.08	.93	1.08	1.48	.61	1.08	4.61	4.31	25.37	3.25	C. L. B.
2 (b)	.96	.99	1.21	1.02	1.11	1.21	2.82	.96	1.05	1.08	1.08	1.48	.59	1.11	4.37	4.31	25.35	3.23	
3 (a)	.99	.78	1.07	.99	.99	.96	2.54	.99	.88	.99	.99	2.11	.78	.99	3.09	4.10	23.27	2.56	N. G.
3 (b)	1.03	.81	1.03	.96	.92	.96	2.57	.96	.85	.88	.99	2.12	.81	.85	2.94	4.08	22.76	2.72	
4 (a)	.92	1.12	1.18	1.12	1.28	1.12	2.61	2.04	.92	1.28	.92	2.61	.74	.92	3.33	5.42	27.53	2.67	G. W. D.
4 (b)	.91	1.16	1.19	1.03	1.23	1.03	2.81	2.08	.91	1.30	1.04	2.80	.68	1.01	3.43	6.54	29.15	3.07	
5 (a)	.94	.94	.94	.94	1.10	.79	2.36	1.10	.94	.84	1.10	2.05	.94	.74	2.66	3.95	22.33	3.17	A. H. G.
5 (b)	.92	.95	.95	.95	1.10	.83	2.38	1.10	.89	.86	1.19	2.09	.92	.74	2.69	4.09	22.65	3.35	
6 (a)	1.00	.75	1.00	.75	.75	1.00	2.50	1.25	1.00	1.00	1.25	2.25	1.00	1.00	3.00	3.00	22.50	2.00	A. B. E.
6 (b)	.95	.86	.90	.72	.90	.99	2.52	1.44	1.12	1.04	1.22	2.25	.90	.95	3.11	2.93	22.80	2.22	

(a). The unknown record given in terms of mm. reduced to per cents. of the average of the six dots contained in it, as in Table II.

(b). A row of per cents. from Table II, selected as representing the unknown sender, because of its greater resemblance to (a).

The letters A, B, C, etc., refer to the several Morse characters.

computed as above. The identification was equally sure. Table III. gives the six sets of results obtained in this way in comparison with the corresponding results from Table II. Of special importance is the fact that the individual results, numbers four, five and six, Table III., were written much more swiftly than the results represented in Table II. by the same operators; for it is thus shown that the individual characteristics persist through different rates of speed. The variation in speed does not, however, leave the ratios between the several characters undisturbed. Examination of Table III. will show that greater speed is gained for the most part by shortening the longer characters. Fig. 1 in Plate I. shows the relations of Table III. graphically.

Third treatment.—By a different method, a single letter *v*

TABLE IV.

OPERATOR.		A •	C	A •	C	A •	C	B̲	E	TOTAL.
H. O. C.	(a)	.099	.093	.105	.099	.116	.092	.231	.165	1.000
	(b)	.098	.094	.105	.098	.116	.094	.230	.165	1.000
G. H. G.	(a)	.101	.101	.105	.105	.121	.091	.258	.118	1.000
	(b)	.097	.097	.104	.106	.119	.091	.258	.128	1.000
G. E. F.	(a)	.063	.073	.059	.076	.055	.054	.236	.384	1.000
	(b)	.067	.067	.058	.081	.058	.058	.230	.381	1.000
A. B. G.	(a)	.067	.114	.060	.109	.042	.126	.265	.217	1.000
	(b)	.069	.118	.063	.105	.043	.128	.260	.24	1.000
N. G.	(a)	.111	.093	.111	.102	.100	.105	.275	.103	1.000
	(b)	.114	.089	.112	.101	.100	.102	.274	.108	1.000
N. H.	(a)	.065	.089	.100	.089	.109	.090	.248	.210	1.000
	(b)	.063	.090	.100	.090	.110	.088	.250	.209	1.000

(a) The ratios of the average length of each element, to the average length of the whole letter *v*.

(b) One of the eight percentages selected at random, the design being to demonstrate its efficiency in identification.

from the word ' via ' was studied. The average length of each element was found, and the ratio of this to the average length of the whole letter was computed. Each of the eight trials for six of the subjects chosen at random were thus treated. The results are given in Table IV., and they show that each of the six may be identified by the characteristics which appear in the single letter.

Variation:—Sixty-nine dots are required to write the message used. An operator wrote the message eight times. It is evident that the sixty-nine dots made in one writing of the message will vary, and also that each of the sixty-nine dots will vary in the eight successive writings thereof. To save circumlocutions, I shall call the first *heterotaxic* variation, and the second *homotaxic* variation. These two sorts of variation were studied in a variety of ways, covering all the material at disposal, and always with the same result. In order to make a sure, quantitative comparison between the two sorts of variation, it was decided to study eight dots, beginning with the first dot in the word ' via. ' Since the message was written eight times, this selection gave eight rows and eight columns, or sixty-eight dots in all, for each of the sixteen subjects. The homotaxic variation was computed as follows: The average, the mean variation $\left(\frac{\Sigma\nu}{n}\right)$, and the per cent. which the latter is of the former were computed for each of the eight columns. The average of these eight results is a measure of the homotaxic variation. The heterotaxic variation was found by two methods. First, the rows were treated in the same manner as that used in finding the homotaxic variation in the columns. Second, the average of each column was found, and then the per cent. of variation in these averages was computed. The reason for this procedure will be given below. Table V. shows the results obtained.

It is evident from the foregoing table that the homotaxic variation is an inverse measure of skill. In every day language, this simply means that an operator can repeat the same action more exactly the more expert he is.

The heterotaxic variation as given in column II. is a resultant of two factors. First, of course, the accidental variation

TABLE V.

OPERATOR.	AGE.	YEARS EXPERIENCE.	HOMO-TAXIC I.	HETERO-TAXIC II.	HETERO-TAXIC III.
C. G. MALLOTTE	22	2	.117	.120	.086
A. B. GUTHRIE	21	5–12	.112	.161	.150
G. E. FELLOWS	43	[1]5	.094	.097	.035
G. W. DYER	60	33	.078	.154	.150
NELLIE GREEN	24	5	.075	.156	.150
C. L. BUCHANAN	57	25	.070	.152	.130
L. A. CLARK	40	17	.062	.078	.053
NOBLE HARTER	37	21	.056	.171	.170
R. C. BROOKS	21	3	.052	.135	.120
Z. M. APPLE	24	5	.050	.090	.072
A. B. EVANS	27	10	.047	.170	.170
C. W. GOODMAN	32	15	.045	.104	.088
H. O. CHAPMAN	27	10	.045	.116	.083
G. H. GODFREY	55	31	.041	.120	.106
W. H. FOGG	26	10	.034	.192	.180
E. B. CASSELL	36	18	.027	.092	.075

enters here as everywhere. Second, the operator *does not intend* to make the same character exactly alike in successive positions. This intentional differentiation corresponds to inflection in speech. A study of Table II. or III. will show clearly these characteristic differences between a character in one position and the same character in a different position. By computing the heterotaxic variation by the second method described, we partially eliminate the element of accidental variation. A comparison of the variations given in columns II. and III. of Table V. shows that the amount of accidental variation thus eliminated is, as might be expected, smaller in the case of the expert men. If we take the results in column III., Table V. as the best attainable measure of variation due to intentional inflection, it appears that this is slightly greater in the more expert men than in the less expert. The average heterotaxic

[1] Has been out of business about 18 years.

variation of the first seven, or the less expert operators, as determined from column III. of Table V. is 106. The corresponding value for the last nine, the more expert men, is 118. The largest two values in the Table belong to two of the more expert men, and the smallest two belong to two of the less expert men.

In conclusion, therefore, it may be said that the accidental variation is a somewhat accurate inverse measure of skill, while the variation for inflection, is likely to be larger rather than smaller with increasing expertness.

Note on the accuracy with which the longer groups of clicks are made by telegraphic operators. A count of the results show in writing.

h (....) 5 errors out of possible 128.

v (...—) 10 " " " " "

q (..—.) 4 " " " " "

3 (...—.) 12 " " " " "

4 (...—) 17 " " " " "

p (.....) 56 " " " " "

6 (......) 91 " " " " "

In order to show the variations in writing the figure 6 (......), and that these variations are not primarily determined by the skill of the operator, the results for the several operators are given.

V. The Curves of Improvement in Receiving and Sending.

Throughout the year of exploration, operators were questioned closely with regard to the rate of improvement with practice at various periods. Operators generally agreed upon certain main facts. Upon the basis of this general inquiry and of his own personal experience as an operator and a teacher of telegraphy, H. drew the curves represented in Fig. II., Plate I. as a rough picture of the facts.

In further verification of the main characteristics of these curves over two hundred operators, ranging in skill from the

Operators.	Years Experience.	Present Position.	Av. No. of Dots in Writing 6.
C G M	2	Student	5.2
A B G	5-12	"	6.0
G E F	5	College Professor	5.6
G W D	33	Ry. Agent	9.2
N G	5	Ry. Operator	10.2
C L B	25	Ry. Agent	8.6
L A C	17	" "	6.1
N H	21	Teacher	7.5
R C B	3	Student	7.1
Z M A	5	W. U. Operator	6.0
A B E	10	" "	7.2
C W G	15	Dispatcher	6.1
H O C	10	"	7.7
G H G	31	Ry. Agent	12.2
W H F	10	Dispatcher	5.0
R B C	18	"	8.7

most expert to those just beginning, have been questioned and have given practically unanimous assent.[1]

For the purpose of gaining not only more, but more definite information, requests were sent to a number of schools of telegraphy. Blanks were sent to such schools with the request that the typical curves of improvement be plotted. In many cases, of course, no reply was received, and in some cases the advertising impulse was the evident inspiration of curves which represented their students as becoming skillful operators in a few months. The manager of Valentine's School of Telegraphy, Jonesville, Wis., wrote : " While I recognize the fact that every student undergoes the experience you have outlined in your letter, I hesitate to furnish you this information without first having systematically obtained it." Seven months later he sent the

[1] One skillful operator denied having experienced the period of non-advancement shown in the receiving curve before reaching the main-line rate. His associates in the office explained this exception as a lapse of memory due to vanity. Their incredulity illustrates the practical unanimity of opinion.

curves in Fig. III., Plate I., which are believed to be entirely reliable, as is also Fig. IV., Plate I. from the Commercial College of Kentucky.

Two schools where telegraphy is taught in Cincinnati were visited personally and arrangements made to have the progress of a representative student in each observed systematically. These results are given in Figs. V. and VI., Plate I. Arrangements were also made to have two reputable operators, well known to H., observe and test the progress of one student in each of their offices, from the time of beginning until proficiency was reached. These results are given in Figs. VII. and VIII., Plate I.

Finally H. was able, during the winter 95–96, to test the advancement of two learners from the beginning until they were both fair operators. Both were students in the Western Union Office at Brookville, Indiana. The operator, Mr. Balsley gave every assistance in his power to make the investigation successful. Will J. Reynolds, one of the students, is eighteen years old and is a young man of more than ordinary ability. Edyth L. Balsley, the other student, is seventeen years old and is a very bright young girl. The former began in August, the latter in September, 1895. The tests were made every Saturday. Forty tests were made with the young man and thirty-six with the young woman.

Ordinarily telegraphic speed is reckoned in terms of so many words per minute. For these tests, however, the letters were counted. Of course sentences were used in each test which had not been used before. Pains were taken to keep the tests of uniform difficulty. On the one hand, many short and easy combinations, and on the other hand, combinations representing unusual difficulty from a telegraphic point of view were avoided. Special pains were also taken to see that the amount of practice from week to week was substantially uniform.

The sending test was made as follows: The learner was directed to write as fast as he could do so, legibly. The observer copied the words as sent as a test of legibility. Some two-minute period was noted by the observer, unknown to learner, and the number of letters sent in that time was afterward

counted.   Several tests were taken and the results averaged.
The variation in the several tests was slight[1].   The receiving
test was made as follows: The observer would try a rate of
sending which he judged would correspond to the learner's
capacity.   The learner was required to name the letters, later
on the words, or, when he had more skill, to copy without naming them.   If he failed to interpret correctly at that rate, a
slower rate was tried.   If he succeeded, a more rapid rate was
tried.   A two-minute period was noted and the letters were
counted as above.

The results of this study are shown in Figs. IX. and X.[2]

Significance of the practice curves.   Certain main facts appear in all the foregoing curves:

1. The sending curve rises more rapidly and more uniformly than does the receiving curve from the beginning of
practice to the learner's maximum ability.

2. The receiving curve rises more slowly and irregularly.
All the results agree in showing a long, flat curve for several
months before the slowest main-line rate is reached; and all the
evidence before us indicates another long flat curve a little
above the rate necessary for the transaction of ordinary office
business, in the case of operators to whom that amount of skill
in receiving is sufficient.   A study of the quantitative results
shown in Figs. IX. and X. shows that there are many short flat
places in the receiving curve followed by relatively rapid improvement.

3. Two of the curves show a fact which usually appears at a
period of the learner's development later than that shown in
these curves, namely, that the receiving rate finally exceeds the
sending rate.   This is almost the universal rule.   A receiving
operator with a typewriter can practically take his ease in taking the most rapid press work.

[1] The M. V. ranged from .37% to 2.3% of the averages.
[1] It is believed that the progress of the learners was materially hastened by
their interest in the tests.   They were forewarned as to the slowness of progress
and they gave special attention to practice.   Both are now (June 1896) able to
transact ordinary business on the main line.   It may prove to be worth while
for certain purposes to study the curves of improvement with more accurate
methods and apparatus, but there can be no doubt that the method used gives a
highly accurate quantitative picture of these curves.

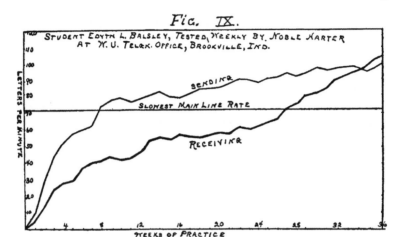

Fig. IX.

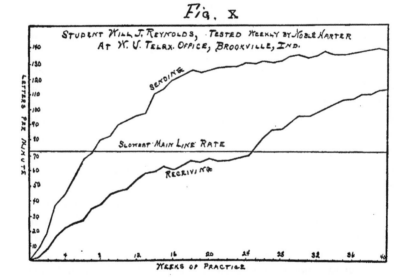

Fig. X.

4. In considering the reasons for the remarkable differences between the receiving and sending curves, the following points may be noticed: (a) The language which comes to the ear of the learner seems to him far more complex than the language which he has to write. When he wishes to *write* the letter *e*, he must have in mind only the making of one quick snap with his hand. When he *hears* the letter *e*, he hears two sounds,

the down stroke and the back stroke, and must take note of the time between them to distinguish the dot from the dash. If we take the more difficult combinations, as k ($—.—$), or j ($—.—.$), the greater complexity of the sound picture with its irregularly occurring back stroke is sufficiently evident. (b) The opportunity for practicing receiving at slow rates is evidently far less than for sending at such rates. It is always possible for the learner to do his slow best at sending, but he must depend upon others for a chance to receive at a rate within his capacity. It is of course true that he hears all that he himself sends, but it is a significant fact that the hearing of his own writing does not improve his power to receive in anything like the same degree that the hearing of other operators' writing does. As the curves show, young operators can, at a certain period, send with fair rapidity for a long period during which they cannot understand a single sentence on the main line. (c) A further significant fact is that learners *enjoy* the practice of sending, but feel practice in receiving to be painful and fatiguing drudgery. For this reason they naturally incline to practice sending a great deal, but must summon up all their resolutions to keep up the necessary practice in receiving. (d) A fact which seems to be highly significant is that years of daily practice in receiving at ordinary rates will not bring a man to his own maximum ability to receive. The proof of this fact is that men whose receiving curve has been upon a level for years frequently rise to a far higher rate when forced to do so in order to secure and hold a position requiring the higher skill. That daily practice in receiving will not assure improvement is further seen in the fact that in many cases inferior operators after being tolerated for years are finally dropped because they do not get far enough above the dead line. (e) One conclusion seems to stand out from all these facts more clearly than anything else, namely, that in learning to interpret the telegraphic language, *it is intense effort which educates*. This seems to be true throughout the whole length of the curve. Every step in advance seems to cost as much as the former. Indeed, each new step seems to cost more than the former. Inquiry at the telegraph schools and among operators indicates that between sixty and seventy-five per cent. of those who begin the study of telegraphy become discouraged upon the plateau of the curve just below the main-line rate. As a rule, ordinary operators will not make the painful effort necessary to become experts. Facts of an analogous character will be recalled from other fields.

The physiological, psychological and pedagogical implications of this conclusion are manifestly important. If in our educational methods in the past, we have often made the pace that kills, there is possibly the danger on the other hand that we shall make school work all play, and so eliminate the intense effort which is necessary for progress.[1]

5. The sending curve conforms approximately to the well-known typical practice curve with the important difference from the curves usually obtained in the laboratory that it extends over a much greater period of time. This difference characterizes the whole curve. If we represent the practice curve by the general equation

$$y = f(x)$$

it is evident that the function of x contains a constant which depends upon the unit of time. So for example, the curve given in the figure would present exactly the same appearance if the same results had been obtained in forty successive hours or forty successive years. Comparison of different practice curves shows that this time factor varies greatly in the development of different abilities. A comparative study of this charac-

---

[1] The conclusion here reached in matters of learning telegraphy recalls the opinion of Senator Stanford upon the training of race horses. In a letter to Horace Busbey (*Scribner's*, June, '96), Senator Stanford says:

"My own idea, and I think it is justified by experience, is to commence working the colt early, developing its strength with its growth. If the exercise is judicious, the colt takes no harm from it. I do not remember a single instance where an animal of mine was injured by early work. When a breakdown has occurred, it has been invariably after a let-up. Let-ups are very dangerous to young fast animals, as their bodies grow during the let-up without corresponding development of strength, and they are very liable to get too much work when their exercise is renewed. My aim is to give the greatest amount of exercise without fatigue, and never to allow it to reach the period of exhaustion. This is secured by short-distance exercise. It is the supreme effort tha develops. If colts are never over-worked they are always willing to try in thei exercise, having no apprehension that they will be forced beyond their comfort."

teristic of various practice curves would have evident theoretical
and practical values.

6. The receiving curve presents many profound interests
and difficulties. It is a quantitative study of apperception. It
represents with a high degree of accuracy the increasing power
which practice brings to interpret a language. The task of the
mind is not in every respect analogous to that involved in listening to foreign speech, for in the telegraphic language, after
a short time, every element is recognized by the learner if he is
given time, whereas in the foreign speech he may frequently
be disturbed by words that are entirely unknown. We have,
however, gained the impression, partly from personal experience
and partly from conversation with teachers of language and
others who have learned foreign languages, that the curve of
practice in learning a language must present at least great
general similarities to the receiving curves here shown. All
agree that just below the ability to understand what is spoken,
there is a long discouraging plateau where many give up in despair; that there is at last a sudden ascent into the ability to
understand most of what is said; finally that the perfect mastery of one at home in the language, comes much later and only
after very persistent work. Of those who undertake the study
of any foreign language, most stop on the first plateau below a
working proficiency; and of those who go on, most stop on the
second plateau, below complete mastery.[1]

7. What is the interpretation of the plateaus in the receiving
curve? For many weeks there is an improvement which the
student can feel sure of and which is proved by objective tests.
Then follows a long period when the student can feel no improvement, and when objective tests show little or none. At
the last end of the plateau the messages on the main line are,
according to the unanimous testimony of all who have experience in the matter, a senseless clatter to the student—practically as unintelligible as the same messages were months before.

[1] The President of the Cincinnati Business College, who prepared estimate
VI., says that the same general characteristics appear in the learning of shorthand. A director of primary work in a western city, after examining the receiving curve, expresses the opinion that it represents the progress of a child in
learning to read. This point will be made a subject of immediate investigation.

Suddenly, within a few days, the change comes, and the senseless clatter becomes intelligible speech.

In explanation of the form of the *motor* curve, one may suppose that it is an asymptotic approach to a physiological limit. In the receiving curve there is also something like an asymptotic approach to a limit; but that limit, whatever its nature, suddenly disappears. What it is that occurs during the period of sensible and measurable improvement, may be represented in various ways according to the standpoint from which the mind and mental growth are viewed. But in every case, one has to account for the great slowing down in the process of improvement. Stated otherwise, the task is to explain the nature of the changes in brain or mind which must be taking place, during the period represented by the plateau, and which yet make no determinable manifestation of themselves. That changes are taking place during this period, which are essential to the acquisition of proficiency, is proved by the fact that no one is able to omit this period.

8. As suggested above, it is probable that the curves which represent the acquisition of the telegraphic language also represent the main characteristics of the curves for many other acquisitions. This should, however, by no means be taken for granted. We should rather require of ourselves a thorough study of the actual curves of improvement for every ability which makes measurable manifestation of itself. The determination and comparative study of these curves would furnish one thing which is always a precious enlargement to any science—an outlay of problems which permit approach by systematic research and which promise results of far-reaching, theoretical and practical importance.

THE INFLUENCE OF INTELLECTUAL WORK ON THE BLOOD-PRESSURE IN MAN.[1]

BY MM. A. BINET AND N. VASCHIDE,

Paris.

I.

Physiologists measure the blood-pressure in animals by applying the monometer to an artery; the height to which the column of the monometer is raised by the blood furnishes the measure of the pressure. A measure of the pressure in man can only be made from the exterior, the methods employed by Vierordt,[2] Marey,[3] Kries, v. Basch, Mosso,[4] Bloch, etc., all consist in suppressing the pulse, or in arresting the circulation in an organ that is easily accessible, *e. g.*, the hand and fingers, and in measuring the minimal pressure necessary for this suppression.

It would evidently be of the greatest value to combine these pressure-results with those which are furnished by the form of the arterial pulse, and by changes of volume in the limbs, in order to determine precisely the influence of intellectual work and of the emotions on the circulation. The question, *e. g.*, whether in any case an active or passive vascular dilation occurs, can only be answered with certitude by the monometer.

We undertook this psychological study in the belief that no one, up to this time, has reached satisfactory results. There are, it is true, some scattered observations in medical journals, on the pressure of the blood during intellectual labor, but the pressure has been generally taken with defective apparatus. The only systematic work on the subject, at least to our knowl-

[1] Translated for the REVIEW from the author's manuscript.
[2] *Die Lehre von Arterienpuls. Braunschweig*, 1855.
[3] *Travaux du laboratoire*, 1876; p. 316,
[4] *Arch. ital. de Biologie*, 1895; p. 177. This work contains a short historical sketch, a discussion of the researches of Basch, and the description of a new apparatus.

edge, is that of Kiesow; we will indicate later on what criticisms should be made on his work. In short, the problem which we have set before ourselves has no history.

Our first care should be the choice of a good instrument to measure the blood-pressure in man. Clinicists frequently employ the sphygmometer of Bloch, more or less modified by Verdin and Chéron; this instrument resembles Cattell's algometer. It is a pressure-dynamometer which obstructs the pulsation of the radial artery; the experimenter interposes his finger between the artery of the subject and the instrument, and receives on his own finger the pressure of the instrument in such a way that with the finger he presses upon and obstructs the artery of the subject, and at the same time perceives the pulsation of the artery; the method consists in gradually increasing the pressure of the exploring finger until it no longer perceives the beating of the artery which it compresses. We did not make use of this instrument; for after having tried it for some time, we rejected it because it involved a subjective element of estimation. We gave the preference to Mosso's sphygmomanometer which has the advantage of indicating its results by tracings.

It is unnecessary to give a description of the numerous parts which make up the apparatus; this description may be found in the work of Mosso and also in the *Année Psychologique*.[1] We will content ourselves with indicating the principle. Two fingers of each hand are placed in rubber finger-tubes, and through these tubes are exposed to the pressure of water; this pressure is varied by means of a piston and measured by a mercury manometer, which registers at the same time the pulsations of the fingers. If we begin with o and increase gradually, we find a regular change in the amplitude of the pulsation; this is very small at first, grows and reaches a maximum, decreases again, aud finally disappears; thus the amplitude does not vary directly or inversely with the pressure; there is a most favorable degree of pressure, equal on the average to 80 mm. of mercury, at which the pulse attains its maximum amplitude; a weaker or stronger pressure have

[1] *Année Psychologique*, II., p. 584.

alike the effect of diminishing the pulse.   The question is how
to measure the blood-pressure with an instrument of this sort.

Marey's opinion was that we must take, as measure of the
blood-pressure, the counter-pressure necessary to obstruct and
suppress the pulse.   Mosso maintained, on the contrary, that it
is the most favorable pressure, about 80 mm. of mercury, which
is equal to the pressure in the arteries.   This disputed point is
of little importance.   What interests us as psychologists is not
the absolute value of the blood-pressure, but the change which
it undergoes by reason of mental processes; in relating our experiences we will have to examine the criteria of both Marey
and Mosso, and to determine which of the two answers best to
the special end which we have in view.

Technique.   It is necessary to give some practical details as
to the manipulation of Mosso's sphygmomanometer.   Two very
different methods may be employed together, since they supplement each other.   A. The first method consists in registering
the pulse with variations of pressure from 0 to 100 or 120 mm.
of mercury, either varying the pressure by sudden jumps, *e. g.*,
from 0 to 10, from 10 to 20, from 20 to 30, etc., or by slow
changes of pressure which are almost insensible.   The latter is
the method recommended by Mosso.[1]   It is very useful when
one wishes to compare the blood-pressure to different hours of
the day; it is necessary then to make the piston of the apparatus move from the minimal to the maximal pressure, in order
to determine the value of the most favorable pressure.   The
differences of blood-pressure at different hours of the day can
in this case be expressed in figures, an expression which is evidently the aim of all scientific research.

Here a parenthesis.   In measuring the pressure with
Mosso's sphygmomanometer, we must not take account of the
absolute amplitude of pulsation, but of the counter-pressure
necessary to give the pulsation its maximal amplitude.   This is
not at all the same thing.   Mosso gives an interesting example
which will make this distinction clear.[2]   One of his subjects,

---

[1] We found it practicable to make the piston revolve automatically with a
weight-motor.

[2] *Op. cit.*, p. 180 f.

Dr. Colombo, has his blood pressure taken in the normal state; the most favorable point of counter-pressure is at 80 mm., of mercury. Then the same subject takes a hot bath, and, on coming out of the bath, without dressing, has his pressure taken again. As a result of the bath the amplitude of pulsation was increased enormously, while the blood-pressure was diminished —it was then only 60 mm., of mercury—as was demonstrated by the most favorable degree of counter-pressure. Hence, he would have made a serious error if, on the basis of the enlargement of the pulse, he had inferred an increase of pressure. It is absolutely necessary to determine the most favorable counter-pressure in order to compute the pressure. This is the method with which it is necessary to begin.

But, on the other hand, this method entails great practical difficulties; we observed three: 1., it is slow, it requires a manipulation which lasts at least 1 to 3 minutes; 2., it produces very clear sensations in the fingers of the subject as the pressure is changed, and these sensations might disturb his attention in a manner prejudicial to the experiment; 3., it causes, by the changes of pressure, certain excitations which may produce reflex phenomena, such as vascular constrictions, in the fingers.

The first of these difficulties, the most serious, shows itself when we study the changes of pressure produced by a phenomenon which lasts only a short time; for example, the result of the concentration of the attention, of a mental calculation, or of a deep breath. Suppose we wish to know whether a mental calculation increases the blood-pressure or not, the time needed to take all the pressures from 0 to 120 is at least 1 to 3 minutes. Hence, it is necessary to see that the mental calculation lasts just so long, and that is not always easy. Moreover, the method can only indicate the blood-pressure at the moment when, by trial, we reach the most favorable counter-pressure. We do not know exactly what the pressure at the beginning of the intellectual labor was, nor how it changed during the progress of the experiment. All this shows that this method is insufficient. But such as it is we believe it to be indispensable, 1., to show whether the average pressure has increased or diminished, 2., to indicate in millimeters of mercury the value of the change of pressure.

In Kiesow's article on the effects of psychic excitations, studied by means of Mosso's Sphygmomanometer,[1] the author almost never employed this method ; he indicates it only once. He employed it on a Privat-Docent to study the blood-pressure after mental work, and noted a deviation of pressure equal to 8 mm.[2] But he does not give the tracing, and the experiment indicates only what occurred afterwards, and not what occurred during the mental work.

B. The second method, much the shorter and more convenient, consists in registering the pulsations with a constant pressure of the manometer, and then producing the mental work and other psychic phenomena studied, without changing the pressure of the manometer. Thus by the first method we change the pressure successively, in order to register the maximal amplitude of the pulsation, while by the second we leave the pressure constant, and observe simply the changes of amplitude of the pulsation which the mental operation produces. For example, we begin by registering the pulsation of the fingers under a pressure equal to 50 mm. of mercury ; then without touching the piston again, we ask the subject to make a mental calculation and observe whether there are any changes in the pulsation, the pressure remaining always at 50 mm. as before the calculation.

What is the advantage of this method? It will be seen at once : 1. We seize the first modification produced by the mental calculation, and all that occurs at the beginning, the middle, or the end of the process. 2. We do not distract the attention of the subject by changes of pressure in the fingers. 3. We do not produce reflex vaso-motor phenomena by changes of pressure.

But this method cannot inform us whether the pressure has changed or in which direction it has changed. It shows us merely—when it shows us anything at all—that the pulse has changed in amplitude. Now, it was mentioned above that the changes of amplitude in the pulse (the case of Dr. Columbo is an example of this), are not a constant sign of changes of pres

[1] *Arch. ital. de Biologie*, 1895, xxxiii, p. 198.
[2] *Op. cit.*; p. 207.

sure; hence it may be that when the pulse becomes stronger, the effect is due to a relaxation of the arteries, to a diminution of blood, or in any case to some cause other than an increase of pressure. Hence, before employing the second method we must employ the first, which shows with certainty whether any change of pressure occurs and in which direction it occurs. The first method gives the principle fact and the second the details. The two are complementary.

There remains one very important question: when the second method is employed, what pressure should be chosen as constant? There is a very simple way of determining it, *viz.*, to compare the two tracings of increasing pressures made, the one in the normal state, and the other during the phenomenon which we wish to study, such as mental calculation. The comparison of these two curves allows us to decide for what counter-pressure they differ most. If the maximal difference is, *e. g.*, at the counter-pressure of 120 mm. of mercury, it is that counter-pressure which we must choose for the method of constant pressure, since it is that which is most favorable for the differentiation of the two curves.

We must here make a criticism of Kiesow's work. This distinguished author has not determined the most favorable counter-pressure, and in his experiments with constant counter-pressure, he has always chosen the most favorable counter-pressure, that which gives the maximal amplitude of pulsation. We do not find in his work any justification of his choice. This choice, it must be admitted, is not the most fortunate, as is shown by numerous tracings (1 to 6) inserted in his work. In these tracings it is impossible to see whether the mental calculation has had any influence upon the blood-pressure, since the pulse-amplitude shows no change. It is possible that among the individuals whom he has studied, intellectual labor produced no effect upon the pressure. We cannot tell. But we believe it more probable that the negative result reached by Kiesow is due to the fact that he chooses as the constant pressure the most favorable pressure; for, on the one hand, the maximal difference between the two curves for rest and mental labor does not occur, according to our own experiments, at the most favorable counter-pressure; and, on the other hand, we observed constantly among the subjects in whom intellectual labor produced an increase of blood-pressure, that this effect is not noticeable when the most favorable pressure is taken as the constant pressure, but is most clearly noticeable when the strongest counter-pressure is used.   These considerations lead us to believe that Kiesow has committed a technical error, quite excusable indeed in an author who is not entirely familiar with the graphic method.

II.

Our experiments were made upon three subjects, but principally upon a young student of psychology, 23 years old, and in good health.   We will speak simply of the experiments made upon him.   Last year we made on him numerous experiments on the effect of mental labor on arterial circulation, and hence he is able to observe himself and concentrate his attention.   His pulse, compared with the others whom we examined, is weak, but his pulsation is well formed; when he makes a mental effort there occurs in him almost always a fine and quite radical vascular constriction, with a diminution in the size of the pulse-curve; then the vascular constriction disappears and the tracing returns to its normal level; this return to the normal may take place before the mental effort of calculation is completely finished, particularly if the subject has been given to solve a very complicated problem which requires much time.   There is, besides, during the calculation an acceleration of the heart and of respiration.   These experiments do not show whether intellectual work increases the blood-pressure.   The vascular constriction of the capillaries which we observed tends to relieve the pressure, as does also the acceleration of the heart, but since we do not know what the work of the heart, what its force was, during this time, we cannot say certainly that the pressure has increased.

The Sphygmomanometer relieved all doubt.   At the beginning, we employed the first method of experimentation, which consisted in taking the pulse under increasing pressure from 0 to 140 mm. of mercury; this test is made at first while the subject is in a state of rest without excitement or preoccupation

of any sort; then the same experiment is made while the subject is absorbed in a difficult mental calculation; in this way
two curves are obtained for comparison; the difference of the
two curves can be attributed to the intellectual labor unless some
. chance circumstance, as an emotion, a shiver, etc., prevents the
two experiences from being comparable. This double test was
made on our subject at five different times so that we obtained
ten curves which may be compared in pairs.[1] The change of
pressure from 0 to 140 mm. was made each time very slowly by
hand in an almost insensible manner, lasting almost always the
same length of time (two minutes and a half); the experimentor regulated the speed of his movement by means of a seconds
watch. The pulsations of the mercury column were not written
by means of a float on a revolving cylinder (Mosso's method),
but were transmitted by means of air pressure to a Marey tambour; a very small escape[2] attached to the transmission tube
prevented the pen from becoming displaced through the influence
of the sinking back of the column or mercury (produced by the
piston), so that the pen traced at approximately the same level
the pulsations of the column of mercury, although the latter
was at different heights, varying from 0 to 60 mm. We found
this arrangement much more advantageous than that of Mosso,
which gives the tracings in steps; by means of ours, one may
perceive more easily the gradual changes of amplitude.

The mental calculation was to last for about two or three
minutes: we did not give the subject a single calculation, because it would have to be very complex and very difficult to last
so long, and the subject, who had no special talent for this sort
of exercise, would have become confused and lost the figures;
and in the end, we should not have been able to get the strong
and concentrated attention which we wished to study. It seemed
better to give to the subject a series of easy multiplications; as
soon as he had finished one, he gave the answer and was immediately given a second, then a third. In general, during the
two or three minutes that the experiment lasted, the subject

---

[1] A much larger number of experiments have been made since these lines
were written.

[2] On the regulation of graphic tracings by means of an escape, see the
Année Psychologique, II., p. 776, 1896.

made three multiplications, each of two figures into two figures. As he was very much interested in the experiments, he always made a vigorous effort, as is shown by the correctness of the answers given. He closed his eyes, knit his brows, and leaned his head a little forward.

We measured exactly the amplitude of the pulse for the ten experiments: they were made at the same hour and under strictly comparable conditions.[1]

We subjoin the results in Table I.

TABLE I.—AMPLITUDE OF PULSE UNDER DIFFERENT PRESSURES DURING A STATE OF REST AND DURING INTELLECTUAL WORK.

Pressure.	Without Intellectual Work.					With Intellectual Work.					Average Without.	Average With.
	1	2	3	4	5	1	2	3	4	5		
20			0	0.5	1			0.5	0.5	0	0.5	0.5
30			0	1	1.5			0.5	0.5	0	1	0.5
40	1	0.5	0	2	2	0.5	1	1	1	0.5	1	1
50	1	0.5	0.5	2.5	3	0.5	1	1	1.5	0.5	1	1
60	1	1.5	1.5	4	5	1	1	1.2	1.5	1	1.5	1.2
70	2	2	2	3	4	1.5	2	3	3	1.5	2	2
80	2.5	2	5	5	5	2	3.5	4	4	2	5	3.5
90	2	2	3.5	4	4	2	1.5	3.5	3	2	3.5	2
100	1	1.3	2	2	0.5	2	0	4	3	2	1.3	2
110	0.5	1	0.5	1.5	0.5	1	0	2	1.5	1.5	0.5	1.5
120	0		0	0.5	0	0.5	0.5	1	0	0.5	0	0.5

Explanation of Table I. The five first vertical columns on the left indicate the amplitude of the pulse during five experiments in the normal state; the amplitude is measured in mm; we begin with an amplitude of 20 mm. of mercury, then 30, then 40, and so on up to 120. The five following vertical columns show the amplitude of the pulse during a series of mental calculations at all pressures from 20 to 120 mm. of mercury. Finally, the two last columns show the average[2] of the results

---

[1] The pressure varies with the hours of the day. We always made alternately the experiments of rest and intellectual work, in order to keep them in comparable conditions.

[2] We give, not the arithmetical mean, but the *median value*, as indicated by Scripture (PSYCHOLOGICAL REVIEW, II., 1895, p. 376, and *Année Psychologique*, I., 1894).

obtained from the experiments in the normal state and during intellectual work respectively.

Let us look for a moment at the left side of the Table (I), containing the results of individual experiments. We are struck with the irregularity of certain series of figures. The amplitude of the pulse does not increase regularly up to the most favorable counter-pressure and then regularly decrease. In experiments 4 and 5 in the normal state, *e. g.*, the figures make several quite unexpected jumps. This is due to the fact that the subject is not an automaton; he has had during the experiment vascular constrictions and changes of blood-pressure which have changed the trend of the curve. Similarly in experiment 2, during intellectual labor the subject has had suddenly near the end of the curve at a counter-pressure of 100, a reflex vascular constriction caused by a rather strong emotion (he noticed that he had given a wrong answer to the problem set). These experiments show that we must multiply the experiments and only preserve the average results, in order to eliminate the sources of error.

Let us now compare the averages from the last two columns of Table I. The differences are evident. First, the curve of pressures of the state of rest has a greater amplitude than that of intellectual work; the maximum amplitude of pulsations in the first curve is 5 mm., that of the second is only 3.5 mm. There has evidently occurred in our subject during all the mental calculation, a diminution of the pulse which results from a vascular constriction that is more or less marked. The position of the maximum point in the two curves is about the same, at 80 mm. of mercury, and, if this fact alone were taken into consideration, we might conclude that the blood-pressure was not modified; but we must hasten to add that when the pressure was increased beyond 80 mm. the two curves acted very differently. The pressure curve for the normal state decreased rapidly; at 100, it fell to 1.3 mm., and at 110 it was practically suppressed; on the other hand, the pressure curve for mental work withstands the stronger pressures more vigorously, notably pressures from 100 to 120. In short, here are two cases which coincide in their maximum, but which differ very much in their resistance to strong pressure. We think that this resistance must be taken into consideration; when one pulse withstands a counter-pressure of 120 and still records, while another pulsation of the same amplitude is checked by this counter-pressure, we must recognize that the former pulsation corresponds to a stronger arterial tension. We are thus led to set aside Mosso's criterion in this particular case, and to accept that of Marey.

The tracings which we have obtained, together with our numerical results show clearly the essential difference between the two pressure-curves.

In determining the complexity of this phenomenon, be it understood, it would be difficult to take account of it with a clinical sphygmometer of Bloch's type, a method which consists in obstructing the radial artery until the finger inserted between the syhygmometer and the radial no longer perceives the beatings of the latter. The experimenter would have to be very skillful in taking exact account of the constriction produced by intellectual work, which decreases the amplitude of the pulsation, and to perceive that in spite of this diminution, which ought to give to the exploring finger a new sensation, the pulsation has greater resistance.[1]

III.

From what precedes, we conclude that, with our subject, a pressure of from 100 to 120 completely suppresses the pulsation of a state of repose as also that of a state of intellectual labor. This observation will help to guide us in the second series of researches, where we will employ a constant pressure; it is clear that to make apparent the difference between the circulation in a state of intellectual labor and that of rest, it is this counter-pressure of from 100 to 120 which must be chosen.

In order to remove all doubts we have made a counter-test in the following manner: Seven times in succession our subject made a mental calculation having his fingers subjected to a constant pressure, and each time the pressure chosen was different; the results also were very different. With a constant pressure of 40 mm., there was no modification produced by the

---

[1]Féré, who made some use of the sphygmometer, noticed that when the artery contracted, *e. g.*, under the influence of cold, the apparatus gave only erroneous indications (*Pathologie des émotions*, p. 14,, note).

fact of mental work; with a pressure of 60, the same negative result; with a pressure of 70 mm. there was a slight augmentation of pulsation; at 80 mm., there was again a slight augmentation, not measurable, but visible to the eye; at 100 to 120 the augmentation is very clear; it varies from simple to double; at 140, all pulsation was suppressed. This shows us very well that the constant pressure chosen ought to lie between 100 and 120. These experiments are a confirmation of those made before: they show anew that if we choose the most favorable counter-pressure, we may obtain results which are as completely negative as those of Kiesow are.

Now let us take a counter-pressure of 110. We first register the pulse with this pressure for about a half minute, then tell the subject to commence a mental calculation. While he is absorbed in his work we watch the pressure with care; for when we give a heavy pressure with the Sphygmomanometer, it tends to diminish; and in order to keep it equal, it is necessary to give a stroke with the piston from time to time. This slight correction ought to be made very gently, so that the subject does not experience any new sensation in his fingers, and does not perceive anything. Excepting this slight cause of error, for which we ought to watch, this method of experiment is much easier than the preceding; one does not disturb the person in the experiment, and, moreover, the change of pressure in the hand is seen in the tracing as soon as it is produced. The experiment carries with it a kind of sensible evidence; as soon as the mental calculation begins, there is an increase in the pulsation.

This experiment was made 11 times upon our subject, always with analogous results. We gave him multiplications of two figures by two figures, and immediately he began the operation in his head. The first three or four pulsations which register themselves are usually of the same character as the preceding, sometimes they are slightly shortened, an effect which is probably due to the vascular constriction which is habitual with this subject at the beginning of intellectual work. Then the pulsation increases, it doubles in size, or becomes twice and often three times as great. This increase in amplitude maintains itself, in general without increase or diminution, and with great regularity during the whole of the mental calculation; when the subject has found the solution and has given it, there is no sudden diminution of pulsation; it may retain its amplitude without change for 15 seconds, sometimes even longer; then the pulsation begins to diminish very gradually; finally it recovers the same amplitude that it had at the beginning of the mental calculation. This return to the original condition is a very significant fact for us, since it shows that the change in amplitude of the pulsation is not due to the apparatus, but to the physiological condition of the subject.[1]

A. BINET.

[1] This is part of a more general study which I am making on the physiological expression of thought, including also my experiments with M. Courtier on capillary circulation and respiration. Some of the results will appear in April, 1897, in the third *Année Psychologique.*

DISCUSSION AND REPORTS.

LANGUAGE AND IMAGE.

With reference to the understanding general concrete terms, like telephone, tree, things, etc., it would be a very natural supposition that it would only be done by imaging. Indeed, what else is or can be the knowing the meaning of words for sensible objects other than a connecting word with image? and the better the word is understood would there not be the more definite imaging? The natural supposition is that the whole function of a vocal sign of a sensible is to call up that sensible as individual or group to the mind, *i. e.*, the production of an image, and that if a word signifies a thing or things it can only do this through image.

However this very natural idea that the understanding of a sense word must be through sense, seems hardly borne out in practice. Did the reader who understood the first sentence of this paper have any imaging when he came to the words 'telephone, tree, thing?' And does he not understand this last without image? A little reflection assures you of no trace of image, and yet you read the sentence with perfect understanding. By far the great majority of readers at least will find this the result of their introspection. And further it will be said that the better the word is understood the less imaging is required till at length there seems to be none at all. The man who is perfectly familiar with the telephone, both the word and thing, does not need to image as does the farmer's boy on hearing the word. And this appears to be true of both common and proper names. Most men on hearing the very familiar name of a near relative as in casually saying ' my wife,' ' my son,' form no image, but on hearing name of some one whom they have seen but once or twice the understanding of the word implies very definite image. Thus if some one asks, ' is your wife here?' and another, ' is Mr. Penn here?' (an acquaintance seen but once) you answer understandingly at once in the first instance without definitely imaging, but not so in the later case. Hence we have the paradox that apprehension of sense meanings is most perfect when senseless.

The interesting problem of how we understand the meaning of ob-

67

ject names without conscious object-reference is certainly not solved by Mr. Stout's remark that 'imageless apprehension' merely is 'the power to distinguish the apprehended object from other objects,' though 'the constituent parts of the object cease to be discernible.' (Analytic Psychology I., p. 84.)   But this surely is not real imageless apprehension, but only the last stage in the imaging apprehension, that is, when we need but one distinctive mark in referring the word to the thing.   Here the image is reduced to a single element, but is as real an image as ever.   But it is obvious to an ordinary reflection that in common conversation and reading we are continually understanding words, and yet not having, so far as we can see, even a trace of image of mere distinctive mark or generic aspect.

But I think the best clue to the mental process in understanding sense words without apparent imaging is given by a study of cognitive process as a whole, by comparing the understanding meaning of a word with the understanding meaning of a thing.   All knowledge of objects is interpretation, is a getting at meaning, and all objects as known are thus signs, and in a large sense constitute a language.   In knowing what a telegraph instrument is when I see it I am aware of its significance, as contrasted with a Hottentot, to whom the object would have no more meaning than the English words designating it. And the interpreting becomes easier with successive experiences of the same things until they are at length known without any interpretation being consciously applied.   Every time I see a chair I know it to be such, though I do not consciously image it in its use as a chair.   I have learned to know it so easily and quickly that the knowing act becomes unself-conscious and so unrememberable, but continues as real act, for it is evident that in the most casual notice of a chair one really appreciates it for what it is.   When you go into a drawing room you will both know the chairs and sit down in them quite mechanically, though if you see some strange piece of furniture, which you have to identify as chair, then there is self-conscious identifying interpreting process which is rememberable knowing.

Now the knowing meaning of a word and thing are quite parallel activities; indeed, word is really kind of thing.   If a very common thing like chair becomes so well known as to be subconsciously known, we might expect the same of its name.   And in fact, let the reader reflect on his understanding of the previous sentences where this word chair occurred, and he will hardly find in any case that he has been conscious of any imaging process and yet he is sure he understood the meaning.   The name chair has, through practice, become so familiar and the process has been made so quick, easy, and abbreviated as not to be in the least intruded on self-consciousness. In general we suspect that the objects which are subconsciously known will have names subconsciously known, that the imaging interpretation is in both cases carried on, though not rememberable. The law of habit, that we get to doing acts so well we are not aware of acting, applies in both the knowing things and names; and the general results of common knowing seems to confirm this. This habit theory is plainly quite different from Hobbes' theory of habit and understanding.

Of course, in the nature of the case, we cannot get direct proof of unrememberable mental process. Yet an illustration of the effect of habit upon knowing is seen in the perception of distance, which we have learned so well in early life by a real judging, which later becomes unself-conscious process; and hence the ordinary theory of space perception is intuitional. Again, another illustration is in reading as a very rapid subconscious spelling, and in thinking as unself-conscious mental pronouncing of words. The poor reader consciously spells, the better reader takes in the spelling of the word and cognizes it at a glance, and is unconscious of any process, and the very best reader grasps by sentences and is unconscious of either letters or words as such. Similarly the poor thinker talks aloud or moves his lips, the practiced thinker only mentally pronounces, and the best thinker is unconscious of using any words. Yet it is undoubted that thought, which has once thoroughly learned words as its instrument, never after becomes really wordless. Thought by means of words cannot get beyond words.

A more direct evidence of subconscious process than these analogies is this: that we sometimes come upon a very common word whose meaning we have to definitely search for, and we rummage our collection of images till we find the right one, and the old faculty is reëstablished. By a constant imaging of thing for word and word for thing, a perfect coördination is formed which is carried on in an under-consciousness—that is a consciousness of which we are not and do not need to be conscious. Again, an evidence of subconscious imaging in understanding meaning is this: that when we have read understandingly several sentences of general sense terms without being conscious of imaging, but are then asked to state the substance in our own words, we immediately begin to marshal the images which we did not directly connect with the words, but which we yet seemed in some way to have had.

Practice, of course, tends to abbreviate the image, and we become satisfied to only partially realize meaning with a dim sense of an indefinite realizability, which for practical purposes we do not need to carry out. There is generally felt to be a great potentiality in the word which we do not stop to measure. When we are told that it is a thousand miles from New York to Chicago, we may understand well enough with a *minimum* of realization, but which we know at the time can be indefinitely increased. A word is a machine which easily moves an unimagined, yet imaginable mass of images and ideas, and it is the very office of words to give us the practical manipulation of these masses without recourse to any but the most general imaging reference, and that often subconscious, yet with a constant sense of unrealized but realizable potentiality.

In helping us to realize the hidden image force, our main reliance is in poetry, which may be defined as the art of using words in such a way as to awaken image to full life. Poetry partly accomplishes this by a special vocabulary of its own, and partly through the dextrous throwing of the word into a new and more striking position, as by inversion, metre or rhyme, or mentally by a trope, and so leading the mind to image.

Poetry revivifies language by bringing out the latent image or inserting a new one. Take Tennyson's expression, ' The rainy Hyades vext the dim sea.' Here each word in itself may evoke no image, but the combination and the figurative use call up a most vivid image, and that vast reach of the imaginable wherein poetry chiefly lies. Even a bare connective, as ' and,' has its latent image evolved when used emphatically, as in the line :

' With rocks, and stones, and trees,'

where a dim visual ' more' is evoked. If the poet uses only the common words of prosaic life, as did Wordsworth, he must have great skill to attain the imaginative effect, and the more common the word the harder it is to give it sensuous force.

We have thus far remarked only upon the understanding of the meaning of the concrete terms, more or less general, but language is plainly more than notation of sensibles. Some words, like ' signify,' ' idea,' for instance, are purely intellectual words, and any infusion of image but distorts the meaning. And many words also relate rather to pain, pleasure and emotion than to the sensible in any form, and must thus be understood. In fact, the first expressive vocal utterance was doubtless a cry of pain, animals otherwise dumb giving in great pain a squeak, which of itself conveys no sensuous image. Primitive language is not a name, but a cry. We know immediately what is meant upon hearing a cry, because it awakens in us some of the painfulness for which it stands. One to whom pain was wholly unknown would be as unable to interpret a pain note as a blind man to interpret the words red, white and blue. It is very probable also that what we take to be vocal signals indicating food are, with the very lowest animals, at least, only signs of eating pleasure, and so do not convey real image of object as food. The eating act, as is evident from observation of very young infants, is carried on at first with little or no consciousness of what is eaten. It might even be maintained that animal language is never properly denominative, and only with the higher species does it become even indirectly denominative. Mere emotion words, like joy, sorrow, hate, etc., are also plainly understood without sense image. Nothing is really imagined, no real objective reference is really made, but the words in their isolation are understood wholly by subjective realization. In some very slight measure the understanding of all pain words gives pain and all pleasure gives pleasure, that is, in revival, just as the knowing the meaning of sense words implies revived sense—that is, image. In understanding meaning of the words joy, sorrow, you experience at least a faint joy and sorrow.

We conclude then that language, as an indicator, can only indicate by suggesting to our consciousness what is indicated, as object, thought or feeling, even in most summary and unself-conscious form to which it is brought by practice, and from which it may be rescued by poetic art to its primitive vividness.   HIRAM M. STANLEY.

LAKE FOREST, ILLINOIS.

UPRIGHT VISION.

Dr. Stratton's paper in the last number of the PSYCHOLOGICAL REVIEW on 'Vision without Inversion of the Retinal Image' calls for some criticism. The first sentence in it shows that he means to discuss the problem of upright vision, and in the same paragraph he announces his purpose to examine the projection and ocular movement theories of this phenomenon. But the course of his experiments and arguments shows, not only that he had no right to talk about upright *vision* in this connection, but that he has not even understood his own problem. Nor does he in reality discuss the two theories mentioned, much less throw any light upon them.

His phrase ' vision without inversion of the retinal image,' especially when taken with the first sentence, where ' upright vision ' is mentioned as the problem, is the main source or evidence of his confusion, as it shows with the later experiments that he has not distinguished between visual perception and tactual or motor adjustment to visual perception. The problem in upright *vision* is to determine how we see objects in a certain way when the image on the retina is inverted. This problem remains the same throughout all of Dr. Stratton's experiments. This is noticeable in the very statements he makes about the effect of the glasses upon what is seen. He concedes the inverse relation between image and apparent object after the glasses are put on, but does not see that this is only a reproduction of the normal relation, and that in so far as *vision* is concerned there is nothing anomalous in the effect. But instead of discussing this question, or getting true upright vision after inverting the normal image, he goes on to study the influence of experience upon motor (not ocular) adjustment to these new conditions and the influence of memory images upon our notion of uprightness. Very well. But this is not a problem in upright *vision* at all. It is merely a problem as to the influence of memory and association upon muscular adjustments, and these *not* ocular movements at that. Dr. Stratton has not analyzed his problem in the least, and his whole discussion will only lead the unwary to think that he has shown the effect of experience, muscular experience and adjustment upon the *ocular* perception of uprightness, when the very fact that he concedes the inversion of the apparent object under the glasses proves that the visual process is as before and is not affected by the foreign factors of either memory or touch. His attempt, whether implicitly or explicitly avowed, is to show that inversion of the retinal image is not necessary to upright vision, but all that he actually shows is that this inversion is not necessary to correct tactual and muscular adjustment and the formation of new judgments for motor movements. That is to say he only shows that we have to invert the memory images at first by an effort of will in order to secure correct movements, and then experience establishes a line of spontaneous connections as prompt as the old ones. But this is no more the problem of upright *vision* than it is one of upright audition. Hence to talk about the projection and ocular movement theories in this connection is simple nonsense, if I may be allowed to use such severe language, and only betrays a misconception and misrepresentation of the problem.

When Dr. Stratton talks about ' vision without inversion of retinal images,' and then discusses motor and tactual adjustments, he ought to have seen either that he was not talking about vision at all, or that the phrase 'without inversion of retinal images' was an equivocal one and leads to complete confusion. It might mean 'without inversion' in relation to the *real* object, which after all is not seen at all, or 'without inversion' in relation to the *apparent* object, which is described by Dr. Stratton himself as representing in fact the inverse relation of normal vision. There is no anomaly in the latter case, which only shows that he does not mean to assert the absence of inversion between retinal images and the apparent objects under the conditions described. Here the visual problem is not altered, but taking the phrase in the first sense, 'without inversion' in relation to the real object (which is not *seen*), the problem is tactual and motor. If at any time he could show an instance of a symmetrical and not an inverse relation between retinal images and real or apparent objects, he might reasonably enough imply or assert that upright vision with inverted images is not an organic but an empirical process. Until he does this, such experiments as he describes in his paper are irrelevant to the problem.   JAMES H. HYSLOP.

COLUMBIA UNIVERSITY.

PSYCHOLOGICAL LITERATURE.

History of Philosophy. ALFRED WEBER, Professor in the Univer
sity of Strasburg. Authorized translation by FRANK THILLY.
from the fifth French Edition. New York, Scribner's, 1896.
Pp. xi + 640. $2.50.

One need not hesitate to pronounce this the best history of philosophy for use as a text-book, and for the purposes of the general
reader. In translating it, Professor Thilly has rendered a not less valuable service than in his translation of Paulsen's *Introduction to Philosophy*.

Professor Weber has an admirable faculty of exposition. He knows
how to select out of a mass of details the points most suitable to his
purpose, and to present them in a lucid, graphic, and interesting way.
His work is less suggestive and original than that of Windelband, but
has the advantage over it of a much more simple and natural method.
He is less detailed in his discussion of systems than Falckenberg, but
the latter treats only the modern period, while the entire development
of philosophy, from the beginning of Greek speculation to the present
time, is brought within the six hundred pages of this volume. The
sense of proportion is, in the main, good, though Greek philosophy
receives less than its due share of attention, being allotted scarcely
more than one-quarter of the space. Too much can hardly be said
in commendation of the literary skill which handles the vast body of
materials, with which a general history of philosophy has to deal, in
such a way that one without previous knowledge of the subject need
have no difficulty in following the narrative with pleasure.

It may be questioned whether the two-fold division, 'the Age of
Metaphysics' and ' the Age of Criticism,' under which both ancient
and modern philosophy are treated, is best adapted to exhibit the relations of the history. The movement of thought may naturally be
conceived as three-fold: first a period of construction or interpretation, then a reaction of sceptical reflection, and then a restatement, in
more systematic form and from a more comprehensive point of view—
this restatement becoming, in turn, the subject of critical analysis, followed by fresh attempts at construction. Windelband recognizes
these stadia in his distribution of the philosophy of Greece proper

into the ' Cosmological,' 'Anthropological ' and ' Systematic ' periods, and in his treatment of the post-Aristotelian, or ' Hellenistic-Roman,' period as one of revolt or decline, and also—largely because of the religious elements in Stoicism and Neo-Platonism—one of positive constructive activity. This is a more discriminating and helpful outlining of the subject than one which includes, in a summary and heterogeneous way, the whole body of thought, from Protagoras to Proclus, under a single rubric. The parallelism between ancient and modern thought is brought out very clearly when we consider each as following this law of development, but the affinities and analogies between the two are obscured when after Descartes, Spinoza, and Leibnitz, regarded as constituting the ' Age of Metaphysics,' we find all other philosophers, from Locke to Spencer, enumerated under the ' Age of Criticism.'

It is hardly just to complain of omissions rendered necessary by the plan of the work. It is, however, of interest to observe that some aspects of the subject are treated more fully than others. The relation between philosophy and science is accorded a good deal of prominence, the speculative bearings of the theory of evolution, in particular, forming the subject of one of the most interesting sections of the book. On the other hand, the relation between philosophy and theology is passed over lightly. Little or no mention is made of the English Deism, the German Illumination, Hume's *Natural History of Religion* and *Dialogues*, the Kantian theory of religion. The effects within the domain of dogmatic and critical theology of Hegel's philosophy of religion are very imperfectly indicated. The highly important philosophic theologian, Schleiermacher, is disposed of in a single sentence. A noticeable omission is that of the series of English writers upon ethics following Hobbes. Political philosophy receives little attention; in speaking of Hobbes, Spinoza, and Locke, their ideas in regard to the origin and nature of the state are not noted; Grotius is not mentioned, or Montesquieu, or Rousseau. The sketch of contemporary philosophy dismisses so influential a name as that of Lotze with a bare mention. These *lacunæ*, however, and others that might be enumerated, are not properly occasion of complaint. It should be said that the footnotes make up, to a considerable extent, for the omissions of the text, since they furnish, in the case of all important authors, sufficiently full bibliographical references. The translator has added much to the bibliography and has contributed an index.

A feature of this work which renders it particularly suitable as an introduction to the subject is the appreciative and positive temper in

which it is written. A historian of philosophy who conceives it to be his function to convict every great thinker of as many errors and inconsistencies as possible is as gravely at fault as the literary critic who occupies himself only with the faults of his author. The discovery of truth and beauty to those who are liable to overlook them is a far more valuable service than the mere exposure of their opposites. Every one who has observed the painful sense of disappointment which is so often the first result of a study of the great speculative systems will appreciate the wisdom of such a treatment of the subject as is indicated in remarks like this: "To the argument (page 594) drawn from the perpetual disagreement of philosophers, we answer that the historian of metaphysics is most impressed with the open or tacit agreement existing between the rival movements and schools. We have discovered such agreement between Plato and Democritus, Descartes and Bacon, Leibnitz and Schopenhauer, Herbart and Hegel." Instead of emphasizing weaknesses, inconsistencies, and disagreements, Professor Weber seeks to exhibit the points of contact between different systems, the elements of truth held by them in common. This is the most effectual way of securing the inexperienced student against the bewilderment and sense of futility which are so apt to overcome him. It is not a defect, but an important merit, of a work which has in view the needs of novices, that it should announce a definite philosophic doctrine. The reader who has patiently followed the long way which European philosophy has traversed may well be reminded at the end that his journey has not been purposeless. A constructive chapter, like that which concludes this volume, is valuable and wholesome, irrespective of the intrinsic merit of its reasonings, as an example of the spirit in which one should study philosophy, and of the fruits one may hope to gather from it.   E. GRIFFIN.
JOHNS HOPKINS UNIVERSITY.

The Power of Thought: What It Is and What It Does. By JOHN DOUGLASS STERRETT. With an introduction by J. MARK BALDWIN. New York, Scribner's, 1896. Pp. xiv + 320.

Introductions by better known men for books written by those who are less known are not *à priori* commendable. As a general rule books had better speak for themselves. That there are justifiable exceptions, however, Baldwin's judgment shows in the present case. For here is a book admirable in many respects, but with a title calculated to make it *caviare* to the very people who alone might be expected to read it. Those whom at first sight the title would 'catch' are again the very ones who would never have the mental patience and courage to read the book through. But if neither the public nor the specially interested read it, it 'falls between two stools.' The association of Baldwin's name will draw the attention of the latter class.

The book is, as I have said, in many respects admirable; it is thoughtful, well-informed and independent in the true sense. There is, too, for the most part, a certain naïve charm about the author's style and his way of putting things. But in spite of this, there is much that is uncouth and barbarous in expression scattered through these three hundred pages—much that is more forbidding than the technicalities of the professional psychologist. After all, when one is writing on science it is hard to avoid technical terms. Those who will read Sterrett's book would read it with more satisfaction if there were a more precise and exacting terminology. The last issue of this RE-VIEW puts the pertinent question: "If one is to traverse a desert, why not ride a camel?" This, to the reviewer's mind, is a fault of the book, causing the author, despite what he says in his preface, to be often diffuse and at times tiresome. Moreover, why wrest from technical terms their customary meaning? Why, to take one instance, keep on talking about physical sensations? "A sensation is but a physical impression in the sensorium, not an idea, not knowledge, not consciousness" (p. 37). For this meaning see also pp. 21, 23, 26, 28, 29, 48, 50, 51, 52, 57, 64, 80, 82, etc. Is it not surprising, then, in the face of all these references, to find the following language on p. 67: "Here, then, is something that touches its soul with a sensation, or a feeling." Are sensation and feeling, then, in any sense equivalents? If they are we are compelled, in trying to harmonize pp. 37 and 67, to consider feeling, too, as physical and extra-conscious! But perhaps the author will say that the context shows that sensation and feeling are not intended as equivalents. Why, then, did he not write *and* instead of *or?* We read again, on p. 191: "And I affirm that the tone and stress of sensation is as much set up genetically by mind as by the exterior potency." Is this not implying that sensation is a conscious as well as a physical perturbation? Can one read such passages without a sense of dumb dismay at this playing fast and loose with terms which ought to have something like a definite meaning?

Notwithstanding, many such defects in execution, Sterrett's general purpose is praiseworthy. His main thesis that mind or thought is power (his popular way of expressing the psychologist's 'mental dynamogenesis'), is worked out from the beginning to the end of the book, with a concentrated and yet comprehensive purpose which ought to prove suggestive to the specialists themselves. This note is sounded in the very first sentence of the first chapter. "To be a free agent man must have the ability to achieve his freedom." And the underlying aim of all the chapters seems to be to prove that he has this ability. No stone is left unturned in the attempted proof of this. It is made plain to the author's mind by a true reading of the conscious life of our sub-human brothers; it is worked out again in an ingenious bit of genetic psychology, where the beginning and organic development of the child's powers are the object of analysis and interpretation; and it finds its final corroboration in the normal life of the mature man.

The most impressive parts of the book to those who are more philosophically than psychologically inclined will be the chapters in which the analysis brings us to close quarters with 'free will.' However, familiar the reader may be with the ins and outs of this question, he will here find much that is instructive. The more fundamental issues are dissected out of the body of the question and stated with a clearness hard to find rivaled. See, for example, Part I., Chap. IV: Mind and Brain, and Part IV., Chap. XIX. and XX. In Chap. IV. are to be found some of what Baldwin calls in his introduction, 'points of view * * * * of the latest scientific investigators.' The reading of it calls to mind at once the names of Romanes, James, S. Hodgson and Baldwin. (See Baldwin on ' Consciousness and Evolution ' in the May, '95, number of this REVIEW.) What the author says about motives is also worthy of special mention—his interpretation reminding one strongly of passages in Green, James and Baldwin. The conflict of motives is not a conflict between separate ideas, each with a distinct activity of its own, and exploding its own gun to compel submission from the others. Such a conception is as imaginary as that ' chimæra bombinans in vacuo '—the freedom of indifference. A motive has no independent existence and means nothing if it is not ' a name for a partial expression of the nature of the agent. ' Very similar, too, to Baldwin's and Hodgson's is his description of the process through which an end passes into volition.

But in spite of all this, which one may cordially applaud, there are occasional lapses from philosophic grace. For example, one fails to feel the force of his method of appeal to 'facts at first hand' (pp. 258 and 260). The writing here is below the author's standard; he seems to be regarding facts as if they were stones to be picked up by the mere reaching out of a hand. What is a fact ? Why did Sir

John Herschel say that there were more false facts than false theories in the world ? Would not a little idealistic analysis do this kind of realistic appeal a great deal of good ! Besides, doesn't the author know the literature on the distinction between ' the sense of freedom ' and ' the fact of freedom ? ' Has he never read Martineau, Hodgson, Chalmers and Mill ! Or, does he ignore them ? Outside of this and a few other lapses, these chapters on freedom are suggestive and convincing.

The book as a whole teaches well the lesson "that we know it" (the world) "not with, as it were, a quasi-detachable intellect only, but with our whole living energy; that we know in so far as we act, nay, that ultimately, only as we will, as we put forth activity, as we act, can we claim fully to be. " (Introduction to Croom Robertson's General Philosophy.) ROGER BRUCE JOHNSON.
MIAMI UNIVERSITY.

The School of Plato. F. W. BUSSELL. New York, Macmillan & Co. 1896.

The author of this book shows unusual insight into the spiritual forces that were at work in that movement of Greek speculative thought, in which Platonism stands central. His aim is to interpret the movement from a special point of view. The title of the book is justified by the discussion as a whole. The author fears in his preface that he may be charged with superficiality and tiresome iteration. He is not open to either charge, though, as to the first, a few more details in places would have been acceptable. He finds his starting point and criterion of interpretation in a study of the philosophical and religious movements of the Roman imperial period, which had their rise in the mingling together of the elements of Greek, Jewish and Oriental culture. These movements profoundly influenced and were in a sense absorbed by Christianity, with which they came in contact. In the union of intellectual and mystical elements, in the current of speculation, and in the aim of the period which was a search for the blessed life, the author sees the true method and end of all philosophy.

The central motive of philosophy, according to Dr. Bussell, is individualism; the self-assertion of the free spirit of man against the universal, whether in the form of nature or society. With this idea in mind the author follows the stream of Greek speculation from its source. His thesis is the rebellion of the individual; his uprising against an environment that seeks to crush him, or, at least, to rob him of his freedom and make him a slave of the universal. The beginning of speculation is the awakening of the individual, and the stages of the Greek movement mark the individual spirit's struggle against nature and society, and, in the later theosophic stages, against an absolute which threatened to swallow up the individual life. According to the author, the supreme end of philosophy is practical, the establishment of a *modus vivendi* by which happiness may be secured. The theoretical and logical are subordinate therefore to the practical and moral.

The author finds the highest organ of philosophy in Platonism, in which the process of knowing is supplemented by mystical intuition. The processes of knowledge are inadequate, and here the author is somewhat agnostic; knowing breaks down or falls at the threshold, and recourse must be had to feeling in order to attain the highest truth. It is through this union of thought and feeling that Platonism obtains its grasp on the truths of religion and the immortality of the soul. The author shows, and this is the most interesting feature of the book, how in the later period the final solution of the problem of philosophy in the ancient world was reached by the reassertion in Neo-Platonism of this Platonic synthesis of thought and mystical intuition.

Throughout the theosophic period, and, in truth, since Aristotle, the pendulum of speculation had swung between the extremes of an immanent naturalism which merged God in the course of the world and a transcendent absolution which removed him beyond the pale of conceivability. Neo-Platonism finds its solution of this problem, and the final one of ancient thought, in the doctrine of emanation which saves the divine transcendence and yet brings God into relation with man and the world, through a chain of mediating beings.

Dr. Bussell characterizes the doctrine of emanation as an honest attempt to overpower the dualism in which stoic cosmogony had ended, but regards the solution as unsatisfactory. What is needed is not so much a theoretic solution of our difficulties as " a divine voice of consolation; something to assure the soul of man of its *intrinsic* worth, of its value in its Maker's eyes * * * something to show us that the practical life and the government of material things is, after all, the highest duty and happiness for us; * * * and above all that God is no palace-secluded sovereign, but a general who fights with us and for us; and this semi-dualistic conception of the efforts, the *painful efforts* of Deity, paradoxic though it may be called, is nevertheless," the author concludes, " a certainty of experience, the supreme consolation and encouragement of the highest thinkers and most devoted believers. And in this lies the significance of the Christian religion."

The author may be characterized as a profoundly Christian thinker who has read and been influenced by Schopenhauer and who is, therefore, somewhat pessimistic, somewhat agnostic and somewhat out of sympathy with modern democratic movements and with what he calls the collectivism of the century. It might be questioned whether the motive of philosophy is not social as well as individual and whether the despair of knowledge need be so profound as it is in the mind of this author; but at all events the theme is treated with insight, the style is stimulating, and the handling of the materials is masterly.

A. T. ORMOND.

PRINCETON UNIVERSITY.

The Development of the Doctrine of Personality in Modern Philosophy. Part I. In. Diss. Strassburg. WM. H. WALKER. Ann Arbor, Mich., The Inland Press. Pp. 80.

This is a careful and creditable study of the subject. The author holds that "the history of the development of the doctrine of personality in modern philosophy is that of a gradual and necessary return to the consideration of the nature and worth of personality from the opposite pole of philosophical thought." The first chapter shows how philosophy "at the Renaissance turned from the inner world to the outer," from the world of scholastic abstractions to the world of reality. Bacon and Bruno "agree that nature is the immediate end of study." Yet indirectly the thinkers of the Renaissance raised the question of personality. "If truth is to be sought for its uses, material or religious, then to whom is it useful, and by virtue of what nature can truth be of use to him?" The second chapter traces the emergence of the problem in Hobbes, Descartes, and the Cartesian school. Political disturbances precipitated the question of "the ultimate unit of society, the legal person." While Hobbes's mechanical philosophy logically implied the denial of personality, his political philosophy found it indispensable. "He not only introduces the concept into modern philosophy, but he also gives it its characteristic modern note. Man is a person because he is accountable for his actions." The Cartesian treatment of the problem is exclusively intellectual; yet, failing to recognize the centrality of personality for knowledge, the Cartesians lose its distinctive character and reduce the subject to the level of the object. The rationalistic dissolution of personality in Spinozism is next indicated (Ch. III.). The author thinks, however, that Spinoza was compelled, "not by the exigencies of his system, but by the logic of facts, to reproduce in the microcosm the scheme of the macrocosm;" for "it would be possible to show that the modes of the attribute of thought are not, after all, ideas, but human spirits." The opposite or empirical dissolution of personality in empiricism is next developed (Ch. IV.). Here Locke's distinction between personal identity and identity of substance is emphasized, and the writer says, in his enthusiasm, that " Kant himself could hardly have defined the transcendental *ego* of apperception in better terms." " Berkeley rises to the higher thought that there is no true unity save in personality." The reference is to *Siris,* but " already in his commonplace book Berkeley writes: ' Nothing properly but persons, *i. e.,* conscious things, do exist. All other things are not so much existencies as manners of the existence of persons.' " Berkely further recognized the essential activity of personality, thus anticipating the new period in the history of the doctrine inaugurated by Leibnitz. " In most of the earlier systems the chief emphasis was laid upon man as a thinking being. That man is also an acting being was added as a subordinate fact." In the new period " the standpoint was reversed, and man was regarded first of all as an active being. Personality was removed from the sphere of thought to that of action." This new standpoint is that of Kant in his doctrine of the Practical Reason, to which the last chapter of the thesis is devoted, and the relation of which to his doctrine of the Pure Reason is admirably shown. Kant is also " the precursor of a new period in which the discussion of the personality of man and the personality of God go hand in hand." To this post-Kantian period, presumably, the second part of the dissertation is devoted.   JAMES SETH.

CORNELL UNIVERSITY.

Our Notions of Number and Space. HERBERT NICHOLS, assisted by WILLIAM E. PARSONS. Boston, Ginn & Co. 1894. Pp. vi + 201.

Dr. Nichols has based upon a series of experiments performed at Cambridge certain views relating, as the title of his book shows, to the origin of our number and space judgments. His book thus presents not merely a statement and explanation of experimental results, but an apparently complete theory, comprised in no fewer than one hundred and nine articles, on the general subjects of space and number—a weighty superstructure to be founded on psychological experiment in its present stage of development.

The experiments from which Dr. Nichols derives his hypothesis were performed with simple apparatus, consisting of rows of pins fixed in cardboard, the number of pins in each row varying from two to five, and the length of the rows varying by half-centimeter stages from one to five centimeters. Other experiments were performed with the same number and distance categories, but with the pins arranged in triangles, squares and circles. Cardboard edges of corresponding lengths were also used, and solid cork triangles, circles and squares for comparison with the pin experiments. Four persons served as reagents. The apparatus was applied by the reagent himself on the locality to be investigated, which was either the tongue, forehead, forearm or abdomen, and the pins were ordinarily 'rocked' back and forth on the skin to facilitate judgment. In the pin experiments the reagent was asked to determine in the same experiment both the number of pins and the length of the row; indeed, where the pins were set in triangles, *etc*, 'figure' judgments were also required; a method which must have produced a certain amount of attentional distraction. A general criticism which suggests itself on a survey of Dr. Nichols' tables concerns his use of sub-liminal values. Many of his inferences are drawn from tables where the percentage of right judgments seldom rises above forty.

The chief results of these experiments may be briefly summarized as follows: (1) When two pins are used, the accuracy of both distance and number judgments increases with increasing distance. (2) When five pins are used, on the other hand, the closer together they are placed, the more accurate is the judgment. This result as regards the estimation of number, Dr. Nichols accounts for by the fact that reducing the distance really increases the uncertainty, but that increased uncertainty means an increased tendency to assign the higher numerical categories, and hence, where the number of pins is actually a maximum, increased correctness of number judgment. Such at least is what the present reviewer makes out of the most difficult passage in the book, whose style is nowhere very clear. (3) The number judgments when the pins are set in triangles, *etc.*, are more accurate than when the same number of pins are placed in a straight line. (4) The number judgments are more accurate when four pins are set in a square than when these are set in an equilateral triangle of the same base. (5) The distance between the pins seems shorter when the pins are set in a triangle or circle than when they are set in a square.

Such being the more important inferences from the experimental results, let us see what the derived space theory is. Since the author's own summary of his doctrine occupies twenty-five pages, only its merest outline can be suggested here, but the gist of it seems to be this: If a combination of nerve endings have been on the whole stimulated oftener together than separately, the resulting presentation will be numerical and spatial unity; if oftener separately than together, we shall have a lineal distance presentation. The length of the distance presentation will depend 'upon the average length of all the time series in which the peripheral line has through life been stimulated.' The further apart two points, the greater the probability of serial rather than simultaneous stimulation; hence the more accurate the distance presentation. If the successive stimulation is discontinuous, the result is a presentation of number. The further apart two points, the more likely they are to be stimulated discontinuously, hence the more accurate the number presentation. The greater the number of points stimulated within a given distance, the less the probability that those points have been previously stimulated discontinuously, hence the less accurate the number presentation. At the same time, the more points touched in a given distance, the more clearly the 'distance tendency' will be recalled, and the more accurate the distance judgment. Three points in a triangle would average more discontinuous stimulation than three in a straight line, and four in a square than four in a straight line; hence we find the number judgments more exact in the experiments with triangles and squares. The fact that number judgments in the case of the square are more accurate than in the case of the triangle is explained by showing that the diagonal points of the square are further apart than any two points on the triangle. In distance judgments with triangles, squares and circles, the sides of a triangle are under-estimated because each corner calls up not only the presentation of the distance between itself and the opposite corners, but the shorter distance presentations between itself and other points on the perimeter, the average 'distance tendency' being thus shortened. Similarly, the diameter of a circle is under-estimated because each end recalls the shorter distance presentations between itself and other points on the circumference. Obviously no such shortening influence is exerted on the sides of a square.

These, as briefly stated as possible, are Dr. Nichols's explanations of his results. There is no space for detailed criticism, but two general observations present themselves. First, it will be seen that the author reduces space to a succession in time. He can hardly mean that it is nothing more, yet he seems to imply that he is giving us a complete theory of space. In a note (p. 155) where he criticises Professor James's doctrine of 'crude extensity,' he expressly says: "Our every notion of extensity is wholly an expression of time extension. * * * I should say that independently of time form there could be no feeling of extensity, while, theoretically, there might be big feelings and little feelings in the sense of more feeling and less feeling." It is surely superfluous to remark that 'time extensity' is not space extensity, and that successive stimulation of different nerve endings could never make them spatially distinct for consciousness unless each one gave a sensation *spatially* distinguishable from that of every other nerve ending. 'Crude extensity,' or a series of local signs in the sense of original spatial differences, one or the other we must have.

Secondly, it is undoubtedly true, as Professor James has told us, that no elements can be analyzed out of a complex presentation unless they have been previously experienced separately. But is it not rather dangerous to claim that two points will not be felt as two unless 'on the whole' they have been oftener stimulated separately than together? When one thinks of the simultaneous stimulation, practically continuous through life, of distant parts of the skin by contact with clothing, one hesitates to say that no points are locally distinguishable save those which have been stimulated oftener separately than together. Is it absolutely certain that the volar surfaces of the ends of the forefinger and thumb average more successive than simultaneous stimulations? Yet on the assumption that the *average* experiences of a peripheral nerve-ending determine the result of its present stimulation rests the whole of Dr. Nichols's theory. MARGARET WASHBURN.

WELLS COLLEGE.

The Education of the Central Nervous System, a Study of Foundations, especially of Sensory and Motor Training. REUBEN POST HALLECK. New York and London, The Macmillan Company. 1896. Pp. 251.

The first four chapters of this work contain a popular statement of elementary facts in the gross anatomy of the central nervous system and in neural physiology. The work assumes that the cortical centers are developed (1) by the exercise of the particular senses whose afferent fibres terminate in them, (2) by practice in recalling sensory images. To these ends an early beginning in the systematic exercise of all the senses, frequent changes of environment, and care on the part of the instructor to exercise the pupil in recalling sensory images, are recommended. The familiarity of great writers with the sensory aspect of nature, as seen in their poetry, is cited to prove, as it seems, that mental superiority is based upon well developed cortical centers corresponding to the special senses. In Chapter X., *How Shakes-*

peare's Senses were Trained, the author's hostility to the study of books reminds one of Rousseau. "No one was ever educated by the study of words" (176). Against 'those who favor going to school chiefly for the purpose of studying books, 'the education of Shakespeare is held up. His superiority is believed to be due to the fact that " he had magnificent sensory training and made the proper motor responses thereto" (180). Chapter XI. emphasizes the necessity of suitable motor responses to sensory stimuli. The last chapter gives pedagogical application to the pleasure-pain theory of Marshall. A convenient index is added to the text.

The style is lucid and very popular, the print clear and the pages handsome. The author offers no new facts, either anatomical, physiological, or pedagogical. The evidence upon which he rests his theory is not the experience of educators, but rather certain assumed physiological facts gleaned from the work of others; while the shadowy evidence upon which some of these 'facts' rest is not mentioned by the author. The precise genesis and function of the 'association' fibres, *e. g.*, as well as the physiological parallel of memory, etc., are problems as to whose solution physiologists can as yet only guess; yet the author cites certain assumed solutions of them and of other psychophysical problems as evidence for his theory. Is the evidence adequate ? We think not; and yet it may be true that pedagogical theory pays too little attention to sensory and motor training in the early life of children. The important question as to how the senses and memory are to be rendered the trained servants of a will which moves toward intellectual, ethical or other practical aims, is not touched upon by the author.   GUY TAWNEY.
PRINCETON, N. J.

The Art of Controversy, and Other Posthumons Papers. ARTHUR
  SCHOPENHAUER. Selected and translated by T. BAILEY SAUN-
  DERS., New York, The Macmillan Co., 1896. Pp. 116. 90
  cents.

The volume is a valuable accession to Mr. Bailey Saunders' library of Schopenhauer. The excellent English translations of the German master have preserved the thought and spirit of the original while in no wise, however, sacrificing the demands of clear, idiomatic English. In the transfer from one language to the other there is in all of these volumes a minimum of loss as regards the impression made of the author's mind and personality. *The Art of Controversy* is one of Schopenhauer's posthumous papers, though a small part of it was pub-

lished before his death in the chapter of the *Parerga* entitled *Zur Logik und Dialektik*. The opening chapter consists of a theoretical exposition of the distinction between Logic and Dialectic, the one a guide in the search for truth, the other a weapon to wield in the quest of victory. This is followed by a practical discussion of the ways and means of securing an advantage over an adversary in debate. This chapter has the significant heading of *Strategems*, and has a vein of irony running through it that gives added force to its many valuable hints. The other essays of this volume are on *Interest and Beauty in Works of Art, Psychological Observations, Wisdom of Life, Genius and Virtue*. The epigrammatic style, the sententious comments upon human nature, and withal an underlying strain of humor, concealed and yet pervasive, render these essays both interesting and suggestive.   JOHN GRIER HIBBEN.
PRINCETON UNIVERSITY.

Zur Theorie der Aufmerksamkeit. HARRY E. KOHN. Halle, Niemeyer, 1895. Pp. 48.

The main contention of this paper is that there is no real difference between the two states of attentive and inattentive consciousness. The difference is only one of degree, and attention is regarded as the intensity coefficient of consciousness. The essential features of attention are discovered in the process of apperception. Different stimuli strive together to possess the field of consciousness, and the victorious inhibit the force of the others, their superior intensity being felt in consciousness as attention. Every change in consciousness or consequent shifting of attention rises from the fusion of a perception-mass with an apperception mass, resulting from the strife of contending stimuli. The writer indicates also as one of the factors in attention, the susceptibility, both original and acquired of the inner nature to certain stimuli in preference to others, thus increasing or diminishing their intensity as the case may be and so further modifying attention. His theory is mainly an exposition of the Herbartian doctrine of struggle and inhibition, and partakes of a like vagueness and artificiality. The constructive portion of the paper is followed by a criticism of the theories of Stumpf, Wundt and James.   JOHN GRIER HIBBEN.
PRINCETON UNIVERSITY.

Dictionnaire de physiologie. CH. RICHET. I. A–B. Paris, Alcan, 1895. Pp. 1044.

Strange to say there has not existed heretofore any special dictionary for physiology. It is a lack which M. Ch. Richet has attempted to fill, with the help of a great number of physiologists of distinction, mainly French. The first volume is now ready, and we find that it treats of physiology in the largest sense. It includes all the sciences commonly known as physics, bacteriology, medicine, chemistry, therapeutics and psychology. To psychology a considerable number of interesting articles are devoted. We may cite Aboulia, Amnesia, Analgesia, Anæsthesia, Apperception, Attention, Áutomatism, etc. These articles are signed by Marillier, Janet, and Richet. They are quite in their place in a dictionary of physiology, but they would be considered too summary in a dictionary of psychology. It is difficult to give a general opinion of these different articles, for they are of very unequal value. Some—as Algesimeter, Agraphia, Audition coloreé—are curiously inadequate; while others—as Hearing—are treatises. But my general impression is that this dictionary is a very useful work, and that it will be of more service to psychologists than the ordinary dictionaries of medicine, in which psychology is altogether sacrificed.   A. Binet.

Paris.

Alterations of Personality. Alfred Binet. Translated by
    Helen Green Baldwin. With notes and a preface by J.
    Mark Baldwin. New York, D. Appleton & Co. 1896. Pp.
    xii + 356.

Hypnotism, Mesmerism and the New Witchcraft. Ernest Hart.
    New edition, enlarged. New York, D. Appleton & Co. 1896.
    Pp. viii + 212.

The appearance of Mrs. Baldwin's excellent translation of M. Binet's monograph, and of a second edition of Dr. Hart's essays, offers an opportunity of giving them mention in the pages of the Psychological Review.

M. Binet's book is divided into three parts—'Successive Personalities,' 'Coexistent Personalities,' and 'Alterations of Personality in Experiments on Suggestion.'

The first part deals with Spontaneous Somnambulism, the exposition of which is based chiefly upon the cases of Félida X. and Louis V.; and with Induced Somnambulism. The latter term is used to designate those secondary states in which the patient is vividly conscious, although they are not remembered in the primary state. Hypnotic states in the narrower sense are scarcely mentioned. The phenomena of post-hypnotic suggestion are then used to prove that the somnambulistic state can survive the reappearance of the normal consciousness, thus constituting a secondary personality.

The conception thus introduced is worked out in detail in Parts II. and III. In Part II. it is used to explain the phenomena of hysterical amnesia, anæsthesia, automatic movement and automatic ideation, while in Part III. the analogous phenomena which can be produced by direct suggestion are interpreted in the same way, including in the latter class 'spirit' writing.

Into the details of M. Binet's reasoning one cannot enter within the limits of a brief review. It is dominated throughout by the notion of a subconscious personality or self, and although he does not hold that this subconscious personality is to be conceived as invariably analogous to the primary self, that it exists in all persons, or that it enjoys a continuous existence, he frequently writes as if he held all these doctrines. There is, in fact, a certain lack of clearness in M. Binet's conceptions, of which his loose interchange of such words as 'unconscious' and 'subconscious,' 'personality' and 'consciousness,' is merely the exponent. Notwithstanding such blemishes, however, the book is an earnest attempt at synthesis in a new field, and as the author is one of the few who can say of the early researches in that field, '*quorum pars magna fui,*' his views are of weight.

Dr. Hart writes in a very different vein. Someone has said that if an Englishman be asked for an opinion upon a subject of which he is ignorant he may for a while be at a loss, but after a half hour's reflection will be found, not only in possession of an opinion, but ready to knock down anyone who fails to agree to it.

Whether this be true on the whole or not, Dr. Hart's mental attitude seems to be of somewhat the same type. In 1850 he began the study of hypnotism and soon satisfied himself that hypnotic states exist, that they are of subjective origin, that will or magnetism has nothing to do with their production, and that the subject is suggestible. He further concluded that hypnotic sleep is due to a reflex inhibition of the cerebral circulation. At that point his powers of assimilation seem to have failed and he has never advanced a step. This, he holds, is the sole and only true faith of hypnotism, which except a man hold faithfully he shall be damned scientifically. All further alleged discoveries are compounds of malobservation and fraud, and those who are engaged in foisting them upon the world are either knaves or fools, mainly, however, fools. For even Dr. Hart can be charitable in his way.

These views are expounded in the first two essays. The third narrates the author's *exposé* of the mehods of Luys and de Rochas. It is good as far as it goes, and so also is the amusing and well written essay on 'The Eternal Gullible.'

The book may be of service to the general public in pruning away some of the absurd notions about hypnotism which are so common. Otherwise it is insignificant. The sole point of importance which Dr. Hart makes is that fraud on the part of the patient is a source of error never absent and seldom provided for, but he probably grossly exaggerates the extent to which this vitiates the results of careful observers. Furthermore, the intemperance of his language and his supreme self-confidence will discredit his work in the eyes of all who value cool thinking, justice and courtesy.   W. R. NEWBOLD.
UNIVERSITY OF PENNSYLVANIA.

Causal-Nexus zwischen Leib und Seele und die daraus resultier-enden psychophysischen Phänomene. HEINRICH METSCHER. Dortmund, Ruhfus. Pp. 179. (No date.)

The first part of this work reviews historically and critically the principal metaphysical theories of the relation of soul and body. All are found unsatisfactory, but no new solution is attempted. Instead, the author, falling back on the general psycho-physical formula as expressing the empirical facts, proceeds, in the second part, to discuss the more characteristic phenomena which exhibit bodily and psychical interdependence. The historical data are almost all at second hand; in the more psychological portions the chief authority is Wundt, cited from the second edition. Wundt is also referred to as one of the leading investigators after Flourens of localization of brain-function. None of the real investigators is mentioned except Flechsig, whose name occurs twice, spelled with an x. In the more metaphysical portions the arguments proceed from the assumption that soul and body interact and from the demand for a theory to explain the fact. No effort is made to unravel the metaphysical implications of this assumption. The author does not consider what light might be thrown on the problem by the application of the critical method, regarding soul and body as terms derived from distinct points of view in the organization of experience, and thence developing the principles on which the experience that yields these distinctions rests. Nevertheless, the book has sufficient merits as a popular exposition. The material is well arranged and the style clear.   H. N. GARDINER.
SMITH COLLEGE.

Die Willensfreiheit. PAUL MICHAELIS. I.–D. Leipzig, 1896. Pp. 56.

Following five pages of introduction, in which the problem is stated, is a sketch of its historical development, four pages being devoted to the Bible, two and a-half to Greek Philosophy, and so on through the Middle Ages and Modern Philosophy till Kant, Kant and his successors being finally disposed of in a little over four pages. The more independent second half discusses the Law of Causality, the Will, Character, Transcendental Freedom, the Development of Moral Will, the Freedom of Moral Will, Ethical Consequences and Education in Moral Freedom, allowing on an average about three pages to each topic. One is reminded of the traditional first sermon, into which the young theologue puts all of the divinity he knows. One's impression of the work, however, improves on acquaintance. Herr Michaelis has evidently not told all that he knew; and while we must regret that he did not confine himself to fewer subjects and develop them in a way which would have made his work of real value as a contribution to the discussion of the main problem, it is fair to say that he has selected his points with good judgment and presented them so succinctly and clearly that one gets from his work as good an idea of what the controversy is all about as from many much more pretentious treatises. The question discussed is the old one of the *liberum arbitrum indifferentiæ*, the *possibilitas utriusque partis*. The author well brings out its ethical and religious bearings. The interest in the question, he says, is not as to whether, when at the cross-roads, we can turn indifferently to the right or to the left, but whether Hercules, at the parting of the ways, can of himself choose ‘the narrow path’ or must wait for assistance from above, that is from without. This possibility Herr Michaelis denies. Our choices are determined. The arguments are the familiar ones and are perhaps conclusive. Few at any rate would contend to-day for a choice without *motive* or deny that the motive essential to choice is determined by circumstances and character. A modern defender of free-will would be likely to say that the question is as to the relation of motive, circumstances and character to will and choice and to maintain that the former, so far from being external forces which determine the will, are elements of it, that choice is determined, to be sure, but self-determined, and that self-determination, as opposed to the mere capacity of transmitting foreign energy, constitutes a freedom whose forms are so various as are the forms of life. The analytic method of Herr Michaelis leads him to overlook the possibility that self-determination may be a valid category and hence, though explicitly recognizing the difference, to really think of psychical causality after the analogy of physical. When, therefore, he himself substitutes a conception of freedom for the older conception, it is not that of self-determination which he gives, but ‘will consciously directed to the moral ideal.' In proportion as the dependence of the individual is insisted on, the function of society is exalted. By nature the individual is unfree. Nor can he free himself. His freedom, *i. e.*, his good moral disposition, which Luther and Augustine believed possible only through divine grace, must come to him from society. The great function of society is to educate its citizens for moral freedom, and to this end belongs, among other things, the education of the criminal and a social-economic condition free from incitements to envy.   H. N. GARDINER.

SMITH COLLEGE.

GENETIC.

Psychic Development of Young Animals and its Physical Correlation. WESLEY MILLS. Parts I. to VI. From the Transactions of the Royal Society of Canada. Dorie & Son, Ottawa, 1894–5.

These papers by Professor Mills consist of a series of diaries of the earliest psychic life of dogs, cats, rabbits, guinea-pigs, pigeons and domestic fowls, followed by some comments. To determine whether a reaction is conscious or reflex, and if conscious, what kind of consciousness, is, of course, more difficult with very young animals than with mature ones. Professor Mills often seems duly impressed with the difficulties of his task, as when (p. 55) he speaks of apparent anger in a pup of 17 days old as possibly merely a reflex. However, he is inclined (p. 53) to believe that a pup of 26 days has a 'sense of fun or humor.' Yet I think it must require a vast deal of very thorough evidence to lead us to believe that so young a pup 'makes believe' in biting play, and thus distinguishes between real and unreal, and so becomes an actor and makes a fiction which is enjoyed as such. So, also the kitten 20 days old, which hisses when called 'puss,' 'puss,' expresses probably fear rather than 'surprise,' as Professor Mills interprets.

Some suggestive remarks are made on the tail-wagging and barking of the dog (pp. 54, 224). But Professor Mills surely goes too far in saying that tail-waggings are to the dog what 'words are to mankind.' Whether the tail is primarily or only secondarily an instrument of expression, and whether it is purposely used, as the voice seems to be, for expression, and how far, these are questions which can only be settled by very thorough observation upon the dingo or wild dog and upon higher breeds. Professor Mills notes that growling precedes barking and that both first occur in sleep. An observation recorded (p. 213) suggests that the bark and growl may be differentiated from some middle tone; but the subject needs to be studied with all dogs from the dingo up to come to any certain result. Professor Mills grants the cat more docility and gratitude than is often allowed. He is much impressed by its relatively long period of psychic immaturity—more than twice that of the dog—and also by its superior persistency, even when very young. This quality, I think, is hereditary, and, being implied in all lying-in-wait and stalking in the feral form, naturally appears very early in the domesticated cat. Professor Mill's observations of the chick practically agree with Professor Lloyd Morgan's. If there is any thing new it is with reference to the sense of support. That most new-born land animals—the prairie dog is a notable exception—evidence a strong reaction on being brought to the edge of a table is, indeed, a marked fact, but just how far it is reflex, and how far a real consciousness as 'sense of support,' is very difficult to make out. Professor Mills shows clearly that length of infancy does not of itself point to higher development. Thus, though the rabbit takes three times as long in coming to maturity as the cavy, yet both are then 'about on the same mental plane.'

While Professor Mills' observations are necessarily somewhat isolated and meager, they appear unbiased, and are of interest and value as a step in the right direction. Complete and exact observations can only be made by those who can give up their whole time to making a full record, day and night for the whole period, and who are thoroughly conversant with the species studied. A thorough method would doubtless lead to the discovery of some temporary and recapitulatory phases of great historical import for mental embryology.

HIRAM M. STANLEY.

LAKE FOREST, ILL.

VISION.

1. Action de la lumière sur la rétine. ED PERGENS. Annales de la Soc. Roy. des Sci. Méd. et Nat. de Bruxelles. V. (3). Pp. 33, 1896.

2. Zur Theorie der Farbenblindheit. A. FICK. Pflüger's Archiv, 64, 313-321.

3. Absorbtion und Zersetzung des Sehpurpurs bei den Wirbeltiren. ELSE KÖTTGEN und GEORG ABELSDORFF. Ztsch. für Psych. und Phys. der Sinnesorgane, VII., 161-184.

*4. Vergleichende Untersuchungen über Raum,- Licht- und Farben-
sinn in Centrum und Peripherie der Netzhaut.* DR. GUILLERY.
Ztsch. für Psych. und Phys. der Sinnesorgane, XII., 243-275.

That the cones of the retina are much shortened under the influence of light was first discovered by Van Genderen-Stort in 1887.
Pergens here confirms the observation, having made use of the latest
methods of staining and preservation. The animal experimented upon
was a fish *(Leuciscus rutilis)*, and great pains were taken to secure
conditions absolutely alike for different individuals as regards everything except exposure to light. After numerous experiments it was
found that the best results were obtained by the rapid method of Golgi ;
sometimes the retina was colored during life by mixing methyline blue
or the Biondi mixture with the water in which the fishes swam. The
amount by which the retina is shortened under the influence of light
was found to be from 170μ to 220μ; this was almost wholly due to a
change in the length of the cones. There was also found to be a diminution in the amount of chromatine in most of the layers of the
retina, and especially in the external granular layer; the author considers that this layer constitutes a reserve of protoplasm and nuclein
in direct relation with the functioning of the rods and cones. The
forward movement of the pigment follows upon the contraction of the
cones, and takes place very much more slowly than that.

2. Professor Fick here produces his 'theory' of color-blindness.
He represents normal color-vision by three curves indicating the excitability of the three kinds of color substance in the different portions
of the spectrum, and considers that, in the different species of color
blindness, one or another pair of these curves become co-incident. He
gives curves of different shape from those usually chosen, and finds
some vague reasons for preferring them; he is apparently unaware
that König's curves have been so chosen, that they *fit* both in the normal eye and that which is color-blind. It is, since König's im-
mensely laborious measurements, no longer a *theory* that the sensations of the color-blind can be represented by a curve which is
the union of two curves of normal vision—it is plain matter of fact;
instead of being vague speculation it is a deduction from observations
of the utmost refinement, *provided* the curves are those adopted by
König—that is to say, provided the fundamental colors are the same
as those chosen by him with special reference to their serving the color
equations of both normal and abnormal vision.

3. The authors here describe, with more detail regarding methods,
than in the brief paper presented to the Berlin Academy of Sciences,

the examination which they have made of the visual purple of a number of different vertebrates, namely, thirteen mammals, three birds, eight amphibians and twenty-seven fishes. They find, as we have before noted, that there are two distinct kinds of visual purple, with no intermediate stages, one which has a faint purplish tinge and is found in all fishes, and another which is not purple at all, but red, and which is found in all other mammals. They also announce the remarkable fact that in all the lower animals the visual purple fades out without going through an intermediate stage of yellow, or that man is the only animal in whom the visual yellow occurs at all.

4. The writer of this paper is concerned to show that the several functions of the retina do not all decrease with like rapidity in passing from the fovea to the periphery, and hence that it is necessary to attribute them to different elements, either anatomical or chemical. He determines with this intention the rate of diminution of the space-sense, the light-sense, and the color-sense.

By space-sense one ought to mean, in the most elementary analysis, the feeling of the *where-ness* of a given sensation of brightness-difference, just as the sense of locality on the skin is the sense of the position in space of a temperature-sensation, or some other skin-sensation; it does not exist as a sensation in the abstract, but merely as a *quale* of another sensation. But Dr. Guillery maintains that the simple perception of a black point on a white surface, without reference to its place, is an exercise of the space-sense, and he gives a long and very ineffective argument to support this claim. He proceeds to determine the physiological point (the size of the just discernible retinal image) for different distances from the fovea, and then the size of the image cast by two points of different brightness when they differ so much as to be just perceptibly different if their image falls upon a single cone of the fovea. He finds that these two functions diminish *pari passu* in proceeding from the fovea the ratio for corresponding points of the retina is—that nearly constant, which does nothing to confirm his theory that they are not one and the same function. The color-sense is naturally a sense which diminishes with a different rapidity from either of the other two; but here the writer's observations would be of greater interest if state of adaptation of the eye had been attended to; there is no indication of his knowing the importance of that condition. His conclusion, in passing, that the sense for blue and yellow (and the sense for red and green) fade out together, respectively, is as nugatory as all the other proofs of this supposed fact; the most that can be determined is that a blue and a yellow, etc., can be found *such that* they fade out at approximately equal distances, but no effort is made to show that the colored papers that happened to be chosen were in any sense of equal value for sensation at the fovea. Of the 'normal' colors prepared by Hegg, for instance, the. red and the yellow would not strike the plain man as at all deserving of the name. The writer is quite unaware of the significance of the recently discussed functions of the visual purple. Christine Ladd Franklin. Baltimore.

Das Einfachsehen und seine Analogien. Sigmund Reichard. Ztschr. f. Psych. u. Physiol. d. Sinnesorg. XL, 286–290. 1896.

This article merely points out that the phenomenon of single vision with identical points of the two retinæ has analogies in the phenomena of single hearing with corresponding nerve-endings in the two organs of Corti, of single smelling with two organs, and of single contact-sensation when two points are stimulated which lie within a single 'sensory-circle;' and attempts briefly to devise a theory of the anatomical development of the retinæ such as would increase the analogy of the visual with the tactile phenomenon.

Ueber geometrisch-optische Täuschungen. Armand Thiéry. Philos. Studien, XL, 307-370; 603-620; XII., 67-126. 1895.

This is a thorough and important contribution to the study of geometrical optical illusions in general. It discusses all the various kinds, gives the results of careful measurements of many of them under various conditions, outlines and criticises the different theories that have been advanced to account for them, and attempts to establish the view that all of them—whether illusions of direction, of size or of curvature—are due to the conscious or unconscious influence of a perspective interpretation of the figures. The following remarks by Prof. Wundt are appended to this article:

"I recognize the great importance of perspective projection for these phenomena, but cannot wholly agree in regarding the perspective idea as the primary cause of the illusions. I believe rather that as a rule the perspective idea itself is to be regarded as the effect of other primary elements, especially of position and movement of the eyes, and it seems to me that the proof of this thesis is itself to be found to a large degree in the observations above recorded. I intend shortly to return to this subject in a special article in these Studien."

Further analysis of Thiéry's views will be delayed until after the appearance of Wundt's article. E. B. Delabarre. Brown University.

FEELING.

Recherches experimentales sur la Joie et la Tristesse. G. DUMAS. Rev. philosophique, June, July, August, 1896.

In spite of the works of Darwin, Spencer, Wundt, Mantegazza, and many others on the emotions, we have, as yet, no adequate experimental researches on the question. With this lack in mind we turn to this work of G. Dumas, who proposes to study joy and sadness in the insane, from the physiological point of view, by registering the capillary circulation, arterial tension, heart-beat and respiration.

In his three rather long articles the author gives us his results. To understand them thoroughly we must recall two laws established by the physiologist Marey, to which Dumas continually returns for the interpretation of physiological phenomena: 1. Vaso-motor constriction, *i. e.*, the contraction of the arteries under the influence of the excitation of a vaso-motor nerve of constricture, produces an increase of tension in the blood-pressure and a slowing in the heart-beat, while dilatation of the arteries, under the influence of the vaso-motor nerves of dilatation, produces the opposite effect. 2. Increase of the action of the heart produces increase of tension; and the reverse.

The author distinguishes six different affective types. 1. *Joy with hypertension;* in general paralytics, the heart-beat is accelerated, respiration likewise, the tension is feeble, the arteries are in a state of dilatation. The author holds that the joy is produced by the dilatation of the arteries; this indeed, according to the law of Marey explains the rapidity of the heart-beat and the diminution of tension.

2. *Joy with hypertension;* in different sorts of insane patients who are very excitable: accelerated heart-beat and respiration, the tension strong, the arteries constricted or dilated. The author holds that in these cases the cause of the changes of circulation is central, in the brain, which excites the heart, and the heart increases the tension. The constriction of the arteries is an insignificant phenomenon.

3. *Sadness with hypertension;* heart and respiration are slowed, tension strong, with constriction. In this case it is the constriction of the arteries which dominates everything; it produces the strong tension and slows the heart.

4. *Sadness with hypotension;* phenomena as in type three, except that the tension is feeble. Here we must hold that the constriction of the arteries does not increase the tension, since the heart is too feeble.

5. *Sadness with hypotension, and acceleration of the heart.*

This occurs in the active sadness of melancholics: constriction, accel-cration of the heart with hypotension. These symptoms seem para-doxical, since in spite of the union of causes which tend to increase the tension, it remains feeble. The author supposes that the heart is not excited, although it appears to be so, and that it empties itself in-completely.

6. *Moral pain, hypertension, acceleration of the heart, vaso-constriction.* These are almost the same symptoms as those of joy of the second type, except that the respiration is more irregular in this case.

This brief account will show that M. Dumas' story is systematic; but when we look at these types we see that some of them are arti-ficially explained, as the second, fourth and fifth.

I may take advantage of this occasion to point out a physiological error made by M. Dumas and all his predecessors, even Lange him-self, whose theories the author criticizes. It is well known that Lange, employing a very simple formula, held that sadness is con-nected with a condition of arterial vaso-constriction, and joy with dilation. It is likely that Lange was led by theory on this point: the theory that in sadness the vessels ought to contract because, in this case, blood would be drawn from the tissues, the temperature would be lowered with lack of blood, paling of tissues, etc. ; and on the con-trary, with vaso-dilation, in joy, the blood circulates more freely, the temperature rises, the skin colors up, vitality is augmented. But these theoretical views do not seem adequate, and it seems that the most favorable condition to circulation is neither dilation nor contrac-tion of the arteries, but a state intermediate between these extremes. Yet I do not now insist on this point, expecting to return to it on another occasion.

The error which I wish to point out consists in attributing to vaso-constriction the loss of blood in the hand, coldness in the extremities, and discoloration of the skin. They are independent phenomena, which may exist with constriction or not. In order to distinguish, it is necessary to study the form of the capillary pulse. If we take an example of true vaso-constriction, such as is produced by the sudden stroke of a bell or by strong inspiration, we find that this constriction shows itself clearly in the form of the pulse-curve ; the tracing de-scends, the curve takes on a smaller size, and its decrotism is less. If at the same time we study the arterial pulse we find that it changes its form in consequence of the effect of the constriction of the arteries upon the flow of the blood; the curve rises, and its decrotism diminishes. The effect is analogous to that which follows pressure on the artery under the sphygmograph. These are the signs of vaso-constriction, which is above all an active phenomenon.

Now, in many circumstances, for example in the fatigue produced by a day of uninterrupted intellectual work, we find the occurrence of coldness, lowering of temperature and discoloration of the tissues. The pulse is faint and difficult to take. If the phenomenon is very accentuated we get only a linear tracing, with no sign of pulse; the respiration is slow, the heart-beat less than usual. Does this indicate vaso-constriction? Is there in this case an active constriction of the arteries? If so it would seem very extraordinary—such activity of the vaso-motors in the midst of the general lowering of the organic vitality. As a matter of fact, the form of the capillary pulse, when it can be registered, gives quite a different indication. We find a feeble pulse, lessened decrotism very high up on the line of oblique ascension; in a word, a pulse indicating weakness, lack of blood and slow circulation.

It is not astonishing that authors heretofore who have described the physiological effects of emotion have confused these two very different conditions of the capillary circulation. The confusion is almost inevitable if the form of the pulse is not registered. Moreover, this slow pulse is very difficult to register without special tambours and adjustible membranes of the kind which we use in the laboratory of the Sorbonne.

In conclusion, I am able to formulate the following practical rule: When the extremities are cold, discolored, we can not conclude to vaso-motor constriction without study of the force of the capillary pulse, and if it is impossible to register this pulse we cannot conclude from this impossibility to the presence of constriction.

As far as I can judge from my own experiments, M. Dumas deals sometimes with slow circulation, and more rarely with true constriction. Consequently, as he does not take account of this source of error, all the effective types which he distinguishes must be revised. There remains from this work the general conclusion, which is very interesting, that in joy there is an acceleration of the heart action, and of respiration, while in sadness these two functions are made slower; but that in active sadness, sharp suffering, the symptoms are almost the same as in joy. This certainly does not lead to a theory of emotion, but it is a useful contribution to the study of the question.

A. BINET.

PARIS.

Zur Lehre vom Einfluss der Gefühle auf die Vorstellungen und ihren Verlauf. GUSTAV STÖRRING. Phil. Studien, xii., Heft 4, pp. 475–524.

Dr. Störring devotes the greater portion of his paper to a philosophical and introspective study of his question. The first part is given to showing that feelings affect ideas through attention. Like Ribot, he believes that feelings determine the fixation of an object in consciousness, and are the basis of attention. This holds both in normal and in abnormal mental life. The second part of the article treats of the influence of feelings on association and reproduction; an idea with a strong feeling-tone is more suggestive, and has, in turn, greater suggestibility. Similar organic sensations may associate two ideas in consciousness.

Störring describes, also, an experimental research into the influence of feelings on the voluntary muscles. After mentioning Féré's similar work, he reviews the experiments of Münsterberg, which showed that under the influence of pleasure (*Lust*) outward movements were made too large, inward ones too small, and, conversely, under the influence of displeasure (*Unlust*) outward movements were made too small, inward ones too large. Störring constructed an apparatus with which the fore-arm swung freely in a horizontal plane, the elbow resting in a cup. The hand carried with it a thin board on which there was an index moving over a graduated scale. This scale was arranged in an arc, with the elbow-cup as a center. Readings could be taken from the scale, or the apparatus could be made self-recording.

The subject was drilled, with closed eyes, in first moving his hand through an arc of 10 cm., it being stopped by a peg at the end; and then in repeating the movement, as accurately as possible, the peg having meanwhile been removed. This imitation-movement was found to have a positive constant error, but comparatively small. When, however, a pleasant or displeasing feeling-tone was created by placing in the subject's mouth raspberry juice or a solution of salt, the constant error, positive or negative, became quite large. Störring found, in the case of a pleasant feeling-tone, a positive constant error for flection of the arm; in the case of a displeasing feeling-tone, a negative constant error for flection, and a positive one for extension. These results are directly contrary to Münsterberg's. Störring seems less interested in a pleasant feeling-tone than in one that is displeasing, not giving any results of arm-extension in the former case. The work appears to have been carefully done throughout; but there seems to have been only one person tested.   LEONARD B. McWHOOD.
COLUMBIA UNIVERSITY.

PATHOLOGICAL.

Le Moi des Mourants: nouveaux Faits. V. Egger. Revue Philosophique, XLII., 337–368, October, 1896.

In reply to Dr. Sollier's criticism of the title under which M. Egger introduced the discussion of this subject (see this Review, III., 236 and 454), the latter explains that the terms used were not medical but psychological; the 'mourant' is one who is such for himself, *i. e.*, who believes himself to be dying, and as to the 'moi,' it does not, he says, exist unless such an one, "already prepared by previous reflections on himself and in full possession of his faculties, resume his past either by a rapid series of recollections or by spoken or written formulas." He further explains that his object in studying the mental states of the dying was to confirm his theory of the *ego*—the *ego* is 'the total recollection,' 'the consciousness of the past as such,' etc. Hence his explanation of the vivid resurgence of memory-images in accident cases as a special illustration of the 'moi vif' analogous to the expressive utterances, of which he gives many examples, in which those about to die sometimes appear to sum up a whole life and character. In other words, the cause of the reaction is held to be logical, not pathological. M. Egger, therefore, while accepting Dr. Sollier's explanation of the beatitude commonly felt at a certain stage of the crisis, namely, that it is the direct consequence of the bodily insensibility, refuses to admit Dr. Sollier's further hypothesis, that the phantasmagoria of memory-images is an indirect consequence of this same bodily condition. He claims, in opposition, anæsthesia without hypermnesia, and, again, hypermnesia without anæsthesia. The last, however, he does not establish, at least for the accident cases, and the cases cited of conscious reflection on the past and reflective anticipations of the impending future on the part of dying persons in full possession of their faculties would seem to belong to a different class from that of the vivid panoramic vision in certain cases which Sollier's hypothesis sought to account for. On any theory, there must, of course, be some sort of an organized past to recur to; M. Egger's theory requires it to be that of a civilized adult. Hence cases like that of Charles Darwin, who, when a schoolboy at Shrewsbury, experienced, during a fall of some seven or eight feet, such an extraordinarily rapid succession of ideas as seemed, he says, to contradict the assertion of the physiologists, that each thought requires an appreciable amount of time—cases like these fall outside of the theory. Darwin, to be sure, does not directly tell us that his ideas were memories. But in one of the new cases here reported we find a person three times in his life in mortal danger, and surveying with extreme rapidity his past in the first experience when less than ten years old, and in the first only. How does M. Egger explain this? He explains it by reference to a ' moi précoce' and distinguishes between the ' moi encombrant' of schoolboys and ' what the psychologist calls a *moi*.' There is no doubt a place for the distinction; only in this connection, while it suggests the sort of self reacting, does it succeed in removing the form of the reaction itself, the hypermnesia, from the need of a mechanical explanation or in disconnecting it from cases like that of Darwin above, and its suggested pathological associates? We think not.

H. N. Gardiner.

Smith College.

Periodische Depressionszustände und ihre Pathogenesis auf dem Boden der harnsauren Diathese. C. Lange. Tr. into German from second edition by Hans Kurella. Leopold Voss, Hamburg and Leipzig, Publisher. 1896. Pp. 52, including Appendix.

This paper was first read before the Medical Association of Copenhagen, in 1886. The second edition (1895) has an appendix of 13 pages.

The author singles out of the classes of diseases known as Neurasthenia and Melancholia a very frequent affection which he calls ' periodic depression.' Although in some respects like the first stage of Melancholia, with which it is erroneously identified, it differentiates itself from it in that (1) the patients have neither fixed ideas nor hallucinations; they never ascribe their suffering to external agents; (2) the periodicity is a constant feature, while in Melancholia it is rare; (3) not one of the many hundred cases studied by the author went further than the supposed first stage.

The most characteristic feature of the disease in an alternation of periods of depression with periods of usual moral tone. The periodicity varies greatly. Generally, the shorter the depression periods the more regular is their reappearance; in some cases the movements of the disease are so regular that the day of their coming can be safely predicted. In more than half the cases that came to his notice it is between the ages of 25 and 35 that the disease made its appearance. It does not show any preference for any particular class of people, but " it is almost powerless with individuals without hereditary taint." In almost every case the author discovered a bad heredity.

The symptoms are those of nervous depression: dullness, sleepiness (not incompatible with disturbed sleep), apathy, inertia. The patient can hardly set to work, but when he has once begun he may experience almost as much difficulty in stopping. Yet there is no appearance of reduced efficiency. He is joyless, affectionless; the expression sometimes used by him, 'geistige Steifheit oder Versteinerung,' mental rigor, describes well his condition. Sometimes anguish is added to the ordinary blank depression. The physiological symptoms have less significance. There is a general expression of fatigue and of sorrow. The patient looses flesh, and this loss is made more apparent by the flaccidity of the muscles. The digestive organs are somewhat sluggish. Menstruation seems neither to influence the disease nor to be influenced by it.

Concerning the pathogeny of periodic depression, the author found in every case, as well during as between the depression periods, a strongly marked tendency to the formation of an abnormal quantity of uric acid sediment. According to the theory he adopts, the uric acid acts directly on the elements of the nervous system to which it is carried by the blood.

In the appendix, Lange answers some criticism questioning the sufficiency of the non-quantitative method with which he established the pathogeny of the disease. He also points to some signs indicating that at last, 'out of the chaos of Neurasthenia, Periodic depression is coming to light.'

The least satisfactory part of this specification of a new type of nervous disease, supported by observations on about 2,000 cases, is the one concerning the symptomatic importance of the presence of an excess of uric acid in the urine of the patients and its supposed relation to the disease.   J. H. LEUBA.

WORCESTER, MASS.

NEW BOOKS.

Abhandlungen zur Geschichte der Metaphysik, Psychologie und Religions philosophie in Deutschland seit Leibnitz. L. STRUMPELL. Hefte, I.–IV. Leipzig, Deichert. 1896.

The Art of Controversy. A. SCHOPENHAUER. Translated by T. B. SAUNDERS. London, Sonnenschein; New York, Macmillan. 1896. Pp. VI+116. $.90.

Genius and Degeneration. W. HIRSCH. From the second German edition. New York, Appleton. 1896. Pp. vi+333. $3.50.

Notes médico-légales. H. J. GOSSE. Geneva, George. 1896. Quarto. Pp. 30.

Das Princip der Entwickelung. H. DINGER. Jena, Kämpfe. 1896. Pp. v+75.

Experimentelle Studien über Associationen. G. ASCHAFFENBURG. Leipzig, Englemann. 1895. Pp. 95. (Sonderab. aus Kraepelin's *Psychologische Arbeiten.*)

Uber den Einfluss von Arbeitspausen auf die geistige Leistungsfähigkeit. E. AMBERG. Leipzig, Englemann. 1895. (From Kraepelin's *Psychologische Arbeiten.*)

Die Willensfreiheit. P. Michaelis, Leipzig. 1896. Pp. 56.

Paidologie : Entwurf zu einer Wissenschaft des Kindes. O. CHRISMAN. Jena, Vopelius. 1896. Pp. 96.

Abhandlungen zur Philosophie und ihrer Geschichte. Edited by B. ERDMANN, Halle a. S. Niemeyer: I. *David Hume's Kausalitätstheorie.* P. RICHTER. 1893. Pp. 50. II. *Andreas Rüdiger's Moralphilosophie.* W. CARLS, 1894. Pp. 51. III. *Hume's u. Berkeley's Philosophie der Mathematik.* E. MEYER. 1894. Pp. 57. IV. *Thomas Hill Green und der Utilitarismus.* G. F. JAMES. 1894. Pp. 37. V. *Zur Theorie der Aufmerksamkeit.* H. E. KOHN. 1895. Pp. 48. VI. *Kepler's Lehre von der Gravitation.* E. GOLDBECK. 1896. Pp. 52. VII. *Der Unterschied der Lehren Hume's im Treatise und im Inquiry.* W. BREDE. 1896. Pp. 50. VIII. *Die motorischen Wortvorstellungen.* R. DODGE. 1896. Pp. 78.

The Development of the Doctrine of Personality in Modern Philosophy. W. H. WALKER. Part I. Ann Arbor, Mich., The Inland Press. No date. Pp. 79.

Action de la Lumière sur la Rétine. E. PERGENS. Brussels, Lamertin. 1896. Pp. 33.

Die Entwickelung des Seelenbegriffes bei Kant. M. BRAHN. Leipzig, Gerhardt. No date. Pp. 66.

Causal-Nexus zwischen Leib und Seele. H. METSCHER. Dortmund, Ruhfus. No date. Pp. 177.

The Psychic Development of Young Animals and its Physical Correlation. WESLEY MILLS. Parts II. to VI. Reprinted from the Trans. Roy. Soc. of Canada, Second Series, 1895–6, Vol. I., Sec. 4. Durie & Son, Ottawa. Pp. 191–252.

Periodische Depressionszustände und ihre Pathogenesis. C. LANGE.
Translated by H. KURELLA. Hamburg and Leipzig, Voss.
1896. Pp. 55.
Report of the Commissioner of Education, 1893-4. Vols. I. and II.
N. W. HARRIS. Washington, Government Printing Office. 1896.
Kategorienlehre. E. v. HARTMANN. Bd. X. of Ausgewählte
Werke. Leipzig, Haacke. 1896. Pp. xv + 556.

NOTES.

MR. R. P. HALLECK considers the review of his book in the last
number of the REVIEW unfair to him. The reviewer, Professor Kirkpatrick, sends the following letter, in further explanation of his criticisms: " Inasmuch as Mr. Halleck thinks my review of his ' Psychology and Psychic Culture' unfair and even ' brutal' in its criticism
of his error in regard to the psychophysical law, I wish to say that I
do not believe that there are *many serious* errors in the book, for that
was the only one found in a careful reading of a number of topics.
That one was of such a nature, however, that no careful reader of
modern psychology could have made it, hence one cannot be sure that
the rest of the book is reliable without a careful examination of every
sentence. I may also emphasize the fact that the author has succeeded
in his aim of making a clear and interesting text book in which many
of the illustrations are peculiarly apt, and that he is to be criticised for
his subordination of other things to that aim rather than as to the way
in which he has carried it out."

AN EXPLANATION.

Prof. H. C. WARREN's appreciation of my *Outline of Psychology*
is so generous, and the tone of his criticism so uniformly moderate,
that I hesitate to offer objection to any of his statements. Indeed, for
his remarks upon the scientific aspects of my work I cannot but be
grateful. As regards what I may call an ethical aspect of it, however,
he is so unfair to what was at any rate my intention that reply seems
called for. He says: " Careful search fails to reveal a single reference to modern psychological literature in the whole book. This is
certainly a most singular omission and is much to be regretted. * * *
(The book) takes no pains to direct into proper channels the desire

for further reading which it will undoubtedly provoke." I have said in my preface (p. vi.) : " The system * * * stands * * * in the closest relation to that presented in the more advanced treatises of the German experimental school, Külpe's *Outlines of Psychology* and Wundt's *Grundzüge der physiologischen Psychologie.* While I have tried to make the present work complete in itself, I have also written with the view of producing a book which should be preparatory to these standard psychologies." I have thus explicitly directed the reader to two modern hand-books of psychology, in both of which he will find copious literary references. E. B. Titchener.

Prof. Titchener's remarks are quite true, and I thank him for pointing out the ambiguity in my statement. What I alluded to were page references, for further reading on special topics; I think this evident from the context. My criticism here was intended to be entirely *practical*, not ethical. H. C. Warren.

Dr. G. A. Tawney, Princeton, has been appointed to the chair in philosuphy in Beloit College, Wisconsin, made vacant by the death of Prof. Blaisdell.

The Review has received Prof. C. Stnmpf's diagrammatic *Tafeln zur Geschichte der Philosophie.* They will be found helpful in the teaching of the history of philosophy. (Berlin, Speyer & Peters, 1896, 80 Pf.)

Schleicher Frères, Paris, announce as in press the first issue (for 1895) of an *Anneé Biologique* described as *Comptes Rendus annuels des Travaux de Biologie générale,* directed by Prof. Ires Delage, of the Sorbonne.

A *Philosophisches Lexikon,* edited by Dr. M. Klein, with the assistance of a number of writers, principally German, is announced by Reisland (Leipzig). It is to be issued in 25 parts (M. 2.40 each). We note the name of Prof. M. M. Curtis, of Cleveland, Ohio, among the contributors.

Professor Flournoy, of Geneva, has published a *Notice sur le Laboratoire de Psychologie de l' Universitè de Genéve,* on occasion of the National Swiss Exposition. It contains lists of apparatus and publications, and interesting remarks on experimental psychology.

Vol. IV.   No. 2.   March, 1897.

The Psychological Review.

PROCEEDINGS OF THE FIFTH ANNUAL MEETING OF THE AMERICAN PSYCHOLOGICAL ASSOCIATION, BOSTON, DECEMBER, 1896.

Report of the Secretary and Treasurer for 1896.

The fifth annual meeting of the American Psychological Association was held in Boston and Cambridge, December 29 and 30, 1896, the time and place having. been chosen with reference to the simultaneous meetings of the American Society of Naturalists and the Affiliated Societies. There were forty-five members in attendance, the largest number since the organization of the Association. Three formal sessions were held, one on the morning of the 29th at the Harvard Medical School in Boston, and two sessions on the 30th at the Peabody Museum of Archæology in Cambridge. The morning session of the 30th was given up to papers of a distinctly philosophical character. The members of the Association for the most part attended the discussion on ' The Inheritance of Acquired Characteristics' before the American Society of Naturalists on the afternoon of the 29th, psychology being represented in the discussion by Professor James, of Harvard. Together with the other Affiliated Societies, the psychologists were present at Mr. Alexander Agassiz's lecture and reception in the evening of the 29th, at the luncheon given by the President and Fellows of Harvard College on the 30th, and at the annual dinner of the Societies at the Hotel Brunswick, Boston, on the evening of the same day. President George S. Fullerton presided at all the meetings of the Association.

At the regular business meeting and in the intervals of the program the following business was transacted: Election of officers for 1897: *President,* Professor J. Mark Baldwin, of Princeton University; *Secretary and Treasurer,* Dr. Livingston Farrand, of Columbia University; *Members of the Council,* Professors Josiah Royce, of Harvard University, and Joseph Jastrow, of the University of Wisconsin. Elected to membership on nomination of the Council: Dr. Ernest Albee, Cornell University; Dr. C. F. Bakewell, Harvard University; Dr. E. F. Buchner, Yale University; Mr. A. F. Buck, Union College; Mr. J. F. Crawford, Princeton University; Professor F. C. French, Vassar College; Dr. Alice J. Hamlin, Mt. Holyoke College; Professor J. G. Hibben, Princeton University; Dr. C. W. Hodge, Princeton University; Dr. David Irons, University of Vermont; Professor R. B. Johnson, Miami University; Dr. C. H. Judd, Wesleyan University; Dr. Robert McDougall, Western Reserve University; Professor G. H. Palmer, Harvard University; Mr. F. C. S. Schiller, Cornell University; Dr. G. A. Tawney, Beloit College.

An invitation was received from the British Association for the Advancement of Science to attend the next annual meeting to be held in Toronto, Canada, as members of the Section of Physiology. It was moved and carried that such members of the Council, including the outgoing members, as are able to attend, be official delegates of the Association to that meeting, and that such members of the Association as may be able to do so accept the invitation to attend as members.

An invitation was received from the American Association for the Advancement of Science to join that Association. It was voted that all members who might feel so disposed are recommended to present their names to the Secretary for election to that Association.

A communication was received from the Director of the Biological Laboratory, at Wood's Holl, inviting the Association to hold an informal meeting at Wood's Holl during some week of the summer months.

The invitation was referred to the Council, which recommended that the question of an informal Summer meeting of the Association be favorably considered, and that Wood's Holl be regarded as an eligible place for such meeting.

The following motions were made by Professor **Witmer, and** were referred to the Council:

1. That the Council of the American Psychological Association be recommended to select only such papers and contributions to the program of the annual meeting as are psychological in subject-matter.

.2. That the Council of the American Psychological Association be recommended to present at the next meeting of the Association a plan for the formation of an American Philosophical or Metaphysical Association, as one of the affiliated or associated organizations meeting with the present Affiliated Societies.

3. That in the election of new members to the American Psychological Association all names nominated by the Council shall be presented to the Association at its opening session in written form, or visibly displayed upon· a blackboard, together with a statement of the contribution or contributions to psychology, in virtue of which the persons named are eligible to membership, and that the action upon such names shall be taken by the Association at the final business meeting.

The time and place of the next meeting were referred to the President, to be determined in consultation with the authorities of the Affiliated Societies.

The Committee on Physical and Mental Tests presented their report, and, after a vote of thanks for the hospitality shown by Harvard University and the Local Committee of Arrangements, the meeting adjourned.

The report of the Treasurer and the abstracts of papers read at the meeting follow:

REPORT OF THE TREASURER:

Livingston Farrand in account with Am. Psychological Association.
Dr.

To receipts from retiring Treasurer......................	$308 09
" Dues of Members...	177 00
" Estimated Interest on Deposits.........................	15 00
	$500 09

Cr. By Expenditures for

    Postage and Stationary.............................$11 90

    Printing and Clerical Work....................... 14 25

    Expressage 40

                                               $ 26 55

          Balance on hand................................. $473 54

  Audited by the Council and found correct.

                                Livingston Farrand,

                                Secretary and Treasurer.

Abstracts of Papers.

The Physiology of Sensation. By E. A. Singer, University of Pennsylvania.

States the fundamental question as : What would be an ideally complete physiology of sensation? The method employed in answering the question would establish an analogy between what has been regarded as progress in the past and what should be sought by a progressive psychology of the future. All the validity claimed for the method rests upon our right to speculate until facts be forthcoming. The result of such an analogy is stated in the following form : wherever we know anything about the physiology of sensation, we find that the correlate of a mental difference is a structural physiological difference. Where we are yet in ignorance as to the physiological counterpart of a mental difference we should assume it to be a difference in structure rather than a difference in functioning of the same structure. This view is to be contrasted with such current opinions as would regard the physiological counterpart of intensity as the greater or less activity of the same nervous structure ; feeling tone as the greater or less disintegration, or as dependent upon conditions of greater or less nutrition of the same structure, etc. Some attempt is made, rather by way of illustration than as framing a completely tenable hypothesis, to suggest a physiology of these so-called properties of sensation that would relate them to quality of sensation. Thus the physiological basis of intensity differences is sought in part in the different end organs affected in greater or less reaction to a stimulus; in part also in special apparatus suggested by the allied nature of intensity and saturation in color sensations. Feeling tone is distinguished from pleasure and pain; the physiology of the former being related to that of the emotion, the physiology of the latter to that of the special senses. Local sign presents the inverse problem as to how sensations conditioned by confessedly different nervous structures should come to be classed together. The answer suggested is that the classing together of locally different sensations and qualitatively similar is conditioned by the formal likeness of the end organs affected, they determining a likeness in the adequate stimuli and in the general way of behaving of the sensation. Recognized likeness and difference of sensations are found to involve psycho-physical reflection.

Intensity of Sensation. By JAMES E. LOUGH, Harvard University.

Sensations forming an intensity series have this characteristic which distinguishes them from a qualitative series: namely, that the intensity series goes towards or from zero—the vanishing point—while a purely qualitative change leads neither to nor from the zero point of sensation. Theories of intensity of sensation may be classed in general under two heads: (a) that the stronger sensation *is* the weaker sensation plus more of the same sensation—following an analogy from the physical world which may prove dangerous and exposing psychology to the troublesome presupposition that our psychic elements (sensations) are compounds; (b) that the intensity series is merely a qualitative series, but ordered in a series towards or from zero by the presence of a second series of sensations, *e. g.*, brightness sensations or muscular sensations.

It would seem much more satisfactory to discover in the nature of the psycho-physical process itself that which shall give to sensations the characteristic of an intensity series. Accordingly, this hypothesis is offered: any sensation of a given quality and intensity that may arise, depends upon a certain physiological condition which is reached only after passing successively through a series of other physiological conditions, each of which is the basis of a sensation of the same quality, but differing in degree from zero to the given sensation. That is, any sensation depends upon the physiological basis which contains, in a temporal series, the bases of all the weaker sensations of this particular quality. The final neural condition, after passing through all the intermediate steps, may be called the maximum effect of the stimulus. By a study of the intensity of sensations produced by a stimulus of a known intensity acting for a time less than that necessary to produce its maximum effect, it is found that this intensity is exactly proportional to the duration of the stimulation. Concerning the nature of the psycho-physical process nothing is postulated save that the basis of the stronger sensation contains that of the weaker in the time series as stated above.

Report of Experiments on the Reduction of the Tactual Double-Point Threshold by Practice, and on the ' Vexirfehler.' By G. A. TAWNEY, Beloit College.

The first object of the following experiments was to examine the view of Volkmann and Fechner that, by daily practicing some one spot of skin in the perception of two points, the threshold for this perception is reduced, not only for the spot actually practiced, but also for the symmetrically opposite spot on the other side of the body. A number of threshold determinations were made on different parts of the body varying in number from six to thirty-two for each subject. One of these spots was chosen for special practice which continued for a period varying from two weeks to a month. At the end of this time, the threshold determinations on the six to thirty-six different parts of the body were repeated, in order to compare them with those at the beginning of the practice series. The instrument used was a simple pair of compasses. The results show unmistakably that where any reduction of the threshold occurs as a result of practice, it occurs over the entire surface of the body; it demands, therefore, a central explanation. The paper further discusses the nature ' Vexirfehler ' (double-point illusion). It was assumed that the double-point illusion is the result of suggestion and it was sought to free a subject, whose threshold formerly could not be determined, from the suggestion involved. The experiments seemed to show that the reduction of the threshold by practice is, to a great extent at least, a result of suggestion. Several series were carried out for the purpose of studying the psychosis underlying the 'Vexirfehler.' The results seem to show that this illusion is mainly due to auto-suggestion, although physiological factors may play a subordinate part.

Comparison of the Times of Simple Reactions and of Free-Arm Movements in Different Classes of Persons. By ALBERT L. LEWIS. (Introduced by Professor Witmer.)

This paper gave the results of nearly 9,000 experiments on American men and women, and on male Negroes and Indians. The relative order of these four classes was found to be in reacting to Sound, arranged from shortest to longest: Indians, American men, Negroes and American women; to Light, American men, Indians, American women and Negroes; to Touch, Indians and American men the same, Negroes third and American women fourth. With regard to the mean variations of the average reaction times, the order was: in Sound, American men, Indians, Negroes and American women; in Light, American men, Indians, Negroes and American women; in Touch, Indians, American men, American women and Negroes. Following this was given a comparison of the flexion and extension movements of both right and left arm. The relative order of the classes was found to be American men, Indians and American women. This order holds throughout the four movements. No report on the Negroes was given, as the experiments on this class were not yet completed. It was noticeable in these experiments that the American men were quicker in their longest movement than the Indians in their shortest, and the Indians were similarly quicker than the women. Not less interesting was the fact that, although all the subjects were right-handed, the flexion movements of the left arm were quicker than the corresponding movement of the right, except in the case of the American men, where the time of the movement was the same for each arm. The conclusions drawn were that there are

characteristic variations in the reaction time and rate of movement of classes of persons; that a close relation exists between
reaction time and rate of movement; that a number of reactions
is necessary to give a characteristic result in each individual case.

*Researches in Progress in the Psychological Laboratory of
Columbia University.* By J. McKEEN CATTELL.

Among the subjects in course of investigation the following
may be mentioned as likely to be completed soon: Mr. W.
Lay, lately Fellow in Philosophy, has for several years been
studying mental imagery by various methods. In addition to
questions such as those proposed by Mr. Galton, others have
been set more independent of immediate introspection and extending to auditory and motor imagery. Among others, including musicians, 100 leading artists have in letters and interviews
described their imagery. Imagery has been investigated by its
effects on memory, and in the compositions of poets and other
writers. Mr. Lay has, finally, given special attention to his own
imagery and associations. Mr. S. I. Franz, Fellow in Psychology, is investigating after-images. He has already published
experiments on the threshold for after-images, and is now studying the duration and nature of the after-image as dependent
on the intensity, duration and area of stimulation. He is able
to correlate the effects of these magnitudes for consciousness
and to analyze physiological and mental factors. The individual differences are of interest, for with the same stimulus the
image differs greatly with different persons. Mr. L. B. Mc-
Whood, Fellow in Psychology, is studying the motor accompaniments of the perception and emotional results of music.
The movements are a series of taps made as rapidly as possible
and a pressure, not a maximum but kept as nearly as may be
constant. The subject decides on his preferences, etc., for the
tunes and combinations used, and these are compared with the
motor effects. Mr. H. E. Houston is studying color nomenclature, with special reference to children, and proposes to extend
his work to other senses. The growth in accuracy and extent
of the color vocabulary in schools has been determined, and the
attempt will be made to find and set a normal nomenclature for

colors and other classes of sensations. Other researches were referred to briefly.

The Psychic Development of Young Animals and its Somatic Correlation, with Special Reference to the Brain. By WESLEY MILLS, McGill University, Montreal.

This paper is based on researches on psychic development and on the development of cerebral cortex in the same groups of animals. As somatic correlation other than that of the brain has been considered in other papers, that phase of the subject was not especially treated in this paper. The main conclusions are as follows: in the dog and the cat there is a period extending from birth to about the time of the opening of the eyes characterized by reflex movements, the sway of instincts and the absence of intelligence. During this time the cerebral cortex is inexcitable by electrical stimulation, so that the psychic condition during the blind period is correlated with an undeveloped state of the motor centers of the cortex of the cerebrum. The advance in movements, first of the limbs and later of the head and face parts, together with the psychic progress associated with this, is correlated with the rapid development of the cortical centres for the limbs in the first instance, and later for the head and face in the period immediately following the blind stage. This is more rapid and more pronounced in the cat than in the dog, and is correlated with the greater control in the cat over the fore-limbs and with certain physiological and psychic developments characteristic of the cat.

Similar conclusions apply to the rabbit, except that the difference in the rapidity of development of head and face movements is correlated with an earlier organization of the corresponding cortical centres, and that there is a greater difference between the fore-limb and the hind-limb, with all of which there are special psychic correlations bound up with certain peculiarities of the rabbit's modes of life.

· The vast difference in physiological and psychic development of the cavy at birth is correlated with the presence of cortical cerebral centres readily excited by artificial stimuli, centres which in a few days reach a practically perfect state of development.

The psychic manifestations of the pigeon and the fowl have not the same sort of cerebral cortical correlates as the animals referred to above.

The Organization of Practical Work in Psychology. By Lightner Witmer, University of Pennsylvania.

Under the designation of practical work in psychology was included: 1. The direct application, whether by professional psychologists, practicing physicians or teachers, of psychological principles to therapeutics and to education.

2. Such psychophysical investigation of mental conditions and processes as may serve to throw light upon the problems that confront humanity in the practice of medicine or teaching.

3. The offering of instruction in psychology, to students of medicine or to teachers, that contains a promise of future usefulness to them in their respective professions.

Thus the plan has a view to the professional practice of psychology, to research and to instruction, as these stand related to the two professions of medicine and teaching.

In order that psychology may become a usable possession of the medical man, details of organization must be perfected that will bring about a union of the department of psychology with the professional departments of the medical school.

The following details of organization are suggested as a part of a plan for the development of research work and instruction useful to the community and to the teacher:

1. The University Department of Psychology should be in close association with all classes and grades of children. Organization is required to make possible the conduction of physical and mental tests upon all children in all grades from the kindergarten up to the graduate department and upon such so-called abnormal children as may be found in special institutions for the feeble minded, the deaf, the blind and the morally defective.

2. A Department of Psychology needs for purposes of demonstration a Psychological Museum equipped with specimens of work done by defective and by normal children with the instruments and apparatus used in teaching them, and affording some

display of the results of special investigations into the physical and mental characteristics of children, exhibited, perhaps, in the form of tables and curves.

3. An experimental training school presenting the following features:

a. Independent schools or homes for such children as can afford to pay for expert psychological and pedagogical treatment.

b. A psychological clinic and dispensary.

c. Special or ungraded training schools for children who are backward or physically defective—these to be organized under the control of the city school authorities but to be in harmonious and effective relation with the Psychological Department of the local university.

4. Instruction in psychology should be adapted to meet the wants of two classes of teachers:

a. The common school teacher of all grades from the kindergarten to the university, who needs, above all else, courses in the practical study of children.

b. The psychological expert who is capable of treating the many difficult cases that resist the ordinary methods of the school room. The pedagogical or psychological expert requires thorough courses in some branches of medicine and in practical psychology. For both classes of teachers, the features just enumerated under one, two and three, will be found of great service in supplying the requisite practical experience in psychology.

Psycho-Physical Tests on Normal School and Kindergarten Pupils. By Miss MARY P. HARMON (Introduced by Prof. Witmer).

These tests form part of a general scheme which proposes the development of a series of tests which shall be applicable alike to the oldest and youngest pupils in all grades from the Kindergarten to the Normal School. The intention is to repeat from year to year a series of experiments of which a few are included in this preliminary report as the children now in the Kindergarten pass through the various grades.

The tests reported upon include family statistics, age, height, weight, lung capacity, simple reaction time to sound and rate of free arm movements.

One hundred girls in the first year of the Normal School were tested. Ninety-five per cent. are American born. Seventy-nine per cent. of the mothers and seventy per cent. of the fathers are American born. The grandparents range from forty-one to forty-four per cent. American born. The average age is 18.2 years. The average height is 62.4 inches, the average weight is 112.8 pounds, and the average lung capacity is 134.4 cubic inches. The average reaction time taking the minimum of five trials is 153 σ. The average quickest movement is for the right hand in extension 114 σ, in flexion 108 σ; left hand in extension 109 σ; left hand flexion 217 σ; the distance moved over was 53 centimeters. Some coördination was noticeable between intellectual capacity and rate of reaction and movement; those girls who stood out as bright being below the average.

Thirty-four boys and sixty-three girls in the Kindergartens ranging from four and one-half to seven years of age give an average height of thirty-nine to forty-four inches. Weight thirty-five to forty pounds. The boys give an average lung capacity of forty cubic inches; the girls of twenty-five. The boys give an average shortest reaction of two hundred and eighty-four, the girls of two hundred and eighty-one. The boys give an average longest reaction of five hundred and thirty-three, the girls of six hundred and eighty-four. The boys move the right arm in extension, the left in flexion, the left in extension and the right in flexion in the following times respectively: 153, 154, 158, 160; the girls make the same movements in the following time: 219, 205, 228, 223. The average shortest time for all movements is 153 for the boys and 192 for the girls. Thus the girls throughout are noticeably slower than the boys, although their reaction time is but a trifle longer. Comparing the Kindergarten children with the Junior Class of the Normal School we find the average shortest reaction of the Juniors is 131 σ shorter than that of the Kindergarten boys and 128 σ shorter than that of the girls. Their rate of movement is 62 σ less than for the boys and 101 σ less than for the girls.

Personal Experiences under Ether. By WESLEY MILLS, Mc-
Gill University, Montreal.

This paper relates the experiences of the writer during and
immediately subsequent to the administration of ether, together
with a later experience which seemed to grow out of the former
and which produced a profound impression.

A Preliminary Study of Memory. By BROTHER CHRYSOSTOM,
Manhattan College.

The paper presented rather a plan of work for the present
scholastic year than results already obtained from experiments
on memory. The immediate end sought was a knowledge of
the relative value of visual and aural memory. The method
adopted is similar to that described by Mr. E. A. Kirkpatrick in
the PSYCHOLOGICAL REVIEW, November, 1894. The two series,
viz., of objects for vision, and of names for hearing, are shown
on alternate days. Both names and objects are familiar, the
names being monosyllables and excluding association effects.
The objects and names recalled with greatest facility are then
noted and classified with a view to determine the cause of this
phenomenon. At this stage the work is again reviewed and
examined as helping to answer the question: "Is conscious
memory a *spiritual* phenomenon?"

Lest the conditions under which the experiments are formed
might be exceptional, a series of thirty questions was prepared
to be answered not only by the subjects of these experiments,
but also by about three hundred boys and young men engaged
in academic and collegiate study in various other cities of the
Union. These questions refer to the signs of attention, the best
time for memory work, the relative difficulty experienced in
memorizing different disciplines, the place of repetition in memory, the means of steadying attention, individual mnemonic devices, and the influence of heredity upon memory.

*On a Method of Studying Cerebral Circulation (the Eye-Pleth-
ysmograph).* An informal communication. By E. C. SAN-
FORD, Clark University.

The method in question is an insignificant modification of

one described by Dr. F. W. Ellis in the *Boston Medical and Surgical Journal* of April 21, 1887, but little known as yet to psychologists. It is in essence a means of taking pulse and blood-pressure tracings from the ophthalmic artery. This artery, which supplies the eye ball and orbit, is anatomically in direct connection with the cerebral system and furnishes an index of its condition.

To secure these tracings a plaster cast is taken of the upper part of the face, extending a little above and below the eyes and a little around onto the temples. In making this cast the eyes are covered with watch glasses, so that when finished, a hollow remains before each eye. Holes are afterward bored

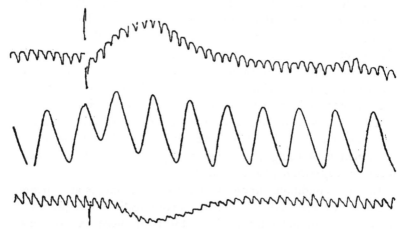

The curves read from left to right. The upper one gives the time in seconds. The next gives the eye pulse; the third the respiration—upward movements showing inspiration, downward expiration; the fourth, the finger pulse—taken from the fingers of the right hand with a small air plethysmograph. The short vertical lines at the left give the relative positions of the writing points during the tracing of the curves. The irregular marks breaking into the ninth pulsation in the second and fourth curves show the momentary dislocation of the apparatus caused by the muscular ' start ' of the subject, on hearing the sound.

The cut is a photographic reproduction, in the size of the original tracings, of a five-fold enlargement of them shown at the meeting of the Association. The enlargement was very carefully drawn for measurements of the curves to 0.1 mm., except in the case of the time line where a curve showing equal seconds was substituted for the actual one which contained 4.29+ vibrations to the second. The greatest irregularity in the motion of the kymograph in any second of the period shown was under one part in forty-seven.

into these hollows and short glass tubes inserted and sealed in place. When the cast is to be used the face is anointed with thick vaseline, to help in making the cast air-tight, and it is further held in place by a bandage about the head. Rubber tubes are slipped upon the glass tubes and their free ends lead away by a Y to a single Marey tambour. Every increase of blood in the orbit now causes a compression of the air in the cavities before the eyes, and an elevation of the stylus of the tambour which can be recorded in the usual way with a kymograph and smoked paper.

During the spring of 1896 this method was used by Mr. G. E. Dawson and the writer, in a study of the relation of certain psychical states to circulation and respiration. The accompanying cut shows a favorable, but by no means unique example of the tracings obtained. In it may be seen the rise of the cerebral blood pressure (second curve from the top) and corresponding fall of pressure in the fingers (fourth curve) caused by startling the subject with a sharp and unexpected noise. A full report of the study is delayed by the great time required for a careful study of the curves obtained.

Color-Blindness and William Pole: A Study in Logic. By Mrs. CHRISTINE LADD FRANKLIN. Read by title.

Philosophy in the American Colleges. By A. C. ARMSTRONG, JR., Wesleyan University.

This paper was based on data obtained from a number of representative colleges and universities with reference to the development of philosophical instruction in recent years. It appeared that this development has been a marked one, although the movement has had a comparatively late origin. The causes of the increase in philosophical faculties and courses were discovered, first, in the general educational advance and the deepening of the national thought; second, in conditions special to the department. The growth of the special science has occasioned a demand for the speculative correlation and interpretation of their results. The progress of psychology, at first as an empirical and experimental science, then in relation to systematic discussions and even metaphysical problems, has given

it a central importance in the philosophical curriculum.   Logic,·
on the contrary, has lost ground in comparison with its position
a generation ago, and ethics, while better maintaining its place,
has become more systematic and less practical, except in that
political and social ethics have been added to the ethics of the individual.   Apart from psychology, the greatest advance has
been made in general philosophy.   Little has been accomplished in the way of detailed historical research, but the history of philosophy, as now taught, gives the student some acquaintance with the history of intellectual progress as well as
with the classical philosophical systems.   Constructive thought
and instruction have been begun, though the propounders of
complete systems are few.   Pedagogy is one of the youngest
branches of the department, but not the least valuable.

With the extent and the content of philosophical teaching,
methods have also changed.   Elective courses have, for the
most part, taken the place of prescribed work.   In psychology
emphasis is placed on experimental inquiry in the laboratory.
Historical, systematic, ethical and religious philosophy take on
a more literary form, with constantly increasing use of methods
found fruitful in other departments.

In fine, philosophy has reëstablished its position in the
American universities and may be expected more and more to
influence our thought and civilization.   [Printed in the *Educational Review* for January, 1897.]

Tests of Current Theory Touching Mind and Body.   By
   DICKINSON S. MILLER, Bryn Mawr College.

The probabilities and presumptions by which alone in this
problem theory can be guided may be strictly tested and gauged :

I. As regards those cited on behalf of the theory of interaction : the evolutionary argument from ‘ the distribution of
pleasures and pains’ is invalid, but the evolutionary argument
from the concomitant variations of mind and cerebral complexity
and the original argument from the testimony of conscious experience do, indeed, yield positive presumption of a causal tie.
Yet the presumption of unbroken physical order is also well-
founded.   Were the two incompatible the latter must give way.

They are, however, consistent. The facts in time or space are presumably as the parallelist states them; the material order is uninfringed; nevertheless one psycho-physical event is the indivisible cause of the next psycho-physical event (the psychical and physical sides being by hypothesis inseparable), and hence the psychosis is part-cause of the total ensuing event, part-cause consequently of the ensuing neurosis. Thus the strict sense of our terms obliges us to admit an *unintrusive causation* on the part of consciousness and so to reconcile presumptions apparently at odds.

II. As regards universal parallelism or panpsychism; the arguments for it rest all upon the need of ascribing ' continuity' or ' uniformity' to the world. There are, however, four reasons for denying that panpsychism would yield such continuity. And even if it did, there prove on analysis to be no such signs of continuity in the world either of naïve imagination, of mechanical atomism, or of strict metaphysics, as to warrant the acceptance of a theory not otherwise evidenced.

The Relation of Mind and Body. By C. A. STRONG, Columbia University.

The object of this paper was to show that parallelism is not necessarily inconsistent with the efficacy of consciousness.

The interactionists usually fail to tell us what they mean by the matter on which they say that the mind acts. But matter means either a content of consciousness or an independent reality symbolized by that content, either object or eject. Furthermore, many idealists deny the existence of ejects; whence the following dilemma.

If ejects be denied, matter no longer remains in any palpable form for the mind to act upon; since it will hardly be maintained that our volitions act directly on the content of our perceptions. If ejects be accepted, there is no reason why our volitions should not act upon them and so deserve, in a sense consistent with Hume's doctrine of causality, the predicate of efficacy.

But such efficacy admits of, if it does not require, a parallelistic interpretation. For consciousness may itself be the eject

which appears to an onlooker as the brain process; and in that
case the phenomenal interaction between the brain process and
other physical events would run parallel to and be the symbol
of a real interaction between consciousness and other ejects.

Is the 'Transcendental Ego' an Unmeaning Conception? By J.
E. CREIGHTON, Cornell University.

This paper is an attempt to indicate some of the permanent
elements of truth in the doctrine of the Transcendental Ego,
taking into account, however, only the theoretical consciousness.
There are two ways of looking at the knowing consciousness.
First, that of psychology, which takes consciousness simply as
a string of states or processes. These, as they first appear, are
found to be complex and capable of resolution into elementary
sensations. Now, the psychologist undertakes to describe the
quality, intensity, extent and duration of the sensations, and to
determine the various ways in which they combine into complexes. This investigation, being concerned only with the conscious processes and their modes of existence, finds no place for
an Ego of any sort. But it is to be noticed, that so far as mental
states are observed, as it were, from the standpoint of an external observer, the investigation deals with their *real*, not
with their *ideal* side. And no description, however exact and
accurate, of the various attributes of sensations, or of the ways
in which they are fused and associated, can stand as an account
of experience. To understand the fact of knowledge, then, a
new standpoint—that of Logic or Epistemology—is necessary.
Consciousness must here be conceived as taking the form of
judgment. For knowledge comes only as the result of a process
of interpretation and evaluation, and in this consists the essence
of judgment. Knowledge, then, is the product of judging
thought. Now the Transcendental Ego must be found in the
judging thought or not at all. Both Kant and Fichte protest
against making the Ego a thing or substance beyond consciousness. The real question is whether thought as we actually find
it possesses the predicates—unity, identity, permanence, etc.—
which the transcendentalists apply to their Ego. After showing
in what sense we can speak of a conscious or ideal activity as

permanent and self-identical, the paper concludes with a statement of the positive grounds which compel us to apply these predicates to what we may call Thought or the Ego. Our experience forms one single system; the world of knowledge which is the product of the activity of intelligence is a whole, or at least *is required to be a whole*, and not a thing of shreds and patches. Now Kant argued from the unity of the Ego to the necessary unity of the Ego's experience. We may reverse the argument, and from the unity of experience infer that the thought which has constructed this experience is itself a single and self-identical principle.

The Relation of Pessimism to Ultimate Philosophy. By F. C. S. SCHILLER, Cornell University.

To show that the question of pessimism is an ultimate one for philosophy. Pessimism is not merely a possible outcome of the hedonistic calculus, but the denial that life is worth living may follow from the despair of *any* ideal of Value, *e. g.*, of Goodness, Knowledge and Beauty as well as of Happiness. It forms an attitude towards judgments of Value and the ultimate ideal of Value resulting from them, precisely analogous to the attitude of Scepticism toward judgments of Fact and the ideal of Truth. In each case there seems to be three possible attitudes : affirmative (gnostic—optimist), negative (sceptical—pessimist), and agnostic (or 'critical'). But the third may be reduced to the second. Further, the question of ultimate Fact is finally subordinate to that of ultimate Value, so that the question of Optimism or Pessimism becomes the final alternative for Philosophy. Pessimism, however, remains secondary. Practically, the recognition of this view would strengthen Philosophy.

The Method and Standpoint of Ethics. By JAMES SETH, Cornell University.

The present tendency to regard Ethics as a science rather than as a part of Philosophy or Metaphysics is a reaction from metaphysical Ethics of Kant, and a return to the sounder view of Aristotle and of the earlier British school. We must, however, distinguish two types or groups of science, the Normative and the Natural. The normative sciences deal with our judgments of worth, the natural sciences with our judgments of fact. To the former class belong Logic, Æsthetics and Ethics. Our several judgments about the value of thoughts, of feelings, and of actions are reducible to a common denominator of Truth, of Beauty and of Goodness; the discovery of this unifying principle and the construction of the system of our intellectual æsthetic and ethical judgments in their organic relation to it, is the business of Logic, of Æsthetics and of Ethics respectively. These sciences must be distinguished, no less than the natural sciences, from Metaphysics, whose province it is to deal with the question of the ultimate validity of our judgments, whether they are judgments of fact or judgments of worth. Both the natural and the normative sciences have to be criticised and correlated by Metaphysics, whose question of questions is that of the comparative validity of the Ought-judgments and the Is-judgments as expressions of ultimate Reality. The distinction here insisted upon between the normative and the natural sciences is not a difference in method, but only in subject-matter. The function of Ethics, for example, is like that of Physics, merely to organize the judgments of 'Common Sense' or ordinary thought. There is a 'Common Sense' of value, as there is a 'Common Sense' of fact; and there is a science of value, as there is a science of fact. It is not possible for Ethics to transcend the sphere of Common Sense, and to discover, beyond that sphere, a Norm or standard by which we can establish or invalidate the judgments of Common Sense. Like all sciences, Ethics is a criticism of Common Sense; but it is an immanent criticism, a self-criticism.

A Generalization of Immedite Inferences. By JOHN GRIER HIBBEN, Princeton University.

When we have given, All *x* is *y*, it is possible to infer immediately:

(1) The Converse, Some *y* is *x*.
(2) The Obverse, No *x* is not-*y*.
(3) The Converted Obverse, No not-*y* is *x*.
(4) The Contrapositive, All not-*y* is not-*x*.

(5) The Obverted Converse, Some *y* is not not-*x*

(6) The Inverse, Some not-*x* is not *y*.

(7) The Obverted Inverse, Some not-*x* is not-*y*.

The above may be tabulated in the following square of Immediate Inferences :

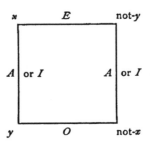

The letters *A, E, I,* or *O* indicate that the two terms between which any of them is situated may be joined in a proposition of the form represented by that letter ; and in every case such a proposition will be a legitimate inference from the original proposition, All *x* is *y*.

Thus between the two upper terms *x* and not-*y*, two propositions of the form *E* may be inferred :

No *x* is not-*y*. *E.*

No not-*y* is *x*. *E.*

Between the two lower terms, two *O* propositions are possible :

Some *y* is not-*x*. *O.*

Some not-*x* is not *y*. *O.*

Reading down the two vertical lines, two *A* propositions :

All *x* is *y*. *A.*

All not-*y* is not-*x*. *A.*

Reading from the lower to the upper two *I* propositions :

Some *y* is *x*. *I.*

Some not-*x* is not-*y*. *I.*

Again when *E* is the original proposition, no *x* is *y*, all **the** possible inferences may be comprehended in a square which **dif-**

fers from the one above only by interchanging the positions of
y and not-*y*.   This is in accord with the fact that an *A* proposition becomes an *E* proposition by obversion, in which process it is observed that not-*y* displaces *y*.   Given no *x* is *y*, we
have :

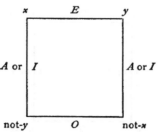

Forming propositions as before we have all the inferences
from an *E* proposition :

No *x* is *y*. *E* (the original proposition).
No *y* is *x*. *E*
Some not-*y* is not not-*x*. *O*.
Some not-*x* is not not-*y*. *O*.
All *x* is not-*y*. *A*.
All *y* is not-*x*. *A*.
Some not-*y* is *x*. *I*.
Some not-*x* is *y*. *I*.

When *I* is given, some *x* is *y*.   We have the *A* and *E* inferences of the *A* square becoming *I* and *O* respectively; also
the horizontal lines are to be read from left to right only; and
no inference is possible between not-*x* and not-*y*.
We have therefore the following :

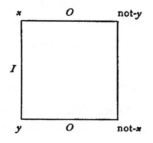

The possible propositions are :

Some *x* is *y*. *I*.

Some *y* is *x*. *I*.

Some *x* is not not-*y*. *O*.

Some *y* is not not-*x*. *O*.

Similarly when *O* is given, some *x* is not *y*, the square is the same as the *I* square with the interchange of *y* and not-y,

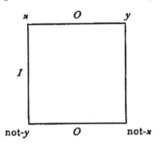

The possible propositions are :

Some *x* is not *y*. *O*.

Some not-*y* is not not-*x*. *O*.

Some *x* is not-*y*. *I*.

Some not-*y* is *x*. *I*.

[NOTE.—When *A* or *E* is inferred, the weakened form *I* or *O* is always possible.]

The Negative in Psychology and Logic. By A. T. ORMOND. Princeton University.

The paper is summed up in the following propositions :

I. That the theory of negation is involved in the general theory of judgment, which must be considered as a preliminary.

II. That all judgment arises out of volitional grounds and maintains the volitional form in its central pulse of assertion.

III. That the differentiating conditions of judgment are : (*a*) the rise of the world of representation as objective, (*b*) the presence of some interest in this objective world, (*c*) the real subject of the judgment which is some body of experience or knowledge, constituting the genus or universal within which the judgment function acts.

IV. That all judgment with the possible exception of the simple existential is disjunctive, in the sense that it is concerned with alternatives in a larger universe in which these are included.

V. That negation arises along with affirmation as a form of the self-assertion of the real subject. The assertion of this subject motives to the affirmation and negation.

VI. That denial arises on the presentation of the incompatible to this subject, and is simply the act of removal or suppression by means of which the subject maintains itself.

VII. That denial does not necessarily presuppose a previous affirmation, actual or supposed, but may arise directly as a reaction against the incompatible, just as we may assert directly the inequality of two lines.

VIII. That the *function* of denial must be distinguished from its *implications*. In its function denial is always removal and can never pass into affirmation. By implication, however, affirmation is involved in various degrees in denial.

IX. The negative affects the copula of a judgment rather than its predicate. The theory that the negative is not copular virtually abolishes negation by translating all judgment into the affirmative form.

X. But thinking cannot get on without denial. In the world of alternatives the incompatible arises. In presence of the incompatible, affirmation is powerless. The pulse of denial is as essential to thought and knowledge as is that of affirmation.

XI. But while the functions of affirmation and denial forever remain distinct, they tend, as the body of knowledge increases in scope and definiteness, to become more and more closely connected in their implications.

This paper will appear in full in THE PSYCHOLOGICAL REVIEW.

Address of the President. Subject: *The 'Knower' in Psychology.* By GEORGE S. FULLERTON, University of Pennsylvania.

An examination of the treatment of the Self in its function of 'knower' by philosophers and psychologists, and a discussion of the meaning of 'knowledge' in psychology. It was an attempt to apply to this problem the scientific psychological method outlined as the true psychological method in two earlier papers read by the author at recent meetings of the Association. It was shown, in a brief historical sketch of the development of the idea of the Self in the history of philosophy, how the abstract and inconsistent notions which usually pass current have come into being. The author then turned to modern psychology, and first criticised the notion of the Self as a self-constitutive activity, which comes to the surface in the writings of the Neo-Kantian school, finding the position of its advocates inconsistent and untenable. He next took up the view of the Self that regards it as a noumenon, or a something to be distinguished from the phenomena of consciousness, and in some sense underlying them, taking as the chief subject of his criticism the recent works of Professor Ladd, which do not, it is true, hold to a noumenal self in a bald and uncompromising form, but which, in his opinion, combine this notion with that held by the Neo-Kantians, and with a third, which he discussed later. He held that this position necessarily leads to difficulties which prove its untenability.

Following this, he referred to a class of thinkers which he described as belonging to the Humian school, using that term in a broad sense to indicate those who repudiate noumena, and accept the phenomena of consciousness and their inter-relations as furnishing the whole material with which the psychologist has to deal. He referred particularly to the later writings of Wundt, and those of Ziehen, Külpe and Titchener. With the general position taken by these authors he expressed himself as in substantial harmony, although he did not regard them as having seen the full significance of their own teachings on the question of the nature of knowledge either for psychology or epistemology.

The latter part of his address, embodying his own positive conclusions, maintained that the attempts to explain knowledge by the intervention of a 'Knower' of either the noumenal or the Neo-Kantian sort are based upon a misunderstanding, and regarded the notion of the abstract and inconsistent 'Knower' still current among philosophers and psychologists as a survival from, **and** development of, the crude notion of the bodily self which precedes the beginning of reflection, and the duplicate of this seen in the animism of savage races.

[The address has been published in full in THE PSYCHO-LOGICAL REVIEW for January, 1897.]

PRELIMINARY REPORT OF THE COMMITTEE ON PHYSICAL AND MENTAL TESTS.

The Committee on Physical and Mental Tests appointed at the last annual meeting of this Association submits the following report:

The committee has drawn up a series of physical and mental tests which is regarded as especially appropriate for college students tested in a psychological laboratory. The same series would also be suitable for the general public and, with some omissions and slight modifications, for school children. The committee has had in view a series of tests requiring not more than one hour for the record of one subject. In selecting the tests and methods the committee regarded as most important those which seemed likely to reveal individual differences and development, but also took into account ease and quickness in making the tests and in interpreting and collating the results.

Each member of the committee selected a tentative series of tests. The report includes these selections, together with brief descriptions of methods. After each test and method are placed the initials of the members of the committee recommending it.*

* We refer especially to two publications for descriptions of some of the tests: *Official Catalogue of Exhibits*, Department M., World's Columbian Exposition, *Section of Psychology*, Joseph Jastrow in charge, 1893; and *Physical and Mental Measurements of the Students of Columbia University*, J. McKeen Cattell and Livingston Farrand, THE PSYCHOLOGICAL REVIEW, Nov., 1896. The following papers on the subject may also be mentioned: "Mental Tests and Measurements," J. McK. Cattell, with an appendix by Francis Galton, *Mind*, 1890; "Zur Individual Psychologie," Hugo Münsterberg, *Centralblatt f. Nervenheilkunde und Psychiatrie*, 1891; "Researches on the Mental and Physical Development of School Children," J. A. Gilbert, *Studies from the Yale Laboratory*, 1895; reported also by E. W. Scripture, *Zeitschrift f. Psychologie*, etc., X., 1896, and THE PSYCHOLOGICAL REVIEW, III., 1896; Der psychologische Versuch in der Psychiatrie, Emil Kraepelin, *Psychologische Arbeiten*, 1895; La psychologie individuelle, A. Binet et V. Henri, *L'Année psychologique*, 1896.

Preliminary Data: B. C. J. S. W.

Date of birth; birthplace; birthplace of father; birthplace of mother; occupation (including class in college, or, if not a student, the last educational institution attended); occupation of father; any measurements previously made. B. C. J. S. W.

Color of eyes; color of hair; right or left-handed. B. C. J. S.

Mother's maiden name; number of brothers; sisters; order of birth; age of parents at birth; birthplace and occupation of grandparents. W.

Two schedules of observations and records to be filled in, one by the recorder and one by the subject, as in the Columbia tests, with such modifications as experience shall make desirable. C.

A blank to be filled in by the recorder, noting asymmetry of head or body, color of eyes and hair, complexion, degenerative or other stigmata of head, eyes, ears, mouth, teeth, hands or feet, posture, gait, manner, coördination and speech, indications of intellectual, emotional and moral characteristics. W.

Physical Measurements: B. C. J. S. W.

Height, weight and size of head. B. C. J. S. W.

Breathing capacity. C. J. S. W.

Height sitting. C. W.

The measurements should be made in the metric system. The weight should be taken in ordinary indoor clothing. The height should have the height of the heel subtracted. At least the length and breadth of the head should be measured. B. C. S.

Keenness of Vision: B. C. J. S. W.

The maximum distance at which diamond (4½ point) numerals can be read with each eye singly. B. C. J. S.

The illumination should be in the neighborhood of 100 candle-meters; about eight out of ten numerals should be read correctly at the rate of about 2 per second. The minimum distance should also be determined, if possible. B. C.

In addition or as a substitute, drawing a series of forms as recommended. J.

Use Snellen Test-types. B. S.

Some other substitute for these tests, to be suggested after satistory trial. W.

Color Vision: B. C. J. S. W.

Select as quickly as possible four greens from a series of wools; measure the time; if long, make further tests. C.

Combine with test of rate of perception by requiring subject to name, as rapidly as possible, a series of colors, either wools or papers. B. W.

Use the chart exhibited at the World's Fair.   J.

Keenness of Hearing: B. C. J. S. W.

The distance at which a continuous sound can be heard with each ear singly. B. C. W.

Use some artificial external meatus if the test is to show small differences in sensibility. W.

The sound should be from a watch reduced to a standard. An arrangement should be used by which it can be periodically cut off without the knowledge of the subject. C. S.

Use for this a stop-watch. B. J. S.

I endorse the stop-watch; it can be manipulated so that the time is recorded, showing how long it took the subject to decide that the watch has stopped. J.

Perception of Pitch: B. C. J. S.

Adjust one monochord or pipe to another, the tones not to be sounded simultaneously. C. J.

Select a match from a set of forks, making a fixed number of vibrations per second more or less than a standard, *e. g.*, standard 500 v. per second; other forks 497, 497.5, 498, 498.5, etc. ; 500, 500.5, 501, etc. B. S.

I prefer the adjustment to the selection method. The test can be made with two Gilbert tone-testers. J.

Fineness of Touch: C. J. S. W.

The æsthesiometer is unsatisfactory; the discrimination of roughness of surfaces and touching a spot previously touched should be tried. C. J. W.

Sensitiveness to Pain: B. C. J. S. W.

The gradually increasing pressure that will just cause pain. The point or points in the body to be used to be agreed upon. B. C. J.W.

Perception of Weight or of Force of Movement: B. C. J. S. W.

Arrange a series of weights. B. J. W. With and without sight. B.

Make movements of equal force and determine the error. C.

The best method still to be developed. J.

Dynamometer Pressure of Right and Left Hands: B. C. J. S. W.

In place of or in addition to the ordinary dynamometer test make movements of the thumb and forefinger and continue as rapidly as possible for fifteen seconds. B. C.

Use mechanical counter for this and take reading at end of every minute. S.

Thumb and finger dynamometer. Record best and worst of five trials. W.

Rate of Movement: W.

Distance of 35 cm. One preliminary trial with right hand in extension, then two trials in succession of R. E., L. F., L. E., R. F. Collate shortest of two trials under each typical movement. W.

Fatigue: B. C. W.

Muscular exertion. B. W. As described above. C.

Intellectual exertion. B. W.

Will Power: W.

The ability of the subject to respond after fatigue has set in to a suggestion of the experimenter with an extra effort of will. W.

Voluntary Attention:

Test by simple mental operations under distraction. B.

Coincident variations in Psycho-physical process. W.

The modifiability of the knee jerk, or of a sustained bodily process, such as rate of breathing or pulsation of a volitional muscular or intellectual process, when the subject's attention is engaged by some mental content. W.

Measure at the same time concentration or distraction of attention. W.

Right and Left Movements: J. W.

The accuracy with which movements are made to the right and left. J. W.

Some such test as this for indication of right and left-handedness. W.

I do not insist on this test as one of great importance. J.

Rapidity of Movement: C. J. S. W.

Taps on a telegraph key. J. W.

Movements requiring force, as described above. C.

Make short marks as rapidly as possible for twenty or thirty seconds, *e. g.*, | | | | |. S.

Trilling with two fingers and with five. W.

Accuracy of Aim :   B. J. S. W.
  Throwing a marble at a target.   J.
  Or striking a point upon the table with a pencil point.   W.
  Touch an insulated spot, as proposed by Scripture.   S. B.   Also
for steadiness of hand.   B.

Reaction-time for Sound: B. C. J. S. W.
  The reaction to be made with the right hand with a signal about
two seconds before the stimulus.   B. C. J. W.
  Five reactions to be made without preliminary practice; after the
reactions have been made, the observer to be asked whether the direc-
tion of the attention was motor or sensory.   B. C.
  It is not much use to ask for direction of attention with most sub-
jects.   W.
  Sensory and motor reaction with instruction, after the above test.
B.

Reaction-time with Choice: B. J. W.
  Use card sorting.   B. J. S.

Rate of Discrimination and Movement: B. C. J. S. W.
  100 A's in 500 letters to be marked or as many as can be marked
in one minute.   B. C.
  One out of a number of geometrical forms to be marked: determine the number marked in 90 seconds.   J. W.
  Or colors, or pictures of objects.   W.

Quickness of Distinction and Movement: B. J. S.
  Rate at which cards are sorted.   B. J. S.
  Combine with reaction with choice.   B.
  With the effects of practice, etc., as proposed by Bergstrom.   S.

Perception of Size: C. J. S. W.
  Draw a line equal to a model line 5 cm. in length, bisect it, erect
a perpendicular of the same length and bisect the right-hand angle.
C. J.

Perception of Time: B. C. J. S. W.
  The accuracy with which a standard interval of time, say ten or
twenty seconds, can be reproduced.   C. W.
  Thirty seconds or one minute.   W.

Memory: B. C. J. S. W.
  The accuracy with which eight numerals heard once can be reproduced and the accuracy with which a line drawn by the observer

at the beginning of the hour can be reproduced at the end of the hour.
C. W.

Line to be identified (not drawn). Ten numerals to be used. B.
Nine numerals. S.

A combined test of memory, association and finding time as described in the catalogue of the Columbian Exposition. J. W.

Accuracy of observation and recollection as proposed by Cattell
and by Bolton. J. W.

Memory-type: B.

Variations in use of 10 numerals; method as follows:

1. Show numerals in chance order and have subject write them
from memory after a small interval.

2. Speak numerals in chance order and have subject write them
from memory after the interval.

3. Show and speak in chance order and have subject write them
from memory after the interval.

4. Show and have the subject speak them and then write them
from memory after the interval.

Compare the results for indications of memory type and kind of
imagery preferred. Question the subject as to his mental material in
each case. B.

Apperception Test of Ebbinghaus. B.

Imagery: B. C. J. S. W.

Questions proposed in the Columbia tests. C.
Methods should be worked out more fully. B. C. J. W.
Cf. Method under preceding head. B.
Make memory span tests, showing and speaking the digits at the
same time, and ask the subject which sense (sight or hearing) he
found himself using, and if either seemed to him a distraction. S.

The committee urges that such tests be made, so far as possible, in all psychological laboratories. It does not recommend
that the same tests be made everywhere, but, on the contrary,
advises that, at the present time, a variety of tests be tried, so
that the best ones may be determined. Those who make tests
which they regard as desirable are requested to send these with
sufficient description to the committee.

The committee hopes that the tests proposed may be dis-

cussed fully at the present meeting of the Association, and asks
that the present committee be continued for another year.

(Signed,)

J. Mark Baldwin,
Joseph Jastrow,
E. C. Sanford,
Lightner Witmer,
J. McKeen Cattell, *Chairman.*

Officers and Members of the American Psychological Association, 1897.

President, Professor J. Mark Baldwin, Princeton University. Sec
retary and Treasurer, Dr. Livingston Farrand, Columbia University.

Council, term expiring 1897—Professor G. T. Ladd, Yale Uni-
versity, Professor J. McK. Cattell, Columbia University; term ex-
piring 1898—Professor E. H. Griffin, Johns Hopkins University,
Professor E. C. Sanford, Clark University; term expiring 1899—
Professor Josiah Royce, Harvard University, Professor Joseph Jastrow,
University of Wisconsin.

LIST OF MEMBERS.

Aikins, Dr. H. Austin, Western Reserve University, Cleveland,
Ohio.

Albee, Dr. Ernest, Cornell University, Ithaca, N. Y.

Alexander, Professor Archibald, 10 W. 54th Street, New York
City.

Angell, Professor J. R., University of Chicago, Chicago, Ill.

Armstrong, Professor A. C., Jr., Wesleyan University, Middletown, Conn.

Bakewell, Dr. C. F., Harvard University, Cambridge, Mass.

Baldwin, Professor J. Mark, Princeton University, Princeton, N. J.

Bigham, Dr. John, DePauw University, Greencastle, Ind.

Bliss, Dr. C. B., University of the City of New York, New York
City.

Boas, Dr. Franz, Museum of Natural History, New York City.

Bryan, Professor W. L., Indiana University, Bloomington, Indiana.

Buchner, Dr. E. F., Yale University, New Haven, Conn.

BUCK, MR. A. F., Union College, Schenectady, N. Y.

BURNHAM, DR. W. H., Clark University, Worcester, Mass.

BUTLER, PROFESSOR N. M., Columbia University, New York City.

CALKINS, MISS M. W., Wellesley College, Wellesley, Mass.

CATTELL, PROFESSOR J. McKEEN, Columbia University, New York City.

CHRYSOSTOM, BROTHER, Manhattan College, Grand Boulevard and 131st Street, New York City.

COPE, PROFESSOR E. D., University of Pennsylvania, Philadelphia, Pa.

COWLES, DR. E., McLean Hospital, Somerville, Mass.

CRAWFORD, MR. J. F., Princeton University, Princeton, N. J.

CREIGHTON, PROFESSOR J. E., Cornell University, Ithaca, N. Y.

DANA, PROFESSOR CHARLES L., Post-Graduate Medical School, New York City.

DELABARRE, PROFESSOR E. B., Brown University, Providence, R. I.

DEWEY, PROFESSOR JOHN, University of Chicago, Chicago, Ill.

DONALDSON, PROFESSOR H. H., University of Chicago, Chicago, Ill.

DUNCAN, PROFESSOR G. M., Yale University, New Haven, Conn.

FARRAND, DR. LIVINGSTON, Columbia University, New York City.

FITE, PROFESSOR WARNER, Williams College, Williamstown, Mass.

FRANKLIN, MRS. CHRISTINE LADD, 1507 Park Ave., Baltimore, Md.

FRENCH, PROFESSOR F. C., Vassar College, Poughkeepsie, N. Y.

FULLERTON, PROFESSOR G. S., University of Pennsylvania, Philadelphia, Pa.

GARDINER, PROFESSOR H. N., Smith College, Northampton, Mass.

GILMAN, DR. B. I., Museum of Fine Arts, Boston, Mass.

GRIFFIN, PROFESSOR E. H., Johns Hopkins University, Baltimore, Md.

HALL, PRES. G. STANLEY, Clark University, Worcester, Mass.

HAMLIN, DR. ALICE J., Mt. Holyoke College, South Hadley, Mass.

HIBBEN, PROFESSOR J. G., Princeton University, Princeton, N. J.

HODGE, DR. C. W., Princeton University, Princeton, N. J.

HUME, PROFESSOR J. G., University College, Toronto, Canada.

HYSLOP, PROFESSOR J. H., Columbia University, New York City.

IRONS, DR. DAVID, University of Vermont, Burlington, Vt.

JAMES, PROFESSOR W., 95 Irving Street, Cambridge, Mass.

JASTROW, PROFESSOR JOSEPH, University of Wisconsin, Madison, Wis.

Johnson, Professor R. B., Miami University, Oxford, O.
Judd, Dr. C. H., Wesleyan University, Middletown, Conn.
Kirkpatrick, Mr. E. A., Winona, Minn.
Kirschmann, Dr. A., University of Toronto, Toronto, Canada.
Krohn, Professor W. O., University of Illinois, Champaign, Ill.
Ladd, Professor G. T., Yale University, New Haven, Conn.
Lloyd, Mr. A. H., University of Michigan, Ann Arbor, Mich.
Lough, Mr. J. E., Harvard University, Cambridge, Mass.
MacDonald, Dr. Arthur, Bureau of Education, Washington, D. C.
MacDougall, Dr. Robert, Western Reserve University, Cleveland, Ohio.
Marshall, Mr. Henry Rutgers, 874 Broadway, New York City.
Mead, Professor George H., University of Chicago, Chicago, Ill.
Mezes, Professor Sidney E., University of Texas, Austin, Texas.
Miller, Dr. Dickinson S., Bryn Mawr College, Bryn Mawr, Pa.
Mills, Professor Wesley, McGill University, Montreal, Canada.
Minot, Professor C. S., Harvard Medical School, Boston, Mass.
Münsterberg, Professor Hugo, Harvard University, Cambridge, Mass.
Newbold, Professor W. Romaine, University of Pennsylvania, Philadelphia, Pa.
Nichols, Dr. Herbert, 3 Berkeley St., Cambridge, Mass.
Noyes, Dr. Wm., Boston Insane Hospital, Pierce Farm, Mattapan, Mass.
Ormond, Professor A. T., Princeton University, Princeton, N. J.
Pace, Professor E., Catholic University, Washington, D. C.
Palmer, Professor G. H., Harvard University, Cambridge, Mass.
Patrick, Professor G. T. W., University of Iowa, Iowa City, Iowa.
Pierce, Mr. Edgar, 3 Thompson Street, Ann Arbor, Mich.
Royce, Professor Josiah, Harvard University, Cambridge, Mass.
Sanford, Professor E. C., Clark University, Worcester, Mass.
Schiller, Mr. F. C. S., Cornell University, Ithaca, N. Y.
Schurman, Pres. J. G., Cornell University, Ithaca, N. Y.
Seth, Professor James, Cornell University, Ithaca, N. Y.
Shorey, Professor Paul, University of Chicago, Chicago, Ill.
Singer, Dr. E. A., University of Pennsylvania, Phila., Pa.
Smith, Dr. W. G., Smith College, Northampton, Mass.
Sneath, Professor E. Hershey, Yale University, New Haven, Conn.
Stanley, Professor H. M., Lake Forest University, Lake Forest, Ill.

STARR, PROFESSOR M. ALLEN, 22 West 48th Street, New York City.
STRONG, PROFESSOR C. A., Columbia University, New York City.
TAWNEY, PROFESSOR G. A., Beloit College, Beloit, Wis.
WARREN, PROFESSOR H. C., Princeton University, Princeton, N. J.
WASHBURN, DR. MARGARET, Wells College, Aurora, N. Y.
WILDE, DR. NORMAN, Columbia University, New York City.
WITMER, PROFESSOR LIGHTNER, University of Pennsylvania, Phila., Pa.
WOLFE, PROFESSOR H. K., University of Nebraska, Lincoln, Neb.

Members will please notify the Secretary of any errors in names or addresses as given in the above list.

UPRIGHT VISION.

BY PROF. JAMES H. HYSLOP.

Columbia University.

The present paper discussing the problem of upright vision directly has been suggested by what I have already said in a previous number of the PSYCHOLOGICAL REVIEW in regard to Dr. Stratton's experiments. I wish here to discuss the whole question on its own merits and without regard to anything that has occurred in that connection, and the first task must be to show just what the problem really is. In order to do this effectively it may be well to look a moment at its origin, after stating the form in which the question is usually put for an answer. It is: "Why are all things seen upright when the image on the retina is inverted?"

Before I get through I shall endeavor to show that this way of putting the question easily leads to an illusion in regard to the nature of the problem, but for the present, taking it as perfectly intelligible, we may further ask how such a question ever came to be put at all? No one ever thought of asking it until the discovery was made that the eye is really a *camera obscura* which inverts its images. The problem created by the emanating corpuscles of Democritus and by the etherial vibrations between the object and the eye did not suggest it, and probably could not, as the formation and inversion of the image was not known until the property of lenses was known. Nothing anomalous in the phenomena of vision was suspected before the fact of refraction was recognized. But as soon as it was discovered that the image on the retina was inverted, the apparent anomaly at once suggested the question why the object was seen upright when the image is inverted, and various theories have been invented to explain the phenomenon. Among them we have the ocular movement theory, the projection theory, the re-inversion

142

theory, and the theory of correction by experience in connection with touch. The last theory holds that in respect of visual functions, the inversion of the retinal image is not necessary to upright vision, but that the conception of uprightness is the product of experience and that naturally we may or do perceive things upside down.

This view of the case, and the question creating the problem or supposing that the phenomenon is anomalous, are founded upon two illusions. The first of these illusions is that, to be intelligible to our minds, the process ought not to involve an inversion of the retinal image. Until it was discovered that the eye was a camera it was natural to conceive the process after the analogy of touch, this conception being modified by the idea of vibrations. There were metaphysical and idealistic puzzles enough in the phenomenon, and perhaps also epistemological problems, but more for psychology or perception as a fact. In touch we were accustomed to a perfect correspondence between the impression upon the sensorium and the object producing it. There was apparent no disparity or inversion of relations. The space relations of impression and object were taken or known to be symmetrical and nothing seemed to be anomalous about them. But as soon as it was found, as a matter of fact, that the retinal image is inverted—that is, its position reversed from that of the real object—the question arose how we could see the object upright.

Now it is to be noted that the question was not, how this retinal image becomes inverted, because we have no immediate knowledge of the fact, and so it could not be a problem. Its existence was simply inferred as a necessary result of what is known of the property of lenses, though it was easily confirmed by experiment after the fact was inferred as a consequence of the nature of the eye. Hence the reason for the inversion of the image was explained before its existence could be demonstrated empirically, or at least it could be explained. Hence the anomaly did not consist in the fact of inversion, but in the relation of this fact to the opposite relation of the object, and the question arose, How does perception take place under these conditions? Or why do we see the object in an upright position when the retinal image is inverted?

But what precisely does the question mean? Does it ask for the explanation of an anomaly? After all, is not the question essentially absurd? It certainly does not appear so to those who ask it. But the reason is an unconscious assumption which creates the whole problem to be solved, but which may have no ground upon which to rest. It is the assumption that in order not to be an anomalous phenomenon the object and the image ought to correspond. The old Democritean view of perception involved precisely this conception of the case: the εἴδωλα imprinted themselves on the eye, we should say retina. The undulatory theory of light hardly altered the conception, except for metaphysics. There was here the idea of correspondence between image and object, whether rightly or wrongly assumed. Of course, as soon as this assumed correspondence was disproved, there would arise the conception of something anomalous, and the question mentioned would arise. As long as the phenomenon of vision did not appear thus exceptional, there would not be anything to suggest that it was a non-natural fact. Upright vision would be taken as a matter of course. But the moment that it appeared as an exception to what it was supposed it ought to be, instead of supposing that this was just as natural as any other process, the assumption was made that we ought to see things the inverse of what we do as a fact, and that experience corrects the illusion. Instead of supposing that the old assumption or conception of the process was an illusion, men were disposed to accept it as the standard by which to judge the anomalous character of the facts, and rushed off to experience to correct or change what was supposed to be the natural perception of the infant!

I do not say that all persons conceived the question exactly in this way; for there were some who still supposed the process to be natural enough, but regarded it nevertheless either as anomalous or as presenting special features which required explanation. Where it was felt to be anomalous, even if natural, it was judged somewhat after the analogy of touch. In this sense the correspondence between the impression and the object was such as to bring into bold relief the opposition in vision; and the natural tendency was either to go to experience for the adjustment of the two sets of phenomena to the same law, or to some anomalous function in sight to compensate for the deviation of the law of touch. This was making touch the standard of what is natural, just as Berkeley did in the matter of space perception. But what right have we to judge vision by any such assumption? Might not upright vision be just as natural with the inversion of retinal images as the symmetrical relation in touch. Why should we judge the law of one sense by that of another? Does not the action of each sense suffice for itself, and is it not an assumption requiring justification that the process of vision may be rendered intelligible by tactual analogies? There is a deep-rooted, and perhaps legitimate, impression that there is some sort of unity between the senses, and this we may be able to establish in the conclusion. But no such unity can be assumed as would either identify their percepts or necessitate the same law of action between them, and as long as this is the fact there will be no intrinsic reason in the fact of inverted images to justify our assumption, so frequently made, that it is anomalous, and contary to our ordinary notion of perception as drawn from the impressions of touch. That this comparison should be made is an illusion, perhaps pardonable enough, but still an illusion.

This illusion is reinforced, perhaps in some cases created, by a very interesting ambiguity. This is in the conception of 'uprightness.' The idea of 'uprightness' denotes a relation to the earth, which is assumed to represent the natural and uniform position of bodies. I might have said a relation to gravitation, which undoubtedly expresses the case for most persons, who come to know that uprightness is merely relative to a point at the earth's center, and determined by gravity, and not an absolute position in space. Now the most invariable of all the experiences by which we estimate the direction of gravity is our own sense of weight. We can determine it by the visual perception of falling bodies, but movements in the visual field, until we learn the ultimate influence of gravity on the bodies thus moving, would hardly suggest gravity so soon or so forcibly as the absolutely constant sense of weight and the limitations upon free personal movement in space. Then the final discovery from the general result of all experiences, that gravitation defines a line of direction or position for all bodies in relation to the earth, creates the idea that 'uprightness' is this line and it becomes convertible with the tactual and muscular sensations which are the constant and surest determinants of it, though vision gives a line of direction which coincides with it. But we conceive it as related to gravitation rather than as any mere fact of the visual field alone. It is true, however, that the idea of uprightness can have the same meaning for vision as for touch, in the sense that it means merely a reference to the direction of gravitation. But this is not because the sensations or experiences determining it are in any respect like each other. It is because one of them may always be taken as the associate of the other, or as an index of its possibility. They become associated by their synthetic unity in perception, and when any question is raised as to the validity of one of them it is natural to refer to its associate as an index of what the one in question means. In this way, when the question how we perceive uprightness under the conditions mentioned is raised, in view of the sceptical implications of the question itself, and the desire to obtain an explanation without simply restating the fact itself in a mysterious form, it was natural to resort to the tactual process for the datum with which the visual sensation is associated and which represents the uprightness. But the fact is that the visual conception of uprightness is just as definite a content of visual experience as the tactual is of touch, and it would never have any connection with the latter but for the uniformities of certain experiences. This aside, however, the fact that vision can determine independently of touch a relation to gravitation, as a notion of uprightness, is sufficient to show that the datum is not necessarily tactual, so that, however valuable it may be to use touch for explaining the synthetic conception of uprightness, it still remains to explain the visual process within the limits of that sense.

But this reference of the term uprightness to the direction of gravity, or the direction which gravity determines, and to the same relation expressed in tactual and muscular experiences of a certain order, leads to an entire misunderstanding of the real question by making us think of uprightness as felt, when the visual problem uses the term, not necessarily to express the direction of gravity in harmony with touch, but the inverted position of that relation in the image, whether it represents a line in reference to gravity or not. It happens in normal experience that the objects we see in vertically linear extension are arranged with reference to the direction of gravity and we call them 'upright.' That is, visual uprightness and the uprightness of gravity coincide, while that of touch coincides with the same objective reality, and when the retinal image appears inverted we ask how the object can be seen in the inverse position under these conditions, but instead of saying 'inverse' we say 'upright' and create the liability of confusion either with tactual and muscular uprightness or with the adjustment of tactual and muscular experience to the visual. The way to avoid this confusion is to examine the phenomena themselves upon which the problem is based and to remark that it can be stated without using the word 'upright' at all. Now when we note the relation between the object and the retinal image we do not require to ask how we see things upright, but how do we see things in a certain relation when the retinal image represents the inverse relation. The term 'upright' does not appear here, nor is there any reference to the real direction which it represents in relation to either gravity or the other senses. In the visual problem, therefore, the term ought either not to be used at all or it must be understood to mean nothing but the inverse of the relation of the image on the retina. In this way we see that all the associated conceptions of other senses are excluded, and there remains nothing but the real or apparent anomaly of opposition between the position of real objects and that of retinal images.

I have dwelt at length on the illusions and the true conception of the problem, because it is necessary to clear away, once for all, all those experiments and theories of the process which are determined by a reference to tactual and muscular adjustments to visual objects. They are designed to prove that the inversion of the image is not normally necessary to the perception of things as we see them, but that when reversed by artificial means we easily learn to adapt ourselves to these new conditions.

The adaptation is true enough as a fact, but it is not relevant to the problem.   Nor in speaking, as I do, of what such attempts at experiment and theory imply in favor of empiricism, do I mean to imply my own denial of the influence of experience in correcting what might be the original appearance of things to sight. I mean only to state the case so that we can see that, however much experience may have to do with the adjustment of touch to the visual field, we have not in this any fact from which we can justly infer that experience corrects the original perception of vision and enables us to *see* things the inverse of what they once appeared, as it would be necessary to maintain if we affirmed the proposition that the inversion of the image is not normally necessary to upright vision.   Within the limits of sight a man may hold what opinion he pleases on the point.   I am not at present denouncing empiricism within such limits, but only the inference from the experiential nature of adjustment to sight to the experiential nature of the process in sight.   Whether the visual process is native or empirical will have to be determined by phenomena wholly within the range of that sense, and it is an entire misconception of the problem to talk about any tactual or muscular adjustments to visual impressions.   Ocular movements might appear relevant, but no others are relevant that involve a visual judgment of co-existence in space.

Now, having shown that tactual experiences are not relevant, but give rise to an illusion in the problem, we may examine the assumption of empiricism wholly within the limits of visual phenomena.   If we assume that experience corrects the original perception of vision by supposing that the inversion of the retinal image is not necessary to 'upright' vision, we imply that originally there was complete correspondence between image and object, as between tactual impression and object.   This is the assumption of a created function wholly supplanted by experience.   But what facts justify such an assumption?   There is absolutely no fact to justify it except the *a priori* idea of the analogy between touch and sight, or those stories which we occasionally hear about the inversion of objects in case of disease, which require to be much better verified and analyzed before they are entitled to use in this connection.[1] We should never suspect the influence of experience in the case were it not for the unwarranted and unjustifiable assumption following in the wake of the theories of Democritus and the undulatory nature of light. Here we took for granted the identity of the relation between impression and object in the senses of touch and sight, and allow an apparent anomaly to convince us of the influence of experience, when we might just as well have abandoned the assumption of the nativity of the correspondence between them. The fact is that it was experience and *a priori* reasoning that led us to suppose that the phenomenon was anomalous at all, when we ought to have seen that it represented the natural condition of things, and that any correspondence in symmetry between retinal images and objects, if possible at all, would have to be either the product of experience or the result of abnormality.

[1] I have often heard second and third-rate stories about persons who, under certain abnormal conditions, actually saw things upside down. But I have to say that all attempts that I have made to secure a perfectly authentic case have utterly failed. Persons who have told me of them could not vouch for them, and I always find them eluding investigation much as do ghost stories. I have never found any reference to them in books, and Dr. Peterson, of the College of Physicians and Surgeons, in connection with Columbia University, allows me to quote him as saying that, in all his study of nervous diseases and reading, he has not met with a single case of it, and would not believe the narrative if he did meet one. Two years ago I thought I had secured a case on the testimony of a physician. On careful interrogation it turned out that his observation had been limited to the fact that a young boy in Brooklyn had been known always to write and read upside down and experienced great difficulty in correcting his habit. This had occurred twelve years before, and the boy could not be traced. But it is evident that he did not require to be traced, because the phenomenon does not present the slightest evidence of inverted vision. I would ascertain nothing about the boy's habits previous to his entrance to the public schools. Children taught the alphabet and to spell upside down will read by holding the book in an inverted position. But this does not prove inverted vision, and I suspect most reported cases are of this kind. Moreover, any reported instances of a pathological kind have to be viewed with suspicion, for obvious reasons. One instance, however, and this an apparent exception to all my experience, came within my knowledge a short time ago. A lady told me that she had often seen things upside down. On interrogation it appeared that she could not give any clear account of her experience. She remarked that the phenomenon was always connected with very severe headaches, which were often almost unendurable and blinding. She said also that she could immediately correct the impression by reaching out to the object with her hand, and that the whole field did not seem inverted, but only

I have dwelt at length upon the analysis of the problem partly for the purpose of limiting it to its proper field, and partly for the purpose of clearing away its imaginary difficulties and defining exactly what an explanation of the phenomenon must do. It is usual with the empiricist to be content with a reference to some fact or process which involves the influence of tactual or muscular experience. He implies, if he does not assert, that we either correct a primary illusion by this process or we never obtain any properly visual *quale* which has a right to be called uprightness. In this way he conceives the whole problem as one regarding the *genesis* of the idea of uprightness in a sense that does not naturally give it or is supposed not to give it. Whatever he thinks about the naturalness of the percept in the tactual and muscular sense, he can only conceive sight as giving signs which may be used as data for inference to the existence of certain tactual and muscular relations. But he construes the whole question as if it were

certain objects in it, though I could not get any satisfactory account of the experience in its details. On the whole, however, I found nothing in the case that might not be explained by an illusion of judgment in connection with the mental confusion incident to severe headache. Now it is to be remarked that if the whole field appeared inverted in the case the fact could not be discovered except in comparison either with a memory image or with disturbed coenæsthesia and memory images together. But this would not require any inversion of the apparent object to vision, but would only show an inversion of the feelings that serve as a criterion of the relation between memory images and those feelings. Moreover, touching the object would not correct the impression of sight if it represented an organic disturbance or inversion of retinal impressions. It would only correct her judgment. This is seen in the ordinary experience with the microscope, where we easily correct our judgment of locality for touch, without altering the *seen* relations of space in the object. It is worth remarking also that in microscopical experiments we should never suspect the inversion of objects, except for the fact of memory images with which they are compared. Moreover, if, in the case under consideration, only the object looked at appeared inverted, this fact and its correction immediately by touch would prove that the case was an error of judgment and not organic inversion of images. Otherwise we should have to suppose organic disturbance for the one object while the remainder of the field was normal, and it would require a great deal of evidence to support such a fact. I have, however, treated this case more seriously than it deserves, but only because it is the single one in my experience which could claim a moment's scientific attention. There is nothing in it which cannot be explained by supposing an illusion of judgment instead of an inversion of visual reference.

merely one between the theories of nativism and empiricism, when, as a matter of fact, this is not the proper way to conceive it. This may be an interesting question, but what we want to know first is the law of sensorial reference which either explains upright vision, that is, the inversion between image and object, or proves it to be anomalous. If we prove it to be anomalous we suggest a reason for resorting to foreign and empirical influences as secondary agencies in the matter. But whether we ever find it necessary to discuss nativism or empiricism in connection with it, it is certain that we should first ascertain, or exhaust every effort to ascertain, the conditions in the sense of vision that may explain the phenomenon. That we are under obligation to do this is shown by the fact that there is an absolute universality of agreement in visual experience regarding the position in which things are seen (barring possibly abnormal cases above referred to). That is, no one ever remembers a time when his visual judgments required correction, except in reference to memory images, and no illusions occur in normal experience, as they should do, if empirical theories were true. The uniformity of experience in the matter, negatively confirmed by apparent exceptions which will not bear investigation, only indicates or proves that we must seek some conditions within the sense of vision to explain this regularity and exemption from illusion.

All such theories as re-inversion of the image or mysterious central agencies may be thrown out of court at once as simply a restatement of the problem at a point where it cannot either be investigated or subjected either to proof or disproof. The two most prominent explanations have been the ocular movement and the projection theories, which represented respectively the empirical and the nativistic points of view, and whose examination will show that they either begged the question or simply restated the question in more mysterious terms.

The ocular-movement theory supposes that we learn the direction of a point in the field of vision, or rather its position above or below, by the movements necessary to bring it upon the fovea. But this supposition will not stand a moment's examination. It has to assume either a perception of the point to which the movement of the eyes has to be directed or a consciousness of the relation between this movement and the tactual percept of position and uprightness. To assume the first of these alternatives is to admit the existence in consciousness of the datum which has to be derived from the muscular sensations in ocular movements. That is to say, it admits a perception of the uprightness before the ocular movements can have any meaning for consciousness at all. The eye may not yet know that the positions perceived correspond to certain directions represented by gravity—that is, it may not have identified visual with tactual uprightness—but the relations are given in the visual percept or manifold which determine the meaning of the ocular movement and are not determined by it. The fact is, moreover, that in all ordinary processes of ocular movement we have no knowledge of such movements directly, but only of the objects across the field of vision. There is not even a muscular sensation to serve as a ποῦ στῶ for judgment, except in extreme or strained positions or movements of the eyes, and it is specially noticeable in these conditions that the perception of direction or uprightness is not made any more evident by it. Hence the fact is that the direction of ocular movement is determined by the previous perception of relations which the theory assumes are determined by the movement, the sense of movement being known only in the changes across the visual field, and not in the muscular sensations. To assume the second alternative, which involves a knowledge of the relations between the movement and the tactual percept of uprightness, is to make matters worse still. For nothing is clearer than the circumstance that we do not learn the fact of ocular movements, or the meaning of any sensation connected therewith, from any knowledge of its relation to tactual percepts, except from its conjunction with a *sure* tactual adjustment or movement on the one hand and a *sure* movement of objects on the other. That is to say, both tactual and ocular movements get their whole conception from visual construction in so far as they are known to be related to it, and do not determine that construction.

The projection theory has secured several forms of expression, which it will not be necessary to consider. But they are all attempts to prove a theory of nativism, and avail only to re-state the problem which they pretend to solve. The most plausible statement of the doctrine is that the eye projects im-ages or objects into space in the direction which the rays of light enter the eye or are thrown upon the retina. This view can get a mathematical representation according to the laws of optics. But the trouble with all projection theories is that their form of statement implies, at least apparently, that a process of translation is required to effect the result to consciousness, when, as a matter of fact, the whole content of perception, magnitude, distance and uprightness is given without the 'projection' of anything. If the terms localization or reference were employed without implying any conception of translation there would be less inherent difficulty in the theory. But when it seems to in-volve the idea of 'projection' into space it implies a distinction between objects as known in space and impressions which it has no right to suppose. And it is worse when mysterious cen-tral activities are imported for reversing the retinal image, when, as a matter of fact, the very distinction between the impression and the object of consciousness may be an illusion. But inas-much as it may create confusion to force the problem of idealism upon attention, we may assume that there is an interesting phe-nomenon requiring explanation, and only protest against the use of central processes which merely repeat the problem at another point and which cannot be verified or suggested by anything except the fact to be explained.

Now when it comes to presenting a positive explanation of upright vision, or of the compensation for the inversion of the retinal image, it will be necessary to avoid misunderstanding of what is meant by 'explanation.' I do not mean to appeal to any known or unknown cerebral functions which involve a peculiar reaction upon impressions, but only to a law of sensorial action traceable in other senses and adapted to the modified con-dition of vision. This explains the process by assimilating it to a known and supposably understood process. "In science," says Professor Le Conte very pertinently, "what we mean by an ex-planation is a reducing of the phenomena in question to a law which includes many other phenomena, and especially the most

common and familiar phenomena."[1]   This statement was made
in a short article or discussion endeavoring to explain the very
phenomena here occupying our attention, but I question whether
many of Professor Le Conte's readers realized fully the value
and importance of his conception thus formulated.   But explanation by a more widely recognized law than the fact in question is distinct in its nature from explanation by an antecedent
fact or process, and is the proper resource in the problem of
upright vision, because it is the only one capable of direct verification.   It will be best, however, to approach my own way of
stating the case through that of Professor Le Conte.

In his work on *Vision* some years ago he stated his theory,
and more recently in *Science,* where he gives a good diagram
in illustration of the process, which may be repeated here.

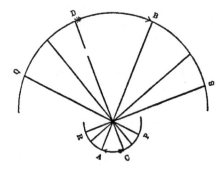

Fig. I.

Prof. Le Conte's explanation of the process is that we refer·
objects back along the ray lines of light, and " thus the external
image is *reinverted in the act of external reference."*   The figure brings out this conception by showing that the light from *B*
falls upon *A* and is referred back to the point *B,* and the light
from *D* falls upon *C* and is referred back to *D.*   And it is the
same with all other points, *2* and *S* and *P* and *R.*   In his
work on *Vision,*[2] Professor Le Conte gives the same explana-

[1]*Science.* New Series, Vol. II., p. 629.
[2]Le Conte. *Vision.* First Edition, p 83.

tion of the phenomenon, though without any accompanying diagram, as above. After stating the problem, he says : " The true scientific answer is found in what is called the ' *law of visible direction.*' This law may be stated thus : *When the rays from any radiant strike the retina the impression is referred back along the ray-line (central ray of the pencil) into space and therefore to its proper place.*"

Before correcting certain misimpressions which I conceive belongs to this way of stating the case, I must mention a personal matter. For a number of years I had supposed this explanation of the phenomenon, though getting very near the solution of it, to be wrong and different from my own, which I had been presenting to my classes. But a year or two ago I had occasion to correspond with Professor Le Conte on this and some experiments in binocular vision, and I found that our conception of the process was essentially the same, and that I had been led astray by his language in the case, which implies a coincidence between the ray and reference line, that appears to be functional, while I wished to separate them functionally, though they might actually coincide. What I shall have to say of his theory, therefore, will be to correct the misconception to which I think it is liable, rather than to object to its real conception and intention.

The objections, therefore, which may be made to Professor Le Conte's formula of the law and mode of illustration are the following : (1) The illustration in Figure I. seems to imply that the horopter or points from which the light comes represent a curved line more or less symmetrical with the retina. This may be a very good theoretical construction of the case, but the same result would hold with a straight line, and this fact requires to be kept in mind. (2) In discussing the theory Professor Le Conte often speaks of ' projection' of the image into space, a form of expression which is misleading, because it assumes space as given and the ' projection' of the point or object into it, as if the percept of space itself were not a mental act essentially a part of the ' projection.' There will be no objection to the language provided we understand this fact. But it is certain that the space percept is an integral part of the total

visual impression, not an independently given datum for consciousness into which it may either 'project' or refer objects.
(3) His statement of the law implies a coincidence between the
reference line and the ray line of light, and most persons reading it would infer that they are essentially connected, and that a
variation of the ray line would be accompanied by a corresponding variation of the reference line. This organic connection I mean to deny, except in so far as evolution may have established an *actual* coincidence which is not necessarily *functional*, and I was glad to discover by my correspondence with
Professor Le Conte that we agreed in our conception of the process. Quite a number of his own experiments in the work on
vision, as well as his comparison of the several senses on the
law of direction, establishes this separation between the actual
and the functional coincidence in normal vision, that is, between
the reference and ray lines, though it is concealed in the formula
for stating the law in vision. Hence my own formulation of
the process in erect vision is designed to keep this distinction
clear, and thus to remove the misconception to which I think
Professor Le Conte's language is exposed.

The following Fig. II will illustrate the process for normal
vision. The light from *P* falls on all parts of the pupil and is

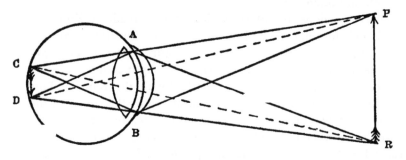

Fig. II.

refracted to the point *D*; from *R* to the point *C*. *P A D* represents the direction from *P* for the ray falling on the upper limits
of the line, *P B D* the ray on the lower limits. Similarly for
R A C and *R B C*. Now either we cannot speak of a single ray

line from any given point such as *P* and *R*, or we should have to call it the average direction of such a ray line. In the former case, which represents the facts, there being any number of ray lines with different degrees of angular incidence between the two extremes *A D* and *B D*, the reference line *P D* cannot coincide with them without multiplying the number of objects to be seen. The law of retinal points determines this, and we simply construct the reference line as determined by this fact and without relation to the ray line. In the second alternative not only is the conception of a ray line arbitrary, but there is no evidence of its coincidence with the reference line *P D*. I would therefore formulate the law of direction without any reference to the ray line, but only in reference to the function of the retina. If we observe the direction of the reference line in Fig. II. and its relation to the retina we can note that it is at least approximately vertical to the surface on which the light falls. Consequently I shall formulate the law of vision upon the basis of this fact. *The law of visual direction or reference is that it is in a line that is vertical to the surface, or point upon which light falls.* This statement implies neither coincidence nor variation from the ray line of light, but it expresses a real or supposed law of the retinal sensorium. Whether the reference line is really or only approximately vertical to the retina it is not necessary to determine. This would have to be a subject for mathematical calculation. But I may state the theoretical form for definiteness and leave any variations from it to be explained by the appropriate causes. It is certain that the reference line sustains actually or approximately the relation to the retina that I have given it, and it remains to give other evidence than the phenomena of normal vision, that will show at the same time both the separation of the reference and the ray lines and the fixity of the reference line, which will be found to be vertical as indicated.

The simple phenomena that prove the law as here formulated are those of phosphenes and Purkinje's experiment. The first of these are produced by the familiar experiment of pushing with the finger against the eye-ball on either side, or above or below, with the eye closed. The bright circles of light thus

produced are not referred in the direction of the pressure, but
in the very opposite direction, at least apparently vertical to the
point of the impression. In Purkinje's experiment a pencil of
bright light may be thrown upon the sclerotic coat at the side of
the pupil by means of a microscope, and if the instrument be
very lightly shaken, the light that passes through the translucent
membrane falls on the retina without refraction, and the shaking
of it gives rise to after images caused by retinal shadows of
the blood vessels either on the retina or in the sclerotic coat, and
these when seen are referred, not in the direction of the light,
but directly in front of us in the background at which we are
looking. The effect of the experiment is illustrated by the following diagram, (Fig. III.) :

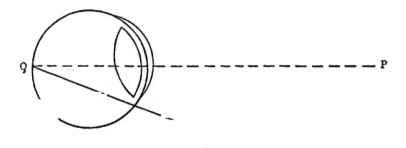

Fig. III.

The line $S\mathcal{Q}$ represents the direction of the light and the
line $P\mathcal{Q}$ the reference line of vision for the retinal shadows.
What is shown by it is the fact that the reference and ray lines
do not functionally coincide, and that the reference line is vertical to the surface of incidence for the light. That is to say, the
reference line for vision is an organically fixed function of
the retina, which has no necessary relation to the direction from
which the stimulus comes. Professor Le Conte ought to have
remarked this fact when he described these very phenomena in
his book, and it might have saved the misconception likely to be
enacted by his statement and diagrammatic representation of
the law. He might have observed this separation of the two

lines very clearly in the experiment regarding retinal shadows, in which he says that ‘while retinal images are inverted, retinal shadows are erect,’ but are seen inverted, the direction of the light, or rather shadow, that causes them not having anything to do with their reference. As the experiment showing this is important for the theory here advanced it may be quoted : “ Make a pin-hole in a card, and holding the card at four or five inches distant against the sky above the right eye with the left eye shut, bring the pin-head very near to the open eye, so that it touches the lashes and in the line of sight; a perfect *inverted* image of the pin-head will be seen in the pin-hole.” [1] The pin creates a shadow on the pupils and lens, and *shadows are not refracted.* Hence their images are erect on the retina, their line of incidence being perfectly straight toward the retina, and the reference actually giving an inverted object of sight, while the lines of incidence and reference cannot possibly coincide. The same fact is shown in the illusion caused by the refraction of light in passing through ‘ the watery meniscus between the two lids and the surface of the cornea.’ These are all Professor Le Conte's experiments,[2] and they simply attest the uniformity of the reference line regardless of the ray or incidence line, and this reference appears in the direction of a vertical to the point upon which the light or image falls. It will be apparent from this how it compensates for the refraction of light and the inversion of the image in normal vision.

Now whether in normal conditions, as represented in Fig. II., the ray line and reference line ever actually coincide, assuming the mean of all that issue from the same point as the ray line, must be decided by mathematical calculation. Evolution may have adjusted the retina with its reference lines to the ray line after refraction, but not because this adjustment is necessary to erect vision. But we must not mistake any real or supposed adjustment for other purposes as evidence of functional connection, because it is easy to show that visual reference has functional stability while the incidence of stimulus varies in all sorts of directions.

[1] Le Conte, *Vision*, First Edition, p. 86.
[2] Le Conte, *Vision*, First Edition, p. 88. *Philosophical Magazine*, Vol. LXI., p. 266, 1871. *Science*, New Series, Vol. II., p. 667.

We have seen now how erect vision is possible in spite of inverted images, and it remains to show that the reference line is only an illustration of the same law in the other senses. Professor Le Conte remarks this fact and describes it so fully and clearly that I need only refer readers to his work. But I may observe that it is only an illustration of the law of 'eccentric projection,' which is used to describe the tendency of touch to refer a stimulus in a direction vertical to the sensorium or point of contact. This may be a theoretical way of putting the case, but it expresses substantially the direction of reference when a stimulus impresses the sensorium. Now accepting Mr. Spencer's conclusion that the sense of touch was the original germ out of which all the senses were developed, among them sight, we can readily see that nature had only to give the retina a curved form, circular, elliptical, or parabolic, in order to adjust the law of 'eccentric projection' to the modified conditions of vision involving refraction of light and inverted images. The law of direction is thus the same for all sensory impressions, though it is undoubtedly vague in smell and greatly influenced by association and experience in hearing. But in the tactual, thermal and visual senses it is very clearly the same. It will be especially interesting to remark here that, with this explanation of upright vision, we at last secure a direct analogy with touch. The assumption, which we said was not absolutely necessary, turns out at last, under a modified form, to represent a connection which, whether necessary or not, is a fact. The analogy with touch, however, which we criticized, was not based upon the conception of the law of direction or eccentric projection, but upon theoretical conceptions about visual impressions, before it was known that there was an inverted retinal image, and these conceptions happened to coincide with the notion of tactual impressions. But with the law of eccentric projection in touch and the adaptation of the retina to compensate for refraction and the inversion of the retinal image, we have the analogy restored and the phenomenon of erect vision explained by a wider law of sense perception which, in the other senses, presents nothing anomalous.

It will be apparent from the law of visual reference thus

established that, other things remaining the same, if the retina were a plane or a convex surface, instead of concave, objects would appear inverted. Thus in Fig. II. if the retina were a plane surface and the law of direction be as formulated, the point P would be seen in a direction vertical to the point D in the plane C D, and so be located or referred to a position somewhere between P and R. If the surface were convex, objects might appear both inverted and magnified. All this, of course, assumes that nature might not make compensating adjustments for such surfaces, and only serves theoretically to show that with the law of direction there is nothing really anomalous in erect vision with inverted images, but that the anomaly would exist in the truth of the experiential theory that tactual and muscular sensations correct the original perceptions of sight. Erect vision with inverted images is the natural and proper thing, while any conclusion that the inversion of the retinal image is not necessary to the present result would contradict the law of direction, and simply create instead of solve a problem. Erect vision is simply a fixed function of the eye, just as is that of corresponding points, and we have only to use this law of reference or direction, as Professor Le Conte does, in order to explain single vision by corresponding points.

There is indirect evidence of natural functions for upright vision in the uniformity of its occurrence and the impossibility of securing pathological cases of real inversion that will bear scientific investigation. But if the theory that the inversion of the retinal image is not necessary to normal vision, and that the impression is derived from tactual experience be true, there ought to be frequent illusions even in normal sight in regard to the position of objects. People's experience varies, and we find in all other fields that the products of experience alone show such a variety of conceptions and opinions contradicting each other that it is the sure origin of illusion and no uniformity of results accompanies it. But there is such absolute agreement in human experience about the fact of erect vision that the presumption in favor of its being a normal and necessary function connected with inverted images ought to be as strong as the belief that perception of any kind is a native function of the retina.

This uniformity is even so great that we cannot be sure about the genuineness of pathological cases which either elude authentication altogether or must stand the ordeal of explanation by illusion of judgment. Moreover, we can raise the serious question whether it would even be possible to prove a case of inverted reference, normal or pathological, when reported. Such a result or experience will depend either upon a comparison with memory images or upon a comparison of simultaneous impressions with each other and with memory images, and here the question of illusions of judgment would arise as a ghost to be laid before we could form any opinion as to real inversion. But, however, this may be the uniformity and universality of human experience in respect to erect vision, attests an organic function for sight which is not consistent with the suppositions of mere experience in touch and muscular adjustment, nor with the liability to illusion in the variability involved in all products of experience. The only way to gain support for possible differences of experience in the matter is to raise the question as to our knowledge that others do not see things the inverse of our own perception. But granting that they may do so, if it is as uniform in their experience as ours, and if they experience an inversion of impressions, whenever we do under artificial conditions we have the same evidence of organic fixity of functions in this case as ours, and nativism stands as against empiricism, while to suppose that there is no inversion between the retinal image and real or apparent objects in such imaginary cases of difference between ourselves and others, is to suppose that the same physical structure and conditions of the eyes are not followed by the same optical laws of refraction. Assuming these laws, however, we should have the relation of inversion between image and object, even if we supposed that the image is erect, that is, in the same relative position to objects as seen by another, but inverted in relation to objects as seen by the subject. We should still have both nativism and the law of vertical reference in such cases. It only shows again, however, that the terms 'upright' and 'erect' create illusions as to the nature of the problem and that we conceive it rightly only when we substitute for them the mere idea of an inverted relation between image and object. In this way tactual conceptions and associations are easily excluded.

But the question of nativism is not the main or first one to be considered. We may view it either as the consequence of the explanation here advanced or as confirming it if independent evidence of nativism be accessible. The real question is regarding the law of normal vision, which will explain the perception of erect objects when retinal images are inverted. This we found to be vertical reference or eccentric projection from the plane or surface of incidence for light. This fact, if it be a fact, shows that inversion of images is necessary to normal visions, and that all experiments to test its nativity by tactual and muscular adjustment are based upon an illusion as to what the problem really is.

THE STAGES OF KNOWLEDGE.

BY PROF. ALFRED H. LLOYD.

University of Michigan.

Knowledge, we are told, is a growth. In conscious experience is to be seen a process that is resolvable into a number of stages. In fact in no science has the evolutional idea taken a stronger hold than in psychology.

The stages of knowledge, as commonly understood, are four, if I may reduce them somewhat. Thus: sensation, perception, conception and intuition. But an evolutional series of this kind, however well it may explain its special phenomena, is really in need of being explained itself. Mayhap it is in its entirety, in its earlier as well as in its later parts, a result of the very evolution that it would explain, and if so, the science depending upon it can hardly be too quick or too thorough in recognizing the fact. Mayhap, I say, but in truth I think the supposition is a fair report of reality, and I think also that the science of psychology to-day needs to be brought to a clearer consciousness of itself in this particular respect. Hence the simple suggestions that follow in this paper. I would reflect in a perfectly general way upon the evolutional series in the growth of knowledge, and expose it, and in the end indicate what seems to me the meaning of the change in psychology that the *exposé* effects.

Psychologists have said of sensation, as the first stage of knowledge, that it is of the material or the physical, of the visible and the tangible and the audible and the like, being a consciousness of what the self is supposed distinctly not to be. They have said that it has for its content only the here and the now and the this, or, in other words, some particular thing in some particular place at some particular time. But the purely passive experience required by this idea of sensation, whereby, to use an old-time distinction, sensation has contained no

164

thought, no universalizing or generalizing tendency, would have to be in unconsciousness; it would be, after all is said, only a hypothetical stage of conscious experience; as soon as it were realized, the account of it would cease to be adequate. So true is this that more recently we have found sensation commonly referred to, not as consciousness or an element of consciousness at all, but merely as an antecedent of actual consciousness, that is, either the external stimulus or the internal possibility. Sensation has come to play the part of a sort of zero of knowledge, a lower 'limit' in the evolutional scale.

Very simple experiments have demonstrated the impossibility of conscious 'sensuous' experience without the quality or meaning of the object being determined by relations beyond its position in space and beyond the moment of its being experienced and beyond individuality or isolation in general. In consciousness, however simple, say of mere color or of pressure or of temperature, other things and other times and other places determine the character of this thing here and now; any simplest object as it enters consciousness gets outwardly reaching relations. The later idea of sensation, then, only marks a retreat in psychological doctrine before this now undisputed law of relativity. But, alas! even science can make the mistake of jumping from the frying pan into the fire, since sensation as outer stimulus or as inner possibility is, if possible, more objectionable than sensation as physical atom or element. Knowledge at zero brings fatal difficulties.

Thus the idea of sensation as stimulus only shows an attempt, very common and doubtless very natural in human thought, to keep the same relations or conditions in unconsciousness that are observed in consciousness. Sensation as stimulus carries the dualism of mind and matter or subject and object into the sphere of life that lies wholly beneath or back of conscious experience. But doing this it robs dualism of all real meaning or content. It makes dualism absolutely formal, a mere hypothesis based upon a questionable analogy. From the point of view of what is without to the conscious self, that is, from the point of view of the object, the psychologist who entertains the notion of an wholly independent stimulus to consciousness

undertakes to present a stage or a state of life in which the distinction between what is without and what is within is quite impossible. That distinction is a development, not an antecedent
condition.

The justice of this criticism is evident also from the compli-
mentary idea of sensation as the subjective basis of possibility,
that is, as a 'sensation continuum' or an originally wholly undifferentiated consciousness, a sensuous consciousness of no distinctions, whether in its object or in the organism, out of which a
highly differentiated experience with organism to correspond is
evolved. But surely one does not need glasses to see that 'sensation continuum' not only is but another name for unconsciousness,
but also, like sensation as stimulus, is a sort of indirect or would-
be dualistic account of a condition in which mind and matter or
subject and object are really not two but one. At least the only
object to which it can claim any right is as thin a ghost as ever
crossed the path of science. Sensation, then, whether as objectively a mere stimulus of consciousness or as subjectively a continuous or undifferentiated consciousness, in so far as to be
regarded the first stage of knowledge, bears witness to an original state of unity or identity between self and not-self.   ,

It sums up the foregoing to say that 'sensation continuum'
and sensation as physical stimulus are, in the first place, opposites or extremes that meet, since the dualism on which their opposition depends cannot stand, and, in the second place, purely
formal ideas, descriptive of the beginning of mental life only
analogically and *retrospectively*. If you must recognize them
call them limits, since, as already suggested, they show knowledge at zero; call them abstract limits, but remember that the
idea of a limit always gives reality rather to a law operating
within the observed members of a series than to a separate
thing or a separate state. A limit never is; only the series
and its law are; the limit, so to speak, only sets the law and so
deepens the reality of each member of the series by making the
series itself an organized whole. In mathematics the infinite
and the infinitesimal are not real as quantities; they are real
only as relationship within quantity or among quantities; they
are quantitative indirections for quality and law. So, again, in

psychology, sensation, at best only the infinitesimal of knowledge, whether as continuum or as stimulus, can not be real as a separate antecedent stage of knowledge ; it must be, on the contrary, the epistemologist's indirection, or apology, for something deeper than mere knowledge and its stages, say for the vital principle itself or for the impulse to self-expression. The epistemologist has been ready enough to be an evolutionist, but he has also insisted on abstracting the knowing or merely cognitive self. Hence his notion of sensation as a first stage, when in reality it is not that. Psychology, in short, is more than epistemology ; it is biology also ; and sensation, as evolutional epistemology has reported it, is, I repeat, an indirection or abstraction for the principle of vital spontaneity.

Just what this principle is, in what terms it must define itself to the new psychology, the foregoing has all but indicated. Thus the law or principle to which the limits, sensation as mere stimulus and sensation continuum, testify or give reality, can have, I think, no better elementary statement than this, namely, that external stimulus and internal motive are one and identical ;[1] and in this identity, which makes knowledge from the start, not a mere consciousness of an outer world, but at once a part of and a means to active self-expression, in brief a something on which depends the freedom of the vital impulse, in this identity lies the first law of knowledge, a law which I would have psychology substitute for its still lingering doctrine of sensation as the first stage and the infinitesimal of knowledge. As a law of knowledge it is, of course, a key to the understanding of positive or conscious sensation, which is obviously quite distinct from sensation as mere stimulus, and of perception and conception and intuition, and to the understanding also of the order that psychology has come to give to them in the growth of knowledge.

Positive or conscious sensation, to which I now turn, involves the reference of some so-called sensuous quality to some external object. In different senses the degree of this objective refer-

---

[1] Certainly, quite apart from what has been said here, one must indeed have difficulty in entertaining the idea of a stimulus so external as not to be also motive or of a motive so internal as not to be also stimulus.

ence varies. For example, it is commonly much greater in the experiences of the eye than in those of the organs of smell or taste, but differences in degree in no wise change the fact or principle, which is our present concern. Conscious sensation is never purely subjective. Psychologists are now well agreed on this point. The experiments alone, already referred to, which have demonstrated the absolute dependence of any sensation for its meaning or quality upon other experiences beyond its own time and place, have left them in no doubt. Some have even imagined that the relationship between different mental states could be mathematically determined; others refuse to go so far; but all accept the general law of relativity. Thus to give Höffding's very conservative wording of the law: "From the moment of its first coming into being the existence and properties of a sensation are determined by its relation to other sensations." That this is a law of the objectivity as well as of the relativity of all conscious sensation hardly needs to be indicated, but, to be perfectly explicit, I may add that 'relation to other sensations' must mean to other sensations in space as well as in time or that dependence of any particular experience for its own special meaning on other moments is also necessarily dependence on other places or positions. If the time relations tend to keep the meaning of the experience subjective, the space relations must make it objective. In other words, the simple law of relativity must be taken as signifying that all conscious sensation is of a spatially external object, or not-self, but of an object whose qualities are in a certain interesting way subjective, in that they must embody by implication, if not directly, the self's past.

But this is not final; for, while the sensuously qualified object, or not-self, must, in the light of the law of relativity, be thought as the past self objectively present to the self, or as the self's objectified past, yet it is clear that the very fact of presentation or objectification points to some change in that past, say to some operation therein performed upon it, and an understanding of exactly what this operation is, is all-important. To get such understanding, however, we must, if possible, get back of the law of relativity or objectivity; we must get back of this law, at least so far as our comprehension of it depends on an application of its principle merely to differences of position in space and time or even of stimuli of measurable quantity or intensity. Relationship, let us reflect, is as much a matter of unity as of difference, of continuity as of isolation, of organic movement as of external ratios, and the objective world must in general owe its reality to something even deeper than 'difference thresholds' or 'threshold values' or than mere quantities of any kind.

The real difficulty is that so far we have been looking rather to what the sensuous object is than to how it is. The law of relativity, as sketched above, binds all experiences into one differentiated whole, and with space and time as the distinct but inseparable bases of the relations a past self as that which qualifies and a not-self as that which is qualified get their definite places in a theory of knowledge, and are seen of course to have most intimate connection each with the other; but assuredly more must be known than the formal bases of the relations. We must get at the living reality, at the vital principle of relationship instead of its formal bases. The theory of knowledge has been tarrying too long at the sign of the formal bases.

And what is the living reality, the vital principle? Plainly it is the impulse to self-expression with its identical aspect of motive and stimulus. Impulse to self-expression, at once differentiating and organizing, since both a wholly random act, an act in general, and a wholly specific act, an act in isolation, are not only unknown but also unthinkable, is a principle that quite transcends the special forms, space and time,[1] and yet that, so far as manifesting itself in motion, is spatially and temporally interpretable. Action, identical with self-expression being neither random nor specific, neither general nor individual, must be as expressive of control as of spontaneity. Accompanying all action, then, there must be a tension, or, the same thing, a consciousness, consciousness being always a tension between control and impulse or spontaneity. Control, however, is just that aspect of self-expression which gives reality to a not-self

[1] One has here to think of Spinoza's self-caused and self-intelligible substance, existing *in se* and *per se*, that transcended thought, the time aspect of law, and extension, the space aspect of law, in that it had infinite other attributes. Spinoza, be it remembered, all but gave Leibnitz his self-acting monad.

with stimulating qualities, while spontaneity, as a positive impulse in tension with control, shows these qualities to be real only as embodying the past, since such qualities must be reminiscent. In short, the not-self, as qualified, does but show the self's past in tension, and whether we approach the matter from the standpoint of self-control or from that of the not-self in whose qualities the self's past is seen to be in tension, the presence of a process of organization, of an organic activity, is beyond question,[1] and the organization plainly is not less of the objective qualities than of the controlled activities or impulses belonging to them. But organization of any particular impulse signifies reduction of it to a pure means wholly adapted to the single end of the organism, or to such a condition that when expressed the whole self can identify itself with it; and organization of all the manifold impulses must signify the development of activities every one of which can and must fully express the self. And on the side of the objective qualities, often called the outer stimuli, a perfectly correlative process, as already said, must take place, in that each individual quality, or sensuous content, corresponding to an individual impulse, must in its function of stimulus appeal to the whole self, not to the impulse as an isolated activity; and must therefore in its qualitative character be determined by a relation to the other qualities. Each qualitative part, or content, of the not-self, in so far as stimulus, must be at the same time, by ' fusion,' if you will, or ' assimilation' or ' association,' the qualitative whole, and just herein we see from the standpoint of impulse to self-expression, which is in action a process at once of differentiation and of organization; just herein do we see what the law of relativity means, how it is a law of objectivity, that is, a principle of control, and in being this is also a law of organic activity, and how, secondly, from the same standpoint, stimulus just in so far as it produces ' reaction' must be absolutely identical with motive.

---

[1] Compare with this account of the origin of the not-self the extremely interesting special case of it in the generally accepted explanation of the idea of space as rising with organization and symbolization (through association of muscular and tactual and retinal sensations) of the motor-impulses. Space as geometrical—that is, as mathematically definable—is the objective correlate of free movement. An exact geometry is possible, ' innate,' only to such as have the power of free movement.

The identity of motive and stimulus, above suggested as the first law of knowledge, very materially modifies a current idea of 'reaction,' as but just now hinted, and gives a notion of environment, heretofore styled the not-self, that has far-reaching consequences alike in psychological and in ethical theory. To add a few words upon the first point, that of the proper conception of reaction, it is evident that identifying stimulus and motive reduces reaction wholly to a process of the self acting upon itself or within itself, or even of environment acting upon itself or within itself, and not to what has been so often assumed, a process of self or mind, as something essentially distinct in nature, acting or reacting in its own peculiar way upon not-self or matter. Indeed, 'reaction' is a term imbued altogether too much with the spirit of dualism to be at all safe in self-controlled discourse. 'Self-activity' is far better, and with the conception of environment here required, whether one means self-activity of environment or self-activity of self is of no importance. "Environment did it" equals "self did it" in all cases of action, since the stimulating quality by reason of its determining relations is environment as a whole and the organically qualified environment as a stimulating whole is one and the same with the organic self and its impulse to complete self-expression.[1]

The notion of environment that our law of knowledge enforces is this: Environment is the self present to itself, in an other-than-it form, the otherness always signifying a tension between control and impulse to act. So much was really implied in what was said in a former paragraph, namely, that the not-self must be regarded as the past self presented to the self, or the self's objectified past, or with regard to its stimulating qualities as the past in tension; but now we have clearly before us the operation performed upon that past, as implied in the very fact of the presentation or the objectification, this operation being nothing more nor less than organization into the present or ad-

[1] Quite another way, and to me a very suggestive way, of putting the foregoing is that the human body is to be looked upon only as a part of 'environment.' The tendency to cherish it, whether in the passing psychology of reaction or in religion—of course the two are related—must give a false idea of activity. In reality the human body is but a part of a physical whole; it is, however, a part whose activity is that of the whole; hence it has mind or soul.

justment to the present, so that environment or not-self proves to be the past made present, its qualification being always a process of adjustment to the present. In other words, environment as differentially qualified and self as organically free and active develop together, not, as some have seemed to think, does environment with stimulating quality exist before a living self with interest in it, nor, as others have maintained, does the living self or soul antedate its environment. God did not *create* the world nor is man in any sense so creative, nor on the other hand is man in the ordinary understanding of the doctrine evolved out of the physical. Both the physical with its qualities, primary and secondary, and the freedom of self expression are evolved together. Evolution of course has been disposed to put the qualified world first in time, and creationism to put the fully developed spirit first in time, and which has committed the grossest anachronism it is really hard to say, since to reiterate, neither came first, or rather both were first and have kept the contemporaneity from the beginning. Thus, to suggest large-written illustrations, I can imagine man, when first assuming the erect position congratulating himself on having relegated so much of his past as was in the going on all fours to a mere object or symbol in his consciousness, and I can even feel the interest he must have taken in the new qualities and the more organic character that his world came to have for him with the change. The wanderer returning after long years to the scenes of childhood and seeing as object with emotional qualities that in which he had once lived, with which he had once wholly identified himself, could sympathize too. But how absurd it would be for either the returned wanderer or the erect man to say with materialistic evolution that out of that object *as so qualified* he had been evolved, or with orthodox creationism that in the object there was evidence of a fall from an ideal state to which, however, he has now at last returned. And yet upon such abstractions, upon such anachronisms, even recent psychological doctrine, in its idea of reaction and in its idea of the stimulating medium very largely relies. True, the past is in the object, or the environment, or the stimulating medium, but because the object is, and is at once organic and relationally differentiated, the present is there too, and if the present also the future. The object is not reminiscent merely; in being object it belongs to the present; it is, again, in so far as qualified and in so far as constructed or ordered literally ' up to date ;' it is a stimulus that is also motive; it is a revelation as well as a reminiscence, the future as well as the past.

. In environment, or object, as now present to our thinking, we have of course the ' perceived world.' The study of positive or conscious sensation has brought us to a comprehension of what psychology knows as perception, the second stage of knowledge. The law of relativity, as also a law of objectivity and of organic self-expression, under which a sensuous consciousness develops into a consciousness of an ordered outer world present to a self-controlled self, under which the world of experience becomes in the technical sense a ' perceived' world, carries with it, as we have found, three things: (1) the persistence of the past or of past experience in any present consciousness, (2) a differential, or negative, qualification of consciousness, by which the objective reference springs up, and (3) an organic activity, whereby consciousness, becoming objective, gets what is commonly called symbolic character, being symbolic of the activity itself. Perception, then, is a process by which the past may be said to move over into the object and to abide there as an important phase of the present, and the percept, the self so present to itself, is the original unity of the self as an organism differentiated and in the differentiation projected as not-self. The percept, accordingly, is not-self, but very much as the band of prismatic colors is the not-self of uuresolved light, or as tools and shop and materials are the not-self of the tool-using mechanic, or finally as a social community, in which labor is divided, is not-self to each one of its members. The percept is not-self, but also the incarnate self. What else can its tendency to symbolic character signify ? Now perception, as the perceived image evolves into mere symbol, becomes conception and intuition. This is technical and abstract. But the meaning of images becoming mere symbols is not far to seek.

Any image in which by virtue of its being objective and

of its sensuous qualities being organized, the past is fully adjusted to the present is become a symbol; it is a *mere* symbol. With the perfect adjustment the image's or object's qualities lose their reminiscent and individually stimulating character; the ' associated ' past, on which the consciousness depends, comes to be so real in the present as no longer to be suggestive of the past; whereupon the reminiscent qualities lose value, except that of the relation embodied in them, and the object as a mere system of relations, an organically relational whole, becomes not an object of sensuous consciousness, but a symbol, that is, *a basis of activity*, and has the same relation to the life of the self in general that language with its ' parts of speech' has to the expression of thought. In an image or object or symbol so developed, the self is set free. No symbol is mere symbol that is not proved so by some action in use of it, and the action of course fulfills motive and stimulus as one.

The term language, so says this psychology, must be extended to include the object of consciousness in this sense of the used symbol. Indeed one has to think of parts of fluent activity in general instead of merely of parts of speech. In parts of fluent activity psychology sees the survival of the sensuously stimulating qualities or elements which in the evolution of experience gradually pass into mere terms in a system of relations. Indeed, in the narrow sense, what is language, if not a complex of ' dying metaphors' or ' material associations,' or ' passing reminiscences', dying or associated or passing in the interest of organization or adjustment or fluency? Yes, the whole world of perception, as it becomes symbolic, as in it the past is adjusted to the present, is essentially linguistic, the basis of fluency in action; it is language that the perceiving self can use, with this limitation that when the self uses it as language, when the self acts fluently in it instead of simply observing it, it is more properly called the world of conception, since the self is then rather conceiving than perceiving reality.

It is common enough in psychology to connect intimately conception and the use of language, but observe that here, as the term language is made to include so much more than it usually covers, there is demand also for a more inclusive idea of conceptual thought. All sensuous images becoming symbols are linguistic; all fluent expression of self, all free activity, is thought in the stage of conception. Language obviously is only another name for the not-self as the self incarnate.[1]

But to some I shall doubtless seem to be denying the very most essential function of language, which is to name or report or describe. Language, I am reminded, enables its user to stand aloof from the physical world and to carry on an abstract activity —with reference to the world, it is true, but quite apart from it. So separate from ordinary activity has language been regarded that it has even been declared to be a gift of heaven, not of earth, an integral part of man's spiritual equipment. But let me say, varying a little what has been said already, that all free fluent activity is abstract or separate in exactly the sense meant. Finding a use of language in all fluent activity is not at all opposed to the orthodox ideas of language. Forsooth, are writing and speaking the only cases of self-activity? Every spontaneous act, every expression of the living self shows, in the first place, an experience organized into a symbol or a past brought into adjustment with a present, and in the second place this symbol as something belonging to the active self, something which mediates the activity, something quite as much motive as stimulus, applied as a 'name,' or a 'report,' if you like, to an outer world. All action, I would assert, from the lowest to the highest, from the simplest to the most complex, is of a self *naming* a not-self. When action is, the object or the symbol is as much the agent as the subject. So, in the sense of language being original, one cannot object to thinking of it even as a gift from heaven; it is as original as activity. Biologically, freedom in an environmont is also freedom of an environment, and organism and environment are one as thinking-self and language are one.

It has not infrequently been a matter of controversy if thought were possible without language, and the solution of the problem seems to be that thought is possible without language

---

[1] On the more general use of the term language compare the short discussion : 'A Psychological Interpretion of Certain Doctrines in Formal Logic.' PSYCH. REV., Vol. III., No. 4, July, 1896—pp. 422-426.

in the narrower sense, that is, written and spoken language, but impossible without language as such, that is, without environment. Do animals think? Do they know relations? Are they addicted to language? Assuredly they are and do, if ever they act in self-expression. What living creature is not ' addicted' to an environment?

The rise of language as such, so our psychology here would lead us to conclude, means nothing more nor less than the mechanicalization of environment or the perceived world. In other words, the pure symbol, used in conception, in so far as a basis of fluent activity, is only a mechanism that the individual has become free to use. And in such mechanism, I would suggest in passing, as objective or physical, is evidence always of the rise of a community of individuals acting organically. In short, the fully developed object of perception is more than mere symbol; it is a mechanism in which is the basis of the life of a social organism. Its character as language, as ' medium of the exchange of thought,' can have no other import than this, since thought itself is organized social life. This intimate connection, moreover, between the rise of language and conception, the mechanicalization of environment, and the development of the social organism, is a most important outcome of the standpoint taken here, but discussion of it is not within the scope of the present article. Motive and stimulus are identical; environment is essentially linguistic; and language is not the medium of the exchange of abstract thought, but the basis of an organized life. That is the whole story in a nut-shell. Simply the linguistic environment makes possible individual self-expression in a social group; or mechanicism, like the *a priori*, which according to Kant makes the experience of it possible, is social.[1]

So far I have insisted on extending the use of the term language to make it include environment or the medium of expres-

---

[1] Social, I repeat, in the sense of free industrialism or of society as an organism; in history the social mechanicalism of Rome is evidently the '*a priori* from' in which modern life as industrial and organically international has been possible. Rome, with her Christian idolatry, her spiritual monarchism, her linguistic formalism, her Jewish finance, only have witness to the *originality of the medium of self-expression*, an idea which the modern individual has naturally enough taken to himself. But, in general, mechanism is the *a priori* condition of individualism and organism.

sion without limitation or abstraction. But, of course, language in the narrower sense, in the sense that limits it to special forms of sounds and shapes, has, even in its very narrowness, an important relation to the activity of thought. In emphasizing the broader view of language, therefore, I have appeared to slight the narrower. Hence I wish to add the following much condensed paragraphs by way of atonement.

It is a generally recognized principle that self-expression brings interpretation or meaning to the impulse expressed, and that meaning, coming so, controls the impulse. In other words, after expression impulse is held for a time, longer or shorter, in abeyance. Impulse in abeyance, however, not only confines the self's activity within the self, but also changes the special centres or organs of consciousness, and the confinement and the change would seem to be what make language in the narrower sense. Thus, to give the most obvious illustration, an impulse of man's in abeyance does not mean inactivity, but activity abstracting itself and identifying itself with eyes and ears, with the writer's hand and the speaker's tongue. Where, indeed, could activity find itself more at home than in these marvellously mobile organs? They are, in fact, but the stage upon which the self rehearses its part. They show the self acting ' to itself,' as we say specially of a child that learns to read without speaking ; that is to say, acting apart or abstractly or reflectively.

Control, then, abstracts activity and develops very mobile organs for the special function so arising, the function of acting to oneself or quite within oneself. But acting to oneself brings the consciousness of environment or. not-self; and, more than this, the environment gets what, in lack of a better account, I have to call a double character. Thus there arises a special consciousness, or experience, inhering in the special organs of the abstract activity and, at the same time, a special consciousness inhering in the organs of the self's complete activity, and, obviously enough, the special object of the former serves as a name or symbol of the latter; the special object of the organs of activity to oneself *names* the special object of the organs of the possible activity to one's world. The self does not talk talks nor see sights, nor hear sounds ; it *names* the not-self.

And, furthermore, in the name, arising as the object or natural medium of the abstracted activity, relationship, that is, relational or organic structure, will far outweigh all consideration of mere size. The name, in short, will be only a sort of after-image of the sphere of the self's original expression of impulse—original, that is, antecedent to the rise of control. That the original expression will have already determined the relations, or given the self an experience of them, is clear enough, since without such determination the expression itself could never have taken place. So the reproduction in an after-image is no miracle, but only shows how realized relationship in experience brings independence of mere quantitative determinations. The theory of language as originating in pictures, reduced reproductions of natural objects, has its limitations, but it will serve here in illustration. Its limitations, after all, are rather in terms of narrow application than of principle involved.

So, in summary, expression of impulse puts impulse in abeyance; impulse in abeyance brings an after-image of the special experience, which, as a relational whole, expression has defined; and, the after-image being a freed image, or the sphere of an abstracted activity, the direct use of it, the use of it with reference to its origin, the controlled, mediated use of it, gives what we commonly understand as the linguistic expression of self.

But we have yet to consider the last stage of knowledge, intuition. Intuition, however, is but the perfect freedom of using language, or of adaptation to environment. It is a stage of knowledge very much as sensation was a stage of knowledge. Thus the used mechanism is, as it were, the limit that the sensuously qualified symbol approaches, and intuition as stage of knowledge is a limit too, being such a limit as we have seen sensation to be and giving evidence of the same law of knowledge. Intuition comes with the completion of the process of mediation; with it consciousness ripens into fluent action; with it thought is set free. If in sensation stimulus and motive are one, in intuition at the other end of the scale developed mechanism as the stimulus and free agent as the motive, in short, language and thought, are one. The mechanism is nothing more nor less than stimulus to the *free* agent's will.

So at both ends of the scale evolutional psychology has erred. It has retained intuition as the last stage of knowledge with the same blind persistence, or rather with the same misunderstanding of the true meaning, that has characterized its treatment of simple sensations or of sensation as stimulus or original continuum. Neither sensation nor intuition is a content of consciousness. The former is the vital impulse to self-expression; the latter is that impulse fully mediated in an act. As stages of knowledge they are limits, the infinitesimal and the infinite respectively, and, so understood, they only show how psychology, bent on keeping knowledge in a sphere quite by itself, has striven to do without physiology and biology. Thus, again, sensation as stage of knowledge is the back-door by which psychology has spirited life into the domain of knowledge; and intuition in its turn is but an epistemological disguise for the ripened act; and if the former is due to the gratuitous construction of retrospection—on the part, say, of self-conscious inactivity—the latter results from a closely related prospection.

And the change in psychology, finally, that recognition of this origin of the evolutional stages of knowledge effects is simply the turning of the old-time idea, or concept, into an act; of self-conscious inactivity into activity; of psychology, science of the soul, into biology, the science of life on earth.

DISCUSSION AND REPORTS.

THE PRESIDENT'S ADDRESS.

In his recently published address (PSYCHOLOGICAL REVIEW, January, 1897) Professor Fullerton, after firing random shots at a full score of ancient worthies and modern colleagues, trains the heavy guns of his critical raillery on my views as to the nature of mind. His reiterated charges of 'obscurity' and 'inconsistency,' made in the lightsome mood to which we have all become accustomed, I am entirely content to let stand for what they may seem worth to those who have carefully read my books. I only wish at present to call attention to two or three misapprehensions. Perhaps, however, even this . may have some bearing upon the charges if, as it seems to me, the misapprehensions are so obvious and on the surface as to show cause *in the critic,* why he should find the views of nearly every one else, with mine, guilty of essentially the same errors.

In the first place, I am charged with having abandoned the standpoint of psychology, because I have insisted that all the phenomena of consciousness must be considered not merely 'content-wise,' but also 'function-wise,' and indeed as forms of self-activity; and also because my analysis of cognition shows that cognition always implicates reality, 'envisaged, believed in, or inferred.' But I find Professor Fullerton himself, in this very address, insisting upon a 'broad and reasonable sense of the word content,' and affirming by it "*I* mean all that is to be found in consciousness, including relations, changes and activities." Moreover, he commends Professor Wundt for treating the subject-matter of psychology in the proper way; although he patronizingly adds in a note that Wundt, too, does not appear 'to fully appreciate the significance of his own position.' But does not all the psychological world know that Professor Wundt makes, in his psychological writings throughout, prominent use of the doctrine of the soul as a conscious self-activity, and that concerning the relation of psychology and philosophy he has even expressly denied the possibility of treating them as independent disciplines. As to knowledge, however, in this very paper also Professor Fullerton repeats, with evident increase of self-satisfaction, what he had to say in a paper of three years ago: The psychologist 'must assume (*sic*) the existence of an external physical world,' of which our ideas are copies that are 'intimately related to particular bodily organisms.' Now it seems to me that any clear and consistent thinker will be forced to exclaim over such a tenet as this: Here is ' belief,' and ontological ' implicates' inferred, with a vengeance. Perhaps Professor Fullerton will sometime free, for us all, his little bit of an 'assumption' from the 'obscurity' and 'vagueness' and 'inconsistency' in which he has left it.

But a much more serious and quite indefensible misapprehension seems to me the only explanation of Professor Fullerton's method of criticizing my views by a kind of see-sawing between the two books, ' Psychology, Descriptive, etc.,' and ' Philosophy of Mind.' He is, indeed, so kind as to admit that I am developing these views in ' the right direction.' But curiously enough, the one which is really the earlier of these two works, but which my critic appears to regard as the later, sets the high-water mark of my poor attempts to be clear and consistent, as well as ' learned and really scholarly,' respecting the doctrine of mind. What, however, is the actual case? The first book *is* what its title signifies, namely, an attempt to describe the development of human mental life in the individual; and, among other forms of development, the growth in clearness and complexity of the conception of Self, just as observation and experiment and scientific analysis find it. With my accomplishment of this task Professor Fullerton has little fault to find. But the avowed purpose of the ' Philosophy of Mind ' is, without abandoning the standpoint of psychology, but by transcending this standpoint and passing on to the standpoints of metaphysics and epistemology, to give speculative treatment to the phenomena of consciousness. In other words, I have made, in this later work, the effort to construct a rational doctrine of the real nature of mind. Now, like any other critic, Professor Fullerton might deny to me the right or the ability to attempt such a task, or he might refute the positions taken in the course of the attempt. But to overlook the relations of the two works; to cite, as my final view, sentences from ¦the former which I have quoted into the latter so as to furnish my speculation with empirical data; to impart meaning into metaphysical terms which I have most expressly guarded against or even rejected, and thus to throw into confusion and inconsistency what is clear and consistent when read in the connection and in the light of the author's intent— this seems to me a style of criticism which is best left to itself to refute.

One more misapprehension I wish to notice. I am accused of teaching a kind of ' diluted' Kantian doctrine of the soul as *ding-an-sich* or *noumenon*, lying behind all actual self-known existence and answering either to a purely negative and limiting conception or to the bare idea 'that it is,' without the possibility of knowledge as to 'what it is.' Shades of the great founder of critical agnosticism! And yet I have been studying carefully over and over again the 'Critique of Pure Reason' for years and with scores of keen and critical minds as pupils and co-workers, and have never discovered my agreement on this particular doctrine with the sage of Königsberg. But since I can scarcely ask Professor Fullerton to read again the 'Philosophy of Mind,' where I have, as clearly as language can and so often as really to run great conscious risk of wearying my readers, tested and rejected the Kantian view, I know nothing better to suggest for him than a revised study of Kant. Perhaps this will lead him to discover unlimited chances for obscurity and inconsistency in his own attempt to place a writer who affirms that *we do know reality*, beyond all power of sceptical idealism or agnostic positivism to shake the foundations of such knowledge, in every act of self-knowledge, and that *all knowledge is, quoad knowledge, essentially transcendent*, agree with the great author of the 'Critique of Pure Reason,' who taught on all these points precisely the contrary view.

Much more might be said about Professor Fullerton's manner of treating those whose names and opinions he is wont to handle with such effective appearance of grace and ease. But I prefer to leave sword-play for the most part to men who like it and who really think it leads to truth, and to content myself with the humbler and less impressive use of trowel and spade.

GEORGE TRUMBULL LADD.

YALE UNIVERSITY.

UPRIGHT VISION AND THE RETINAL IMAGE.

Professor Hyslop's recent objection to my article on 'Vision without Inversion of the Retinal Image,' in the November number of this REVIEW, is a welcome criticism of the bearing of my experiments, even though the form in which he has seen fit to express his objection is, perhaps, needlessly brusque. He says, in substance, that I have missed the real problem of upright vision in taking it as a problem of the harmonious interorganization of motor, tactual and visual experience, and that the real problem is an exclusively visual one. According to his view, the question of upright vision is: How do apparent objects get a spatial position inverse to that which they have in the retinal image? And since my article, to his mind, shows clearly that during the experiment the position of apparent objects was still the reverse of their position in the retinal image, my experiment has nothing to do with the problem of upright vision.

I am glad that Professor Hyslop has taken the trouble to show that the problem, as I understand it, is quite different from this problem which he counts the true one. The two problems have hardly anything in common, and it is well that everyone should see that mine is not his. For his problem is, I feel sure, an illusory one and vanishes as soon as one sees the true relation which vision, as a whole, bears to the retinal image.

It is sometimes said that one never has an experience of his own retinal image. This is perhaps strictly true, and yet it is often misleading, in that it is understood to mean that the retinal image is outside my experience and yet not so alien, but that somehow I can compare its position with that of my visual experience. The fact is, the retinal image is, by representation, made a part of my experience, just as all things which I represent become thereby parts of my experience, even though I do not directly perceive them. And only by thus representing my retinal image and definitely assigning it a position within the world of things actually visible to me does any comparison of its position with that of other objects become possible. It is visualized, or otherwise represented, in definite spatial relation to those parts of the world which I see, and thus becomes an integral part of my larger world of visual and visualized experience, built out beyond and in between the objects of actual sight. My brain, for instance, becomes a part of my visual world because I assign it a definite position within the visual total, though I have never seen it. I represent my brain, not as enveloping my experience nor as having lines of direction independently comparable with those of my visual world, but as itself a part of that total visual world and as having for me no position nor direction except as within that total and as relative to the other parts of the whole. Its position in my world of experience is nothing absolute, but is determined merely relatively to the internal lines of direction and points of reference of that experience. Likewise my retinal image is an integral part of my visual world. Its place is within my visual total, and its position and direction are determined only by making use of the directions of reference within that total. Why it should have the position and direction there which it does have; in other words, why the rest of my visual world and that small portion of it, which I call my retinal image, should have the peculiar spatial relation they do have, is a matter of optics and vertebrate morphology, not a problem for psychology.

The position which, from our knowledge of optics, we assign the visual image within our visual world does not mean that our visual experience bears an inverse relation to something *external* to that visual experience, as Professor Hyslop seems to think. This relation is in no sense a relation between two heterogeneous terms, one of them a system of visual experiences, and the other an alien counterpart inverse to these. Since our only way of comparing the image with our visual perceptions is by representing it relative to their position, and as embedded in their larger system, its relation to the rest is no indication of the relation of the whole system of visual perceptions, or of the visual process as such, to something else. It does not give us the slightest warrant for holding that the visual process includes, for instance, a process of spatial transposition of objects into some other direction or order than that given in the immediate retinal stimulus. The *interrelation of objects*, not the absolute position of objects, is what we wish to know by sight, as by touch. Even if we could make absolute position at all intelligible, a knowledge of it would be of no earthly use to us, except in so far as it might guide us to a knowledge of the relative situation of things. Now our vision gives us this *interrelation of objects* exactly as their images are interrelated in the retinal image. We see things in the very same relation to our body that the images of those things bear to the image of our body on the retina. Later on, the reflective mind wishes to add into its visual system of objects other objects not given in vision, and among the rest interpolates one small item not appearing among the images on the retina, namely, the retinal image itself. The fact, that I represent among my objects a smaller inverted image of some of them, seems to me no better evidence than, for instance, an inverted chair among my visual objects would be that transposition or reversal takes place in the process of vision itself. If Professor Hyslop really thinks that the position of visual objects with reference to the visual image reveals a peculiar character in the visual process itself, such as to constitute a problem, there must be for him a still more serious problem in the fact that our visual objects appear to be in front of our head, though the real organ of vision is in the occipital cortex.

Vision as a whole and by itself is indeed neither inverted nor upright. Objects *within* the visual system may be inverted or upright with respect to other objects in the system; but the whole cannot by itself have either of these characteristics. For this reason there can never be a purely visual problem of upright vision. And since visual experience cannot be compared with things-in-themselves, nor consequently with the retinal image-in-itself, upright vision must mean a vision which gives us objects upright with reference to some non-visual experiences which are taken, for the time being, as the standard of direction. Upright vision, in the final analysis, is vision in harmony with touch and motor experience; and the only problem of upright vision is one concerning the necessary conditions for a reciprocal harmony in our visual and tactual or motor perceptions.

Now the actual conditions of vision make it seem, to a person who takes an uncritical common-sense view of things, a matter of surprise that there is harmony between these different kinds of perceptions. Since the retinal image of any object lies in a direction inverse to the object as a touch experience, the nervous basis of vision seems to be in discord with the system of tactual perceptions; how does it come about, then, that there is mutual harmony in the two forms of perception? The theories which may be roughly styled the projection and the eye-movement theories answer this question by stating, each for a different reason, that vision reverses the retinal direction of objects. The real visual direction, as distinct from the merely retinal direction, is thus, according to these theories, identical with the touch direction, and the problem is solved. But an implied corollary of either of these theories is, that if the retinal image were *not* inverted with respect to the tactual position of things there *would be* discord between the two kinds of perception. For the same mechanism which hitherto had produced a reversal would remain; the reversal ought, therefore, to take place persistently, and visual objects would in that case be spatially the inverse of their tactual counterparts. These theories tend, therefore, to the result that an inverse relation between tactual direction and the direction of the retinal image is one of the necessary conditions for a harmony between touch and sight.

My experiments make it extremely probable that the harmony rests on no such condition whatever; and this probability is still farther strengthened by later and more extended experiments, of which I hope soon to give a detailed report. Both sets of experiments go to show that when the retinal direction of objects becomes identical with their tactual direction the discord in the experience is only temporary. In fact, the experimental results confirm the truth of the view stated near the beginning of this paper, that we have no reason to suppose that there even is a reversal or transposition of directions in the visual process. *A fortiori*, we need no theory to explain the reversal.

Professor Hyslop, however, points with assurance to certain passages in the report of my preliminary experiment, as proof that such a reversal was present even under the conditions there described. What I have already said of the relation of visual experience to the retinal image, is, it seems to me, a sufficient answer to his interpretation of the facts. But even from his own point of view the passages he refers to are innocent enough, when one distinguishes carefully between that portion of my experience which was based on the older visual conditions and that portion which was being constructed under the new (experimental) conditions. I stated in my paper that when I artificially turned the retinal image upright I saw things at first upside down. Now, since the retinal image was turned 180° and visual objects, in consequence, were turned 180°, this means to Professor Hyslop that the normal inverse relation between image and objects still held, and that my experiment is only an additional evidence of how persistent this relation is. I admit that in my mixed experience at the beginning of the experiment, and in general throughout the experiment (for the experience to the end was a conflict between old and new), this relation existed. But it existed simply because the experience was a mixture of old and new perceptions, and the directions of reference were largely still the old ones. My 'real' body was, in general, localized as I had seen it in my pre-experimental vision. The retinal image was localized with reference to this older visual position of my body, and not in the way which a complete submission to the new visual experience would have required. As long as my body was localized according to the old experience, and other things in sight were localized according to the new, the two standards for localizing my retinal image were in conflict; so that the image's correct relation to one of these standards meant its inharmonious relation to the other. An entirely harmonious organization of the new experience, based on a full knowledge of the laws of light, would have required that the retinal image should be localized among the objects of my experience, in an upright position with respect both to my body and to the objects represented in the image. But since my body was, in general, still localized by recalling pre-experimental perceptions of it, a localization of the image in proper relation to this old position of the body made the image inverted with respect to the things I saw. And if, on the other hand, I localized the image in proper optical relation to the things it imaged, the relation between the image and my body was incorrect. In general, I no doubt remained faithful to my body and let the outer contradiction take care of itself.

But all this is only a transitional state of consciousness. Suppose that the partial reharmonization of my experience had given place to a complete harmony of tactual and visual perceptions and to a suppression of my old localizations brought over from the earlier experience—a result toward which the experiments surely point;—I would then feel and see my body unreservedly in its new place in the visual field, and in the same relation to the new objects around my body, as existed between my body and surrounding objects in the older experience, viz., my feet on the ground, my head toward the sky, etc. The proper localization of my retinal image according to the laws of experience, would now produce no such contradiction as was inevitable during the earlier, transition state. I could localize the image—and a self-consistent organization of my new experience would force me to localize it—upright with respect both to my body and to the objects pictured in my image. The inverse relation between my retinal image and the objects perceived would here have disappeared.

The result toward which the experiment points has thus a most definite bearing on the problem of upright vision, even in Professor Hyslop's sense of the term. And instead of adding testimony to the persistence of the inverse relation between image and objects, it really shows that this inverse relation is a psychologically non-significant accompaniment of the peculiar lens-arrangement of the eye, and would disappear could we but change the eye in that regard alone. If our eye had contained a more complex system of lenses instead of the simple arrangement we actually have, there would have been no hint in our experience, and certainly none outside of our experience, of any mutually inverse relation of objects and their retinal images.

Through the courtesy of the editor, I have been permitted to read advance sheets of Professor Hyslop's article in the present number of this REVIEW. The grounds upon which he denies the pertinence of my experiments to the question I had in view are fully covered, it seems to me, by what I have already said. Nor do I see that he has yet produced a single fact to show that the interrelation of visual objects is not *identical* with the interrelation of their retinal stimuli. Since visual objects have no absolute position or direction, but only relative position and direction, there is no evidence that vision reverses or transposes anything, until some one shows that vision gives us objects in some different order or interrelation from that which their images or stimuli have *among themselves* on the retina. Only a reversal of this sort would give us a visual problem. And since no such reversal or transposition occurs, there is no exclusively visual problem of upright vision, as Professor Hyslop supposes.

UNIVERSITY OF CALIFORNIA.   GEORGE M. STRATTON.

THE ORIGINALITY OF ÆSTHETIC FEELING.

In the September number of this Review, Dr. Livingston Farrand has deserved well of all interested in the philosophy of art, by calling attention to Grosse's *Anfänge der Kunst.* Agreeing, as I do, with his high estimate of the book, I wish to point out briefly the significance of some of its conclusions. As the title indicates, the author has limited himself to the historical and descriptive treatment of his subject, but his results seem to have some bearing upon the nature of the æsthetic impulse itself. Is the beautiful a variety of the useful? Does it exist in and for itself, or has it an end beyond itself? Can we analyze our feeling for it into yet simpler elements, or is it an immediate and ultimate judgment of value? The bearing of Herr Grosse's work upon these questions is what I wish to discuss in this paper.

The author's conclusions are best considered with reference to the particular divisions of the arts made by him, for the results vary slightly in the different arts. (1) Personal adornment holds the first place in his classification; does this show an immediate feeling for beauty or is it undertaken for ulterior ends? Apparently it serves a two-fold end, that of attraction and that of repulsion. Primitive man adorns himself either to attract his mate or to terrify his enemy. Even the most primitive form of dress seems to have this external end, rather than the more immediate one of serving as a protection from the cold or as a concealment of the person. The main purpose of early adornment was the same as that found in animals, the furtherance of sexual selection. Early art in this most primitive form had thus an important function in the development of the race. It was not a mere accident of evolution, but one of its forces, a means to the survival of the fittest. (2) Again, the ornamentation of weapons and domestic implements in most cases seems to have been undertaken for utilitarian reasons. Their smoothness and polish were a direct advantage to their owner. Moreover, their symmetry and proportion were not necessarily due to æsthetic feeling, but were the result of the inherent possibilities of the instrument itself or due to imitation of nature. The laws of mechanics are accountable for much apparently æsthetic purpose in nature. (3) As we might expect, painting and carving give more direct evidence of æsthetic feeling. The fact of their existence as distinct objects shows that to some extent they have their end in themselves. Of course, many of these apparent pictures are examples of picture writing, drawn, not from delight in the forms, but in order to give information to friends. Others, again, are religious symbols, but the majority must be classed as products of pure æsthetic feeling. Wherever the faculties of observation and execution are well developed there they are sure to find expression in an activity having its end in itself in the pure delight of creative activity. A remarkable illustration of this is given in the fact that the hunting tribes, although inferior in general culture to others, are the ones in which drawing and carving seem to have reached their greatest development, the hunter's eye and hand having been abnormally trained by virtue of his occupation. (4) The function of the dance is largely religious and social. It gives expression to the emotions of the performers and rouses those of the spectators. The fact that the primitive dance is not a performance of individuals, but of the whole tribe or village indicates its nature as an integrating agency in society, uniting the tribe among themselves and making them more effective against external foes. (5) Early poetry is undoubtedly an æsthetic phenomenon, arising as it does out of pure delight in the story or as the natural outlet of emotion. It also had an undoubted social significance and value in binding together the shares of the common literature and song. (6) Finally, music seems to be the one art of purely æsthetic origin. It seems impossible to assign to it any end beyond itself. It is the furthest removed from all considerations of practical utility. Mr. Darwin, it is true, would derive it from circumstances connected with sexual selection, but his explanation is an obvious *petitio principii.*

These conclusions may perhaps be summarized under these three heads: (1) All primitive peoples have some form of art. (2) These art forms are not always due to purely æsthetic impulses, but have a utilitarian purpose. (3) The function of early art is social preservation. With reference to our subject these results might seem to point to a negative conclusion in regard to the originality and independence of the æsthetic impulse. If art can be shown in so many cases to serve ends beyond itself, why may it not have done so universally? Why may not utility have been the mother of the arts and the essence of their meaning? And if æsthetic appreciation is thus a secondary product, reached late in the process of development, this fact is in some way interpreted to the disadvantage of art. Its naturalness is questioned, and with its naturalness, its value in itself.

On the contrary, it is necessary to note, in the first place, that art cannot be used as a means until it first exists as an end. The utility of art arises from its æsthetic quality, rather than its æsthetic quality from its utility. Unless ornament and decoration were already at tractive to the primitive female they would have no value as an element in sexual selection. It is because they already please the eye that they play the part they do in early social life. The social function of art is dependent wholly on its æsthetic character. This holds in music, poetry, and the dance, as well as in the plastic arts. Mr. Darwin's explanation of the origin of music leaves unexplained the essential point, the cause of the agreeableness of the elementary cries. It may be contended in reply to this statement of the relations of art to utility that it takes no account of the many cases in which it has been proved that æsthetic pleasure in objects has arisen from long experience of their utility, that is, from association of non-æsthetic pleasures. This is quite true, but it is because this point involves a different problem, a problem which may be quite as important, but which is yet perfectly distinct. The one concerns the conscious nature of æsthetic feeling, the other involves the history of its unconscious conditions or origins. The one is within the sphere of art itself; the other is wholly outside these limits. The worth or dignity of art does not depend upon any theory of its origin; these pre-artistic beginnings cannot depreciate in any degree the value of the completed product. Art is distinct from its causes or antecedents. It is the same question which has been so often fought over in the history of thought, nature *versus* origin, but it is continually cropping up again in new forms demanding repeated consideration. Whatever may have been the origin of art, it exists now as an independent expression of man's nature. The only way in which its value might be questioned would be through the proof that it exists as art only by virtue of its relation to an ulterior end. Just as the ethical value of man depends upon his autonomy and his right to exist as an end in himself, so the æsthetic dignity of art consists in its sufficiency to itself. It may further social unity, must do so if it is to exist permanently, but it does so by virtue of its inherent nature. Its use as a means presupposes its value as an end, and this fact Herr Grosse's conclusions only serve to confirm. They show that art is useful, but not that utility is the essence of art.

Again, this fact may be brought out more clearly by considering the distinction between art forms and æsthetic pleasure in them, or between forms which may at one time be artistic and another time not so. The fact that certain forms once served utilitarian ends, and that the same forms at a later period gave pure æsthetic pleasure, by no means indicates identity of nature in the subjective appreciation. Identity of the object does not imply identity of feeling for it. What anthropology can do for æsthetics is to trace the history of these objective forms, thus showing the antecedents of art, but this history of forms is not a history of the subjective feelings for art. In the truest sense consciousness has no history. Its states are eternally themselves; there is succession of these states, but they themselves remain in nature self-identical and distinct from one another. Hence it may very well be that a form which has later become known as an art form existed originally for other than æsthetic ends. It may have been useful for hunting, or clothing, or agriculture, or it may have been but an accidental variation grown dear by custom, or it may have presented a peculiarly pleasant stimulation to our perceptive powers, but it is not an object of æsthetic appreciation until ulterior ends have been lost sight of, and it is enjoyed for itself alone. The feeling for beauty is simple and not to be analyzed, whatever may have been the history of its becoming, or of the objects which arouse it. That is to say, it shares the nature of all feeling in being immediate. It is a self-evident, though apparently often forgotten, fact that all mediacy presupposes the immediate. Utility is only a secondary notion acquiring its meaning from its relation to an end. This is true both in ethics and æsthetics. The beautiful as well as the good carries us back to the nature of man as an ultimate standard beyond which explanation cannot go. The original judgment of value must, therefore, have been a simple and irreducible one, a feeling of immediate satisfaction in some action or passion congruent with the human organism. Into this instinctive judgment the question of utility cannot enter, since it in turn is founded on it as its presupposition and standard. Between this instinctive feeling and the most highly developed æsthetic appreciation there is no difference in kind; hence, unless we are prepared to deny the existence of any such immediate satisfaction, we must admit the originality of the æsthetic judgment. Herr Grosse's results, therefore, while giving us valuable information as to the conditions of primitive art, are not to be taken as furnishing any derivation of the æsthetic feeling itself, since these earliest art forms, so far as they evidence æsthetic appreciation at all, indicate that the feeling for the beautiful was as simple then as now.

NORMAN WILDE.

COLUMBIA UNIVERSITY.

PSYCHOLOGICAL LITERATURE.

Agnosticism and Religion. JACOB GOULD SCHURMAN. New York, Charles Scribner's Sons, 1896. 16°. Pp. 181.

Two addresses (one being to the students of Cornell University) and an essay, all written in the broad rich oratorical style of which President Schurman is a master. He defends theistic religion against agnostic denials, on the one hand, and against the dogmatism of theologians, on the other. Since Kant this attitude, which is unquestionably that of wisdom, has been gaining strength; but so ardent is man's love for sharp conceptions that such vague belief as this little book expresses will, so far from being universally greeted as a happy *via media*, probably gain for its author the reprobation of influential circles on both sides. The theologians will doubtless express themselves most strongly, and in these days of wariness in official position President Schurman is to be praised for the courage with which he exposes himself to their ire. The work makes little pretence to originality of argument. The first essay is an interesting account of Huxley's career. The author yields him hearty praise, but complains, first, that he never treated religion as if it too could be a positively evolving thing; second, that he failed to see through the absurdity of the Kant-Hamilton dogma that God must be essentially unknowable to man; and third, that he too trustingly assumed that the scientific investigator as such must be the chief authority in all things, even those of the spirit. The second essay is a defence of man's knowledge of the Divinity that expresses itself in the Universe, as against what the writer calls 'the farce of nescience playing the part of omniscience in setting the bounds of science.' The last paper eloquently rejoices in the evolution of our Christian churches towards non-doctrinal theism. "If a true Christian discovers that the creed of his church is no longer tenable, his plain duty * * * * is not to leave the church, but to let his light so shine that others may come to a knowledge of the fact that the church is not the mere embodiment of a creed, but the plastic organization of a life which is spiritual. His insight into the real situation of affairs forbids desertion, even though he is aware that fidelity may be rewarded by banishment or persecution" (p. 170). The little book deserves a wide success. W. J.

192

Studies in the Hegelian Dialectic. J. M. E. MacTAGGART. Cambridge, University Press, 1896. Pp. xvi + 259.

By these *Studies* Mr. McTaggart leaps at one bound into the foremost rank among the interpreters of Hegel, and in the course of his exegesis he displays so much ingenuity and subtlety that his book cannot but prove extremely stimulating to all who read it. It is, of course, impossible to follow him through all the depths and ramifications of his argument, but an idea of his main results may be attained by considering his answers to three of the leading questions about the Hegelian Dialectic. They are: I. What is the aim it sets before itself? II. What is its relation to experience? III. What is the significance in it of Negation?

I. Its aim, according to Mr. McTaggart, is to show that only in the Absolute Idea can the ultimate explanation of anything be found and that all other principles of explanation are necessarily inadequate. And the sole postulate it requires in order to refute scepticism and to establish all knowledge upon this impregnable rock, is the existence of experience, *i. e.*, the validity of the idea of Being, from which the Dialectic sets out. If Being is admitted, the nature of thought is such that all the other categories follow, and not even the extremest scepticism can deny that something is. But Being is the most abstract of the categories and in restoring to science the category of the Absolute Idea the Dialectic corrects the error of a course of abstraction which has been driven to equate Being with Nothing.

II. It is a mistake to suppose that the Dialectic is independent of experience or tries to reduce the universe to pure thought. When it is called a process of pure thought, that only means that it is " dependent not on experience being thus and thus, but only on experience existing at all. And the existence of experience cannot be called an empirical fact. It is the presupposition alike of all empirical knowledge and of all pure thought." And this general nature of experience is the passive basis of the dialectic movement, which is " due exclusively to that element of experience which we call pure thought" (p. 19). This indispensable but passive condition of the working of 'pure thought' forms an immediate element in knowledge (p. 41), but is not in itself knowledge. In this sense, then, Hegelism is 'without presupposition.'

III. With regard to the place of negation in the Dialectic, Mr. McTaggart holds that, so far from denying the law of Contradiction, it is essentially based on it. And, moreover, though at first and in the case of the lower categories the antithesis negates the thesis and has to be reconciled to it by the synthesis, yet, as we pass to the higher categories, the sharpness of the opposition is gradually mitigated, until at the end we progress almost continuously. "The really fundamental aspect of Dialectic is not the tendency of the finite category to negate itself, but to complete itself" (p. 10). It follows that the Dialectic, as depicted by Hegel, does not at first fully express the nature of thought—its own nature (pp. 138-9) is in a sense subjective and represents only the way in which the human mind proceeds from error to truth. But that only brings out into clearer relief the fact that the whole truth and the sole truth is nothing less than the Absolute Idea. Mr. McTaggart somewhat hesitates to claim Hegel's approval for these inferences from his method, and admits that " the change in the type of the process is not sufficiently emphasized in Hegel," but he regards it as necessary, " since it is only by the aid of some such theory that we can regard the system as valid at all" (p. 158).

After this comes a chapter on that sorest of vulnerable points, the relation of the Dialectic to Time, concerning which I have had my say elsewhere,[1] and two chapters on the final result and application of the Dialectic. In these latter McTaggart drops the rôle of reverent discipleship and in his own name reaffirms objections against which he had elaborately defended Hegelism in the earlier chapters, denying, e. g., that pure thought and the philosophy which systematizes it is an adequate expression of the whole nature of the Spirit, and that the applications are the really valid part of Hegel's system (p. 238). Some of his conclusions here seem strange emotional exotics to grow upon the arid and alien soil of Hegelism, e. g., that all reality consists of *spirits* which are individual (p. 222). But after all the main questions suggested by his book are : (1) Will his interpretation of Hegel stand? And (2) if it will, what does Hegelism amount to?

Of the first of these questions it would be unbecoming to essay a decision while life-long students of Hegel show the reticence and caution observable in Professor Wallace's review in *Mind* (N. S. No. 20). And after all science is more concerned with the validity of Hegel's plea as presented by Mr. McTaggart than with the actual meaning of a writer who certainly neglected many opportunities for speaking out clearly. Hence the second is the question of more pressing importance, and an answer will probably be most facilitated by a critical discussion of the three characteristics of Mr. McTaggart's interpretation stated above.

[1] *Mind*, N. S. No. 13. *The Metaphysics of the Time-process.*

· I. It may be pointed out, to begin with, that only a very accommodating sceptic would assert Being in such a sense that the whole Dialectic can be extracted from it. The ordinary kind would probably óbject that Mr. McTaggart's argument most palpably involved the characteristic Hegelian confusion of essence and existence, and that the admission of a (possibly illusory) appearance of existence did not carry with it the validity of the *idea* of Being.

As to II., it is very hard to construe the independence of experience which Mr. McTaggart ascribes to 'pure thought.' The Dialectic is a process of 'pure thought' which is represented as the active principle in knowing, whereof it monopolizes the credit. Yet it is admitted to be abstract (*e. g.*, p. 18, 105, 233), *i. e.*, the product, together with pure sensation, of a merely logical analysis of the actual process of knowledge which alone is a concrete experience. We are expressly warned (p. 74) that "the importance lies only in the concrete whole," and that "this reality is not to be considered as if it were built up out of thought and sensation." It follows that "pure thought" "never really exists except as an element in experience" (p. 105), *i. e.*, it is never found as a fact at all. How then can the Dialectic be a description of any actual process of knowledge?

Further, it is doubtless true that the 'lower' categories are abstract and very far from the concreteness of the actual. But is this any less true of the highest category, of the Absolute Idea itself? Mr. McTaggart talks as if it were concrete, but it is concrete only in the sense of coming at the end of an unavailing effort to transcend the abstractness of all thought. To become really concrete, the Dialectic would have to get back to the concrete individuality from which abstraction started. Why, if it has such a horror of abstraction, did it ever abandon it? That is a vital question for all such schemes of thought. For they are all rendered superfluous by the recognition that knowledge serves a purpose, that it is always necessarily abstract, that the abstraction is useful, and progressive because it is useful. In the whole process it is only the first step which costs, the step that takes us from the concrete individual to the abstract universal. But after that everything is plain sailing, requiring no justification; we proceed gaily to the highest abstractions, nay to the idea of Being—a symbol so abstract that its content cannot be distinguished from nothing—whenever such abstraction is needed for our calculations. Such is the state of things which Hegelism so elaborately misunderstands that it feels bound to prove, by an (unsuccessful) reduction to their starting point, the validity of instruments of thought which are

fully sanctified by their usefulness.   And all for what?   To justify,
it is said, the use of 'higher' categories.   But is it not simpler to defend their validity by recalling that the lower originally proceeded out
of them by progressive abstraction?   The Dialectic undoes the abstraction of science—but had science no reasons for its abstractions,
and if it had, will it not suffice to remind it of those reasons?   What
need then for the Dialectic?

III.   The same question is echoed by Mr. McTaggart's conclusions
as to the subjective element in the Dialectic.   If " the opposition of one
idea to another and the consequence negation and contradiction do not
mark any real step towards attaining the knowledge of the essential nature of thought" (p. 147), if the Absolute Idea alone is adequate, then it
is surely better never to lose sight of it than to recover it by a dialectic
process which, in spite of Mr. McTaggart's utmost elucidations, remains
an enchanted forest in which the babes in philosophy are sure to lose
their way.   To admit that not the Dialectic itself, but only its result,
can pretend to absolute truth, is surely to reduce it to a pedagogical
method due to the infirmity of human intelligence.   And not only is
the method bad pedagogically, but no cause is shown why it should
be the only method.   If the Absolute Idea (or better still, as shown
above, the concrete individual) is to be reached, the shorter and
simpler the method the better.   And better methods readily suggest
themselves.   The necessity of ultimately recognizing the anthropo-
morphic basis of our interpretation of our experience—for that according to Mr. McTaggart is what the Dialectic demonstrates—may easily
be made clear both directly and indirectly.   Directly, by showing that
none of the categories used in science or ordinary life ever free themselves from their human reference; indirectly, by showing that the
lower categories annul themselves when taken as independent.   Both
these methods would seem far preferable to the illusory starting point,
the paradoxical phrasing, the cumbrous and obscure progression of the
the Dialectic, which seems nothing but a highly contentious way of
reaching assumptions which in science and ordinary life we accept
without contention and in philosophy can justify far more simply.
So that to me at least it seems not the slightest merit of Mr. McTaggart's work to have given fresh urgency to the question: What, then, is
the good of the Hegelian Dialectic?

F. C. S. SCHILLER.

CORNELL UNIVERSITY.

S. Kierkegaard als Philosoph. HAROLD HÖFFDING. Stuttgart, Frommann, 1896. Pp. x+170.

This brochure is the third in *Frommann's Classiker der Philosophie*, a series similar to *Blackwood's Philosophical Classics* which is being issued under the editorial supervision of Prof. Falckenberg of Erlangen, already well known through his *Grundriss der Geschichte der neueren Philosophie.* Besides the present work, volumes on *Fechner* by Professor Lasswitz and *Hobbes*, by Professor Tönnies have already appeared. Among the notable announcements of numbers to come are Riehl's *Hume*, Paulsen's *Kant*, Höffding's *Rousseau*, Lasson's *Hegel* and the volume on *Lotze* by the editor. The series will be of especial value because of its additions to our list of standard compendiums on the classical writers and systems.

Kierkegaard (1813-1855) finds a place in the series as the foremost thinker which Denmark has produced (p. 2) and as a notable personality in the philosophico-religious movements of the century. Professor Höffding leads up to his subject proper by chapters on *Die romantisch-spekulative Religionsphilosophie* (Schleiermacher and Hegel), *Kierkegaard's ältere Zeitgenossen in Dänemark* and *Kierkegaard's Persönlichkeit.* Then follows the discussion of Kierkegaard's philosophy under the two principal heads of epistemology and ethics. This forms the body of the work, which concludes with a somewhat briefer explanation and criticism of the philosopher's attitude toward the Christian faith and his breach with the 'weakened and softened Christianity' of the Church. Central in the whole development and of great psychological interest is the influence of Kierkegaard's temperament upon his speculation. Possessed by an inherited melancholy tendency, extremely conscientious, and with a dialectical gift which forbade him to glide over antinomies, he reproduced in his thinking, especially in his ethical and religious conclusions, the lonely individualism, the unceasing inner conflict, the paradoxical outcome of his life. In the beginning he is satisfied neither with Hegel's speculative theology and its impossible iteration of the threefold rhythm nor Schleiermacher's easy renunciation of a direct knowledge of the absolute. As he frames his own ethic, he emphasizes freedom and the essential individualism of moral culture, only to void morals of all social content and, by giving them an exclusively transcendent basis, to reduce morality to asceticism. Toward the close of his life he feels himself compelled publicly to censure the existing Christianity as a degenerate travesty of the pure religion of Christ and to demand a return to the unworldly simplicity of the primitive Christian community. Then, worn out by his labors and his sufferings, he dies when only forty-two, after profoundly affecting the thought of his time and country.

The book is written with the customary skill of its author. The touch is so deft that the reader wishes it were possible to read the Danish original of Professor Höffding instead of the German translation; and so sympathetic, in spite of grave differences of position between the subject and the writer of the work, that he is ready to agree with the opinion expressed in the preface by Schrempf, one of Kierkegaard's principal German admirers: *Dass hier ein Philosoph der Continuität den Irrationalismus Kierkegaard's darstellt und auf seinen wirklichen Wahrheitsgehalt prüft, kann auch der Verehrer Kierkegaard's nicht bedauern, sondern nur mit Freude begrüssen.*

A. C. ARMSTRONG, JR.

WESLEYAN UNIVERSITY.

Ueber physische und psychische Kausalität und das Prinzip des psycho-physischen Parallelismus. MAX WENTSCHER. Leipzig, Barth, 1896. Pp. x+122.

The two essential elements of modern psycho-physical parallelism are stated by the author to be: first, the assumption of a uniform parallelism between any given psychical process and its corresponding cerebral process; and second, the affirmation of an entire absence of any causal interaction between these two kinds of processes. Wundt lays greater emphasis on the second part of the doctrine, but concedes the impossibility of consistently maintaining an absolute independence of the individual consciousness. This principle, which is advanced by its supporters merely as an expression of empirical facts, is in reality a metaphysical doctrine, for it goes beyond experience in all its teachings, and if it were really based on observed facts it could serve only as a preliminary formula and would require some explanation.

A study of physical causation shows the impossibility of proving that we are here dealing with a closed, independent system of processes. We can discover only the phenomenal aspect of causation; its essential nature is beyond the reach of our observation. That any description of phenomena by the physical sciences should seem to support the doctrine of an independent physical causation follows from the circumstance that only physical facts enter into the discussion. The extension of the principle to realms in which other kinds of facts enter in, is not justified by its apparent confirmation in the physical sciences. But in the natural sciences themselves, even if we admit the assumption that the amounts of energy in the cause and in the effect are equivalent, we are by no means forced to admit that no outside agent can enter into the process. Take, for example, a case of potential energy which is converted into kinetic energy. The moment at which this stored up energy shall begin to discharge is not determined by the energy itself. It is determined by circumstances which do not depend on the expenditure of any physical energy. If some liberating cause sets the process in operation the energy of this liberating cause is not destroyed in the act of bringing about the discharge, but its energy is added to that of the efficient causes, and its equivalent appears in the effect. The determination of the moment at which a cause shall operate may thus be effected by some agent without the expenditure of any physical energy. In this way we have a reasonable explanation of the frequently observed fact that the psychical processes determine the moment at which certain physical processes shall take place, without there being any demand for additional physical energy either in the cause or in the effect.

Living organisms exhibit individual peculiarities. We have here in the physical world certain groups of processes obeying laws which are peculiar to themselves. Such organisms may well be regarded as mediators between pure physical processes and processes which are non-physical in their nature.

Psychical causation is limited to certain individuals of a unitary character; their unity consists, not of some objective relation of parts, but of immediately perceived unity in consciousness. Such individuals are capable of communicating with each other only through the physical world. The question arises, are these circles of individual, unitary consciousness entirely closed to the action of any external cause? In their origin they can not be regarded as independent. Breaks in the temporal continuity of the series of processes and the appearance of new processes, such as sensations, can not be explained from the foregoing conscious states or conditions, but require the action of some outside agency. Psychical activities are not determined by the temporal relations of outside causes, but by the relations which exist between the actual contents of processes resulting from these causes. It is the logical, ethical or æsthetic relation between contents of consciousness that leads to volition. The subject thus determined by relations of content may, in the manner indicated, influence the temporal order of physical processes.

Instead of parallelism between two independent series of processes we have, then, a form of interaction which may be called causal. The attempts to avoid the word cause by using the term occasion are mere verbal evasions. This kind of an explanation, formulated in the spirit of Lotzean philosophy, seems to the author to meet the observed facts and metaphysical requirements involved, better than any form of parallelism.

CHAS. H. JUDD.

MIDDLETOWN, CONN.

Grundriss der Geschichte der Philosophie. JOHANNES REHMKE. Berlin, Duncker; New York, G. E. Stechert, 1896. Pp. 304. This is a compendious volume covering the whole range of European philosophy from Thales to Lotze. It differs from many of the recent Outlines in its almost entire exclusion of bibliographic material, titles of works of the authors discussed as well as specific references to these works being rarely introduced, and no reference being made to other histories or to monographs covering the same ground. It is not a ' manual,' therefore, in the sense of being a guide to study beyond itself; its value lies in its own individual interpretation of the systems of which it treats. It differs also markedly from some of the smaller and many of the more extended Outlines in that it does not attempt at any point to give the general historical setting of the philosophical movement, but confines itself rigidly to an account of the substance and relations of systems of philosophy proper—*wissenschaftliche Philosophie.* So complete is this abstraction that even the specific contributions of Christianity and the influence of the modern scientific movement alike receive no recognition. It may be questioned whether such a method of treatment can be in the fullest sense true; and, from the pedagogical point of view, one may doubt whether it conduces to the best philosophical culture. At the same time, it is but fair to judge a book by what it *does* give us within the limits it has set for itself, rather than by what it purposely does not give. And we find, on examination, an unusually clear, vigorous and interesting presentation of the leading systems and schools from ancient to modern times. The author's interest is evidently strongest in the direction of Metaphysics and *Erkenntnisstheorie.* He has given much more than a bare statement of principles and doctrines; rather we find a sympathetic and thoughtful interpretation, and occasionally, when the author gives himself room, a fine logical and psychological analysis and development of the problem in hand. This is notably the case in his account of Kant. The treatment is ' objec tive' in the best sense, with frequent reference to the relations, positive and negative, which one system bears to its predecessors. Only now and then does the author let fall a criticism or suggestion which indicates his own point of view, *e. g.*, pp. 24, 250, 295.

Dr. Rehmke divides his work into Ancient and Modern philosophy. Notable here is his inclusion under the former head, not only of the philosophies of the Hellenistic period, but also of Scholasticism and the philosophy of the Renaissance, on the ground that these are essentially only pupils of the Greeks. The Christian Middle Ages is treated very briefly, only 15 pages. Modern philosophy is divided into Pre-Kantian, Kantian and Post-Kantian. Naturally a large place, 46 out of 200 pages, is given to the exposition of Kant, while Post-Kantian philosophy gets a space of only 44 pages. The chapter on Kant shows the author at his best, and is decidedly a fine piece of work. Naturally a considerable preponderance is given by the author to Continental and especially German thought. The more recent English thought is omitted entirely.

A few minor errors have caught the eye in a somewhat rapid reading: on page 4 (l. 26) Anaximander stands instead of Anaximenes; on page 84 the date of Philo is given wrongly; on page 103 Bacon's famous simile for final causes has strayed from its original connection.

JAMES SIMMONS, JR.

IOWA COLLEGE, GRINNELL, IA.

Die Impersonalien. M. JOVANOVICH. Belgrade, 1896. Pp. 143.

After a short introduction in which he deals with the history of previous investigations, Jovanovich presents his point of view and then enters upon the consideration of his subject proper, the impersonal judgment, under the three heads—origin, function, limits.

Previous investigators mistakenly isolated the grammatical and the psychological-logical points of view. On the one side an identity of thought and language was maintained; on the other there was a discrepancy. The representatives of both views fell into hopeless confusion and contradiction. A true estimate does not admit the identity of thought and language nor a discrepancy between them.

Anthropology forbids us to maintain that impersonal judgments are the original embryonic forms out of which all others have been differentiated. Animism as expressive of the earliest form of experience teaches us that primitive man interpreted all outer occurrences in terms of his own personal life; the clouds and heavens 'rained.' In the mythological age these personal activities were generalized; Jupiter, Zeus, Indra, 'rained.' Finally, when thought freed itself from personification, the causes of certain experiences became completely undetermined and unknown. At this stage the impersonal 'It' arose.

The function of impersonals was and is that of indicating a subject which is altogether unknown, but which, nevertheless, the mind must still think.

From this also the limits of the impersonal are clear. All endeavor to determine the subject, in whatever degree this determination may be presented, is artificial and arbitrary. It inevitably leads to confusion and perversion of meaning. Our only method of classification must be based solely upon the different kinds of experience which are referred to the unknown subject.

So much for Jovanovich's own treatment; the monograph is, throughout, dependent entirely upon Wundt's interpretation. In fact; the author's deference to his master, and his confident assertion of the falsity of views differing from his own, do not seem to be consistent with the supposed impartiality and scientific thoroughness of the German student.

The investigation is indicative of the difficulty which has met all enquirers in this field from the time of the Greek grammarians. The impersonal judgment has been considered an anomaly which must be dealt with from the standpoint of certain presuppositions. Underlying Jovanovich's treatment I find these: (1) All experience is objective; (2) the fundamental relation is that of subject and object; (3) judgment consists in the uniting of thought and reality, *i. e.,* it is discursive.

The mere statement of the first two presuppositions will suggest the criticisms likely to be made. The third is the most important. If we admit that all judgment is discursive then a subject must be sought for the impersonal. Predication without a subject of predication is a contradiction. But, on the other hand, no subject has been found for the impersonal. Is the controversy then to be continued forever? The difficulty might suggest that it would be profitable to lay aside our presuppositions, in order that we might understand the impersonal not as a judgment, nor as having a subject or a predicate, but as an experience. This point of view leads, in my own opinion, to the following result. The impersonal presents us with a situation immediately recognized as such. It distinguishes itself from intuition in that the impersonal is vague, schematic, while the intuition is clear and definite. Again, certain forms of the impersonal indicate a breaking-up of this immediate recognition and a reference to a vague whole not immediately grasped. Now in as much as reality is grasped, differentiated or measured in the impersonal, we may rightly call it a judgment. But it is a judgment in which subject and predicate do not appear. This analysis leads us to believe that the essential nature of judgment is recognition or differentiation, not reference. In the impersonal and intuitive forms recognition is immediate; in the ordinary discursive form it is mediate.

This view is supported by child psychology in which we find definite situations or realities recognized before there is any use of noun and verb. Again, comparative philology shows that the noun cannot be derived from the verb and *vice versa*, but it points (as Jovanovich admits) to a stage in thought where they were simply implicit. Finally, when we recognize that in the child's consciousness the use of noun and verb, and the recognition of a self as opposed to an object, arise together, we see how our theory fits in with the necessity felt by Romanes of getting a connecting link between the perceptive processes of animals and the conceptual processes of man. The impersonal recognizes the facts which Romanes brought forward and frees his position from the logical entanglements which it presents, in giving us percepts apart from concepts.

Thus as the immediate recognition (though in a vague schematic way) of reality and the beginning of a reference to a mediately recognized whole, the view of the impersonal above presented unites the various conflicting theories. As immediate recognition there is neither subject nor predicate; as a vague reference to a larger whole a subject is found in varying degrees of determinateness. Finally, when the "It" represents merely a shorthand way of indicating a familiar object, we have the singular judgment.

S. F. MacLennan.

University of Chicago.

Quelques Remarques sur L'irréversibilité des Phénomènes psychologiques. E. Halévy. Rev. de Met et. de Mor., Nov., 1896.

M. Halévy's article is, in the main, a criticism of the attempt made by psychologists of the Association School to apply to mental phenomena the principle of mechanical reversibility. In a purely quantitative science like geometry all terms have the same *logical* value, and may be defined in the same manner with *change of sign*. If all Force be reduced to modes of motion the same doctrine will hold in the case of the physical sciences.   But does it hold when we come to deal with mental phenomena? Is the past interchangeable with the future, and can memory be substituted for will? Psychology cannot be classed among the purely positive sciences until this seeming irreversibility of its phenomena is explained.   Hence the attempt made by M. Ribot and others.   These theories M. Halévy examines.

The one postulate of Associationism is 'a succession of states following one another according to the laws of resemblance and of contiguity.' A series of states related to one another by these laws would be completely reversible. If 'past' and 'future' as psychologic states follow this same order, one can be substituted for the other.   Memory and will also become psychologic functions, one the inverse of the other.   Associationism has to explain their apparent difference.

Suppose we say that the difference is that between a *present* state and the associated state *not present*, that does not tell us why the not-present is named sometimes future, sometimes past.   We do not dispose of the difference by proving that the psychological *process* is the same (association) when a state is referred now forward, now backward.   Again, M. Ribot seems to give up the problem when he assumes that the present state has duration—hence a beginning and an end, giving rise in present consciousness to an immediate intuition of past and future.

But suppose the distinction is, in part at least, a function of will. The past is that which is determined, the future is dependent in part upon my undetermined volition.   If this be true it remains for Associationism to explain their apparent difference—they must become reversible; likewise the distinction between ' me ' as cause and ' thing ' as cause.   Volition differs also from foresight (prevision).   If this difference be abolished, freedom of the will becomes identical with foreknowledge.   " To be free is to *know* what one will do and why one will do it."   This complete convertibility of phenomena demanded of Associationism, M. Halévy concludes, is impossible.

In the second part of the paper he takes the ground that while ' past ' and ' future ' are irreversible in the sense of being convertible, yet that both may be reduced to terms of logical succession.   There is a distinction to be made between the order of desire (*vouloir*) and the order of perception (*percevoir*).   In the first case we proceed from *end* to means—D C B A.   In the other we proceed directly from means to end—A B C D——.   There is a sense in which the series A B C D is completely irreversible, and of this Associationism fails to take account, viz, in the order of *logical* representation the conclusion cannot precede the premise. But this series may be interpreted in time, either in the order of will or in the order of perception, one the inverse of the other. Thus there is no contradiction between psychic reversibility and logical irreversibility. Synthesis, for example, represents an interpretation in the order of perception, which is the same in direction as the logical order. Analysis, on the other hand, corresponds to the order of volition.

M. Halévy rejects the associationist's identification of past and future, and rightly. But can they be reduced, as he thinks, to terms of logical succession? In the first place, the logical order does not involve time, and is interpreted as *succession*, only when the idea of time has arisen from some other source. Again, the order of perception of phenomena is not always logical, yet they get referred to their appropriate places in the time-series. So the arrangement of events in the future by imagination does not follow always their logical order. Genetically the child remembers before it reasons; the time order does not depend on logical sequence. We are inclined to think that the reference of things forward and backward is as fundamental as perception itself.

PRINCETON UNIVERSITY.   J. M. TROUT.

EXPERIMENTAL.

Observations sur quelque Types de Reaction simple. TH. FLOURNOY. Geneva, Librairie Ch. Eggiman & Cie., 1896. Pp. 42.

The object of the series of investigations of which the present monograph is a report is to determine how many clearly-marked types of simple reaction there are and what are the characteristics of each. By a type of reaction Professor Flournoy means the way in which a comparatively unpracticed subject reacts in the shortest time. In the course of the experiments he tested about seventy students of both sexes. The number of reactions obtained from each subject is very unequal, but unity of method makes the results comparable. The reactions were all taken with the d'Arsonval Chronometer and are, therefore, not reliable for absolute time. Their value lies in the comparison of group averages. The tests were made in series consisting of two, and sometimes more, groups of about fifteen reactions each, in which the direction of attention was the only factor varied from group to group. To avoid the possible effect of fatigue, the temporal order of the series was varied from group to group. The stimuli used were tactual, visual and auditory.   The response was the closing of a key by the index finger.   Careful notes were kept upon the bodily attitude and the subjective experiences of the reactor during each group of reactions, upon whose importance Professor Flournoy lays great stress.   From the results thus obtained, Professor Flournoy differentiates four principal types of reaction, two of which are divided into sub-types.   They are: 1, the motor type, consisting of (a) the natural motor type and (b) the forced motor type; 2, the central type; 3, the indifferent type, and 4, the sensory type; subdivided into (a) the visual motor type and (b) the kineso-motor type. The criterion for the separation of the principal types is the shortness of reaction time; that for the separation of the sub-types, the subjective condition of the reactor.   Each type is named from the direction which the attention takes when the reaction time is shortest.   In all cases, except the forced motor type, the shortest reaction was also the one naturally adopted, the easiest and the most automatic.   Professor Flournoy does not consider his enumeration of types exhaustive.   It includes only those which have come out clearly in his experiments. Mixed and indeterminate cases of his own, as well as the logical possibilities of the case, make him think that further research may differentiate more types.   Beside the data mentioned, Professor Flournoy has kept a record of the nationality of the reactor, the branch of work he was pursuing and his type of mental imagery.   It is to be regretted that detailed results from only seven of his seventy subjects are published and that we are not told what proportion of them belong to each type.

Although Professor Flournoy expressly states that his work is not intended as an interference in the long and heated discussion about the existence of simple reaction types other than the type of Lange, and the relation of reaction type to mental imagery, his investigations deal directly with both these questions and cannot but have a bearing on them.   In opposition to the Leipzig investigators, he finds that there are types (in his sense of the word) of simple reaction other than that investigated by Lange.   Whether or not these types could be reduced to the Lange type by indefinitely long practice, he leaves an open question.   With the amount of practice he gave his subjects, he finds no indication that the other types of reaction approach the motor.   On the contrary, practice, as far as he has observed it, tends to reduce the time of the typical reaction faster than it does the times of the other reactions, with the result that the characteristic difference in time is lengthened and the types become more distinctly marked.   In so far as Professor Flournoy's results corroborate the type theory of reaction, they agree with those obtained in the laboratories of Princeton and Chicago. But his observations on the effects of practice are just the opposite of the Princeton and Chicago results. Professor Baldwin, who is motor in type, noticed incidentally that his sensory time approached his motor time with practice. Professor Angell and Mr. Moore, whose primary interest was in the effect of practice on reaction time, found in all three cases which they investigated that the non-typical reaction approached the typical with practice. According to the theory of reaction type advanced by Professor Angell and Mr. Moore the effect of practice would necessarily be to decrease the difference in type. The facts at command are insufficient for any dogmatic statement. Professor Flournoy gives statistics on the effects of practice for only one case. The other four cases for which we have statistics on this point (Professor Baldwin and the three subjects tested at Chicago) all give results opposed to Professor Flournoy's. In the tests made at Chicago it was found that it took some practice for the two types to emerge clearly, but that after they were once clearly differentiated they began to approach. In as much as in Professor Flourney's isolated case the two reaction times were at first practically identical (sensory 137, 5 σ, m. v. 22; motor 140, 2 σ, m. v. 28, 3) and the reactor found great subjective difficulty in getting a genuine motor reaction at all, it is at least possible that it took a much greater amount of practice than usual for the two types to become differentiated; that his results stop with the differentiation of the type, and that further practice would have made them approach one another. The number of reactions, however, is as great as the number which, in the tests made at Chicago, sufficed for both differentiation and approach of type.

From the statistics which Professor Flournoy kept with regard to the type of mental imagery of his reactors he agrees with Professor Baldwin that the general tendency of the individual to use sensory or motor images corresponds with his reaction type. But any assertion that reaction type corresponds to mental imagery so closely that one can be determined by the other he thinks is more than the facts at present warrant. The mixture of type and fluctuations of imagery found in a single individual, and the large variety of possible sensory-motor coördinations, make it seem improbable that any hard and fast relationship between the two can ever be formulated. Professor Flournoy makes the suggestion that nationality may prove to be as much of an index of reaction type as mental imagery.

HELEN B. THOMPSON.

UNIVERSITY OF CHICAGO.

The Effects of Odours, Irritant Vapours and Mental Work upon the Blood Flow. T. E. SHIELDS. The Journal of Experimental Medicine. Vol. I., No. I. 1896.

The author, in summarizing his results, tells us that " the most important outcome of this investigation has been the completion of various improvements in the construction and use of the plethysmograph, by means of which numerous errors attending the use of the instrument have been eliminated." It is, in fact, a far way from the apparatus employed by Fick, Mosso and Lehmann to the elaborate contrivances described in this dissertation; and in view of the many problems whose solution has been sought in this line of work, the more important of these modifications deserve notice.

With earlier forms of the plethysmograph it was doubtful whether the changes recorded were due to variations in the volume of blood or to movements of the enclosed arm and fingers. This source of error Shields eliminates by means of an arm-holder which, without hindering the circulation, keeps the arm rigidly in place and prevents panting of the elastic sleeve. Again, in the records hitherto obtained, the pulse and the gross volume changes were shown in the same curve and tended to mask each other. To separate these, the vasomotor effects are registered by a suspended test tube (Bowditch), while the pulse effects are taken care of by an air cushion which responds to smaller waves from the arm cylinder and transmits them to the Marey tambour. The volume and pulse changes, along with the pneumographic and time curves, are inscribed by frictionless glass pens upon a horizontal kymograph so constructed that a continuous record of any desirable length may be obtained. For psychological purposes the main advantage of this arrangement is that a whole series of reactions may be studied in their mutual connection, and without the disturbance occasioned by change of kymograph drums.

In the first class of experiments of which an account is given, various odors were administered to the same subject through tubes ending in an odor plate, and were controlled by electric valves in such a way that nothing could be known of the stimulus except through the sense of smell. In a second series of experiments, twelve subjects were tried. In addition to the effects produced by odors and vapors, other changes were noted and attributed to ' mental activity,' but the precise character of the stimulation which called these forth is not sufficiently indicated.

The results, illustrated by plotted curves at the close of the dissertation, show that olfactory sensations, irritant vapors and mental 'work cause a diminution in the volume of the arm. "Whenever the stimulation (odor) occasions an increase in the volume of the arm, as sometimes happens, it seems to be due to acceleration of the heart rate, which, of course, tends also to increase supply of blood to the brain." But no support is afforded to the view "that pleasant sensations are accompanied by a diminution of the blood supply to the brain and unpleasant sensations by the reverse effect." In the statement of these conclusions and throughout the dissertation, there is a cautious tone which in no way lessens the value of the work.

E. A. PACE.

CATHOLIC UNIVERSITY, WASHINGTON.

Attention: Experimental and Critical. By FRANK DREW. American Journal of Psychology, VII., 533–573. 1896.

The experimental part of Dr. Drew's study consists of three distinct lines of work: *A*, measurements of reaction and association times of various degrees of complexity under various conditions of distraction; *B*, a qualitative study of association by Galton's method (*Human Faculty*, pp. 185 ff.) with concentrated and distracted attention; and *C*, a study of the recognition of the order of nearly simultaneous stimuli with voluntarily directed attention.

Though many reactions were taken for *A* and the general results were in substantial agreement with those of other observers, they were not regarded as satisfactory and no use is made of them here except as they furnished introspective and other casual observations.

In *B* the question was: What effect, if any, is produced in the normal run of association by distraction? Tests were made in parallel series: in one the experimenter looked at the stimulus word and then gave himself up to securing as many associations as possible within a fixed interval, at the end of which those gotten were noted; in the other he tried to do the same thing while adding a number of digits requiring an approximately equal time. Four sets of 100 stimulus words each were used and each set was gone over twice at intervals of a month, the repetitions being sometimes arranged to duplicate the first conditions and sometimes to alter them, as shown in the following little table.

	First time.	Second time.
1st Set:	Distraction	Distraction
2nd Set:	Concentration	Concentration
3rd Set:	Distraction	Concentration
4th Set:	Concentration	Distraction

In this way over 3,000 associations were collected and treated statistically. The most striking result is the relatively small effect produced by the adding.[1] There is a somewhat larger proportion of fresh associations in the second trial of sets first gone over with distracted attention than in those first gone over with concentrated attention; the sets with concentrated attention show more associations from the last three-fifths of life (excluding the immediate past); there is an indication that word jingles and purely verbal associations are interfered with by the adding, probably because the language apparatus is partially taken up by that activity; but in almost every case the percentage of difference is small. This result, though at first surprising, is not so strange when the conditions of the experiment are regarded. It seems likely, on the one hand, that the haste of getting the greatest number of associations in a limited time and from a single word is a distraction in itself, and on the other that many associations in the series with adding are secured in momentary wavering from that task. Two incidental observations are of some interest, namely, that the first thing to follow the sight of the stimulus word (when the novelty of the experiment had worn off) was almost always a mental pronunciation of it which furnished the nucleus from which the associations developed; and second, that almost all associations were given a ' spatial setting' or localization in motor or visual-motor terms. This latter was often the first thing to come and was tardily followed by the other elements of the association.

The third line of experiments had to do with the time order of nearly simultaneous stimuli, and the question took this form, namely: Given a pair of stimuli (two clicks, for example, addressed one to each ear) so near together that their order can just be recognized, will any change be produced by voluntarily attending to one or the other ? A very little work on this matter had already been done by Dr. Alice J. Hamlin (*American Journal of Psychology*, VI.), but with negative results. The stimuli used by Dr. Drew were telephone clicks (one to each ear), electric shocks (one to each hand) and a click and shock to ear and hand; the interval for the first two pairs was 0.024 sec. and for the click and shock 0.031 sec. Parallel series with balanced attention and attention concentrated on one side or the other were taken in considerable variety, chiefly upon two subjects. The

---

[1]This experiment was made by Drew on himself. A similar series under slightly varied conditions was undertaken by the writer at the same time and the statistics partially worked up. Drew's general negative result is supported by them.

following are the most important results: With two clicks concentration of attention is a positive hindrance, fewer right judgments being made on the average, and still fewer (relatively) when the stimulus arrived first on the side to which attention was directed, due possibly to an unconscious change in the manner of judging. To test whether the criterion by which the order was judged was one of intensity, experiments were made with loud and faint clicks, and it was found that both subjects tended to call the fainter the earlier. With shocks it was found (contrary to the click results) that attention to one side or the other favored the stimulus received on that side. With strong and weak shocks the fainter again seemed earlier, but the tests on this point are few and not fully accordant. When the subject was distracted from both shocks by being required to read aloud, there was in no case a decrease in accuracy and sometimes a decided gain. The experiments with disparate senses (ear and hand) show, with balanced attention, a strong bias in favor of the order shock-click, which renders difficult the interpretation of the results with directed attention. Both subjects show gain with directed attention, but disagree as to whether it is more advantageous when directed toward the leading stimulus or the other. Such biases were also found at other stages of the work and add greatly to the laboriousness of the experiments and the complexity of the results, especially as they were not constant, but underwent slow changes as the research continued. Introspection under the conditions of the experiment was also singularly difficult and threw little light upon its real nature.

To make a generalization which shall unify these varying results is hardly possible until further experiments have established more fully the effects of several of the factors involved. While not undertaking to do this, Dr. Drew makes many suggestions and presents a theory of perception, apperception and attention which was developed in considerable part by these experiments. It is an extreme example of those that would reduce mind almost or quite to kinæsthetic terms. For the detail of it the reader must consult the paper itself, though with the warning that in parts the thought suffers much from obscurity of presentation.

CLARK UNIVERSITY.   E. C. SANFORD.

ANTHROPOLOGY AND CRIMINOLOGY.

Psychologie der Naturvölker. Ethnographische Parallelen.
JACOB ROBINSOHN. Leipzig, Friedrich, 1896. Pp. i + 176.
This is a very comprehensive title for a rather contracted work.

ANTHROPOLOGY AND CRIMINOLOGY.

The author has made a creditable compilation of records regarding the primitive conception of the soul, but his work was anticipated twenty-five years ago by Tylor and in a much more thorough and philosophical spirit than that exhibited in the book before us. There is hardly a single point brought out by Herr Robinsohn that is not treated in Tylor's chapters on animism in his well-known 'Primitive Culture' and, while the amplification of evidence is welcome, there is not much more to be said for it.

There is, on the other hand, a good deal to be said against the waste of energy on an already well-threshed subject while so many fruitful ethnological fields are left untouched. This is not an argument against rehandling an old topic, especially in a new light, but our author has neither new light nor new methods, yet his book appears with all the air, though not the express claim, of an original and valuable contribution to ethnological knowledge. Further, as already implied, the title is misleading. One opens the book expecting naturally a treatise, good or otherwise, on comparative psychology, but it is a sad day for our science if the psychology of primitive man is to be confined to primitive man's conception of his own non-bodily self, which is what we are offered here.

By way of praise, it may be said that the subject-matter is well arranged and well handled, the bibliography is useful, and the whole would be a capital piece of work if it had not all been done before. As it is, it is a very good guide-book to Tylor.

LIVINGSTON FARRAND.
COLUMBIA UNIVERSITY.

The Female Offender. C. LOMBROSO and W. FERRERO. With an Introduction by W. DOUGLAS MORRISON. New York, Appleton, 1895.

In the present volume, one of the 'Criminology Series,' edited by Douglas Morrison, Lombroso's '*La Donna Delinquente*' has been made accessible to the English speaking public. The work is a typical example of Lombroso's acute observation, but also of the entire inadequacy of his statistical methods. No variation from the normal type escapes his notice, but the comparison of the frequencies of their occurrence among various social groups is entirely unsatisfactory, because it is based on very small series of observations. To give an instance: Plagiocephalism is found in 42% of 66 male criminals; in 17.2% of normal women; in 28.8% of 55 criminal women. Therefore, the error of mean squares of the first group is about 6.3%, that of the last group 6.7%. The difference between these two groups is 13.2%, but its error amounts to 9.1%. Therefore this difference of frequencies of occurrence is very uncertain. The theory of probabilities proves that we might expect these results to be fundamentally changed if the number of observations were increased. In the instance given here the differences of observed values are great; in most cases they are entirely inside the limits of errors. We hold, therefore, that Lombroso has not succeeded in establishing the validity of any of the characteristics of the criminal type which he claims to have discovered.

It is true that signs of degeneracy are frequent among criminals and that a correlation of degeneracy and of criminality exists which may be directly physical, but which is likely to be, to a great extent, social. A consideration of the fact that these signs are not confined to the criminal classes shows that it is an incomplete correlation with which we have to deal. That is to say, signs of degeneracy are sometimes, not always, connected with criminality and, *vice versa*, criminality is sometimes, not always, connected with degeneracy. Therefore the problem, in order to be satisfactorily solved, should be treated in a manner differing from that applied by Lombroso. Setting aside the necessity of basing descriptions on much more extensive series which would enable us to prove that differences are not merely accidental, both aspects of the correlation should be investigated. We must not only gain systematic knowledge of the characteristics of the criminal classes, but also of the general distribution of each of these characteristics among a variety of classes not criminal. Only in this manner can we hope to understand their significance.

While Lombroso will always deserve the credit of having forcibly called attention to the physical and psychical characteristics of abnormal man, his statistical methods are so unsatisfactory that very few of his results can claim to be well established, and I believe hardly a single one in the volume under review can be considered as proved by the material offered.

COLUMBIA UNIVERSITY.   FRANZ BOAS.

CHILD PSYCHOLOGY.

Paidologie. Entwurf zu einer Wissenchaft des Kindes. OSCAR CHRISMAN, In Diss., Jena, 1896. Pp. 72+24 pages of bibliography.

This is a sketch of 'Paidology' by the original inventor of the term. The introduction is a general plea for the recognition of paidology as a university study. The author would have it pursued as a pure science and wants everything relating in any way to children to be included in the work, whether it has any practical bearing or not. The short History of Paidology, which follows, consist mainly of mere names and titles of works, but gives no statement of results ·or summary of ideas contained in the authorities quoted. Everything is made to seem equally valuable.

The system of Paidology is sketched as follows:

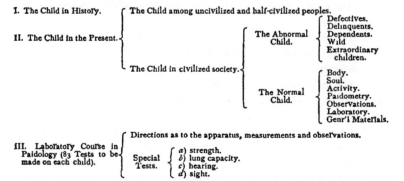

The laboratory course consists of the usual tests of experimental psychology. Certainly the most valuable part of the pamphlet is the list of ´522 books and articles relating to children and catalogued in the appendix.   HERMAN T. LUKENS.

L'instinct de la conservation chez les enfants. PAOLA LOMBROSO. Revue Philosophique, Oct., 1896. Pp. 379–390.

Children may be compared to the little infusorian animalculæ which are all the more tenacious of life the more microscopic they are. As if conscious of the fragile character of their existence, they maintain their grip with all their force. This is seen as follows:

1. In the *physiological* development of children. Their respiration, circulation and changes in tissues are more rapid, and, in proportion to their size, they eat twice as much as adults. Like savages, they are less sensitive to physical pain than civilized man, and their wounds heal more easily and more quickly. In fact, children of less than two or three years can seldom locate a pain definitely, and their attention is readily diverted from it.

This innate tendency to the protection of their ego characterizes as well their whole psychic life; and, since effort consumes tissue and produces fatigue, children may be said to follow the *law of economy of effort*, which, in subordination to the law of self-protection, is the great law of psychic life in childhood.

2. In *learning language* children adopt those forms easiest to them, using instinctively gestures before words and, later, imitating the sounds of objects in onomatopœsis, which is itself a sort of oral gesture. The so-called generalizations of children and their sometimes striking association of ideas are all owing to the repugnance on their part to making the effort necessary in using new terms. To keep, applying old terms to new objects is often easier than to learn new words, and hence children continue using the same word for objects, sometimes the most disparate, which however have happened in their mind to be associated in some far-fetched way.

3. In all his *conceptions* and *thinking* the child tends to economy of effort. His ideas and images are concrete, because the concrete is easier to grasp than the abstract. He repels instinctively the idea of infinity and immortality, because these require too much effort in thinking them. For the same reason he hates innovations, likes to hear the same story over and over again without the change of a single phrase, and must be put to bed with the same ceremony every night. This ' misonéism ' is very serviceable to the child in helping to establish habits of routine and to give a certain settled equilibrium to his ideas.

4. The *sensibilities* and *feelings*, when excited, are still more wasteful of vital energy, and here too the children tend to conserve their strength. They are ' myopic to pain and presbyopic to pleasure.' Anything may serve them as a plaything and the most commonplace happenings of their everyday life may delight them. Their imagination turns reality into a romance and, since wishes do become horses, beggars may ride. But the joys and sorrows of childhood are only skin deep, and the caresses and jealousies of children are often only an exaggerated mimicry of the affections. The tendency of childhood, therefore, is, not to love, but to be loved; because this gives pleasure and protection; while, on the other hand, to sympathize with others and share their joys and sorrows would consume vital energy.

5. Hence the young child is scarcely susceptible to real *love* at all. That this is true is shown by the rarity of cases in which children fall in love, *e. g.*, Berlioz at eight years, Rousseau at eleven, and Marie Baskirtseff at twelve. These exceptions to the rule serve only to show what an enormous expenditure of nervous energy accom-

panies the presence of deep passion and how important it is that children should be preserved from it, as, indeed, they usually are by the
very superficiality of their affectionateness.

6. Even the *moral sense* is subject to the 'law of the least effort.'
A child is naturally prone to resentment, readily lies, easily becomes
conceited, and thinks the whole world was made for him. In morals,
he is essentially an egotist, but gradually puts himself into accord with
us and learns to respect the rights of others, because he receives more
caresses and bonbons by so doing.

In a word, the same 'law of least effort' that governs all the phenomena of sociology and psychology necessarily governs all the phe-,
nomena of child life likewise. Before birth, the foetus, like a para-
site, draws off to itself from its hostess all the materials it needs for its
growth and development, utilizing all the maternal organism, blood,
respiration, and everything to its own advantage without giving any-,
thing in return. The selfishness of the young child is but a continuation of the same process of unconscious parasitic assimilation of its
environment.

HERMAN T. LUKENS.
BRYN MAWR COLLEGE, PENNA.

PHYSIOLOGY AND BIOLOGY.

An American Text-book of Physiology. Edited by WILLIAM H.
HOWELL. Philadelphia, W. B. Saunders, 1896. Pp. 1052.
$6.00.

A standard text-book of physiology is, perhaps, more important for
the student of psychology than a handbook of psychology. Each of
us must form his own apperceptive system of psychology based on
data gathered from many sides, but physiology is essential to us, and
here we are, to a certain extent, dependent on compilations. We have
been fortunate in having such excellent works as Foster's *Text Book*
and Hermann's *Handbuch.* Foster has an extraordinary insight into
the essential bearings of physiological research and great ability as an
expositor. For purpose of reference, however, his book is defective,
because it gives no references and not sufficient facts. Hermann's
Handbuch dates from 1879, and the intervening years have witnessed
great progress in physiology. There is consequently room for a new
text-book useful to the psychologist.

The work before us is called an American Text-book, which may
be taken to indicate that it is written by American authors and per-

haps that it contains frequent references to research carried out in America. The coöperation of ten of our leading professors of physiology sets an example to other sciences, and the result shows that this example should be followed. With the progress of science specialization and coöperation become equally needful. There is no physiologist so competent to cover the whole field of the science as to write on a subject selected by him. The fact that there is some overlapping and some diversity of opinion as to methods and results will probably be stimulating to the student and give him a correct idea of unsolved problems and recent progress.

The introduction and the parts on secretion, chemistry of digestion and nutrition, movements of the alimentary canal, bladder and ureter, and blood and lymph are written by the editor, Professor Howell, who shows the clearness of exposition of Professor Martin, his teacher and predecessor at the Johns Hopkins University. Circulation is treated by Professor Curtis of Columbia University and Professor Porter of Harvard University; respiration and animal heat by Professor Reichert, of the University of Pennsylvania; reproduction by Professor Lee, of Columbia University, and the chemistry of the animal body by Professor Lusk, of Yale University. These sections are likely to be of special interest to the psychologist, as he is most ignorant of the subjects. The exposition is clear throughout, and the reputation of the authors is a sufficient guarantee of its accuracy.

The section on general physiology of muscle and nerve is by Professor Lombard, of the University of Michigan, and that on the central nervous system is by Professor Donaldson, of the University of Chicago. The latter occupies 139 pages, and will be found to be of great value for reference. The author treats separately the nerve cell, the groups of nerve cells and the nervous system taken as a whole. This article, as others in the book, is well illustrated by tables, curves and illustrations.

The article on vision by Professor Bowditch is, I think, the best we have, with the exception of the large works by von Helmholtz and Aubert, and these are less contemporary. Within the limits of 64 pages the more important facts of physiology and psychology are shown in excellent perspective, with due regard to the more recent advances. The psychological part of the article on hearing by Professor Sewall, of the University of Denver, does not seem to me so good. We are told that "sound, in its physiological meaning, is a sensation which is the conscious appreciation of internal changes occurring in certain cells of the cerebral cortex;" that loudness depends on 'amplitude or the extent of motion of the air molecules,' of 'the middle C of the piano * * * representing 132 vibrations,' etc.

The editor holds that "consciousness is a property of the cortical nerve cells," as contractility is a property of muscle tissue, and that psychology is a province of physiology; but he admits that consciousness is a fact which physiology 'cannot as yet explain.' As a matter of fact, psychology is, as a rule, excluded from the book, which does not interfere with its value to the psychologist. I believe that the student of psychology should have followed a regular course in physiology, and should keep such a work as this at hand. In turn, I think that the physiologist and the physician, especially now, when ophthalmology, otology and neurology are important departments, should have followed a course in psychology, and should subsequently not neglect his handbook of psychology.

J. McKEEN CATTELL.

Charles Darwin and the Principle of Natural Selection. E. B. POULTON. Century Science Series. New York, The Macmillan. Co., 1896. Pp. viii+224. $1.25.

This is a remarkably clear, direct and modest account of the life and work of Charles Darwin, by the Oxford exponent of Natural Selection. Professor Poulton has known how to give the truest relief to the portrait of a great man, the relief which is secured by simplicity· of statement and the unadorned narration of facts which are in themselves their own glory. One rises from the perusal of the narrative with a sense that science is not easy even to the man to whom it comes easiest—to the man of the industry, good judgment and ability which constitute the most normal and sane genius—and that it is inapproachable to, the man to whom the secrets of nature are tools to be juggled with or stones for the building up of systems. Indeed, the two things which impress the student of the work of Darwin are, to my mind, his freedom in the use of hypotheses and the soundness of the 'judgments of value' which he passed. upon the facts of nature. Professor Poulton marks both of these lessons, and they are both needed in this time when one school decries the use of imagination. which constitutes the life of science, in the interest of the sort· of. cataloging of facts which the child in the nursery does before he begins to think, and the other shows little sanity of judgment in dealing with the value of this fact or that for the purposes of synthesis. There will always be classifiers by trade and systematizers by passion; but it is just the nature of true science that she bars the gate of·

her kingdom to both of them and opens it to the man whose vision of a fact is at once also a sound judgment of its meaning and value.

Thatsächlich, the one thing on which there may be difference of opinion among those who believe in natural selection, is Professor Poulton's treatment of it as a causal or, as he says, a 'motive' principle. I say among those who believe in natural selection, for, of course, there is no gain in anticipating the criticisms of those who do not. But speaking strictly *entre nous* to the Darwinians themselves—can natural selection be spoken of in these terms? It gives the enemy cause for stumbling, for they immediately fall to asking: "How can a thing be selected before it is produced? And if it is first produced, there is your motive, your causation, already accomplished before natural selection comes in at all." I believe this position is quite invalid; Professor Poulton shows it so over again: but the general question familiar to psychologists as between the efficient and the formal cause comes to mind. The form of the result, as, for example, in Darwin's own illustration of the house as given in this book (page 116) is due to natural selection in the sense that without natural selection it would not have been what it is. Here there is no dispute among Darwinians. But the efficient or real motive principle is to be found rather in the positive forces of life which enables the creature selected to live and beget his kind, under the recondite laws which issue in continued variations; these are the positive things, and the the operation of natural selection is absolutely dependent on their continued working. Suppose, for example, they should be right who seek to prove that there is an impulse toward certain preferential lines of growth and reproduction in the life processes themselves, then natural selection would remain exactly the same principle that it is now; it would still state the conditions which limit the survival, and so the perpetuity of kinds. I think Darwinians should recognize this; for it is only when they do that they will put an end to the senseless criticism which they get in the terms of the pseudo-quotation above. .

And the need of insisting upon it goes farther, since it is in this assumption that natural selectionists sometimes get their air of 'claiming the earth,' so to speak. It is clear that there is an immense amount of research ahead in the defining of the positive principles of life and development, in accounting for the quantity and distribution of variations, in ascertaining the positive qualifications which some creatures may have over and above others, whereby the former are constituted as the fittest to survive under the operation of natural selection. And each statement of a positive qualification is a real addition to the theory of evolution, although it leave natural selection exactly where it was before, only defining its sphere of application as wider or narrower, as the case may be. None of these new determinations, it seems to me, can ever overturn natural selection, since that is a statement simply of the difference of fate which must overtake organisms as long as there are different conditions of living, differences of endowment, and different phases in the cycles of life. But just in as much as these determinations truly describe the creatures which survive, it is they, and not alone the mere ordeal which they may have survived, that is of positive value for evolution science.

In conclusion, it is of interest to note—and of very peculiar interest to psychologists to note—as Professor Poulton does, that both Darwin and Wallace declare in their correspondence, each for himself, that it was the study of Malthus on population which led to the discovery of the principle of natural selection.

J. MARK BALDWIN.

VISION.

Eine neue Theorie der Gesichtswahrnehmung. K. UEBERHORST. Ztschr. für Psychol. u. Phys. der Sinnesorgane. XIII., 54–65. 1896.

The author proposed a new theory of visual perception in 1876, which he now perceives to be erroneous; and, in the course of years, he has composed the one which is here published and which was read before the International Congress of Psychologists at Munich last summer. He states his present theory at once, and in these terms: Visual perception, like perception in general, is neither sensation nor knowledge, but the product of a special psychic activity, whose essence consists in the binding together into a peculiar unity of a sensation given by an organ of sense with another sensation, idea, or memory image which is present to the soul at the same time, which two factors are conceived by the unconscious intelligence as signs of one and the same object. When we enter a room that is well known to us perception proceeds far more rapidly and completely than if the room is unfamiliar; this is usually explained by saying that in the former case a crowd of memory-images are called forth by the present impression and unite with it, and thus a clear idea of the content of the room is produced. This explanation is near to being the correct one, but nevertheless it does not exactly hit it off; the supposed fusion is not what takes place, but the real process is that, first, an intelligence which is unconsciously present in us, or, in Kantian phrase, an *à priori* knowing, refers the present impression and the memory image to one and the same object; thereupon the intuition function becomes active and produces out of the two the new form, the present clear perception, as a peculiar unitary thing. The author admits that this thought will not instantly dawn upon one, but he believes that the reader will be convinced of its truth and value by the consideration of those illusions by which we see certain plane drawings as solid forms. He discusses a number of these illusions, but it seems to the reviewer that he underestimates the difficulty of leading the reader to see that his explanation differs, except in words, which represent fictions, from the explanation usually given. All this, he says, after describing a number of common illusions, is a union effected by the Unconscious Intelligence between the present sensation and the idea which is in the mind; but it is difficult to see that there is anything in the instances chosen which throws light upon the question at issue—whether the fusion is effected by the Unconscious Intelligence, or whether it just takes place, without the aid of that mythical creation. The idea that there is something in the mind which does everything is not so much in favor among the psychologists as it was once, and merely stating it as a belief is not enough to carry conviction. Nor does it seem well-advised to devote a good portion of a paper to a diagram for showing that two points which are, to a single eye, in the same direction when looked at directly are not so when looked at peripherally—a point which most text-books (that of Norris and Oliver, to mention the latest) are content to dispose of in a line; moreover, the difference is so slight that it can only be effective for points which are very far removed from each other, and it is certainly of no moment in determining the solidity of ordinary objects, and cannot therefore furnish the complete basis for our notion of the third dimension. In conclusion, the author affirms that, since Hartmann's *Philosophie des Unbewussten*, no one has any right to doubt the existence of the Unconscious Intelligence, and hence that no one can find it unjustified if he seeks to take cognizance of its activity in the production of the perception.

Ueber Erythropsie. ERNST FUCHS. Archiv für Ophthalmologie, xlii. (4), 207–292.

This is an extremely careful piece of experimenting and also of reasoning, and, on account of its connection with recent theory, it is worth while to report it at some length.

It has been known for some time that persons who have been operated upon for cataract frequently see things in a red light; this happens after an injury which permanently increases the size of the pupil, or after the loss of the lens, and particularly when both defects occur together. These are circumstances which predispose to true, typical erythropsia, but the immediate cause is exposure of the eyes to a dazzling light; sunlight reflected from large fields of snow is sufficient to cause it even without these favoring circumstances, but much more so if the snow fields are at a high altitude. The red color is particularly noticeable upon entering a hut after some hours of mountain climbing among the Alps, and it was upon such an occasion that it first attracted the author's attention. Its extreme brightness at this time was, doubtless, owing to an unusual amount of ultra-violet rays in the light reflected from the snow, for severe sun-burn was also experienced, and sun-burn has been shown by Widmark to be due to the ultra-violet rays. In spite of the certainty of its occurrence, this erythropsia of the normal eye has received hardly any mention in ophthalmic literature.

Fuchs' experiments were conducted partly on a mountain near Vienna and partly after widening the pupil of the eye by homatropin, in both cases by means of looking for a rather long time at bright snow, which does not need, however, to be of a blinding brightness. They were confirmed by several observers, some of whom were able to obtain the effect without either of the preliminary steps. It was found convenient, upon entering the moderately darkened room, to look upon a chessboard of alternate white and black squares. At the first instant one sees nothing, then there is a brief period of seeing green, and then the red color appears, upon the bright squares much sooner then upon the dark, to remain for three or, at the most, four minutes. With some persons the red is preceded and followed by a flash of orange and citron-green. But within a region of from three to five degrees at the center of the field the phenomenon is entirely wanting (except with certain persons upon one or two occasions). Peripherally, the red color does not reach to the limit of vision, but it does extend beyond the usual field for red. In color-tone, it is complementary to a slightly yellowish green. Looking at the snow through variously colored glasses did not in the least change the color of the erythropsia, but with glass of the same color the phenomenon did not occur at all.

Fuchs proceeds to discuss the cause of the phenomenon. The color of daylight is reddish, and that of snow-light approaches violet;

the green that precedes the red may, therefore, be the after-image of this color, though that is not quite certain. The erythropsia itself is certainly not an after-image, either positive or negative, of the ordinary kind. It bears many resemblances, however, to what Fuchs calls the after-effect of dazzling, concerning which he offers a large number of new observations, but it also differs distinctly from this. He comes to the rather doubting conclusion that it is the entoptic vision of the visual purple, but his readers will certainly feel that this hypothesis has everything in its favor. The subjective color is exactly the same as that of the so-called ' visual purple.' [It is, of course, not *purple* at all, in English, but crimson; *purple* is a piece of shockingly bad translation; nor is it by any means made out that the substance is a visual substance. I am glad to see that my name for it, rod pigment, is becoming accepted.] Usually the color is invisible to us, like any color which is unchanging and which covers the whole field of view; but after it has been thoroughly bleached out the eye is sensitive to its sudden re-appearance. Even though the rods do not perceive color, it would be sufficiently reflected from them upon the cones to become visible, and there may easily be enough of the substance in the pigment of the epithelium to account for the rare cases in which it is seen in the fovea. That red glass prevents its occurrence corresponds with the fact that red light does not bleach out the rod pigment; and that it is most vivid after blinding through green glass is in accordance with the fact that the maximum absorption of the rod pigment is in green. Ewald, Tait and Boll believe that they perceived the rod pigment entoptically on first waking up in the morning, and by these painstaking experiments of Fuchs their supposition is made probable beyond a reasonable doubt.

CHRISTINE LADD FRANKLIN.

BALTIMORE.

PATHOLOGICAL.

Manuel Pratique des Méthodes d'Enseignement spéciales aux Enfants Anormaux (*Sourds-muets, aveugles, idiots, bégues, etc.*). HAMON DU FOUGERAY et L. COUËTOUX. Préface du DR. BOURNEVILLE. Paris, Progrés Médical, 1896. Pp. 288.

This volume appeals to such physicians, teachers and professors as are especially interested in the questions of the care and education of certain classes of defective children. The book is divided into five parts, the first of which is concerned with deaf-mutes, the second with

the blind, the third with idiots, the fourth with stammerers and stutterers, and the last with individuals presenting combined anomalies,
such as the deaf-mute-blind, the deaf-mute-idiotic, the blind-idiotic
and the deaf-mute-blind-idiotic. Under each heading we are given an
historical account of the condition described, statistics of the disorder,
details as to institutions existing in France for the care and treatment
of these classes of cases, a summary of the legislation relating to them
and a résumé of the methods of pedagogic treatment employed.

In the instruction of deaf-mutes the authors, after presenting the
arguments *pro* and *con*, express themselves wholly in favor of the
pure oral method of inculcating language and opposed to the mimetic
method or mixed oral and mimetic method. The chapter describing
the pure oral method is based on the work of Goguillot. This method,
in brief, consists of a preparatory course of education of the sight,
touch and muscular sense, followed by touch-studies of the action of
the respiratory muscles, then of the lips, tongue, buccal cavity and ·
larynx. After this comes the emission of sound, and by proper placing of the muscles of articulation, under direction of the teacher and
with the help of a mirror, the pupil acquires first the words, then the
consonants, and finally the combinations in syllables and words.

The chapter on the instruction of idiots is simply a reproduction
of the writings of Bourneville upon that subject, the methods employed at Bicêtre and fully described in the various reports issued
from that institution during the past sixteen years.

For stammering and allied disorders of speech the authors recommend and detail, at some length, the Chervin method of treatment.
Chervin began to apply his method in 1846 and published a book
upon the subject in 1895. The method does not differ essentially
from the rational physiological systems in vogue all over the world at
the present day.

*Récherches cliniques et therapeutiques sur l'Epilepsie, l'Hysterie et
l'Idiotie, compte rendu du service des enfants, idiots, epileptiques
et arrièrés de Bicêtre pendant l'année 1895.* Par BOURNE-
· VILLE, médecin de Bicêtre, avec la collaboration de MM. Bon-
· court, Comte, Dardel, Dubarry, Leriche, Lombard, J. Noir,
Pilliet, Ruel, Sollier, Tissier. Vol. XVI., avec 31 figures dans le
texte et 8 planches. Paris, Progrès Médical, 1896. Pp. 254.

This is the sixteenth volume of the famous studies made by
Bourneville and his assistants at the several hospitals united under the
name Bicêtre. These annual reports are a rich field for the searcher

after facts in the domains of pathology, thereapeutics and pedagogy as applied to epilepsy, hysteria and idiocy. The first part of the volume for 1895, as in former years, is devoted to a history of the service during the year, and in this we note the creation of special classes for the feeble-minded and a chapter on the medico-pedagogic treatment of abnormal children. The second part consists of clinical and pathologico-anatomical studies of thirteen cases of idiocy and epilepsy, containing a valuable addition to our repository of facts relating to these subjects. The third part gives us the result of observations upon the effects of certain remedies. Three cases of cretinism treated by extract of the thyroid gland exhibited marked improvement in the intellectual sphere as well as nutritive changes, such as loss of weight and increase in height. In regard to the matter of nutrition, Bourneville shows in a number of other cases the value of the thyroid juice in diminishing obesity. A chapter on the exhibition of bromide of camphor in vertiginous epilepsy demonstrates its great utility in that form of the disorder.

FREDERICK PETERSON.

NEW YORK.

Grundriss der Psychiatrie in klinischen Vorlesungen. Theil I.: Psycho-physiologische Einleitung. Theil II.: Die paranoischen Zustände. C. WERNICKE. Leipzig, Thieme, 1894–6. 8°. Pp. 178.

Drily written and, though clear, not easy reading, Professor Wernicke's book, short as it is, is already the weightiest of the attempts, of which several have lately been made, to apply psychological laws to the unravelling of what happens in disordered mental function. Part I. is a synopsis, many pages of which deserve to become classic types of exposition, of that modern scheme of cerebro-mental action of which Wernicke by his little work on Aphasia was himself one of the founders. The great lucidity of the statement now made shows us once more how surely protracted meditation on a subject makes a man its master. For psychiatric purposes the chief result of this Part is that the insanities (being diseases of the cortex, which is the organ of association) should psychologically all be explicable as disorders, defects, excesses or perversions, as the case may be, of the associative function.

In Part II. the author applies this notion to delusional conditions, his account of which is entirely unconventional and reveals the man of original perceptions on every page. For most of his new distinctions

and classifications—unfortunately all with Greek names—the reader
must consult the original. I will confine myself to a brief notice of the most important thing in the book, which is the explanation, by a single underlying cause, of the whole complex of delusional symptoms. How is it possible to find such a mass of false
ideas at war with each other and with reality, such a loss of the
sense of probability, such hallucinations, such inter-current emotional
states and motor tendencies, in one patient? Professor Wernicke
answers by what he calls his *hypothesis of sejunction* or dissociation. A pathological process has loosened the firmly connected
system of associations, so that a large number of those originally
there have become impossible, and a 'disintegration of the personality' results. Confusion in perception and dementia are evidently
nothing but gaps in normal association, replaced or not by associations
that are non-normal. But our author explains the phenomena of excess, the impressed thoughts and hallucinations by his theory, as well as
the phenomena of defect. The two run together, excess in the processes that stand over being the consequence of the loss of such other
processes as may have disappeared. Defect is thus primary and excess
secondary, as in the ordinary theory of dreaming and the theory by
which the present reviewer[1] and Mr. Parish[2] have treated illusions
and hallucinations. . Professor Wernicke applies the theory of sejunction very ingeniously to a large number of symptoms, sensorial,
ideational and motor, and of course dilates at length on delusions as
explanatory theories by the patient of his elementary disturbances.
The false connection with himself (*Beziehungswahn*) which the patient finds in so many different experiences, the distortions of memory,
the distinction between presently active and residual morbid processes,
all come in turn to be suggestively discussed.

I cannot help thinking, for my own part, that the explanation of
irritative phenomena (or *Reizerscheinungen*) by defects of association
(or *Ausfallserscheinungen*) has to bear somewhat too heavy a burden in Professor Wernicke's pages. If the mere stoppage of associa-
tion-paths be by itself enough to heighten any process at which the
stoppage may occur, then, whenever we hesitate for a word, we ought
to get the last cue-word in the shape of an hallucination of hearing
—of what W. calls a *phonem*, rather than as a mere verbal *idea*.
But I can discover no tendency to such sensorial vivacity in the last
idea reached in such cases, and this fact, I must confess, has given me

[1] Principles of Psychology, II., 122 ff.
[2] Ueber die Trugwahrnehmung, München, 1894, p. 105 ff.

some uneasiness about the theory of hallucination suggested in my own book. It seems now time for the 'discriminating stage' of criticism to be applied to that theory, and of course the field of paranoia presents itself as the place *par excellence* for working the discriminations out. The great lucidity and rationality of many paranoiacs, their freedom from any speech disturbances or other *Heerderscheinungen* in the way of directly perceivable defect are hard to reconcile with the view that their 'false voices' (which would seem to be *Heerderscheinungen* of excess) are secondary rather than primary symptoms. In many important respects there are analogies between patients with delusions and cases of hysteria such as those that Janet, Brewer and Freud have explored, and this would suggest that it might be well to search for parasitic systems of subconscious ideas as a possible source of some of the trouble in the former cases. In one way ('disintegration of personality') Wernicke's 'sejunction' formula coincides with Janet's, yet Wernicke ignores altogether the notion of subconscious ideas; and indeed it is evident that if they exist we need quite new methods of finding them out. But be all this as it may, it is still certain that Wernicke's hypothesis of sejunction or dissociation opens a new era of interpretation in mental pathology and gives to all observers of the insane a new task in the way of something definite to verify, complete or refute. This is a great service and the book that has performed it ought to be translated without loss of time.

W. J.

NEW BOOKS.

Psychologie der Naturvölker. Ethnographische Parallelen. JACOB ROBINSOHN. Leipzig, Friedrich, no date. Pp. 176.

Lehrbuch der Psychologie. F. JODL. Stuttgart, Cotta'sche Buchhandlung, 1896. Pp. xxiv+767. M. 12.

Outlines of Psychology. W. WUNDT. Trans. by C. H. JUDD. Leipzig, Engelmann; New York, Stechert, 1897. Pp. xviii+342. $1.75.

Theorie der Begabung. R. BAERWALD. Leipzig, Reisland, 1896. Pp. x+289. M. 5.

Das konträre Geschlechtsgefühl. H. ELLIS and J. A. SYMONDS. Bibliothek der Socialwissenschaft. Ed. by H. KURELLA, No. 7 (original Ausgabe). Leipzig, H. Wigand, 1896. Pp. xi+308.

Atlas of Nerve Cells. M. A. STARR. With the coöperation of
OLIVER S. STRONG and EDWARD LEAMING. New York, The
Macmillan Co., 1896. LIII. plates, 13 diagrams. Pp. 79, 4to.
$10.00

Das Ideal des 'ewigen Friedens.' LUDWIG STEIN. Berlin, Reimer,
1896. Pp. 65. M. 1.20.

Die Freiheitslehre bei Kant und Schopenhauer. D. NEUMARK.
Hamburg and Leipzig, Voss, 1896. Pp. xii+89. M. 2.

Die Autonomie der Moral. K. B. R. AARS. Hamburg and Leipzig, ? 1896. Pp. 121. M. 3.

Die Psychologie in der Religionswissenschaft. E. KOCH. Frei-
burg and Leipzig, Mohr, 1896. M. 2.80.

The Cell in Development and Inheritance. E. B. WILSON.
Columbia Univ. Biolog. Series, IV. New York and London,
The Macmillan Co., 1896. $3.

Dritter internationaler Congress für Psychologie in München
(Aug. 4–7, 1896). München, Lehmann, 1897. Pp. xliv+490.

Studien zu Methodenlehre und Erkenntnisskritik. F. DREYER.
Leipzig, Engelmann, 1895. Pp. xiii+223. M. 4.

*Addresses and Proceedings of the National Educational Associa-
tion, Buffalo, N. Y.* Published by the Assoc., Chicago
University Press, 1896. Pp. viii+1088. $2.

Manual of Logic. J. WELTON. University Tutorial Series. Vol. I.
Deductive, 2d ed., revised. Vol. II. Inductive. London,
W. B. Clive; New York, Hinds and Noble, 1896. Pp. xxii+
411 and xiii+292.

Manual of Ethics. J. S. MACKENSIE. University Tutorial Series.
2d ed. London, W. B. Clive; New York, Hinds and Noble,
no date. Pp. xxx+355.

Matière et Mémoire; essai sur la relation du corps à l'esprit.
H. BERGSON. Paris, Alcan, 1896. Pp. iii+279. Fr. 5.

Charles Darwin and the Theory of Natural Selection. E. B.
POULTON. Century Science Series. New York, The Macmillan
Co., 1896. Pp. viii+224. $1.25.

Christianity and Idealism. JOHN WATSON. Publications of the
Philosophical Union of the University of California. Edited by
G. H. HOWISON. Vol. II. New York, The Macmillan Co.,
1897. Pp. xxxviii+216. $1.25.

Problems of Biology. GEORGE SANDEMAN. London, Sonnenschein; New York, The Macmillan Co., 1896. Pp. 213. $2.

AN EXPLANATION.

My attention has been called to the fact that a meaning, far other than any intended, might be put in certain words of mine, in my estimate of Mr. Sterrett's book in the January issue of the REVIEW. It is suggested that a reader might take my words (p. 78) to mean that Mr. Sterrett's results were not reached independently and that he had used the work of recent investigators without giving them due credit.

I wish to prevent any such misinterpretation by saying that when I wrote, I had no such thought in mind and that I have good reason for knowing that Mr. Sterrett's results are the outcome of his own insight and independent reflection. In pointing out the agreement of his thought with that of the authors mentioned in my review, the real intention was to emphasize the healthiness of his originality.

ROGER BRUCE JOHNSON.
MIAMI UNIVERSITY.

NOTES.

DR. JAMES WARD has been appointed to the new Professorship of Mental Philosophy and Logic in Cambridge University.

WE regret to record the death of Professor W. Wallace, Professor of Moral Philosophy in the University of Oxford, who was killed on February 19th by a fall from a bicycle.

WITH the current issue the *Vierteljahrsschrift für wissenschaftliche Philosophie* begins a new volume (XXL), with a somewhat enlarged programme, under the editorship of Fr. Carstenjen and O. Krebs, to whom the editorial care had been transferred by Avenarius before his death.

THE same issue of the *Vierteljahrsschrift* announces a prize (of 500 M.) for the best essay on the subject: *Nachweis der metaphysisch-animistischen Elemente in dem Satz der Erhaltung der Energie und Vorschlag zur Ausschaltung dieser Elemente.* The length is to be 3 to 4 forms of the *Vierteljahrsschrift*, the language German, and the limit of time October 1, 1897. The essays may be sent to either of the editors, to Professor E. Mach, of Vienna, or to Professor A. Riehl, of Kiel.

THE firm of Ruether u. Reichard, of Berlin, announce a *Sammlung von Abhandlungen aus dem Gebiete der pädagogischen Psy-*

chologie und Physiologie, to be issued in complete essays, 6 to 8 per year. The series is to be edited by Professor H. Schiller, of Giessen, and Professor Th. Ziehen, of Jena.

WITH the number of December, 1896, the *Revue Philosophique* issues its second general Index (1888 to 1895, pp. 91, Fr. 3), prepared by J. Clavière. As it contains an analytical table of matter, as well as an index of names, it will be serviceable as an index to the important literature of that period.

WE have received the annual 'Addresses and Proceedings of the National Educational Association' for 1896 (University of Chicago Press), and the 'Report of the Commissioner of Education' for 1893-4 (2 vols.), and 1894-5 (2 vols.); Washington, Government Printing Office, 1896; both valuable repositories of information for students of education.

PROFESSOR JAMES SETH has been added to the editorial staff of the *Philosophical Review.*

L'Anthropologie states that a government School of Science has been established at Madrid with twenty-seven professorships, one of them being a chair in physiological psychology to be occupied by Professor Simmara.

WE may call attention to the full description (with cuts) by Professor Mosso, of his new Myotonometer (for studying the tonicity of the muscles in man), in the *Arch. Ital. de Biologie*, XXV., fasc. 3, 1896.

THE *Psychological Index* for 1896 will be issued about the middle of March. The arrangement whereby it is also published in the *Année Psychologique* is continued, and the *Index* will hereafter have the coöperation of M. N. Vaschide, of the Sorbonne, in the preparation of the French titles. We are glad also to announce that, by coöperation between the REVIEW and the *Zeitschrift für Psychologie u. Physiologie der Sinnesorgane*, an interchange of titles between the English and German bibliographies has been arranged, so that, beginning with the *Index* for 1896, the two will be in these respects substantially alike. A difference in the number of titles in favor of the German bibliography will, however, still be probable in view of its later date of publication.

This issue of the REVIEW is enlarged to accomodate the Proceedings of the American Psychological Association.

VOL. IV.   No. 3.   MAY, 1897.

THE PSYCHOLOGICAL REVIEW.

THE NEGATIVE IN LOGIC.[1]

BY PROFESSOR A. T. ORMOND.

Princeton University.

Historically the negative has occupied the attention of logicians since the first beginnings of the science. Aristotle gave it a prominent place in his reflection and in modern times it has been discussed by all the masters in this field; by Leibnitz and Kant, by Hamilton, Lotze, Sigwart, Wundt, Bradley, Bosanquet and Benno Erdmann. It is not my purpose in this paper to review the work of these thinkers, even in outline, but rather with their results in mind to attempt a statement of what I conceive to be the most important features of an adequate theory of logical negation. In the first place it is clear, I think, that the logical negative is very closely implicated in the general theory of judgment and that a radical treatment of it must go to the roots of judgment itself. For this reason a considerable section of this paper will be devoted to judgment with a view to seeking its psychological and logical grounds.

In treating judgment psychologically we must conceive it as a conscious function, and this, followed back to its very first presupposition, would involve the question of the origin of the consciousness in which the function arises. But whatever the responsibility of psychology may be for the genesis of consciousness, logic is free I think to assume the medium in which the functions it is interested in are found. A question, however, which does, indirectly at least, concern the foundations of logic

[1] Read in abstract at the Boston meeting, American Psychological Association. The discussion is mainly psychological.

is that of the organic conditions in which consciousness operates. The tendency of the genetic thinking of the time is to go back of the psychological to the biological in order to discover the first laws or conditions of conscious activity. And this is, I think, on the whole, a healthy disposition, inasmuch as the vital and the psychic activities cannot be separated in an organism which has once become the bearer of consciousness. I do not mean that there are none of the activities of such an organism that are not psychic, but that within the circle of the conscious, the vital and the psychic are one and the same. To omit all detail, the important question here is, how, for our purposes, shall the relation of the biological to the psychic be conceived? There are two view-points that are to be kept separated in our thinking : the external or physical and the internal or psychic. From the physical standpoint, which is the biological, we view consciousness as something in the organism and superadded to the organic functions, whereas, from the psychic point of view, which is that of mind itself, consciousness is not simply in an organism or an appendage to its activities, but it is *comprehending term, the medium in which the existence of everything is realized, and in which the organism, in order to get itself recognized among existent things, must somehow become immanent as part of its content. Realizing this point of view we will be led to regard that duality which constitutes the mould of organic activity in general, the interaction of organism and environment, as immanent and structural in the sphere of conscious activity, and from the same point of view the biological laws of habit and accommodation will become immanent laws of consciousness. I mean by this that consciousness does not simply contemplate the biological functions as external and conditional to its own activities, but that when conscious activity arises, say, as will, the laws of habit and accommodation are taken up into consciousness and become constitutional principles of volitional activity.

Assuming, then, that the vital conditions the psychic in its own sphere by becoming immanent and constitutional to it, our notion of psychic activity will resolve itself into that of *conscious* vital function transforming and yet obeying the life categories

which have been taken up into the conscious sphere as immanent laws of psychic activity. Nor will it be difficult from this
point of view to realize the ground on which the first conscious
activity may be characterized as volitional, inasmuch as it will
take the form of conscious reaction of the organism upon its
environment, which, operating under the laws of habit and accommodation, it gradually assimilates and absorbs into itself.
The general concept which I have sought to emphasize at this
point is the immanence of the vital from the psychic point of
view and the consequent necessity for translating the biological
categories into internal and structural principles of the conscious activities.

If we regard the conscious organism simply as acted upon
by its environment, that is, as a recipient of stimulations, there
is no ground for ascribing will to it. It is only when we conceive it as active and as reacting upon the ground of stimulation
that we can think of it as will. What we call will can, in these
early psychic activities, be nothing but the conscious responses
by which the organism effects its assimilative and adaptive movements. We may call them *pulses of self-assertion*, by which
the organism wreaks itself upon the ground of stimulation, and
the acts will be acts of self-conservation and will fall under the
general category of survival.

These earlier acts of volition will not be primarily motived by
any idea or representation, but rather by some feeling of pleasure
or pain, most likely one of pain, since mere pleasure feeling could
not serve as a motive for activity, but, on the contrary, in itself
and without some accompanying idea or representation which
would translate it into teleological terms, would tend to arrest
motion. If we assume then that the very first motive-impulse,
logically considered, is painful feeling we may conceive the
primal impulse of volition as some want or unsatisfactory
condition which *impels* the conscious organism to escape from
its present state into one that shall be less intolerable. We have
then the conception of a will motived in a negative sense from behind, but, so far as this element of motivity is concerned, blind as
to what is before it and having no other guidance than the specific
quality of the painful impulse, to enable it to pick its way among

the pleasant and painful stimulations of the environment. But by the pain-motive, which is a principle of *avoidance*, we may conceive the organism as feeling its way with a certain degree of selective intelligence, it being understood that the pleasure-motive becomes also active, and that representation when it arises attaches itself to both pleasure and pain as a teleological principle of positive and negative selection.

The will of such an organism would be an active function of appropriation and avoidance moving under the guidance of the selective motives, and the special question which arises here from our point of view is how the volitional activity comes to take on an intellectual character and become what we call judgment. To answer such a question in detail would involve a wide excursion into genetic psychology. The following statement must suffice at this point. The conscious organism not only collides volitionally with the grounds of its stimulations, but out of these collisions arise representations (the spatial no doubt arising first) which are to be conceived as elements of form under what these grounds appear to us as *objective* and *intelligible*. Let us suppose this process as completing itself in the presentation to consciousness of the objects of a world in the midst of which its functions are performed. So that what was blindly and vaguely realized before through feeling now stands out in a representation. If from this representation we subtract the volitional pulse we have simply a world presented but not affirmed. But if we restore this pulse as a conscious reaction upon the presentation we have the simplest assertion of the object; that is, judgment in its most elemental form. This is essential. In all judgment the central thing is a volitional pulse. To this as genus certain differentiæ must be added in order to constitute judgment, and the next section must be taken up with a determination of these differentiæ.

From the genetic point of view there are originally only two kinds of judgments : *existential*, or judgments which assert simple existence, and *relational* judgments, which assert relations among existents. The elements of the existential judgment are : (1) the *objective* representation of something to consciousness; (2) the act of *positing*, which is virtually our willing the existence or non-existence of the thing. But between the representation and the volitional fiat, let this thing be, there must intervene the motive of the fiat, which is some interest. This interest must coalesce with the representation in order that the volitional pulse may be stirred to utter itself in the let this thing be or not be. Thus arises the simple existential judgment. It is more than mere perception; we must perceive and then do something to our perception before the content or object may exist to and for us. Interest must fall upon the object represented, and there must be that pulse of self-commitment which has been translated into the let this thing be, before the judgment of existence can be said properly to arise. The judgment thus puts a kind of personal stamp of endorsement on the object of perception.

The relational judgment is more complex. Its prototype will be found in volitional alternation, or that process by which the animal or the young child selects out of conflicting, or at least competing means, those which will serve its end. Thus the chick, whose end is food and whose alternatives are cinnabar caterpillars and other caterpillars, will choose the other caterpillars, rejecting the cinnabar species. This process ceases to be purely volitional and takes on judgmental complexion when the alternatives are consciously conceived, or become related in thought as alternative means of satisfying the volitional end; that is, when a body of experience or knowledge becomes the guiding principle of selection. In the chick's case the selective principles are all below the level of *thinking*. The end, food, although not conceived in any intellectual terms, yet functions in the chick's consciousness as a limiting and guiding principle. The chick's universe is one of food, and the included alternatives are food-alternatives. The body of experience acquired by the chick thus conditions its selective activity. The motives of selection rise to the plane of thinking when they themselves become the objects of representation. The child performs a judgment of relation when it pronounces an object good or selects it because it is good. In such an act the relation of the object to some end sought by the child is seized and affirmed. This is the simplest kind of judgment of relation. The more complex forms arise when the less obvious relations on which classifications proceed come into consciousness. In this progress the immediate relations of the object to the survival of the subject gradually drop into the background and the activity takes on a more purely intellectual form. The principal differentiæ of the judgment of relation may then be stated as follows : (1) a body of experience or knowledge which determines the sphere or universe of existential relations; (2) the appearance in this universe of a number of competing alternatives whose relations to some interesting end also rise into consciousness and specifically determine the judgment. These are the differential features of the act in which the volitional pulse of assertion is central and which takes the form of appropriation or rejection of some among the included alternatives.

Now, it may be asked at this point, do we not beg the question when we postulate a universe which includes all the alternatives as a *condition* of the judgment of relation? How else, it may be asked, than through a process of judgment could such a universe arise? We answer that our first universes arise in perceptual experience. Judgment is never without presuppositions. The chick no doubt learns from experience what objects are food for it before it is able to select among the objects presented to it. Our logical universes may be and no doubt are in the later stages of experience, products of logical processes. But this is evidently not the case at the point where judgment first arises. The first universe must be one that is supplied by extra-logical experience. When arrived at, however, the judgment function will operate within it in the manner indicated.

We have then the two distinguishable types of judgment— the Existential, which asserts simply existence, and the Relational, which is more complex and selects among alternatives included in a broader genus or universe of existent relations. If, now, we leave the first species out of view as being for our purposes relatively unimportant, we may say that the judgment function is a *disjunctive operation within a larger genus or universe.* Bosanquet recognizes this character in his doctrine that every judgment involves as its presupposition a larger comprehending judgment. The comprehending term need not, however, as we have contended above, be a judgment. It may be some body of experience which for the time being functions as the real subject of judgment. In other words, the ground of the disjunction may be purely psychological.

To summarize the discussion up to this point, judgment rises out of volitional gounds. It is informed by the motive of volition and it includes the volitional pulse as its central essence. All judgment then is volitional in its nature. The volitional pulse becomes a pulse of judgment when a field of representation arises to which some interest attaches. The simple judgment of experience is the first result. The subject of a logical judgment need not be logical; it may be purely psychological, a body of extra-logical experience. The judgment of relation preserves the volitional character and simply adds other differentiæ. We have seen that the ground of this judgment is a genus which comprehends, and at the same time limits, the alternatives about which the judgment is pronounced, and that the judgment itself is essentially disjunctive. But the comprehending genus need not be a judgment; it may be psychological and not logical. Now this conclusion is the one that might be anticipated from the point of view of logical immanence.[1] For just as the vital is immanent in the psychic so in the region of the logical processes the later comprehends the earlier which acts as its inner motive and the psychologial is immanent in the logical. We see at this point how the psychological universe, which is the concrete universal of the Lotzean school of logicians, becomes the immanent motive and spring of logical processes, so that it is not necessary to postulate an infinite series of logical universals, but experience passes by insensible gradations from the pre-logical into the logical stage.

The fact that every judgment either affirms or denies led Aristotle to regard affirmation and negation as coördinate moments in judgment. Modern logicians have tended rather to subordinate negation to affirmation, and some have gone so far as virtually to deny the reality of negation. Without delay-

---

[1] The doctrine of immanence set forth here is not identical with Erdmann's. What it means is the internal activity of psychological content as a motive in logical processes.

ing on historical details, however, we may seek an answer to
two questions concerning the negative: (1) How does negation
arise? (2) What is its function in judgment? If we bear in
mind the relation of judgment to volition we will be ready to
agree, I think, that all judgment is positive. There cannot be
a judgment in which something is not asserted. All judgment
is, therefore, positive and assertative. The distinction between
affirmation and denial must then be a distinction between two
kinds of positive assertion. So much seems clear. But it is
not so clear what an assertion that is neither affirmative nor negative can be or how such assertion can be real. How shall we
render the question intelligible? In the first place, it is clear,
I think, that when I say in a negative existential judgment, for
example, that no griffin exists, the nominal subject, griffin, is
not the real subject which motives the assertion. The real
subject is something known; some conception of reality which
necessitates the denial. Now the assertive force of the judgment lies in the self-conserving force of this backlying knowledge or conception which simply maintains itself against what is
incompatible with it. Every existential judgment may then be
regarded as the self-assertion of its real subject, *pro* the compatible, *contra* the incompatible. There is always a positive;
the self-assertion of the real subject which conditions both affirmation and negation. Suppose, for illustration, that this were
not the case and that griffin were the real subject of the judgment, the function of the denial would be to remove its own
subject and thus commit logical suicide. The real subject is
that which necessitates the denial and is some backlying knowledge or conception of reality which is incompatible with the
existence of griffins. The real subject maintains itself against
its incompatible. Thus the negative judgment arises. We see,
then, how the negative existential judgment rests on position.
It is not pure destruction and removal, but something establishes
itself in and through it.

   If we take the judgment of relation the same fact comes out
even more clearly. We have seen that the judgment of relation is disjunctive and that it presupposes a genus or universal
that is either logical or psychological. Take the judgment:

men are not infallible. Here the real subject which necessitates the denial is some backlying knowledge or conception of human nature with which the notion of infallible men is incompatible. Let us suppose that this is not the case, and see what follows. The denial simply sweeps away the notion of infallible men and leaves nothing behind. There is thus no motive for further progress. We can escape this irrational result only by identifying the real subject of the judgment with the knowledge or conception of reality that necessitates the denial. This need not be a definite affirmation that men are fallible or even the knowledge of that fact, but rather some knowledge or conception of human nature that is incompatible with its infallibility. This real subject it is that asserts itself in every judgment and renders it positive, whether its form be affirmative or negative. And this it is, and this alone, which enables judgment to make progress through denial as well as through affirmation.

How, then, are affirmation and negation related? The answer cannot be given without recognizing the position of the real subject as the condition and motive of both affirming and denying. Some logicians, as Sigwart and Bradley, take the ground that a negative judgment presupposes an affirmation or an attempted affirmation of the opposite. This is also substantially the view of Benno Erdmann. But it is clear at this point, I think, that what the denial does presuppose is the position, the self-assertion of the real subject. The real subject maintains itself and necessitates the specific denial or affirmation, as the case may be. This real subject is always related to the judgment as the genus or universal within which the affirmation or denial falls. It is this larger assertion, and not a specific affirmation of the thing denied, that is necessarily presupposed in the negative judgment.

In what sense then are . affirmation and denial related to each other? We do not inquire here what the actual relation between any two given affirmations and denials may be, for a denial *may* be the contradiction of a previous affirmative assertion; but rather what is the essential and necessary relation between affirmation and denial *as such?* If we bear in mind that it is the real subject that necessitates the judgment which is in its nature, an appropriation of what is compatible or a rejection of what is incompatible with its actual content, it would seem not to be necessary that even proposed or suggested affirmation should precede denial, as is the contention of Bradley and Bosanquet. For if the real subject which is the genus or universe within which the judgment functions, necessitates the affirmation or denial on the ground of compatibility or incompatibility, it would seem to follow that inasmuch as the relation of incompatibility may be directly apprehended, like the inequality of two lines, therefore denial may be direct and unmediated by any suggested or attempted affirmation. It seems gratuitous for us to say that we cannot deny without having first gone through the form of affirming. Limiting the implications of the relation to the requirement of necessity, I cannot see any sufficient justification for the doctrine that negation is mediated by affirmation. On the contrary, so far as the logical relations of the two moments are concerned, they seem to be perfectly coördinate. The real subject approaches the alternatives contained in the limiting genus without logical pre-possession and affirms or denies them with direct relation to itself and without regard to their relations to one another.

But from another point of view there is a difference. We have seen that the real subject gets on through both affirmation and denial. But it gets on directly by affirmation, while its progress through denial is only indirect. The organism maintains itself through the avoidance of what is hurtful, as well as by the assimilation of what is beneficial; but the two functions do not advance it in the same way. It is directly benefited by food, but only indirectly and mediately by the avoidance of the hurtful. The same is true of affirmation and denial. While logically they are coördinate in the sense that neither is mediated by the other, yet affirmation ministers more directly to its subject than does negation. Naturally, then, the interest in affirmation will be stronger than that which attaches to denial and, therefore, psychologically, if not logically, negation will be forced into a secondary place.

To the question, then, of the necessary relation of affirmation and negation we answer that logically they are coördinate and inconvertible modes of assertion, and that the real subject of discourse advances through denial as well as through affirmation. The first part of this conclusion seems, however, to be contradicted by double negation, which by common consent of logicians is held to be identical with affirmation. Now, it is true that the denial of a denial leads up to an affirmative judgment. But this is not the same as to say that double negation and affirmation are identical. The truth is the denial of a denial simply sweeps the first denial away and leaves the ground clean for an affirmation which immediately follows. But this affirmation is a third judgment. That this is true will appear not only from an inspection of the movement of thought in such cases, but also from the consideration that a denial of a denial contradicts it, and leads, therefore, by a process of immediate inference to the assertion of the contradictory affirmative. Double negation is not affirmation, then, but simply prepares the way for affirmation by destroying the negative that blocks its path. It is one of the modes by which the real subject necessitates an affirmative judgment. Logical analysis thus fails to lend any support to the idea that affirmation and denial are not perfectly distinct mental functions, or that there is any point where they tend to lose their difference and become identical.

There has been great difference of opinion among logicians as to whether the negative ought to be referred to the predicate or to the copula of a judgment. If we distinguish at all between predicate and copula, which seems to me to be a doubtful performance, then the predicate will be the name of something that is conceived to affect the subject in some way and the copula will stand for the mode of this affection. The copula may then be regarded as a conceived relation between the subject and the predicate matter. Let us take the judgment, men are not fallible. If the negative belongs to the predicate, then, as Benno Erdmann points out, the judgment becomes affirmative, men are non-fallible and the distinction between affirmation and negation is virtually abolished. But if it belongs to the copula the negative maintains itself and a certain conceived content is rejected by the subject on the ground of incompatibility. Benno Erdmann holds that the negative is to be referred to the copula,[1]

[1] *Logik, Erster Band,* § 57, 348.

and in this I think he is unquestionably right, and would only take issue with him on the point that what the negative copula sweeps away is an affirmation or a proposed affirmation. It has been shown, I think, that all that is necessarily involved in negation is the presence of an alternative that is equally open to affirmation or negation and that whatever more than this may be involved in any given case must be determined by the context of the judgment. The denial removes an alternative that might have been affirmed had it been compatible, and it removes it as a whole out of the sphere of possibilities. The function of denial is thus always removal, sublation.

The *implications* which the negative judgment may contain is a consideration that is to be carefully separated from that of the meaning of denial. The implications of the denial when it has once performed its function are to be determined in view of the relations of opposition which subsist between it and other conceivable judgments involving the same terms. Denial contradicts affirmation in the sense of wiping it out completely. This insight is as old as Aristotle. But when the denial is taken as a judgment form then it stands related differently to other judgment forms, affirmative and negative. Thus if we say all regular students are eligible to college honors, we, in effect, say that any regular student is eligible. The denial of this implies that there are regular students who are not eligible. This gives the traditional opposition of all are and some are not. But the negative judgment may be denied by others which are not contradictory. Thus all are will be denied by none are. But it is not necessary to enlarge on a topic so familiar. The important point of the discussion here is the necessity for distinguishing between the meaning of denial and the implications of the judgment in which the denial is incorporated.

Benno Erdmann's doctrine of the immanence of the predicate in the logical subject makes it possible for him to speak more profoundly than most logicians on the subject of negation. Every denial, he says, rests on the failure of immanence of the predicate in the subject.[1] This is true. But Erdmann does not, I think, develop the full implication of his own doctrine. If we

[1] Logik, Erster Band, § 57, 353.

take the subject in the narrow technical sense in which it is ordinarily used, then no question of immanence can arise and the denial simply sweeps away a possible synthesis, leaving nothing behind. Thus if we deny that men are infallible we remove the notion of infallible men and leave nothing in its place. Thinking is thus brought to a standstill with no motive for any further progress. In order to avoid such a disaster the real subject of the judgment must be something that survives both affirmation and denial. It must be some universe or piece of knowledge lying in our consciousness which asserts itself in the removal of the incompatible or in the assimilation of the compatible. The real subject survives the denial and gets on by means of it. And it is this subject alone which has immanent in it all the real alternatives on which affirmations might be founded, while denial in such a case indicates a failure of immanence in the sense that what it denies is no real alternative at all. It does not exist within the confines of this larger subject. This amendment I would suggest to Erdmann's doctrine of the immanence of the predicate in the subject; an amendment that would be perfectly consistent with his refusal to allow to denial any independent significance. Denial always, on this view, points back to a larger self-asserting subject, in relation to which it is the cancellation of an affirmative possibility, and although it does not as definitely point forward to affirmation as Erdmann thinks, it does, in fact, prepare the way for the more definite self-assertion of the real subject.

The fruitful question regarding the function and value of the negative is, as Bosanquet says, why in knowledge we cannot do without denial? A full answer to such a question is, perhaps, impossible. But if we have rightly conceived the relation of judgment to the volitional processes which underlie it, an equivalent question would be, why cannot volition do without rejection? The obvious answer here is that the environment contains things that are incompatible with the organism's survival. And just as we have reason to think that pleasure without pain could not supply an adequate stimulus to volitional activity, or a principle of selection that would enable it to avoid the hurtful, so for analogous reasons we have grounds for thinking that knowledge could not get on with simple affirmation. The infinite sphere of alternatives that may confront any given subject will contain the incompatible as well as the compatible. Now, before the incompatible, affirmation is powerless. There is needed a selective principle which will enable the subject to assert itself against and in spite of the incompatible. Hence the necessary function of negation. Knowledge makes progress as much by denial as by affirmation. But it progresses in a different way through denial, and at no point can the two modes be identified.

Denial we have seen to be a selective principle in the activity of knowing. In practice, however, it possesses various degrees of selective value. To begin at the bottom of the scale the value of negation is at its minimum in what Kant has called the infinite judgment. This judgment definitely assigns the negative to the predicate of the judgment. When we say, for example, virtue is not four-cornered, we assign virtue to the infinite universe of non-four-cornered things where it has stones, vegetables, caterpillars and other things for its companions. The negative is at its lowest terms here because it is most indeterminate; it has simply expelled virtue from the province of four-cornered things, but otherwise leaves it to wander at large in an undetermined universe. If we leave out of view the infinite judgment and connect denial where it properly belongs, with the copula of the judgment, its value will be found to vary indefinitely. Its function is uniform, the removal of a false alternative, but what this removal does for knowledge is variable. The point on which I wish to put emphasis in this connection is that the significance of negation will, other things being equal, vary with the extent and richness of the real subject, which necessitates the denial. The denial of the scientist means more for knowledge than that of the unlearned, though both denials be equally valid. The denial of the child is less significant than that of the man. The savage looks out on the stars and shakes his head; the trained astronomer, looking through his telescope, makes the same sign. The difference in significance is vast, and why? Because the denial is necessitated by knowledge, and just in proportion as this knowledge is rich and exact will the denial be definite and specific. The astronomer's denial, perhaps, brushes aside a false hypothesis, or removes the only obstacle in the way of a great discovery, while that of the savage signifies, it may be, only the failure of some combination which has a superstitious import to his mind. Some of the later writers on logic represent this tendency of negation to become more specific as approximation to the significance of affirmation. Or, to put the same thing in different language, denial tends to become the equivalent of affirmation until at the highest point it has the same value. It seems to me, however, that these logicians state a truth in language that is misleading. In order to say anything intelligent about the value of denial we must first distinguish between its function and its implications. The function of denial is always and invariably removal. As such it is as unique in its character as affirmation. We have also seen that in its relation to the knowing process it is a principle of selection. In this regard it is also unique, and not to be merged in affirmation. But the implication of denial will in most instances, at least, be something positive. It will at least limit and define the sphere of alternatives by removing the false and incompatible. And as knowledge becomes richer and more specific a denial will come to point with greater and greater precision to an affirmation which will be involved in it by some relation of opposition. It is incident on the growth of knowledge that the system which it immanates becomes more closely knitted together and that the judgment functions become more specific. If knowledge could once complete itself we would then have a subject whose every affirmation would exclude a specific negation and whose every denial would lead by direct implication to a specific opposite affirmation.

CONTRIBUTIONS FROM THE HARVARD PSYCHO-LOGICAL LABORATORY.

COMMUNICATED BY WILLIAM JAMES.

A. DISCRIMINATION IN CUTANEOUS SENSATIONS.

BY LEON M. SOLOMONS.

It is well known that the power to discriminate between a touch from two points and that produced by one is susceptible of great improvement by practice. But the process by which this comes about, as well as its general bearing on the origin of cutaneous perceptions, has been considered only speculatively. At the suggestion of Professor James I undertook an experimental investigation of this problem.

My first object was to determine whether it was a simple question of exercise, like the growth of a muscle through use, or whether there was a distinctly mental element of an educational nature, allied to such processes as learning to read. For this purpose two subjects were selected and each regularly practiced in the discrimination of touches made with dull compass points on the fleshy part of the forearm. But one, S, was regularly told whether he was right or wrong, while the other, G, never was. At the start both distinguished two points as two at about a distance of an inch and a-half. After a few weeks' practice the one who had been told when he was right and when wrong, S, had reduced the distance to about one-fourth inch, while the sensitivity of the other, G, remained practically the same. To make sure that this was not due to individual differences the second subject was then for a while told when he was right and when wrong, whereupon he improved rapidly. The subjects were always touched with one point about as often as with two, care being taken to avoid any kind of regularity in the alternation. The tendency to call one two was often as marked as the tendency to call two one.

From these experiments I concluded that the process of training was essentially a mental one, a real learning, a formation
of new associations.

The next question then was, what peculiarity of the sensation produced by two points causes them to be recognized as
such. This seemed to resolve itself into two lines of inquiry:

1. What other judgments as of distance, area, locality, etc.,
seem to be related to this?

2. How must the sensations from two points, and the conditions of their application, be varied in order to have them apperceived as one and similarly, *mutatis mutandis*, for one point?

Along the first line experiment soon developed the following:

(*a*) The impression of area-covered which accompanies a
judgment of one, is often greater than that accompanying a
judgment of two in the same neighborhood; so we cannot suppose the judgment of twoness to be based upon the impression
of area. In other words, when we judge the points to be double it is not because they seem to affect us over more than a certain area, which area we take to characterize the contact of a
single point.

(*b*) In a subject trained to discriminate two points from one,
the ability to *localize* touches, that is, to touch with the other
hand the place touched, was no better than the average, and not
nearly so accurate as the discrimination. That is, the error in
localizing, measured by distance, was much greater than the distance apart necessary for discerning two points to be two.
From this it would appear that judgment of doubleness does not
depend upon separate localization of the different points; that we
do not know the touch to be caused by two points by perceiving
them as in two different locations.

(*c*) When touched in one place and then in two others, an
untrained subject's ability to tell which of the second touches
was nearer the first, was much more accurate than his ability
to detect simultaneous doubleness, measuring accuracy by distance as before. A difference of less than one-half inch between the distance of the two *successive* touches from the first
was readily perceived by a subject whose discrimination of
simultaneous doubleness required a distance of one and one-

half inches.   This would seem to shut out any theories trying
to explain the detection of simultaneous doubleness through a
feeling of 'distance-apart.'

Along the other line of inquiry, the first thing tried was expectant attention.   The subject was told beforehand what the
stimulus would be, but requested to make judgment entirely independently of this knowledge, so that the effect of the suggestion upon the actual feeling might be judged.   The result
was that two points were felt as two when so near together that
without the expectation they would certainly be perceived as
one.   The judgment was fully twice as delicate when aided in
this way.

Then the subject was told that he might be deceived—that
when told that the stimulus would be two, it might really be
one.   He was to put himself in the condition of expectation for
the stimulus as it was told him it would be, but to take care he
was not deceived when it came to judging.   The result was
always as in the previous experiment.   That is, the influence
of the expectation predominated, so that when touched by one
point he would perceive two if he had been led to expect two;
and when touched by two, set farther apart than was necessary
for perceiving them as two ordinarily, he would perceive them
as one if told to expect one.

Judgments of two might often be changed into judgments of
one by inserting a dull pencil point between the compass knobs.
Similarly a judgment of one could often be changed into two by
touching the arm in some other place.   The extra touch seeming to suggest the doubleness of the stimulus without itself being clearly perceived or localized.

The absence of connection between the judgment of twoness
and other judgments—area, position, etc.—as well as its great
susceptibility to suggestion, both direct and indirect, seemed to
point to the whole thing being nothing but a matter of simple association.   We learn that a certain kind of sensation means two
points, just as we learn that certain marks mean the letter H,
that another group of sensations means 'book,' etc.   If this
were true it ought to be possible to establish any arbitrary association desired—to train a person so that he would call one two

and two one. To test this the following experiment was tried:
Beginning with the points far enough apart to be readily perceived as two, the subject is practiced in discriminating this sort
of contact from that of one point. The touch from two points
is made by a rather sharp blow, and in one region of the arm;
while that from one is made more by a pressure, and in an adjoining portion of the arm. Gradually the double points are
brought nearer together. The moment the subject shows a tendency to call them one they must be separated farther again
and approached more gradually. When the two points have
in this way been brought very near—I always waited until
they were within one-fourth inch of each other—the position and character of the touches are reversed. That is, the
double points are now *pressed* down, and in the place where
the single point was formerly applied, while the single touch
is made with a blow, and in the place where at the start the
double touch was made. Under these circumstances the judgment reverses, two is called one, and one two. That is, the
peculiarities of the sensation due to the method of application, and the locality, have completely superseded those due to
the number of points, as a basis for the judgment. Generalizing, we might say: any cutaneous sensation may give rise to a
perception of two contacts, if the past experience of the individual has established the proper associations. That we commonly do not make errors in this regard is due to favorable past
experience. An artificial environment might educate us entirely
otherwise.

Coming back to our original question—the process by which
improvement comes about, and its general bearing on the theory
of cutaneous sensations—we may say that it cannot be traced to
a refinement of our power to localize, or to a refinement of, or
an establishment of relations with, our judgments of distance or
area. Simple direct association between the sensation produced
by two points, and the idea of two points has been shown to be
perfectly capable of explaining the phenomena. That it actually
is the cause is a conclusion that seems almost forced upon us.
But this particular judgment is so intimately connected with other
cutaneous judgments—position, area, etc.—so probable is it that

what holds for one holds also for the others, that it would seem well to postpone a verdict until they have been similarly investigated and shown to obey similar laws. This I hope to be able to show in the near future. Meanwhile we may give a provisional answer, at least, to the second of our questions. Since any cutaneous sensation may be judged two if the proper associations are established, then our *perception* of *two-touches,* even though obtained through sensations of touch only, must involve other elements. The elements of number and space which enter into the complete presentation must be non-cutaneous, that is, associated with the activity of a different portion of the brain from that immediately connected with the nerves from the skin.

B. STUDIES IN SENSATION AND JUDGMENT.[1]

BY EDGAR A. SINGER, JR., ASSISTANT.

I. DIFFERENTIATION OF SENSE ORGANS.

A group of coördinated experiments was conducted with the view of determining how far the process of differentiating the physiological bases of sensation could be carried. These included the sensory fields of touch, pain, temperature, taste and sight. The limits of the present contribution compel us to confine ourselves to the first three of these fields as perhaps the most interesting.

a. Touch and Pain.

The results of Goldscheider, Frey, Nagel, Dessoir and others have given a decided impetus to the investigation of the peripheral apparatus connected with the senses of touch and pain.

---

[1] This and the following studies are the partial outcome of a course given to the undergraduates of Harvard University during the Winter and Spring of 1896. In permitting them to be published I am conscious of the comparatively elementary character of the work and of the little that it offers in the way of real conclusions. Nevertheless, it occasionally presents new points of view, and, where this is not the case, the care with which the experiments were performed renders them, I think, worthy of consideration as confirmatory evidence in fields where such is greatly needed.

E. A. S., JR.

With these results before us, a series of experiments was instituted with a view to the answering of the following questions:
1. Can points be found possessing consistently different thresholds of touch, and, if so, how great a difference of threshold
is to be found? 2. A precisely similar question with respect
to pain. 3. Do points bearing similar threshold relations for
touch and pain coincide? For example, is a point sensitive to
touch also sensitive to pain, and so on? 4. Can the threshold
values of touch and pain be made to vary independently? 5.
Are there any constant conditions of distribution?

Two groups of experiments were conducted: the first rather
preliminary in nature and broader in scope, but accurate enough
to deserve mention; the second conducted with greater refinement and confining itself to the pain-sense. The apparatus in
the two series was the same, to wit: a delicately poised balance
beam, on one end of which was fastened sometimes a bristle,
sometimes a fine jeweler's needle. The arcs through which the
beam swung were marked upon a graduated scale. By dis-
placing the beam through a constant arc, releasing it and allowing it to swing freely toward a position of equilibrium, very
constant conditions of applying the stimulus were obtained.
The portion of the body operated upon (the back of the hand,
or the volar surface of the arm) was laid in a clay cast and
held firmly in such a position that the end of the bristle or the
point of the needle would just make contact with it when the
balance was in equilibrium.

In the preliminary series above mentioned a small portion
of the skin (a rhomb of 4 x 6 mm. about) was selected on the
back of the hand. In this region eleven spots were located by
minute peculiarities of the skin, for the most part revealed only
by the use of a lens. No ink was used in marking these
points on the hand: the spots were plotted on paper and
designated by numbers. This region was gone over in two
ways: first with a bristle and then with a jeweler's needle.
Each point was stimulated from fifteen to twenty times in each
way; the experiments extending over a number of days. The
series was completed with one subject only, although the
experiments performed on other subjects gave no cause to

doubt our main conclusions. When the bristle was used, various arcs of fall were first tried until one was found (2° 30′) which sometimes yielded a sensation, sometimes remained unfelt. When the needle was used, several arcs (10°, 7°, 5°) fulfilled these conditions; and all were used, the average result of the three being taken. The results obtained may be graphically represented as in Fig. 1. The numbers on the horizontal line

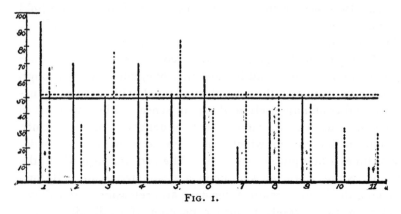

FIG. 1.

stand for the eleven points selected for investigation. Of the two lines corresponding to each point the full line represents the percentage of times the application of the bristle yielded a sensation of touch; the dotted line, the percentage of times stimulation by the needle yielded pain. The horizontal full line represents the average percentage of times the bristle yielded a sensation at the points touched; the horizontal dotted line, the average percentage of times the needle produced pain at the same points. We may take these percentages as measures of the sensitiveness of the points to touch and to pain stimuli respectively. The threshold of each kind of sensation and the mean of these are only capable of comparison *inter se.* All that we wish to determine is whether points possessing more than average sensitiveness to touch coincide with those possessing more than average sensitiveness to pain and *vice versa.*

It is exceedingly difficult to obtain consistent results when we vary the conditions of time as they should be varied, keeping only the points touched as nearly as possible constant. The latter presents a most difficult problem, and is, probably, the chief source of variation. The results, therefore, must be accepted with all the reserve that is naturally inspired by an average of considerably varying elements. Nevertheless, until we obtain more satisfactory evidence, the following view of the problem may be conservative enough, and within the limits of observation. To our first two questions we should say that differences of threshold of pain and touch respectively do exist corresponding to fixed points of the skin, and that these differences are considerable enough to be easily noticeable. To our third question we should answer : the minimal and maximal thresholds of touch and of pain respectively cannot be readily shown to coincide locally and probably do not coincide.[1]

As the most general formula for the results so far obtained we might say : the sensitiveness to touch and the sensitiveness to pain are not identical functions of position. Our fourth question raises the query as to whether the sensitiveness to touch and to pain respectively are similar functions of some other variable. One variable factor that at once suggests itself is the condition of the skin. The variation of this factor with the location of the point touched (*e. g.*, location in a furrow, or on a ridge), we shall discuss later. But it can be made to vary artificially for the whole region by softening the skin with warm water, soap and glycerine. Under these conditions the threshold for touch was quite noticeably raised, though apparently not for all points. The few experiments tried on the threshold of pain under these conditions showed it to be lowered. A more complete research in this direction is needed; but these results were fairly marked. If they are correct we could answer our fourth question in the affirmative. The sensitiveness to touch and to pain respectively can be made to vary independently; the sensitiveness to touch varying inversely, that to pain directly with the softness of the skin covering the parts affected.

---

[1] An exception should be made in the case of the point marked 1. This point was sensitive both to touch and to pain. It was, however, a singular point, lying at the base of the longest hair of the region and at the junction of several furrows. It could be compared with points described by Goldscheider and interpreted by him as being the seat of a number of close-lying points of different specific nature, such as at other locations we find separated.

In the second series of experiments (conducted by Messrs. Kline and Parker) a refinement was introduced in the method of mapping the surface experimented upon. To this the 'buttered' side of a glass slide covered with melted paraffine was applied. The paraffine froze upon striking the skin, and not the slightest furrow escaped the paraffine 'print.' The print was then transferred to paper by means of a pantograph, thus being enlarged to any convenient size. The general method of experimenting was the same as before, only the jeweler's needle being used and only the threshold of pain investigated. We need therefore only describe the conclusions reached after a large number of experiments.

1. After increasing the intensity of the stimulus beyond the threshold of touch, one of two results was obtained. Either (a) the increased intensity gave only touch even after blood was drawn, or (b) the touch sensation merged into pain.

2. Points exceedingly sensitive to pain gave this sensation with an intensity of stimulus very slightly above that which marked the threshold of touch.

3. The points sensitive to pain were distributed in a characteristic way. Calling those points that gave only touch with considerable intensities of stimulus (corresponding to areas of from 15°–22°) non-sensitive, and those points that gave pain for low intensities of stimulus (5°–10°) sensitive points, the following facts of distribution were revealed: 97% of non-sensitive points were on the elevations of the part investigated, 3% were in the furrows; 73.5% of the sensitive points were in the furrows, 26.5 were on the elevations. Thus it will be seen that sensitive points are more numerous in the furrows of the skin; non-sensitive points mostly confined to the elevations.

To these definitely objective results may be added those which depend upon the introspection of the subject. In this way the following points were brought out:

1. In the field of touch it is perfectly possible to distinguish between ordinary touch and pressure (the 'kernel-like' feeling of Goldscheider). We did not succeed in obtaining consistent results showing these sensations to be permanently attached to definite points, but it is not improbable that a more extended

research would prove them to be so. However that may be, the difference was only such as could, in the opinion of the subjects, be explained by the structure of the skin at the point affected.

2. The qualities of pain produced at sensitive points were quite different. They were called 'acute,' 'aching,' 'numbing,' 'pricking,' 'tingling.' These different qualities were fairly characteristic of the point touched and did not replace each other to any great extent.

3. Nearly every pain was preceded, or succeeded, or both, by an itching or tingling not to be found in touch points. Sometimes the tingling would remain alone without pain, but usually at a point that was in the habit of yielding pain.

4. Pain could thus follow touch or tingling after a considerable interval, but when it was of the 'acute' kind seemed to be just as immediate as touch.

No theory of the physiological basis of touch and pain could be deduced from such results as the preceding alone. Such a theory must, we feel, take into account a much larger range of facts, notably those connected with the independent variation, under pathological conditions, of the touch and pain senses. It may be well, however, to point out a few theoretical inferences from our experiments: 1. From the fact that the threshold of touch is raised for some points by softening of the skin, while that of the pain points is lowered; from the fact that pain points are more numerous in the furrows where the skin is softer; and, if Goldscheider's observation is true, from the fact that touch points are more numerous on the elevations where the skin is harder; it would seem that touch is dependent, not only on the nervous equipment of the skin at any point, but also upon its ability to conduct the stimulus to surrounding points. Thus touch might quite well be possible at a point from which pain (under proper conditions) was absent, without showing that a nerve could be sensitive to touch that was not sensitive to pain. 2. On the other hand, any theory that tried to identify the nerves of touch and of pain would have to show that the points of greatest sensitiveness to the one sensation were also unusually sensitive to the other. For while the fact that conditions of the skin which render it a better conductor of stimuli may increase the sensitiveness to touch of certain points not provided with nerve endings (much as a small coin placed on the skin would transmit a slight pressure better than would a bit of dough under the same conditions), yet it does not seem plausible merely to identify touch points with points of best conduction. It would not, for example, seem probable that a point supposed, on the ground that it was unusually sensitive to pain, to be provided with an easily stimulated nerve-ending, would be less sensitive to touch than some hard part of the skin which yields touch by transmitting the stimulus to several nerve-endings. It would seem to require greater energy to set all this machinery in motion than to affect one slightly protected nerve-ending.

So far as our experiments go, then, we regard them as pointing toward a discreteness of the end apparatus of touch and pain. The explanation of the different ' timbres' of pains (their ' acute,' 'tingling,' 'aching' etc. character,) would require a much more general discussion than would be here in place. We can only suspect that we are here dealing with a more complex sensation than mere touch or mere pain, but that it is not yet necessary to suppose a specific apparatus to explain these peculiarities of sensation.

b. Temperature-sense.

The now well-known results of Goldscheider[1] formed the basis of a series of experiments on the temperature sense. While the grosser results of this investigator are now largely accepted, those who have tried to confirm his more refined (and perhaps more important) conclusions have realized the difficulty attending such an effort—a difficulty that has been recently expressed as an impossibility by Dessoir.[2] In such a field the testimony of many observers is needed.

After trying various kinds of apparatus the original metal cylinders of Goldscheider were found to afford the most satisfactory means of applying the stimulus. These cylinders were heated in water at 36° C. for locating warm spots, and cooled

---

[1] Goldscheider, Archiv f. Physiologie, '89.
[2] Dessoir, Archiv f. Physiologie, '92.

in a similar way to 3–4° C. for locating the cold spots. The surfaces investigated were on the back of the hand and on the volar surface of the arm.

The investigators (Messrs. Marsh and Mathews) found the arrangement of the spots as Goldscheider has described it. The spots radiate from centres at which they are relatively numerous. The centres of the cold spots usually lie close to, or coincide with, the centres of the warm spots. The cold spots are, on the whole, more numerous, they react more quickly and are more easily located. Again, both cold and warm spots seem to vary *inter se* in the strength of their reactions. Their sensitiveness differs at different times.

The investigators regard as the chief interest of their experiment the results of applying mechanical and electrical stimuli to the spots already located by a temperature stimulus. The mechanical stimuli used were the metal cylinder before described, but kept at a mean temperature, and a slender wooden splinter, with a cork tip of the same size as the blunt point of the metal cylinder. By a slight pressure upon the temperature spots already located (and marked in Goldscheider's way with dilute ink), warmth and cold were experienced at the warm and cold spots respectively. The same success attended the experiments with electrical stimulation. The stimulus was applied by means of an electric needle, the point of which was brought lightly in contact with the temperature spot; a weak current, just failing to give the usual tickling sensation, being employed. Both mechanical and electrical stimuli were tried only on the spots that had before proved most responsive. In every case, however, in which they were tried, they succeeded.

Finally, the analgesic nature of the temperature-spots was investigated. In every case one point within the spot was found which would bear a heavy weight on a stimulating needle without yielding pain. The needle point being, of course, much smaller than the spot of ink marking the temperature spot, it was necessary to experiment within this area for some time before an analgesic point was found. In no case, however, did the investigators fail to find such a point.

As a result of their experiments the investigators feel that

Goldscheider's results are generally reproducible. It is beyond the scope of the present communication to comment upon his deductions from these data.[1]

II. Intensity.

With the advance of psychology more and more attention is being given to questions relating to the nature of Intensity of sensations. Not only have the meanings of 'threshold' and of 'difference threshold' frequently been discussed (of which later), but the nature of the concept of intensity itself has been treated in new ways (*e. g.*, by Münsterberg). Experimental psychology has so far had little to do in the discussion, which has remained theoretical in character. It is possible, however, that the laboratory, by investigating the conditions upon which variations in the judgment of intensity depend, may contribute something to the settlement of the problem.

The facts that find expression in some such law as that of Weber, whatever may be their ultimate meaning, at least reveal this : that between the point at which a stimulus is administered, and that at which a judgment of its intensity is pronounced, a certain factor enters into the result which, for brevity's sake, we may call ' subjective.' The search for this subjective factor has largely confined itself to imagining ways in which the energy represented by the physical stimulus might be lost before setting in motion the apparatus of judgment. It seems plausible, however, to suppose that the physiological effect of every stimulation is not merely to excite some special sensory nerve, but to produce a profound change in the entire organism, and, further, that the judgment of the nature of the stimulus must have for its physiological basis these secondary effects of stimulation as well as the primary one of the specific sensory excitation. It is impossible to say, *a priori*, how fully such secondary effects as these represent that which we have above called the ' subjective '

---

[1]One must always hesitate to say that suggestion has played no part in such experiments as those here described.   A subject sufficiently trained to be a reliable observer of the delicate phenomena involved must also have become familiar with the results of past workers in the field.   We can only say that, so far as a conscientious effort to be unbiassed effects freedom from suggestibility, the experiments here recorded are as reliable as can well be hoped for.

factor in the judgment of intensity. It cannot be without interest, then, to examine the way in which variations of the physiological reaction to a stimulus affect the judgment of the intensity of the stimulus. The reaction must, of course, be a very general and a very subtle one. Nevertheless, we may take simple types of it in the form of pronounced and readily measurable reflexes. A series of experiments along this line we shall proceed to describe.

Judgment of Intensity as Affected by Involuntary Reactions to Stimulus.

In this series, conducted by Messrs. Dearborn and Gaylord, use was made of the well-known phenomenon of the knee-jerk. The apparatus, being similar to that used by all experiments in this line, needs no description. The jerk in the vertical plane was selected as being most convenient for the purpose. About 300 experiments were made, each consisting of a pair of stimuli, one being kept constant, the other being made equal to, greater or less than this normal. The subject was directed to estimate the intensity of the second stimulus with respect to the first. The experiments were made upon three subjects, one of whom was throughout ignorant of the object of the experiment. Sometimes the squeezing of a hand dynamometer was found useful for increasing the general innervation. The specific object of the investigation was to find how far the relative lengths of the jerks accompanying the two stimuli determined a subject's judgment of the relative intensities of the blows.

In examining the results there are two cases to be considered. Either (1) the relation of the second kick to the first was the same as the relation of the second stimulus to the first, or (2) the relation of the second kick to the first was different from that of the second stimulus to the first.

Examining now the distribution of the right and the wrong judgments, the following facts are revealed: (1) Of the right judgments, 71% were in cases in which the relations between the stimuli were the same as the relations between the kicks; in 29% they were different. (2) Of the wrong judgments, in the cases in which the relations between the stimuli were different from the relations between the kicks, 93% were in accord with the relations between the kicks, only 7% were contrary thereto. In brief, then, an agreement between the relations of the stimuli and those of the kicks increases the percentage of right judgments; in the case of a disagreement between the two the judgments, under the conditions of the experiment, showed a far greater tendency to be determined by the relations of the kicks than by those of the stimuli.

There are three possible interpretations of these results. Either (1) the physiological conditions that favor a greater kick include the conditions of a heightened sensibility, or (2) the association between a larger reaction and a more intense stimulus being established, the influence of the kick upon the judgment of intensity involves a more or less direct inference from our psychological experience, or (3) our concept of intensity contains as an immediate element, the muscular sensations arising from our adaptation or reaction to the stimulus.

The first explanation finds nothing to support it in what little we know of the physiology of the knee-jerk. While it is not at all an impossible hypothesis, it is not a necessary one, and confirmation of it can scarcely be hoped for. The second hypothesis is a perfectly possible explanation, and finds analogies in many of our psychological experiences. For example, when a large object of the same weight as a small one is judged to be heavier we have the influence of an association of this kind. The third hypothesis must exist for the present as a mere speculation, and our attitude toward the phenomenon will depend, for the present, largely upon the theoretical stand we take respecting the nature of intensity in general. It can only be said that the phenomenon would be of the nature we should expect if one of the chief 'subjective' factors in our judgment of intensity were the reaction of the organism to the stimulus; for here we find the variations of that reaction to be the chief determinant of variations of the judgments.

III. Judgment.

There is, perhaps, no problem calculated to throw more light upon the psychology of judgment than that of the nature of a difference threshold. Attempts to fix the meaning of the term have robbed it of that confidence reposed in it by the older psycho-physicists. The essentially relative nature of the concept has been insisted upon by Wundt[1]; in a still more thorough-going way by Fullerton and Cattell[2] and a mean position, seeking to define in more careful terms the meaning of the much used term ' just noticeable' stimulus or difference of stimuli has been adopted by Schumann[3]. We have found it helpful to treat the judgment simply as a reaction. The organism is affected by a certain kind of stimulus. We find the organism reacts in several ways to the stimulus, one of which ways may be the expression of a judgment. Between these two objective facts lies a chain of events within the organism of which we know little, but whose nature we may be led to suspect by introducing new factors and noting the variations resulting. One form of variations concerns the time elapsing between stimulus and the reaction, which reaction may express, in some form or other, a judgment. Another variation concerns the amount of stimulus that is required to produce a given kind of judgment. So far we are not dealing with theory, but simply trying to obtain a general expression of the facts of the case.

Our work was confined to the judgment of differences. This is only an apparent limitation, since all judgments are judgments of difference. Whether we say that there is a difference in intensity between two tones presented to us, or that a book is before us, we are in both cases dealing with judgments of difference. Only, in the latter case the judgment is more complex, involves more comparisons, some of them with that which is not immediately given. Turning then to the problem of the judgment of difference as the most general that we can consider, the question arises as to the nature of a threshold. Evidently our only objective criterion for the fact that a difference is perceived, or rather what we mean by a difference being perceived, is that the subject reacts to it correctly. Thus, he says that a difference is be-

---

[1] Wundt, Grundzüge. 4 te Auf. V. 1, p. 397.

[2] Fullerton and Cattell, Perceptions of Small Differences, p 11.

[3] Schumann, Zeitschrift f. Physiologie u. Psychologie d. Sinnesorgane. V. 6, p. 476.

fore him, or he imitates the difference in some way, or he indicates a difference a certain percentage of the times that one is presented. Now it does not follow that all these kinds of reaction are ' set off,' or discharged, by the same degree of difference between the stimuli. To say that a subject reacts rightly, although he does not perceive the difference presented, means that one kind of reaction is set off by less difference than is another (the vocal expression of a judgment, for example). The various ways in which the judgment is expressed give in turn, as is known, different values for the threshold.[1]

Just such variations as these are significant. It would be a wrong conception of the nature of a threshold to suppose them to be accidental errors to be eliminated, or to suppose that any one result came more near to being some ' real' threshold value than any other. The discrepancy arises from the fact that what we call a judgment of difference is not of the same psychological nature in each case. If we analyze the intra-organic elements that enter into a judgment-reaction we may roughly divide them into the centripetal (sense organs, directly or sympathetically involved, conducting tract, etc.); the centrifugal (*e. g.*, motor coördination involved in expressing a judgment); and the central (the perceptive background upon which the stimulus falls). The first two factors interest us only in so far as we must keep them constant while examining the third. Our problem is: How may the central apparatus of judgment be varied?

a. Preperception.

An element that has been found to affect the quickness of our reaction to a stimulus suggests itself as probably having an influence upon the sensitiveness of this reaction. This element it is convenient to call *preperception, i. e.,* an expectation, the psychological elements of which we need not stop to analyze, of the kind of stimulus that is to be presented. Experiments involving this factor can be arranged in a great variety of ways. We confined ourselves to a very simple and, therefore, a very difficult case. Ordinary series of experiments for the purpose

[1] Cf. the extensive work of Merkel on psycho-physical methods. **Wundt's** Phil. Stud.

of determining the difference-thresholds of intensity and of pitch of sound were instituted. In a number of successive sets the kinds of difference presented, and hence the possible kinds of judgment, were increased in variety. There were four types of experiments including :

I. Difference of intensity in one direction; *i. e.*, the subject knew that the test stimulus would be always greater (or always less) than the normal.

II. Difference of intensity in two directions (*i. e.*, greater and less).

III. Difference of pitch in two directions (*i. e.*, higher and lower).

IV. Difference of intensity and difference of pitch, each in two directions:

It will be seen that in I there was only one possible judgment of difference. In II and III there were two; in IV there were four possible judgments of difference. The subject was always asked to compare the two stimuli in all the respects in which they could differ. The apparatus used was a tuning fork (Ut₄) the prong of which was struck by a rubber hammer falling through a vertical arc. The intensity was varied by changing the arc, while the pitch was altered 2 or 4 vibrations per second by placing a piece of wax on the prong. The experiments were performed on two subjects, whose results we shall give together, since they are of the same kind. In each series the similar stimuli and each kind of difference were given in equal numbers. The number of experiments was not equal in all the series, the lowest number being 250 in series III. The following table gives the percentage of right judgments of sameness and difference in each series :

| | Intensity. | | Number |
	Same.	Different.	of Possibilities.
I.	71.5	57.5	1
II.	61.0	56.3	2
IV.	41.3	44.5	4

| | Pitch. | | Number |
	Same.	Different.	of Possibilities.
III.	79.0	49.8	2
IV.	71.8	32.5	4

From this table it will be seen that the greater the number of possibilities of judgment the less the accuracy of the judgment or the higher the threshold. To present this as a set formula we might say: the sensitiveness to differences between stimuli varies inversely with the number of possibilities of judgment presented. A parallel formula has already been stated connecting the quickness of discriminating reactions with the numbers of possibilities presented. And the two would seem to have similar theoretical explanations. Every perception involves a combination with the stimulus of a concept prepared by past experience. A stimulus is above the threshold that is sufficiently strong to set in motion the central mechanism that corresponds to this concept. Usually the number of concepts likely to be aroused by any stimulus is only limited by the context of events into which the stimulation has entered: in the experiment we still further limit this number. In proportion as we limit it do we lower the threshold value of the stimulus. In our present experiment it is, of course, with the difference between stimuli, each of which is perfectly noticeable, that we are dealing. The concept in question, then, is that of a kind of difference, and it is the number of these concepts likely to be awakened that we limit. But as before stated, the fact that the judgment is given as a judgment of difference does not change the nature of the problem.

b. *General and Specific Judgments.*

The last experiment, showing the effect of the psychological factor of preparation, leads to a new question. However great the number of differences presented in such a series as the preceding, *i. e.*, however numerous the possibilities that offer themselves to a subject at every choice, there yet remain two factors constant throughout, to wit: sameness and difference. The question arises whether, in case we could in some way obtain judgments that correspond to difference in general and compare with these judgments of particular kinds of difference obtained under the same conditions of stimulations, we should find the two classes to possess different threshold values. It was with this question that we sought to deal.

A few observations drawn from every-day life may be appropriate by way of introduction. It is well known that where differences exist, comparatively slight in nature, between objects of considerable complexity of structure (such as human faces) one may be quite aware of a difference without being able to tell in what the difference consists. And this is not merely owing to our lack of a name for this particular kind of difference, for we may afterwards recognize it in the color of the eyes, the size of a feature, etc.,—differences that are easily describable. Have we here a mere anomaly, or a phenomenon deeply pervading our mental life?

Again, one may quite frequently, when expecting a certain kind of difference, react to another kind. The reaction is right in so far as there is some kind of difference presented; it is wrong in judging what that kind is. A series of experiments will illustrate and confirm this statement. With a small dynamometer provided with a blunt point, the skin on the volar side of the arm was pressed. The series of 250 experiments upon a subject unacquainted with the object of the experiment included 100 in which there was no difference between a normal stimulus and a second stimulus which the subject was asked to compare with it; 75 in which there was a slight difference of pressure, and 75 in which the same pressure was administered at a slightly different point. Both of these differences were below what is ordinarily called the threshold. The subject was informed that the experiment was designed to determine the threshold of difference of location, and that the stimuli would sometimes be the same and would sometimes differ in location. The judgments were always given as same or different in location. The following table gives the percentages of judgments of sameness and difference :—

Judgments.

		Same.	Different in Location.
	Same.	69.	31.
Stimuli.	Dif. in Location.	40.	60.
	Dif. in Pressure.	57.	43.

There were then 43 % of the stimuli that did not differ in location, but differed slightly in pressure, that were judged to

be different in location. But so were there 31 % of stimuli
that differed in neither that yet were judged to be different in
location. The difference between these, viz. 12 %, represents
the percentage of times in which the subject was led by the
presence of an unexpected difference to judge that an expected
one was presented. This judgment was right in its general,
wrong in its particular character. Examining the subject afterward revealed the fact that she was ignorant of any differences,
save those of location, having been present.

　The problem of the relation between the thresholds of general
and of specific judgments of difference may be approached in
several ways. The simplest way that suggests itself would be
to conduct two series of experiments,—in one of which the subject would be asked to judge whether or not a difference were
present, in the other of which he would be required to pronounce upon the kind of difference; several different kinds
being included in each case. This would, of course, presuppose
an ability on the part of the subject to distinguish consistently
between the awareness of difference and the awareness of a
special kind of difference. It must be confessed at the outset
that the absence of such an ability would by no means settle
the question. Still, since it is impossible to pronounce upon
such a question *a priori*, a series of experiments was conducted
with the view of seeing how far such a distinction between
general and specific judgments was possible.

　The experiments were conducted by Messrs. Holt and
Southard, the apparatus used being the same tuning fork struck
by a falling hammer that was before described. Differences
of intensity were obtained, as before, by varying the arc of fall,
differences of pitch by placing a small piece of wax at different
heights upon the prong of the fork. The subject was asked to
judge between the stimuli varying in intensity and in pitch.
There were two subjects; upon each of which were performed
400 experiments, arranged to eliminate the effects of practice
and of over-estimation. They were divided into two sets,—in
the first of which the subject was asked to decide simply whether
the stimuli were alike or different; in the second of which he
was required to pronounce upon the specific differences presented

(*i. e.*, greater or less intensity, higher or lower pitch, in any combination). Calling the first set general judgments, the second specific, the results may be classified as follows, the figures giving the percentages of correct judgments.

Subject.	General.	Specific.
S.	70.0	74.0
H.	74.4	82.7
Mean.	72.2	78.4

It would seem from these results that, so far as a voluntary attempt to distinguish between the general and the specific elements in judgment is concerned, the advantage of sensitiveness is somewhat in favor of the latter. The introspective testimony of the subjects may suggest a reason for this. " It would seem to both subjects that to look for general differences and not to perceive specific was as easy as looking for a star with the eyes voluntarily closed. The subjects could not voluntarily assume the attitude of mind for perceiving general differences. The subject asked to make general judgments really made specific. All he could do to assume the ' attitude ' was to think vaguely of nothing and to relax his attention. Thus the less accuracy of the general judgment as compared (in the above table) with the specific is accounted for."

But, though a voluntary effort to distinguish between the general and the specific element in judgment may not, in general, be successful; yet it does not follow that a subject may not react more sensitively to difference in general than to specific difference, although every reaction, taking the form of an articulate judgment, should assume in consciousness a specific character. With a view of investigating this question another plan was adopted.

Three series of experiments were made: the first including differences of intensity and of pitch of sounds; the second, differences of pressure and of location of touch; the third, differences of color, of size, and of form of figures drawn on cards. The subject was made aware of the kinds of difference that would be presented to him and was asked to pass judgment, comparing the stimuli in all respects in which they could differ.

There are, then, five kinds of judgment with which an analysis of the results obtained must deal:

1. Similar stimuli judged to be the same.
2. Similar stimuli judged to be different.
3. Different stimuli judged to be the same.
4. Different stimuli judged to be different, including those in which the specific nature of the difference was wrongly judged.
5. Different stimuli judged to be different and in which the specific nature of difference was rightly judged.

If the vertical columns contain the judgments, the horizontal lines the relations of the stimuli judged, we may represent the five classes in the following way:—

Judgments.

Stimuli.	Same.	Different.	Spe. Diff. rightly judged
Same.	100–*a*	*a*	
Different.	100–*b*	*b*	*c*

a=percentage of similar stimuli judged to be different.

b= " " different " " " "

c= " " " " in which the specific difference was rightly judged.

If *b*=*a* the difference between the stimuli is too slight to be noticed.

If *c*=*b* the difference between the stimuli is so great as to be always distinguishable.

In general a series can be arranged in which *b* will be greater than *a* and less than *c*. This simply shows that the difference between the stimuli influences the judgment to some extent and that mistakes as to the kind of difference sometimes occur. But the fact that such mistakes occur does not of itself prove that the presence of a difference has influenced the judgment, while the specific nature of that difference has remained without effect. For the varying conditions, physiological or other, that would make similar stimuli appear different might (and generally would) also be sufficient to make one kind of a difference appear as another. We have, however, a datum that enables us to eliminate this factor. For we know the percentage of times that objectively similar stimuli are judged to be different in a certain specific way, and this percentage, whatever the cause of its existence, must be at least as great as that which represents the proportion of perverted judgments of difference. For example, a sound would be judged to be greater than another sound of the same objective intensity at least as often as would a sound of less intensity. The only class, then, of perverted judgments of specific difference that we can use in showing that differences may produce a correct reaction when the specific kind of difference remains without influence on the judgment, is that which remains after we have subtracted the percentage to be accounted for by mistaken judgments of similar stimuli.

From these considerations we derive the following formulæ —in which x stands for the general judgments of the nature sought; p for the correct particular judgments not explainable by chance; n for the number of possible judgments of difference presented; a, b and c having the same significance as before:

$$b = a + p + x$$
$$c = \frac{a}{n} + p + \frac{x}{n}$$
$$\text{then } x = \frac{n}{n-1}(b - c) - a$$

The experiments conducted yielded the following results:

I. Series including differences in pitch and intensity.

		Judgments.		
		Same.	Different.	Right Part. Dif.
Stimi.	Same	56.3	43.7	
	Different	26.1	73.9	46.4

Substituting in the above formula 43.7 for a, 73.9 for b, 46.4 for c, 2 for n (since difference in intensity and differences in pitch were the only judgments possible) we find x to be 11.3.

II. Series including differences in pressure and in location of touch.

		Judgments.		
		Same.	Different.	Right Part. Dif.
Stimi.	Same	47.5	62.5	
	Different	27.8	72.2	37.1

Substituting in formula as before (n again being 2) we find x to be 77.

III. Series including differences in form, color and size of figures. This series, carried out by Messrs. Hackett and Thorndike, required somewhat special apparatus. Figures of more or less complex shape were drawn on cards. The figures were either exactly alike, or differed in size, shape, color, or any combination of these. It would have been difficult to make the differences sufficiently slight to have yielded any considerable percentage of wrong judgments if the subject were allowed an indefinite time in which to formulate his judgment. The plan was preferred of making the differences fairly apparent, exposing them for a small fraction of a second only. This was done by fixing the card behind a pendulum provided with a screen; the screen being perforated by a window. The time of exposure was kept constant by keeping the pendulum-arc constant. The figures to be compared were exposed simultaneously. In 90 experiments the figures were alike; in 320 they differed in one of the above respects. The series yielded the following results:

Judgments.

		Same.	Different.	Right Part. Diff.
Stimi.	Same	84	16	
	Different	30.6	69.4	49.1

Since there were three possible judgments of difference, n in this series is 3, whence $x = 14.5$.

It will be seen then that in each of the above series there is a certain percentage of right judgments of difference which cannot be explained as due to chance and to complete appreciation of the particular differences presented. We may refer to this as the pure general judgment of difference. This is not the place to attempt any further interpretation of this factor. That there can be an actual content corresponding to such a factor—a mere feeling of difference in general—seems introspectively clear from observations of every-day life. That such a content was alone present in the percentage of cases that we have called pure general judgments of difference we cannot pretend. All that we can say is that the subject judged as he would have judged had this factor alone been present and had the particular determination of the judgment been an arbitrary addition of his own, not dependent upon objective conditions of stimulation. In this sense we may say that the general judgment of difference has a lower threshold than the particular.

If we ask now: What light do these facts throw upon the theory of the threshold? the following answer may be given. The main standpoint of the early psycho-physicists will seem to involve the assumption that when two stimuli were presented there was only one sense in which they differed, as also there was only one way in which this difference could be expressed by the subject. Their problem was: How great must this definite difference be in order that it may call forth this definite expression from the subject? With closer investigation of the psycho-physic methods it became apparent that a 'just noticeable' difference might mean quite a number of things, the meaning being dependent upon what was regarded as the expression of a judgment on the part of the subject. Some, like Fullerton and Cattell, would be willing to say that there was no difference so slight but that in some sense it was noticed by the subject. As the result of our own researches we feel justified in going a step further. Not only may a difference be noticeable or not, according to the way in which we define 'noticeable,' but, for any given criterion of noticeability, a difference may be noticeable or not, according to what we may mean by 'difference.' Mere difference may be noticeable at a point at which the specific kind of difference may be unnoticed. And finally, with the same criterion of noticeability, a specific kind of difference may be noticeable or not, according to purely mental preparedness of the subject to receive it. With these facts recognized, the problem of psycho-physics awaits a re-statement.

THE IDENTIFICATION OF THE SELF.

BY DR. SMITH BAKER.

Utica, New York.

While watching certain clinical cases my attention became attracted to the tenacity with which the sufferer would sometimes hold on to seemingly undesired, and many times actually harmful, strands of morbid experience. Why one should ever do that which, whether he be well or ill, will prove, in every way and all along, to be, not only detrimental, but distressing and dangerous, is, so far as I can ascertain, one of the problems of the Self not yet solved.

As the problem seems to be closely associated with, if not clearly involved in, that of self-identity, it appears probable that its successful study may be made in this vital connection, if anywhere.

The study of the process of the identification of the observed Self necessitates, primarily, the recognition of some fixed point, or permanent line, or 'innermost center within the circle,' of the normal self, from which departure can be noted. But to what phase or aspect of psychical experience shall we look for such a point of departure? The Self, when normal, seems capable of experiencing every sort and degree of conscious life, without necessarily disclosing the principle of its identity, or the limits within which it is circumscribed. But notwithstanding this, it seems to be commonly appreciable also, that there is actually somewhere in the personal summation a prime characteristic, which always focusses all the other, even wayward features, to a more or less stable density; and, moreover, that so long as this comes to pass, the Self actually stands out as a satisfactory realization—a persistent Identity not to be trespassed on, and likewise demanding notice and record. This focussing characteristic is discussed, usually, under Attention,

272

Memory, Unity, Resemblance, Synthesis, Selective Industry of the Mind, Continuity, etc.

Of the ways by which the focussing ability and its processes are accounted for in psychology, two seem to be worthy of especial consideration in this connection. One is described by saying that, upon proper stimulation, the elements of consciousness seem to ' fall together' around some one or more central characteristic, as if by their own or by its own attraction. Thus in the presence of a sensation or an idea or a motor suggestion, say of a coin, all the elements of consciousness having any predilection so to do are said to ' fall ' or ' drop' into line ; while, someway out of this process of precipitation, there arises the notion of a Self, identical with the one realized at previous times, in connection with other coins. As revealed by observation of the adult mind, this may possibly be the case, especially after the self-notion has become an automatic affair of many experiences. But the suspicion arises that, in reality, this is only a reminiscence of the early impulsive, and instinctive activities, becoming more vivid and more impressive as the later, more actively self-energizing processes are developed. And I take it that the actual worth of such a foundation of self-identity is very small in the ordinary adult life, so full of variableness, both within and without. Morever, the question as to whether one would ever have attained to a complete notion of self-identity, had this been the all of individual experience in this connection, is legitimate.

The other way in which the Self is said to become identified by itself is through some process of actual effort with which there is always associated a more or less distinct ' feeling of effort.' Here, instead of the elements of the Self simply falling together, at the suggestion of appropriate stimuli, they are determinedly pulled or forced together, by the Self, in conscious or possibly infra-conscious activity. The feeling of effort thus experienced is that of a real energizing in accordance with some preconceived purpose, or plan of self, or method of finding the self, in the midst of all the multitudinous affairs of consciousness ; while the assurance of selfhood results from the conceived possibility of searching for and successfully finding it, whenever it is designedly or necessarily thought of or needed. As such an assurance of self, it may be treated objectively, as a most important interest, and presented and represented in whatsoever way may seem most conducive to the furtherance of the interest in hand. Thus, if for a moment, the Self becomes lost, in no matter how complex a maze of experiential factors, and then has occasion to recover its identity, in order that its realization may be at the moment complete, it seems to be able to accomplish this very surely, instead of being obliged to wait the assurance which comes involuntarily, and always, as an heritage probably, of antecedent, purposeful experiences.

Psychology must necessarily deal with this phase of active energizing, no matter what its theory of origin, process, or of relative importance; for it enters into all *conscious* experience, and undoubtedly is the vital element in what is understood by volition, as distinguished analytically from other phases of psycho-motor activity. Latterly the tendency seems to have been to affirm the sense or active energizing or 'feeling of effort,' as being exclusively recognizable after, instead of before or during the event. It does not appear to be quite inclusive enough, however, to simply say that only as we are finishing, or immediately at the finish, of a volitional experience are we able thus to retrospectively cognize the feeling of effort. In every conation we seem to energize invariably and actively from the very moment when the focussing and fixating of attention begins to be effected; and as a matter of fact we are conscious from the very first of the processes involved. Immediately the ideo-motor need is responded to, whether the processes of respouse are, broadly speaking, automatic and not so clearly recognizable, or initiatory and willed, and so, more fully conscious, the feeling of effort keeps pace with the effort itself, and correspondingly feature by feature is cognized as such. Archaic as this may appear, I confess after reading and experimenting and pondering so far as I have thus been able to, my utter inability to see that any other conclusion is in accordance with the facts, at any rate as revealed in my own consciousness. Logically, how can one talk about the elements of consciousness 'falling' together, if one does not recognize the commotion engendered? But the commotion itself has in it the element of effort—admitted by everyone; the point of difference being, as to initiation, or the place in the conative processes where it emerges into consciousness.

Conceiving, then, that the elements of consciousness may either fall into or 'accrete round' an attention-focus (automatism), or else be actually brought to such a point, by conscious effort (volition), it follows that the content of the attention-focus and of the conative processes will depend largely on the degree and kind of satisfaction, which either may be anticipated in the result or purposely required of it. Probably anticipated satisfaction is never realized from purely effortful activity alone recognized as such; always there are present certain reminiscent factors, derived from past experience, and now become incorporated in the self-feeling. But volition to be volition must always include the conscious energizing for something, which something may be added to, and so be made to contribute to, the completeness of the result so largely expected as being chiefly of a ready-made character. This something—this fresh element, which we ever seek to add to the ideo-motor activity, in order that it may be satisfactorily extended and recognized—is not a Wil-'o-th'-Wisp simply luring us on so much, as a native impulsion, a central and centering line of force, or central 'line of selective industry of the mind,' inherent in our being and constituting the assurance of a 'never-lapsing ownership,' always to be recognized as such (under ordinary conditions).

Trying now to trace and describe this central-most line-point of permanent and positive energizing, one finds it very difficult to do so in one's own normal condition, for here the psychophysical mechanisms all run so smoothly and in such accurate balance that only as one for a time abnormalizes himself, as it were, can he catch even a glimpse of it, and then he is not very sure that what is revealed is not an illusion simply. It seems scarcely possible to observe accurately the normal self in this respect, save in the light of abnormality.

Letting oneself, then, postpone the hour for conclusions, until he shall have had an opportunity to study the problem in connection with his own relevant morbid experiences, and the more permanently morbid states in others, clearer visions of the innermost Self and of the processes by which it characterizes itself may possibly result, even though this source may not give one the ability to formulate what one sees or to express it fully. This certainly has been my own experience, and for that matter it is obvious enough that I am not relieved of the difficulty yet. For long, as I suppose it may have been the case with many others, I caught glimpses, more or less satisfying, of the identical and identifying Self, in the very midst of its so mysterious processes of self-identification; and many times did I find myself trying to put what I had observed into appropriate language. But it was not until while conducting a series of experiments to ascertain the ordinarily warm element of different individual minds that such glimpses became assurances that there might be obtained actual evidence of a universal, more or less graspable, something, which had no business to forever escape clear apprehension and description. Granting latitude for individual type influence, people seemed to resemble one another in the way by which they bring about the attention focus; and also in the way by which they lose the ability to bring it to pass in abnormal conditions. If "the only point that is obscure is the act of appropriation itself" (James), then it began to seem to me that this very act was submitting itself to observation and was challenging some one to see and understand.

Would the studies of Professor Royce on 'Imitation' and those of Professor Baldwin on 'Mental Development' apply here; and likewise would more detailed studies of some of the patients which I happened to have on hand throw any light on the subject of the principle or process of personal identity, normal or abnormal? Whether so or not, I soon found myself under the spell of these discussions and groping about in the psychological field for cues and confirmations and helps of every kind so much needed. Applying the principle of imitation to many of the phases of misery under observation, and seeking etiological information under its guidance, and then trying to bring about curative results in the same way, I soon had to confess that never before, had things worked so easily and with such clearness of view. Conceiving that through imitation of outside copies the mental processes were always being effected in definite ways, and in a centrifugal manner, so to speak, why not conceive that imitation of a self copy, derived secondarily from the primary not-self copy, should constitute, through a centripetal determination, the very act of appropriation, the self-identifying act which was the object of search? Especially did this notion seem to be required in connection with the origin, development, and course of certain diseases, and even more so still in connection with the most obstinate non-response to therapeutical measures, encountered so frequently. Here it sometimes becomes very apparent, that each section of the self-experience stream determinedly hugs to itself, and adopts and incorporates, not only whatever happens to be imitable from without, but likewise something called up, as it were, from within, and patterned after as closely as attendant circumstances admit. This, that is called up, serves as a veritable copy (or if not, why not?). The trigger pulled by suggestional impact, all the explosive energy of the Self endeavors purposely, if you please, to mimic the last, or, if not this, then some other past self-summation, in just as close feature as possible. The Process of Energizing, if we could personify it, might be said to actually call up the characteristics of the past-self, and to imitate them accordingly. And this process of energizing, this actual mimicry of Self, might be said to really constitute the process, the fact of self-identity, everywhere and always, and moreover to be recognizable as such.

The outcome of this was embodied in a paper read by abstract before the American Neurological Association and now published in full,[1] and which elucidates this general conclusion: that imitation of an extra-personal copy constitutes the initiation of many disease processes; while imitation of a self-developed and self-summated copy constitutes the process by which they so persistently and so obstinately perpetuate themselves either continuously or recurrently. This idea of the perpetuating of a self-set copy derived primarily from a non-self copy, in an imitation series, prolonged either until the original impelling force is spent or until inhibited, deviated, or overcome by the counter-

---

[1] *The Journal of Nervous and Mental Diseases*, New York, March, 1896.

acting influence of some more forceful copy originally derived
in its own turn from without, has grown with subsequent observation, and seems to be especially applicable as thus noted to
instances of hysteria, neurasthenia, hypochondria, psychalgia,
imperative conceptions, and impulses, and the like, and likewise to be of much service not only in comprehending their development and nature, but in instituting and conducting methods
of treatment.

But observation in this lump sort of way and under pressure
of clinical necessity is not exactly of the modern experimental
kind, and I suppose no psychologist gives much attention to results obtained in this way. So the need of more accurate experimentation came to be appreciated; and this prompted to
various attempts to either verify, modify or annul, if need be, a
conclusion so taking and seemingly so serviceable.

In order to do this I trained the attention to focus itself upon
the feeling of effort when coupled with the feeling of satisfaction derived from effort of the right kind; for I conceived this
to constitute the ' me-feeling,' the personal assurance, the innermost indication of normal psycho-physical activity, in myself, if
not in others of a different type. At first I simply watched for
that element in the passing multifarious self-experience which,
common to all, might appear always to savor most thoroughly
of the self-fact; and naturally I looked for evidence of unity
as probably being this most surely. But soon it did not seem
that *unity* of consciousness was what I would better search for
after all, for in me, at any rate, there were to be noted, even during
my most active moments, unquestionable gaps; in fact, that between the succeeding pulses of consciousness, so far as introspection could determine, there were unconscious blanks which
must be included in any attempt to account for a continuing persistent self-identity. Of course, this does not deny conscious
unity to others, or the most persistent sub-conscious activity in
myself; but it does affirm that in my own consciousness blanks
are to be discovered and recognized as such retrospectively,
and that if each section or pulse of consciousness actually en-
gages in 'hugging to itself and adopting the past selves'
(James) it does so across certain definite hiatuses, and so does

not admit of my saying exactly that the Self as ' a closed individual' is evidenced by consciousness in this particular way. ' The inexplicable tie' is in me not of this order seemingly, so far as I have been able to discern, and continuity of self-assurance does not thus express itself as a fact.

Admitting, then, tentatively the introspective revelation that each nascent thought appropriates the past thought across an unconscious chasm, and that consciousness is at best made up of a series of waves passing and touching and being realized by crests only, and not by conscious coalescing, it becomes pertinent to investigate the manner in which the chasm is either traversed in outline or bridged over, in order that the past thought may become merged into the present, and so made to be a most serviceable part of it.

If the chasm be traversed depth by depth we may be pretty sure that at some particular depth the process ceases to be conscious; and so again we are forced to the conclusion that the only way by which past and present can be made to marry is by their being brought together over a route a part of which is always in the dark. What there is in this dark portion of the route of course does not concern scientific psychology. What was recognized on the past side of it, however, and what is recognized on the present side of it, and how these are consciously related, as they normally always seem to be, are matters of such deep concern that without solution, in some universal sort of way, self-identity itself must remain unaccounted for. From what happens, in my own experience at least, I seem justified in affirming that immediately the Self emerges from the chasm between the conscious past and the now-becoming-conscious present—emerges from momentary latency into potency—it is aware of the past as possessing certain characteristics which it would now again live over, in more interesting realization. Or if there be failure on the part of the past to be present, or on the part of the present to discern in it a definite set of features for re-living, then imagination not only rich with reminiscent elements, but with expectant ones also, furnishes them; and in either case there sets in a conscious activity toward a satisfactory realization of the self-like copy thus presented. Mostly this is done so automatically and so smoothly that no notice is or can be taken of it. The past-thought features, or the imaginative-prospect features, or the present-extra-self features so quickly and harmoniously glide into position, either more or less separately or colligated into a composite whole, that the re-living, the re-producing (re-realizing), takes place before one can be aware of it. 'Caught on the fly,' however, especially when favored by some phase of abnormality, one discovers that, from the moment of projection from the nascent point, there becomes manifest, more and more clearly, an ambitious purpose and activity to imitate the self-copy in as close feature as the varying past, present, and prospective elements admit, changing in accordance with the weight of influence exerted by each respectively. What is held up, or rather what appears during each moment or phase of consciousness as a self-copy, becomes the inspiration of a process of re-living or re-realizing it, which, if not mimicry, is close to this in fact.

A concrete illustration of this idea was timely afforded by a personal experience with 'toothache.' A hard bite upon a resisting substance gave a decided hurt at first, which was followed duly by a slight tenderness. After a number of days, exposure to bleak winds induced an irregularly recurrent pain, with comfortable spells between. Occasionally, for an hour or two, there would be no distress whatever, or a night would be passed in undisturbed sleep. Then would recur a succession of strokes, or pulses, or waves of pain varying in intensity, according to exciting circumstances, or its own essential rhythm.

What was the usual attitude of my feeling, thinking, acting Self toward this intruder? A portion of the time it was one of more or less vivid expectancy; and when this was the case much confusion as to the threshold between actual pain and not-pain was always experienced, while the self-reaction differed widely according to the intensity and degree of conscious recollection of previous twinges. Always noticeable, however, was the tendency of the neuro-muscular mechanisms to assume very similar tensions and activities with the recurrence of each attack. When the pain came unexpected, either because of a lack of premonition or else on account of pre-occupation, it was very evident that both mind and body sought to strengthen the lines of endurance and defence, by practicing such of these reflexo-automatic devices as had been more or less usefully established in former experiences—in fact, by imitating the steps assumed under similar provocations. The involuntary fixating of chest walls, of jaws, of eyes, of attention, of emotion, of thought, and then the relaxing and subsequent seeking for relief, constituted a copy-cycle which certainly dominated largely and in detail the successive experiences, expressed most truly in terms of mimicry. Here was evidence to show that I am this moment the same Self that I was during the last, seemingly, because my innermost activity is to be during this moment similar, in a general way, to what it has been in the immediate past, or during all the series of past moments, not simply in that I have remembered the features of the past, or in that I recognize outside copies just now that were fascinating just then, or in that I imagine certain attainments possible to the future—not these alone or chiefly, but in that I can take whatever past, present or future presents, and *actively* imitate it, feature it, realize it in every possible here and now of my normal conscious existence—this it is, which gives me most assurance of my own Self, as being capable of satisfactory identification whenever needful.

Occasional needs of self-identification become sufficiently prominent to awaken notice, in connection with almost every intense experience. Marked joy, grief, anger, moodiness, depression, cerebral or muscular tension, pain, insistent ideation, active engagement, inventive exercise, reverie, etc., are instances from which to select a field for experimentation. Selecting one that promised vivid results, it occurred to me that two series of experiments, one representing the inhibitory and resisting side of life, and the other the stimulating and aggressive side, would lead on to such eventually. The toothache suggesting bodily pain for the field of inhibito-resistant experimentation, I was interested to see what would be my constant and repeated attitude toward it, both when attended to expectantly and when suffered unexpectedly. For the former I applied a drop of weak acid to the semi-abraded skin, and awaited the somewhat slow but certain development of the smart. How I felt; how I strove to blot it out mentally, by certain shrinkings, resistances, diversions; how I lapsed into simple endurance more and more, until finally fleeing to remedial relief, all together made up a striking, composite self-experience, not describable but certainly most appreciable. One experiment after three days' practice came near to being a failure because of the unexpected intrusion of a friend, whose suggestional influence was sufficient not only to largely overcome the sensational effects of the acid, but to interfere with the responsive adjustments of the self-characteristics in a natural way. And so with some of the others. However, before the ten every third-day series was concluded, I was afforded a rather convincing insight into the way in which my behavior was regularly but simply an endeavor to live over again the motions, tensions, thrills of the first and succeeding experiments. Moreover I frequently noticed a very definite dissatisfaction when, for any reason, I was prevented from doing this. As the experimentation proceeded, it became almost amusing to note the sort of strife, as it were, between the two lines of dissatisfaction—the one which came from the suffering proper, and the other arising from incomplete realization of all the self-commitance, usual to pain. But the latter always secured dominance and sort of lorded it over the former until its sway became supreme. In other words, in spite of the smart proper, the self *would have* its own total realization in the direction intended, even though the total suffering was increased thereby. The realization of the awakened Self appeared to be the very chiefest business all along. Another thing came to pass, namely: with each successive experiment the Self aimed, so to speak, to live over again not only the results of the painful experimentation, but also some of its former dire experiences not experimentally imposed. On the whole, I brought to light much that seemed to show that in the presence of pain expectantly developed, I as a self actually endeavor to reproduce all the concomitance previously associated with pain of every sort; and that my self is best satisfied when this is accomplished most accurately and fully. " If I am to have pain," says the Self, "I want it my own way—I demand the liberty to imitate, re-live the pain-mind-body copy developed beforehand, as I please."

Arranging a mechanical device by which a smart blow on the back of the hand was given at irregular intervals and simultaneously occupying the attention as absolutely as possible, I was enabled to study the effect of pain received unexpectedly. My conclusion after the experimental series was concluded was, that repeated irregular unexpected hurts always lead in the direction of a cumulative self-copy, even if the Self does become calloused in the process; and that this more and more determines the devotion, so to speak, of the succeeding imitative Self to its own copy; and that each pulse of painful consciousness is related to the consciousness of self, through the tie which imitation itself furnishes. With attention reminiscent, expectant or held in abeyance, the disturbed self immediately flies to cover in an active mimicry of that before found most vivid, satisfactory, or otherwise determined.

Finally, my experimentation included an observed series of errors or tendencies to error while attempting to play the zither. Having but little musical knowledge or skill, any new piece of music furnished material for prolonged study. Upon first trial certain notes and strains would be played accurately and with some sort of positive satisfaction. But always there were many others upon which both fingers and ears bungled and halted most disastrously. Of course, some of the previous errors would be repeated and others corrected with each succeeding trial. In time the number would be greatly reduced and the character of each error or tendency to error would be more accurately defined. A persistent study of these latter chiefly furnished the data for the conclusions eventually arrived at, namely : that the fingering, the interest in success, the fear of failure, the general pleasure or displeasure, the expectation of pleasing others, the memory of other zither music and performers, etc., all had to do in a most egoistic way in forming a statuesque copy of variable proportions and vividness concerning which, upon each trial, all that was within me struggled to reproduce in terms of most vital and persistent mimicry; and that, in the lasting instances of error, the error-element was the most striking characteristics of the self-copy. Repeatedly at times there was actually more satisfaction in making an error than in playing the music properly. And not until the imitable copy had become infused sufficiently with the influence of some lucky play, for instance, or of some ideational conception of success, or some anticipated applause mayhap, or some other vital and determining characteristic, did the imitation process manifest improvement.

So on many hands, seemingly, have I found tentative resort to a mimicry of a self-copy, ever renewed and ever renewable in the imitation product. And furthermore, it has appeared, more or less convincingly, that the Self is sure of itself normally, only through the bridging over from one pulse of self-sciousness to another, by the active play of imitation; and that the 'inexplicable tie,' the 'act of appropriation,' the most elusive characteristic of self, is possibly this very ability to, at any time, actually realize (*i. e.*, in the present), to a more or less recognizable degree, all that I was and as I was then (*i. e.*, in the past). And that, when the consciousness of this self-same ability is lost, no matter to what extent, nor in reference to what particular feature, always to just such an extent and in just such a way, is the possibility of self-identification gone. Normally, we can to-day imitate the self-copy of yesterday with satisfactory success. Abnormally, this ability is abridged, perverted or lost.

A side conclusion came into view; namely, that much of our so-called identity is simply fictitious, founded seemingly on our ability to imagine and affirm instead of that to prove it thus.

SHORTER CONTRIBUTIONS.

SOME MEMORY TESTS OF WHITES AND BLACKS.

The tests were made on 1,000 children in the fourth and fifth grades in the Washington Schools equally divided between the two races. The average age of the whites was eleven years, with extremes of eight and fourteen. Of the blacks, 12.57 years, with extremes of eight and eighteen years.

The tests adopted consisted of a recitation by the writer of one of four simple verses written for children by Mr. Eugene Field, followed by an explanation of all the possibly difficult words, and the recitation in concert, twice repeated, by the 20 or 40 children gathered (but never exceeding the latter number).

Each child was afterward required to repeat the verse separately in private. The degree of proficiency was marked by the system in use in the schools: E. indicating excellent, G. good, F. fair, P. poor. To obtain the average E. was valued at 100, G. at 75, F. at 50, and P. at 25.

The verses employed were the following:

No. I.   "Give me my bow said Robin Hood,
         An Arrow give to me;
         And where 'tis shot, mark then that spot,
         For there my grave shall be."—(*Field.*)

The average of memory retention obtained by the blacks in this number was 63.22 in a possible 100 with a minimum of 48.63 and a maximum of 71.25 in the different schools, and by the whites an average of 62.54 with a minimum of 60, and a maximum of 66.

No. II.   "I once knew all the birds that came
         And nested in our orchard trees;
         For every flower I had a name,
         My friends were woodchucks, toads and bees."—(*Field.*)

In this number the blacks obtained an average of 62.86% with a minimum of 33.75%, and a maximum of 73.43%. The whites an average of 58.92%, with a minimum of 48.02% and a maximum of 79.37%.

No. III.   " One night a tiny dew drop fell
                Into the bosom of a rose;
                Dear little one, I love thee well,   ˙
                Be ever here thy sweet repose."—(*Field.*)

In this number the blacks obtained an average of 65.64%, with a
minimum of 61.25%, and a maximum of 78.75%. The whites an
average of 54.54% with a minimum of 35.81% and a maximum of
66.37%. Possibly the simpler language, the more familiar ideas, and
the pleasing cadence of this number will account for the great superiority of the blacks.

No. IV.   "My Shepherd is the Lord my God,
                There is no want I know;
                His flock He leads in verdant meads.
                Where tranquil waters flow."—(*Field.*)

                (Paraphrase of the 23d Psalm.)

In this number the blacks obtained an average of but 32.93% with
a minimum of 5% and a maximum of 54.40%. The whites an
average of 42.14% with a minimum of 38.76% and a maximum of
45.52%. One would naturally suppose that in the verse so closely corresponding to a familiar psalm, that both races would have made a
much better record than that obtained in the other numbers which
were unfamiliar. It will be observed that in one black school there
was nearly a complete failure (5%) and that the average obtained
was 30.97% less than the combined average obtained in the other
numbers, while in the whites, the percentage was but 16.52% less
than the combined average. The difficulty appeared to consist chiefly
in the rather abrupt changes or want of continuity in the ideas, and
the use of three unfamiliar symbols. Verdant, Meads, and Tranquil,
which were supported by no visual or other sense presentations, and
possibly, because of the familiarity with the first line there was a
failure to keep the attention alert.

The renderings given the lines were in some instances not only
grotesque, but indicated an ignorance of the meaning of simple
words, an entire absence of the sense of rhythm and rhyme, and a
confusion of ideas. I quote a few of these renderings:

Line I.   My shepherd is the Lord my God.
                " The Lord God is my Shepherd."

Line II.   There is no want I know.
                "There is no one I know."
                "There is no one I love."

Where the only one I know.
" There is no other God before me."
" I know there is one."
" There is no one like me."

Line III.   His flock He leads in verdant meads.
" He leads His flock in vast fields."
" He leads his flock in needant fields."
" He feeds His flock by night."

Line IV.   Where tranquil waters flow.
" Where vast waters flow."
" Where trinkling waters flow."
" Where trennikel waters flow."
" Where peaceless waters flow."
" Where tremble waters flow."

As may be inferred, the false renderings were more frequent in the blacks because of their more limited vocabulary and feebler comprehension of the language.

In confirmation of the theory that the capacity for intellectual achievement depends very largely upon the acquired control of the attention and the degree of memory susceptibility or concentration, I find striking evidence in the close correspondence of the average markings for study rank, made by the different teachers and the markings for memory rank made by the writer.

The average obtained by the blacks in studies, being 64.73 in a possible 100, and in memory 58.27, and by the whites, 74.32 in studies, and 58.09 in memory. In making comparisons allowance must be made on the one hand for excessive and insufficient marking on the part of teachers, and on the other for the fear and embarassment caused by reciting to a stranger.

I am, however, convinced that if the study and memory markings were made by one person that they would correspond still more closely; and that it is possible to determine by the memory test the capacity of the teacher to instruct, as well as that of the pupil to acquire; as memory depends upon the habit of attention, to the growth of which the intelligence is proportionate (Ferrier). Another feature in the results obtained is the very remarkable and unexpected correspondence in the memory rank of each race, 58.09 in the whites, and 58.27 in the blacks; from which, in the absence of any data for comparison, nothing can be positively assumed.

To summarize the results, the average age of the whites was 11 years, of the blacks, 12.57 years, a difference in favor of the blacks of 1.57 years. The average obtained by the blacks in study rank was

64.73, in memory rank, 58.27, a difference of 6.46%. The average obtained by the whites in study rank was 74.32, in memory rank 58.09, a difference of 16.23%. The average obtained by both races in study rank was 69.52, in memory rank, 58.18, a difference of 11.34%; in study rank the memory rank of both races being equal.

If Ribot is correct in the opinion that voluntary or controlled attention in distinction from " spontaneous or instinctive attention, is a product of civilization, an instrument that has been perfected," we have, in these races as found in Washington, an apparent equality in development.—(The Psychology of Attention.)

No positive conclusions can be drawn from these tests as to the increase or decrease of mnemonic capacity in the whites, as to my knowledge, there is no standard of comparison of the same number and ages. In both races, of course, the memory is in decadence from primitive conditions, but as the blacks are much nearer those conditions I naturally expected to find a much greater auditory mnemonic ability than is possessed by the whites.

The decadence in the blacks is serious enough to be easily recognized by those familiar with the race in slavery, or in the early days of freedom, or with the isolated communities of illiterate negroes of purer blood still to be found in portions of the South.

The enfeeblement of the memory is accompanied in both races by a parallel decline in the powers of sight and hearing, and is apparently due to neglect in training the attention and of compulsory exercise of the memory, to educational methods which foster an increasing dependence on technical aids to mental effort, to the abnormal increase in visual presentations to the memory, until they exceed and displace all other sense presentations, to the neglect of mnemonic training, and to the mental paralysis consequent upon a too complex and overloaded curriculum.

The children selected from the blacks for this test were the darkest to be found in the schools. Of these, 72% were classed as ' dark,' 22.80 % as ' medium,' and 5.20% as ' light'; but such a classification is extremely arbitrary, as the degree of admixture of blood cannot be determined by the complexion, and negroes of absolutely unmixed blood are rare in our large centres of population.

It would be interesting to have examinations made in smaller communities of blacks of much purer blood, in isolated districts like the sea islands on the Atlantic seaboard. The memory rank of those subjected to this test is, undoubtedly, lessened by the admixture of blood, which tends to equalize the conditions; but, as will be observed, their memory rank in its decadence much more frequently exceeded the study rank than among the whites—an excess also due to their acknowledged racial deficiency in reasoning power.

The intellectual deficiency of the blacks as compared with the whites is more particularly shown by the average ages at which the grades were attained by both races; the blacks having attained the fourth grade at 12 years, and the fifth grade at 13.14 years, while the whites attained the fourth grade at 10.63 years, and the fifth at 11.40 years, a difference in favor of the whites of 1.37 years in the fourth, and of 1.74 years in the fifth grade, differences which indicate the value of heredity in racial culture even if ability to memorize be equal.

It is not within the purpose of this paper to deal with educational methods, but rather with results.

In studying the latter, it is painfully apparent "that the fundamental, discouraging and almost insurmountable difficulty in the education of the Negro is his ignorance of our language; in his home and in the field, in the church and school, he speaks a *patois* without a literature, and with a very limited vocabulary. The great mass of the Negro population of the country very rarely hears the English language spoken in its purity, and the children fortunate enough to be taught by one of their race who has acquired it, only hear it in the school room or in the houses of their white masters." (Article, 'The Negro and the Church,' by the writer, *Prot. Epis. Rev.*, July, 1896.) In both races there is a better knowledge of the signs or symbols than of the things signified, or an imperfect mastery of the language. Among the blacks, it will especially be found that many words in very simple prose and verse convey no conception of the thought or object represented. They also exhibit a decadence of the observing faculties from earlier conditions.

In both races there is a too great reliance on exterior aids, and a neglect, deficiency, or failure in habits of thought or the ability to think clearly, which makes it difficult for a child to use its own natural mental gifts, and which ultimately results in a loss of brain power and an inability to assimilate, or to determine the general principles to be derived from the great variety of particular knowledge presented in our school curricula.   GEORGE R. STETSON.
WASHINGTON, D. C.

EXPERIMENTS ON MEMORY TYPES.

It has been said that "the great mystery of memory lies in the mind's apparent power to transcend time and bring itself into contact with the vanished past." It is not the purpose of the present paper to solve the ' mystery of memory,' but to show how memory, under certain conditions, acts. This article will give the results of experiments tried upon auditory and visual memory.

Auditory-Memory. The following experiment was tried on public school children, students in a commercial school, and juniors and seniors in a college. Three groups of numbers were chosen, each group consisting of ten numbers. The first group was read at the rate of one number per second. The second group was read twice, and the third group three times, each number being pronounced at the same rate as those of the first group.

The purpose of the experiment was to find how much the memory would be strengthened by the second and third reading. The experiment was tried several times upon a class of seventh grade pupils and the results were as follows: They numbered 52% of the total number with one reading; 50% with two readings, and 58% with three readings. Sixth grade pupils gave the following: 42% of the total number with one reading, 41% with two, and 54% with three readings. The experiment tried upon the commercial students varied a little from the sixth and seventh grade pupils, giving these results: one reading 36% of total number; two readings 37%, and 54% with three readings. The experiment which was tried upon a class in psychology at San José College, gave the following results: One reading 58% of total number; 44% of total number with two readings, and 66% of entire group with three readings. Some results obtained from a class in psychology at Napa College were as follows: 48% of total number with one reading, 40% with two readings, and 65% with three readings; or, to put them in tabular form, they would be as follows :

Class.	I.	II.	III.
7th Grade.	.52	.50	.58
6th "	.42	.41	.54
Com. Stud't.	.36	.37	.54
S. J. C.	.58	.44	.66
N. C.	.48	.40	.65

These figures seem to indicate that two readings nearly always—there being but one exception—weakens the memory. I noticed in trying the experiment that after the group was pronounced once and was being pronounced again there nearly always appeared a look of confusion in the faces of the pupils. In the first reading associations would be formed, associating certain numbers together and giving them a certain order, such as might be suggested as they were being read. But, when they were read the second time, new associations would be formed, and some of the former ones lost, thus making a confusion in their thought and causing them to lose all the associations they had made.

In every case there was a decided improvement with three readings. This may be because the third reading harmonized the associations made in the two previous readings and thus the confusion that was caused was dispelled.

The data obtained shows that the power of retaining or recalling the memory-image varies with different persons. Some were able to recall the entire list while others could only recall two or three numbers. But the fact that one person is better than another in reproducing memory-images, it does not indicate that he has a better mind, as is thought by some people. Usually the boy or girl with a ' parrot-like memory' pleases everybody, while he who has to cognate and con over what he wishes to remember does not stand very high in the popular estimation.

It was found that younger pupils nearly always reproduce the numbers without any hesitation, while college students always hesitated and required more time to reproduce the list. This would seem to indicate that pure spontaneous memory depends on the degree of impressibility, while a cultured intellect depends more upon the power of reason. Young children are superior to men in impressibility, in the power of retaining the memory-image, and in spontaneous recollection, while the latter have gained more power of voluntary acquisition and recollection. Hence the training of memory should not only be to increase the power to recall an image, but the power to determine *what* shall be recalled.

Some experiments seem to indicate that the power of recognition is nearly double that of recall, that is, if some of the numbers not reproduced be mentioned, they are recognized in nearly every instance.

Visual-Memory. Two lists of words, consisting of fifteen each, were chosen, care being taken in the arrangement of the words.

They were as follows:

I.	II.
Bottle	Table
Pen	Man

I.	II.
Coat	Book
Floor	Room
Gun	Cat
Picture	Desk
Stove	Spade
Ring	Ship
Tree	Knife
House	Carpet
Rock	Lamp
Sun	Pencil
Bridge	Window
Hill	Fan ·
Chair	Mouse.

The two lists were placed upon the blackboard and covered. The cover was taken from the first list and it was exposed for thirty seconds. The second list was exposed at the rate of one word every two seconds, the word being erased at the end of that time.

The object of the experiment was to determine which was stronger, successive or simultaneous memory.

It was tried upon pupils of a public school, ranging from eight to fifteen years of age, and the following results were obtained:

Age.	Sim.	Suc.
8	.11	·33
9	·32	·49
10	·33	·49
11	·44	·52
12	·55	·56
13	·53	·54
14	·56	·56
15	·51	·52

The table seems to indicate that successive visual-memory is much better for the younger pupils than simultaneous visual-memory; but as they increase in age they improve in the power of the latter, there being a difference of 22% at the age of eight, while there is a difference of only one per cent at the age of fifteen.

It will be noticed that the increase in the power of recall is not uniform throughout, those thirteen years of age being below those of twelve, and those fifteen less than those of fourteen. This is owing to some idiosyncrasies of the individual pupils, but does not effect the general result.

The reason the younger pupils recall more of the second group is, probably, because their power of association is not so great. Their power of reproducing the words depends upon their powers of retention and the degree of impressibility, while the older pupils depend more upon association for retaining the words and their volitional powers to recall them. In the second group the opportunity offered for association is not so great as in the first, and hence, more are remembered by the younger pupils.

A similar experiment was tried on a class of commercial students, but numbers were used instead of words. They varied from fifteen to twenty years in age, and it was found that simultaneous was much stronger for them than successive visual-memory, there being 42% of the entire list reproduced when the fifteen numbers were exposed thirty seconds, and 39% when each number was exposed two seconds.

This seems to indicate that older students and those more advanced can recall more objects when exposed simultaneously than when shown successively. It is owing to the fact that the power of association is stronger in the older than in younger persons.

Visual- and Auditory-Memory. This experiment was tried on public school children. Two groups of names were used, each group consisting of ten words. The first group was read at the rate of one word every two seconds. The other group was placed on the blackboard and covered. Each word was then uncovered at the rate of one every two seconds and erased at the end of that time.

The object of the experiment was to determine which was the stronger, visual or auditory-memory.

The data obtained seems to indicate that generally auditory-memory is much stronger for younger pupils than visual-memory. The following results were obtained:

Age.	*Auditory.*	*Visual.*
8	.42	.30
9	.54	.57
10	.57	.54
11	.69	.66
12	.80	.65

There is but one instance in the above table where the visual-memory excels the auditory, and this was probably due to a lack of attention by a few pupils.

The younger children are accustomed to a large amount of auditory work, and it is natural that they should remember spoken better than written words.

It is probably true that the auditory-memory is associated with the visual. I noticed, in trying the experiment upon some pupils, that they pronounced the words softly as they were exposed. Thus, if "when the two senses act together in recollection they hinder each other," we must observe this in accounting for the fact that visual is weaker than auditory-memory.

A similar experiment was tried upon a class of commercial students, ranging from fifteen to twenty years in age, gives 28 % of the total number reproduced in auditory and 45 % in visual-memory. This would seem to indicate that visual-memory is better for older students than auditory-memory. The reason is because visual-memory is employed more by them than auditory.

CHAUNCEY J. HAWKINS.

YALE UNIVERSITY.

THE PROPAGATION OF MEMORIES.

One essential condition of the continuity of individual consciousness in our present state seems to be the persistence of impressions in the substrate, or, in other words, the retention of vestiges. It is apparently usually implied, if not stated, that this persistence is due to the survival of the cells (of the cortex presumably) in which the original impression issuing in consciousness was made. Were this theory correct the destruction of a given cell or generation of cells would banish forever their vestiges and destroy the power of reproduction in so far. It is, however, a notorious fact that the events of a very early period of life are remembered and vividly conceived of even in very late life, and it is not unusual for the earlier events or experiences to crowd out the later ones which ought, by reason of their freshness, to be most prominent. Any theory of memory which depends on the persistence of the original elements is weak, in view of the theoretical consideration mentioned, and is contradicted by facts of observation. In the first place, the law of substitution and restoration of function is well intrenched in the data of pathology and experiment, and, in the second, we have every reason to believe that the individual cell of the cortex has its birth, adolescence and period of decline, like any other cell, and it follows that its vestiges, as such, disappear with it.

Recent investigations show that a comparison of a given number of ordinary brains with those of insane persons reveals little or no difference (if cases of general paralysis and alcoholism be excluded). In other words, there are nearly as many cells showing pigmentary degeneration and vacuolation in one series as in the other. Any section of the cortex will contain some cells evidently beyond their prime. With this phase of the subject is associated another; viz, the power of multiplication. Some years since the writer described a process of proliferation by which the cerebellum in particular is supplied with a germinative zone which, by constant subdivision of its elements, gives rise to the definitive cells. The announcement met with incredulity on the part of critics, but has recently been fully corroborated by several independent investigators. At the same time the writer suggested that, in many groups, germinative or proliferating areas or nuclei persist, and from these cells arise from time to time to supply later needs. The details of this mechanism remain to be studied, but Professor Howard Ayers recently corroborated the existence of subdividing cells in the mature brain, and similar cases are reported by others. So far from exciting surprise, this may be expected. Many histologists have expressed surprise at the comparatively new doctrine of nervous transmission by contiguity rather than continuity, but it is not difficult to see that this method of non-exclusive reaction of cell upon cell is exactly adapted to permit the graceful withdrawal of a cell as its age approaches, while a younger element gradually ingratiates itself into the sphere of influence of the other by the growth of its fibrous arborizations. True, there doubtless are latent cells in the cortex, and it is not necessary to suppose that rapid proliferation is continued throughout life. All that is insisted on is that the mental life of the person is not coextensive with that of the cells in the cortex.

If it be granted that the individual memory outlives any single generation of cortical cells it is evident that a theory of consciousness is called for other than that commonly in vogue. I have elsewhere outlined such a theory. Briefly, it is presumed that the unity of consciousness is not due to the flickering of some extraneous illumination upon part after part of the cortical reservoir of vestiges, but that the individual consciousness at any time is the totality of the interrelated activities or the associational equilibrium. The histological mechanism of the cortex leaves no opportunity for doubt that an excitation of one region does habitually produce the most extensive set of interreactions with other regions, and we may best conceive of the outcome as a neurological equilibrium, always varying, but always a single, though complex, correlation. The metaphysical concomitants of this view may be passed over here, though of vast importance to monistic thinking.

If, then, it be admitted for the argument's sake that consciousness is a unit of equilibration on its neurological side, it may be farther understood how the early vestiges may be propagated beyond the life of the first generation of cells, *i. e.*, those which first received a given vestigeal impression. When, *e. g.*, a certain event is recalled, a succession of equilibriated states occur to which the several cells concerned contribute each its share. When a new cell is gradually interpolated in the cortical associational system it participates in this kind of an equilibrium, at first passively and afterwards by reproduction of the secondary vestige due to its early functioning. It being of the same order as the cell which is now aging, it reacts after its kind, *i. e.*, in a manner suitable to its position as to the other cells and avenues of discharge. Thus, in time, we conceive that a nearly complete substitution for an old cell may be affected without our perceiving any difference in the tone of memories. That there is such change is unquestionable. What the man recalls of his boyhood is something very different from the memory of the same events soon after their occurrence.

It is no longer difficult to understand why in old age the events of youth may re-emerge in memory. The earlier events have their relations with the simpler, broader forms of association, and when the subtle, later connections fall away, older forms of equilibrium reappear. To be more explicit, in the first few years of the child's life the avenues of association are relatively few and they are increasingly complicated with every new element introduced into experience. The tendency of all early experiences is then to follow lines already open. The little events of childhood are superposed upon the elemental associations. Now, when the more complicated associational paths are destroyed, suggestions tending to awaken vestiges are shut up to a few lines of association, and these are just the ones on which the childish experiences were based. It is not necessary to pursue this line of reasoning further. It is believed that most of the hitherto unreconcilable facts of memory are consistent with this theory of propagation of vestiges.

C. L. HERRICK.

DENISON UNIVERSITY.

NOTE ON 'REACTION TYPES.'

The following observations are of so fragmentary a sort as to seem hardly worthy of publication, yet the results are so striking and suggestive and it being impossible to complete a more careful series, it has seemed best to present them and let them stand for what they are worth.

During a visit to the laboratory in November, 1896, of the well-known pianists, Rosenthal and Sieveking, who were at that time giving concerts in New York, their reaction-times to sound were measured with a Hipp chronoscope. The signal was the tap of a metal hammer, and they were told to raise the first two fingers of the right hand as quickly as possible, no instructions as to direction of attention, etc., being given. It may be said that neither of the gentlemen had ever seen a reaction-time apparatus previously, and the tests were made on each without the knowledge of the other, thus precluding the possibly disturbing intervention of professional jealousy. A series of seven records on Rosenthal resulted as follows (times in σ) ; 110, 118, 119, 112, 119, 123, 123, giving an average reaction-time of 117.7, and an average variation of only 3.8. When questioned as to the direction of his attention during the tests he stated emphatically that it was entirely directed toward the signal and doubted, whether he could hold his attention upon the reacting fingers. When requested to do so a series of four reactions resulted as follows: 250, 230, 270, 268, an average of 254.5, and average variation of 14.5 *i. e.*, an average reaction-time of more than twice that of the first series, and an average variation of about four times that of the first. A second series of seven reactions with the attention upon the stimulus resulted as follows: 105, 107, 106, 101, 106, 110, 114, an average of 108.4, and an average variation of 3.9.

But one series of five observations was made with Sieveking and, as in the former case, without instructions as to attention. The results were 114, 114, 117, 120, 118, an average of 116.6 and an average variation of 2. When questioned as to attention, Sieveking was as emphatic as his rival but declared that his attention was entirely concentrated on the reacting hand, indicating the interossei of the first and second fingers as the muscles used; which statement while anatomically incorrect was psychologically entirely satisfactory. When asked to react with the attention turned to the signal, he attempted to do so but declared it impossible and declined to proceed.

It is greatly to be regretted that the observations could not have been pushed further and carried out systematically, but circumstances put it out of the question and it must be said also by way of apology that the experiments were made more to exhibit the apparatus than to obtain results and without the idea of publication. Nothing could have been more striking, however, than the clearness with which both gentlemen grasped the point at issue and described their states of mind. It would be interesting with longer series to interpret them in the light of the peculiar musical training and characteristics of the two artists which are said to be diametrically opposed.

As it is, one can only say that, so far as single observations are of value, their reactions argue vigorously for the affirmative in the debated question of the existence of types of reaction.

LIVINGSTON FARRAND.

COLUMBIA UNIVERSITY.

As Professor Wundt devotes many pages of the fourth edition of the *Physiologische Psychologie* to sensory and motor reactions, I hope that he will find space in the fifth edition to include cases such as these. He writes in the fourth edition " Cattell (*Phil. Stud.*, viii, S. 403) * * * könnte weder bei sich, noch bei einigen andern Personen einen von der Richtung der Aufmerksamkeit abhängigen Unterschied finden." But of the three cases reported by me in the article published in Professor Wundt's *Archiv*, one had a motor reaction nearly half again as long as the sensory form with corresponding differences in the mean variations. Professor Wundt indicates that I was not competent to react in a sensory fashion. He writes further " Dies schliesse ich aus der Vergleichung meiner eigenen Versuche, in denen ich sensoriell reagirte, mit denen Cattell's, der sich offenbar der muskulären Reactionsweise bediente."[1] Now Professor Wundt can evidently make an *'experimentum crucis'* for his own case by going to his laboratory, directing attention to the movement and reacting in half the time and with half the irregularity of his early experiments.

Of Dr. Farrand's cases Rosenthal is a performer of extraordinary technical expertness. His fingers are so perfectly trained that he does not need to give them the least attention. Sieveking, on the other hand, is impulsive and emotional. I do not think that we should be justified in concluding from these experiments that Rosenthal is an ' audile ' and Sieveking a ' motile.' It seems to me rather that my or-

---

[1] As a matter of fact my reactions are not ' motor.' They are ' sensory ' when the stimulus is very weak or very strong, but in general the attention is diffused, but little being directed to the experiments.

iginal suggestion is supported—namely, that people react most quickly and regularly in the way in which they are used to reacting, and that when the reflex character of the reaction is disturbed the times become longer and more irregular.

J. McKeen Cattell.

It may be added that Professor Wundt's position remains unchanged in his later published *Outlines* (pp. 198 ff.), while Professor Warren has indicated (Psychological Review, Nov., 1896) the same attitude in Professor Titchener's excellent *Outline.* It seems worth while to say this since cases *galore* have now been reported (by Flournoy, Angell and Moore, and myself, besides those reported above, and under more exact experimental conditions) ; and they seem fully to meet the call for ' facts' made by the last-named writer, at least, several times over (see his *Mind* articles). The existence of ' types' of simple reaction can no longer be ignored by any one.

J. Mark Baldwin.

PSYCHOLOGICAL LITERATURE.

Lehrbuch der Psychologie. FRIEDRICH JODL. Stuttgart, Cotta'sche
Buchhandlung, 1896. Pp. xxiv+767.

Here is a new systematic work on psychology, 750 pages strong.
It is by Professor Jodl, now of the University of Vienna, but for many
years of the University of Prague, well known in this country for his
ethical writings and as one of the editors of the International Journal
of Ethics. The reader observes, first, and not without a quickly
smothered feeling of gratitude, that the book has not a single illustration, not a curve nor a diagram, not even a chart of the brain, nor a
cut of Zöllner's figure. The second striking feature is the wealth of
references to psychological literature. After every subject and after
every subdivision of a subject, there follows a paragraph citing the
special literature upon that subject. At the end of the book there is
a collected bibliography of all the works cited, comprising almost nine
hundred titles. Not only by his references, but also by his discussions, the author shows himself to have an accurate acquaintance not
merely with German psychological literature, but also with that of
France, England and America. This is especially true of English
and American works, by which the author has evidently been much
influenced, and he delights in comparing German and English terminology.

The work is divided into two parts. The first, introductory, treats
in three chapters of the scope and method of psychology, of the relation of body and soul, and of the classification and description of conscious phenomena in general. The second part is divided into nine
chapters, as follows: IV. Sensations: their forms, laws and methods of measurement. V. Special sensations: organic, kinæsthetic,
cutaneous, smell, hearing and sight. VI. Feelings of the primary
order: sensuous feelings and elementary æsthetic feelings. VII.
Elementary phenomena of will. VIII. Secondary phenomena:
memory, association and representative attention. IX. Most important products of the imagination: time, space, subject and object. X.
Language and thought: origin and spirit of language, word and idea,
judgment and reasoning. XI. Feelings of the second and third order:

feelings of personality, æsthetic and moral feelings, etc. XII. Phenomena of will of the second and third order.

In reading or reviewing Professor Jodl's book it is necessary to remember that it is a *text-book*, written for purposes of instruction. If, therefore, it should be found to contain little that is striking or original, this would be its greatest merit. It is often asked whether psychology is yet a science. Nothing could be so discouraging to those who have cherished a hope that it is, as the *individual* character of the various outlines, elements and text-books that have appeared during the last ten or fifteen years. So many books, so many sciences of psychology. Some are mainly physiological, some scorn to mention physiology. Some attempt no general classification of mental phenomena, all the others give different classifications. Some are mere picture or story books apparently designed to astonish the reader. Many of these works are extremely valuable contributions to psychology, presenting new experimental methods and results, new schemes of classification, and new criticisms of former errors, but they are contributions merely and not text-books. They are indicative of the formative stage of a science. The present work by Professor Jodl is less characterized by new and striking features. The material brought forward is, with some exceptions, that which is common to all schools. If this is not indicated in the following review, it is, of course, because it would be apart from the purpose of a review to dwell on tiresome details.

In the first chapter, after defining psychology as the science of the forms and laws of the phenomena of normal consciousness, which appear in the adjustment of living organisms to their environment, the author describes the various methods by which psychology may be studied. Then follows an interesting chapter of 50 pages on soul and body. It contains the briefest statement of the structure and form of the nervous system, a single paragraph on localization, and a long discussion on the nature of consciousness and its relation to the body. The standpoint is thoroughly monistic. Mind is not a substance, nor anything that can outlast the body or even outlast peculiar cerebral conditions of which states of consciousness are inner aspects. Mind is a convenient term for the sum total of these states. Conscious states are not, however, to be identified or confused with physical states or physical beings. The parallelism between them is not that of two different series, but of two aspects of the same series. There is no dualism of body and mind; the dualism is one of perception. But the author does not admit an inner aspect to all physical being and calls panpsychism a new mythology. Consciousness belongs only to organized living bodies, accompanying certain conditions of cerebral development. Without organic life, no consciousness. But the reverse does not follow. No causal relation exists between mind and body. Causal relations exist only between neurological processes on the one hand and conscious processes on the other. But, indeed, we must not think of it as if there were two series. There is one only. In our description, we may follow either the outer objective aspect, *i. e.*, the brain changes, or the inner, subjective aspect, or conscious states, as now one, now the other is more permeable. At present, we are largely confined to the latter method, owing to the extremely backward condition of cerebral physiology. The endless difficulty about unconscious mental states disappears in a minute when we consider consciousness as an attendant phenomenon upon neurological processes, which is present under definite conditions only, but which always presupposes nervous activity. All unconscious mental action may be relegated to physiology. On the whole, concerning the author's presentation of the relation of mind and body, a 'materialist' would have to be of the so-called 'crass' order to find much in it that would be highly objectionable.

In the third chapter follows a more critical analysis of the meaning of consciousness and its forms. The opposition of subject and object is the fundamental postulate of all consciousness. Presentation (Wahrnehmung) is the very essence of consciousness. In general what we mean by consciousness is a succession of such presentations with the various relations between them. In this connection, the author discusses the question whether the ontogenetic development of consciousness is an abridged recapitulation of the phylogenetic, and concludes that the evidence for such parallelism is yet insufficient. Sleep, somnambulism, and hypnotism are briefly discussed in this connection, but with a curious neglect of their cerebral accompaniments, which ill accords with the author's theoretical standpoint.

Under the title, elementary forms of consciousness, the author discusses the problem of classification. After criticizing the attempts of Horwicz and Spencer, Schopenhauer and Wundt, Münsterberg and Lehmann to find the primary elements of consciousness in feeling, will and idea respectively, he decides upon epistemological grounds for the three-fold division into sensation, feeling and will. (Empfindung, Gefühl, Strebung.) The basis of this division is found in the antithesis of subject and object which is the very condition of consciousness. It gives us action (sensation), reaction (will), and the connecting central excitation with its accompanying pain or pleasure (feeling). This classification, thinks our author, conforms to the functioning of the nervous system itself. In sensation we have the mental accompaniment of a stimulus from without by way of the sensory nerves. In feeling we have the *value* of the stimulus for the good or ill of the organism. In will we have the reaction expressing itself in movement through the motor mechanism.

Sensation, feeling and will being thus designated as primary phenomena, we may denote all reproductions of these as *secondary* phenomena. Under this head is included the memory-image of every kind, and for this memory-image or mental state of the second order, we may reserve the term Vorstellung. Finally the author distinguishes phenomena of the *third* order, namely those highest mental processes resulting from the fusion and elaboration of phenomena of the first and second order, such, for instance, as conception, thought, and the constructive imagination.

The first part closes with a description of ' the objective spirit '—a phrase which, rescued from its empty Hegelian meaning, the author uses in the later scientific sense of Lewes, Lilienfeld, and Carus. It signifies our mental environment, the spirit of the age as expressed in human thought, art, science, etc. It is this objective spirit, together with the organic inter-relation of successive generations which presents the element of truth in what has appeared in ancient and modern mythology as the idea of personal immortality, an error which has arisen from mistaking a mere abstraction, the soul, for a real spiritual being or substance.

In the second part, two hundred pages are first devoted to sensation. The distinction which modern English psychology makes between sensation and perception, is recognized under the form of the receptive and spontaneous consciousness. In the relating, comparing, and discriminating spontaneity of consciousness we have not to recognize any new or mysterious ' powers ' of mind. That which is originally given in consciousness is not a series of isolated sensations which may be related and compared, but a complex of related sensations which may be analyzed. The doctrine of the specific energy of the nerves in its older form is severely criticized and the oft-repeated teaching that electrical or mechanical stimulation of the end-organs of taste, smell, or even of sight or hearing, is directly followed by their specific sensations, is declared to be doubtful. Synæsthesia is found to be an incorrectly named phenomenon and to have a purely psychical explanation. A section on the psychophysic law follows. This is a mere discussion of the validity of the law and its meaning. There is no detailed description of experimental methods. The results of late experiments in the value of psychophysical constants for the several senses are not given. The author rejects the psychological interpretation of Weber's Law given by Wundt and does not decide between the other two.

Then follow 140 pages devoted to special sensations, namely, organic and cutaneous sensations, and sensations of movement, taste, smell, hearing and sight. No mention is made of the semi-circular canals as organs for sensations of equilibrium. The reader is referred to other works for all details of experiments and experimental methods. The section on visual sensations is particularly exhaustive. The author, following Hering, Stumpf and James, strenuously maintains that a spacial quality, even tridimensional inheres in visual sensations in their native purity. The empiricists are not altogether wrong in emphasizing the educating influences of other factors in completing our conception of spacial relations, but they are wrong when they give to inference or judgment, which are secondary mental processes, the mystic power of creating something, *i. e.*, the space idea, out of nothing. Indeed, he distinguishes in sensations of sight three distinct elements, intensity, *i. e.*, brightness or darkness, quality, *i. e.*, color, and extension. He admits pure quantitative changes in color sensations without change of quality.

After sensations, the author treats of feelings of the primary order, *i. e.*, sense feelings. Pleasures and pain are their essential qualitative marks and each of these can only be graded quantitatively. They are both positive. Sense feelings, cutaneous pain, for instance, are not to be confused or compared with sensations. They are totally different forms of consciousness, accompanying and interpreting the sensations, and appearing later. The author does not consider or even mention apparently serious objections to this theory, such as have been educed by von Frey, Griffing and Nichols.

In the section on the elementary æsthetic feelings, it is shown that, apart from all representative or associational processes, pure æsthetic pleasure is derived from colors, tones, and from harmony, rhythm and proportion. In the last analysis, the pleasure may be traced to that condition of nervous activity lying between excessive and deficient stimulus. This is very good, but the law is merely mentioned in this general form and no attempt is made to carry the analysis further after the manner of Helmholtz or Grant Allen. This is an example of a certain tantalizing tendency, shown throughout the whole book, to stop just short of the final analysis.

This failure to grapple seriously with psychological problems is still better shown in the next chapter on the primary phenomena of will. According to the author's division of mental processes, the primary phenomena of will are to be distinguished from *feelings* and from *sensations*, including of course all muscle sensations. As they are *primary* states, they are also to be distinguished from all representative elements, *e. g.*, motor images. After these exclusions, one wonders just what there will be left to constitute the primary phenomena of will. Of course, they must be purely psychical conscious phenomena, and when the author refers to them as *movements*, as he often does (*e. g.* in III., 64), we must suppose that he is referring merely to the objective correlates of the purely mental processes. Pure and simple *effort* (Streben) is the final result of this analysis, and this is an ultimate primary phenomenon of will. But when the author attempts to describe this, it becomes as difficult to separate it from phenomena of feeling and sensation, as it is indeed difficult to do so in our own inner experience. In fact, he naively admits that effort is a general term for those mental states characterized by the feeling of bodily needs and the reactions consequent upon them. We cannot but think that the author's attempt to find in will any primary psychical phenomenon is a failure. His loose and careless treatment of the will is illustrative of the treatment of this subject in nearly all the psychology books of the day, and in striking contrast to the incisive and analytic treatment of it in Külpe's *Grundriss*.

Exposition of the secondary phenomena is begun in Chapter VIII. Reproduction, Memory and Association are clearly and fully treated with satisfactory recognition of the physiological principles involved.

On the whole this is the best systematic work on psychology that has recently appeared in Germany. Its purpose does not admit of comparison with Wundt and Külpe. It may be compared with Höffding whose work it will supersede. It is, to be sure, a compilation, but a most valuable one. The author is evidently neither a physiologist nor an experimentalist, but he is in sympathy with experimental methods, and he handles his subject with a fairness and a wideness of vision, with which a life spent upon the details of laboratory work would hardly be consistent. One notices also a grateful freedom from long and tiresome discussions of disputed questions.

G. T. W. PATRICK.

UNIVERSITY OF IOWA.

Elements of Psychology. GEORGE CROOM ROBERTSON. Edited
from notes of lectures delivered at University College 1870-1892
by C. A. FOLEY RHYS DAVIDS. New York, Charles Scribner's
Sons, 1896. Pp. xvi+268. $1.00 net.

Robertson was a man whose influence was greater than his reputation. Natural ability of the highest order, trained by thorough study,
wide reading and careful thought, was subordinated to a character
conscientious and generous to a degree not only rare, but in my own experience unapproached. On a sick bed recovering slowly from painful
surgical operations or traveling in the vain effort to regain health, he was
always able to give more than he asked. Carrying for twelve years the
burden of a disease that must prove fatal, devoting his best energy
to teaching his classes at University College, to helping his friends
and forwarding scientific and social movements, editing each number
of *Mind* as though it were a newly discovered MS. by Aristotle, it
is no wonder that the amount of his published work was small.
Neither is it surprising that the friends and students of such a man
should wish to preserve all that he left, even the oral instruction
to his classes, existing only in the notes of students.

These lectures on psychology and the second series on philosophy would have been viewed by Robertson himself with mingled
feelings. He would have appreciated the piety which lead to their
compilation, but, careful and conscientious to an extreme in all that
he wrote, he would scarcely have sanctioned the publication of ex-
temporary remarks preserved by the notes of students. A book such
as this can scarcely be judged by ordinary standards. As a memorial
volume it will be dear to Robertson's friends; it shows that his teaching was stimulating to an unusual degree. The contributions to psychology as a science are not great. Robertson follows his teacher
Professor Bain; even his use of the German psychology and his own
ideas are often brought forward as criticisms of Bain's writings.
Probably Robertson would have regarded as his most important contribution the elaboration of a theory of perception through the muscular sense, but this is not likely to maintain a permanent place in
psychology. There are, however, many apt thoughts and suggestions,
which with the general point of view—that of traditional English
psychology brought in touch with the latest continental work—make
the book one that will be read with profit by all teachers of psychology.

The notes are, however, called 'Elements of Psychology,' and the
book is placed in a series of text-books. At first sight it seems to be
unsuited to this purpose. The lectures are based on and presuppose

other text-books—Bain, Sully, Murray, or Höffding. The style is colloquial as reported verbatim by students and pieced together by the editor, with occasional interpolations in a very different style from Robertson's manuscript notes. There are repetitions and awkward phrases and even mistakes. Yet in spite of all this, when the work is compared with our most recent text-books, as Wundt's *Outlines* or Titchener's *Elements* it shows great freshness and originality. Perhaps there is no better introduction to psychology.

J. McKeen Cattell.

The Philosophy of Theism. Alexander Campbell Fraser. Gifford Lectures Before the University of Edinburgh. Two Volumes. New York, Scribners; Edinburgh, Blackwoods. First Series. 1895. Second Series. 1896.

These two volumes should be read and reviewed as a single work. Indeed, in the preface to the second volume, Professor Fraser expressly urges that the two volumes 'be looked at as a continuous inquiry, not as a series of isolated discussions.' Taken thus as a whole, these Gifford Lectures are a singularly interesting expression of a long life of scholarship and faith. For sixty years, Professor Fraser, as student and teacher, has been associated with his university. He succeeded Sir W. Hamilton as long ago as 1859, and now, in his ripe old age, he offers this testimony to the reasonableness of religion. His volumes do not pretend to maintain new points of view or to enter far into philosophical controversy. They are, as he says: "An honest exposition of results already reached in a life devoted to similar pursuits." No one can thus receive from this veteran, well known through his earlier studies of Berkeley and of Locke, this final *Apologia pro fide sua* without grateful reverence. It is a book which invites not so much criticism as appreciation; and it will be sufficient to describe its methods and its conclusions.

In the first volume, as Professor Fraser remarks, "the voice of the sceptic was prominent; in the second, faith makes itself heard." At the outset, and with great gravity and dignity, he defines the 'final problem' of all thought. "Is religion an intellectually legitimate state of mind?" "What sort of a universe is this in which I find myself?"; and he 'articulates' this ultimate problem as holding three factors of universal experience—the material world, the subjective self and the spiritual reality of God. He is then led on to consider the three forms of monism thus suggested—the life of God and man interpreted through materialism; the life of God and matter interpreted in terms of subjective idealism; and the life of matter and mind as absorbed in Deity. In the first case he concludes that even reason itself, and its product, science, are lost in the flux of things, and even "materialism itself disappears in the abyss of universal nescience." In the second case, while affirming the superior claim of idealism, he urges its strictly individual limitation. "Individual Egoism is eternally confined in the individual Ego." The third possibility, that of Pantheism, detains him longer, as a faith "which has brought peace to millions of human minds;" and his discussion of this faith is the most weighty section of his first volume. Finally, there remains to be negatively criticized, the attitude of absolute scepticism; and here he reviews the agnosticism which, he believes, should be identified not with modern men of science but with Hume.

Science itself, Professor Frazer concludes, is finally an act of faith, not of reasoning, and the "agnosticism that retains science is not really a protest against faith; it is only an arrest of faith."

At this point in the first volume begins the positive treatment which the second volume completes. A spiritual interpretation of the universe, he goes on to affirm, is, at least, not inconsistent with the facts of Nature, but it is disclosed with far greater fulness by the self-consciousness of man. Man as a moral being brings us into relation with the supernatural. Cosmic faith is the assurance that the natural world will not put us to intellectual confusion; moral faith is the assurance that those who strive for goodness shall not be put to permanent moral confusion. Many mysteries of the universe remain unexplored, but its fundamental character is indicated by the spiritual life of man. *Homo mensura.* The second volume studies, in greater detail, this moral and spiritual man in the midst of a moral and spiritual universe. The working postulate of human life is found in this assumption of a spiritual relation to reality. This moral faith alone permits us to interpret the causation and the design of nature. "The presence, throughout the whole, of latent meaning and moral purpose is not indeed a conclusion that can be logically drawn from the few physical or moral phenomena that are actually offered to us in our experience; but the assumption is warranted * * * * * * as the needed condition of our escape from speechless and motionless Pyrrhomist despair." Finally, there is dealt with the special fact which seems most flatly to contradict this impression of spiritual design. "How can a universe of suffering and sin be a revelation of omnipotent goodness?" To this final difficulty the two-fold answer is given; that it is a world of moral discipline and education, and that its full interpretation is postponed to another life. Very soberly and with much reserve the mystery of death is faced. "Faith in the persistence of morally responsible persons is not the indispensable postulate of all reliable intercourse with the universe of things and persons; but its disintegration would disturb the theistic trust and so leads to universal doubt." " It is the irrational alternative in the dilemma that makes optimistic trust the highest philosophy."

Such is this veteran's philosophic faith: "the natural trust that nothing can happen in the temporal evolution which can finally put to confusion the principles of moral reason that are latent in man."

FRANCIS G. PEABODY.
HARVARD UNIVERSITY.

A History of European Thought in the Nineteenth Century. JOHN THEODORE MERZ. Vol. I, Introduction; Scientific Thought, Part 1. Edinburgh & London, William Blackwood & Sons. 1896. Post 8vo. Pp. xiv+458.

Alike in science and philosophy it has ever been a marked characteristic of English thought to be served by independent as well as by professional workers. Priestley, Davy, Wollaston, Young, Dalton, Faraday and Joule were, like Bacon, Locke, Berkeley, Bentham, the Mills, Grote, Buckle and Mr. Spencer, outside the pale of the universities. Among this distinguished company Mr. Merz (long known favorably to a limited circle of the cultivated at Newcastle-on-Tyne, and to the philosophical specialist as the author of the excellent little monograph on *Leibniz* in Blackwood's philosophical series) now takes his place by right of achievement. Should he continue his *History* to completion as he has begun, he will rank not far from the most eminent of the non-academic writers.

At the present juncture criticism would be beside the mark, and it may serve meantime to call the attention of thinkers to the plan and execution of this most valuable book, to preparation for which Mr. Merz has given no less than thirty years. The author speaks in his preface of the encouragement derived from friends during his long period of self-suppression; he will now be borne up through the rest of his self-imposed task by the universal expectation of all who take real interest in either scientific or philosophical pursuits.

The present volume consists, *first*, of an Introduction, in which three main points are discussed;—the necessity for such an undertaking and its timeliness; the reasons for confining attention to European culture, especially as wrought out by the three great nationalities of

Britain, Germany and France, and the general groundwork of the entire undertaking, which may eventually extend to four or five volumes. The last alone need trouble us now. Mr. Merz' general standpoint may be gleaned from the following: " Unless I believed that our age was elaborating a deeper and more significant conception of this unity of all human interests, of the inner mental life of man and mankind, I do not think I should have deemed it worth while to write the following volumes, for it is really their main end and principal object to trace the coöperation of many agencies in the higher work of our century; the growing conviction that all mental efforts combine together to produce and uphold the ideal possession of the race; that it is not in one special direction nor under one specific term that this treasure can be cultivated, but that individuals and peoples in their combined international life exhibit and perpetuate it." (p. 33.) The plan of the work, as outlined at p. 63 sq., is to treat first of science—' thought as a means to an end.' In the second part, "we have to consider it as its own object, as a reflection on itself, carried on with the object of knowing its own origin, its laws, its validity. This discipline may, as a whole, be called philosophy." So far as I am able to gather from Mr. Merz' statement, two volumes are to be devoted to the first section; a volume to the second, and another to the ' unmethodical thought,' which he groups under the name of religion. Following this scheme, the *second* part of the present volume contains three introductory chapters on the Scientific Spirit in France, Germany and England, respectively; and two systematic chapters, one on the Astronomical View of Nature, the other on the Atomic View of Nature. It will be of interest to readers of this REVIEW to learn that the second volume will present a similar conspectus of the Psychological View.

I can only add that, in my judgment, this work bids fair to rank as a classic. It is suggestive, its learning is admirably balanced and unified and its objectivity is wholly unusual. Everyone ought to obtain it as an indispensable *vade mecum.*

R. M. WENLEY.

UNIVERSITY OF MICHIGAN.

Gustav Theodor Fechner. KURD LASSWITZ. Frommanns Klassiker der Philosophie, edited by RICHARD FALCKENBERG. No. I. Stuttgart, Frommanns Verlag. 1896. Pp. 207.

The author presents, not only the life and writings of Fechner, but also his view of the world. He believes the study of this view will be helpful to present and future thought. The presentation is condensed and systematic; the style clear and touched all through by an enthusiastic admiration of the man and his work. The book may be said to ' read itself,' and one comes to feel that Fechner was both a hero and a genius as a result of this glowing treatment.

The subject is divided into two parts: (1) Life and Works, and (2) View of the World. The first part is divided into three periods. The work of confirming Ohm's law and extending its application to the many possible variations of conditions was Fechner's. As the author of the ' Comparative Anatomy of Angels' and other similar pieces he ranks high as a humorist and a lover of belles-lettres. His work in psycho-physics, experimental psychology and æsthetics is well known and of acknowledged permanent value. Fechner's life is made interesting by the author's accounts of his struggles with poverty, sickness and defective eyesight, as well as by his scientific successes.

Fechner's view of the world is presented in two parts: (1) the Theory of Motion and (2) that of Consciousness. The ingenious and mathematically beautiful effort of the philosopher to state the phenomena of the material universe in terms of the motion of a system of things impresses one as rich with suggestion. The most interesting point is the demonstration that the law of attraction which, when stated as it usually is, in terms of force, fails to explain the phenomena of cohesion and chemical affinity, stands, when stated by Fechner in terms of motion, in perfect accord with these phenomena. This enables him to extend the law to the organic realm, and he conceives the earth itself to be simply a universal organism.

As to consciousness, the physical and the psychical are identical, not two aspects of the same thing or causes the one of the other; they are the same thing looked at from two different points of view, just as the same curve is convex from without and concave from within. There is but one consciousness, as there is but one earth, and individual minds are simply points at which the universal divine consciousness ' crops out,' the 'threshold' of its appearance being a certain degree in the complexity of the individual organism. His view of attention is psychologically interesting. The principle of stability seen in the external world is the principle of the tendency to harmony in the inner— '' the world strives toward a maximum of pleasure " for the universal, divine consciousness. His ethic is hedonistic but not altogether empirical, for its highest good is the pleasure of a consciousness which transcends that of man. The will is determined from within by its own nature, and is therefore free. Man is '' a part of the divine con-

sciousness and, between men, the World is not dark and dumb, rather
she sees and hears with the mind of God."

G. A. TAWNEY.

BELOIT COLLEGE.

Habit and Instinct. C. LLOYD MORGAN. New York and London,
Edward Arnold. 1896. 8vo. Pp. 351. $4.00.

Principal Morgan is known as the author of two excellent books,
and his new volume will go far towards increasing his reputation as an
interesting and original writer. He is a disciple of Darwin, a pupil
of Huxley, and a follower and friend of Romanes. His book bears
clearly the traces of these three men's influence; it is written from the
evolutionary standpoint, it is based on the observations of a naturalist,
and its theme is psychological. A considerable body of new observations, of entirely fresh facts are presented. The immediate object of
the author was to ascertain for some of the higher animals the limits
of instinct. He accordingly devoted himself to a prolonged and
patient study by observation and experiment on the ways of young
mammals and birds, chiefly the latter, as offering a more favorable
field, since they can be readily reared away from the parents.

The main result of the book may be indicated by saying that the
author demonstrates the predominating control of experience and its
educational power during the young life in fixing adult habits. It is
the detailed, keenly analysed evidence of this which imparts to the
volume its chief value and originality, and renders it very refreshing
after the great mass of uncritical writings on animal psychology. Of
wider interest are the concluding chapters, which are devoted to a
broad discussion of the admissibility of the Neo-Lamarckian doctrines
in the author's field of evolutionary enquiry. The distinction which
Morgan draws between modification and variation is a welcome addition to clearness of thought, but the coöperation between the two,
which he seeks to establish with a view of making a compromise between the theory of the Neo-Lamarckians and that of Darwin, can be
regarded as hardly more than an offer to capitulate the Lamarckian
position if the honors of war are allowed.

With the material which he had on hand the author could have
written a paper, which, published in some psychological journal,
would have made his work known to his professional colleagues in a
very much briefer form. He has chosen, on the contrary, a more
popular method, and has based his book upon a course of lectures
delivered before the Lowell Institute in Boston. He has thus become

more readable, and ought to reach a wider public, though to the scientific reader the sacrifice is considerable. The author's presentation of his subject is excellent and his style very clear, though his habitual use of 'would seem' when he means 'seem' grates on the reader's ear. In the numerous critical passages he is calmly impersonal, although much that has been written on animal psychology might easily call forth sarcastic criticism. It may not be amiss to add that the book is made pleasanter to read by the occasional cropping out of a vein of quiet humor.

The work must be recommended very warmly to psychologists and ornithologists. The latter are probably past redemption, for an ornithologist is most rarely a bird-lover and seldom does the ornithological mind conceive a bird as more than a species with a Latin trinomial. To psychologists this book should bring much. As a naturalist, it has seemed to me that the naturalist's method has an immense future in psychology. The method includes two main factors: the observation of details and the comparison of homologous phenomena in different forms of life; and the method starts always from the standpoint of evolution. There need be no restriction, of course, upon the three aspects of psychology, which have heretofore prevailed, the metaphysical, introspective and experimental, but there should come soon and with revolutionary power, not merely enlarged interest in and sympathy with comparative evolutional psychology, but more than that, eagerness to enter this field of inquiry and to share in harvesting it. Those who follow the new trend can hardly begin better than by making acquaintance with Principal Morgan's recent volume, which illustrates how to begin and shows that there are substantial rewards for those who will investigate soberly and scientifically the mighty problems of psychological homologies.

CHARLES S. MINOT.

HARVARD MEDICAL SCHOOL.

SOCIAL PSYCHOLOGY.

The Crowd: A Study of the Popular Mind. GUSTAVE LE BON. New York, The Macmillan Company, 1896. Pp. xxiv+320.

We call attention to this (slightly clumsy) translation of a book already noticed in these pages, because, in spite of its grave defects, it is almost the first scientific attempt to treat a subject of supreme importance, and ought to be read by everyone who is interested in the problems which popular government presents. With public opinion ruling more and more the world, the psychology of public opinion, the sources of its strength and weakness, its pathology and hygiene, and the causes of its stability and of its alterations, ought to be studied with ever-increasing care by those interested in the welfare of mankind. It can hardly be doubted that M. Le Bon's little books will communicate a serious stimulus to study of this sort. He is a many-sided person, physiologist, anthropologist, traveller and historian, and knows the outside world as few Frenchmen know it; but of human life he takes a purely biological view, devoid of every sentimental or metaphysical ideal, and his results are misanthropic and pessimistic in the extreme. Man's worst enemy, it would appear, is man himself; for whilst nothing great can be done except by men in concert, it happens that all the feelings that move men together, all the patriotic, religious and philanthropic ideals which they will obey in crowds and collections, are more or less irrational and insane. Rationality indeed would, on M. Le Bon's view, seem necessarily confined to the isolated man of science or individual critic, and the only ideal permissible to *him* would be that of sound skin and safety from physical danger, for himself in the first place, and thenceforth for as many fellow-creatures as circumstances allow to be embraced. Anglomania is the practical result of all this—a result shared by the entire school of Frenchmen who follow the lead of Taine. For in England and America, whatever minor inferiorities these countries may show, the individual is left more to himself and his affairs are on the whole more safe. France, M. Le Bon seems to fear, is rushing blindly to a destiny which, being the outcome of ineradicable ideals of equality and centralization, will hardly stop short of complete socialism, with everyone at once a slave and a pensioner of the State.

It is curious for us Americans, who are just beginning to idealize less our national ways, to hear them so much idealized by foreigners. Meanwhile, in a sense, it is, of course, true that man's worst enemy is himself; the worst enemies of some ideals are other ideals, and men in crowds, even though those crowds be called deliberative assemblies, are often terribly unwise. But it is only from the standpoint of some one ideal held for true that all other ideals can be tried and condemned, and the great trouble with books like M. Le Bon's is that whilst they are inspired by very distinct ideals these are not expressed in them in frank teleological form. To a reader even half-respectful of the socialistic ideals of the present generation, it seems rather a *reductio ad absurdum* of the pretension of Science to look down upon all such ways of thinking as essentially crazy, to find that her own last word of practical wisdom about human life is to advise her votaries to dwell on the frontier and have bonds invested in many countries, so that when that insane beast Man 'breaks out' in one they may get into another escape. M. Le Bon does not give this advice in so many words, but it exhales somehow from his pages; and, *Lebensweisheit* for *Lebensweisheit*, it hardly seems obvious that, in comparison with this last rational outcome of Science, the religions and the philanthropies, with all their tendency to insanity, make such an inferior show.

Let it not be thought that our author's contempt for religious and other mob-swaying ideals, and his respect for Science, involve any snobbish deference to ' scientists' as a caste. He is, on the contrary, singularly free from all caste deference. Witness his defence of juries, to the irrationality of whose opinions in criminal cases he has devoted a chapter:

" Many writers, some of them most distinguished, have started of late a strong campaign against the institution of the jury, although it is the only protection we have against the errors, really very frequent, of a caste that is under no control. A portion of these writers advocate a jury recruited solely from the ranks of the enlightened classes, but we have already proved that even in this case the verdicts would be identical with those returned under the present system. Other writers, taking their stand on the errors committed by juries, would abolish the jury and have it replaced by Judges. * * * We should cling vigorously to the jury. It constitutes, perhaps, the only category of crowd that cannot be replaced by any individuality. It alone can temper the severity of the law which, equal for all, is bound on principle to be blind and to take no cognizance of particular cases. Inaccessible to pity, and heeding nothing but the text of the law, the Judge, in his professional severity, would visit with the same penalty the burglar guilty of murder and the girl * * * driven to infanticide. * * * Being well acquainted with the psychology of castes and also with the psychology of other species of crowds, I do not know a single case in which, wrongly accused of a crime, I should not prefer to have to deal with a jury rather than with magistrates. There would be some chance that my innocence would be recognized by the former but not the slightest chance that it would be admitted by the latter. The power of crowds is to be dreaded, but the power of certain castes is to be dreaded yet more. Crowds are open to conviction; castes never are " (p. 188).

In future books of this sort the objective psychology and the subjective teleology of the author will have to be kept more distinct, and the latter made more explicit. But the present volume, with all its faults, is a most honest and vigorous production which should be widely read.

W. J.

Psychologie du Socialisme. G. LE BON. Rev. Philos. December, 1896.

The author proposes to apply the principles developed in his previous works to the phenomena of ' socialism,' comprising under this term "the aspirations, wants, beliefs, ideas and reforms which are to-day the profound passion of many minds." To appreciate the power of socialism we must consider it not from the political or economic standpoint, but as a *belief*, and the student of the psychology of beliefs will understand why argument is quite in vain against the collective belief of a multitude.

In its fundamental principles socialism is but a repetition of tendencies which emerged in Hebrew, Greek and Roman life, and reached an actual triumph in early Christianity, only to be abandoned when Christianity became itself a conservative institution at present, although the actual condition of the poorer classes is much superior to that of former times, yet their wants and desires have increased so rapidly that the ratio is more on the side prompting to discontent than ever before. Add to this the prevalent egoism, demoralizing devotion to wealth and indifference of the ruling classes, the pessimism of thinkers, the half-heartedness of the defenders of the present social order, comparable to the weakness of the defenders of dying paganism, and, above all, the decay of the great dominant beliefs of the past which leaves men ready and eager for some new and inspiring belief, and the marvel is not that a new religion like socialism progresses so fast but that it does progress faster. To understand this we must recur to the psychological laws of the evolution of beliefs.

Man is guided in life by two classes of conceptions, *ancestral conceptions*, or *sentiments* on the one hand, and *acquired* or *intellectual conceptions* on the other. The former are the great motives in conduct. They are the atavistic influence to which is due the real conservatism of crowds, often masked as this may be by temporary agitations. The acquired or intellectual conceptions remain almost without influence upon actual conduct until, by repeated hereditary accumulation, they have penetrated the depths of the unconscious and become sentiments. Buddhism, Christianity, Islam were no new faiths. Christianity triumphed not because it was new, but because it embodied the sentiments of Greek and Egyptian and Persian as well as of Jew. At the very beginning a belief may have roots in the intelligence, but when it becomes the actual motor it becomes rather the regulator of the intelligence, the touch-stone of judgment. The mind can receive only what conforms to the new belief. Philosophy, literature and the arts all receive its impress, as in the middle ages, or among the Arabs. All new conceptions and perceptions must be unconsciously shaped by these ancestral conceptions before they can gain entrance to the mind. This is strikingly illustrated in the changing meanings attached to words from age to age, or as used by different races and sexes, a suggestive subject for psychological investigation. On technical subjects there may be intellectual discussion and agreement. But in morals, politics and religion agreement, or even mutual understanding is possible only for those of a common origin. In conference on these themes " it is not the living but the dead who discuss." Ordinary psychology assumes that all men experience identical sentiments under the influence of like stimulation, but nothing is more erroneous. A common well-rooted belief becomes thus the source of common ideas and the greatest factor in the creation of a national soul and will, and so of a characteristic orientation for all ideas.

The psychology of the apostles of the new faith is instructive. Although alienists usually regard the advanced socialists as belonging to the ' criminal-born' type, this is quite a mistake. They are rather actuated, not as the true criminal, by selfishness, but by motives the reverse of selfish, leading to acts quite opposed to their own interests. Like the apostles of past faiths, the men of the Inquisition, the followers of Mahomet, the men of the Convention, their zeal prompts them to destroy first institutions, then all who resist. Their philanthropy is as sincere and as intolerant of opposition as that of former apostles. They may be regarded as hypnotized by two or three formulas constantly brooded over.

Sociology and Philosophy. B. Bosanquet. Mind. January, 1897.

Sociology is coming to be regarded more and more from the point of view of social psychology, the point of view of Plato's *Republic.* This enables us to see its relation to social philosophy. Like individual psychology it is now interested in asserting its claim to be a natural science, and as such to treat all phenomena in its field impartially. The 'laws of association' are the object of investigation, without regard to the logical, ethical or social *value* of the product.

But just as in the concept of apperception we recognize that the mind is not merely a machine, unaffected by its content, but is very different according to the reality which it thinks of, so, in social psychology, when it has ceased to be necessary or worth while to direct our attention solely to the fact that there is a common element in all social groups, we shall inquire into the differences as well. From this the transition to the consideration of the relative social value of the different groups or forms of organization is an easy one, and this is the province of social philosophy. The service of social science to social philosophy may then be similar to that of psychology to logic, ethics and æsthetics, but it would be for the advantage of the sociologist to familiarize himself far more intimately than he has yet done with psychological conceptions and principles, for which he now seems to be vaguely groping.

J. H. Tufts.

University of Chicago.

NEUROLOGY AND PHYSIOLOGY.

The Cell in Development and Inheritance. Edmund B. Wilson. Columbia University Biological Series, IV. New York and Lon don, The Macmillan Co., 1896. Pp. xvi+371

Within recent years the problems of biology have centered more and more largely in the cell. As long as morphologists were chiefly concerned with the evidences and probable course of organic evolution interest gathered around questions of homologies of organs and affinities of organisms, but now that the paramount problem is the *cause* of evolution the old methods are generally found to be of little service. What light could homology or phylogeny throw upon the nature and causes of assimilation, growth, metabolism, inheritance or development? And yet upon these very questions hangs the causal explanation of vital phenomena in general, including evolution. In almost every case these problems have been found to be at bottom questions as to the structure and function of the cell, and in attacking them morphology has of necessity become physiological. In the life of the cell are centered most of the present philosophical problems of biology.

The appearance, therefore, at this time of a general work on the cell is of more than ordinary interest, not alone to the biologist, but to all persons of liberal ideas. Professor Wilson's work is not the first in the field, though I think it may be said to be easily the best. Hertwig's splendid treatise, *Die Zelle und die Gewebe* (1893), was really the pioneer volume in this field; it treats the subject in a more general way than Wilson's work, taking in the non-developmental as well as the developmental cell phenomena, but it is, of course, far less rich in references to recent important literature. The only other work which deserves to be compared with Wilson's is Henneguy's *Leçons sur la Cellule* (1896). This volume is in typography and illustration a work of art, but, like so many other modern French works on biology, it is in large part a huge, encyclopedic compilation and is too technical and diffuse for the general reader.

Professor Wilson has wisely limited his work to the developmental cell phenomena in which at present knowledge is most advanced and interest most intense. After an introduction which gives a brief historical sketch of the cell theory and its relation to the evolution theory, there are taken up, in successive chapters, a general sketch of cell structure, cell division, the germ cells, fertilization, chromatic reduction, some problems of cell organization, cell chemistry and cell physiology, cell division and development, and finally some theories of inheritance and development. In addition there is appended an excellent glossary and a general list of literature.

The book contains a large amount of Professor Wilson's own work and that of his pupils, some of which has not heretofore been published, but such a general work must of necessity be to a large extent founded upon the work of others. The author has brought together, under one point of view, the isolated observations and frequently conflicting views of a multitude of writers. In this he has graciously and entirely avoided the old museum idea of collecting material without reference to its use; although he summarizes almost every important work of recent years bearing either directly or indirectly upon the cell, yet the book is no mere encyclopedia of facts or theories—all is treated in a critical spirit as so much material to be builded into a system. The labor involved in this sifting of literature and collation of results must have been prodigious and all future workers in these lines will owe Professor Wilson a debt of gratitude for the service which he has thus rendered.

The limits of this notice will not allow a review of the conclusions of the author on the many subjects discussed. Those, however, which are of the most interest to the general reader are contained in the final chapter of the book and may receive brief mention here.

The author indicates that all present discussions of development revolve around two hypotheses, both of which are regarded as embodying fundamental truths. The first is the *Germinal Localization* hypothesis of His, the second the *Idioplasm* hypothesis of Nägeli; the former asserts that the cytoplasm of the egg contains in definitely localized areas the germs of future organs ('*organbildende Keimbezirke*'); the latter regards inheritance as the result of the molecular organization of a peculiar kind of living matter, the *idioplasm*, which is now generally identified with the chromatic substance of the nucleus. With regard to the application of these principles to development there are two widely different views. The Roux-Weismann theory of development holds that cytoplasmic differentiation is due to nuclear differentiation and that the latter arises from qualitative divisions of the nuclear substance. The opposing view of Driesch, Hertwig and others is that divisions of the nucleus are always quantitative, never qualitative, and that the progressive differentiation of the cytoplasm is the result, not of the progressive differentiation of the idioplasm, as Roux and Weismann hold, but of the relative position of cells with reference to each other. More recently both Driesch and Hertwig have been compelled to supplement this view by granting that chemical and physical differences exist in different regions of the egg-cytoplasm and that subsequent differentiations arise through the reaction of these different substances upon the nuclear idioplasm which constantly remains the same. With the main points of this hypothesis Professor Wilson is in hearty accord; however, he adds this further very important conception that the specification of the cytoplasm, induced by the nucleus, reacts upon the latter, bringing about a specification of the idioplasm, so that in the end there is a differentiation of nuclear material, though not brought about by qualitative divisions.

The specific character of the development with its orderly course of events is regarded, as in almost every modern theory of heredity, as the result of the *structure* of the idioplasm. The nature of this structure, as Professor Wilson points out, involves the old controversy of preformation and epigenesis, "a controversy which now has little meaning apart from the general problem of physical causality. Despite all our theories we no more know how the properties of the idioplasm involve the properties of the adult body than we know how the properties of hydrogen and oxygen involve those of water." The problem of the historical origin of the idioplasm ' is merely the problem of evolution stated from the standpoint of the cell.' "Whether variations first arise in the idioplasm, as Weismann maintains, or whether they may arise in the body cells and then be reflected back upon the idioplasm, is a question upon which the study of the cell has not thus far thrown a ray of light."

Finally, Professor Wilson considers the nature and origin of coördinated *fitness* as the fundamental problem of biology. In this regard there is an enormous gap between the lowest forms of life and the inorganic world which the study of the cell has only served to widen. With Wigand and Driesch the author thus, apparently, returns to a form of vitalism which, for the present at least, seems the only justifiable course.

The book is written in good literary English, an unusual thing in recent biological works, and, although dealing with some very abstruse and obscure themes, it is remarkably clear and logical throughout. Professor Wilson's style is that of a teacher at his best, precise, concise, enthusiastic. In typography and illustration the volume is a model of excellence; many of the figures are entirely new and few of them have ever before appeared in a general work of this character.

Considering the great amount of ground covered there are remarkably few errors in the volume. Perhaps the most important one is as to Van Beneden's view on the origin of the centrosomes of the first cleavage spindle (pp. 156-7). This Professor Wilson has already corrected (*Science*, Jan. 1, '97). Another error, of minor importance, however, is the statement (p. 113) that the amœboid egg cells of Cœlenterates probably do not ingulf other cells.

To me it seems that the feature which is most open to serious criticism is one which gives the work one of its particular charms, *viz*, its enthusiasm and, in some places, its controversial spirit. Professor Wilson frequently uses strong language, sometimes stronger than seems to be justified. He speaks of a certain abandoned theory as having been 'absolutely proved to be a myth.' He says the Roux-Weismann hypothesis of qualitative nuclear divisions "is as complete an *a priori* assumption as any that the history of scholasticism can show and every fact opposed to it has been met by equally baseless subsidiary hypotheses." Examined in the light of the facts "the improbability of the hypothesis becomes so great that it loses all semblance to reality" (p. 307). And yet a few pages further on (p. 321) he strongly supports the most fundamental part of the Roux-Weismann theory, *viz.*, that *nuclei progressively become qualitatively different throughout the development.* Since the only point of difference, therefore, between Professor Wilson and the Roux-Weismann theory is as to the method by which these qualitative differences of the nuclei arise, such strong statements as those just quoted scarcely seem justified.

Again, in the matter of the origin and significance of the centrosomes in fertilization he goes much farther, I think, than the facts warrant. It is true that in the majority of known cases the centrosomes of the first cleavage spindle come from the spermatozoon, and Professor Wilson has been most active in establishing this fact, but there are cases in which these centrosomes are known to come from the ovum, and, until we know whether the centrosome is really a permanent cell organ or not, it is too soon to assert that the point of origin of the centrosome is a matter of primary significance or that "the centrosome is the fertilizing element proper."

These are, however, criticisms of minor significance. As a whole the work is a remarkably able and comprehensive presentation of the most important biological problems of the day and it easily takes first rank among books of its class.

E. G. CONKLIN.

UNIVERSITY OF PENNSYLVANIA.

Atlas of Nerve Cells. M. ALLEN STARR, M.D., PH.D., With the coöperation of OLIVER S. STRONG, A.M., PH.D., and EDWARD LEAMING, M.D., F.R.P.S. With fifty-three plates and thirteen diagrams. New York, Columbia University Press, Macmillan, 1896. Pp. 78.

The revolution in methods of nervous histology brought about by Golgi's discovery of the possibility of defining nerve cells and processes by a precipitation of metallic salts about the elements has been followed by an activity in research in that field which has hardly a scientific parallel. As might be expected, we are now reaping the results and without regarding the rather startling speculations as to cell function which have made their appearance during the last twelvemonth, the fairly well established and probably valid conclusions arrived at are of great interest and importance. We are no longer to consider the central nervous system as made up of nerve cells and nerve fibres but of units, each consisting of a nerve cell with its processes, of which one is greatly prolonged and is our old nerve fibre while the shorter cell processes which were formerly delegated to the uninteresting duty of nutrition are now elevated to the dignity of auxiliary receptive functional parts. We no longer have our cell with its axis cylinder and protoplasmic processes but have a 'neuron' as our unit, made up of a cell with its 'neuraxon' and its 'dendrites.'

More interesting still is the demonstration of lack of continuity between these units, the nervous impulse traversing the series of neurons by contiguity. This anatomical independence, while perhaps not proven beyond cavil, may at least be accepted as highly probable. These facts together with the demonstration of the collateral branches of the neuraxons are the essentials of the discoveries of the last few years and need only be mentioned to obtain recognition of their importance as furnishing a scientific basis for physiological and pathological theory.

In the superb atlas before us, Dr. Starr has undertaken to show by photographs the state of things at the present day. It may as well be said at once that, considering the methods used, little criticism can be offered. Dr. Strong, who is responsible for the preparations, has attained a perfection of technique that leaves nothing to be desired, Dr. Leaming's mastery of micro-photography is well known and Dr. Starr's explanatory text is characteristically clear and comparatively conservative. The shortcomings of the work are the limitations of the methods. No photograph can show more than one level of a section and it can focus but a small area and as a consequence much that is strikingly evident upon a single turn of the adjustment of the microscope must be taken on faith. In other words, one good slide under the microscope is worth all the photographs in the world in acquiring an idea of the object. This is, of course, a difficulty inherent in the means and the authors have been very judicious in their choice of levels of the sections which would minimize the disadvantage. Further, the Golgi method, valuable as it is, is gross. It blots out details of cell structure in the most ruthless way and we are still in need of a cell stain for finer work on which to base functional conclusions. The object of the atlas is, of course, mainly anatomical; at the same time Dr. Starr's text does not neglect the physiological aspect of the question and there are numerous digressions on that side which deserve notice. Particular attention is called to the brief discussion of the mechanism of reflex action in the cord on pp. 24 and 25, in connection with the function of 'collaterals' and the length of the reflex arc which may extend and, as a matter of fact, probably normally does extend several segments up and down the cord from the point of entrance of the sensory impulse. This is the clearest statement of this phase of reflex action which has come to the notice of the writer and it is a phase too much neglected by contemporary writers on general physiology. To sum up, the work is good in all its aspects and the obvious question whether it is all worth while is not to be answered by any individual. It is not so much an original contribution as a resumé of progress already made and, as indicated above, so far as that can be shown by photography it is admirably done. As a specimen of book making the atlas is magnificent, but the price is prohibitive for students and probably for many laboratories. It would be a great service if the plates could be reproduced by a cheaper process and sold separately to aid class room demonstration.

LIVINGSTON FARRAND.

COLUMBIA UNIVERSITY.

VISION.

Ueber die functionellen Verschiedenheiten des Netzhaut-Centrums und der Nachbartheile. PROFESSOR V. KRIES. Archiv für Ophthalmologie, XLII., (3), 95–133.

Professor v. Kries here replies to Koster (see this REVIEW, Vol. III., p. 108 and p. 231) who doubts the conclusiveness of the considerations which go to show that the cones are the seat of color-sensation, while the rods furnish us with sensations of gray of different degrees of brightness; he makes a very strong showing in favor of the thesis which he defends, and his able summing up of all the evidence can hardly fail to carry conviction.

V. Kries finds that the Purkinje phenomenon (the increased relative brightness of blue in a faint light) does not occur in the fovea; that Koster differs with him on this point is plainly owing to the fact that he is unaware of the extreme difficulty of looking at anything with the fovea when the light is faint,—there is an almost irresistible pull in favor of using an adjoining part of the retina on account of its superior efficiency. The strongest of all the arguments is that two grays composed of different complementary colors, if made to look equally bright at an ordinary illumination, no longer look so in a faint light,—it is difficult to believe that only a single apparatus is involved in furnishing the sensation at the two extremes, if adaptation works so differently upon lights of different composition; when both terms of the comparison are of the same quality, gray, the difficulty which is always felt in comparing different light-qualities in respect to their intensity does not arise, and hence the experiment in this case is of a peculiarly convincing nature. Recurrent vision v. Kries has already attributed to a distinct functioning of the rods, and he finds now that a patient who was suffering from night blindness (which had already been made out by Parinaud, in 1883, to be due to a lack of visual purple) wholly failed to get the recurrent image. Koster found a discrepancy between the extent of the fovea and the area of the space within which adaptation does not occur; v. Kries has now measured the functional fovea (as this latter retinal space may be called) by several different methods and finds an extremely good agreement with the size of the anatomical fovea as lately determined by Koster. The diameter of the functional fovea, when projected to a distance of one meter from the observer, was found by the different methods to be :

By Purkinje phenomenon, . . .	59 mm.
By same for two dichromates, . . .	35 mm.
By recurrent vision, ...	36 mm.
By same for another observer, . . .	52 mm.

Koster's anatomical determination gives for the rodless space 33 mm. and for the space within which the rods are very few 53 mm. The coincidence is, therefore, very close; it is also possible that a better method may yet be devised for the determination of the functional defective area.

C. L. FRANKLIN.

BALTIMORE.

Über kompensatorische Raddrehungen der Augen. W. A. NAGEL. Zeitschr. f. Psych. u. Physiol. d. Sinnesorg. XII., 331– 354. 1896.

When the head is inclined sideways, do the eyes rotate about the sagittal axis in the opposite direction, or do they retain their normal positions in the head without rotation? This question has been argued much on both sides. It had been practically settled in favor of rotation until 1894, when Contejean and Delmas again disputed it. Nagel again proves the existence of rotation by several methods. It can be seen directly on the eye of another person, or on the reflection of one's own eye in a properly arranged mirror, by observing the position of the radial lines of the iris. Care must be taken to prevent change in the direction of the line of regard, that there may be rotation only about it. The ray-like figure, due to irregular astigmatism, seen proceeding from distant luminous points, will also demonstrate the rotation if the direction of its rays, which show the eye's position, be compared with lines on a spectacle-lens whose position is fixed relatively to the head. A third method makes use of after-images. The denial of rotation above mentioned was based on measurement of the position of the blind spot, determined by suitable diagrams for different positions of the head. Nagel uses this same method for quantitative measurements. When the head is inclined 20°, he finds $\frac{1}{6}$ of this compensated by rotation; the proportion grows gradually less up to 80°, where it is $\frac{1}{10}$.

Experiments on animals show similar movements of rotation in many cases. Animals whose eyes are placed in the side of the head and have no common field of regard show rotation when the head is inclined not sideways but in the sagittal plane. It varies in degree from full compensation in case of guinea pigs to its entire absence in some birds, where it is replaced by compensatory head movements. The mechanism for initiating these movements of rotation is situated in the labyrinth.   E. B. DELABARRE.

BROWN UNIVERSITY.

EXPERIMENTAL.

Die motorischen Wortvorstellungen. RAYMOND DODGE. Halle, Niemayer. 1896. Pp. 78.

Mr. Dodge gives an admirable introspective study of his own verbal imagery, analyzing it in all its varieties. Silent thinking in words is for him mainly an inner speaking. But reproduced articulatory images are not the only element. Connected with each word it is possible to represent vaguely the essence of all that the whole sentence is intended to express. Although he can never represent clearly two words at once, or even a single word in all its parts, yet the shadowy sentence-image is made up of many simultaneous verbal images of lesser clearness, and is not identical with the speechless meaning or concept, which the full sentence expresses. The characteristic elements of the words themselves are reproductions of the movement-feeling which arises in actual speaking; derived mostly from lips, tongue and throat, less clearly and characteristically from breast and thorax. Contact and vibration sensations are present, but not essential, as was shown for the former by producing through cocain a strong anæsthesia of lips, tongue and throat. Stricker's assertion, that no sensory elements are present in his motor verbal images, and that they consist in innervation-images, is shown to be indefensible. It is impossible that sensory motor images can be entirely lacking, whether innervation-feelings exist or not; and D. can find by intro-spection no trace of the latter. Peripherally aroused sensations from actual articulatory movements are not essential for inner speech; their reproduced images suffice. When present, they raise the mental presentation of words to greater clearness. Unusual and incompatible positions of the mouth disturb the mental presentation of a sound for a moment only; and show not that particular peripheral sensations must be present, but that strong peripheral sensations of another kind may inhibit for a moment the desired verbal image.

In addition to the reproductions of motor sensations, there must be other elements in the verbal image. For articulatory movements alone, unpreceded by the idea of expressing a word, do not necessarily awaken a verbal idea. The latter possesses a filling, a fullness which can be given only by a sort of unlocalized, faded-out auditory imagery, which never attains an independent, clear and recognizable reproduction. No trace of visual elements can be detected in any recognizable characteristic of the word-image. It is shown, however, that they must be aroused to a certain extent, unconsciously influencing and controlling the conscious imagery. Images derived from writing movements cannot be detected or inferred, unless when a word is spelled. In short, motor images are prominent, and are recognizable as such; auditory images are not recognizable as such, but furnish a recognizable portion of the content; visual images cannot be detected in any conscious feature of the content, but their presence is evidenced by their control.

Similar thorough analyses, with inferences as to the brain-paths used, are given of the verbal elements present, prominently or vaguely, in speaking aloud, in hearing, in reading and in writing. Whichever one of the four kinds of word elements is most prominently aroused, its firm association with the others arouses them also, though not all with equal distinctness. Where they are not consciously distinguishable, yet their unconsciously aroused traces influence the conscious content. The motor images are always of demonstrably greatest importance, in motor speech for determining it, in sensory for understanding it. Auditory, visual and motor types of individuals do not exist in the sense that one or the other element is present exclusively in any of their verbal images; they consist only in the prominence of one element over the others, all of which must be present.

E. B. Delabarre.

Brown University.

Ueber das Gedächtniss für Sinneswahrnehmungen. W. von Tschisch. Dritter Internat. Congress f. Psychologie. (Munich, J. F. Lehmann, 1897.) Pp. 95–109.

This paper, read at the Psychological Congress, is a report of several investigations upon memory carried on at the Dorpat Laboratory. The questions taken up were the space sense (Raumsinn), position sense (Ortssinn), active and passive muscle sense, active movement, sight, sound intensity and tones. These were studied by different investigators, under the direction of Professor von Tschisch, who took personal charge of the one on sound intensity.

The method pursued, with two exceptions, was that of Right and Wrong Cases. For the sense of space, distances on the skin were used as stimuli; for the muscle sense, weights; for sight, light impressions of different intensities; for sound intensity, sounds of the same pitch but different intensities; and for tones, sounds of the same intensity and different pitches. The stimuli were given in pairs; the subject was required to designate the louder, higher, brighter, etc., as the case might be. The proportion of right answers to wrong was noted, judgment of equality being ruled out.

Having determined a pair of stimuli which could be distinguished correctly by the subject in about 70 cases out of 100 when given in close succession, this pair was adopted for subsequent tests, in which an interval of time was made to elapse between the two stimulations. The interval, at first short, was increased by empirical steps (which varied in the different investigations) until some marked diminution of the percentage of right answers, usually below 50%, was obtained. When necessary to prevent the memory from lingering over from one trial to the next, different pairs of stimuli were used alternatively in the same series. The interval of time at which a marked falling off in the percentage of right answers occurred was taken as measure of the strength of memory in each case.

In two investigations in which the method of Mean Errors was used, the same general procedure was employed; the interval of time at which a marked increase in value of the mean error occurred was made the measure of the strength of memory.

The space sense was investigated by means of a pair of compasses, the place chosen being the right forearm. 70 mm. was taken as normal distance, but tests were made for greater and lesser distances as well. For the sense of position, the left forearm was chosen; a point was touched by the experimenter with a pencil, and the subject endeavored to touch the same spot with another pencil held in his right hand; a screen prevented the arm from being seen by the subject, who was allowed to 'feel around' for the spot after touching. In this investigation the method of Mean Errors was used. The muscle sense was investigated by means of copper cylinders, of uniform size and varying weight. For the passive muscle sense these were laid upon the palm of the subject's hand for the space of three seconds and then removed; for the active muscle sense they were placed by the investigator between the subject's thumb and fore-finger, and raised by him. Active movement was investigated by requiring the subject to move his hand slowly to the right or left. A thin stick attached to the hand, with a pointer extending upward to a scale, served to mark the angle of flexion; in the first of each pair of experiments the length of movement was regulated by a knob which the hand encountered; this obstruction was then removed, and the subject required to repeat the movement. The method of Mean Errors was employed here also. The investigations in sight made use of the shadow cast by a steel bar upon a white surface, with varying distances of the light-source. For sound intensity, steel balls were dropped from varying heights on a wood surface. The last study was one on tone differences; five tuning-forks were employed, which differed by four vibrations, from 436 up. For musical subjects differences of four vibrations were used; for unmusical subjects differences of eight vibrations were chosen, as this was nearer their perception threshold.

Comparing the results of the several investigations, Professor von Tschisch finds the memory for space to be weakest; it falls off in exactness the soonest. Memory for position and the muscle sense is somewhat better developed. Memory for active movement and the higher senses is decidedly stronger. The memory for sight and sound, and in the latter sense for intensity and quality, appears to be about the same; in these three the percentage of right answers falls from 70 to about 50 in 15 minutes, for normal individuals.

H. C. WARREN.

PRINCETON.

Experimentelle Studien über Associationen. I. Theil. Die Associationen im normalen Zustande. GUSTAV ASCHAFFENBURG. Leipzig, Engelmann. 1895. Pp. 95.

Dr. Aschaffenburg's aim in his experimental study of association is the establishment of a method of diagnosis in cases of nervous disease. The published part of his work deals with normal associations as basis for the later study of neurasthenic cases. The methods employed are the simple ones of older experimental tests. A word is pronounced to the subject who responds by writing down or by pronouncing the first suggested word; or (in one form of the experiment) by writing down, as quickly as possible, the first hundred words occurring to him. There are 4,400 single cases of association, with

17 subjects, in series usually of 100, but occasionally of 200 or of 50 words. In 2,300 of these single cases the associated word is pronounced, and the time intervening between beginning of stimulus and beginning of reaction is measured by the use of Cattell's lip-key, connected with a Hipp chronoscope. Verbal associates only are studied, without reference to the accompanying images, usually visual, whether these amplified the suggested words or differ from them.

Dr. Aschaffenburg's theory and terminology are frankly Herbartian; his classification is first the ordinary distinction of what Wundt calls External and Internal Association, and then a more detailed division, mainly on the basis of that of Kräpelin. The problem of the experiments is the assignment of every associated word to its proper class, and the author emphasizes, with praiseworthy iteration, the absolute need in work of this sort of the coöperation of the subject, who alone can decide whether a given association is, for example, one of 'subordination' or of 'predicative relation.' The results of this detailed classification are, however, very meagre and justify no definite conclusions, as Dr. Aschaffenburg, who is most modest in his claims, very freely acknowledges. This failure supports the writer of this review in the conviction that the results of such minute classification of material so elusive, are always incommensurate with the doubts and difficulties of the undertaking. On the other hand, the experiments clearly justify the ordinary observation that associations of the concrete, matter-of-fact variety predominate strongly over the more focalized and abstract, for an excess of external over internal associations is noticed with every subject and in every form of experiment. A slight decrease in time also distinguishes these external associations.

The most significant outcome of the experiments is perhaps their demonstration that the absolute reaction-time of a subject affords no important psychic test, since the reaction-times of different normal individuals vary in so marked a degree (p. 67). While, for instance, the average association-time of eight subjects varies between 1,180σ and 1,426σ, it falls in the case of one subject to 927σ, and rises with another to 2,151σ, though the conditions are the usual ones, and though there is no marked individual eccentricity to explain the divergence. Dr. Aschaffenburg properly insists, therefore, that length or brevity of reaction-time cannot be supposed to distinguish the diseased from the sound subject or the abnormal from the normal state. Conditions of fatigue or of emotional disturbance do, however, affect the associations by occasioning interruptions in the continued series, and by augmenting the tendency to associate words through their sound—

alliterative or rhyming words—and to respond by mere disconnected repetitions of former words. From the consideration of these characteristics of association Dr. Aschaffenburg will proceed to his study of association in abnormal subjects. Incidentally, the monograph treats other topics: community of associations, accepted as an evidence of the lack of originality (p. 92); the difficulty of assigning with certainty the period of life to which associated images date back (p. 87); and finally, the grammatical type of associations (p. 82). The associated words, as Kräpelin had indicated, are chiefly nouns, but three of the thirteen subjects respond with a large number of verbs, while another often associates adjectives. The author is unable, however, to trace these types, which correspond with those suggested by Münsterberg (Beiträge, IV.), to any characteristics of individual thought.

Mary Whiton Calkins.

Wellesley College.

Ueber die Wahrnehmung von Druckänderungen bei verschiedenen Geschwindigkeiten. George Malcolm Stratton. Philosophische Studien, Band XII., Heft 4.

Dr. Stratton's experiments seem to have been carefully made, and are discussed with considerable acumen. Were it not for what is, perhaps, a fundamental error in the interpretation of results, the work would be far above the average thesis in psychology.

The first of the three sets of experiments made by the writer was on the accuracy of momentary pressure changes. The method used was that of minimal changes. The stimulus was applied by a system of levers to the little finger. The results of 560 determinations show clearly that a change in the pressure could be perceived before the direction of the change, and that the perception of an increase of pressure is more accurate than that of a decrease. Weber's law was found to hold for 75–200 g.

In discussing these results Dr. Stratton concludes that the process involved is similar to that of absolute threshold perception rather than that of difference discrimination. The greater accuracy of perception for increase of pressure is ascribed to the intensifying effect of attention, the writer rejecting the fatigue hypothesis of Hall and Motora, who had observed the same phenomenon.

In interpreting his experiments Dr. Stratton assumes that the stimulus is pure pressure, and goes so far as to regret that movement cannot be entirely excluded. Does he suppose that a sensation of pressure is possible without movement? The fact is, as can be shown by the simplest experiments, that constant pressure, if below the pain threshold, soon ceases to effect consciousness. Pressure without movement cannot, therefore, be considered a stimulus at all, or classed together with other sensory stimuli. Gustatory and olfactory stimuli, it is true, seem to lose their effect gradually, but this phenomenon is easily explained by fatigue. Fatigue cannot, however, be caused by a pressure so small that we can hardly perceive it. Dr. Stratton's assumption is all the more remarkable in view of his recognition of the resemblance of the process to that of threshold perception. He himself observed that the change in pressure seemed to him but a slight touch of the stimulated surface.

In another series of experiments the writer investigated the effect of variations in the rate of change on the accuracy of perception. The rate of change of the stimulus was regulated by the application of Archimedes' law of fluid pressure, as in the other experiments. The method of minimal changes was used. The least perceptible increase was found to be inversely related to the rate of change, a result exactly the opposite of that obtained by Hall and Motora. But instead of rejecting contemptuously the work of the previous investigators, as many experimental psychologists would have done, Dr. Stratton repeated the experiments of Hall and Motora and got the same results. The discrepancy between the results of the two sets of experiments must, therefore, be due to the methods employed. The increase of the threshold from decrease of the rate of change is explained by the effect of attention and the conditions of the observer's reaction. In support of this view the writer offers considerable evidence. The opposing results he explains on the supposition that differences are more easily perceived, the closer the objects to be compared. How this applies to continuous changes is not clear. Had the writer not started with what is, I believe, a radical misconception of pressure phenomena, he would not have rejected so hastily the physiological interpretation.

HAROLD GRIFFING.
NEW YORK.

Mesure de la Clarté de quelques Representations Sensorielles. M. FOUCAULT. Revue Phil., Dec., 1896.

The problem set out for investigation is the determination of sensible discrimination for weight or pressure. The method employed is that of right and wrong cases. Small boxes of uniform size were used, in which the different weights were placed. The experiments were tried on the back of the hand, always in the same place during same series. The subject was not permitted to see the weights, the results were withheld from him, and the order in which the different weights were tried was made irregular. By clearness of a representation is meant the degree of certainty with which it can be distinguished from any other representation. Expressed quantitatively; if v represent the right cases, and d the wrong cases, the clearness will be expressed by the formula $\dfrac{v - d}{v + d}$. The clearness of the representation is not the same as its intensity. It varies with the fatigue, degree of attention, etc., and not always in the same direction as the intensity. The functional relation between clearness and intensity has not been determined experimentally, but it may be said that, in general, the greatest clearness is obtained from *mean* excitation. M. Foucault's problem then is to establish a ' clearness-scale,' proceeding from the point where the two weights are not accurately discriminated. The utility of such a series of experiments is: (1) the determination of the variability of sensible discrimination. (2) A clearness scale will afford a means of comparison between senses qualitatively different. (3) "The determination of the mean clearness for a certain kind of perception, will furnish also a measure of sensibility for that stimulus." (4) Such a study furnishes an analysis in quantitative terms of different mental functions. Here we determine the function directly by the relative ease with which the mind discriminates. (5) Lastly, we shall determine the type of the subject. In this series of experiments M. Foucault makes out two distinct types of imagination.

The results are as follows: I. *Determination of mean clearness.* There were eight subjects. Four series of experiments were taken (540 ex. in each series, 240 on each subject). The weights varied from 18 to 20 gr. and were tried in two directions. 1. (The clearness varies for different subjects.) 2. This difference (1 to 4 gr.) is in all the cases less than one-third of the original excitation, which Fechner thought the threshold of difference for pressure. The proportion of right cases, and consequently the clearness, increases according as the excitation increases from 1 to 4. According to Fechner's theory the difference should be imperceptible. This confirms the results of Jastrow and Pierce. 3. The results present a number of negative cases, but even for the smallest difference of excitation the excess of right cases is appreciable so that the negative instances may be considered the exceptions, due to individual differences of the subjects, etc.

II. *Variation of clearness due to relative size of stimulus dif-*

ference. There are two cases: 1, where the difference increases; 2, where the difference decreases. In both cases "the mean clearness is greater according as the relative difference is greater."

III. *Determination of sensibility for pressure differences.* This is on the assumption that the relative clearness determined by the method of right and wrong cases will be a measure of discriminative sensibility as found ordinarily by the gradation methods. The results are obtained here by combining those of the previous experiments. It is a question whether they are exact enough to be of any great value. The sensibility of the two hands was not found to be appreciably different. Whence the conclusion is drawn that pressure sensibility does not depend at all upon the fineness of muscular development.

IV. *Conclusion relative to the imagination.* The subjects divide themselves into two classes: 1. Those who detect a decrease of stimulus most readily; 2. Those who detect an increase best. Throughout the experiments, in no case was the first stimulus replaced, so that always the judgment was between the second weight and the memory-image of the first. The sensibility is found to vary in either direction. It is not found to be greatest for the augmenting series, as Jastrow insists. (*Am. Jour. of Psy.*, Vol. I., 271 ff.) To explain this difference of type, M. Foucault proposes the following hypothesis: In the change from the perceived image to the memory-image, the latter will be sometimes greater, sometimes smaller than the original image. This change is due to the imagination. There are then two types of imagination, one tending to enlarge memory images, the other diminishing them. The coefficient of this variation is determined as follows: If Ca represent the mean clearness for the increasing series and Cd for the decreasing series, $\frac{1}{2}(Ca + Cd)$ will be the mean clearness of perception. In the case where Ca is greater than Cd, on the hypothesis the Cd clearness is less because the comparison image is diminished. So the imagination coefficient will have a negative sign and will equal $Ca - \frac{1}{2}(Ca + Cd)$ or $\frac{1}{2}(Ca - Cd)$. The reverse case will be where the Cd clearness is greater than the Ca clearness and the coefficient will equal $\frac{1}{2}(Cd - Ca)$. No direct relation is discoverable between the mean clearness, or sensibility, and the coefficient of imagination-variability, so that as one (mean clearness) increases the other tends to disappear. Conditions of fatigue, distraction, practice, etc., which affect sensibility, do not influence appreciably the imagination coefficient. This was tested carefully for practice.

This positive and negative character of imagination enables us to explain the negative cases which have been mentioned. The person who has a tendency to an enlarged memory-image will perceive with most clearness differences which are in the negative direction, and will have, consequently, a tendency to more false cases in the augmenting series, where the differences will be in favor of the *first* impression. And conversely, where there is a tendency to diminish the image, the greater error will be in connection with the diminishing series, where the difference will be in favor of the *second* impression.

J. M. Trout.

Princeton University.

LOGICAL.

Manual of Logic. J. Welton. 2d Edition. London, University Correspondence College Press. New York, Hinds and Noble. 2 vols. Pp. 411, 292.

This is a second edition of this work, revised and largely recast. Much of the historical matter of the first edition has been omitted. The author has endeavored also in this edition to give greater prominence to the distinctions of thought which underlie the distinctions of language with which the traditional logic is concerned. The two volumes cover the ground of deductive and inductive reasoning in a very exhaustive manner, dealing with the important questions of the theory of logic as a careful exposition of the technical rules and praxis. This treatise should prove a valuable help to teachers of Logic. It is adapted for such a purpose rather than for use as a textbook. The author's very thorough elaboration of his subject has lead him, at times, to rather a diffuse treatment, notably the chapters on Opposition, on Eduction, on Figure and Mood, and, in general, the more technical parts of formal Logic.

Ueber die sogenannte Quantität des Urtheils. Otto Sickenberger. München, 1895.

This is a Doctor's dissertation presented to the University of Munich. It is, in the main, an historical survey of the logical doctrine of the quantity of the judgment. The author traces the discussion from Aristotle to the present, with special mention and criticism of the positions of the modern logicians, especially Lotze, Brentano, Sigwart, Wundt and Erdmann. He concludes with a short chapter outlining his own position, being the constructive portion of his work, which is evidently secondary to that of historical exposition and criti cism. He divides judgments primarily into universal and individual, with an intermediate class, which, as Lotze, he designates by *this* A etc., to distinguish from all A's and some A's.

In this intermediate class he finds an illustration of a principle which he regards as fundamental to the true conception of judgment, namely, that the distinction between universal and individual lies in thought and not in the objects themselves. For the judgment of the form this A etc., may be regarded as universal or individual, according as the point of view is shifted from the individual to the universal aspect. Moreover, some objects essentially different may, in thought, be the same if regarded exclusively from the standpoint of their identity, disregarding completely their differences; so, also, one and the same object may be represented in thought as two instead of one, as it is regarded, first in its individual, then in its universal character and relations. There is, however, an impression left upon the reader that there is a sundering of concept from reality. Differences in thought, owing to a shifting of the subjective point of view may, nevertheless, be referred to the reality whence they emanate. The abstract must have some basis of reference which rests upon the real and concrete. The hypothetical universal may swing clear of reality in a sense; that is, that its expressed condition may never be realized. Yet the ground of the hypothetical relation thus expressed in thought must have a reference to reality; otherwise it may be only an imagi- native connection, which, even if the conditions were to be realized, the alleged result would not follow.

Dr. Sickenberger's analysis of the various judgment forms is clear and exhaustive. On the whole, the chief value of the dissertation lies in its historical contributions.

JOHN GRIER HIBBEN.

PRINCETON UNIVERSITY.

Outlines of Logic and Metaphysics. By JOHANN EDUARD ERD- MANN. Translated from the Fourth (revised) Edition, with Pre- fatory Essay, by B. C. BURT. New York, The Macmillan Co., 1896. Pp. xviii + 253.

In view of its well-known relation to the Hegelian school, of its first publication fifty-two years ago, and of the immediate interests peculiar to readers of THE PSYCHOLOGICAL REVIEW, it is probably unnecessary to enter here upon a detailed discussion of the contents of this work. Other considerations, however, present themselves. In face of them it is not easy so to review the book as to do justice to the solid work expended upon it by the translator. For, on the one hand, Dr. Burt's translation is careful and accurate, though far too literal to admit of freedom from stiffness, so indispensable in an introductory manual. Further, his prefatory essay is a competent piece of writing, displaying commendable intimacy with the alterations upon the Hegelian logic made and proposed by disciples of the first generation, like K. L. Michelet, J. E. Erdmann, Rosenkranz and C. H. Weisse. On the other hand, it may very well be questioned whether the book was the right one to translate. Written within a decade after Hegel's death, it bears abundant traces of the atmosphere from which it sprang. And, in these circumstances, it is a very open question whether the student's purpose would not be better served by study of the smaller logic of Hegel in Professor Wallace's translation, especially as it is presented with so much valuable apparatus in the way of elucidatory comment. Yet again, modern logic has not been stationary, and a satisfactory ' Introductory Text-Book ' ought to bear a date later than 1864, that of the edition from which the present version is made. On the whole, then, it must be said that between the classical work of Hegel himself and Dr. Bosanquet's recent *Essentials of Logic*, no place remains for this translation. Moreover, its terminology is as harsh as Hegel's own, and is not lit up by those illustrative flashes which the reader expects from the author of the *Phänomenologie*. Of course, criticism of this kind raises the whole question of translating. And it must be said that sufficient discrimination is not always shown. The translator needs common sense for his selection as well as knowledge for his rendering. Dr. Burt has the latter in plenty; one cannot think that he has in this case weighed the circumstances which will certainly militate against his work as a students' manual. It ought to be added that the ' get up ' of the book is little creditable to the publishers; and in this matter Messrs. Sonnenschein, of London, and not the Macmillan Company, are to blame.

R. M. WENLEY.

UNIVERSITY OF MICHIGAN.

NEW BOOKS.

Education and Patho-Social Studies. A. McDonald. Reprint from Report of Commissioner of Education. Washington, Government Printing Office. 1896.

L'Attenzione e i suoi disturbi. S. de Sanctis. Rome, Unione Coop. Editrice. 1896. Pp. 46.

Genetic Studies (I.-II.) J. Mark Baldwin. Princeton Contributions to Psychology, I., 4. Princeton, University Press. Sept., 1896.

Emozione e Sogni. S. de Sanctis. Reggio Emilia, Calderini. 1896. Pp. 27.

Studies in the Hegelian Dialectic. J. M. E. McTaggart. Cambridge Univ. Press; New York, Macmillan Co. 1896. Pp. xvi + 259.

Physische und psychische Kausalität und das Princip des psychophysischen Parallelismus. M. Wentscher. Leipzig, Barth, 1896. Pp. 10 + 122. 4. M.

Die Impersonalien: eine logische Untersuchung. M. Jovanovich. In. Diss., Leipzig. Belgrad, Koen., Serb., Staatsdruckerei. 1896. Pp. 142.

Ueber die sogenannte Quantität des Urtheils. O. Sickenberger. In. Diss. Munich. München, Wolf. 1895. Pp. 217.

The Will to Believe and other Essays in Popular Philosophy. William James. New York and London, Longmans, Green & Co. 1897. Pp. xvii + 332.

Die physiologische Beziehungen der Traumvorgänge. C. M. Geissler. Halle, Niemeyer. 1896. Pp. 47.

A History of European Thought in the Nineteenth Century. John Theodore Merz. Vol. I. Introduction; Scientific Thought, Part 1. Edinburgh and London, Wm. Blackwood & Sons. 1896. Pp. xii + 458.

Contributions to the Analysis of the Sensations. E. Mach, Translated by C. M. Willams. Chicago, Open Court Co. 1897. Pp. x + 208. $1.25.

The Survival of the Unlike. L. H. Bailey. New York and London, Macmillan. 1896. Pp. 515. $2.00.

Handbuch der physiologischen Optik. H. v. HELMHOLTZ. Zweite umgearbeitete Auflage, mit 254 Abbildungen u. 8 Tafeln. Hamburg u. Leipzig, Voss. 1896. Pp. xix + 1334. M. 51.

Philosophy of Theism. A. C. FRASER. Gifford Lectures, second series. N. York, Scribners; London, Blackwoods. 1896. Pp. xiii + 288. $2.00.

NOTES.

THE American Psychological Association has joined the Naturalists and Affiliated Societies in accepting the invitation of Cornell University to hold the next annual meeting in Ithaca.

PROFESSOR J. G. HIBBEN has been made full Professor of Logic on the Stuart foundation, and Mr. J. F. Crawford has been appointed Demonstrator in Experimental Psychology, both in Princeton University.

THE *Année psychologique* may hereafter be had from Mr. G. Stechert, the New York bookseller (9 E. 16th St., N. Y.), who will act as the American agent.

HERR CARL WINTER will issue, from the Universitätsbuchhandlung in Heidelberg, a jubilee edition of the *Geschichte der neuern Philosophie* of Kuno Fischer, who celebrated his 50th anniversary in March, 1897. The nine volumes will appear in 40 monthly parts at 3 M.

WE are glad to announce that Professor Hugo Münsterberg, who is one of the coöperating editors of the REVIEW, is to resume the duties of his position at Harvard University in the autumn.

THE members of the American Psychological Association are reminded of the summer meetings of the American Association for the Advancement of Science in Detroit, Mich., beginning August 9th, and of the British Association for the Advancement of Science in Toronto, Canada, beginning August 17th. Provision is made by both Associations for papers in experimental psychology, under Section H (anthropology) of the American Association and under Section I (physiology) of the British Association. By action of the authorities of both associations the members of the American Psychological Association are cordially invited to attend the meetings and become members. All members wishing to join the American Association are requested to notify Professor J. McK. Cattell, Columbia University, New York City, who will furnish information regarding that Association.

All members intending to present papers at the meeting of the British Association are requested to send abstracts of their papers before May 15th to Dr. A. Kirschmann, University of Toronto, Toronto, Canada, Secretary of Section I, from whom full information regarding the meeting can be obtained.

WE record with regret the death, on April 11th, of Professor Edward D. Cope, professor in the University of Pennsylvania, editor of the *American Naturalist*, President of the American Association for the Advancement of Science, and eminent for contributions to paleontology, zoölogy and a wide range of natural science. Professor Cope was greatly interested in psychology, and, as is well known, made much use of psychological factors in his contributions to the theory of evolution.

PROFESSOR J. MARK BALDWIN has been awarded the gold medal offered by the Royal Academy of Arts and Sciences of Denmark for the best work on a general question in Social Ethics. There were nine memoirs in the competition written in four languages. Professor Baldwin's work was entitled ' The Person Public and Private' and is in part the volume of ' Social and Ethical Interpretations of the Principles of Mental Development' which has been announced for early publication by The Macmillan Co.

DR. W. B. PILLSBURY has been promoted to an instructorship in experimental psychology in Cornell University.

THE interest of the Frohschammer fund of the University of Munich, amounting to $400, is offered for an essay on ' A Psychological Analysis of the Facts of Volition,' which must be presented before October 1st, 1899.

CHARLES SCRIBNER'S SONS have in press a work on *Philosophy of Knowledge*, by Professor G. T. Ladd, Yale University. The supjects treated may be seen from the titles of the chapters, which are as follows: I., The Problem; II., History of Opinion; III., History of Opinion (continued); IV., The Psychological View; V., Thinking and Knowing; VI., Knowledge as Feeling and Will; VII., Knowledge of Things and Knowledge of Self; VIII., Degree, Limits and Kinds of Knowledge; IX., Identity and Difference; X., Sufficient Reason; XL, Experience and the Transcendent; XII., The ' Implicates' of Knowledge; XIII., Scepticism, Agnosticism and Criticism; XIV., Alleged 'Antinomies;' XV., Truth and Error; XVI., Ethical and Æsthetical ' Momenta;' XVII., The Teleology of Knowledge; XVIII., Knowledge and Reality; XIX., Idealism and Realism; XX., Dualism and Monism; XXL, Knowledge and the Absolute.

VISION WITHOUT INVERSION OF THE RETINAL IMAGE.

BY PROFESSOR GEORGE M. STRATTON.

University of California.

In the November number of this REVIEW, I gave a short account of some preliminary experiments on vision without inversion of the retinal image. Brief as the experiments were, they gave certain definite results and hinted at others which would probably be obtained if the artificial conditions were continued for a longer time. The course of the experience also showed that problems much wider than that of upright vision were involved, and that a careful record of a longer test might throw light on these also. I was strengthened in this view that the experiment bore on other problems at least as important as that of upright vision, by the remarks of Professor Titchener when the paper was publicly read; while the questions of Professor Münsterberg, on the same occasion, suggested the need of more careful observations in regard to dizziness and the localization of sounds.[1]

The earlier paper was thus necessarily vague or silent on a number of questions in regard to which a more careful and extended experiment could hardly fail to produce something of interest—on such questions as, for instance, whether the reconstruction of the directions, right and left, proceeded exactly parallel to that of the directions up and down; what the connection of visual and tactual localization really is, which enables the one

[1] See the *Berichte* of the Third International Congress for Psychology. Munich, 1897, p. 194.

to influence the other; and, finally, what were the more definite conditions under which the harmonious accommodation to the abnormal sight-perceptions waxed and waned. It was also necessary that a nicer distinction should constantly be observed between acts or ideas arising as a result of deliberate volition and those which arose effortless and unpremeditated. In other words, the account should clearly distinguish at any given stage of the experiment between processes which occurred spontaneously and those which could be called up only by force of will.

The present experiment was conducted under almost the same conditions as those of the preliminary experiment. I myself was again the observer, and the apparatus was the one described in the earlier article, except that a thin cloth-lined plaster cast of the region about the eyes was substituted for the padded paste-board case which before had held the tube of lenses. In making the cast a small mass of non-adhesive material was placed directly over each eye, and afterwards removed from the cast; so that during the experiment the inner lining of the case did not press on the eyes, nor interfere in the least with their free movement. In front of the right eye there was an opening in the cast, into which the tube of four lenses before described fitted exactly. This tube was carefully focussed and set at such a distance from the eye as to give a clear visual field of about 45° compass. The cast could then be bound to the head by a set of tapes, and although somewhat heavier than the paste-board case, was nevertheless much more comfortable, because it pressed evenly over a large surface of the face. By this device all light was excluded, except such as came through the lenses into the right eye.

The time was not spent, as before, entirely indoors. Besides the free range of the house, I could walk in a secluded garden; and since the experiment fell at a time of bright moonlight, I took, every evening but the first, a long walk through the village, accompanied and, when there was need, guided by a companion. The experiment lasted, this time, from noon of the first day until noon of the eighth day—a net period in all (after subtracting the time during which the eyes were blindfolded), of about 87 hours, as against 21 ½ for the previous experiment. The actual record for the eight days is as follows :

DAY.	HOUR OF PUTTING GLASSES ON.	HOUR OF TAKING GLASSES OFF.	LENGTH OF TIME GLASSES WERE WORN.
1st	12 m.	9 p. m.	9 hrs.
2d	9 a. m.	9 p. m.	12 hrs.
3d	9 a. m.	9 p. m.	12 hrs.
4th	9 a. m.	9 : 45 p. m.	12 hrs., 45 mins.
5th	9 : 50 a. m.	10 : 30 p. m.	12 hrs., 40 mins.
6th	9 : 50 a. m.	9 : 45 p. m.	11 hrs., 55 mins.
7th	9 : 15 a. m.	9 : 45 p. m.	12 hrs., 30 mins.
8th	8 a. m.	12 : 10 p. m.	4 hrs., 10 mins.
			Total, 87 hrs.

At all times when the glasses were not worn, the eyes were thoroughly blindfolded. Careful notes were made every day, to record as exactly as possible the actual state of the experience at that time.

Before I attempt a narrative of the experience under the experimental conditions, a word or two as to the terminology will be necessary. One has constantly to make a distinction between the appearance of an object as seen through the reversing lenses, and either the appearance it had before the lenses were put on, or the appearance it would have had if the lenses were removed and normal vision restored. This appearance just described is called in the narrative the ' older,' the ' normal,' often the ' pre-experimental' appearance of the object; while the appearance through the lenses is called its ' newer' or ' later' appearance. Similar distinguishing terms have also to be used with reference to the mere representation or idea of an object, as contrasted with its actual perception.

It is perhaps unnecessary to state that the accommodation to the artificial conditions was, in my case, probably more rapid than it would have been, had I not retained some of the effects of the practice gained in the earlier experiment, about five months before.

The experience from day to day was as follows :

First Day.—The entire scene appeared upside down. When I moved my head or body so that my sight swept over the scene, the movement was not felt to be solely in the observer, as in normal vision, but was referred both to the observer and to objects beyond. The visual picture seemed to move through the field of view faster than the accompanying movement of my body, although in the same direction. It did not feel as if I were visually ranging over a set of motionless objects, but the whole field of things swept and swung before my eyes.

Almost all movements performed under the direct guidance of sight were laborious and embarrassed. Inappropriate movements were constantly made; for instance, in order to move my hand from a place in the visual field to some other place which I had selected, the muscular contraction which would have accomplished this if the normal visual arrangement had existed, now carried my hand to an entirely different place. The movement was then checked, started off in another direction, and finally, by a series of approximations and corrections, brought to the chosen point. At table the simplest acts of serving myself had to be cautiously worked out. The wrong hand was constantly used to seize anything that lay to one side. In pouring some milk into a glass, I must by careful trial and correction bring the surface of the milk to the spout of the pitcher, and then see to it that the surface of the milk in the glass remained everywhere equally distant from the glass's rim.

The unusual strain of attention in these cases, and the difficulty of finally getting a movement to its goal, made all but the simplest movements extremely fatiguing. The observer was thus tempted to omit all those which required nice guidance, or which included a series of changes or of rapid adaptations to untried visual circumstances. Relief was sometimes sought by shutting out of consideration the actual visual data, and by depending solely on tactual or motor perception and on the older visual representations suggested by these. But for the most part this tendency was resisted, and movements were performed with full attention to what was visually before me. Even then, I was frequently aware that the opposite, the merely represented, arrangement was serving as a secondary guide along with the actual sight perceptions, and that now the one factor and now the other came to the foreground and was put in control. In order to write my notes, the formation of the letters and words had to be left to automatic muscular sequence, using sight only as a guide to the general position and direction on my paper. When hesitation occurred in my writing, as it often did, there was no resort but to picture the next stroke or two in pre-experimental terms, and when the movement was once under way, control it visually as little as possible.

The scene before me was often reconstructed in the form it would have had in normal vision; and yet this translation was not carried to such an extent as at the beginning of the first experiment. The scene was now accepted more as it was immediately presented. Objects of sight had more reality in them— had more the character of 'things,' and less that of phantasms —than when the earlier trial began. Objects were, however, taken more or less isolatedly; so that inappropriateness of place with reference to other objects even in the same visual field was often, in the general upheaval of the experience, passed by unnoticed. I sat for some time watching a blazing open fire, without seeing that one of the logs had rolled far out on the hearth and was filling the room with smoke. Not until I caught the odor of the smoke, and cast about for the cause, did I notice what had occurred.

Similarly, the actual visual field was, for the most part, taken by itself and not supplemented, as in normal vision, by a system of objects gathered and held from the preceding visual experience. Sporadic cases occurred, in which some object out of sight was represented as it had just been seen; but in general all things not actually in view returned to their older arrangement and were represented, if at all, as in normal sight. Usually this was the case also in picturing an unseen movement of some part of my body. At times, however, both the normal and the later representation of the moving part spontaneously arose in the mind, like an object and its mirrored reflection. But such cases occurred only when actual sight had just before revivified the later memory-image.

As regards the parts of the body, their pre-experimental representation often invaded the region directly in sight. Arms and legs in full view were given a double position. Beside the position and relation in which they were actually seen, there was always in the mental background, in intimate connection with muscular and tactual sensations, the older represention of these parts. As soon as my eyes were closed or directed elsewhere, this older representation gathered strength and was the dominant image. But other objects did not usually have this double localization while I looked at them, unless non-visual sensations came from the objects. Touch, temperature, or sounds, brought up a visual image of the source in pre-experimental form.

Anticipations of contact from bodies seen to be approaching, arose as if particular places and directions in the visual field had the same meaning as in normal experience. When one side of my body approached an object in view, the actual feeling of contact came from the side opposite to that from which I had expected it. And likewise in passing under a hanging lamp, the lamp, in moving toward what in normal experience had been the lower part of the visual field, produced a distinct anticipatory shrinking in the region of the chin and neck, although the light really hung several inches above the top of my head.

Whether as a result of the embarassment under which nearly all visually guided movements were performed, or as a cousequence of the swinging of the scene, described above, there were signs of nervous disturbance, of which perhaps the most marked was a feeling of depression in the upper abdominal region, akin to mild nausea. This disappeared, however, toward evening; so that by half-past seven it was no longer perceptible.

Second Day.—This feeling of nervous depression, just mentioned, returned the next forenoon. Movements, though, had in many respects grown less laborious, and were performed more on the basis of the actual sight-experiences, and less by excluding these as a means of guidance. Once at least, in the afternoon, I noticed that in washing my hands I had given myself up completely to the actual scene; but at the next instant inappropriate movements occurred, and with the consciousness that I had thus given myself up the old pre-experimental translation of things returned.

Unseen objects could, by force of will, be represented in harmony with things in view, more easily than on the preceding day. I could, for instance, voluntarily bring before me, in consistent relation to the visual field, the general outline of the room in which I was sitting. My own body, however, was much less tractable; at best I could get only my legs and arms appropriately represented, and this only by an effort not required by other objects. And even an unseen object of this latter sort, when felt in intimate connection with some part of the body which stubbornly held its old ground, could not by effort of will be vividly represented in terms of the newer sight.

There was much evidence of a rigid interconnection of experiences, by which the place or reality of one thing decided the place or reality of something else. The vividness with which a part of the body could be localized by visual representation, was influenced to some extent by the consistency of this representation with the actual perceptions of sight. Thus in swinging my clasped hands above my head, although I was aware of the direction of such a movement in the pre-experimental visual field, yet the actual disappearance of my hands *below* the lower border of the field, and the free continuance there of the movement, involuntarily made the region seem, for the time, visually vague and empty where I had hitherto represented my chest and shoulders. Likewise, in walking through the room, the disappearance of a low-hanging electric globe toward the space in which my chin and neck were represented, and the immediately following contact of the globe with the top of my head, tended to disturb the place of representation of both my chin and scalp; while attention to the ceiling disappearing, as I walked along, in what was normally the lower part of the visual field, weakened the connection of the image of my feet with this place in the field. There was thus a suggestion of more than one way of appropriately knitting some item into the body of experience. This not infrequently led to two representations of a single thing, both of which had a sort of reality; although not to such an extent as to give an actual illusion of two objects where there was really only one. The unseen fire-place in the room where I was sitting could be vividly represented according to the new set of visual relations, but the crackling of the fire was involuntarily referred to another direction, and in that direction there was also a dim image of the fire-place. And even when I looked directly at some part of my body, there was an acceptance of the seen thing as the real thing, and yet there was an accompanying transposed representation of it which also possessed a certain reality of its own.

As to the uprightness or inversion of things, the general feeling was that the seen room was upside down; the body of the observer, represented in pre-experimental terms, was felt as standard and as having an upright position. But different circumstances produced a different shade of feeling. When I looked out over a wide landscape, the position in which I felt my body to be and the position of the scene before me were surely discordant and unnatural. Yet I could not, as I had the day before, take either the one or the other unreservedly as standard. It seemed as if an abnormal position of my body in viewing things might just as well account for the facts as would an inversion of the scene. The very expanse of the landscape in comparison with the size of my body no doubt tended to subordinate the latter and render it less unreservedly a norm for judging of correctness of position. But even when, indoors, the view was almost completely filled with the dining-table and its furnishings, there was no striking and obvious feeling that the scene was upside down.

During a rather long walk in the evening I was unable to recognize my surroundings most of the time, although normally they were quite familiar. Recognition evidently depended largely on external relations of position and direction, and, with a disturbance of these, the objects themselves seemed strange. I could voluntarily feel my feet strike on the ground seen in the upper part of the visual field. But my companion, who held my arm, I could not represent on that side of me which, I knew, a harmonious construction of the visual field would require.

On being blindfolded for the night, there was an immediate and involuntary recurrence to the older way of picturing things. Only rarely could anything be represented in terms of the later sight.

Third Day.—I was now beginning to feel more at home in the new experience. At no time during the day did any signs of nervous distress appear, and the hours passed more rapidly than on either of the preceding days.

Walking through the narrow spaces between pieces of furniture required much less care than hitherto. I could watch my hands as I wrote, without hesitating or becoming embarrassed thereby. Yet I often stretched out the wrong hand to grasp a visible object lying to one side; right and left were felt to be by far the most persistently troublesome relations when it came to translating visual into tactual or motor localization. An involuntary feeling of dissatisfaction with the new visual perceptions in some cases produced movements which, although intended to be corrective, were really the contrary. For instance, while holding my hands in water running from the customary faucet, in the wash-bowl, I had repeatedly to suppress involuntary movements of the hands toward the wrong faucet which now occupied a visual position identical with that formerly held by the right one in the normal experience. The visual hands were not in the visual place approved of by the older experience; spontaneous efforts to rectify the misplacement followed, although the motor perceptions were entirely appropriate to the scene, had this been translated into pre-experimental terms. The corrective movements were therefore evidence that a translative reconstruction of the scene had not taken place. And yet the older criteria of inappropriateness of visual position were still active in the new experience. Instead of a reconstruction or translation of this new experience into terms of the old, I now occasionally became aware of an opposite process—a spontaneous translation of some pre-experimental memory-image into the form of the later vision.

Head-movements were still accompanied by a slight swinging of the scene, although in a markedly less degree than on the first day. The movement was referred more to the observer, so that it seemed to be more a moving survey of stationary objects.

It is difficult to describe my attitude of mind toward the inverted scene. Little more can be said than that there was clearly an abnormal relation between the general localization of

my body and the position of the scene as a whole ; but, as when
looking at the landscape the day before, it was not clear which
of the terms was standard and normal and which was thereby
condemned.   I had, however, a distinct consciousness that the
feelings connected with certain positions in the visual field were
by no means what they had been in the normal experience.
What had been the old 'upper' position in the field was beginning to have much of the feeling formerly connected with
the old 'lower' position, and *vice versa*.   Once as I stood before
the fire-place, watching the fire, an odd sensation came over me,
as if I were looking at the fire out of the back of my head.

Contacts in walking past objects had hitherto for the most
part been surprising, because the contact was felt in a different
place from the one anticipated.   But to-day I noticed that expectation was coming more into harmony with the actual experience.   It was also evident that this expectation, when joined
with a vivid representation of the region of the body in question,
had a perceptible influence upon the direction in which the contact was actually felt.   If, for example, I walked up to a low
railing which came against my abdomen, the sensations of pressure seemed to come from the new visual position of the abdomen if I called up a vivid image of this part of my body in its
new position and expected the sensations to come from there.
But the unexpected contact of the railing with my arms (then
out of sight), which had not been represented in their new position, was referred only in the old way, until these too were distinctly imaged as the abdomen had been.   But even when the
localization was in accord with the new visual experience, there
was still a subordinate, background localization after the old
manner.

Other factors besides volition or even recency of visual perception were observed to have an effect on the direction in
which unseen objects were represented.   The position of the
shadow of my body in the visual field, for instance, involuntarily
strengthened the new representation of my body.   Shadows had
also a marked influence in determining where I must think the
window or the sun to be.   And movements of my hands in
front of my eyes to some part of my body which I could not see,
gave the clue to the new visual position of the part.

In this way and from other influences, there was coming to be a more vital connection between my actual perceptions and the larger visual system of merely represented objects. It was becoming easier to follow a line in the field of sight and, continuing the line into this larger system of things, to know what it would lead to. The rooms beyond the one I was in, together with the scene out of doors, could be represented in harmonious relation with what I was actually looking at. Such representations, however, were more or less a matter of voluntary effort; the spontaneous pictures were usually on the pre-experimental basis. But I was now able for the first time to produce even voluntarily a vivid representation of those parts of my body which could not be brought to view, in proper relation to my sight-perceptions. This was much easier when my legs and arms were in sight, but even otherwise the new representation could still be made. The representation in the old way, though, was the spontaneous one, and doubtless was always at least in the background. But in this older representation there was an unusual paling and weakening of the image of those parts which had most often been seen during the course of the experiment. By bringing my legs and arms into view, the older representation became a sort of torso, the filling in of the seen parts refusing to appear, except in the vaguest way, even by an effort of will. When objects other than the body were in sight, they were not accompanied by any background representation of them on the older basis, unless they gave some sound. In such a case, the sound was localized according to pre-experimental relations, and its source was dimly pictured in accord with this localization.

That the new experience was getting a more stable place in my mind, was perhaps shown by the involuntary recurrence of scenes in their new visual relations, after actual perception had ceased—when I closed my eyes, for instance, or in the evening when my glasses were removed and my eyes were blindfolded.

Fourth Day.—By the fourth day the new experience had become even less trying. There was no sign of bodily discomfort, and for the first time during the experiment, when nine o'clock in the evening came I preferred to keep the glasses on, rather than sit blindfolded—which had hitherto been chosen as a welcome relief.

During the day, actions appropriate to the new visual perceptions frequently occurred without any conflict or apparent tendency to react by a misinterpretation of visual positions. My hands, in washing, often moved to the soap or to the proper position in the basin, without premeditation or any need of correcting the movement. At one time in the morning, before the bandage was removed from my eyes, I pictured the basin and its appurtenances before me in pre-experimental terms. But my actions were the opposite to those which would have been appropriate to this image. Here I reacted in the new way on an old system of relations, instead of reacting in the old way on a new system of relations— a mode of reaction frequent in the earlier part of the experiment, and by no means fully suppressed even yet. But the more common form of inappropriate reaction now was a movement of one hand when the circumstances really required a movement of the other; as when I reached with my right hand to pick up a book on the floor to my left. I happened to discover, however, a simple means of obtaining without calculation the use of the proper hand in picking up things on the floor —a means which I used thereafter with almost invariable success. If, with one of my feet near the object, I gave a tap or two on the floor before I stooped to pick it up, the proper hand immediately came into play. Curiously enough, it was easier at this time to start the proper foot than to start the proper hand. But there had also been great progress in the suitable use of my hands, shown particularly in the lessened difficulty in serving myself at table, although this was still far from easy.

The sight of objects other than my body, was not accompanied by a representation in the form of the normal experience. The character of the representation of things not actually in sight was influenced by the recency of their visual perception and by the closeness of their relation to things in sight. Objects in sight called up the ideas of neighboring objects in harmonious spatial relation with the things I saw. When I looked down the room in which I was sitting, the ideas of the other rooms of the house were apt to arise in appropriate relation to my sight perceptions. But if I tried to represent the other rooms without first surveying the room before me and obtaining afresh a powerful 'apperceptive mass,' the spontaneons image of the other rooms was more frequently in terms of pre-experimental vision. And yet the spontaneous representation of things when all sight-perceptions were shut out by closing or blindfolding my eyes, or by darkness, was far from being an inevitable return to the older form of vision. More than once on shutting my eyes, for instance, the room was involuntarily represented as it had just been seen; or in walking after dark into an unlighted room, its general arrangement and more prominent objects rose of themselves before me in the later form of sight. And even in the morning, before I had put on the lenses and refreshed the new experience, the flow of ideas was not purely in the form of the older experience but was strongly mixed with forms of the new. This was also the case on removing the lenses in the evening.

The mode of representing the parts of my body differed with circumstances. On entering the unlighted rooms spoken of above, the movements of my legs and arms were, without my willing it, imaged in terms of the newer sight. As far as I could make out, this quite obscured the older form. At other times, the older representation of my legs striking against the floor was apparent, but seemed dim and unreal as compared with the new. Thus not only was the spontaneous visualization of these parts becoming a mirror of the new visual experience, but the spatial reference of the touch-perceptions was following with greater vividness the direction given by the new visualization. The feeling of contact of things on one side of my body was likewise becoming more spontaneously referred to the proper place in the new visual representation. Hitherto the proper lateral reference had probably always been an afterthought, or reflective reconstruction; the wrong localization was first suggested and then rejected. Now the wrong localization, it is true, still came, but often no sooner than the correct one, and in subordination to this. At other times the older reference alone was suggested. For instance, it occurred that two objects of different shape, one in each hand, when brought into view, had just the transposed position, as regards right and left, from what I had expected to see them have in the visual field. The touch sensations were here localized in incorrect visual terms.

Sounds coming from objects out of sight were localized as of old, except when the object was vividly represented in the new way. In the latter case, the old localization of the sound was not the exclusive one, but was accompanied by a distinct solicitation to refer the sound to the place where the object was visualized. When the object was in plain sight, the sound seemed to come from the direction in which the object was seen.

The feeling of the inversion or uprightness of things was found to vary considerably with the strength and character of the representation of my body. When I looked at my legs and arms, or even when I reinforced by effort of attention their new visual representation, then what I saw seemed rather upright than inverted. But, if I looked away from my body and gave exclusive force to its pre-experimental image, then everything in sight seemed upside down. Especially was it noticeable that during active movements of the body, as in brisk walking or in coping with objects whose arrangement was relatively unfamiliar, the feeling of the uprightness of the scene was much more vivid than when the body was quiet. During such active operations there was at times a surprising absence of incongruity in the appearance of things. In the evening, during my outdoor walk, I called up a picture of my body in its old visual position, outside the field of view; I had the distinct feeling that such a position was upside down. The outer scene and the new arrangement were clearly at this time the standard.

The swinging of the scene during movements of my body seemed greater or less, according to the way in which I represented to myself this movement of my body. When I pictured the movement in terms of the new visual experience, the movement seemed to be a survey of stable objects. But when I lapsed into the older way of visualizing the movement, then the scene itself seemed to shift before my eyes.

Fifth Day.—At the thought of putting on the lenses, in the morning, there was an influx of ideas in the new visual form. I even noticed in many cases that there was a reconstruction, in the new terms, of objects which I had just before been thinking of in the old way.

At breakfast, with the lenses on, the inappropriate hand was rarely used to pick up something to one side. The movement itself also was easier and less wayward; seldom was it in an entirely wrong direction. When hand and object were both in sight I did not, as a rule, have to calculate or try to find the direction and extent of movement necessary to reach the object, but merely fixed my attention on the thing, and the hand was laid upon it without more ado, except for an occasional slight correction of the direction.

In walking I did not so often run into obstacles in the very effort to avoid them. I usually took the right direction without reflecting and without the need any longer of constantly watching my feet. When the doors were open I could walk through the entire house by visual guidance alone, without holding out my hands in front of me to warn in case of a misinterpretation of the sight-perception. For the first time, I dared to turn and sit down on a chair without beforehand assuring myself with my hands that I had placed myself aright. My movements were of course still cautious and awkward. And often the question of right and left was troublesome; for example, I wished to grasp the handle of the door beside me, and must hesitate a moment before it was clear which hand to use. But I found that the appropriate hand often came to the appropriate side of the visual field directly and without the thought (frequently necessary before) that *that* visual side meant the *other* side in motor or older visual terms. An evidence of the growing ease with which simple movements were coming to be done is given by the fact that I took a sheet of my notes and laid it upon a shelf in another part of the room, all the while intent on something entirely foreign to the matter in hand.

When I rocked myself in a chair the downward and forward movement of my body was primarily and spontaneously felt as a movement toward the actual visual floor; that is, toward the *upper* region of the visual field, to express the direction in terms

of normal vision. And the backward, upward movement was
likewise felt entirely in accordance with the actual visual experience. In this way the rhythmic variation of the visual field
during the rocking seemed a harmonious and natural result of
the rocking itself, and not, as formerly, a shifting of the scene,
unnatural, and therefore suggestive of illusion. And on other
occasions, there often was no immediate feeling that the position
of the object seen—the position of a person, for instance, with
whom I was talking—was incongruous; only after reflection
was I aware that the scene was reversed from what it had been
before the experiment began.

But in general the most harmonious experiences were obtained
during active operations on the scene before me. In rapid,
complicated, yet practiced movements, the harmony of the
localization by sight and that by touch or motor perception—the
actual identity of the positions reported in these various ways—
came out with much greater force than when I sat down and
passively observed the scene. During such a passive observation I still involuntarily represented my head, shoulders, and
chest in the old pre-experimental relation to the actual things in
sight. I could, however, by an effort of will fill out the entire
form of my body upon the foundation of the parts then seen,
but such a visualization was felt to be forced; the spontaneous
image of the unseen parts of my body as I sat quiet was thus
what it had been during the older experience, and did not at all
fit the actual localization of the parts I saw. For these latter
were felt to be where they appeared in sight. But even they,
when no longer actually in view, often lapsed into the older
mode of representation; so that with my two feet pointing in
the same direction, but with one in sight and the other
outside the visual field, they sometimes felt as though pointing
in diametrically opposite directions; the seen foot pointing forward while the unseen one pointed backward, to express the
directions in terms of the new visual experience. If I took a
fresh look at the hidden foot, however, and then let it pass out
of sight, its image remained for some time in accord with the
recent perception. But that the older way of representing my
body was losing ground, even in the case of the unseen parts,

was evidenced by the disappearance of that anticipatory " drawing in " of chin and chest when a solid object passed through the visual field in the direction which in normal vision would have meant a blow in the chest, but which now suggested a free passage overhead. The clear knowledge that the object would not strike me, had been of no avail on former days to prevent some sign of practical distrust.

Localization in cases of unseen contact often went astray, mainly in that the wrong visual side was first suggested, but corrected before I turned my eyes on the thing touching me. Localization of sounds was various, and at times gave a sudden and surprising turn to the experience. Thus, as I sat in the garden, a friend who was talking with me began to throw some pebbles into the distance to one side of my actual view. The sound of the stones striking the ground came, oddly enough, from the opposite direction from that in which I had seen them pass out of my sight, and from which I involuntarily expected to catch the sound. I unhesitatingly accepted the visual directions of throwing and of the stones' movement, but the auditory spatial suggestion was in complete discord with these.

During the usual moonlight walk it was evident that differences of light and shade could not so readily as in normal vision be translated into differences of elevation of the ground.

When blindfolded, after the glasses had been taken off, representations in the form of the new vision were a more vivid constituent of my train of ideas than on any previous night. After I went to bed, while still awake, they came in concrete and colored scenes.

Sixth Day.—In walking about the room blindfolded for a few moments in the morning, images in form of the pre-experimental vision were almost exclusively present. Once or twice at this time a strange indecision and confusion came over me when I did not immediately lay hands on an object which I knew was within reach. I doubted whether I was not using the opposite hand from the one intended. A moment's hesitation, the bewilderment for some reason gave way to assurance, and the movement went on its way. In putting on my shoes—the lenses were now in place—the problem of right and left, which had hitherto rendered this operation difficult, was unreflectingly solved by making a direct visual comparison of the contours of foot and shoe and seeing whether they matched.

Movements of the head or of the body, which shifted the field of view, seemed now to be in entire keeping with the visual changes thus produced; the motion seemed to be toward that side on which objects entered the visual field, and not toward the opposite side, as the pre-experimental representation of the movement would have required. And when, with closed eyes, I rocked in my chair, the merely represented changes in the visual field persisted with the same rhythmic variation of direction which they would have shown had I opened my eyes. I tried to *make* the imagined objects take the opposite course—the course they would have taken in the older vision during such movements of the body; but only after some moments of effort could I get even a faint suggestion of such changes, and these were immediately supplanted by those in accord with the new visual experience, the instant I ceased my attempt to reinstate the old by force.

When I sat passive, either the old or the new position of my unseen body could be brought prominently forward by act of will. When the old representation was thus reinforced, the actual scene seemed inverted. But when the new representation of my body was emphasized, then the scene felt right side up. During active operations on the visual surroundings, however, the older image of my body became, in many cases without my willing it, weaker than the new, and at times faded completely away.

Variations of touch-localization under different conditions of sight were clearly observable. I felt that my legs were where I saw them, or where they were vividly represented, if they were out of sight. If I tapped upon my knee in plain sight, the contact was localized only where sight reported it to be. But if I tapped while not looking at my knee, the contact was referred to both the old and the new visual positions, the reference according to the older visual experience being probably the stronger. I then placed my two index fingers in view before me, at equal distances from my body, and resting on a paper tablet in my lap. The right finger now was in that position in the visual field, which in normal sight would have been occupied by the left and *vice versa;* though, of course, the direction in which the fingers pointed in the visual field did not similarly correspond with the old. In many cases, now, a contact (the touch of a pencil point, for instance, by an assistant) on one of the fingers could at will be felt in either of them; at times, indeed, the contact could be referred to both fingers at once. When there actually was a contact with both fingers at once (for instance, a pencil point on one, and the assistant's finger tip on the other), the voluntary transfer of the localization of the pencil's contact from one finger to the other was much easier. And in this case, the contacts, although qualitatively distinguished with ease, and spontaneously referred to their distinct and proper places in the actual field of sight, could nevertheless voluntarily be felt as coming from the same finger at the same time. A movement of one of the fingers, such as a slight bending and straightening of it, while the other remained passive, produced a marked difference between the two fingers, both as to their visual appearance and as to the character of the tactual sensations just mentioned; and this movement rendered the arbitrary reference of the two contacts impossible. Each contact could then be felt only in the place where it was seen to be.

Likewise the substitution of a thumb for one of the fingers (the right thumb for the right index, or the left for the left) prevented a voluntary control of the localization. In the case of the two fingers, however, such a control was still possible when the positions of the fingers in the visual field did not exactly correspond each to that of the opposite finger in pre-experimental sight, or when the contacts fell on relatively different spots on the two fingers, that is, on spots which did not mutually correspond. With the thumb and forefinger, as above described, it is true that, when attention was somewhat withdrawn from vision and given more to touch, I could voluntarily feel my thumb on the opposite visual side from the one on which I saw it; yet there was no reference of the two sensations of contact to the same member, or an identification of the felt thumb with the seen finger, as was usually possible with the two index fingers. In several cases, though, the visual perception of the source of the peculiar sensation of contact kept also the touch-sensation fixedly on that side where its source was seen to be; or even gave a sudden and surprising reversal to the whole localization, when this had been based on only a vague and partial report from sight. This reversal of localization occurred several times when I was not directly experimenting on the matter, and furnishes an interesting parallel to the results more deliberately obtained. More than once, as I sat with both hands in sight, holding a tablet of writing-paper, a sensation coming from one hand—the feeling of a single loose sheet projecting beyond the others—was involuntarily referred to the visual perception of the *other* hand. But as soon as I saw where the cause of the sensation visually lay, then the touch sensations immediately went over to this latter position, changed hands, in other words, and could not even by effort of will be felt as at first.

Localization of sounds, when the source of the sound was in sight, followed in most cases the visual position of the source, provided I did not voluntarily recall the older position of the object. And since the compass of the visual field was about 45°, the actual divergence from the older localization of the sound could thus be about as great as the diameter of the field of view. For when the source of sound was seen at the border of this field, its older localization would have been on the opposite side of the field and at an equal distance from the center. When the source of the sound was out of sight, a much greater divergence of localization was possible. For in walking I actually felt my feet striking against the floor which I saw extending into the (old) upper side of the field of view before me; and the sound of my steps seemed to come from the place where I felt my feet strike—in this case a divergence of 180° from the old direction of the sound. But when I felt my feet in the old place, the sound too seemed to come from that direction.

In the evening, after I was blindfolded, the play of imagination was almost exclusively in terms of pre-experimental vision.

(To be concluded.)

THE PSYCHOLOGY OF SUFFICIENT REASON.

BY DR. W. M. URBAN.

Princeton University.

§ 1. Among those who make earnest with the idea of genetic psychology it seems to be taken for granted that in some sense the relation between utility and knowledge is a close one—that the extension of the doctrine of Selection into the sphere of knowledge processes, whether as natural selection or selection of a peculiar sort, is warranted. That there is wide difference of opinion, however, as to the nature of that selection and of the accommodations that result, a moment's glance at the literature will show. The uncertainty and differences in the answer to this problem arise mostly from the natural difficulty of keeping the philosophical and psychological sides distinct, in which direction Spencer set an unfortunate example. It seems to be equally unwarranted, however, to consider the question definitely settled either positively or negatively by a one-sided consideration from the point of view either of psychology or of a theory of knowledge. The following paper has therefore nothing more in mind than a consideration of some psychological phenomena which point to a process of selection according to the principle of utility in the sphere of the higher knowledge processes.

§ 2. Genetic psychologists prefer to designate the adaptation of consciousness to its environment by means of intelligence as 'sufficient,' rather than 'necessary,' as in the case of lower psychic organisms. By that distinction they mean to indicate the element of 'subjectivity' which distinguishes the selection in the case of higher will acts from the outer necessity which controls the lower instinctive reactions. Thus Spencer makes a distinction between the 'necessity' of the organized reactions of instinct and the 'sufficiency' of the less stable rational reactions

growing out of the correspondence of ideas to external reality.[1]
So also Professor Baldwin: " The principle of sufficient reason
is subject to a corresponding genetic expression on the side of
accommodation. Sufficient reason in the child's mind is an attitude, a belief, anything in its experience which tends to
modify the course of its habitual reactions in a way that it must
accept, endorse, believe. This has its sufficient reason, and he
must accommodate to it."[2] With a consideration of the nature
of subjective sufficiency is included, therefore, the elements for
the solution of the problem of accommodation among intellectual
processes.

§ 3. Sufficiency in the sphere of intelligent processes does
indeed include much more complex elements than the simple
necessity of reflex movement. If the hypothesis of a positive
selective factor, over and above the negative function of natural
selection, is necessary, as it seems to be, even for the explanation of accommodation in the sphere of reflexes, still more is this
positive factor, in much more developed form, a primary requirement in the higher spheres. For, though both are alike in that
they are reactions upon environment, they differ materially in
the nature of that reaction.

In reflex movement there are two terms, the stimulus and the
reaction, between which at least the scientific criterion of *likeness*
of cause and effect may be found. They are both objective
terms and experience tends to prove the constancy of the relation of stimulus to reaction on the pleasure-pain hypothesis.
The higher apperceptive functions, on the contrary, have three
terms, the stimulus, the supervening ideal and emotional complex which gathers about the stimulus, and the motor reaction
which follows in the will act. Here an entirely new relation
meets the eye. Instead of the relative constancy of the relation
between stimulus and reaction, instead of the relative constancy
of outer conditions, appears a practically absolute inconstancy.
The number of possible complexes of ideas and emotions that
gather about the stimulus is, to all intents and purposes, infinite.
For the stimulus does not work directly as outer reality; but in

---

[1] Spencer, ' *Principles of Psychology*,' Vol. I., Chap. 7.
[2] Baldwin, *Mental Development*, p. 323.

its place enters the complex 'motive,' which, though it stands in the place of outer reality, does not necessarily correspond to it, but oftener does not. The pleasure-pain hypothesis is not directly applicable, for the reason that pleasure and pain do not enter necessarily into these complexes, but are oftener merely suggested.

§ 4. We may, therefore, express the relation (*a*) between the 'motives' and the will act, or (*b*) between the subjective ground of a judgment and the judgment itself as sufficient reason, but not as necessary cause as in the relation of stimulus to reflex movement. This infinite variability of motives which allows us to speak of them as subjectively 'sufficient' but not as causally necessary is evident if we consider with what difficulty 'motives' objectively necessary are found for the simplest will acts.

The consequence of this uncertainty is that we confine ourselves to simple primal effects such as love, hate, etc., which we have, in a manner, objectified as real forces, or at best we make hypotheses on the analogy of our own experience. The personal equation of sufficiency is further observable in spheres not directly connected with the will—in the æsthetic and intellectual judgment. In all thought products the sufficiency lies not in the logical texture, but in the ethical and æsthetic feeling sources of the production. Almost every bit of original thought, especially where it is of the genius rank, must suffer the elimination by critical thought of just those subjective elements in which for the thinkers the sufficiency lay. The same is true in the reaction of the individual upon race beliefs and customs, speech, etc.; the personal equation is always the source of the sufficiency which determines his reaction. 'Characterologie' is, however, notably the despair of empirical science simply because of this law of infinite variability. To be sure, it has been sought to construct a psychology of metaphysical systems, but scarcely with success, even in the case of the non-school philosophers who carry their hearts on their sleeves. The important point is that if the law of selective accommodation is carried up into the sphere of intellectual functions, as a principle of explanation for the existence of our knowledge, the problem becomes extremely complex, because (*a*), as has been shown, the reaction is no longer upon simple reality, but upon an intervening *motive* complex which shows infinite variations from reality, and (*b*) as a consequence of this infinite variability, instead of the law of simple ' autogeneity ' of ends in instinctive reactions, we have the law of heterogeneity of ends as the governing principle of the higher psychological processes.

§ 5. If it were asked what in the nature of our psychological organism gives rise to this divergence of the motive, which takes the place of the stimulus, from the known reality from which the simple stimulus arises, the answer would come from almost every reader, the presence of the imaginative processes. To these is due the presence of such a law as that of the infinite heterogeneity of ends. If the simple stimulus, unmodified by imagination, was reacted upon, the conditions could be comparatively constant as in instinctive reactions. By imagination is meant, of course, not the vulgar conception of the phantasy which confines it to the sphere of the æsthetical shine nor of the narrow view of some psychologists which restricts it to a particular kind of apperceptive processes, but rather is it a term for that general *element in all apperceptive processes of a complete nature which selectively projects ideas before conciousness* in an emotional unity and sufficiency more complete than that of the merely associational relations. This conception is in full accord with the doctrine of Wundt which describes all those unitary complexes of ideas and feelings (*Gesammtvorstellungen*) which precede either judgments or will acts as the products of ' *Phantasie-Thätigkeit* ' and its ' *schöpferische Synthese* ' which he will have recognized as a thoroughgoing principle of all psychological processes.[1] That this general element of imagination is the source of the divergence of the motives as ideal content from reality is clear from the nature of these processes, by means of which our stimulus may bring about an infinite variety of imaginative complexes dependent upon the nature of the psychological organism.

§ 6. But it is exactly this characteristic of the imaginative processes which suggests them as a possible basis for a doctrine of accommodation. It is true that in imagination we see the

---

[1] *Grundriss der Psychologie* (1895) p. 367.

source of the divergence of motives from the real environment for which they stand; but in this very divergence is likewise seen the possibility of new adaptation, for this law of the heterogeneity of ends which has its root in imagination offers at least the material for new selection, if only there exists a principle of selection adequate to the demands made upon it. For this principle we need not look beyond the imaginative processes themselves; in their activity lies also a principle of selection which counteracts that element in imagination which works as a source of estrangement from the outer environment, or, if the expression be allowed, uses it as an element in a higher synthesis. The imaginative processes stand in marked contrast to the associations from which they rise in two particularly noticeable characteristics.

a. While the associations pass in succession, according to immanental causal laws, the imaginative processes are governed by a law relatively superior to the associational flow of ideas, by an immanental teleological principle, which, although it expresses itself in the already mentioned law of heterogeneity of ends, yet is at bottom ruled by one motive, namely, the reproduction of reality or the production of experiences analogous to reality. This '*Imaginatio*' is a struggle to reproduce reality by an imitation on the basis of the scattered feeling, and idea, memories which already exist in consciousness. The result of this is a feeling and ideal complex which possesses as its ground tone a 'reality feeling' very like to that of an actual experience.

b. As a consequence of its being governed by this motive, the process of imagination is marked by a certain wilfulness with which some associations are selected and others rejected, according to the criteria of this reality feeling. With this wilfulness comes a certain increase of motor energy, an excess which tends to express itself in actual will acts.

§ 7. A little reflection will suffice to show that these imaginative processes, thus described, are spendid attempts at association in a complete sphere of manifold association. These associations in their mechanical state, if not organized in the form of instinct, stand rather as a barrier to direct reflex accommodation to environment. They must first be brought into a unitary complex of feelings and ideas, which shall at least relatively reflect the reality which comes to consciousness in the form of stimulus. The ruling criterion is the feeling of reality with which the imaginative complex, this imitation of reality, is clothed. This sense of reality, or 'sufficiency,' it is evident, belongs alone to the feeling side of the complex, for the necessary relations of the ideas come to light first through reflection upon the results of the process, either in the judgment or in the will act, and its relation of advantage and·disadvantage in the environment. Until the judgment or will act actually takes place and is reflected upon as a part of objective knowledge or of actual objective reality, that is *retrospectively*, it appeals to consciousness only as subjectively sufficient. For the sense of reality which attaches to the imaginative processes, as background to the judgment or act, arises from the fact that there has been reproduced in consciousness the same organic state (or at least with only slight modification) as existed at an earlier time when reality was directly reacted upon. This means, of course, that the same general affect tone, together with the particular feelings of that experience, have been reproduced by a new stimulus, and consequently that stimulus, by reason of the emotional complex gathered about it, is sufficient to bring about the habitual reaction or one nearly like it.

From these considerations arises a distinction which is fundamental to the whole problem of genetic psychology, namely, the difference between the motor side, which has its source in the feelings, and the immanental relations among the ideas; a distinction which is to be made in every psychological process, especially in the imaginative processes. Both the idea and the motor expression are parallel results of the one psychological process, but stand in no relation of cause and effect. The ideas are not motives to the will act, much less are they causes of the affect side of the process, but both are results of a common, more primal process of imagination.

§ 8. With this distinction, between the 'affect' or force side of the process and the ideal complex, we have a principle by means of which we may more clearly understand the motor expressions which result upon the imaginative processes. When once the imaginative intuition of reality, with its affect of 'sufficiency' and reality, has come into existence under the influence of the motive of accommodation to the stimulus, the 'motor excess' of this process may express itself in either of two ways. Either the stimulus upon which the imagination followed appeals so directly to the pleasure and pain feelings, or the reality feeling is of such intensity that a will act follows as its expression, or else these conditions do not exist and the motor excess is turned upon the ideal content in a series of apperceptive analytical processes which determine the relations of the ideas among themselves. In the first case the 'force' of the process has found vent in a will act which brings the organism into direct relation to outer reality, in the form of accommodation; in the latter this natural expression has been retarded or prevented, and the energy is expended upon an analysis of the ideal complex, where the theoretical relation of the ideas to each other becomes the problem. The important point is that both of these widely different results spring out of the common primal term— the Imaginative Processes. Out of the union of ideas and emotional elements which takes place under the motive of the imitation of reality, the 'sufficiency' of both the will act and the judgment arises. The 'sufficiency' lies, in both cases, in the affect side of the complex; the coming into prominence of either the motor expression in the will act, or of the theoretical judgment upon the relations of the ideas, is dependent upon laws which we have now to consider. For just here lies the problem of Selection; if like imaginative processes which work under the teleological norm of an imitation of reality at one time pass over into motor accommodation to environment and again fall back upon their own ideal content, on what principle is the selection made as to which complex shall result in will act and which shall not?

§ 9. Here, it would seem, is the place to call in the simple principle of utility, and properly understood, it seems to us to be the solution of the problem. The subjective 'sufficiency' of the motives of will acts and of the 'grounds' of judgments alike was seen to lie in the affective side of the imaginative processes which precede them. The characteristic of this

affect is that it is a strong sense of reality, made up of the
memory feelings of prior experiences. All of these complexes
have the feeling of reality, closely related to the reality of perception in some degree, but not all have the affect side predomi-
nant, in the sense that it appeals directly to the fundamental feelings of pleasure and pain, as a direct stimulus, and therefore
not all are brought directly into relations to the principle of utility. In the place of the more definite sense of utility or disadvantage which attaches to the ' motives,' or the imaginative
processes which result in motor reactions upon environment, in
those complexes which result in judgments upon the ideas, the
concept of general worth or value must be substituted. That is,
the reality feeling of the imaginative complex is of such a nature that it is handled as of value or worth to consciousness, but
not as so intense as to bring forth a will reaction—that is it does
not involve a suggestion of immediate pain or pleasure to the
organism.

§ 10. The problem of Selective accommodation may then be
stated as follows : How is it possible that from motor reactions,
which are based entirely upon their utility to the organism—that
is, will acts of accommodation to environment—imaginative complexes may arise which have only the predicate ' worth ;' that is,
which result not in immediate reaction upon environment, but in
judgments as to the relations of the ideas? How, in other
words, is the abstract concept of *truth* to be connected with the
concrete utility of the particular experience.

The answer to this is to be found in the nature of the imitative process of Imagination. The primary type of this process
is that in which the affect side prevails and the consequent
motor reaction follows. As a matter of fact, all observations
tend to show that the less developed the psychological organism
the greater the number of completed will acts in proportion to
those which are not allowed to follow their course. The more
developed the psychological state the greater the degree of
selection manifested in the will acts, that is, the less the emotional complexes are allowed to have their natural motor discharge. It follows that we must look upon all imaginative processes as originally ending in will acts; only gradually did

imaginative complexes arise in which the attention was turned upon the ideal complex which gathers about the stimulus, instead of the stimulus itself.

§ 11. Definitely formulated then, a theory of selection which adjusted itself to these facts would read somewhat as follows : Reaction of the organism to its environment in the sphere of intelligence does not take place directly upon the stimulus, but through the mediation of ideal complexes which stand for the external reality. These complexes are of the nature of imitations of external reality in that they are the result of imaginative processes which gather together the experience of the past under the teleological criterion of reproduction of the reality feelings of the past. All of the infinite number of complexes thus possible tend to go over into motor expressions in will acts, that is, in accommodation to environment. Some of these are favorable, that is, the imaginative complexes correspond to reality, and some are not favorable, have not corresponded to actual reality. Gradually the number of imaginative complexes which go over into will acts becomes proportionately smaller by means of this selection, and the number of those which are prevented because they have proved themselves not to be in harmony with the external reality, the reaction upon them having failed to be accommodative, becomes proportionately larger.

Thus arises gradually a sphere of imaginative processes which express this motor energy only in appreciative analytical acts upon themselves in the manner previously described. These relations thus developed are of general worth or truth instead of immediate practical advantage or disadvantage.

The nature of the selection becomes clearer from the consideration of certain pathological cases. Hallucination and illusion are conditions where, or account of hyperæsthesia, imaginative processes retain their reality feeling, although repeated motor reactions upon them fail to be accommodative. The immediate reality feeling, growing out of the intensity of the emotion is so strong that the disadvantages (often the *pain*), of reaction upon the external world fail to modify or destroy the imaginative complex. The normal imaginative complex is, however, subject to modification from the feelings which arise

as the result of the reaction.   And herein lies the possibility of
new accommodations.

§ 12. But how, it will be asked, can such a theory of selection account for the logical and *a priori* relations among the ideas
which tend more and more to segregate themselves from the
direct accommodations.   Surely they are not the products of
selective accommodation and yet an extension of the principle
of selection to the sphere of the intellectual processes, must be
on the basis of the principle : that only *those ideas are true
which have proven to be of utility.* A little reflection will suffice
to discover a fallacy in this principle.   Ideas are never of utility ;
only feelings and states which are consequent upon accommodations are of utility.   Ideas are only signs for psychological
states.   To speak of ideas as being of utility implies a point of
view which overrides the boundaries of psychology, and falls
into the fatal error of Spencer, of basing the whole of genetic
psychology on the metaphysical hypothesis of a correspondence
between the ideas and reality.   This distinction between the
' force' side and the ' ideal' side of the imitative processes,
which is expressed in the sentence " the idea does not work but
only the process of getting the idea," enables us to separate completely the dynamical and utility side of psychological processes
from the logical relations of the ideal content that results.   And
this is an absolutely necessary presupposition of any genetic
study.   The fundamental laws of the ideal side of our conscious
complexes are laws of relations based upon the analytical criteria
of ' clearness and distinctness.' They belong distinctly to the peculiar sphere of ideas and have nothing to do with the problem
of organic accommodation.   In the latter sphere the criteria, as
we have already seen, are distinctly affective, growing out of the
feeling of reality and the pleasure and pain which accompany
it.   The ideal relations as such lie, accordingly, entirely outside
the line of direct accommodations.   They work only indirectly
in future accommodations, in that when consciousness is gathered
together again in a new imaginative complex for a new motor
reaction, the ideal content appears in more distinct and perhaps
modified relations, but again the ' sufficiency' and the accommodation will lie in the affect side.

§ 13. But is not the fallacy in the preceding expression that "only those *ideas* are true which have proven themselves to be of utility" the stumbling block to any application of genetic selection in the intellectual sphere; a final barrier to any connection between utility-selection and truth ? Were it not better to say : *our ideas must be true, that is correspond to outer reality, if the acts based upon them are to be advantageous?* Here the correspondence between our ideas and outer reality is assumed and the utility of our acts concluded from the assumption. The primacy of immanental *a priori* relations among ideas is taken for granted as the source of a necessary accommodation to an environment corresponding to these ideas. On the contrary, it could be claimed that ideas must prove themselves useful, before they can obtain a permanent place in the content of our consciousness, they must be seen by actual practice to correspond to reality before they can be distinguished as permanent truth from the mere fictions of the imagination. This apparent antinomy which so often stands in the way of reconciliation of empirical and *a priori* theories of knowledge rests upon different ways of looking at a single process or fact. In the first part of the antinomy is expressed an objective attitude toward accommodations after they have actually taken place. We conclude from a favorable accommodation on the part of a particular psychological organism as a consequence, to a knowledge of the true relations of things in this consciousness as ground. On the other hand, if we say that the ideas must be of utility to be true, we conclude from the subjective ground to an objective consequence, because from our standpoint, as practical agents, it is alone those ideas which appeal to us as of worth which correspond to this practical accommodation which we have made in will act.

§ 14. This difference in attitude corresponds to a distinction which can be made in the general body of truth. The relations among individual elements of scientific truth are true in a sense that the whole of truth is not, for they are analytically determinable according to the logical criteria immanent in the ideas themselves. The whole truth, however, has no such criteria as Descartes clearly saw when he made the whole of the truth de-

pendent upon the certainty of the intuition of the self, that is
upon a psychological term of belief. The self cannot be
doubted because there are no higher criteria according to which
it can be proved. The reality feeling of the self is, therefore,
the criterion of the truth of all the content in the conciousness
of the self. So also in this case the relation may be expressed
epigrammatically in the sentence : *The whole of truth rests upon
utility which goes back to the psychological affective side, its
parts, however, upon analytical and logical necessity.* This
contradiction finds its psychological solution, and that is all that
concerns us, in the reduction of both terms to a more primal
term, the imaginative processes. These are found to be the
background of will acts and judgments alike. The ' sufficiency' of the ' motive' as well as that of the psychological
ground of a judgment lies in each case in the affective side of
the imaginative complex. Of these two possible results of the
imaginative processes, the will expression is the more primal.
The relation of the practical will side of consciousness to reality
is closer and more fundamental than that of the ideal. In its
accommodation, therefore, is to be found the source of all new
content in consciousness. The reflective processes which are
the result of the turning of the motor force or attention upon the
ideal content are the secondary results when the natural reaction
is hindered or retarded. Thus arises gradually a sphere of
segregated truth, which is first of all of theoretical and general
worth, and only indirectly of practical utility. The individual
acts of will which are based upon the utility to the organism
whose reactions upon environment they are, must tend in the
long run to fix the results as necessary for the race. When,
however, these results are so recognized, they become parts of
a settled and independent body of truth, which has its own laws
outside the sphere of the utility reactions which first brought it
into being.

§ 15. A study of the development of child consciousness and
of primitive peoples would present a mass of material which
tends to prove that intelligent accommodation to environment,
proceeds upon the principle of a selective *reduction* of imaginative reactions upon given kinds of environment to permanent

bounds. That is in the proportion that *extension* of the possibilities open for the imagination is reduced, in equal proportion, is the *intension* increased. In the young child or in the primitive man the imagination clothes elements of environment of the most divergent nature with the same attributes, mostly personal, and reacts upon them accordingly, or again the same stimulus is at different times reacted upon with different imagination content, simply because the reality feeling does not work definitely and certain. Thus arise the phenomena of superstition—the freedom from which is a continuous process of accommodation to environment, and which, when completed, may leave behind a new science as illustrated in the development of chemistry from alchemy. When such a stage is reached where a definite amount of theoretical material is segregated by the selective reduction of the number of the possible reactions or imaginations, the imaginative processes, though restricted in extension to this material, grow in intension, and the process is then continued in the form of scientific hypothesis. But all this leads us into the sphere of comparative psychology, while our only object was an analysis of the psychological processes which point to a doctrine of selective accommodation.

In closing, the interesting fact may be noted that both Kant and Herbart find the subjective sufficiency of judgments to lie in the imaginative processes. Kant, in his subjective deduction of the categories finds in the transcendental synthesis of imagination the ground of the union of the sense intuition and the logical forms. Herbart likewise finds the psychological grounds of sufficient reason in the imagination. With both, however, the imagination is at bottom a metaphysical term, and, consequently, though both gave valuable suggestions as to the nature of the psychological grounds of judgments, it is only suggestively that their doctrines of imagination can be referred to in this connection. The above developed principle of selective accommodation rests alone on the analysis of the psychological processes called imagination.

SOME FACTS OF BINOCULAR VISION.

BY DR. CHARLES H. JUDD.

Wesleyan University.

Some interesting experiments in binocular vision were reported a few years ago by Professor Hyslop and Professor Venn in *Mind*[1] and in THE PSYCHOLOGICAL REVIEW.[2] The unusual conditions of vision under which these experiments were performed—both observers are able to carry out the adjustments of ocular accommodation and those of ocular convergence independently—seem to have prevented their conclusions from receiving the usual critical treatment which comes from general and extended experimental observation. A little practice has enabled me to follow the experiments of both, and while I am able to corroborate the results in general, important considerations prevent me from adopting the conclusions which Professor Hyslop reaches in his last paper. These conclusions may be summarized in Professor Hyslop's own words as 'looking to a central explanation of both distance and magnitude, independent both of peripheral conditions and motor impulses.' It is the aim of this paper to report certain experiments which seem to point in a different direction, and it will be possible, I think, to show where the error has crept in.

The apparatus for the experiments consists of two plane mirrors mounted in two frames which are hinged together in such a way that the mirrors may be inclined at various angles. Let ad and bc be the mirrors. (Fig. 1.) They may be folded so as to come into the positions $a'd'$, $b'c'$, or so that their positions are $a''d''$, $b''c''$. The whole may be held in the hand at a convenient distance from the observer's eyes. At the beginning of the experiment the mirrors are held in the same plane $adbc$, The eyes are converged in the directions me and nf, so as to

[1] *Mind*, Vol. XIII., p. 499; Vol. XIV., p. 251 and p. 393.
[2] PSYCHOLOGICAL REVIEW, Vol. I., p. 247 and p. 281.

receive the reflected rays from a luminous point *o*, the relative positions being so chosen that the pencil of light entering the right eye comes from the right mirror, and that entering the left eye from the left mirror. The points seen will be referred to a distance behind the mirror as great as that of the real point in front of the mirrors. If now the frame be slightly folded so as to bring the mirrors into an inclined position, with the angle of

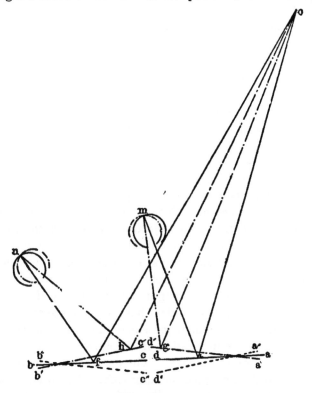

Fig.1.

inclination turned toward the observer, as *a'd'* and *b'c'¹*, the points of incidence of the rays entering the eyes will travel from *e* to *g* and from *f* to *h*. The effect of this movement on the apparent distance of the point in depth will be imperceptible, as can be shown by closing one eye while the mirrors are being inclined. When, on the other hand, both eyes are fixed on the point, as the mir-

¹ The angle is exaggerated in the figure.

rors are slightly inclined, the point behind the mirrors is distinctly seen to approach the observer. The eyes must be converged in the directions *mg* and *nh*, and the fixation point evidently lies very much nearer the mirrors than when the optical axes were in the positions *me* and *nf*. A very slight inclination of the mirror produces a marked effect. Just the opposite phenomena follow an inclination of the mirrors when the angle of inclination is turned away from the observer. Here the point is seen to recede during the movement of the mirrors. The point of intersection of the optical axes also recedes. The whole series of phenomena is evidently explained by the fact that objects requiring a greater degree of convergence are judged to be nearer, and those requiring a smaller degree of convergence are judged to be more distant. It is to be noted that the judgments of position are certain only during the actual movements of the mirrors. As soon as the movement ceases the point seems to have that same sort of indefinite location in depth which is so characteristic of our judgment of the distance of the stars.

New and important experiences appear if an object is used instead of a luminous point. When the mirrors are now inclined into the positions *a'd'*, *b'c'*, the object, as the point before, seems to approach the observer, but it also grows very distinctly smaller. This diminution in the size of the image can evidently not be due to the fact that the points of incidence travel from *e* to *g* or from *f* to *h*, for if this slight change has any effect at all, and it is so slight that it doubtless has no such effect, it would be in the opposite direction, for since the object is virtually brought nearer by the inclination of the mirrors, its retinal image is thereby increased in size. The decrease in apparent size is connected with the apparent approach. The whole matter will be clear if we recall the ordinary facts of perspective. If two objects unequally distant give the same sized retinal image, the more distant object will be the larger and a long series of experiences has taught us to judge in accordance with this fact. In ordinary experience, then, when an object approaches an observer the convergence will increase and, at the same time, the image on the retina will grow larger. But, under the conditions of the experiment, the retinal image remains constant (or, if anything, grows only slightly larger), while at the same time the convergence is increased. The lens does not change its degree of accommodation, so that the case is not complicated by any factor besides those of retinal image and convergence. There is evidently only one objective phenomenon which could give this unusual combination of retinal image and convergence, and that would be the approach of an object which was rapidly becoming smaller in size. The result is that we actually perceive an object in the mirrors which approaches and at the same time grows smaller. The converse may be seen by folding the mirrors slightly away from the observer; the object now seems to recede and to grow larger. The explanation is of course similar.

While the convergence is actually changing the appearances of movement in the object are very apparent; as soon as the movement of the eyes ceases the absolute distance of the object in space becomes more indefinite, just as in the case of the point in the first part of the experiment. The diminished size of the object, on the other hand, remains unmodified. This justifies us in concluding that the apparent magnitude of objects is due to the combination of retinal images and sensations of convergence under the general law that *of two objects requiring different degrees of convergence and yielding the same sized retinal images, the one requiring the greater convergence will seem smaller.* It will also appear nearer unless associated factors from past experience come in to disturb the localization. These associated factors are not strong enough to affect the judgment while sensations of movement are actually coming into consciousness, but may have some influence when the only sensations from convergence are the somewhat weaker sensations of position. In any case the effect of the two peripheral conditions, namely, retinal images and motor sensations (including sensations of mere position) are the determining factors. These factors, being combined in unusual relations, give rise to unusual perceptions. But the perceptions are in accordance with the ordinary rules of perspective as shown above.

All the above described facts may be easily observed by any one. The following experiments require in their second modification some ability to dissociate the closely related processes of convergence and accommodation, but an observer with strong eyes and a little practice can soon acquire the ability to perform them. The same pair of mirrors is employed, but they are so inclined that the angle towards the observer is considerably less than two right angles, as *ad, cb* (Fig. 2), and the eyes are so located that the only ray from the luminous point *o* which is visible in the left eye is incident on the right mirror, and

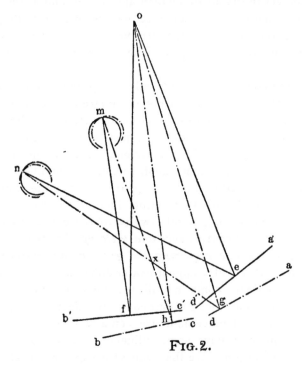

FIG. 2.

the pencil entering the right eye is incident on the left mirror. The only way in which the two images can be made to appear single is by converging the two eyes so that their optical axes shall intersect at the point where the two pencils of light intersect, that is, at *x*. The two eyes must be converged in the directions *mh* and *ng*. If this is done the point will be seen as single, but its location in space will not be at all definite. It seems to be behind a third mirror situated between the two original mirrors which are visible in indirect vision. If the angle towards the observer be made smaller, as $a'd'$, $b'c'$, the point will be distinctly seen to approach the observer. The points of incidence will travel along the mirrors from g to e and from h to f, but this change can be entirely neglected as in the earlier experiment. The opposite effect will be observed if the angle toward the observer is gradually increased; the point will then recede in a very noticeable degree. A reference to the figure will show how the change in angle of the mirrors is accompanied by a change in the degree of convergence. In all the cases described active movement of convergence is always accompanied by a decided appearance of change in the distance of the object in the third dimension, and this change in apparent distance always follows the rule that the greater the convergence the nearer the object. The rule holds without exception for relative degrees of convergence; when, however, the absolute distance is to be judged, other factors enter in and the object seems further away than the real point of fixation. This false reference of the point of fixation is doubtless due to the conditions which arise from the imperfect reflection of the mirror which gives added sense data, and to the conflicting sensations of accommodation to be discussed more fully in the next modification of the experiment.

As in the first series of experiments, important factors are introduced when we make use of an object rather than of the luminous point. A new complication arises in the fact that when the eyes are converged to the point x they will, under the ordinary circumstances of vision, also be accommodated so as to focus rays of light diverging from x. If an object whose rays of light are less divergent, as in the case of the real reflected object, is to be seen in clear outline the accommodation must be changed so as to adapt it for a point whose distance is greater than the point of fixation. That is, the accommodation must be for distant objects while the convergence is for a near object. This is difficult for the unpracticed observer and may be impossible for some. When the ability to accommodate and converge independently is once acquired, however, the object can be seen very clearly and sharply defined, even while the eyes are converged to the nearer point. If now we start with the mirrors in the position *ad*, *bc*, (Fig. 2) the object will be seen as very much smaller than the image in the plain mirror when observed with the single eye. Its relation to the position before convergence took place will be rather indefinite, but seems at first somewhat greater than before. If the angle is made smaller, as *a′d′*, *b′c′*, the image seems to grow very much smaller and approaches decidedly. As soon as the movement stops the location of the object again becomes indefinite, and it may appear at the same or even at a greater distance than before. The conditions are very much involved and yet the results all obey the principles that during active movement of convergence the greater the degree of convergence the shorter the apparent distance of the object, and, the retinal image remaining the same in size, the smaller the apparent size of the object. Here again, when the movement ceases the diminished size remains constant while the localization becomes less definite. The fact that the distance seems to be about the same when the mirrors are at rest, whatever the size of the object, speaks for the influence of the sensations of accommodations which are of no very great importance in the estimation of depth, but probably play some part. We shall find evidence later for assuming that accommodation has some influence in perception. The more important fact that while the relative position corresponds to the convergence, the absolute localization is not at the point of fixation, furnishes a greater difficulty, but here again it is to be noticed that the mirrors seen in indirect vision are smaller and the illusion of greater distance could easily arise, as it often does, when a concave lens is held before an object; the object is seen smaller and further away until the attention is called to the true relation of the image to the object.

There is only one point in which this series of experiments differs from the first, and that is in the dissociation of convergence and accommodation. The size of the retinal image here remains constant just as in the former series. This follows from the fact that the image is sharply focused on the retina, and since the rays from the object are equally divergent whatever the position of the mirrors, the lens must remain constant if the rays are always to be brought to a focus. That the size of the aperture in the pupil can have no influence on the size of the image followed from the general law of refraction that a part or the whole of a lens casts exactly the same sized images.

We turn now to the discussion of Professor Hyslop's experiments and conclusions. The earlier series differs from those which have been reported in this paper, in the fact that the figures were there drawn on paper or glass and the possibility of comparing a large number of successive experiences was thus lost. The experiments here described furnish important additions to the general body of fact which may be used in explanation, but even the less elaborate experiments with fixed figures seem to lead to conclusions which are favorable rather than adverse to the motor-sensation theory. In fact similar results have been used by Aubert,[1] Professor Le Conte,[2] Professor Martins,[3] and Dr. Rivers,[4] to establish the same conclusions that I have drawn from my experiments. Professor Hyslop's experiments are in brief as follows: Two circles are drawn at a distance of a few inches apart, and the eyes are converged so as to fuse the images, either by crossing the eyes or at a point nearer than the plane of the paper, or by distant convergence at a point beyond the plane of the paper, as represented in figures 3 and 4. A and B, A' and B' are the circles in profile. In order to get clear images at C and C', of course the accommodation must be unnatural. The result of crossing the eyes is that C is seen in direct vision considerably smaller than the original circle, and nearer to the observer's eyes. A and B are seen in indirect vision somewhat larger than C, but smaller than the original circle, not so near the observer's eyes. All of these results I am able to corroborate fully. I find also the converse of these facts when the eyes are converged at a point beyond the plane of the paper, as does Professor Hyslop. There is another important observation which has evidently not escaped Professor Hyslop, since it appears in his figures, but which he seems to have made

[1] *Physiol. des Netzhaut*, p. 330.
[2] *Sight*, p. 158 seq.
[3] *Philosophische Studien*, Bd. V., p. 601 seq.
[4] *Mind*, N. S., vol. V., p. 79.

no use of in his explanations. This is the observation that the distance between A and B, as seen in indirect vision, is very greatly increased; in fact, just about doubled, so that if we

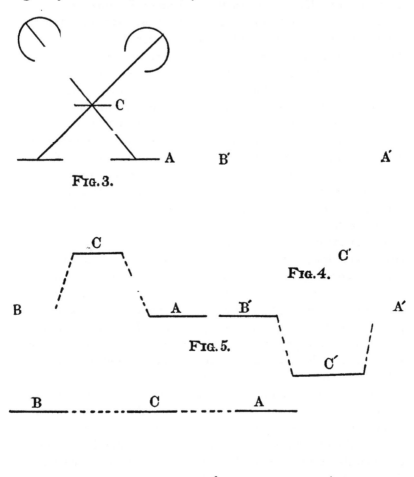

Fɪɢ. 3.

Fɪɢ. 4.

Fɪɢ. 5.

Fɪɢ. 6.

think of C as lying between A and B, the distance AC and the distance BC are about equal to the original distance AB. Furthermore, Professor Hyslop, while he has been at great pains to discuss all of the possibilities of some change occurring in the size of the retinal image, seems to have overlooked the possibility of an explanation without the assumption of any change in the size of the image. But, since the image is sharply defined on the retina, the lens must be accommodated as it would be in monocular vision. There is therefore no ground for the long discussion as to the possible changes in the image due to accommodation. Still less is there reason for refuting the supposition that difference in aperture would affect the size of the image. The oblique distances from the eyes to the circles in both cases (Figs. 3 and 4), are slightly different from the perpendicular distances, but the differences are not appreciable and have no perceptible influence. The smallness of C in the first case and the increased magnitude of C' in the second case offer no difficulties in the light of the explanation given of the results with the mirrors. The retinal image is constant in size, the convergence is different, and the object which is, on account of the convergence, perceived as nearer in the first case is interpreted as smaller, while in the second case it is more distant and interpreted as larger. The estimation of absolute depth is very indefinite, but may be made clearer by bringing up some small object, such as a pencil, in the plane of the paper. The difference in the size of the circles in indirect vision and the central images furnishes a more complex phenomenon. It is necessary to bear in mind that we are dealing here with a case, which is essentially a case of monocular vision. Yet the binocular influences are present and must play some part in determining even this monocular perception. That the binocular and monocular tendencies are in conflict, appears from the fact that the circles are pushed farther away from each other, that is, the distance AB in indirect vision is very much increased. This increased distance will seem to grow shorter if the attention is turned toward one of the circles visible in the indirect field. Professor Hyslop has pointed out that the distance in depth of the central circle and of those in indirect vision is apparently different; the indirectly seen circles appeared to be nearer the plane of the paper. The apparent increase in the distance apart is due to an illusion, as the result of which the perspective distance is mistaken for the horizontal distance. What is really seen is represented in Fig. 5, what is thought to be seen is represented by Fig. 6. This illusion is due to the indistinctness of indirect vision and tends to disappear when attention brings out the perspective. The differences in size of the indirectly seen circles when compared with the original circles may be explained largely, if not completely, as the influence of the accompanying binocular sensations on the monocular perception. The circles are seen as somewhat nearer and consequently smaller in the first case, as more distant and larger in the second. Apart from the special complication here pointed out, these phenomena are perfectly analogous to those which appeared in the experiments with the mirrors. The explanation may be extended so as to include certain other cases which Professor Hyslop uses in his criticism of the association and motor-sensation theory.

The case of after-images remarked by Professor Hyslop and independently reported by W. Scharwin and A. Novizri in the *Zeitschrift für Psychologie und Physiologie der Sinnesorgane,* Bd. XI, Hf. 5, furnishes a striking parallel. An after-image appears larger the more distant the plane on which it is projected.[1] The retinal image is in such a case exactly the same size whatever the distance of the plane may be. The change in apparent size is to be explained in the same way as in the cases described.

Other facts, derived from the fusion of stereoscopic figures under various conditions, furnish, in Professor Hyslop's view, insurmountable difficulties for the motor-sensation theory. If two stereoscopic figures made with circles in such a way as to give the frustum of a cone when fused by crossing the eyes, be drawn on separate pieces of paper so that the distance between the figures can be changed by moving the papers further away from each other, or nearer to each other in the same plane, the results will be the following. " Thus we move the circles farther apart while increasing the convergence to retain fusion, the frustum shortens while its magnitude diminishes. On the other hand, as they approach each other and the fusion is sustained,

---

[1] I find the fact mentioned by Aubert as a discovery of Lehot (Fechner Repertorium, 1832).

the frustum lengthens and the magnitude increases, and all this while the figures occupy the same plane." The increase in

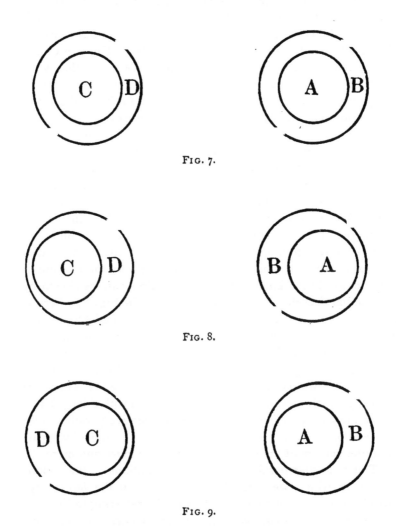

Fig. 7.

Fig. 8.

Fig. 9.

magnitude of the circles offers no difficulty in this case. The actual change in the distance of the figures from the eye as they are moved in a given plane may be of some slight influence but this factor is not appreciable; the retinal images are practically constant in size. The variation of the fixation point, which recedes when the figures approach each other and advances towards the observer when the figures are drawn apart, sufficiently explains the change in the apparent size of the circles. The length of the frustum is another matter. Under ordinary circumstances this decreases as the object recedes, so that when an object recedes to an infinite, or even to a very great distance, all appearance of solidity is lost. In the case in hand, the object in question does really recede when the figures approach each other. The spaces between the circles will share in the enlarging effects of this receding movement, but when the frustum is spoken of as lengthening reference is not made to this increase in length taking place concomitantly with the other dimensional changes. The length of the frustum increases relatively more rapidly than it should to preserve the original proportions. This increase is still more important when we think that under normal conditions the frustum would naturally become proportionally even smaller. The explanation of this change in the length of the frustum is to be sought in the binocular parallax. This can be shown by the familiar fact that four circles drawn as in Fig. 7, where *A* and *B*, and *C* and *D* are concentric, when united by crossing the eyes give no stereoscopic effect whatever; the binocular parallax is practically zero. When the binocular parallax is positive, as in Fig. 8, the result is a frustum of a cone with the small circle towards the observer; when the parallax is negative as in Fig. 9, the result is a frustum of a cone with a large circle nearer the observer. As the positive or negative parallax is increased the frustum grows longer as may be shown by separating the centers of the circles *AB* and *CD* more and more.

The binocular parallax under the conditions of the experiment with which we started, increases when the figures approach the median plane as will be seen by referring to Fig. 10, where the angles *anb*, *bnc* and *cnd*, are larger than the corresponding angles *a'nb'*, *b'nc'* and *c'nd'*; *abcd* represents here the profile of two such circles as are represented in Fig. 8. The first position *abcd* lies nearer to the median plane than the second position *a'b'c'd'*. The point *n* represents the nodal point in the eye. The size of the retinal image will undergo some changes also when the circles are moved away from the median plane, but these changes are not of importance when the distance through which they are moved is small. *The lengthening of the frustum is therefore a function of the visual angle and increases when the figures approach the median plane.* A similar result appears when the object recedes in depth from the observer, the binocular parallax will decrease as the distance

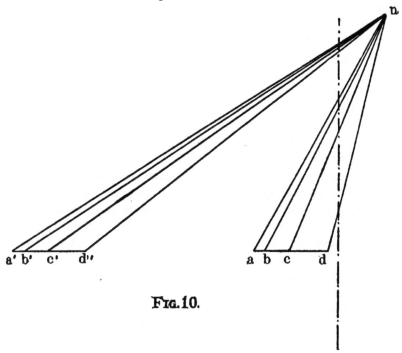

FIG. 10.

from the eye increases. Of two equal variations, however, one in the lateral direction, the other in the third dimension, the former will have the greater influence in modifying the binocular parallax. This proposition can be mathematically demonstrated for all distances great enough to come into consideration for our experiment. These established results explain another series of facts which Professor Hyslop has described. If two stereoscopic figures are drawn at a given fixed distance and moved backward and forward in the third dimension, the relative size of the circles will remain constant, but the frustum will increase in length as the figures move away, and it will grow shorter as they approach. The fact that the size of the circles seems to remain constant is what we should naturally expect. When fusion once takes place the size of the image is determined by the relation of the size of the retinal image and the degree of convergence. If now the figures are moved away, the convergence and the retinal image vary just as they would if a real object at the point of fixation were being moved away. The relative size, therefore, seems to remain constant. Not so with the binocular parallax. The figures are at a fixed distance apart, and when moved away from the eyes they will approach relatively nearer to the median plane. At an infinite distance they would be on the median line, and near at hand their distance from that line reaches its maximum. This approach to the median plane when the figures move away gives a relatively smaller decrease in the binocular parallax, a result which is in contradiction to all ordinary experiences, for usually when an object moves further away the binocular parallax decreases without this counteracting influence. Here again, we are confronted by a series of conditions which seem contradictory to experience. The interpretation of the sense data will, however, be fully determined by peripheral conditions. The object observed will seem to change, for that is the only possible objective condition under which the unusual combination of sense data could possibly be presented.

All of the results from these various experiments furnish ground for accepting the association and motor-sensation theory of visual space rather than the contrary as Professor Hyslop concludes. The sense-data presented in every case are interpreted in accordance with past experiences. Where such combinations of data arise as are not in conformity with any single past experience, the interpretation immediately permits the assumption of a change in the object itself; the size of the object changes or the position of its parts in the third dimension seems to vary. The relation fixed by past experience between the various sense-data is more constant than the belief in a single particular case, so that, although we know that the object remains constant in size, it is interpreted as changing, this perception being more readily adopted than any modification of the fixed relation between the various kinds of sense-data. The light thrown by this fact on the general theory of space perception as well as on the question of perception in general requires more discussion than can be allowed after the detailing of these empirical facts. In general, however, the conclusion is to be emphasized that analysis of the phenomena furnishes striking evidence in favor of the motor-sensation theory rather than against it.

SHORTER CONTRIBUTIONS.

BLOTS OF INK IN EXPERIMENTAL PSYCHOLOGY.

The chance characters made by the compression of one or more drops of writing fluid between two small squares of paper seem to have a varied usefulness in experimental psychology. Rectangular pieces of paper twice as long as wide are folded transversely in the middle. Six centimetres by three is a convenient size for use when large series are employed. Small drops of rather thick common ink are then placed near the centre of one of the squares, and the two halves firmly pressed together with the moving fingers until the fluid has been absorbed. The shape and size of the blot may be determined to some extent by the finger and by the amount of ink applied; several small drops make more various blots than a large single drop.

There being no proper top or bottom to these characters, mere partial or complete reversal changes their apparent nature. Thus the two originals may be used as reverses of each other directly, or by quarter, half, or three-quarters turning of one of them, three other relative characters may be produced. If circular bits of paper instead of square be employed, theoretically infinite combinations are at the command of the experimenter. Direct reproduction of any character may be made by tracing its outline and filling this in with a brush and pen. If many reproductions are required, photography is the best means, and the negatives used in that process may be useful as stencils, behind which variously colored papers can be placed somewhat as in the ambrotypes of fifty years ago. If the blots be required in series, they are best made on heavy gummed paper squares and stuck upon sheets of the required shape and size. Paper not too smooth is best for the blots, that they may dry quickly and be colored uniformly. If copies larger or smaller than the original are desired they may be made with the pantagraph. Colors, of course, are as easily used as black, and variation in the way of shading is also unlimited.

The characters may be exposed behind a Münsterberg pendulum, attached by rubber bands to a kymograph cylinder, through an aperture, and used in many other ways.

It is suggested that these characters may be of use in at least the following psychological researches: In the study of the content of consciousness as regards the relative ease of recognizing an object and its reverse, either when seen alone or in various series. In studies of memory, by measurements of the length of time after which a given blot, straight or reversed, may be recognized; also by the relative power of reproducing after an interval the outline of an exposed character. In the study of Imagination, qualitatively, in various ways, and quantitatively, by measurements of the relative times required for a presented suggestive blot to bring to mind its obvious likeness. In determinations of reaction time with choice. In study of the discrimination of minute formal differences. In the study of after-images of various colors, and positive or negative. In studying Association.

The advantages of blots or characters thus made seem to be these; The practical infinity of their variety; the ease, rapidity, and cheapness of their production in black or colors; the facility with which exact reverses are made; the lack of associational suggestiveness of many of them, and on the other hand the ease with which suggestive ones may be obtained; and the unlimited range in size.

HARVARD UNIVERSITY. GEORGE V. DEARBORN.

THE IMAGERY OF ONE EARLY MADE BLIND.

I became blind at the age of five years and one month, in August of 1877. My home was then in New Brunswick, Canada. I have an image in my mind of many of the scenes which I saw before losing my sight. I remember how the trees looked across the river where they seemed to disappear into the sky and I believed they supported the sky. I remember how the small ships which used to come up the river looked. I also have a vivid picture of the falls in the river. I used to sit on the edge of the bank overlooking the falls and gaze down about fifty feet at the water. In fact I remember almost everything which I saw during the last summer while I possessed my sight.

My Idea of Space.—When I contemplate a geometric proposition, it is presented to my mind ras aised on a piece of paper. When I studied geometry I had all the diagrams used to prove the proposition raised on paper. Thick pasteboard was used so that the figure would endure. Any geometric proposition, therefore, appears to me raised on such a figure as I then used.

When I wish to represent to myself something infinitesimally small, I take a thin piece of paper and tear it in halves; then I tear one of the halves in halves and continue this process until I have the smallest piece of paper which I can hold in my hands; then I consider that sub divided as many times as I subdivided the original piece of paper, and then again what is obtained by that subdivision again subdivided, and so on until I can think no longer of the subdivisions for mere infinity of numbers, and still I do not feel satisfied when geometricians make a leap in the dark from this smallest conceivable to zero. I can not understand how zero can ever be reached in this way. The longer the piece of paper which I at first divided is the more thoroughly can I approach to the minutest possible in the repeated subdivisions.

When I wish to represent to myself the infinitely long I consider myself in an extended body of water with a life preserver on. I have sometimes been in the water in such a manner; and if I can hear no one on the shore, there comes to me some idea of what infinity is. My home is on the shore of Lake Superior and when in that body of water facing away from the land, there comes to me some idea of infinity.

I consider infinity going away just as I would swim away from the land. I might swim and swim and still I would never come to a stopping place in that body of water; and infinity would go on before me to the opposite shores of the lake four hundred miles away and still it would continue beyond that point an infinite number of times. Or again, I represent infinity to myself as the rails of an extended rail-road track. When I wish to represent to myself two parallel lines which, however, far produced will never meet, I consider the lines of the track. I have frequently followed these rails for a long distance, fourteen miles being the farthest I have ever gone at once; and from this distance I can consider those rails continuing on in that same line with that same distance between them for an infinitely greater distance than I have ever walked.

Of course I was not old enough when I lost my sight to consider infinity, but I do remember looking up into the sky and wondering what was beyond that and how far it went. I distinctly remember seeing a ball thrown up into the air as far as I could follow it with my eyes, and from that I got my only seeing conception of infinity. I lost my eyes with scarlet fever, and before the sickness came on they were as perfect as any eyes.

I cannot consider in my mind at once a figure of more than six sides. If I wish to consider more sides than that, I have to consider them in parts of three or four sides at a time. I have to go round the figure in my mind slowly. I cannot conceive in my mind at once a polygon of an infinite number of sides, nor can I imagine how a polygon of an infinite number of sides could ever merge into a circle.

YALE UNIVERSITY.   ALEXANDER CAMERON.

DETERMINATE EVOLUTION.[1]

I. ORGANIC SELECTION.

Admitting the possible truth of either of the current doctrines of heredity, yet there are certain defects inherent in both of them. Natural Selection, considered merely as a principle of survival, is admitted by all. It fails, however, (1) to account for the lines of progress shown in evolution where the variations supposed to have been selected were not of importance enough at first to keep alive the creatures having them (*i. e.*, were not of 'selective value'). The examination of series of fossil remains, by the paleontologists, shows structures arising with very small and insignificant beginnings.[2] Further, (2) in cases where correlations of structions and functions are in question, as in the case of complex animal instincts, it is difficult to see what utility the partial correlations could have had which would necessarily precede the full rise of the instinct; and yet it is impossible to believe that these correlations could have arisen by the law of variation all at once as complete functions.[3] These two great objections to the 'adequacy of natural selection' are so impressive that the Neo-Darwinians have felt obliged to deal with them. The first objection may be called that from 'determinate evolution,' and the latter that from 'correlated variations.'

On the other hand the doctrine of use-inheritance or Lamarckism is open to equally grave difficulties in my opinion. (1) It is a pure assumption that any such inheritance takes place. The direct evidence is practically nothing.[4] No unequivocal case of the inheritance of the normal effects of use or disuse has yet been cited. Again (2) it proves too much, seeing that if it actually operated as a general principle it would hinder rather than advance evolution in its higher reaches. For, first, in the more variable functions of life it would produce conflicting lines of inheritance of every degree of advantage and disadvantage, and these would very largely neutralize one another, giving a sort of functional 'panmixia' of inherited habits analogous to the panmixia of variations which arises when natural selection is not operative. Again, in cases in which the functions or acquired habits are so widespread

---

[1] Matter added in the foreign editions of the author's 'Mental Development in the Child and the Race.'

[2] Cf. the statement of this objection by Osborn, *Amer. Naturalist*, March, 1891.

[3] Cf. Romanes, *Darwin and after Darwin*, II., chap. 3.

[4] See the candid statement of Romanes, *loc. cit.*; and Morgan, *Habit and Instinct*, Chap. XIII.

and constant as to produce similar 'set' habits in the individuals, the inheritance of these habits would produce, in a relatively constant environment, such a stereotyped series of functions, of the instinctive type, that the plasticity necessary to the acquirement of new functions to any great extent would be destroyed.   This type of evolution is seen in the case of certain insects which live by complex instincts; and however these instincts may have been acquired, they may yet be cited to show the sort of creatures which the free operation of use-inheritance would produce.   Yet just this state of things would again militate against continued use-inheritance, as a general principle of evolution; for as instinct increases, ability to learn decreases, and so each generation would have less acquisition to hand on by heredity.   So use-inheritance would very soon run itself out.   Further, (3) the main criticism of the principle of natural selection cited above from the paleontologists, *t. e.*, that from 'determinate evolution,' is not met by use-inheritance; since the determinate lines of evolution are frequently, as in the case of teeth and bony structures, in characters which in the early stages of their appearance are not modified in the direction in question, during the lifetime of the creatures which have them.   And, finally, (4) if it can be shown that natural selection, which all admit to be in operation in any case, can be supplemented by any principle which will meet these objections better than that of use-inheritance, then such a principle may be considered in some degree a direct substitute for the Lamarckian factor.

There is another influence at work, I think, which is directly supplementary to natural selection, *i. e.*, *Organic Selection*.

Put very generally, this principle may be stated as follows: acquired characters, or modifications, or individual adaptations—all that we are familiar with in the earlier chapters under the term *Accommodations*—while not directly inherited, are yet influential in determining the course of evolution indirectly.   For such modifications and accommodations keep certain animals alive, in this way screen the variations which they represent from the action of natural selection, and so allow new variations in the same directions to arise in the next and following generations; while variations in other directions are not thus kept alive and so are lost.   The species will therefore make progress in the same directions as those first marked out by the acquired modifications, and will gradually 'pick up,' by congenital variation, the same characters which were at first only individually acquired.   The result will be the same, as to these characters, as if they had been directly inherited, and the appearance of such heredity in these cases, at least, will be fully explained. While the long continued operation of the principle will account for ' determinate ' lines of change.

This principle comes to mediate to a considerable degree between the two rival theories, since it goes far to meet the objections to both of them. In the first place, the two great objections as stated above to the ordinary Natural Selection theory are met by it. (1) The 'determinate' direction in the evolution is secured by the indirect directive influence of Organic Selection, in all cases in which the direction which phylogenetic evolution takes is the same as that which was taken by individual modifications in earlier generations. For where the variations in the early stages of the character in question were not of selective value, there we may suppose the individual accommodations have supplemented them and so kept them in existence. An instance is seen in the fact that young chicks and ducks which have no instinct to take up water when they see it,[1] and would perish if dependent upon the congenital variations which they have, nevertheless imitate the mother fowl, and, thus by supplementing their congenital equipment, are so kept alive. In other fowls the drinking instinct has gone on to perfection and become self-acting. Here the accommodation secured by imitation saves the species—apart from their getting water at first accidentally—and directs its future development. Farther (2) in cases of ' correlated variations '—the second objection urged above to the exclusive operation of Natural Selection—the same influence of Organic Selection is seen. For the variations which are not adequate at first, or are only partially correlated, are supplemented by the adaptations which the creature makes, and so the species has the time to perfect its inadequate congenital mechanism. On this hypothesis it is no longer an objection to the general origin of complex instincts without use-inheritance, that these complex correlations could not have come into existence all at once; since this principle gives the species time to accumulate and perfect its organization of them.

Similarly, the objections cited above to the theory of use-inheritance can not be brought against Organic Selection. In the first place (1) the more trivial and varied experiences of individuals—such as bodily mutilations, etc.—which it is not desirable to inherit, whether good or bad in themselves, would not be perpetuated in the development of the race, since organic selection would set a premium only on the variations which were important enough to be of some material use or others which were correlated with them. These being of

---

[1] See Morgan, *Habit and Instinct*, pp. 44 f. and his citations from Eimer, Spalding, and Mills.

such importance, the species would accumulate the variations necessary to them, and the individuals would be relieved of the necessity of
making the private adaptations over again in each generation. Again
(2) there would be no tendency to the exclusive production of reflexes,
as would be the case under use-inheritance; since in cases in which the
continued accomplishment of a function by individual accommodation
was of greater utility than its accomplishment by reflexes or instinct—
in these cases the former way will be perpetuated by natural selection.
In the case of intelligent adaptations, for example, the increase of the
intelligence with the nervous plasticity which it requires is of the greatest importance; we find that creatures having intelligence continue to
acquire their adaptations intelligently with the minimum of instinctive
equipment.[1]   There is thus a constant interplay between instinct and
accommodation, as the emergencies of the environment require the
survival of one type of function or the other.   This is illustrated by
the fact that in creatures of intelligence we find sometimes both the
instinctive and also the intelligent performance of the same function;
each serving a separate utility.[2]

(3). The remaining objection—and it holds equally of both the current views—is that arising from the cases of structures which begin in a
very small way with no apparent utility, such as the bony protuber-
ances in places where horns afterwards develop, and in certain small
changes in the evolution of mammalian teeth; which afterwards progress regularly from one generation to another until they become of
some utility.   While it is not clear that Organic Selection completely
accounts for these cases, yet it is quite possible that it aids us in the
matter; for the assumption is admissible that in their small beginnings
these characters were correlated with useful functions or variations,
and that the Organic or Natural Selection of the latter in a progressive
way has secured the accumulation of these characters also.   The facts
of correlation are so little known, while yet the correlation itself is so
universal, that no dogmatism is justified on either side; the less, perhaps on the side of the paleontologists who assert that these cases can
not be explained by Natural Selection even when supplemented by
Organic Selection; for when we enquire into the state of the evidence
for the so-called ' determinate variations ' which are supposed in these
cases, we find that it is very precarious.[3]

[1] Groos (*Die Spiele der Thiere*, p. 65 f.) has pointed out the function of
imitation as aiding the growth of intelligence with the breaking up of instincts
under the operation of natural selection.

[2] Baldwin, *Science*, Apl. 10, 1896.

[3] For example, the only way to establish ' determinate variations ' would

We come to the view, therefore, that evolution from generation to generation has probably proceeded by the operation of Natural Selection upon variations with the assistance of the Organic Selection of co-incident[1] variations (*i. e.*, those which reproduce congenitally the acquisitions of the individuals). And we derive a view of the relation of ontogeny to phylogeny all through the animal series. All the influences which work to assist the animal to make adaptations or accommodations will unite to give directive determination to the course of evolution. These influences we may call ' orthoplastic ' or directive influences. And the general fact that evolution has a directive determination through organic selection we may call ' Orthoplasy.'[2]

As to detailed evidence of the action of Organic Selection, this is not the place to present it. It is well-nigh coextensive however with that for Natural Selection; for the cases where natural selection operates to preserve creatures because they adapt themselves to their environment are everywhere to be seen, and in all such cases Organic Selection is operative. Positive evidence in the shape of cases is however to be found in the papers of the writer and others on the subject.[3]

be to examine all the individuals of a given generation in respect to a given quality, and compare their mean with *the mean of their parents—not with the mean of all the individuals of the earlier generation.* For some influence, such as Organic Selection, might have preserved only a remnant of the earlier generation, and in this way the mean of the variations of the following generation may be shifted and give the appearance of being determinate, while the variations themselves remain indeterminate. And again, the paleontologists have no means of saying how old one of these fossil creatures had to be in order to develop the character in question. It may be that a certain age was necessary and that the variations which he finds lacking would have existed if their possessors had not fallen by natural selection before they were old enough to develop this character and deposit it with their bones.

[1] A term suggested by Professor Lloyd Morgan.

[2] These terms are akin to 'orthogenic' and 'orthogenesis' used by Eimer (*Verh. der Deutsch. Zool. Gesell.*, 1895); his terms are not adopted by me however, for the exact meaning given above, since Eimer's view directly implicates use-inheritance and ' determinate variations ' which are here rejected. On the use of these and other terms see *Science*, Apl. 23, and *Nature*, Apl. 15, 1897.

[3] It may be in place to recall something of the history of this suggestion as to Organic Selection and cite some of the publications bearing upon it. The present writer indicated it (only) in the first edition of this work (Feb. 1895), presented it fully with especial reference to the origin of instinct in *Science*, March 20, 1896, and developed it in many of its applications in an article entitled ' A New Factor in Evolution,' *American Naturalist*, June and July, 1896 (reprinted in *Princeton Contrib. to Psychology*, I., 4, September, 1896). Professor H. F. Osborn expressed similar views briefly in an abstract in *Science*, April 3, 1896, p. 530; and more fully in *Science*, November 27, 1896.

II. The Directive Factor.

We have now seen some reason for the reproduction of individual or ontogenetic accommodations in race progress. The truth of Organic Selection is quite distinct, of course, from the truth of any particular doctrine as to how the accommodations in the life of the individual are effected; it may be that there are as many ways of doing this as the usual language of daily life implies, *i. e.*, mechanical, nervous, intelligent, etc.

Yet when we come to weigh the conclusions to which our earlier discussions have brought us, and remember that the type of reaction, which is everywhere present in the individual's accommodation, is the 'circular reaction' working by functional selection from over-produced movements, we see where a real orthoplastic influence in biological progress lies. The individuals accommodate by such functional selection from over-produced movements; this keeps them alive while others die; the variations which are represented in them are thus kept in existence, and further variations are allowed in the same direction. This goes on until the accumulated variations become independent of the process of individual accommodation, as congenital instincts. Thus are added to the acquisitions of the species the accommodations secured by the individuals. So race progress shows a series of adaptations which corresponds to the series of individual accommodations.

It may be remarked also that when the intelligence has reached considerable development, as in the case of man, it will outrank all other means of individual accommodation. In Intelligence and Will (as will appear below)[1] the circular form of reaction becomes highly developed, and the result then is that the intelligence and the social life which it makes possible so far control the acquisitions of life as greatly to limit the action of natural selection as a law of evolution. This may be merely indicated here; the additional note below will take the subject further in the treatment of what then becomes the means of transmission from generation to generation, a form of handing down which, in contrast with physical heredity, we may call 'Social Heredity.'

Professor *C.* Lloyd Morgan also printed similar views, *Science*, November 20, 1896, and in his book, *Habit and Instinct*, November, 1896. The essential position was reached independently by each of these writers and has been developed by correspondence since their first publication of it.

[1] *I. e.* in the volume, *C*haps. X. to XIII.

III. INTELLIGENT DIRECTION AND SOCIAL PROGRESS.

The view of biological evolution already brought out has led us to the opinion that the accommodations secured by the individuals of a species are the determining factor in the progress which the species makes, since, although we can not hold that these accommodations, or the modifications which are effected by them, are directly inherited from father to son, nevertheless by the working of Organic Selection with the subsequent accumulation of coincident variations the course of biological evolution is directed in the channels first marked out by individual adaptations. The means of accommodation were called above orthoplastic influences in view of the directive trend which they give to the progress of the species.

It was also intimated, in the earlier section, that when the intelligence once comes to play an important part in the accommodations of the individuals, then we should expect that it would be the controlling factor in race-progress. This happens in two ways which may now allow of brief statement.

1. The intelligence represents the highest and most specialized form of accommodation by 'circular reaction.' With it goes, on the active side, the great fact of volition which springs directly out of the imitative instinct of the child. It therefore becomes the goal of organic fitness to secure the best intelligence. On the organic side, intelligence is correlated with plasticity in brain structure. Thinking and willing stand for the opposite of that fixity of structure and directness of reaction which characterize the life of instinct. Progress in intelligence, therefore, represents readiness for much acquisition, together with very little congenital instinctive equipment.

It is easy to see the effects of this. The intelligence secures the widest possible range of personal adaptations, and by so doing widens the sphere of Organic Selection, so that the creature which thinks has a general screen from the action of natural selection. The struggle for existence, depending upon the physical qualities which the animals rely on, is largely done away with.

This means that with the growth of intelligence, creatures free themselves more and more from Natural Selection. Variations of a physical kind come to have within limits an equal chance to survive. Progress then depends on the one kind of variation which represents improved intelligence—variations in brain structure with the organic correlations which favor them—more than on other kinds.

2. The other consideration tends in the same direction. With

the intelligence comes the growth of sentiment, especially the great class of Social Sentiments, and their outcome the ethical and religious sentiments. We have seen in earlier chapters how the sense of personality or self, which is the kernel of intelligent growth involves the social environment and reflects it. Now this social sense also acts wherever it exists, as an ' orthoplastic ' influence—a directive influence, through Organic Selection, upon the course of evolution. In the animal world it is of importance enough to have been seized upon and made instinctive: animal association acts to screen certain groups of creatures from the operation of Natural Selection.

In man the social sentiment keeps pace with his intelligence, and so enables him again to discount natural selection by coöperation with his brethren. From childhood up the individual is screened from the physical evils of the world by his fellows. So another reason appears for considering the course of evolution to be now dominated by the intelligence.

But, it may be asked, does not this render progress impossible, seeing that it is only through the operation of Natural Selection upon variations—even allowing for Organic Selection—that progress depends? This may be answered in the affirmative, so far as progress by physical heredity is concerned. Not only do we not find such progress, but the researches of Galton, Weismann and others show that there is probably little or no progress, even in intelligence, from father to son. The great man who comes as a variation does not have sons as great as he. Intermarriage keeps the level of intelligent endowment at a relatively stable quantity, by what Galton has called ' regression.'

Yet there is progress of another kind. With intelligence comes educability. Each generation is educated in the acquisitions of earlier generations. There is in every community a greater or less mass of so-called ' Tradition' which is handed down with constant increments, from one generation to another. The young creature grows up into this tradition by the process of imitative absorption which has been called above ' Social Heredity.'[1] This directly takes the place of physical heredity as a means of transmission of many of the acquisitions which are at first the result of private intelligence, and tends to free the species from the dependence upon variations—except intellectual variations—just as the general growth of intelligence and sentiment tends to free it from the law of natural selection.

[1] P. 361 and 364 (as in the first edition). See article on ' Consciousness and Evolution,' Science, August 23, 1895, reprinted with discussion by Prof. E. D. Cope and the writer in the Amer. Naturalist, Nos. from April to July, 1896.

These general truths can not be expanded here; they belong to the theory of social evolution. Yet they should be noted for certain reasons which are pertinent to our general topic, and which I may briefly mention.

First, it should be said that this progress in emancipation from the operation of natural selection and from dependence upon variations, is not limited to human life. It arises from the operation of the principle which has all the while given direction to organic evolution; the principle that individual accommodations set the direction of evolution, by what is called Organic Selection. It is only a widening of the sphere of accommodation in the way which is called intelligent, with its accompanying tendency to social life, that has produced the deflection of the stream which is so marked in human development. And as to the existence of 'Tradition' and 'Social Heredity' among animals, recent biological research and observations are emphasizing them both. Wallace and Hudson have pointed out the great importance of imitation in carrying on the habits of certain species; Weismann shows the importance of tradition as against Spencer's claim that mental gains are inherited; Lloyd Morgan has observed in great detail the action of social heredity in actually keeping young fowls alive and so allowing the perpetuation of the species, and Wesley Mills has shown the imperfection of instinct in many cases with the accompanying dependence of the creatures upon social, imitative and intelligent action.

Second, it gives a transition from animal to human organization, and from biological to social evolution, which does not involve a break in the chain of influences already present in all the development of life.

J. MARK BALDWIN.

PROFESSOR LADD AND THE PRESIDENT'S ADDRESS.

In his discussion of my late address before the American Psycho logical Association, Professor Ladd makes three definite criticisms, viz.,

1. That I misunderstand Professor Wundt's position as to the nature and functions of the mind.

2. That I confound his own earlier and later books, and thus seem to find inconsistency where it does not exist.

3. That I unjustly place him in the same category with Kant, when he (Professor Ladd) claims that " we do know reality," and that "all knowledge is *quoad* knowledge, essentially transcendent" (PSYCHO-LOGICAL REVIEW, March, 1897, pp. 180–182).

Regarding criticisms 1 and 3 I shall say little. It appears to me that Wundt's later utterances justify what I have said. I referred in my address to the last edition of the *Grundzüge* and to the lectures on ' Human and Animal Psychology.' As to classing Professor Ladd with the noumenalists, I think that is no injustice. Kant himself kept talking about noumena as though he knew enough about them to at least talk intelligently upon the subject and to contrast them with phe-nomena. Had he been quite consistent in denying us any knowledge whatever of noumena, I think he would have dropped the subject alto-gether. Moreover, I have nowhere charged Professor Ladd with being a good Kantian, but I think he is enough like Kant and a num-ber of others whom I would call Noumenalists, to be properly de-scribed by the use of that term. He contrasts ' phenomena' with ' reality.' He holds (sometimes) to a reality which is not phenomenal. It matters little whether we accept his term, or that which Kant has made familiar to us, he (sometimes) treats this something, I believe, in a distinctly ' noumenal' way. He does not treat it in precisely the same way in all his books, being, as I indicated in my address, less of a noumenalist in his later works than he was in his earlier. I shall give two or three references to prove this later.

As to the second criticism made by Professor Ladd, in which he states that I have been guilty of the ' quite indefensible misapprehen-sion' of confounding his earlier and his later works, and thus of doing him a certain injustice, I will speak a little more at length.

Professor Ladd has quite misunderstood my reference to his earlier and his later works. It would never have occurred to me to thus characterize two books published in the same year (1895), even though the preface of one of them bore the date of the year before. For all I know to the contrary, that preface may have been dated on the last day of the year, and the preface of the other on the first day of the year following. By Professor Ladd's earlier works I meant his 'Elements of Physiological Psychology,' published in 1887, and his 'Introduction to Philosophy' published in 1890. It surprises me that Professor Ladd should have fallen into error upon this point, for in his discussion of my address at the time when it was delivered, he referred to these earlier works, and in my response I stated that I had read them, and that, in comparing his later works with them, it appeared to me that he had undergone a change of mind. I still think that an examination of these works will show that he has undergone such a change.

And as I did not arrive at the opinion that Professor Ladd has modified his views, by comparing his 'Psychology' with his 'Philosophy of Mind,' so also I did not infer his inconsistency from an illegitimate comparison of the statements made in the two volumes, leaving out of consideration the difference in their aim. To prove this, let me take a single volume. An examination of the eleven references that I have made to his 'Psychology' will reveal that, in that one book, he is:

1. A Noumenalist: pp. 215, 513 and 511–517.

2. An adherent of the doctrine that mind is a self-activity within consciousness—a doctrine akin to that of the Neo-Kantians: pp. 532, 638.

3. An Empiricist, who holds that all objects of knowledge, including the self, are, psychologically considered, states of consciousness or psychoses; and that the self in consciousness does not come into being until consciousness has attained a considerable development: pp. 508, 509, 510, 519, 523, 531 and 532.

Thus the self is, according to this one book, at one and the same time the object of a metaphysical faith, an activity in consciousness, and an empirical psychosis.

As to Professor Ladd's change of faith, I will ask the reader to compare the statements of his earlier books with the two upon which I dwelt in my address. Let him, for example, read Professor Ladd's criticism of Metaphysics on page 611 of the 'Elements of Physiological Psychology' (1887). He there criticizes Metaphysics on the ground that " it has often declared that we have an immediate and indubitable knowledge of the mind as one and the same real being in all acts of conciousness," maintaining that " *consciousness carries with it no immediate knowledge of any real and self-identical* being—not even of that real being which we call Mind, and, with good reason, assume to exist as the ground or permanent subject of mental phenomena." He states that Metaphysics treats of those *assumptions* that underlie all of our experience with what we call reality, and he draws a parallel between the hypothetical beings called atoms, which we assume to account for physical phenomena, and the real unit-being called the Mind.

In his 'Introduction to Philosophy' (1890) Professor Ladd regards 'knowledge' as the presence in consciousness of certain complexes of mental elements accompanied by a belief (pp. 230, 234, 235) or persuasion (p. 237) or conviction (p. 230) that there exists beyond consciousness (pp. 204, 225, 251) a something called 'reality' in relation to them (chapters VIII. and IX. passim). We get reality as an inference from experience (pp. 224, 233), and this inference is not rational but 'blind' (pp. 234, 235, 247, 251) and 'instinctive' (p. 251). It is true that in the same volume Professor Ladd, in speaking of the knowledge of the self, uses the verb 'to know' as synonymous with 'to be conscious of' (p. 226), but I think that is only a slip. The general argument of the volume is to the effect that reality is something that I think I may justly call noumenal, and not something immediately known.

In the two books to which I made so many references in my address, Professor Ladd finds the reality of the self to be involved in every act of knowledge 'as an immediate datum of experience,' and he no longer describes the metaphysical faith which gives us reality as 'blind;' as a Neo-Kantian, he makes the real self a self-activity in consciousness; as an empiricist, he makes it an empirical psychosis. I think I have not been wrong in believing that he has modified his views.

I cannot help thinking the tone of Professor Ladd's communication a trifle sour. He speaks of my criticism as 'raillery,' and intimates that I have dealt with the works of various philosophical writers in a spirit of levity. I have carefully re-read what I have written and I cannot see that it is not courteous and in sufficiently good taste. My address contained but one jest, and that one was borrowed from Professor Ladd himself and merely adapted. If it has annoyed him I of course regret having used it, for it is no part of the work of a critic to needlessly hurt the feelings of the person criticised. I wrote with all seriousness. I believe that Professor Ladd's utterances are conflicting, and it seems to me that anyone who points out this fact does him a real service.

GEORGE STUART FULLERTON.
UNIVERSITY OF PENNSYLVANIA.

VISCERAL DISEASE AND PAIN.

In a series of papers published between 1893 and 1896, Dr. Henry Head has treated 'Disturbances of Sensation with Especial Reference to the Pain of Visceral Disease.'[1] The starting point of his investigation is the well-known fact that visceral disorders are frequently accompanied by cutaneous tenderness, the pain occasioned by organic disturbance being 'referred' by the patient to an area on the surface of the body. Dr. Head has carefully mapped out these areas, designating in his first paper those which lie below the first dorsal segment, and in his second paper those which are found on the head and neck. His third paper deals, not with the topography of the areas, but with the pain caused by diseases of various organs. His report contains a vast amount of clinical evidence interspersed with theoretical considerations. The value of his contributions to pathology, anatomy and physiology has been duly recognized. And, quite naturally, the results which he obtained and which certainly throw light on an intricate problem, have been pressed, with some eagerness, into the service of psychological theory.[2] Whether there are separate nerves for pain is a question which cannot be fully discussed here; but the evidence in favor of the affirmative view supplied by Head's research is such as to deserve examination.

It seems to be fairly established that in cases of visceral disease certain skin-areas are affected in such a way that they show increased tenderness, increased reflexes, and one or more maximal points to which the pain is referred and to which the tenderness is limited as the disturbance subsides. The tenderness can be tested by applying a pin to the sensitive area, in which case the rounded head causes as sharp a sensation as the point causes on normal surfaces, while the application of the point gives rise to excessive pain. Quantitative data as to the amount or duration of pressure are not furnished in Dr. Head's report.

[1] *Brain*, XVI., 1893, p. 1; XVII., 1894, p. 339; XIX., 1896, p. 153.
[2] *Pain Nerves.* Herbert Nichols, PSY. REV., May, 1896, p. 309.

What is, perhaps, of greater importance, he has shown that the eruptions in *Herpes Zoster* occupy areas which have the same distribution and the same maxima as the areas of tenderness in visceral disease.

From these statements it must not be inferred that the topography of the areas of tenderness is a simple or easy affair. At times only the maxima can be determined; in nearly all cases more than one area can be pointed out; and certain areas of the body which are rarely affected, appear, when they do become tender, in combination with others.

With these facts as a basis, Dr. Head proceeds by way of elimination to show the significance of the areas. They bear no relation to cortical distribution, nor do they correspond to the distribution of peripheral nerves. Do they represent the supply from posterior nerve-roots? To this question a negative reply is given. The areas supplied from the roots overlap, whereas the areas of cutaneous tenderness and of herpetic eruption do not overlap. Hence the inference that each of these latter areas represents the supply from a single segment of the cord. And since the touch nerves issue from several segments and, in their distribution, overlap, it would seem to follow that there are separate paths for touch and for pain.

So much stress is laid, in deductions of this sort, upon the way in which the zones are mapped out, that one may be permitted to look more closely at the facts of distribution. To begin with, it must be noted that the proofs for the overlapping of the touch-areas and the proofs for the limitation of the pain-areas, are not of precisely the same character. Sherrington found that when, in the monkey, a single posterior root is divided, there is no absence of sensation; and Head, in some few cases, observed the same thing in man. The same area, therefore, must be supplied from several roots and fibres from these must interlace. But in mapping out the areas of tenderness, Head observed a large number of subjects, locating an area in this patient and another area in another patient and so on. His criterion is this: "If they overlapped to any considerable extent, like the areas of common sensation, the extent of skin covered when any one was present must necessarily be greater than that left unaffected when the areas on each side of it were tender. That is to say—supposing Nos. 1 and 3 were tender, the skin between their borders, which was unaffected, must of necessity be of smaller extent than that affected when No. 2 only was tender." Whatever be the accuracy of this method, it is obviously less direct than the method employed to demonstrate the overlapping of touch-zones. Dr. Head himself does not contend for an absolute definition of the areas of tenderness; he admits more than once that there is some overlapping, though this is slight as compared with the overlapping of zones supplied from the posterior roots. It is a 'difference of degree.' Another investigator, Dr. Mackenzie, is more emphatic. He tells us: "From the study of cases of *Herpes Zoster* and of the hyperæsthetic areas associated with visceral disease, I have come to the conclusion that there is distinct overlapping of the fields of cutaneous supply in individual nerve roots, of pathic, thermic and trophic fibres as well as of those of ordinary sensation." [1] This divergence suggests that further investigation may be necessary before the argument from overlapping as against sharp definition can be securely formulated.

Much depends, of course, upon what is meant by 'different areas of distribution.' Experiment has shown that on the skin there are points for heat and points for cold; whence it is reasonable to infer that there are separate paths for these two kinds of stimulation. If the areas in question were simply expansions of similar points, each having its special and exclusive function, the evidence in favor of separate nerves for touch and for pain would be strong. There might be irregularities in the distribution and different degrees of sensibility in the various areas; but once the work of mapping out had been accomplished, we would be able to indicate, for any given area, its particular function. It will hardly be claimed that our topography of the skin has attained this ideal accuracy, so far as zones for pain distinct from touch-zones are concerned. In particular, the results published by Dr. Head do not establish any such clear demarcation. Consequently, it is not in this strict sense that Dr. Nichols must be understood when he states as a fact that "the zones of distribution for pain, heat and trophic nerves cover markedly different fixed areas of the skin from the zones of distribution of the touch-nerves."

It is possible that we are exacting too much—insisting on proofs that will never be forthcoming. In fact, different areas of distribution may be conceived after a less rigorous fashion. Different functions might occupy in part the same area, though their respective zones have different boundaries. It might be shown, for instance, that in a total area which we will call 12, the zones 1–9 are sensible to tactile stimuli and the zones 3–12 are sensible to painful stimuli. In this case, we should say that the zones for touch overlap the zones for pain, or vice versa, without admitting that one touch-zone overlaps another touch-zone, or that the zones for pain overlap one another. Under such conditions, the argument for separate pain nerves would be a more

[1] *Brain*, XVI., 1893, p. 349.

labored one. Nevertheless, it would have a weight of its own—provided that areas of this sort could be marked off on the normal subject.

There is more reason for doubt where difference of distribution hinges upon a change from normal to abnormal conditions. The argument might then take on several forms, one of which may be mentioned simply to show that the phrase 'markedly different fixed areas' needs careful interpretation. From the diagrams furnished by Dr. Head, it appears that the areas of cutaneous tenderness in visceral disease are quite large, extending in some cases in broad bands around the body or along the limbs. If the 'fixedness' could possibly imply that these areas are in all cases, normal no less than pathological, reserved for pain, the markedly different areas for touch would be rather limited. The likelihood of such a misconception is not great where one merely compares the normal condition of any organ with its abnormal condition. But at present we are dealing not with local, but with referred pain. The disease is visceral; the skin is supposed to be normal—or at least to be affected in only a roundabout way. Accordingly, one might infer, in consequence of the markedly different areas, that considerable portions of the skin are set apart for painful stimulation, and that they enter upon this function when the necessary condition, visceral disorder, is realized.

A more plausible form of the argument: areas supplied from the posterior roots and serving the function of touch overlap in normal conditions, whereas, in visceral disease, areas are marked off which serve the function of pain and do not overlap. This brings us in view of the question whether the same fibres which, under normal conditions transmit tactile stimulation, do not serve as pain-paths in visceral disease. It will be remembered that, according to Obersteiner's observations, there are diseases in which tactile stimulation of one portion of the skin gives rise to a sensation which the patient localizes in another portion. This allocheiria is due to a lesion in the central nervous system. According to Dr. Head, "the phenomena of allocheiria and of referred pain in visceral disease are in nature and explanation essentially the same. Both depend for their appearance upon the law that where a painful stimulus is applied to a part of lower sensibility in close central connection with a part of much greater sensibility, the pain produced is felt in the part of higher sensibility rather than in the part of lower sensibility to which the stimulus was actually applied." This explanation bears directly upon the transferred localization of tactile and painful stimuli; but it will also account, I think, for the painful feeling itself. As a result of visceral disease there is a heightened excitability at the point of central connection; hence the **exag-gerated** reflexes which characterize the affected skin-areas. A stimulus which, under normal conditions, would produce only a sensation of touch, passes into the modified center and is referred, in painful phase, to the stimulated area. Or again, stimuli originating in an internal organ and producing ordinarily unconscious reflexes, are referred, in the altered condition of the cord, either to a superficial area or to the diseased region itself, as is the case when the serous cavities of the body are affected. On this hypothesis, the difference between parts of higher sensibility and parts of lower sensibility might, to some extent, be explained. The higher sensibility of superficial areas is more easily understood if we suppose the same fibres to conduct tactile and painful stimulation. Frequency of tactile stimulation and transmission would increase the sensibility of the skin areas, whereas, on the hypothesis of separate paths, it is difficult to see why the skin should be more sensible and why the pain should be referred to it rather than to the seat of disease.

Should this view prove correct, the difference of distribution would cease to be a primary factor in the problem. The effect of stimulation would depend, not so much on the number of segments in the cord that it reaches, as on the condition of any or of all the segments. Whether the areas of cutaneous tenderness in visceral disease are sharply defined or distinctly overlap, is at best an open question. Its final settlement, no doubt, will be hastened by painstaking research along the lines of Dr. Head's investigation. One may fully appreciate his work without feeling bound to declare, in the words of Dr. Nichols, that it ' must set this dispute at rest forever.'

E. A. PACE.

CATHOLIC UNIVERSITY, WASHINGTON.

PSYCHOLOGICAL LITERATURE.

Analytic Psychology. G. F. STOUT. London, Swan, Sonnenschein &
Co.; New York, Macmillans, 1896. 2 vols. Pp. xi+289 and 314.
There can be no hesitation in pronouncing this the most important
work in general psychology by a British author since Ward's *Brit-
annica* article of a dozen years ago. That article marked an epoch
in British psychology by its complete break with the traditional Associationism : it was a proclamation of independence. Mr. Stout's work
shows that the independence has been won. "It may be said," he
writes, "that at present the psychological world is divided into two
camps; on the one side are the champions of Association, on the other
the champions of Apperception. * * * I have definitely sided with the
second party" (ii., p. 41). What Oxford has done for metaphysics, that
Cambridge has accomplished for psychology. And both movements,
the psychological no less than the philosophical, stand evidently under
the commanding though modified influence of the same man, Kant.

The 'Analytic Psychology,' however, follows, as its title indicates,
the traditional English method. At the same time it suggests a contrast to another *genetic* psychology, and Mr. Stout's main interest is,
he tells us, with the latter. But just as the geologist acquires knowledge of the nature of geological changes by observation of the changes
that are going on now, so for investigating the origin and growth of
mental products, it seemed necessary first to analyze the developed consciousness and to study the laws of mental process in present experience. In pursuing this method, Mr. Stout avoids the infelicities of
an 'evolution' of mental life on the basis of imaginary 'principles of
psychology,' and succeeds in giving a strong impression of what our
mental life really is and of the principles which actually govern it, at
least in those forms of it here considered. For, in the opinion of the
author, some products of mental life can be more profitably studied
from the point of view of their development, and their consideration is
accordingly reserved for a future work. The number of topics
omitted in the present work is certainly striking, but judgment on the
special wisdom of the omissions may be deferred till the promised
'Genetic Psychology' is also before us for comparison.

410

The general plan of this treatise is as follows: An introduction on the scope and method of psychology is followed by two books, the first of which contains the general analysis, the second a more detailed examination of processes. Book I., after discussing the principle for the division of ultimate mental functions (Chap. I.) and the possibility of their analysis (Chap. II.), distinguishes the fundamental forms of the cognitive consciousness (Chaps. III.–V.) and concludes with a chapter on feeling and conation (Chap. VI.). Book II. follows a similar arrangement. Beginning with a discussion of the conception of mental activity (Chap. I.), it then examines, in a general synthetic order, the cognitive processes (Chaps. II.–XI.) and concludes with a chapter on pleasure and pain (Chap. XII.)

Psychology is defined as 'the positive science of mental process' (p. 1), including mental development (p. 9), in individuals (p. 7). Its data are distinguished as (1) products of past process, (2) the process itself as introspectively and retrospectively observed and (3) certain external signs. Specially valuable among the first is the material furnished by philology and anthropology; Mr. Stout thinks that the contributions from these sources may ultimately prove of at least as much importance for psychology as those yielded by physiology. Of greater interest is the author's adoption of the hypothesis of 'psychical dispositions' as a means of connecting present conscious process with the results of conscious process in the past. This conception controls the whole of his psychology. He considers it and, indeed, shows it to be distinctly preferable to the hypothesis of subconsciousness and more practicable than the corresponding physiological hypothesis. Our ignorance of the precise correlation of mental process and physiological process is such, he says, that physiology cannot be made the sole basis of psychology. Under certain assignable conditions, the two sciences might be merged in one; but the realization of those conditions appears at present infinitely remote. Even when it is recognized that a 'psychical' disposition is a 'physiological' disposition also, it is still very often necessary for the sake of clearness to separate the purely psychological side of the process from corresponding physiological data and hypotheses.

As a positive principle for the division of ultimate mental functions, Mr. Stout adopts Brentano's—the mode in which consciousness refers to an object; but he criticizes Brentano's use of it, especially in identifying the 'object' with the immediate conscious content. According to Mr. Stout, there is present in all 'noetic' experience, over and above the presentation as modification of the individual consciousness, a unique thought-reference to something which, as the thinker means or intends it, is not a present modification of his individual consciousness. "The object of thought is never a content of our finite consciousness" (p. 45). It is difficult to follow Mr. Stout here. The above statement, for example, taken literally, would seem to make psychology itself impossible. This, of course, is not meant. "The point is that the object as we mean or intend it, cannot be a modification of our consciousness at the time we mean or intend it" (p. 46). But is this really so? It is true that the process of cognition is distinct from its object, but it does not follow that the object is not immanent. Mr. Stout says, indeed, that in thinking of a sensation, I qualify it, as an event in my mental history, by reference to other ex-·perience not present, and that in considering abstractly a content as such, I generalize it, regard it as one of an indefinite series. But clearly, if for psychological purposes I attend to a visual appearance, as such, whatever reference to an 'external' object or to other portions of my experience may be implied, what I mean and intend is not those objects but just this present modification of my visual experience. It may be said, perhaps, that a modification of consciousness is continually changing, and that to be conscious of it, I must be conscious of it as a process, but that the parts of a process cannot possibly be all present together, and that consequently in grasping the unity of its successive phases, I necessarily transcend the immediate present. The reply to this is, that there is no evidence that modifications of consciousness form a succession of timeless instants. What we mean by a present modification of consciousness is a modification in the 'specious' present. The evidence has yet to be given that a present content of consciousness cannot be an object of thought while it and the process of attending to it lasts.

In the second chapter, the theoretical objection against the possibility of analyzing presentations, viz.: that a discriminated content cannot be identical with one that is undiscriminated, is met by the rejoinder of irrelevancy; it is not necessary that the two contents should be identical, but only that the undistinguished differences present in the original experience should be adequately represented by the analytic distinctions in the new. A similar explanation is given of the analysis of dispositions. Here, to be sure, the discovered distinctions do not actually exist prior to their discovery; they are, however, determined by a mental condition other than the process of fixing attention.

Sentiency as a mode of consciousness was briefly referred to in the general analysis of 'noetic' experience in Chapter I.; but this side of experience receives scant consideration in the present treatise. Mere sentiency would be 'anoetic.' Chapters III. and IV. deal with modes of simple apprehension. Emphasis is placed on the apprehension of form of combination, corresponding to the German ' *Gestaltqualität*,' as a unique mode of consciousness distinct from the apprehension of the matter and from the apprehension of relations, both of which presuppose it. Besides these modes of explicit apprehension, there are modes of implicit apprehension, which appear in all cases of ' psychic fringe' and one special case of which is that mental state we call understanding the meaning of a word. Mr. Stout's admirable discussion at this point forcibly illustrates the picturesque remark of Professor James in a similar connection that " introspective psychology must here throw up the sponge." Stout himself falls back on unconscious mental process.

Chapter V. follows Brentano in treating judging or believing as distinct from simple apprehension. The expression ' judging *or* believing' is misleading in that it suggests that the two are identical, and the comment on it on p. 98 is not, we think, altogether happy. However, the point is that judging, as implying belief, is a unique attitude of consciousness towards objects. Mr. Stout calls it ' the Yes-No consciousness.' Might we not, perhaps, call belief the psychical modality of judgment? Certainly, apart from emotional coloring, degrees of assurance seem to be, as Mr. Stout says, ' degrees of firmness or fixity rather than of intensity' (p. 110).

The cognitive consciousness has thus been analyzed into the three fundamental modes of sentience, simple apprehension and belief. Chapter VI. analyzes the volitional consciousness into feeling (pleasure or displeasure) and conation (desire or aversion). Specially noteworthy is the treatment of striving in ' noetic' consciousness as a mode of attention, the two being distinguished in dynamic reference only as the direction of mental activity to an end is distinguished from the activity itself in the successive phases of its realization (p. 126). From this point of view aversion is regarded as attention constrained.

The Second Book opens with an explanation of the conception of mental activity. Accepting Bradley's view that ' activity' implies a self-determined process in time, Mr. Stout finds physical analogues for the psychological conception in movement under the law of inertia, where the continued motion of a body is traceable to its own previous motion, but particularly in the reactions designated by Avenarius *vital series*, where the process not merely perpetuates itself, but adapts itself to an end, and is directly and indirectly self-developing. The analogue is most striking in the central nervous system, where the physical process is actually correlated with the mental. The proof that the mental process is self-determining is (1) that it initiates the changes on which its propagation immediately depends, and (2) that the brain-substance in which these changes take place has been rendered capable of them only through previous psychophysical process in which it has taken part. The fact that its self-determination is indirect is no reason for regarding it as a fiction. In the sense, therefore, in which ' activity' can be referred to physical process, it can be referred to mental process. The point in which all physical analogies fail is that the mental process feels its own current. James, Baldwin and Bradley are wrong in identifying the activity of consciousness with certain selected aspects of the process. The distinction between its passivity and its activity is relative. The whole process is active. Mr. Stout seems at times to say that we have an immediate experience of its degrees (see, e. g., pp. 160 f). He finds no meaning in the attempt to *place* the feeling-aspect of the consciousness in organic or muscular sensations. But suppose the question is put in this form: Could a disembodied spirit actually *feel* his conscious life as distinguished from being conscious of it?

The special analysis of mental process takes up, first, (Chaps. II., III.) attention, which is regarded, not as a ' special activity,' but as a process coincident with noetic consciousness generally. The treatment is masterly from every point of view. It has the prevision, the sureness of touch, the finish of a skilful demonstration in anatomy or, let us say, of a performance by a great artist on the violin. Stress is laid on the systematic complexity of the process, on its character as a prospective attitude, on its relation to mental development, especially in its dependence on preformed dispositions. Its teleological aspect— its tendency to go on until the end is reached and then to stop—is excellently considered, as is also its inhibitive aspect, for which a purely psychological explanation is found particularly in the systematic unity of the process and its relation to preformed dispositions. As to the physiological correlate of attention, some such conception as that of higher and lower level centres (Hughlings Jackson) is preferred to that of special centres of attention (Wundt) as corresponding more closely to the features of the psychological process. Wundt's postulate rests on the grave psychological error of separating the activity of attention from its content. Among other points of interest in the chapter are the conception of interest as the hedonic aspect of attention (p. 225), the careful discussion (pp. 225–236) as to whether attention is ever determined by pleasure and pain, as such—which is seriously doubted—and the refutation of the other common opinion that attention makes its object clearer and more intense (pp. 244 ff). Exception may be taken to this statement or to that, but the analysis as a whole is carried through with remarkable strenuousness and consistency. It would be easy to point parallels to every single feature of the doctrine, but as here worked out, it is, we think, a distinct advance on anything that has been written on the subject hitherto in English. This is particularly to be said in view of certain applications of it in the sequel.

Chapter IV. deals with the more mechanical aspects of conscious process, retentiveness, habit and association. The well-worn subject of habit receives new light from the suggestion that the transition from volitional to automatic action is due, not merely to the effect of repetition, but also to the teleology of attention (p. 265).

Chapter V. deals with the synthesis of presentations in the reference of thought to a single object. 'Noetic synthesis' implies "the introduction of a distinct kind of mental factor, the apprehension of the whole which determines the order and apprehension of the parts" (ii., p. 41).

In Chapter VI., with explicit reference to Bradley's criticism of Associationism in his *Principles of Logic*, Mr. Stout dwells on the constructive synthesis which pervades even the lowest phases of mental process. While associationists tend to represent the whole as due exclusively to the combination of the parts, the thesis here maintained is that every new synthesis results from the further determination of parts within a pre-existing whole. The special aspect of the process treated in this chapter is 'Relative Suggestion,' *i. e.*, the continual spontaneous readaptation of already acquired experience to novel conditions. There is no such a thing as a mere 'literal resuscitation, revival or reinstatement' of former associations.

Chapter VII. on 'Conation and Cognitive Synthesis' developes the counterpart of the doctrine that all conation is attention, namely that all mental process is, as such, conation. From this point of view cognitive synthesis is regarded, not as a web which conative tendencies spin, but as a further defining and differentiation of those tendencies themselves.

Then comes the great chapter (VIII.) on Apperception in which all the preceding discussion is brought to a head. This emphasis on apperception is new in British psychology. Mr. Stout's conception of the process is also new. He has been greatly influenced by the Herbartians and it is in Herbart's sense rather than in that of Leibniz or of Kant that he uses the term. But he differs from Herbart primarily in his conception of the preformed mental system as an organized whole involving noetic synthesis—this as opposed to the conception of a mere apperception-mass of presentations—and then in regarding the entire process as an evolution in which neither the appercipient nor the apperceived factor is at any time either exclusively passive or exclusively active. He defines it as " the process by which a mental system appropriates a new element, or otherwise receives a fresh determination " (p. 112). It expresses the growing point of mind and is a feature common to all understanding, interpreting, subsuming and the like. Among the important features of the doctrine are the conceptions of ' negative' and ' destructive' apperception, the former occurring where the effort to incorporate a new element is defeated, the latter where " one system by appropriating a new element wrests it from its preformed connection with another system." The effect, however, in either case is to develop an apperceptive system of some sort. In the case of 'negative apperception,' for instance, though the system incorporates no new element, it receives a fresh determination and the process can never be repeated under precisely the same conditions again, while as part of a more comprehensive process, it directly conditions positive mental development. Of even greater interest, if possible, is the working out of the conceptions of the coöperation and competition of apperceptive systems, of the conditions which determine their strength and of their conflict and its issue. These topics are all skilfully handled with abundance of acute observation and illustrative detail. The hypothesis of psychical dispositions formed under the influence of attention from which they derive their systematic complexity—the conception of such preformed dispositions reacting on the further process of attention thus becomes, in the hands of the author, a powerful instrument for analyzing the most intricate of mental processes, the process of mental organization and growth. Doubtless much remains to be done in exhibiting the mechanical aspects of the process, and the unity of apperception which appears as an ultimate datum of the analysis constitutes an important and difficult problem. But the thorough and comprehensive treatment of the subject here given is likely to remain for long a standard of reference. One word as to terminology. Is it necessary or desirable to speak of the process of the further determination of a content of attention as a process in which one idea, group or system

' apperceives' the idea which it appropriates or by which it is otherwise determined? We do not say that the idea of red ' perceives' the idea of hardness. The Kantian terminology is here, we think, decidedly preferable to the Herbartian because it relates ' apperception' to that consciousness of self as subject which, whether contributing anything or not to mental process, is certainly very much in evidence and moulds and colors the significance of common speech.

The chapters on ' Comparison and Conception' (Chap. IX.) and on ' Thought and Language ' (Chap. X.) deal especially with the problem of the universal. Conceptual thinking is thought of the universal, as such. Psychologically the universal is the apperceptive system with its universal objective reference. The problem is, to get this into the foreground of consciousness; its solution is chiefly by comparison and by language. The great function of language is to fix and detain, and so render capable of further manipulation, apperceptive systems by means of expressive signs (p. 192). The way language does this is very carefully explained.

Chapter XI. is on ' Belief and Imagination.' Belief is regarded both as a condition of activity and as a result of the limitation of activity. An illustration of the latter principle is the belief in external reality. The brief summary of the author's controversy with Dr. Pikler on this point (pp. 245–248) leaves, however, a rather confused impression. And, as regards the former principle, while it is no doubt true that the acceptance of a proposition means that I *can* make it a starting-point or a link in a process of reasoning ultimately affecting conduct (p. 238), it is by no means clear that I always must. A large number of our theoretical beliefs, accepted on mere authority, appear to yield themselves in fact to no further theoretical uses and to have no direct bearing on conduct.

In the final chapter of the work, the author applies his general conception of mental process as activity tending to an end to the theory of ' Pleasure and Pain' (Chap. XII.). Pleasure, it is held, arises where the activity is unhindered, pain where it is for any reason thwarted or checked, the intensity of the affective state depending on the intensity and complexity of mental excitement and the degree of its hindrance. The theory is abundantly illustrated, and the first part of it, at any rate, may be regarded as fairly well made out for all cases susceptible of psychological analysis. The second part—Mr. Stout unfortunately does not make the distinction—is more doubtful, for it is obviously impossible to compare directly with any accuracy, degrees of intensity of affective states or degrees of complexity of the processes concerned in them. There is, besides, a difference between intensity and amount of feeling, *e. g.*, in the pleasure of indolence as compared with some other pleasures, and this difference requires to be accounted for. In its psychological form, the theory is admittedly inadequate to account for the so-called pleasures and pains of sense. At this point, Mr. Stout translates the principle into physiological terms. Following the clue of the psychological analysis and, assuming that the tendency of mental process is correlated on the physiological side with a tendency of disturbed neural arrangements to equilibrium, the thesis is that "pleasure and pain depend respectively on the uninterrupted or interrupted course of the vital series" and that "intensity of pleasure or pain depends on the intensity and complexity of the pleasant or painful excitation." The theory is then applied to the affective states connected with various classes of sensations, Mr. Marshall and the 'nutrition' theorists coming in for a good deal of effective criticism by the way. His own theory recommends itself to Mr. Stout, in the absence of any positive knowledge of what the physiological process really is, by its comprehensiveness—it assumes that pleasure and pain are produced in all cases in the same way—and because of its basis in psychological experience. It should be noted, however, that the psychological basis is the teleology of the process of attention. The pleasures and pains of sense, on the other hand, have to do directly with 'anoetic' consciousness. And here the process may be quite different. Certainly, as Mr. Stout himself admits, the conception is quite vague when applied to cutaneous pain, especially, we may add, when its purely sensational character is admitted and even the possibility of special pain-nerves.

Though but a fragment of a larger whole, the present treatise is as complete in itself as—may we say?—Schubert's 'Unfinished Symphony.' In each case the intention of the author is completely worked out and in both the execution is finished in the highest degree. Mr. Stout elaborates his thought through all the intricacies of its movement with masterly freedom, sustained power, copious illustration and in the classic style. The book is extremely well written. Severely rigorous in analysis, fixing and defining the most subtly evanescent and baffling of phenomena, it rarely happens that the thought is not clearly expressed. It is one of the books that will live. It will take its place among the great works in the history of English psychology.

H. N. GARDINER.

SMITH COLLEGE.

Contributions to the Analysis of the Sensations. ERNST MACH. Translated by C. M. WILLIAMS. Chicago, The Open Court Publishing Co. 1897. Pp. xii+208, 37 cuts. $1.25.

In the present condition of psychological literature in English an important translation is more of a contribution than any except the best of original work, and such a contribution has certainly been made by the translation of this little book of Mach's. Its distinguishing feature is freshness of view. Instead of the glorification of physics as the ideal toward which psychology should strive which is now and then heard from psychologists themselves, Mach tells us in his preface that he is profoundly convinced " that the foundations of science as a whole and of physics in particular, await their next greatest elucidations from the side of biology and especially from the analysis of the sensations."

How this can be is made clear by the first two chapters. The first develops the general standpoint of idealistic, or, more exactly, sensational monism; the sensations are the 'elements of the world' and their interrelations the subject matter of all science—this standpoint being held, of course, not as a permanent philosophy but as a working hypothesis. The second chapter, on the Chief Point of View for the Investigation of the Senses, advocates a rigid psycho-physic parallelism—no sensation without a corresponding physical change; like sensations, like changes; if space is tridimensional, the underlying neural process will also be found threefold. Such a parallelism follows more or less naturally from the monism of the introduction.

The next three chapters are devoted to an analysis of spatial vision: the first chiefly to physiological similarity and symmetry, the second chiefly to illusions of movement, and the third to normal and illusory perceptions of perspective and the like. The first emphasizes the motor factor in visual space; the second leads up to " the will to perform movements of the eyes, or the innervation to the act," as the essence of that space; and the third offers as a tentative explanation of the phenomena treated, certain habits of the eye, largely independent of consciousness and a result of race experience, which favor seeing according to the greatest probability. Something of this kind, though very differently formulated, is at the bottom of Thiéry's recent explanation of geometrical-optical illusions, and something of the kind seems necessary to bring order into this rather confused field.

The chapter on Time which follows is less interesting—in part perhaps because of its greater difficulty and in part because Mach himself has done less original work in this field.

Sensations of tone are considered in the seventh chapter, the most important sections being those in which the author explains pitch on the basis of only two specific energies instead of the very large number often assumed, and those in which he suggests a hypothetical explanation of the positive character of harmony which musicians have generally declared that Helmholtz neglected in his theory.

The final chapter deals with the philosophy and psychology of science from the monistic standpoint of the introduction. The psychology of the acquisition of knowledge, of judgment, abstraction, concepts, natural laws, mathematical space and physical time are all briefly considered. To the text of the German edition a good number of notes, two appendices, and a full index have been added.

The book is hardly one which the general reader will master easily in all its details, but as a book in which special students who have passed the stage of the text-books and laboratory practice may make the acquaintance of some of the open questions of sensation, and, at the same time, take a lesson in the charm of scientific modesty and reasonableness, it can hardly be excelled.

E. C. SANFORD.

CLARK UNIVERSITY.

Consciousness and Biological Evolution (*I, II.*) *The Religious Instinct. The Function of Religious Expression.* H. R. MARSHALL. Four articles. Mind, July, 1896, to April, 1897.

The first two articles of this series, proceeding upon the assumption of a Spinozistic parallelism of the physiological and psychical, seek to set forth two correspondences, that of instinct to biological constancy and conservatism, and that of reason to biological variation in its highest aspect. As to the first point, Mr. Marshall says that instinct as lapsed intelligence means merely "that as habit becomes more fixed, neural action becomes more thoroughly organized; and that correspondingly the psychic elements coincident with the neural activities become less and less emphatic in the pulse of the preëminent consciousness with which introspection acquaints us." But Mr. Marshall does not make clear why, as neural activities are organized, 'preëminent consciousness' lapses. On the contrary, parallelism would suggest that the more organized the neurosis the more organized the psychosis, and so not its failing but strengthening. Parallelism would say that only upon the supposition that neural organization means 'less emphatic' neurosis will psychosis appear as 'less emphatic,' that is in instinct form. But this supposition is obviously untrue. Further Mr. Marshall by his definition, which he defends at length, of instinct as organized activities, and then explaining instinct by organization simply refers instinct to itself. The question will doubtless occur to many why instinct should be restricted to conservatism. Are not 'cranks,' originals and geniuses a type proceeding from organization? Do not such tendencies run in families?

Mr. Marshall later gives an interesting but by no means conclusive account of social instinct in relation to the individualistic and specific.

As to variation Mr. Marshall emphasizes it as independent activity, 'an element of an aggregate' acting as 'isolated entity.' But while variation is obviously independent activity, it is not necessarily, as seems implied, wholly individualistic. On the contrary, variation is mainly toward the aggregate, it is the initiation of organization. Indeed, as in radical clubs, variation may be said to be organized. The general trend of variation is toward solidarity and centralization. But changeability and volatility may become so constant a characteristic of a race, *e. g.*, the French, as to be a certain kind of conservatism. That reason is in man the chief variant process hardly needs 'argument.' In Section 16 Mr. Marshall thus sums up his doctrine of variation: "The suggestion then which it seems to me biology may gain from this special psychological view in reference to the nature of variation is that organic variation is probably due, in large measure at least, to the tendency of elements in organic aggregates to react as though they were isolated entities, rather than integral parts of a complex systematized unity; acting thus whenever the force reaching them from their environment is so emphatic that it overcomes the forces inherent in the organism of which they are elements, or compels reaction before sufficient time has been allowed for these organic forces to become effective." This, in plain English, equals "variation is due to a tendency to vary." Here then, as in the case of instinct, Mr. Marshall travels in a circle.

The last two articles deal with the religious instinct and its expression as an example of biologic conservatism, the first article being a deduction of religious instinct as a necessary function to socialization, and the second article being an induction from the facts of seclusion, fastings, self-torture, initiation, prayer, sacrifice, celibacy and pilgrimage, as religious practices, that religion has actually exercised this function of restraint of individualism and promotion of sociality. It would take us much too far afield to consider these articles more closely at this time, but while they are suggestive, we think that the sketch is too summary to satisfy most readers. We hope they serve the author only as an outline for an extended research and discussion yet to appear.

HIRAM M. STANLEY.

LAKE FOREST, ILLINOIS.

RECENT WORKS IN PHILOSOPHY.

Christianity and Idealism. By JOHN WATSON, LL.D.   The Macmillan Company, New York and London.   1897.   Pp. 211.

The Life of James Mc Cosh.   Edited by WILLIAM MILLIGAN SLOANE.   New York, Charles Scribner's sons.   1896.   Pp. 287.

Professor Watson's book is the first publication, though second in the series, resulting from the laudable enterprise of the Philosophical Union of the University of California.   Passing over the first part of the volume, on account of space limit, we come in the second part to the discussion of special interest to philosophical readers, that of the relation of modern Idealism to the Christian ideal of life.   In his preface Professor Watson includes under the term Idealism such different systems as those of Descartes and Hegel, Kant, Spinoza and Lotze.   The fundamental principle of idealism is expressed in the proposition, the real is rational.   The departures of any of the above thinkers from pure idealism is to be measured by their departure from this principle.   Now broadly conceived, the rationality of the real is held by many who are not accounted as idealists.   But the school of idealism, with which Professor Watson is most in sympathy, tends to identify the real and the rational in the sense that reality in its last analysis reduces to the activity of thought.

Under the influence of this presumption which tends to narrow the principle of idealism to the tenet of a school the author proceeds to interpret the content of Christianity in accordance with the rational categories.   But in this effort both elements are subjected to a severe strain.   The central category of Christianity, whether we view its historical content or that of the living christian consciousness of the present, is, without doubt, that of concrete, personal spirit.   The difficulty of Professor Watson is that of reconciling this category with the principles of a philosophy which tends to reduce the real to ultimate terms of thought.   That by the application of force a species of adjustment may be effected is no doubt true.   But the only satisfactory treatment of the relation would consist in such an exhibition of essential unity between the content of Christianity and the principles of Idealism as would make it appear that Christianity itself, when it becomes reflective, naturally and normally expresses itself in the terms of the idealistic creed.   Now it is one thing to say that the reflective Christian consciousness will be broadly idealistic, but quite another to maintain that it will find its most adequate expression in the ready-made principles of any of the idealistic schools. Professor Watson speaks as the mouthpiece of a special form of idealism, and his is perhaps the most eloquent and persuasive voice of his school. But there are those, and among them I am forced to count myself, who are not convinced that the main contention of the author has been successful, and who believe that complete unity between Christianity and Idealism would involve more than thinkers of Professor Watson's school are willing to concede.

No one who reads Professor Watson's book will fail to be impressed by its great ability and its positive merits. It is written in the author's best style and it rests on the firm belief that the vitalest problems of philosophy are those of religion and that a philosophy which takes a negative attitude toward religion, or attempts to shirk its problems, proves recreant to its most pressing duty. Professor Watson's faith in the ultimate unity of philosophic and religious truth is also reassuring in view of the hesitating tone of so many of our thinkers. And that he has made a noble contribution to the religious thought of the time none will be more ready to admit than those who are not convinced that the specific aim of the last section of his book has been completely attained.

The life of James McCosh is mainly autobiographical, taken from notes written down by him during the last years of his life. But these notes were incomplete and at times fragmentary and the editor, Professor Sloane, has performed a difficult task with the masterly skill and tact of an experienced literary craftsman. The record embraces the boyhood and youth of McCosh, his university career at Glasgow and Edinburgh, his experience as a minister during which he played his part in the memorable disruption and the establishment of the Free Kirk of Scotland, his career as a professor at Belfast and a leader in the national education of the Scotch and Irish, closing with the splendid chapter which his twenty years at Princeton added to the educational history of that university and the country. The whole story gives a strong impression of the simplicity as well as the greatness of the man and will enable the public to understand the secret of his immense influence at Princeton and the profound impression which he was able to make on the educators of his generation. Space will permit only an allusion to the educational services of Dr. McCosh and we must hasten to notice his work as a thinker and philosopher. Some of the most important of his services in this line have been rendered as a leader in a movement of transition and adjustment. Such, for example, was his attitude toward evolution which, as a religious thinker, he adopted and defended as an ally rather than a foe to religion, at a time when evolution was generally regarded as atheistical. Such also was the service he rendered the new physiological psychology at a time when traditional methods were almost universally prevalent. Although not distinctly experimental, Dr. McCosh's method was largely observational and his works are treasuries of facts and shrewd observations. In philosophy Dr. McCosh stands in line with the best Scottish traditions. He was a stout champion of a realistic epistemology and an intuitional metaphysics. His real contribution to philosophy consists, however, not so much in any special doctrines which he may have taught as in certain fundamental convictions, metaphysical, ethical and religious, which inspired all his work. In his advocacy of these he was able to exert a profound influence upon his age and, at the same time, to make an important contribution to its thought.

PRINCETON.   A. T. ORMOND.

Contemporary Theology and Theism. R. M. WENLEY. New York, Charles Scribner's Sons, 1897. Pp. 197. $1.25.

We congratulate Professor Wenley and the public upon the happy thought which prompted him to mark his advent to an American university by the publication of this little book, part of the material for which was originally presented before the Theological Society of Glasgow University in the form of an address. Professor Wenley is favorably known as the author of *Socrates and Christ* and *Aspects of Pessimism*, and as a contributor to the philosophical journals. The present volume, like the earlier ones, is, in the main, critical and expository rather than constructive, but the constructive element is sufficient to define the author's position among contemporary students of the philosophy of religion. In the brief space here available one can do little more than cordially commend this essay to all who are interested in contemporary Theology and Theism—to the lay reader as well as to the professed student of these subjects.

The author's purpose may, perhaps, fairly be said to embrace a threefold aim, viz., to show the influence of philosophical theory upon current theological thought, to offer some criticism of the theology resulting from an inadequate philosophy *overriding* facts and warping their interpretation, and finally to ask whether theology can not in its turn add something to philosophy, and so contribute toward the formation of a more adequate philosophy of religion. The first half of the volume furnishes cogent illustration of the historical, as well as of the logical, inseparability of philosophy and theology—a fact which should not, but which does, need ever fresh iteration—and offers some acute and valuable criticism of the two main currents of contemporary theological thought which have been chiefly determined by their respective philosophical presuppositions. The speculative school is that which, building ultimately on Hegel, construes the historic facts of religion, and of the Christian religion in particular, in accordance with the logical necessity of the Hegelian dialectic; which the Ritschlian school, building on Kant and Lotze, so separate philosophy from religion, dogma from fact, that it holds a Christianity divorced alike from metaphysics and from history, and resting on no objective basis of fact. These two schools do not of course adequately represent contemporary theology, since there are also the ' mediating ' theologians and the conservative school to be noted. In this regard, therefore, Professor Wenley's title is bigger than his book, and to this extent it is misleading. But his exposition of the two theological tendencies with which he deals is clear and fair; his criticism of their defects is acute, and the reader who is not particularly acquainted with the movements of recent theology will doubtless retain a more vivid impression from this bird's-eye view of two of its phases than he would from a more expansive and detailed presentation.

The latter half of the volume deals with 'the theistic problem.' The question is, " Can theology, accepting the metaphysical first principles which spiritual inquiry of necessity involves, so react upon philosophy as to produce a less inadequate solution of difficulties?" Professor Wenley answers, yes. There are at least three regions where theology can assist and correct philosophical speculation. These are " the questions of the personality of God, of the creative or originating power which marks the divinity of Christ, and of the relation of man to sin." It is with the first of these three, or with the theistic problem proper, that the remainder of the book is chiefly concerned—at first by way of criticism of the agnostic and gnostic positions respectively, and then in offering some constructive suggestions toward the solution of the problem. Possibly the most important sections of this portion of the book are those which contain the very discriminating and appreciative estimate of Hegel, and the suggestion that the key to the solution of the theistic problems may be found to lie in a more perfect analysis of the idea of personality. The *Hauptproblem* is how ' to preserve the requisite balance between immanence and transcendence.' The author thinks he finds the clue to the resolution of this difficulty in the finite self, which combines the qualities of immanence and transcendence, and so furnishes an analogy for the nature of God. The hint here let fall seems to us full of suggestiveness, but Professor Wenley has not worked it out sufficiently to make his meaning altogether plain. We close with an expression of the hope that he may yet be able to do this for us in the more systematic and constructive work of which we trust the present essay is the precursor. Meanwhile it may perhaps be worth noting that his general point of view is not unlike that of Professor Fraser in that he too starts from man and man's experience as the clue to the nature of divine personality. GEORGE L. PATTON.

PRINCETON UNIVERSITY.

PEDAGOGICAL.

Ueber eine neue Methode zur Prüfung geistiger Fähigkeiten und ihre Anwendung bei Schulkindern. H. EBBINGHAUS. Ztschr. für Psychol. u. Phys. der Sinnesorgane, XIII., 401–459. 1897.

In 1895 the city authorities of Breslau applied to the Hygienic Section *der Schlessischen Gesellschaft für vaterländische Kultur* for an opinion and report on the advisability of holding school sessions five hours long. The secretaries of the Section, Professors Flügge, H. Cohn and Jacobi, added to their number several other physicians and educators, including Professor Ebbinghaus, who has given us the above account of the preliminary labors of the commission.

The method of Burgerstein with addition and multiplication of simple numbers, that of Sikorski and Höpfner with long dictation exercises, and that of Richter with easy algebra and Greek conjugations, were all objectionable since they did not preserve sufficiently the normal character of a recitation period. They aimed to measure fatigue but vitiated the results by the monotony and lack of interest due to their methods.

A second set of investigators, recognizing this, have avoided interfering with the normal school-work, but apply an appropriate test from time to time, to determine the amount of fatigue due to the regular work. Thus Griesbach tested pupils at different periods in the course of the day by measuring their sensibility to touch, and found that it varied with their mental fatigue.

The Breslau commission determined to combine the best features of both methods; they allowed the ordinary school work to take its regular course, but tested the pupils before school and at the end of every period by having them spend 10 minutes in (1) adding or multiplying (arithmetic test), or five minutes in (2) writing numbers of from 6 to 10 places from dictations (memory test), or (3) filling in omitted syllables and words in a specially prepared text (combination test). The tests were made in a gymnasium and in a girls' school, on three different Wednesdays a fortnight apart.

The second test, that of the memory span for numbers, showed most remarkable variations from period to period and seemed least reliable when the tests were not all made by the same teacher so as to insure uniformity in rate, rhythm, tone, etc., in giving out the numbers.

The third test was intended to go deeper and test intellectual fatigue. The omitted syllables were indicated by dashes and pupils were required to restore the omissions as rapidly as possible, but always *so as to make sense.* In general this test brought out greater differences in the several classes than either of the other two methods. By this method of testing Untertertia accomplished more than twice as much as Sexta and made an average of less than one-third as many mistakes, whereas by the arithmetic test the difference was less than 25% increase in these three years.

The three methods showed interesting differences within each class as well as from class to class. For this purpose each class was divided into three groups according to their ranking in scholarship. The memory test showed quite as good results, or even better among the duller pupils than among the brighter ones. The arithmetic test placed the duller pupils midway between the brighter and the mediocre ones. The combination test, however, reflected with great fidelity the rank and scholarship of the pupils. The quantity of work as well as the quality of it increased regularly in every class from the duller to the brighter pupils. The differences between the three groups were much greater in the lower classes and least in the highest classes.

In the lower classes the girls were without exception behind the boys in all three tests, but in the higher classes the sixteen year old girls had completely overtaken the boys of corresponding age.

The memory test showed no sure signs of fatigue at the end of five hours of school work. The arithmetic test brought out evident weakening in effectiveness and accuracy, while the combination method gave no sure signs of fatigue in the upper and middle classes at all. Pupils of 10 to 12, however, undoubtedly fatigued much more rapidly. Whether this fatigue is *harmful* or *useful* is not shown by these tests and would require other tests to determine the fact. It is to be hoped the Commission will carry out these further investigations, for it is certainly a very effeminate pedagogy that is going to try to keep the dear children from ever getting tired.

Lastly, the results were worked over to compare the effects of different branches of study. After language lessons in the classics the combination test showed considerably better results both in quantity and quality, than after lessons in any other branch, *e. g.*, science, arithmetic or drawing; notwithstanding that these subjects afforded less mental strain of attention and consequently probably less fatigue.

The Pedagogical Seminary. Edited by G. STANLEY HALL. Vol. IV., 2 and 3. December, 1896, and April, 1897.

' A Study of Dolls,' by Mr. Ellis and Dr. Hall gives the substance of an extensive and laborious collection of data, tabulation of statistics and rare suggestions of applications. The chief topics are: material of which dolls are made, substitutes and proxies, psychic qualities, doll's food and feeding, sleep, sickness, death, funeral and burial of of dolls, doll's names, discipline, hygiene and toilet, doll's families, schools, parties, weddings, accessories and furnishings, miscellaneous anthropological notes.

The doll passion seems to be strongest between seven and ten and reaches its climax between eight and nine, and the parental instinct is far less prominent in doll play than is commonly supposed. However disconnected the words doll and idol, some psychic connection cannot be doubted. Idols may, perhaps, be valuable object lessons in religion for children at the pagan stage and may yet have a rôle to play in elementary religious training. The small scale of the doll world focuses and intensifies affections and all other feelings.

Although doll play educates the heart and will even more than the intellect, many school subjects are also helped by it. Children with French dolls incline to practice their little French upon them; can this tendency be utilized in teaching a foreign language to young children? Some children thus learn to read, sew, knit, do millinery work, observe and design costumes, acquire taste in color and even prepare food, they make their dolls represent heroes in history or fiction and take them on imaginary journeys into foreign lands, and sometimes the doll serves as an ethical ideal and helps them to be good. Dolls are an excellent school for children to practice all they know of rudimentary sociology, ethics and science. Would not dolls and their furnishings be among the best things to make in manual training schools? Why are dolls, which represent the most original, free and spontaneous expression of the play instinct, so commonly excluded from kindergartens, where they could aid in teaching almost everything?

" There should be somewhere (*a*) a doll museum, (*b*) a doll expert to keep the possibilities of this great educative instinct steadily in view, and (*c*) careful observations upon children of kindergarten, primary and grammar grades should be instituted as at an experiment station in order to determine just what is practicable."

Mr. Small's study of the ' Suggestibility of Children ' presents a great deal of concrete material, partly experimental and partly observation notes in answer to a syllabus. He concludes that in healthy children a high degree of suggestibility is a universal condition and largely within the control of any one in sympathy with children. Hence the necessity of removing from the public schools, stutterers, emotional prodigals, and nervous defectives; greater prominence of motor element and dramatic instinct in learning; a possible use of the social instinct as it crops out in school fads to awaken interest in history, literature and science; a hint at the natural method of child discipline in suggestion as children use it; and the strong influence of the attitude of the teacher upon the tastes and ideals of the pupils.

Mr. Dawson's ' Study in Youthful Degeneracy ' gives us the results of a difficult and embarrassing study of sixty juvenile delinquents, comprising carefully selected types of (1) thieves, (2) incendiaries, (3) assaulters, (4) sexual offenders, and (5) general incorrigibles.

In the April number Mr. Street reviews the chief methods of language teaching and Mr. Croswell summarizes the ' Courses of Study in the Elementary Schools.' Mr. Burk has worked over a great many returns to a questionnaire on ' Teasing and Bullying ' and believes that ' these are to be classed more as crystallized instincts than as conscious and voluntary activities.' He suggests that the movements involved are ' the racial form of all exercise,' and that as such " they are the only possible forms of exercise upon which progress in physical development, and mental development, of the individual rests."

Mr. Partridge has contributed two short articles on ' Second Breath ' and ' Blushing,' and Miss Frear, of Stanford University, has worked out in a series of six charts a number of general conclusions based on the material in Mr. Russell's book on imitation.

The work in these two numbers of the *Seminary* is based almost entirely on the returns to President Hall's Child Study Syllabi, and the authors have taken advantage of this rich concrete material for copious use in illustrating all the points brought forward. Notwithstanding the able and thoroughly practical conclusions of most of the papers, the chief inspiration of it all lies in the plain, unvarnished observation notes that formed the raw material for these studies and might form the basis of dozens of still other 'conclusions.' The advantage of publishing the original material is obvious in affording opportunity for further interpretations.

HERMAN T. LUKENS.

BRYN MAWR COLLEGE, PENNSYLVANIA.

VISION.

Ueber intermittirende Netzhautreizung. FR. SCHENCK. Pflüger's Archiv, Bd. LXIV., 165–179, 607–628.
On Intermittent Stimulation of the Retina. Part I. By O. F. F. GRÜNBAUM. Journal of Physiology, XXL, 396–403.
An Account of Certain Phenomena of Colour Vision with Intermittent Light. G. J. BURCH. Journal of Physiology, XXL, 426–434.

Much interest has been aroused by the method of photometry introduced by Professor Rood in 1893 (Am. Jour. Sci., XLVI.), which is based upon the fact, first observed by Plateau, that there is a definite relation between the intensity of two alternating light-sensations and the rate of frequency of repetition necessary to cause them to become fused, that is, to cause 'flicker' to become extinguished The less the difference of intensity of the two excitations, the less rapidly do they need to alternate in order to produce a homogeneous intermediate sensation; if a disc is half white and half black, it must rotate more rapidly to extinguish flicker than if it is half a light gray and half a dark gray, and the less the difference in the grays the less is the rapidity of rotation that is required. This circumstance gives an evident foundation for a method of photometry, which is of particular advantage for the estimation of the brightness of different colors, since the color constituent is found by most people to be very disturbing in estimating relative brightness by plain inspection; by this method it is only necessary to select from a number of grays of known brightness the one with which the color in question will most readily fuse.

Schafhäutl (Münch. Akad. Abh., VII.) had already proposed in 1855 a photometric method based upon the extinction of flicker, which should give absolute intensities and not simply comparative ones; he looked at a bright surface through a hole behind which a small screen was caused to vibrate which alternately shut out and let through the light from the surface to be examined. He assumed that the rapidity of vibration of the spring would be proportional to the square root of its length (which would not be the case when the spring carries a weight) and that the intensity of the light when flicker just ceased would be proportional to the square root of the rate of vibration of the spring (which is also not known to be true).

Schenck proposes, in his second communication, a modification of the method of Rood, by which the color to be tested is placed upon a color-disc on which there is a gray which goes gradually, from the center outwards, from white to black; this is secured by painting black upon a white surface in such a way that the amount of black at any given narrow ring of the disc is proportional to the distance of that ring from the center. He then looks at the rotating disc through a small hole in a piece of cardboard, and determines at what distance from the center fusion takes place with the lowest possible rapidity of rotation; this will be the position of that black and white mixture which is of equal brightness with the color which is being tested, and the proportion of black and white in it will be given by its distance from the center. Outside and inside of this ring, flickering is still going on, because the gray is either too dark or too light to fuse with the color at so low an intermittence frequency. The method was found to work well. It was tested by determining the brightness of each of two complementary colors, and then the brightness of their resulting gray light and comparing this last with the brightness computed for the two colors when mixed in the proportion necessary to give gray; the coincidence was very close. This method of testing was of course made use of by Rood, and described by him in his first communication. But the curious circumstance developed itself that when the brightness of the papers was determined by direct inspection—by choosing the gray which seemed to look equally bright with a given color—very different results were obtained. The two brightest colors, yellow and green, were given as much too bright by the intermittence method, yellow especially so, while all the other colors, and particularly red, were given as too dull. No explanation has been found by Schenck for this discrepancy. The idea of Hering that complementary colors have an opposite and compensatory specific brightness effect does not apply, because here yellow and green belong in one category, and red and blue in the other. Moreover, there is no extinction of the color in this experiment, it is merely spread in a thinner layer over a larger retinal surface; therefore, there would be no sense in assuming that the intermittence method determines the white-valence alone, and by the test already referred to, it is evident that there

is exactly determined by the intermittence method that element of
brightness (whatever it may be) which goes to the formation of the
brightness of the gray produced by the mixture of two complementary
colors; from which it results that Hering's idea of the specific brighten-
ing and darkening power of the four colors is as meaningless and confusing when it comes to a practical application as it is in theory. The
mere inability to detect by direct inspection the relative brightness of
two different colors seems to be also no sufficient explanation, because
it would appear that *some* definite affection of sensation is got by this
means which is common to different observers and to the same observer
at different times. The subject would apparently repay further investigation.

A curious circumstance was first noticed by Filehne, in 1885, in
connection with the fusion into one mean sensation of two rapidly
alternating sensations. If two discs are prepared, one of four alternate equal black and white sectors and the other of sixteen, and if
the first be given a rotation velocity four times as great as that of the
second, then the rate of alternation of black and white excitations upon
a given point of the retina is alike in both cases, but, nevertheless, the
conditions are not equally favorable for fusion; the rapidly rotating
disc will present a fusion of sensation at a time when flicker is still
persisting in this disc of many sectors. Mere linear velocity seems
in some curious way to assist the fusion. Thirty alternations per
second suffice to produce fusion in the one case, while if the sectors
are numerous and the disc rotates in the same proportion slower, flicker
may persist with over seventy alternations per second. Fick found
that when parallel lines were drawn on a drum which rotated about
an axis parallel to the lines, as many as 170 alternations a second
might be necessary to produce fusion, but that if the moving lines
were looked at through a slit, flicker ceased at forty per second. He
suggested that this discrepancy was owing to the fact that when the
speed of translation is slow the eye more readily follows the moving
contour of the sectors, and the alternating excitations do not fall in
order upon exactly the same part of the retina, but that the use of a small
aperture for observation prevents this movement of the eyes. Schenck's
first paper is devoted to upholding this view as against Marbe, who
maintained that the slow contour movement in itself is enough to re-
tard fusion. He does this first by experiment, and he then shows with
much skill that the theoretical considerations by which Marbe has
sought to deduce his view as to the effect of contour motion from his
theory of Talbot's law are ineffective, and also that his theory is at

bottom not different from the usual theory, and especially not so well stated as by Boas (Ann. d. Phys. u. Chem., N. F. XVI.). To sum up, the moments which affect fusion favorably are these:

1. Diminution of the duration of the double period.
2. Increase in the difference of duration of the two separate excitations.
3. Diminution in the difference of intensity of the two excitations.
4. Increase of the absolute mean intensity.
5. More rapid contour motion (in the case of rotating discs).

Marbe's explanation of the effect of the first four of these circumstances is the same as that of Boas. His explanation of the last, which is that it is due to contrast, is counter-indicated by an experiment of Baader's, in which a disc is prepared of alternate black and white half rings, and it is found that fusion takes place just as well as with solid half circles of black and white, in spite of the fact that adjoining rings upon the retinal surface are in the first case constantly in opposite phases of excitation, and hence favorable to the production of contrast. Schenck himself seems to think that, when fusion is prevented by reason of eye-movements, it is by means of a psychical effect, *ein deutliches Erkennen der Conturen;* does he not here overlook the very evident fact that when the eye follows the contour a given part of the retina is exposed for a longer time to white and respectively to black and that there is, therefore, a physical effect which is exactly the same as if the disc were rotating more slowly?

Mr. Grünbaum's paper presents a degree of obscurity in the description of a sufficiently simple experiment which one would have to go far to see equalled; in grammar even it is not above reproach. His experiments show apparently that even the use of an aperture does not do away with what we may call the Filehne anomaly, described just above, *unless* there is a constant relation between the size of the aperture and the cross-section of the black and white disc-sectors which are sweeping past it. Consider for a moment what would be the effect of a non-constant relation between the two quantities just named: let a and b be two equal discs, each with alternate equal black and white sectors, but let the individual sectors of b be ten times as large as those of a, and at the same time let them rotate ten times as rapidly. If they are looked at through apertures at the same distance from the center of each disc, then the conditions as regards any given retinal point will be alike in both cases, it will be subjected to alternate black and white excitation in periods of the same duration. But there will be a difference as regards the square surface of the retina as a whole upon which the image of the aperture falls. If the black and white sectors are no wider across at the point examined than is the aperture, then there will be no perceptible time during which *the whole aperture* is black or is white, but if the sectors are the large and the rapidly moving ones, then the whole aperture will be a good part of the time exposed wholly to either black or white. The former case, according to Grünbaum, is favorable to simultaneous contrast, and hence the difference in physiological intensity of the two stimuli is increased, and fusion is interfered with. He refers to Sherrington's paper (about to be noticed) for proof of this effect of contrast; but Sherrington found, under favorable circumstances, that contrast caused 34 rotations per second to be essential to fusion when without it 22 were sufficient, while Grünbaum gets, for changing breadth of sector (everything else remaining the same) a change of number of rotations from 43 to 225. It is difficult to believe that such a difference as this could be due to contrast. Moreover, are not the conditions as favorable to successive contrast in the latter case as they are to simultaneous contrast in the first? Grünbaum considers it improbable that 'when an aperture of 5 mm. is used and the eye focussed for a cross drawn upon the screen' (by which he doubtless means to say that the center of a cross is fixated) any movement of the eye can occur. One might equally well say that, under these circumstances, very small movements of the eye, which are known to be unavoidable, would be sufficient. He neglects to say that his explanation is the same as that given by Marbe, and criticised as above by Schenck.

Burch experimented with spectral light, which he made intermittent by means of a rotating screen pierced with holes. His double period consisted of a short duration of very bright light and a long duration of darkness. When the dispersion was wide, so that the field of view of the spectroscope was sensibly of one color, and when the rotation was too slow to produce fusion, he detected patches of darkness of the same shape as the interstices between Purkinje's figures. With a very short duration of the flash, the yellow spot of the retina became subjectively evident; under certain circumstances "upon looking steadily at the part inside the bend of the absorption band between C and D, it is seen to be occupied by an irregular group of brilliant red dots on a ground of beetle-green or steel-blue." When the flashes were of very great intensity, instead of a continuous spectrum there were seen three bands of color, red, green and blue, upon a brightly illuminated whitish background. The explanation given of this latter phenomenon by Mr. Burch is very ingenious, and, as it happens, it fits in very well with my theory, in fact, it is much the same as the explanation that I have given, under simpler circumstances, for the lesser purity of the portions of the spectrum between the fundamental colors in general. It is this: a given color-decomposition (if we speak in chemical terms, for the sake of clearness), will be effected chiefly by a certain oscillation frequency of light, which we may call its optimum period, but it will also be effected to a less extent by other rates on either side of this. Now when the light employed is very intense, a maximum decomposition will be effected by periods at some distance on either side of the optimum period. With a steady illumination, this would make the whole spectrum whitish, and very bright, but with an intermittent illumination, the resulting sensation is not so intense as to prevent the observer from recognizing the greater apparent brilliancy of those portions where two color-sensations overlap, and accordingly those parts look brighter than the rest and have the pale tints of binary color-blends. The author apologizes for this explanation on account of the fact that it posits red, green and blue (in opposition to Hering) as the primary colors. (He saw violet, under certain circumstances, as very bright also, but an easy explanation lies at hand for this— there are only a few red-producing rays at that end of the spectrum with which to diminish the purity of the blue.) This is, however, an element in its favor, and he has moreover other observations, not yet published, which will confirm this view.

C. L. Franklin.

Baltimore.

Neue Versuche über intermittende Gesichtsreize. Karl Marbe. Phil. Studien, XIII., 1. 106–115.

The author investigates the relations between the critical period of duration of intermittent visual stimuli and the average brightness (Helligkeit) of the stimuli. "For two visual stimuli which fall upon the retina successively and periodically, there is a certain short period of duration in which they produce a constant sensation." This the author calls the critical period of duration. According to Baader, the critical period grows for two colorless stimuli, as the difference of brightness between the two sensations decreases. This is true alike when the average brightness increases with the increasing difference between the stimuli, and when the average brightness is constant. Kleiner showed that, with a difference of stimuli increasing from o on, the critical period decreases at first very rapidly, then slower and slower, until finally the decrease almost ceases. The author asks and answers the questions whether the conclusion of Kleiner holds for all cases of increasing stimuli, indifferent whether the average brightness of the stimuli increases, is constant, or decreases; and whether, if this is the case, the regularity is determined by the differences in the stimuli.

Author used 40 gray pieces of paper of different degrees of brightness determined photographically, as described in the Zeitsch. f. Psych. u. Physiol. d. Sinnesorgane, Bd. XII., S. 62f. The brightest piece reflected about 13 times as much light as the darkest, the determinations being made by the Kirschmann photometer. Degrees of brightness between white and black were determined as follows: A white and a black disk of 16cm. diameter were placed on a Maxwell color-mixer. Concentrically over these was placed the gray disk whose intensity was to be determined. Then the white and black disks were adjusted to give the same brightness as the gray disk, starting first from a mixture which was clearly brighter, then from one which was clearly darker than the gray disk, and taking the average of the two determinations, which is given in the tables. The method by which the rapidity of rotation was determined which is necessary to give a constant sensation from the two stimuli, is described in Phil. Studien, Bd. IX., S. 389ff. Driving force was produced by an electromotor with an Ad. Fick regulator.[1]

The author's conclusions are as follows: (1) With increasing difference between two stimuli the critical period of duration decreases at first very rapidly, then more slowly, and finally almost none at all. (2) This holds indifferently, whether the average intensity increases or decreases with increasing difference of stimuli. (3) The values of the critical periods of duration are determined, for the most part (*im wesentlichen*), by the objective, not by the subjective, differences between the two stimuli. (4) To equal objective differences correspond about equal critical periods of duration.

The article includes five tables and three curves. The account of the experiments is somewhat condensed and brief, but probably a more detailed account is unnecessary. The subjects were the author and Professor Külpe.

G. A. TAWNEY.

BELOIT COLLEGE.

---

[1]Described by Bradt: Ueber die Wärmebildung bei summirten Zuchungen des Muskels. Wurzburg, Etlinger's Buchdruckerei. 1893. S. 13ff.

VOLITION.

The Psychology of Effort. JOHN DEWEY. Philosophical Review, VI., 43–56, January, 1897.

Professor Dewey here presents a theory of the psychology of effort in harmony with his theory of the significance of emotion (this REVIEW, II., 13 ff). Accepting the sensationalist view of the consciousness of effort, he finds the specific quality of this consciousness in the rivalry between the sensation of motor adjustment and the sensori-motor idea of the desired end, with the accompanying disagreeableness due to failure of habit. The scandal of the assertion that awareness of effort is a sense of changes of breathing, of muscular tensions, etc., is removed, he thinks, when it is explained that "these sensations report the state of things as regards effective realization." The theory explains the increase of the sense of effort in fatigue psychologically—it is due to the introduction of new distracting elements; other theories fall back on the exhaustion itself, an extra-psychical factor. It also explains certain facts in connection with the mastery of novel acts; in learning to ride a bicycle, for example, if the more habitual motor adjustments fail to get transformed so as to correspond with the image of the desired balancing, the sense of effort may be at a maximum, but if the movements become utterly unregulated, so that the consciousness of the end aimed at disappears, then, notwithstanding the mass of muscular sensations, the sense of effort vanishes also. Dewey denies that the sense of effort arises from an activity struggling against resistance. The appearance of such a struggle he explains as due to the importance attached to the motor adjustment as means. If this fail, then all lying outside it is regarded as resistance. "The real state of things is that there are two acts mutually opposing each other during their transformation into a third new and inclusive act." He also opposes the view that it arises from the self endeavoring to overcome obstacles. The whole process is one of divided self-activity, not that of an active 'self' on the one side as over against muscular resistance on the other.

As in the theory of emotion, the 'scandal' of the sensationalist view appears to the present writer to lie not so much in the assertion that the sense of effort is the feeling of bodily sensations as in the isolation of these sensations and the appearance of treating them as though they existed in the experience itself in the same form in which they exist for our psychological abstraction. Admit them as in actual experience elements in a specifically related mass of conscious contents, admit them as the feeling, the sense-awareness of a struggle of adjustment in which the actual self of the moment, self-divided, is seeking expression in a complete action, and who is there that cannot subscribe to the theory?

H. N. GARDINER.
SMITH COLLEGE.

Über willkürliche Vorstellungsverbindung. STEPHAN WITASEK. Zeitschrift für Psychol. u. Physiol. d. Sinnesorgane, XII., 3 und 4, Oct., 1893.

A difficult and interesting topic is handled by Witasek after a somewhat inadequate and an unduly diffuse fashion. His subject is the nature of *willkürliche Vorstellungsverbindungen*, that is, of volitions which have as their ' objects' psychic facts, not bodily motions. How, for instance, can one be said to ' will' to imagine a three-fourth rhythm, or the ' color designated by the Frauenhofer line B?' Anticipatory image of color and of rhythm there must be, or there is no volition, yet the anticipatory image can not be precisely like the intended one, else the supposed volition will coincide with its object. Witasek answers by distinguishing the anticipatory image as un-perceptual (*unanschaulich*), from the concrete image which is the result of volition, while he observes that they are alike in referring to the ' same thing'; since, however, such a sequence of un-concrete upon concrete may be an affair of purely involuntary association, he emphasizes the additional consciousness of the relation between the two. He proceeds to analyze the solution into four psychic factors: (1) the act of will (*Willensakt*), (2) the unperceptual anticipatory image of the object, (3) the relation between the anticipatory image and (4) the concrete image which is the object of the act of will.

Witasek's exposition of this analysis discloses its weak features. There is in the first place, no justification whatever of its first moment, the ' act of will' which proves to be a perfect fifth wheel to the coach (see p. 211). The ' relation' between (2) and (3) is another contraband article in modern psychological writing; it might better be treated after Dr. James' fashion as a ' transitive element' of the anticipatory image itself. In fact, the greatest value of the discussion is its recognition of the problem of inner volition, its emphasis upon the difficulty of the distinction between volition and object of the volition, when the latter is itself a fact of consciousness. The real nature of the distinction, however, is only suggested by the description *unanschaulich*, which, if one may judge from the illustrations offered, virtually means 'verbal.' On the other hand, the different emphasis of attention in the case of anticipatory and of resultant image is not adequately considered, for (in the opinion of the writer of this notice) attention is the *x* in terms of which the problem must be solved.

MARY WHITON CALKINS.

WELLESLEY COLLEGE.

EMOTION.

The Sense of Beauty, being the Outlines of Æsthetic Theory GEORGE SANTAYANA. New York, Charles Scribner's Sons. 1896. Pp. ix+275.

Perhaps the first thing to be mentioned about this book is its perfection—if the word be not too cruelly pressed—its flawlessness. It is an unpadded little masterpiece—it fills its covers as an athlete fills his skin, it 'pays' its way sentence by sentence down the page. It makes ' no pretentions to originality beyond that of putting together the scattered commonplaces of criticism, under the inspiration of a naturalistic psychology'; but the inspiration has been sincere, and the commonplaces have been not only reset, but recut, and the 'cutting' is often, in its unobtrusive way, exquisite. Granted its point of view, it is all thought out with an extraordinary quietness and completeness and uninsistent finish; and the artistic imagination has everywhere been discreetly busy with its phrase.

It ' contains the chief ideas gathered together for a course of lectures on the theory and history of æsthetics given at Harvard College from 1892 to 1895.' It consists of a brief ' Preface,' from which the foregoing sentence is quoted; of an ' Introduction,' on the ' Methods of Æsthetics'; of four ' Parts,' on the ' Nature of Beauty,' the ' Materials of Beauty,' ' Form,' and ' Expression' respectively; and of a concluding chapter. There is also an analytical table of contents and an index. The ' Method' recommended (it has been indicated already), is the psychological, as distinguished from the historical and from the didactic. Æsthetics is the theory of a certain kind of ' values,' and values are subjective. " We desire nothing because it is good, but it is good only because we desire it." " Things are interesting because we care about them, and important because we need them. Had our perceptions no connections with our pleasures, we should soon close our eyes on this world; if our intelligence were of no service to our passions, we should come to doubt in the lazy freedom of reverie, whether two and two make four."

The problem of the 'Nature of Beauty,' therefore, is simply to distinguish the æsthetic pleasures from the non-æsthetic. And this distinction does not lie in the supposed 'unselfishness' of æsthetic pleasures. Selfishness and unselfishness are not of the essence of any pleasures whatever, they are accidental, extrinsic. "There is no reference to the nominal essence called oneself in one's appetites or in one's natural affections; yet a man absorbed in his meat and drink, in his houses and lands, in his children and dogs, is called selfish because these interests, although natural and instinctive in him, are not shared by others. * * * I care about myself because *myself* is a name for the things I have at heart. To set up the verbal figment of personality and make it an object of concern apart from the interests which were its content and substance, turns the moralist into a pedant and ethics into a superstition."

Neither does it lie in the supposed universality of æsthetic pleasures. "The pleasures of the senses have, it is said, no dogmatism in them; that anything gives me pleasure involves no assertion about its capacity to give pleasure to another. But when I judge a thing to be beautiful, my judgment means that the thing is beautiful in itself, or (what is the same thing more critically expressed) that it should seem so to everybody." But preference of every sort is ultimately irrational and it is simply unmeaning to say that what is beautiful to one man *ought* to be beautiful to another. If their senses are the same, their associations and dispositions similar, then the same thing will certainly be beautiful to both. If their natures are different, the form which to one will be entrancing will be to another even invisible, because his classifications and discriminations in perception will be different, and he may see a hideous detached fragment or a shapeless aggregate of things in what to another is a perfect whole. It is absurd to say that what is invisible to a given being ought to seem beautiful to him. Evidently this obligation of recognizing the same qualities is conditioned by the possession of the same faculties. But no two men have exactly the same faculties, nor can things have for any two exactly the same values.

The distinction lies, paradoxically enough, in the accomplished objectivity of æsthetic pleasures. "Every sensation we get from a thing is originally treated as one of its qualities. The qualities which we now conceive to belong to real objects are, for the most part, images of sight and touch. * * * But emotions are essentially capable of objectification, as well as impressions of sense; one may well believe that a primitive and inexperienced consciousness would rather people the world with ghosts of its own terrors and passions than with projections of those luminous and mathematical concepts which, as yet, it could hardly have formed."

In process of time, however, such concepts are formed, and the list of pleasures objectified is retrenched—mainly on the ground of their association with some particular organ of the body, like the palate. "The pleasures we call physical, and regard as low, * * * are those which call our attention to some part of our own body, and which make no object as conspicuous to us as the organ in which they arise." The residue, the pleasures that are unreclaimed, those whose 'organs' are transparent, are the æsthetic. "The scientific idea of a thing is a great abstraction from the mass of perceptions and reactions which that thing produces; the æsthetic idea is less abstract, since it retains the emotional reaction, the pleasure of the perception as an integral part of the conceived thing."

Beauty, therefore, is 'pleasure regarded as the quality of a thing.' The 'Materials of Beauty' are to be found in the various susceptibility of the human frame to pleasure, in especial, among others, to the pleasure that unites the sexes. "The capacity to love gives our contemplation that glow without which it might often fail to manifest beauty; and the whole sentimental side of our æsthetic sensibility, without which it would be perceptive and mathematical rather than æsthetic, is due to our sexual organization remotely stirred." For individuals that "need not unite for the birth and rearing of each generation, * * * it would not be necessary that any vision should fascinate, or any langour should soften, the prying cruelty of the eye. * * * Sex is not the only object of sexual passion. When love lacks its specific object, when it does not yet understand itself, or has been sacrificed to some other interest, we see the stifled fire bursting out in various directions. One is religious devotion, another is zealous philanthropy, * * * but not the least fortunate is the love of nature and of art; for nature is also often a second mistress that consoles us for the loss of the first." Beauty of 'form' is essentially bound up with the intrinsic agreeableness of certain kind of muscular tension, and beauty of 'expression' is a special case, simply, of psychological suggestion.

This is the main thread of the argument, but the pages abound in the discussion of minuter points and in that *exercise méthodique du discernement* which has been declared to be the essence of criticism.

ALFRED HODDER.

BRYN MAWR.

*Æsthetische Untersuchungen in Anschluss an die Lippssche
Theorie des Komischen.* I. and II. G. HEYMANS. Zeitschrift
für Psychologie u. Physiologie der Sinnesorgane. XI., 1 and
5–6, April and July, 1896.

Heymans finds in the Lipps theory of the comic[1] what he calls the
'final and definitive solution of the old problem,' but nevertheless
discovers certain inadequate features on which he comments in his first
paper. Lipps holds that the consciousness of the humorous is roused
when a high degree of psychic force is lavished upon a trivial or un-
essential content of consciousness, and with this statement Heymans
is in full agreement; but he denies the universality of the second form
in which Lipps states his theory, the assertion that the humorous object of consciousness is always a meaningless one following upon one
which is significant. Many cases of the comic, of course, fall within
this class, but the real contrast involved is between a content attended-
to—that is, in the Herbartian terminology of Lipps and Heymans, a
content requiring an expenditure of 'psychic force'—and another
which makes no such demands upon the attention. Therefore, the
earlier object need not be in itself significant, but may be attended to
merely because it is unexpected. Heymans illustrates by misprints,
which are never funny when the incorrect words are wholly meaningless,
but only when they appear to be *bona fide* words, so that the contrast is
between the surprised attention to a word, however unimportant, at
variance with the context and the sudden *intuition* of the word intended which needs no special emphasis.

Heymans also instances cases to show that Lipps is mistaken
in requiring that the contrast occur between contents which are
qualitatively alike. The paper is least effective in the explanation
of laughter following on sudden relief from deep-seated feelings
and impulses, for here Heymans yields to the temptation of making
laughter a certain indication of the feeling of the comic, whereas
it is surely often a mere physical reflex, and, at other times, an accompaniment of surprise untinged with the comic consciousness.

In his second paper Heymans develops a suggestion of Lipps
into the theory that the beautiful is the object of facile attention. The
object of the æsthetic consciousness thus calls forth the same psychic
energy as the preceding content of consciousness, and is distinguished
from the comic object, which demands less psychic force, and
from the terrifying object, which calls for more. Heymans attempts

---

[1] Psychologie der Komik. Theodor Lipps, Philosophische Monatshefte,
XXIV & XXV.

to prove his case by an analysis of traditional classifications of the beautiful, discovering that the 'formally beautiful,' by its unity in manifoldness, and the 'typically beautiful' by its conformity to the habitual, do really facilitate attention. Two other classes of the beautiful are considered; the 'imitative,' which, however, at once reduces to one of the other classes, or else turns out to be no form of the beautiful at all, and the 'associatively beautiful.' Heymans correctly defines the associated element of the æsthetic object as that which itself has a tendency to associate, and thus to emphasize, the perceived part of the object, but he seems not to realize that by this analysis he really opposes the association-theory of æsthetics, since he admits that a percept is beautiful, not because it is associative, but because it absorbs attention so completely that associated elements, if they occur, are unattended to. The comparison of the 'interesting' machine, with the 'beautiful' landscape, clearly shows that the presence of associated factors—images of utility and result—which draw the attention from the object itself, hinders æsthetic apprehension.

A closer examination than Heymans gives would prove that one main characteristic of the 'beautiful' objects is its isolation, its unrelatedness, its entire separation from any considerations of utility or any definite reference to past or future. But Heymans admits enough of this to endanger his entire theory, since he really shows that not every object of attention, but only the perceived or imaged object of direct attention, is beautiful; attention is indeed then an important characteristic, but not as he teaches, the essential feature of the æsthetic consciousness.

MARY WHITON CALKINS.

WELLESLEY COLLEGE.

La Timidité, Étude Psychologique. L. DUGAS. Revue Phil., December, 1896.

This article is chiefly an analysis. The term timidity is used broadly to designate the emotion caused by inhibition of action, confusion of thought, or feeling, which arises generally when others are present. It is distinguished from fear by the fact that it is always caused by persons, whereas fear is an emotion connected with things as well. Nor is timidity a physiological feeling purely, though some of its forms approach this type, thus, for example, the trembling occasioned by the mere presence of an audience or crowd. But even here the emotion depends upon the character of the crowd quite as much as upon its number, the circumstances, etc. The timidity which seems most purely physical depends largely upon the *ideas* which the crowd evokes in the mind of the individual; that is, the influence which the crowd, as a crowd, exercises is secondary to the feeling which arises from the *thought* of it.

Timidity is not to be regarded as a psychic state of special or determined kind, but is rather a form which affects different states of mind, a sort of malady, or temporary derangement of the *will*, the *intelligence* and the *feelings*. In connection with the will, it is due to the momentary inability to produce certain movements or failure to direct them properly. (gaucherie.) All the while the *timide* thus affected is intensely conscious of both the movement he desires to make, and of his inability to execute it. This consciousness constitutes the emotion. This momentary aboulia never attacks the automatic functions of the body. The *gaucherie* seems to be due to the effect produced directly by the *presence* and *regard* of others. The inhibition may not be entire, affecting only the direction of the movements. The inhibiting effect of the presence of others affects the mind, disturbing its functions. M. Dugas calls this form of it *stupidité*. It may be either complete or partial. The first is often taken for lack of intelligence ; thus the frequent confusion of pupils in the presence of their teachers. The second type is that of mental confusion, where all direction of thought is lost. There is a total failure of mental adaptation to the occasion or question in hand. On the affective side timidity takes the form of mental stupor. (stupeur.) As described by Rosseau and others, this inhibition may be so intense as to cause a complete suspension of the regular intellectual functions, where the subject becomes lost in a purely affective state of pure feeling, or, as in the other two cases, it may be only partial, resulting in a sort of chaos of feeling.

This timidity-feeling is intensely subjective. Not only is the *timide*, *gauche* and *stupide*, he is intensely conscious of it in addition. This is not true in the case of awkwardness and stupidity that arise from ignorance. What then is the relation of timidity to consciousness? Both are due, M. Dugas thinks, to mental incoördination. That is, if adaptation were perfect, we should be reduced to automata, and consciousness would be impossible. But consciousness is the *normal* accompaniment of such mental incoördination, while timidity-feeling is abnormal, being the presence of an *undue* consciousness of this non-adaptation. Timidity-feeling may be of two kinds. It often becomes reflective; more generally, it is spontaneous and involuntary. Thus the falsehoods told by a person in this state of excitement are not reprehensible, as those told deliberately, since the man speaks before he can reflect. The judgment function is more or less inhibited. All acts and thoughts under the influence of this social inhibition are impulsive, like those of the hypnotic subject.

In its last analysis timidity is found to be due to a lack of sympathetic correspondence between the individual and his social environment. " The subject is not responsive to social magnetism, unable to divest himself of his own peculiar ways of life and thought." In short he is unable to imitate others. He may be intensely conscious of the defect and may feel keenly the need of the sympathy which he fails to exercise and to receive. This lack of responsiveness to social suggestion shows itself in several ways. First, in the attitude of the *timide* toward the *crowd*, further in his treatment of those whom he judges his *superiors*, and lastly in his general unwillingness to *confide* in others. This spontaneous timidity-feeling, which M. Dugas calls *intimidation*, to distuinguish it from reflective timidity, is ʻdue to the distress arising from the realization of the lack of sympathy between ourselves and our environment.ʼ Reflection is apt to create a certain exaggeration of this feeling, so that the person affected ʻbegins to despise himself, to exaggerate his perplexities, and to pet his anger.ʼ He is apt to isolate himself intellectually. While his thinking may be original, it will lack social adaptiveness. On the affective side there is a tendency to conceal sentiments of his own, and to distrust the sympathy of others. Hence the reserve that is characteristic of timidity. He may be further affected by a certain *maladie d'idéal*, or tendency to despise the things of ordinary life in comparison with his fancies. On the volitional side his acts are apt to be impulsive, and are often incomprehensible to himself, mainly because he no longer has the power of deliberate judgment.

Finally, in its spontaneous form timidity marks a normal state in mental growth, that stands midway between the pure reflex life of the child and reflective mental life. Between the more abnormal form and genius a possible relation is suggested. The exclusiveness which the *timide* seeks, while it cannot of itself inspire art, may give occasion for its development.

J. M. TROUT.

PRINCETON UNIVERSITY.

The Popular Aesthetics of Color. JOSEPH JASTROW. Pop. Sci. Monthly, January, 1897. Pp. 361–368.

This is an application of statistical methods to the determination of color preferences. The material for the study—about 4,500 records—

was collected in connection at the Psychological Laboratory of the World's Fair. By means of a convenient system of cards those who were sufficiently interested to stop recorded age, sex, favorite color, and favorite combination of two colors. Twenty-four single colors were displayed from which to choose : red, orange, yellow, green, blue and violet, with six intermediate, and the twelve lighter shades of these. Twenty-four combinations were also shown, presenting as wide a range as possible. The most important as well as the most interesting results are these :

1. The general favorite of all colors is blue, more than one-fourth of the voters choosing this. Red holds the second place, though it is preferred by less than half as many. Then follow lighter blue, blue-violet, red-violet, lighter red (pink) and violet, while the least favorite colors are orange and its shadings toward red and yellow.

2. Darker colors are decidedly preferred to the lighter shades of the same colors, and primary colors (red, orange, etc.) to intermediate (red-orange, orange-yellow, etc.).

3. The difference between the average male and female chooser is striking. The women's favorite color is red, the men's is overwhelmingly blue : " of every thirty masculine votes ten were for blue and three for red ; while of every thirty feminine votes four were for blue and five for red." Men confine their choice to relatively fewer colors and have a much less marked tendency than women to choose the lighter and daintier shades.

4. Among the combinations of colors the two most frequently chosen are red with violet, and red with blue ; and the most generally avoided are orange with green, violet, or lighter blue. In these combinations the same colors, on the whole, are preferred and avoided as in the single color-preferences.

5. Preference according to age shows (*a*) that blue is least selected by the youngest group (below 18 years), decidedly preferred by the oldest (over forty years), and equally chosen by the groups between these ages ; (*b*) that violet is gradually avoided as age increases ; (*c*) that lighter red is the preference of the young girls ; (*d*) that relatively more persons between twenty-five and thirty than at any other age have ' no choice.'

J. O. Quantz.

Wisconsin University.

PATHOLOGICAL.

Das konträre Geschlechtsgefühl. HAVELOCK ELLIS and J. A. SYMONDS. (Bibliothek für Socialwissenschaft. 7 Band.) Leipzig, Wigand, 1896. xvi + 308.

It would not be right not to enter a protest against the appearance of such a work as this in a library intended primarily for popular reading. Even Krafft Ebing, although writing solely for the medical profession, has been severely and justly criticised for the unnecessary emphasis and importance he has given this subject by his articles on the perversions of the sexual sense, and nothing but harm can follow if popular scientific literature is to suffer a similar deluge. Medical literature of the last few years contains altogether too many histories of these unfortunate individuals who have only discovered themselves to be abnormally afflicted after reading a description of their condition in one of the many monographs or medical journal articles, and the alienist has come to look regularly for a series of sexual pervert autobiographies after the appearance of each new monograph.

If an intelligent understanding of his condition could ever lead to an amelioration of it we might endeavor to endure in silence, but his attention invariably returns to his case and the sexual pervert merely establishes a bond of sympathy between himself and his fellow sufferers; and the world is the worse off in that the sum of morbid introspection has been increased without any corresponding gain whatever. Apart from its influence on the perverts themselves no healthy person can read this literature without a lower opinion of human nature, and this result in itself should bid any writer pause. The writers of the present volume have done their work well, from their point of view, and have threshed over the literature most thoroughly from Bible times down, adding three hundred more pages to a literature already too flourishing.

WILLIAM NOYES.

BOSTON INSANE HOSPITAL, MATTAPAN, MASS.

Ueber Spaltung der Persönlichkeit. (Sogenanntes Doppel-ich.) VON SCHRENCK-NOTZING. Vienna, Holder. 1896. Pp. 22.

Human personality consists of a complex of elements blending into a unity in the form of self-consciousness; it is, therefore, in constant flux. Besides conscious memory, the seat of which is in the cortex, we must discriminate an organic or hereditary memory (innate reflexes etc.) and a memory for acquired reflexes (walking, etc.) which is probably seated in the basal ganglia. We may also discriminate various grades in consciousness from the clear and focal to the dim and marginal, but, to be conscious at all, a mental state must belong to that one complex, for the word ' conscious' has no other meaning. Félidia X and the other classical cases of successive personality are to be regarded as springing from the addition to, or subtraction from, the sum total of psychic processes which constitute a personality of sundry elements, especially the acquired reflexes. Hence the disorder is manifested in a bewildering variety of forms, the only constant trait being the partial or total destruction of the memory bond between the successive complexes. Pierre Janet's ' geistreiche Auffassung' of hysteria is, in the main, in accord with this view, and it is in no way inconsistent with such a conception of the unity of consciousness as has before been outlined. That *simultaneous* personalities can exist is, however, strenuously to be denied. The cases so interpreted differ from those above described only in this: that two independent thought trains, instead of succeeding one another at long intervals, shift from focus to margin in such rapid succession that the observer is unable to detect any lapse in the movements controlled by each, and, as the memory bond is broken, the patient claims that he is aware of one only, ignoring the other; hence the observer infers a sub-conscious personality to account for the movements which the patient denies producing. Dr. von Schrenck-Notzing adduces no specific evidence in support of this view, but rests his case solely upon the supposed impossibility of admitting that two foci can exist in one and the same organism, or that incoherent, dream-like states may exist out of all relation with any focus.

Telepathy and the Subliminal Self. R. Osgood Mason. New York, Henry Holt & Company. Pp. 336.

This book is designed to serve as an introduction to ' Psychical Research' for the use of the general reader. The author writes, on the whole, in a sober vein, the greater number of his cases being very carefully chosen from the publications of the Society of Psychical Research, and his professional position as a physician in good standing will doubtless give his words a weight which they would not otherwise possess. It seems, therefore, of the more importance to call attention to a certain laxity in his sense of the value of evidence, of which illustrations occur more than once and which seriously impairs the value of his book. The earlier series of experiments with the Creery sisters surely cannot be quoted in proof of telepathy, in view of the fact that the children confessed to the use of signals in the later series. The visions of Elisha, the responses of the Delphic oracle, the marvels told of Pythagoras, the wonders and portents narrated in the pages of ancient historians can have no weight in any cautious mind. More extraordinary still is the statement that Apollonius' vision of the assassination of Domitian rests 'upon the best of ancient authority,' for that same excellent authority, that is, Philostratus' historical romance, narrates, among many other even more extraordinary marvels, how Apollonius detected the plague prowling about Ephesus in the guise of a beggar and caused him to be stoned, whereupon the beggar, dying, changed into a huge black dog of the size of a lion and the plague was stayed. (*Philostr. Vit. Apoll. IV, 10.*) In quoting such cases as evidence, Dr. Mason's zeal seems to have run away with his discretion. This is the more to be regretted because he gives several original observations of phenomena, with reference to which sound evidence is much needed and which would be of great value were their accuracy unquestionable. Especially to be noted is the case on page 71 of the 'magnetization' of water; the one on page 125 of successive personalities and the planchette case on page 159.

By way of explanation the author merely propounds the doctrine of a subliminal self, to which he ascribes all phenomena otherwise inexplicable. Spiritistic conceptions are carefully excluded and the few cases given which would suggest such an interpretation are referred to the agency of the subliminal self telepathically exerted.

WILLIAM ROMAINE NEWBOLD.
UNIVERSITY OF PENNSYLVANIA.

NEW BOOKS.

Telepathy and the Subliminal Self. R. OSGOOD MASON. New York, Holt. 1897. Pp. viii + 343. $1.50.

Hypnotism. ALBERT MOLL. Fourth ed. revised and enlarged. London, Walter Scott. 1897. Pp. xiv+448. 3s.6.

The Theory of Socialization. A Syllabus. F. H. GIDDINGS. Brochure. New York, The Macmillan Co. 1897. Pp. xii+ 48. $0.60.

Notes on Children's Drawings. Edited by ELMER E. BROWN. University of California Studies, Vol. 2. No. 1. Berkeley, California. 1897. Pp. 75.

Sight. J. LE CONTE.   Internat. Sci. Ser. 2d ed.   New York, Ap-
pletons. 1897. Pp. xvi + 318. $1.50.

The Logical Copula and Quantification of the Predicate. ED.
ADAMSON. London, Nutt. 1897. Pp. 19. 1s.

De la Spiritualité de l'Ame. G. DE CRAENE. Vol. I. Louvain,
Institut Sup. de Philosophie. 1897. Pp. 351. Fr. 3.50.

Philosophy of Knowledge. G. T. LADD. New York, Scribners.
1897. Pp. xv + 614. $4.

Schopenhauer's System in its Philosophical Significance. W. CALD-
WELL. New York, Scribners. 1896. Pp. xvii + 538. $3.

Aristotle and the Earlier Peripatetics. E. ZELLER. Trans. by B.
F. C. COSTELLOE and J. H. MUIRHEAD. London and New
York, Longmans. 1897. Two vols. Pp. xi + 520 and xiii +
512. $7.

Essays. G. J. ROMANES. Edited by C. LLOYD MORGAN. London
and New York, Longmans. 1897. Pp. 253.

The Theory of Contract in its Social Light. W. A. WATT.
Edinburgh, Clark; New York, Scribners. 1897. Pp. xii + 96.
$1.25.

Introduction to Sociology. A. FAIRBANKS. New York, Scribners.
1896. Pp. xv + 274. $2.

Mind and Matter and Monism. G. J. ROMANES. Edited by C.
LLOYD MORGAN. New Ed. London and New York, Longman's.
1896. Pp. vii + 170.

Contemporary Theology and Theism. R. M. WENLEY. New
York, Scribners. 1897. Pp x + 202. $1.25.

The Ethics of J. S. Mill. Edited with Introductory Essays
by CHARLES DOUGLAS. Edinburgh and London, Blackwood.
1897. Pp. cxxvi+233.

Principes de Metaphysique et de Psychologie. PAUL JANET.
Paris, Delagrave. 1897. Two vols. Pp. viii + 650 and 620.

Christianity and Idealism. JOHN WATSON. New York, Scribners. 1897. Pp. 211.

Sulla cosidette Allucinazioni antagonistiche. S. DE SANCTIS and
M. MONTESSORI. Roma, Società Editrice Dante Alighieri.
1897. Pp. 17.

I fenomeni telepatici e le allucinazioni veridiche. E. MORSELLI.
Florence, Salvadore Landi. 1897. Pp. 58.

Sull'importanza delle recerche relativa alla storia delle scienze.
G. VAILATI. Turin, Roux. 1897. Pp. 22.

Der Stundenplan. H. Schiller. Sammlung v. Abh. d. pæd. Psych. u. Phys., heft I. Berlin, Reuther u. Reichard. 1897. Pp. 65. M. 1.50.

Was ist Philosophie. Inaug. Rede in der Univ. Prag. A. Marty. Prague, Calve. 1897. Pp. 35.

Allgemeine Pathologie des Gehirns. Th. Ziehen. Sep. Abd. from Lubarschs Ergeb. d. All. Path. Wiesbaden, Bergmann. 1897. Pp. 591–630.

Empfindung. Th. Ziehen. Sep. Abd. from Eulenburg's Real-Encyc. der gesammte Heilkunde, 2te ausgabe. Vienna, Urban u. Schwarzenberg.

Zur Frage der Kausalität. Ed. Pfleiderer. On occasion of Weizsäckers Jubiläum. Tübingen, Armbruster. 1897. Pp. 77.

University of Iowa Studies in Psychology. G. T. W. Patrick and J. A. Gilbert, editors. Vol. I. 1897. University, Iowa City, Iowa.

The Psychology of the Moral Self. B. Bosanquet. London and New York, Macmillans. 1897. Pp. viii + 132. $1.25.

La studio dell' attenzione conativa. S. de Sanctis. Rep. from atti della società Romana di Antropologia, IV., fasc. 2. Pp. 19.

The Lumleian Lectures on Some Problems in Connection with Aphasia and Other Speech Defects. H. C. Bastian. Reprinted from the *Lancet* (London), April and May, 1897. Pp. 115.

L'Année Psychologique. A. Binet. Third year, 1896. Paris, Schleicher Frères. 1897. Pp. 825. Fr. 15.

Geschichte der neueren deutschen Psychologie. Max Dessoir. 2te völlig umgearbeitete Auflage. Erste Halbband. Berlin, Duncker. 1897. Pp. 356.

NOTES.

American philosophy has been honored by the appointment of Professor Josiah Royce, of Harvard, Gifford Lecturer in the University of Aberdeen for two years beginning 1898–1899.

Dr. W. B. Pillsbury, of Cornell University, has accepted the Instructorship in Psychology and the direction of the psychological laboratory in the University of Michigan.

THE time during which abstracts of papers for the physiological section of the British Association may be sent in has been extended to July 1st. (Dr. A. Kirschmann, Sec., Univ. College, Toronto, Can.)

IN *The Open Court* for May will be found an article on ' The Prophet of Pessimism ' by the editor, Dr. Carus, together with a reproduction of the original model of the famous bust of Schopenhauer by Elizabet Ney. This model has been acquired by the Open Court Co., and they offer for sale at the very low price of $15 a 'limited number' of life-size plaster casts made from it. The undersigned has secured one of these, and finds it admirable in every respect. Philosophers should have it, whatever their attitude toward Schopenhauer; optimists from charity no less than pessimists from loyalty.   J. M. B.

A MOVEMENT is on foot to establish a laboratory for experimental psychology with instruction in the subject, in University College, London. A committee, including Francis Galton, E. A. Schäfer and others, are soliciting funds. Professor James Sully is secretary of the committee.

A LECTURSHIP in Physiological and Experimental Psychology has been recommended by the Board of Studies of Cambridge University.

PROFESSOR H. K. WOLFE has resigned the chair of Psychology in the University of Nebraska.

MR. F. C. S. SCHILLER, now at Cornell, has been elected Fellow and Tutor in Philosophy in Corpus Christi College, Oxford.

MR. S. I. FRANZ has been appointed Assistant in Psychology in Columbia University.

W. M. URBAN, PH.D. (Leipzig), has been appointed Reader in Philosophy in the Graduate Department of Princeton University; he will give courses in Æsthetics.

PROF. A. C. ARMSTRONG, of Wesleyan University, has been appointed to a chair in History in Princeton University.

DR. W. C. HODGE, of Princeton, has been appointed Associate Professor of Philosophy in Lafayette College.

DR. C. E. SEASHORE, of the Yale Psychological Laboratory, has been made Assistant Professor in the University of Iowa.   ·

E. M. WEYER, of the University of Leipzig, and M. Matsumoto, of the University of Tokio, Japan, have been appointed assistants in the Yale Psychological Laboratory.

THE prospectus has been issued of a new *Revista Italiana di Sociologia*, edited by a board on which Professor G. Sergi will represent psychology. The address is: Rome, 42 Piazza Poli.

VOL. IV. No. 5.   SEPTEMBER, 1897.

THE PSYCHOLOGICAL REVIEW.

STUDIES FROM THE HARVARD PSYCHOLOGICAL LABORATORY (VIII).

COMMUNICATED BY PROFESSOR E. B. DELABARRE.

INVOLUNTARY MOTOR REACTION TO PLEASANT AND UNPLEASANT STIMULI.

BY GEORGE V. DEARBORN AND FRANK N. SPINDLER.

Study of the emotions, in one way or another, has had a conspicuous place in the work carried on in the Harvard Psychological Laboratory. In this field of all others, perhaps, the investigator gains easiest access to the goal of physiological psychology—the determination, namely, of the quantitative and qualitative relations obtaining between those wonderful correlates, mind and body.

That elementary organism, the amœba, when jarred by its environment or more directly stimulated, contracts and tends to take the spherical form. On the other hand, all its movements of self-gratification are processes of expansion or extension. This observable double tendency seems to be the type, almost symbolically expressed, of a deep biologic law which science has shown to exist with almost infinite adaptation to circumstances and habit, in every organism. Experiment proves that, like other impulses of the lower animals, it exists persistently in man.

Professor Münsterberg has advanced the hypothesis that stimuli which cause action of the extensor muscles are as a rule agreeable, while stimuli which cause action of the flexor muscles are as a rule disagreeable. This tendency we should naturally expect to find more fully and simply expressed in the case of the lower animals than in that of the higher. In early organisms such a correlation is necessary to ensure the survival of the organism and the possibility of evolution. For in the lower forms of life there should be such a strict correlation between the agreeable and the advantageous on the one hand, and between the disagreeable and the disadvantageous on the other, that the advantageous would be the agreeable and would be accompanied by expansion and movement towards the stimulating object, while any disadvantageous and consequently disagreeable stimulus would cause contraction and withdrawal from the stimulating object.

This correlation, however, would be more true in animals and savages than in civilized man. In our civilized state we have lost our primitive simplicity. We are still mal-adjusted to many civilized conditions, owing to our change of environment from the savage to the cultured state. By immediate inheritance and habit we have learned to control our motor reactions, to suppress the outward signs of our feelings. We often, perhaps mistakenly, think that even to ourselves as physical organisms, the disagreeable is advantageous and the agreeable is disadvantageous. We often enjoy pain and dislike pleasure. We have a thousand contradictory tendencies that run counter to any such simple rules of motor reactions as that above stated.

Yet in spite of these complications it is plausible that there exists the correlation claimed by Professor Münsterberg, showing itself strongly in the midst of conflicting tendencies. It was to test the validity of this hypothesis that the following research was conducted during the college year 1895–96.

It might be expected that a less educated class of subjects than those we have had would give more marked results, as far as reactions are concerned. Young children or savages would surely show motor reactions more strongly marked to disagreeable or agreeable stimulations. But even in our results, we have found a plain tendency in favor of the theory mentioned.

It must be mentioned that with many subjects we could get no perceptible reactions to the sensory stimuli. Some subjects seemed constitutionally averse to any motor reaction. The

stimulus would generally be pronounced either pleasant or unpleasant, and yet the subject would show no motor reaction
whatever. This lack of reaction was very marked in some
cases. In a few instances the subject pronounced the stimulus
indifferent, yet often reacted to it one way or the other.

Some subjects were very sensitive and seemed to go all to
pieces on any disagreeable stimulus, and would show most surprising and seemingly contradictory reactions. These points
we will try to bring out fully in our statement of the results.

Method of Experiment.

The emotional stimuli mostly employed were odors, but
sounds and variously colored lights were also used, to a much
less extent. It was greatly desired that the stimulus in each
case should give an effect as purely painful or pleasurable as
possible. Many subjects were employed and the stimuli were
given often several times to each, on which accounts odors
seemed the most fitting of possible agents. These furnish about
the only means, indeed, of causing a constant pleasurable
stimulation in the practice of the laboratory. Odors have the
further advantages of being unlimited in number and in action
independent of the subject's power of imagination. It was
much more difficult to find for each subject a positively disagreeable odor than a positively pleasant one, students of chemistry
being especially hard to suit with a sufficiently unpleasant smell.
Constant care was needed and employed to suit the tastes of
the various subjects in this regard, the objects being to employ
types of pleasure and of pain.

The particular olfactory stimuli employed were kept in ounce
vials on a stand made for them. It is hardly possible to make
any classification of them as pleasant or unpleasant. Roughly,
however, they may be arranged in the following order of agreeableness to the greater number of the subjects employed,
the most pleasant first, but the middle ones varying greatly in
this regard. Naturally the most emphatic members of the series
were those most used. Oil of bergamot, cologne water, helio-
trope, methyl acetate, oil of cloves, tincture of musk, ethyl
iodide, spirits of turpentine, xylol, eugenol, oil of eucalyptus,

iodoform, cider vinegar, bisulphide of carbon, ethyl bomeol and camphor, sulphuric ether, toluidin, allyl alcohol, tincture of as-afœtida, diamylamine, acetic acid, ammonium valerianate. A few subjects avowed no pain from any of these, and for these ammonia was employed in place of a real odor. It will be noticed that ' disgusts' are not included in our list, associations not being desired in these experiments, but only pure affective tones.

Panes of glass a foot square, colored red, blue, green and orange were used for subjects with color taste highly developed, the panes being held before their eyes. Similarly, for musical subjects, such sweet tones as tuning forks can give were applied as stimuli, with harsh noises for a contrary effect.

The hands and the head were chosen as the bodily parts most suitable for reaction, these being the most sensitive to motor stimuli and the most convenient. According to the theory in question, the hands should relax and the head drop back under agreeable stimulus, while under disagreeable stimulus the head should drop forward and the hands contract.

The mechanical plan employed for the direct registration of the flexion and extension of the head and hands was as follows : The subject was seated in a comfortable arm chair. A tightly-fitting pasteboard cap was placed on the head, from the center of which a strong thread extended over an easy-running pulley to the extremity of the lever of a Marey tambour. Because the antero-posterior movements of the head were sometimes considerable this lever arm was about twenty-five centimetres in length. By a careful centering of the pulley in the circle of head movements, record of the occasional lateral motions of the head was avoided, account of these not being desired. Pneumatic pressure transferred in the usual way the rise and fall of the receiving tambour's arm to the pen of another Marey tambour, writing on smoked paper on a revolving drum.

The apparatus adjusted to the left hand consisted of a bulb small enough to be fairly grasped in the closed fist. It was at first difficult to find a bulb without so much resistance to compression that the subject's constant attention was necessary to keep it in the state of partial compression needed to secure record of the extensor movements of the fingers. But at last a bulb made of a soft sponge from which the center had been cut, enclosed in thin rubber dam, was hit upon, and this served as a most sensitive and, indeed, adaptable instrument; for sponges may be found or cut of any desired degree of resiliance. The varying pressure of the hand was pneumatically carried to a receiving tambour and recorded on the smoked cylinder at the left of the tracing from the head.

To register the movements of the right hand in states of organic pleasure and displeasure a different form of instrument was employed. About the second and third fingers, as the most sensitive and most powerful, a comfortable ring of brass foil was fastened. This was attached directly to the lever of a tambour and as close to the fulcrum as possible, that all motion might be emphasized; and it was adjusted so that when the fingers were partially flexed the tambour rubber was plane. Comfort of the hand in this case was found important in order to avoid voluntary attention to it and its reactions. The flexor and extensor movements of the two fingers were as before transmitted to a pen tracing on the right of the record of the head.

To secure constant pressure at the start in the three sets of apparatus, the open ends of branches from the three conducting tubes were arranged side by side convenient to the operator, and fitted with clips so as to be simultaneously closed when all was ready and the kymograph in regular motion. The speed of the recording drum was such that one revolution was made in about five minutes. The cylinder was 14 cm. in diameter and 25 cm. long, suitable for two records such as these without change of paper. Straight normals for the better measurement of the curves were regularly run round the drum by stationary pens.

Record of the various conditions of each experiment was written with a stylus on each sheet, including name of subject, temperament, subjective experiences, stimulus, nature of effect whether pleasant or the contrary, date and direction of muscular movement indicated in each reaction. The subjects were mostly Seniors and Juniors of Harvard college and of Radcliffe college and graduate students working in the laboratory.

Their number was nineteen. Inquiries as to emotional likes and dislikes were regularly made and as to musical and 'artistic' education.

RESULTS.

1. Under Pleasant Stimulation.

Taking each movement or lack of movement, whether of head or of either hand, as a separate case, we have recorded 500 effects of sensory stimuli which were considered pleasant by the subjects. Of these, 118, or 23%, were cases of flexion of hands or forward movement of the head, 134, or 27%, were cases of no reaction whatever, and 248, or 49.6%, were cases of extension of hands or backward head movement. Considering the cases of actual reaction alone, there occurred 67% of movements of extension and 32% of flexion—a proportion of more than two to one. The tendency under pleasant stimulation is therefore strongly toward extension.

The two hands and the head did not necessarily act together in the same way. The left hand seems much more sensitive and more given to expressive motor reaction than the right, and as our subjects were mostly right handed, it would seem justifiable to infer from this that the right hand is more civilized and more under control and less naïvely expressive than the left. If the idea stated in the beginning is tenable, that civilized man is more likely to inhibit emotional expression than a savage, then we might expect the right hand to be the more inhibited and the less likely to react.

Counting the cases of pleasant stimuli where the left hand showed no reaction, we have for the left hand under stimuli pronounced agreeable results as follows : Flexion 21%, extension 60%, no reaction 19%. Out of 184 stimulations the left hand shows flexion 37 times, extension 112 times, no reaction 35 times. If we compare the left hand with the right, the percentage of 'no reactions' is seen to be much less for the left hand, while that of both flexions and extensions is greater. Under pleasant stimuli the right hand showed, flexion 20%, extension 40%, 'no reaction' 40%. That is, in a total of 130 cases, the right hand flexed 27 times, extended 52 times, showed 'no reaction' 51 times. The left hand then was indifferent 19% when the right hand was indifferent 40% ; it extended 60% where the right hand extended only 40% ; and it flexed 21% where the right hand flexed 20%. Leaving out the cases of 'no reaction,' the right hand flexed 34% and extended 65% while the left hand flexed 25% and extended 75%.

As for the head under pleasant stimuli, it was found that it flexed, or came forward, 29%, showed no reaction 26%, extended or drew back 45%. That is, in a total of 186 pleasant stimuli, the head came forward 54 times, drew back 84 times, showed no movement 48 times. Comparing the flexions with the extensions alone, the head under pleasant stimuli was flexed 39% of the times, and extended 61%. The head was more indifferent than the total averaged results, but more expressive than the right hand.

It will be noticed, however, that the head shows more of a tendency to flexion under pleasant stimuli than either hand, viz., 29% flexion to 20% for right hand and 21% for left hand. This was one of the surprises of the experiments. In many cases under pleasant stimulus the head would move forward even where both hands relaxed. At first it was thought this was true only of smells, as the odors were necessarily presented suddenly and in front of the face, but the same thing was true of colors and sounds; the head often flexed when these stimuli were, agreeable. This must have been an adaptive movement; for often, after this forward movement, the head would drop back during the continuance of the pleasant stimulus.

2. Under Unpleasant Stimulation.

If we now examine the head movements in response to unpleasant stimuli, similar differences of reaction will be seen. Here it flexed 42%, showed no reaction 19%, extended 38% ; or in a total of 168 stimulations it moved forward 72 times, showed no movement 32 times, dropped back 64 times. Taking flexion and extension alone, we find flexion 53% compared to extension 47%. Even more marked here is the tendency for the head to extend or draw back under an unpleasant stimulus than it was for it to come forward under a pleasant stimulus;

while both hands often, and indeed generally, flexed. Yet for the head also flexion predominates, thus supporting the theory by a slight percentage. Comparing the hands as to their reaction to unpleasant stimuli, we find the right hand here also, markedly more inhibited or indifferent. The left hand shows flexion 66⅔%, no reaction 14.5%, extension 18%; or in 165 cases it flexed 110 times, showed no reaction 24 times, extended 31 times. Leaving out the cases of 'no reaction,' it showed 78% flexion, and 22% extension.

The right hand, however, flexed only 49.5% of the times, while it showed 'no reaction' 29%, and extended 21%. Comparing flexion and extension cases alone the right hand flexed 69% and extended 30%. The right hand, therefore, shows more of a tendency to indifference and extension under disagreeable stimuli than does the left hand. We find then, in the hands a marked preponderance of flexions under disagreeable stimuli, 78% of the movements in the left hand and 69% of the movements in the right hand being flexions.

Combining the cases of the reactions of head and hands under unpleasant stimuli we get 53% flexion, 20% 'no reaction,' 26% extension; or, in 450 cases we have flexion 240 times, 'no reaction' 90 times, extension 120 times. Leaving out cases of no reaction we have 66⅔% flexions to 33⅓% of extension—a proportion of 2 flexions to 1 extension.

3. Under Indifferent Stimulation.

In the cases where the stimuli were pronounced indifferent, that is, neither agreeable nor disagreeable, we find some interesting results. Even here the left hand reacted more than the right. The left hand under indifferent stimuli shows flexion 34%, no reaction 31%, extension 34%; or in 32 cases flexion 11 times, no reaction 10, extension 11 times. It is interesting that flexion and extension are here exactly equal.

The right hand under indifferent stimuli was more immobile. It shows flexion 30%, no reaction 50%, extension 20%; or in the 20 cases of indifferent stimulation the right hand flexed 6 times, showed no reaction 10 times, extended 4 times. Leaving out the cases of no reaction it flexed 60%, extended 40%.

The left hand showed only 31% of 'no reaction' under indifferent stimuli while the right hand showed 50%. The head under indifferent stimuli showed 30% flexion, no reaction 30%, extension, 40%; or flexion 43% to extension 57%, if we disregard cases of 'no reaction.'

The total results of the hands and the head for indifferent stimuli are 31.7% flexion, no reaction 35%, extension 32.9%; or disregarding the 'no reaction' cases, flexion 49% to extension 51%. Extension and flexion here are almost equal with a slight percentage in favor of extension, probably due to adaptive efforts. This is what we should expect under indifferent stimuli. We find also here more cases where there was no reaction than occurred when the stimulus was pronounced pleasant or unpleasant, viz., 35% here to 26% under pleasant and to 20% under unpleasant stimulation.

4. *Summary aud Additional Observations.*

The foregoing results may be summed up in the following table. It includes only the actual reactions to stimuli, 764 in number. The cases where stimuli were applied without resulting reaction numbered 253.

	UNDER UNPLEASANT STIMULI.	UNDER PLEASANT STIMULI.	UNDER INDIFFERENT STIMULI.
Flexion	66.6	32.2	49
Extension	33.3	67.8	51
Proportion	2 to 1	1 to 2 +	Nearly equal.

These experiments afford, therefore, a striking confirmation of Professor Münsterberg's theory, that there is a strong tendency to expansion under agreeable, to contraction under disagreeable, stimuli. Other tendencies are present, however, some of which conflict with this one: such for example as the tendency to move toward an object which attracts attention; the tendency to move away from a disagreeable object; the tendency to make particular movements of adaptation to stimuli; etc. A further influence of great interest is revealed upon examination of the records of the separate individuals who, as subjects, took part in these experiments. If their reactions to stimuli which they pronounced indifferent be examined, it will be seen that some show a temperamental tendency to make movements of flexion more often than of extension; others, the opposite; and others still to make both in nearly equal proportion. These temperamental tendencies show themselves clearly in their influence on reactions to agreeable and disagreeable stimuli. The 'flexion' temperament shows, through the greater predominance of flexions, a greater difference in the proportion of the two movements under pleasant stimuli and a nearer approach to equality under unpleasant stimuli. The 'extension' temperament shows the opposite results, and the indifferent temperament exhibits proportions more nearly those given in the above table.

Temperamental differences then work together with the other special tendencies mentioned above in modifying the tendency to contract under disagreeable and to expand under agreeable stimuli. While, therefore, this latter is clearly established by this research as a real and strong tendency, it is at the same time shown to be only one tendency acting among many.

VISION WITHOUT INVERSION OF THE RETINAL IMAGE.[1]

BY PROFESSOR G. M. STRATTON.

University of California.

Seventh Day.—In the morning the flow of ideas while I was blindfolded was like that described for the evening before. But I noticed in bathing that the old representation of those parts of my body which I had so frequently seen (at least in their clothing) during the experiment, was decidedly less vivid, the outline more blurred, the color paler, grayer, more 'washed out,' than of the parts which had never come within the limits of the visual field.

Later, with my lenses on, it seemed at first as if the experience was in all respects the same as on the previous day. But when I began to pace rapidly up and down the room, I felt that I was more at home in the scene than ever before. There was perfect reality in my visual surroundings, and I gave myself up to them without reserve and without being conscious of a single note of discord with what I saw. This feeling of complete harmony throughout, lasted as long as I kept my legs either within or near the borders of my field of view. Otherwise the older, inappropriate representation of my body arose at times, but faded, while the new representation revived, as soon as some passing object was seen to enter the region into which the older image of my body extended. The absence of any tactual experiences such as a real body in that position would imply, cast, for the moment, an illusory character over the older form of representation.

To what extent objects in view suggested the idea of other things in harmonious relation with the seen things is best shown by the following cases: As I walked into my bedroom and saw the bedstead, I involuntarily thought of the windows, repre-

[1] Concluded.

463

senting them in the appropriate direction fixed by the position of the bed. The general outlines of the room, and the more important points of reference, arose in harmony with the new sight-perceptions. But the detailed filling of this outline was far less complete than is usual in my case in normal sight. A large number of important things in the room simply did not arise in my mind until their relation to the field of seen things had been brought home afresh by perception. During the first days of the experiment ideas of objects frequently arose in opposition to the new sight-perception; now they either did not arise at all, or came in the newer form. The idea of the sofa or chair on which I *passively* sat did still come up in discord with the general experience, together with the dim feeling of my shoulders and of the upper parts of my back. But these were now a comparatively isolated group, and not a vigorous *Apperceptions-masse* to call up a host of surrounding things in orderly relation to itself.

In regard to movements, the most striking fact was that the *extent* of the movement now was inappropriate, movements in the wrong *direction* being comparatively rare in the case of the hands, and even still rarer in the case of the feet. My hands frequently moved too far or not far enough, especially when coming from beyond the visual field to something in sight. In trying to take a friend's hand, extended into the (new) lower portion of my visual field, I put my hand too high. In brushing a speck from my paper in the (new) upper portion of the field I did not move my hand far enough. And in striking with my index finger the outstretched fingers of my other hand the movement was much less accurate when I looked at my hands than when I closed my eyes and depended on motor guidance. The actual distance that my hand moved, in such cases, would, under the normal conditions of sight, doubtless have been appropriate to bring my hand to the desired spot. But an object in what had before been the upper part of the field was now at a shorter distance from my hands than formerly; the movement, under the influence of the habitual interpretation of the visual position, would therefore go too far. And, *vice versa*, a movement to an object in what had formerly been the lower part of the visual field would now fall short of its destination. For the visual position would now require a more extended movement of the arm than formerly, in order to reach it.

When I watched one of my limbs in motion, no involuntary suggestion arose that it was in any other place or moved in any other direction than as sight actually reported it, except that in moving my arm a slightly discordant group of sensations came from my unseen shoulder. If, while looking at the member, I summoned an image of it in its old position, then I could feel the limb there too. But this latter was a relatively weak affair, and cost effort. When I looked away from it, however, I involuntarily felt it in its pre-experimental position, although at the same time conscious of a solicitation to feel it in its new positiou. This representation of the moving part in terms of the new vision waxed and waned in strength, so that it was sometimes more vivid than the old, and sometimes even completely overshadowed it.

The conflict between the old and the new localization of the parts of my body was shown in several instances. The mistaken visual localization of a contact in the palm of one of my hands, and the sudden reversal of even the touch-localization when I detected by sight the true source of the sensations, occurred as on the preceding day. Somewhat similarly, when I moved a heated iron with my right hand to that border of the visual field just beyond which, according to pre-experimental localization, my left hand would have been lying, I involuntarily felt an anticipatory shrinking in my unseen left hand, as if it were on the point of being burnt; although the iron in my right hand was actually several feet from my left, and was moving away from it. When I put my left hand in sight, or looked at it afresh to make sure where it was, the hot iron caused no premonitory feeling whatever on approaching the visual locality which had before been so suggestive of danger.

Seated by the open fire, I happened to rest my head on my hands in such a way that the fire shone directly on the top of my head. I closed my eyes, and the image of the fire remained true to the recent perception. But soon I noticed that I was

representing the fire in pre-experimental terms, and I finally discovered that the change was caused by the growing sensations
of warmth on the top of my head.   My hair and scalp were
persistently felt in their older position, no doubt because I never
directly saw them in any other.   And the old localization of the
fire was the only one consistent with this old localization of the
hair and scalp.   But by passing my hands rapidly back and
forth before my open eyes, ending the movement each time with
a touch upon the top of my head, it was not difficult to produce
a vivid localization of my scalp in harmony with the new sight-
perceptions.   And with this change the old localization of the
fire was suppressed.   During the walk in the evening, I enjoyed the beauty of the evening scene, for the first time since
the experiment began.   Evidently the strangeness and incon-
venience of the new relations no longer kept me at such a tension as hitherto.

On removing the glasses, my visual images relapsed into
their older form, with a constant interplay and accompaniment,
however, of the new.

Eighth day.—Before putting the glasses on, representations
of the older sort held sway.

During the morning, after the glasses were in place, I
noticed that as far as the unseen portions of my body were
concerned, the relation of right and left was, for the most
part, a reproduction of the older visual right and left; that is to
say, a contact on the right side of the body at some point beyond
the reach of sight was felt and visually represented on the (old)
visual right side.   Occasionally the opposite visual side was
suggested, but the sensations were rarely indeed felt there.   The
case was quite different as regards the seen parts of my body,
although even here uncertainly and sudden alteration of reference occurred.   The illusion of contact on the opposite hand to
the one actually touched, arose as on the two preceding days.
I often hesitated which hand was the appropriate one for grasping some object in view, began the movement with the wrong
hand and then corrected the mistake.   If I was attentive
to the new visual representation of some part of my body
which was about to be touched, and expected the contact

there, the contact was felt in the new position and no change of reference occurred. Immediately afterwards there usually arose a sort of tactual after-image on the other visual side. When the original contact was unexpected, the visual image and the tactual localization might simultaneously be both old and new, or might be old alone, with perhaps a merely visual image in the new direction, although without any real reference of the touch-sensations to this image.

Localization of sounds varied, being different when the source of sound was in sight from what it was when this was out of sight, and also in the latter case differing with different directions of attention, or with different suggestions as to the direction from which the sound came. The fire, for instance, sputtered where I saw it. The tapping of my pencil on the arm of my chair seemed without question to issue from the visible pencil. Even when I tapped on the wall to one side, out of sight, if in making the stroke I invariably passed my hand and pencil before my eyes and in the direction of the unseen part of the wall, and attempted to picture the contact in harmony with this movement, I actually heard the sound come from the new visual direction, although not with full and unequivocal localization. There was a strong temptation to localize the sound on the other side also. And this rival localization rose into full life the instant I ceased to keep before me the image of the pencil striking on the new visual side.

The influence of the suggestion coming from recent and repeated movements before the eyes was likewise apparent in localizing parts of my body which could not be brought into the visual field. Thus the involuntary inattentive localization of my forehead and hair was the old localization lasting from pre-experimental sight. But a series of visible movements of my hand to my hair, together with fixed attention on the goal of these movements, made the sensations of touch temporarily come, without difficulty, from this new direction. Sensations of contact on the lips, however, were not so readily dislodged from their old position. In eating at table, the movements of my hands and of pieces of food across the visual field, constantly suggested that my mouth must lie between the line of

sight and the new position of my legs.   But the actual contact
on my lips instantly dispelled this suggestion and located my
mouth definitely and indubitably on the other side of the line of
sight.   The place of the actual contact and that of the merely
suggested contact were thus in striking contrast.   But when I
did my best to visualize my lips in the direction of the suggested contact and strained my attention in this direction, the
actual contact did not dissipate this image or carry it to the old
position of my mouth, but the touch-sensations seemed to come
from the new direction.   Without such a willful visualization
and strain of attention the actual contact always reversed the
involuntary suggestion coming from the visible movements
toward the new position of my mouth.   Even when my forehead and hair temporarily seemed to lie on the (new) upper
side of the line of sight, this did not prevent my mouth from
being felt on the *same* side.   But the new localization of forehead and scalp undoubtedly had a tendency to drive the mouth
out of its old localization; for I found that less effort of attention and visualization was required to make the tactual sensations of the lips come from the new position, when the top of
the head had already been carried over to its new position,
No doubt there was a disturbing incongruity in having both my
mouth and the top of my head on the same side of the line of
sight; consequently the re-localization of one tended to carry the
other to the opposite side of the visual line.

In other cases the re-localization of bodily parts that were beyond the reach of sight was brought about by the suggestive influence of such movements as I have just described, without any
voluntary attention or visualization of the parts whatever.   As
I rocked in my chair, I found that by throwing my arms up
through the field of sight into the visual region in which my
shoulders, according to the old experience, were wont to be
localized, the repeated feeling of the unimpeded motion of my
hands through this region destroyed the old representation of
my shoulders and back, and gave them a localization in harmony
with the new visual experience, except that (as I noticed) my
head seemed too deep-set in my shoulders—in fact, seemed
buried in them almost up to my ears.

The harmonization of the new experience and the suppression or subordination of insistent remnants of the old were always apparent during active operations in the visual surroundings, as has been described for several of the preceding days. While I sat passively the old localization of unseen parts of my body often came back, or perhaps was the usual form in which they appeared. But the instant I began to rock my chair the new position of these parts came prominently forward, and, except in the case of my shoulders and back, readily felt more real than the old. And in walking, when hands and feet rhythmically made their appearance in the visual field, the old representation, except perhaps for some faint inharmonious sensations in the back, was fully expelled without employing any device of will or of attention whatever. The attempt to represent my body in its older form or position ended in a faint, lifeless outline, deficient, as far as I could make out, in those parts which (in a different direction, of course) were actually in sight. The sight of these parts made it impossible to represent them in harmony with the older experience. If in walking I allowed my feet to remain outside the field of view and they relapsed into their older localization, they returned, although still unseen, to their new position as soon as I approached a step or other slight obstacle on the floor.

As long as the new localization of my body was vivid, the general experience was harmonious, and everything was right side up. But when, for any of the reasons already given—an involuntary lapse into the older memory-materials, or a willful recall of these older forms—the pre-experimental localization of my body was prominently in mind, then as I looked out on the scene before me the scene was involuntarily taken as the standard of right directions, and my body was felt to be in an inharmonious position with reference to the rest. I seemed to be viewing the scene from an inverted body.

* * * * * * * * * *

When the time came for removing the glasses at the close of the experiment, I thought it best to preserve as nearly as possible the size of visual field to which I had now grown accustomed; so that any results observed might be clearly due solely to the reversion of my visual objects and not to a sudden widening of the visual field. Instead, therefore, of removing the plaster-cast from my face, I closed my eyes and had an assistant slip out the brass tube which held the lenses, and insert in its place an empty black-lined paper tube that gave about the same range of vision. On opening my eyes, the scene had a strange familiarity. The visual arrangement was immediately recognized as the old one of pre-experimental days; yet the reversal of everything from the order to which I had grown accustomed during the past week, gave the scene a surprising, bewildering air which lasted for several hours. It was hardly the feeling, though, that things were upside down.

When I turned my body or my head, objects seemed to sweep before me as if they themselves were suddenly in motion. The 'swinging of the scene,' observed so continously during the first days of the experiment, had thus returned with great vividness. It rapidly lost this force, however, so that at the end of an hour the motion was decidedly less marked. But it was noticeable the rest of the day, and in a slight degree even the next morning.

Movements which would have been appropriate to the visual arrangement during the experiment, were now repeatedly per-formed after this arrangement had been reversed. In walking toward some obstacle on the floor of the room—a chair, for in-stance—I turned the wrong way in trying to avoid it; so that I frequently either ran into things in the very effort to go around them, or else hesitated, for the moment, bewildered what I should do. I found myself more than once at a loss which hand I ought to use to grasp the door-handle at my side. And of two doors, side by side, leading to different rooms, I was on the point of opening the wrong one, when a difference in the metal work of the locks made me aware of my mistake. On approaching the stairs, I stepped up when I was nearly a foot too far away. And in writing my notes at this time, I contin-ually made the wrong movement of my head in attempting to keep the centre of my visual field somewhere near the point where I was writing. I moved my head upward when it should have gone downward; I moved it to the left when it should have gone to the right. And this to such a degree as to be a serious disturbance. While walking, there were distinct signs of vertigo and also the depression in the upper abdominal region, noticed during the earlier days of the experiment. The feeling that the floor and other visual objects were swaying, in addition to the symptoms just mentioned, made my walking seem giddy and uncontrollable. No distinct errors in localizing parts of my body occurred; I was more than once surprised, however, to see my hands enter the visual field from the old lower side.

Objects in the room, at a distance of ten or twelve feet from me, seemed to have lost their old levels and to be much higher than they were either during the experiment or before the experiment. The floor no longer seemed level, but appeared to slope up and away from me, at an angle of perhaps five degrees. The windows and other prominent objects seemed also too high. This strange aspect of things lasted (as did also the swinging of the scene, the feeling of giddiness, and certain inappropriate movements) after the plaster cast had been removed and the normal compass of the visual field was restored. In the dim light of the next morning, the upward slope of the floor and the unusual position of the windows were distinctly noticeable.

It is clear, from the foregoing narrative, that our total system of visual objects is a comparatively stable structure, not to be set aside or transformed by some few experiences which do not accord with its general plan of arrangement. It might perhaps have been supposed beforehand that if one's visual perceptions were changed, as in the present experiment, the visual ideas of things would without resistance conform to the new visual experiences. The results show, however, that the harmony comes only after a tedious course of adjustment to the new conditions, and that the visual system has to be built anew, growing from an isolated group of perceptions. The older visual representations for the most part have to be suppressed rather than reformed.

Why then do the old visual ideas persist in their old form, and not come immediately into accord with the new perceptions?

If their position were merely relative to the sight-perceptions, they undoubtedly would come into harmony with these perceptions, at least after the first moments of dismay were past. But the fact that the ideas can for some time refuse spatially to conform to the new experience, shows that their position and direction is fixed with reference to something other than the immediate perceptions of sight. What is it which caused the older visual images to preserve a spatial arrangement whose lines of direction were opposed to those of the actual field of view?

To say that the older visual directions persisted because the older tactual directions remained in force, is certainly no sufficient answer unless we can show that visual direction is dependent on tactual direction. But the preceding narrative furnishes strong evidence against such a view. If there is any dependence either way (which I doubt), the evidence seems to favor the primacy of sight.

However that may be, the facts in the present case are more accurately described when we say that the discord was not between tactual directions and visual directions, but between the visual directions suggested by touch and the visual directions given in the actual sight. The real question then is : Why did touch-perceptions so persistently suggest visual images whose positions and directions were in discord with the actual scene? The answer is found, I think, in the familiar doctrine of 'local signs' in touch and in sight, and in the farther assumption that a system of correspondence exists whereby a sign in one sense comes to be connected with and to suggest a particular sign in the other sense.

In the organized experience, a perception in one sensory field not only has in it that peculiar qualitative or intensive character which is its own 'local sign,' but, through this local sign, suggests in the other sensory field the local sign which is most intimately associated with the first. A perception in one sensory field suggests, therefore, in terms of the other sense an image in that place whose local sign is most strongly associated with the local sign of the original perception. According to this view, the local signs of sight correspond to the signs of touch, and *vice versa*; so that each member in this system of *corresponding*

signs has its particular correlate in the other sensory field. The
correspondence here indicated, does not, however, consist in any
spatial or qualitative identity or even similarity of the particular
signs which correspond, but only in the fact that both have
come to mean the same thing. They have occurred in connection with disparate sensory perceptions whose times of
appearing and whose 'curve' of change have been so continuously and repeatedly identical that the perceptions themselves
come, in time, to be referred to the same source, or, in other
words, give the perception to the same object. The perceptions of the two senses are thus identified; and, at the same
time, the disparate local signs (in the different senses) which
are simultaneously aroused in the perception of the one object
come to have the same spatial meaning. This correspondence
of local signs is no doubt an important condition for our perceiving one and the same thing in different sensory fields. And
the persistence of this correspondence between the signs, when
once the power of mutual suggestion has become established, is
the explanation of the fact that during my experiment the
translations of touch-perceptions into terms of sight continued
so long in contradiction to the actual visual experience; and
that, on the other hand, the visual perceptions so long suggested
tactual or motor images not in accord with the tactual or motor
perceptions.

For, whatever the local signs of vision may be—whether
differences in the qualitative or intensive character of the muscular sensations, or differences of sensation connected with different parts of the retina, or intricate combinations of both of
these materials—the reversion of the retinal image would so
alter the conditions of sight that the tactual perception of an
object and the simultaneous sight of the same object would no
longer call into play the pair of local signs which hitherto had
had the same spatial meaning, but a pair of signs which had
come to have opposed spatial meanings. Suppose, for illustration, that any two tactual local signs,[1] *a* and *b*, have in my nor-

---

[1] For convenience sake let us speak of the signs as though they could be
simple. Of course they are really complexes of sensations from joints and
muscles and skin. Similarly of the visual signs.

mal experience the same meaning as the two visual local signs m and n, respectively. A single object which is both seen and touched will arouse the synonymous signs a and m, or subsequently the pair b and n, supposing that the object changes its place. If I merely touch the object, in such a place that a is aroused, this suggests by associative correspondence the visual sign m; and when subsequently I look at the object, m is actually aroused, and the place of the visual object is seen to be identical with the visual place suggested by touch. Touch in this case suggests a visual experience which the visual perception confirms. Likewise a visual perception whose local sign was n would suggest, and afterwards be followed by, a tactual experience whose local sign was b. And in these cases the spatial character of the perceptions by the different senses would be harmonious.

But suppose, now, that the retinal image is changed, as in the experiment. An object which arouses the tactual sign a will no longer give a visual experience containing the sign m, but will give one containing, say, n. And the visual experience containing the local sign m is no longer accompanied by a tactual experience containing a, but by one containing, say, b; and *vice versa*. By the long previous experience, however, a touch-perception containing the sign a has come to suggest a visual experience containing the sign m, and will consequently continue for some time to suggest such a visual experience. But the actual sight of the object will show it in a different place from what touch suggested ; for the visual experience will now actually contain n and not m. And likewise this visual experience whose local sign is n will for some time continue to mean a tactual experience whose sign is b, in a different locality from the real touch of the object, which now contains the sign a. Each sense will in this way suggest experiences which the actual perceptions of the other sense will contradict. Thus touch and sight will be in mutual discord.

According to the view here presented, this discord will continue as long as the local sign a suggests the local sign m, and *vice versa*. But when a, by repeated connection, suggests only the visual position implied in the local sign n, and this latter in turn means only the touch locality whose sign is a; and when m and b have come to have an identical meaning, or are in correspondence; then the total experience will again be harmonious. Each sense would then suggest only what the other sense would confirm. We would see things where we felt them to be, and we would feel them where we saw them to be. But until this reharmonization has been brought about, visual ideas in the older form will continue to arise at the suggestion of tactual experiences, and there will be discord between the things in sight and the wider system of visual representations. The persistence of the old inter-sensory correspondences accounts, therefore, for the long opposition of visual ideas and visual perceptions, during the experiment.

We are now enabled also to see what the harmony between touch and sight really is. The experiment clearly shows that an object need not appear in any particular position in the visual field in order to admit of a union or identification of the tactual and visual perceptions of the object. The visual position which any tactual experience suggests—the visual place in which we 'feel' that an object is—is determined, not by some fundamental and immutable relation of tactual and visual 'spaces,' but by the mere fact that we have constantly seen the object there when we have had that particular touch-experience. If this particular touch-experience were the uniform and exclusive accompaniment of a visual object in some different visual position, the two sensory reports would mean the same thing, and the places of their object would be identical. Of course, the harmony of touch and sight also implies that visual appearances have the same relations to one another as tactual appearances have to one another; so that a given object in sight must have the same spatial relation to the rest of my visual world as the accompanying touch-object has with respect to the rest of my tactual world. But this harmony does not require that the visual manifestation of a tactual object should be just here and not there, or in this direction and not in that.

The inverted position of the retinal image is, therefore, not essential to 'upright vision,' for it is not essential to a harmony between touch and sight, which, in the final analysis, is the real meaning of upright vision. For some visual objects may be inverted with respect to other visual objects, but the *whole system* of visual objects can never by itself be either inverted or upright. It could be inverted or upright only with respect to certain non-visual experiences with which I might compare my visual system—in other words, with respect to my tactual or motor perceptions.

The reharmonizing of touch and sight, in the experiment, consisted therefore of a double work. Visual objects and ideas, which were at first isolated, had to become a system whose parts had the same relations among themselves as the parts of the tactual system, or of the older visual system. Not until the construction of a visual system enveloping and supplementing the actual visual field, would sight have something corresponding to the touch-system brought over undisturbed from the older experience. But the completion of this work was dependent on the progress of the second work, namely the perfecting or entire reconstruction of the process of translating from sight into touch and from touch into sight. Until this reconstruction was complete, each sense would suggest experiences of the other sense which this other sense would flatly contradict. Their reports would therefore necessarily seem discordant. But the restoration of harmony between the perceptions of sight and those of touch was in no wise a process of changing the absolute position of tactual objects so as to make it identical with the place of the visual objects; no more than it was an alteration of the visual position into accord with the tactual. Nor was it a process of changing the relative position of tactual objects with respect to visual objects; but it was a process of making a new visual position seem the only natural place for the visual counterpart of a given tactual experience to appear in; and similarly in regard to new tactual positions for the tactual accompaniment of given visual experiences. New associations had to develop, and new forms of expectation had to arise; in a word, new correspondences had to be brought about. But the tactual perceptions, as such, never changed their place. They simply got a new visual translation.

The especial obstinacy of the old representation of the body requires no extended comment. It is what we would expect when the cause of the persistence of the older images in general is understood. If visual suggestion from touch, based on the pre-experimental set of correspondences between touch and sight, was the chief cause of the persistent return of the older images, then of course the conditions were peculiarly favorable for a continuance of the old visual representation of the body. For in this case touch was ever-present; and moreover the body was seen only in part. Head, neck, shoulders, and the upper part of the trunk, could not be directly seen at all. Shadows, reflections, etc., had some influence in bringing to mind the new visual place of these parts; but such indirect agents lacked the force of direct and continued perception. So that the possibility of bringing about new correspondences was confined, for the most part, to my arms and legs. But there is, doubtless, a solidarity of the body, and when so large a part could not be reached by the new experience, the rest also was affected but little. The body hung together as a unit, and refused to go with the new, unless all of it could go.

In the daily experience during the experiment, localization of parts of the body to one side (right or left) of the visual field of representation was more persistently in discord with the new visual experience, than was the vertical localization of these parts. The explanation of this is found, I think, in the fact that both tactual and visual differences in the body are much more striking at different levels of the body (passing up and down) than on different sides of the body. I frequently saw one of my hands and took it for the other, but of course I never looked at my foot and thought it was my hand. So, too, I erroneously localized in one of my hands an object which was in contact with the other hand, but I never localized in my foot a contact that was really on my hand, nor *vice versa*. The experience itself was thus, as far as lateral relations were concerned, comparatively ambiguous, but not ambiguous at all with respect to vertical relations. When, through the touch-experience, a visual image was called up in the old lateral relations, this image was not so violently in discord with the new visual experience, as a mistake in vertical reference would have been. For the image of my right arm or leg would also serve fairly well for that of my left. And in actual sight nearly the same objects were seen now on one side and now on the other. This hindered a fixed association of a particular image with a particular visual side, such that when a contact occurred the part of the body which it suggested must be referred to this side and not to that, if the contract were to fit into the visual total at all. The fact that the new visual experience was tolerant of a localization on either side almost indifferently was therefore favorable to a continuance of the old lateral localization. But the new vision unequivocally pronounced against an error in vertical localization; the uniform contradiction tended therefore to break up the old suggestions, and to build anew the vertical system more rapidly than the lateral.

It is not improbable that the persistence of the old lateral localization of the body was the main cause of the relative permanence of the old localization of sounds. For, vertically, wide changes in localization of sounds readily came by spontaneous suggestion; but not so the lateral changes. These came rarely except by strong effort of attention and voluntary vizualization. The chief basis for determining the side from which a sound comes—the relative intensity of the sound in the two ears—would lead us to expect exactly this result as long as the two sides of the body were involuntarily represented as of old. If a sound was localized with reference to a particular ear or side of my head, then it would be localized in the old way as long as these were localized in the old way; and not until the localization of the two ears or sides of the head was transposed into harmony with the new experience would the auditory localization, at least in its lateral aspects, come into harmony with that experience. The cases in which the lateral localization of sound did accord with the new sight were no doubt due to a momentary strengthening of the influence of visual suggestion to such a degree that the usual dominant factor in lateral localization became subordinate. The fact that the sound of my footsteps conformed to the tactual and visual localization of my feet, and that in general the sight of the sound's place of origin carried with it the localization of the sound, shows to what an extent our auditory localization is influenced by suggestion.

It was repeatedly noticed in the course of the experiment that the total experience was much more harmonious during active movements of my body than when I inactively looked out upon the scene. This becomes intelligible when one sees how such movements gave additional vivacity to the new visual experience and to all that was in harmony with it, and tended to suppress those images of the body which did not accord with the new relations. The movements of my arms and legs into and through the visual field emphasized their new visual position more than their motionless appearance would have done. They caught and held the attention, and by the vigor of their appearance suggested the rest of the body in harmony with themselves. Moreover the movements of the field of view, when I nodded my head, or moved up and down in walking, or rocked in my chair, were such as harmonized with the movement of my body only when my body was thought of as in its *new* visual position. Otherwise the objects passed through the field of view in the wrong direction,—in a direction which the felt movement of my head or body did not at all explain. And, finally, the new localization of the body was the only one which was *practically important* when the visible environment had to be actively encountered. My actions could be guided, not by keeping in mind the pre-experimental localization of the body and noticing its relation to objects in sight, but only by accepting the new position of my body as *real* and constantly watching its relation to surrounding things. The scene itself became more my own by acting upon it, and this action reacted to bring the representation of my body into harmonious relation to the scene. As a result of these various influences, the whole experience was cleared of inner discord to a degree seldom if ever attained during a time of repose.

At the close of the experiment, after the lenses had been removed, windows and other prominent objects, as the narrative recounts, seemed too high. This was puzzling enough until I discovered that, when my apparatus was on my face, objects in the centre of the field of view were slightly lower than when seen without the lenses. The axis of the cylinder containing the lenses was in fact not exactly the same as the line of sight when the eye was directed to the centre of the field. The displacement this caused in the apparent position of things was the less noticeable because of the general transposition of objects by the inverting power of the lenses. But a careful examination showed that the downward displacement at the centre was about equal to the apparent upward displacement on removing the lenses. No exact comparison could be made, for I did not notice this peculiarity of the apparatus until several days after the close of the experiment. So that I had to depend on my inexact recollection of what the extent of the illusion had been. It is, of course, barely possible that the illusion was in some way a direct consequence of reinverting the retinal image. But more probably the general displacement of objects, by reason of the position of the tube, had grown so familiar that. their normal position on removing the glasses seemed as much too high as their position during the experiment had been too low.

But to return to the more significant features of the experiment. These are, without doubt, found in the results bearing on the relation between touch and sight, and through them on the interrelation of the senses generally. The experiment makes it clear that the harmony between sight and touch does not depend on the inversion of the retinal image. The spatial identity of tactual and visual objects evidently does not require that there should be a visual transposition of objects or that they should be given some special direction in the visual field. The chief reason for the existence of the projection theory is therefore taken away. Nor, on the other hand, are the visual directions made known to us and determined through our perceiving the 'absolute,' or pure motor, direction of the movements which alter the line of sight. The facts all go to show that the direction of movements of the head or eyes is not judged on purely muscular evidence, independently of the simultaneous changes in vision itself. On the contrary the movements are soon felt as having a direction opposite to that of the objects passing through the visual field. During the experiment, for instance, I often felt my eyes turn toward the sky and away from my feet, although they really turned toward my feet. The felt direction of the movement is therefore relative to the direction of the movement of visual objects, and the ' absolute' muscular direction cuts no decisive figure in the perception at all. This will no doubt seem a hard saying to those who have been pinning their faith more and more on the unimpeachable witness of muscular sensations. It certainly makes the eye-movement doctrine of visual directions of little practical assistance for understanding the harmony between sight and touch.

This harmony, as was said, seems rather to be an accord of the *ideas* suggested in terms of one of the senses, with the *perceptions* of the same sense. When touch and sight agree, it means that the perceptions of sight are spatially identical with the visual suggestions produced by touch, and that the perceptions of touch spatially identical with the tactual suggestions produced by sight. The doctrine of a correspondence of local signs, stated some · pages back, makes it easy to see how such a harmony could grow up ; and, at the same time, how a reharmonization of touch are and sight is possible, whatever may be the position of the retinal image. The view makes provision, therefore, for the special results of the experiment, as well as for the normal course of our experience ; which the current doctrines concerning the interplay of touch and sight seem hardly able to do.

THE PSYCHOLOGY OF SOCIAL ORGANIZATION.

BY PROFESSOR J. MARK BALDWIN.

Princeton University.

The object of this paper is to present in outline a way of conceiving of the general fact of human social organization in line with the tendency which has proved itself fruitful in the last few years mainly in France; the tendency to recognize the psychological character of the *motifs* at work in society. It seems to me to be a permanent advance that the biological analogy is giving place to a psychological analogy, and that this is leading the writers in socalled ' sociology ' to examine the psychological processes which lie wrapped up in the activities and responsibilities called social. The point of view sketched in the following pages reproduces some parts of a work entitled ' Social and Ethical Interpretations in Mental Development,' which is now in press.[1]

§ 1. The hard questions, to the thinker about society, seem to me to be two, each of which should have a two-fold statement. The first question concerns the *matter* or *content*, of social organization; what is it that is organized? what is it that is passed about, duplicated, made use of, in society? When we speak of a social phenomenon in its lowest terms, what is it all about, what is the sort of material which must be there if society is there? This question has had very acute discussion lately under the somewhat different statement: what is the criterion or test of a social phenomenon? But the question which I ask under this head is more narrow, since, in all sorts of organization, a further question comes up in addition to that of the matter—the further question, *i. e.*, as to the processes, methods of

---

[1] Macmillans. Seeing that this paper was prepared, in the first place, for a sociological Journal (the *Rivis. Ital. di Sociologia*) the more purely psychological parts of the work are not given much notice. The psychological chapters consist, however, partly ʻof further developments of points of view contained in my earlier work *Mental Development in the Child and the Race*.

functioning and laws of organization of the social content or material. It has been the weakness of many good discussions of late, I think, just as they did not set these questions separately, *i. e.*, (1), the matter, and (2), the functional method.

Let us take an illustration. Some of the animals show a certain organization which appears to be social. But on examination, in certain instances, we find that the actions involved are purely hereditary, congenital, each animal doing his part, in the main or altogether, simply because he is born to do it whenever the organism becomes ripe for these actions under the stimulation of his environment. Now let us contrast with this the intelligent coöperative performance of the same actions by a group of men or children who deliberately join to do them in common. In these cases it is clear that the matter of organization is different; one being a purely biological and instinctive, the other a psychological and acquired action. The results to the observer may be the same, and the question may still remain as to whether the functional method be the same or no, but there is no doubt that the matter is different in type. These two questions may therefore be distinguished at the outset with so much justification.

§ 2. But each of these two questions allows of a two-fold requirement. If we assume that the distinction between habit (with relative fixity of function) and accommodation (with relative plasticity of function as seen in all progress in learning or acquisition) holds of society, then both the matter and the method or process of social organization must allow of these two modes, and working together must besides produce them. If, for example, we take an individual and find that he has a habit of acting in a certain way, and at the same time improves upon his action from day to day, we yet say that the action remains the same in its content or meaning throughout the entire series, from the fixed habit to the skilled variation. Our determination of the content of the action must have reference to just the possibility of the entire series of statements, from fixed repetitions of habit to the extreme variations of accommodation, through all the intermediate stages. In other words, the fact of growth by a series of accommodations must be reckoned with in all the determinations of social content. And statements of *progress* must go with the definitions of the actual content at any given stage of social organization.   In other terms, the content of social life is a changing growing content, and the definition of the material of social organization must take account of this character.

And so must the theory of the methods of functioning also. The process of social organization results in a growing developing system.   Progress is real, no matter what its direction, provided it result from the constant action of a uniform process of change in a uniform sort of material.   This we find in social life, and this is the prime requirement of social theory both in dealing with matter and in dealing with function.

§ 3. It may suffice to bring these distinctions and the problems which emerge more clearly to the light, if we note briefly some of the later attempts to deal with the social organization · from a psychological point of view.   I shall cite types of theory, referring to particular writers merely as illustrating these types and without going into the details of their positions.

The Imitation Theory, illustrated by M. Tarde.   This view of social organization has very much to commend it, from the point of view of method; indeed, as will appear in the sequel, I think it is with modifications of statement the true, and possibly the final solution of the question of type of social function. As a complete doctrine of society, however, it fails signally, since it gives no answer to the question of matter.   M. Tarde does not tell us what is imitable, what is capable, through imitation, of becoming fixed as social habit, and also of being progressively modified in the forms of social progress.   He does seem to become more aware of the need of answering this question in his later work, *La Logique Sociale*, and introduces certain elements of content as ' beliefs and desires,' to supply the lack.   This, however, means simply a departure from his earlier theory, in which the phenomenon of imitation was treated as an answer to the question *qu'est ce qu'une société?*   Apart from M. Tarde's personal views, it may be said that the case of imitation at its purest is just the case in which the social vanishes. Imagine a room-full of parrots imitating each other in regular sequence around the area, and let them keep it up *ad infinitum*, and with as much individual variation as they may; where is the social bonds between the parrots? In so far as the imitation is exact, in this case a thing of congenital instinct, in so far we might substitute tuning-forks for the parrots, and let them vibrate together after striking one of them a sharp blow. Indeed, in his treatment of the final nature of imitation in his *Lois de l'Imitation* M. Tarde brings it into a sort of cosmic correlation with undulatory repetition in physics. I can not see that the mere presence of imitation would avail anything, without tacit or explicit assumptions of two kinds: first, that the material of social organization is essentially imitable material; and second, that through imitation this material would take on the forms of organization actually found in society.

2. Another type of theory which is open to the same criticisms in effect is represented by the 'constraint' view of M. Durkheim. To this view the essence of social organization is the constraining influence of one person upon others. It is in line with the extreme 'suggestion' theory of society, which makes the crowd acting under the suggestion of the strongest personalities in it the type of social organization as such. The weakness of this type of doctrine appears from the striking analogy from hypnotic suggestion which its advocates employ. And the element common to such a view with that of M. Tarde is evidenced in the use which he makes of the same analogy. The analogy seems to me to be quite correct; to this view the extreme and the purest instance of social organization would be hypnotic *rapport*. Here constraint is well nigh absolute, imitation is perfect, subordination is unquestionable. But it is only necessary to state this to see that in hypnotic rapport the social has completely evaporated. It gives no criticism or criterion of social material; the hypnotic subject or the generally suggestible subject tends to take all suggestions as of approximately equal value, to obey everything, to understand nothing, to be the same sort of an instrument of repetition as the parrot and the tuning fork. How there could be any organization as distinct from repetition, of progress as distinct from arbitrary caprice, I am quite unable to see. It may be, as a matter of history, that the first social man

became so because he was knocked down by a stronger, and so constrained to be his slave; but further progress from such a state of constraint, in the direction of coöperation, would be possible only in proportion as there was a ' let-up ' or modification of the one-sided constraint. In other words constraint—or rather the imitation to which it may be reduced as soon as it ceases to be one-sided and becomes *mutual*—may have been the method and may continue to be the method of social organization, but the lines of progress actually made by society would seem to be determined by certain inherent possibilities of fruitful coöperation and organization in some particular spheres. These spheres must be defined, and that raises the quite different question of matter or content. The constraint theorists, I know, take as type of constraint not that of force but that of suggestion; and it is just this tendency which brings their view into line with the imitation theory and makes it available as an important, but less important, contribution to that theory.

3. There is another way again of looking at social organization, a way which, however, may be called psychological only with some latitude. Dr. Simmel, of Berlin, may be taken as representing it in a part of his treatment of society. It consists in attempting, by an analysis of social events and phenomena, to arrive at a statement of the formal principles which each section or general instance of social life presents. Such formal principles are division of labor, altruistic endeavor and coöperation, etc. This is a very serviceable undertaking, I think, and must result in a certain valid social logic—a system of principles by which social phenomena may be classified and which may serve as touch-stones of particular cases of organization. The objection, however, to building a science of sociology upon it is just that the principles are formal; it would be like building the psychology of concrete daily life upon the formal principles of logic. Principles which get application everywhere are not of concrete use anywhere. They also lack—or the system which seeks them out lacks—the genetic point of view. Granted the establishing of these principles by the analysis of social events, the question would still remain as to the original form which they showed in primitive societies. It is

easier to deal with the simpler and work up than it is to reverse this procedure; and from this point of view it would seem quite possible to treat all such principles as developments from imitation and suggestion. Apart from this, however, the essential criticism to be made upon this type of thought is that it deals only with form and functional method and assumes certain sorts of matter of social organization. The principle of division of labor, for example, assumes conscious *thought*, in such division and its constant application by the members of society.

4. Another class of doctrines have the merit of being genetic, those which found the social life of communities upon certain primitive emotions, such as sympathy. These theories are ex emplified by Mr. Spencer, M. Novikow and the English moral philosophers. This is possibly the oldest form of social theory, having its roots in Aristotle, and has all the accumulated authority of age. Its forms of statement are also so numerous that I cannot take them up. From the pure 'sympathy' theory we pass to the 'altruistic theory' which makes social life a derivative of ethical; to the social instinct theory, which says that man is natively social, and sympathy and altruistic feeling are evidences of it; and finally we reach the climax of descriptive vagueness—in a formula wide enough to include all the rest—the 'consciousness of kind' recently propounded by Professor F. Giddings.[1]

As a class it may be said of all these theories that they constantly confuse the questions of method and matter in social organization. In regard to method of function the imitation theory comes in at once to supplement these earlier points of view. But apart from this lack it may be said that the life of feeling and instinct does not furnish the requirements of matter for social organization. There are two sorts of sympathy, two sorts of social instinct, two sorts of consciousness of kind. This appears when we press the requirement indicated above that the matter of social organization should be such as to allow the formation both of social habit and of the adaptations seen in social accommodation and growth. The life of instinct as such

[1] In the third edition of his *Princ. of Sociology* (Preface), however, Professor Giddings defines 'consciousness of kind' more in terms of sympathy.

and of the emotions which come with instinctive activities—*e. g.*, organic sympathy, impulsive altruism, manifestations of kind, such as maternal affection, etc.—all these are race habits. To the degree in which they fulfill the requirement that society live by its stock of habits, to that degree do they fail to enable society to modify its habits and grow. If we sympathize with each other by pure instinct, and act on the movings of sympathy, new organization would be as far off as if we fought tooth and nail; for action would be as capricious. So also, merely to feel socially inclined would not beget differential forms of social organization. To be conscious of others as of the same kind would in itself not determine, in the slightest degree, the sort of thought or action which should be fruitfully recognized and developed within the habits of the kind. If we assume an adequate content, a common material, in short, if we assume social organization already, in the groups which for convenience *after they are made up in nature*, we call kinds, then of course it is the simplest thing in the world to say that what the members have in common is their consciousness of kind; but is no more an explanation than is the phrase ' love of drink ' an explanation of inherited tendency to alcoholism.

It is only when we come to see the second or higher sort of sympathy, social instinct, consciousness of kind, etc., that the requirement that social organization be progressive becomes more apparent, because only there is it possible of fulfillment. We do not find instincts getting much organization apart from certain fixed and congenital forms of association. The higher emotions and actions which arise when consciousness becomes in some degrees reflective as opposed to instinctive, take on aspects which are differentiated from one another according to the mental content which they accompany. There is a reflective sympathy, a reflective sociality, a reflective consciousness of kind; and it is just their value that they now afford some criterion—a material criterion—over and above the mere fact of feeling and instinct. This point is the main business of this paper, so I need not dwell upon it here; but it leads us to see that the theories which deal in such general descriptions of social organization as the terms mentioned carry, are quite inadequate, since they leave the real question of matter unanswered: of the ' what ' of social organization—the ' what ' of such questions as "what does society fruitfully imitate?" " what feeling and acts of sympathy yield results of social value and permanence?" "what is the something found sometimes in the consciousness of kind which in these cases leads to the sort of progress characteristic of an ethical society as opposed, let us say, to a school of fish?" Of course I am not intending to draw lines, even between the ethical society and the school of fish. It is a further question, after we determine the what of social organization, to find how far it is present also in the behavior of the school of fish. But what is it?—' that is the question.'

§ 4. This brief characterization of theories, all aiming to be psychological, enables us to see our problem. I have introduced them only for this purpose; and the inadequacies of presentation will, I hope, not be construed as inadequacies of appreciation. The way the emerging problems appear, in consequence of our review so far, may be shown in certain more formal statements to which the remainder of the paper may now be addressed.

1. There is entire justification for the distinction urged by Tönnies between what have been called in English respectively ' colonies,' ' droves,' ' schools,' ' herds,' etc., in particular cases, and ' societies.' Tönnies distinguishes between the *Gemeinschaft* and the *Gesellschaft*. The difference—to put it in my own way, from the point of view of a current psychological and biological distinction—is this, *i. e.*, between the relatively unvarying, relatively definite, and relatively unconscious organization which has its extreme instance in animal instinct, and the relatively varying, progressive, plastic and conscious organization seen in human life. I shall distinguish these types as ' companies '[1] and ' societies.'

2. The distinction just made is mainly one of matter or content, seeing that the method of interaction (*i. e.*, granting that

---

[1] The word ' community ' might be used for this, as a translation of *Gemeinschaft*; but that word has another significance in English. The term ' colony ' is also inappropriate, I think, for a similar reason.

it is imitation) is substantially the same in the two types of organization.

3. The first problem is, therefore, the determination of the facts regarding the 'what' of social life. What is it that is both common to all *societies* and also capable of progressive organization in each society?

4. The assumption that imitation is the method in both colonies and societies is made on the strength of recent work of various writers. Imitation may, however, be brought to a further test in connection with the problem of matter, since after having determined the sort of matter with which we have to deal, we must then ask whether the imitative method of organization adequately explains the actual forms which this material shows. To my mind the strongest proof of the claim for imitation as type of social function is derived from its effective application after the nature of the material is determined. It thus loses the casual empirical character which social observation so often shows, and becomes wrought into what may then be called, in a figure, *social morphology*. The psychological portions of my work are devoted to a detailed exposition of the imitative development of the social consciousness.

5. Finally, the determination of phenomena as social is only possible under this two-fold requirement as to matter and method. To fail in either of these is to fail entirely; on the one side it would be like determining life by morphology alone, with no necessary exclusion of crystals and plough-shares, provided they were the right shape; or, on the other hand, by physiology alone, which would not exclude a cunningly-devised india-rubber heart or an air-pump-breathing machine, provided it worked.

§ 5. Coming, therefore, to the question of the matter, the 'what,' of social organization, I shall state a general result, and then indicate certain lines of evidence for it.

This result may be put in the form of a thesis as follows: *the matter of social organization consists of thoughts; all kinds of knowledges and informations.* And in the way of further anticipation and description of the mechanism of social organization, we may add that these thoughts or knowledges or informations, originate in the mind of the individuals of the group, as inventions, or more or less novel conceptions. At their origin, however, there is no reason for calling them social matter, since they are particular to the individual. They become social only when society—that is, the other members of the social group, or some of them—also thinks them, knows them, is informed of them. This reduces them from the individual and particular form, to a general or social form, and it is only in this form that they furnish social material. It is evident that much of this is not new; my main interest in presenting it lies in certain psychological principles by which it gets relatively new confirmation, and the resulting characterization given below of the *sort of thought* which is socially available.

§6. The general considerations upon which this opinion is based may be given in contradistinction from special lines of evidence. These general considerations will be seen to arise in connection with the general requirements of social theory as stated in the foregoing pages.

1. It is only thoughts or knowledges which are imitable in the fruitful way required by a theory of progressive social organization. It has been said by some that beliefs and desires are thus imitable. It is clear, however, to the psychologist that beliefs and desires are functions of the knowledge contents about which they arise. No belief can be induced in one individual by another except as the fact, truth, information believed is first induced. The imitator must first get the thought before he can imitate belief in the thought. So of desire. I can not desire what you do except as I think the desirable object somewhat as you do. And if it be a question of imitative propagation or reproduction from one member of a social group to another, the vehicle of such a system of reproductions must be thought or knowledge. The only other psychological alternative is to say that the imitative propagation takes place by the simple contagion of feeling and impulse. This, however, takes us back to the question already raised above, *i. e.*, the question of possible progress by society. We found that the reign of imitative feeling and impulse, whether it be by instinct or by suggestion, would make possible only the form of organization

in which fixed habit is all, and in which no accommodation, movement, progress, would take place. This we found to characterize certain animal companies in distinction from true societies.[1]

2. It is only in the form of thoughts, conceptions, or inventions that new material, new ' copies for imitation,' new schemes of modified organization can come into a society at any stage of its development. This seems evident from the mere statement of it. If we ask how a new measure of legislation, a new scheme of reform, a new opinion about style, art, literature, even a new cut to our coats or a changed height of hat—how any one of these things originates, we are obliged to say that someone first thought of it. *Thought* of it, that is the important thing. Feeling and desire might have impelled to thought; urgent need may have prompted the invention; decaying modes may have made reform a matter of necessity; but with all the urgency that we may conceive, the measure, the reform, the new style, has to originate somewhere in the form of a concrete device, which society can take up and spread abroad. This particular form is then the thought of someone; and society afterwards generalizes the thought. Just how this generalizing is done by society—that is spoken of below; at this stage we may simply say that society is the ' generalizing force,' in social organization, meaning that society as such does not make inventions, nor think original thoughts, much less make progress without original thoughts or, as some teach, without thoughts at all. Assuming the new thoughts originating somewhere, it is the function of society to make them available and to give them social currency; this we may call society's *generalization.*[2]

Then we may say that the individual *particularizes* over

---

[1] The biological view which considers the unit-person, as such, the material of social organization may be refuted in a word. It is as *persons* that persons come into social relationships, and the differences of persons are just in the psychological part. One physical body is as good as another before the law. The distinction between things in groups and persons in society is that there is a 'give and take' in the latter case. The object of social study is thus the 'giving and taking,' and the material is that which is 'given and taken.'

[2] It is really a generalization, since to be thought by minds generally each such invention must be stripped of what is peculiar and characteristic of the first individual's thought.

against society. By this we mean simply that the particular forms in which new thoughts first come, in order that they may afterwards be generalized by society, originate always in an individual's mind. Just what this amounts to—how far the individual thinks from the platform of earlier social generalization—that we can not now discuss.[1] Here we may simply say that it is the individual who thinks all the new thoughts that are thought, and thinks them first in the particular form which constitutes their novelty in contrast with what is already spread abroad in society; and that of all the individual's doings, it is his thoughts which are the socially available factors of his life. Of course there is a form of social propagation which takes its origin in the actions only of this man or that, whether any thought be discoverable in the action or not. But apart from the fact that such actions have to be thought by the imitators, however spontaneous or accidental they may have been on the part of the original actor, it is evident that this form of social origination on the side of accident, mere habit, social convention or mob action is lacking in itself of any fruitfulness in the production of new phases of social progress.[2]

With these general considerations in mind—which are enough in themselves to justify a closer examination of the position that thought or knowledge is the matter of social organization—we may proceed to cite two lines of evidence which support this view. One of them is drawn from the facts of the child's social development, and the other from the corresponding facts of the social and ethical man's relations to the historical institutions of society. These are the two spheres in which the consideration of the psychological factors involved in social organization would lead us to expect reliable results.

§ 7. I. Special evidence from the child's social development. The general method of the child's social development has been worked out on the basis of more or less extended observations

---

[1] My article on 'The Genius and his Environment' may be referred to: *Pop. Sci. Monthly*, July and Aug, 1896.

[2] The newer works in the psychology of crowds seem to show that these represent a disorganizing and down-grade factor rather than the reverse. I think mob-action shows a bye-product or excess-play of the principles of imitation and suggestion.

of my own and other children in my earlier volume. I may quote the conclusion briefly from that work?[1]

" One of the most remarkable tendencies of the very young child in its responses to its environment is the tendency to recognize differences of personality. It responds to what I have called ' suggestions of personality. * * * I think this distinction between persons and things, between agencies and objects, is the child's very first step toward a sense of the qualities which distinguish persons. The sense of uncertainty or lack of confidence grows stronger and stronger in its dealings with persons—an uncertainty contingent upon the moods, emotions, *nuances* of expression, and shades of treatment, of the persons around it.   A person stands for a group of experiences quite unstable in its prophetic as it is in its historical meaning. This we may, for brevity of expression, assuming it to be first in order of development, call the '*projective* stage' in the growth of the personal consciousness, which is so important an element in social emotion.

" Further observation of children shows that the instrument of transition from such a ' projective' to a subjective sense of personality is the child's active bodily self, and the method of it is the function of imitation. As a matter of fact, accommodation by actual muscular imitation does not arise in most children until about the seventh month, so utterly organic is the child before this, and so great is the impetus of its inherited instincts and tendencies. But when the organism is ripe, by reason of cerebral development, for the enlargement of its active range by new accommodations, then he begins to be dissatisfied with ' projects,' with contemplation, and so starts on his career of imitation. And of course he imitates persons. * * * But it is only when a new kind of experience arises which we call effort—a set opposition to strain, stress, resistance, pain, an experience which arises, I think, first as imitative effort—that there comes that great line of cleavage in his experience which indicates the rise of volition, and which separates off the series now first really *subjective*. * * * The subject sense, then, is an actuating sense. What has formerly been ' projective' now becomes ' subjective.' The associates of other personal bodies, the attributes which make them different from things, are now attached to his own body with the further peculiarity of actuation. This we may call the *subjective* stage in the growth of the self-notion. * * * Again, it is easy to see what now happens. The child's subject sense goes out by a kind of return dialectic, which is really simply a second case of assimilation, to illuminate these other persons. The project of the earlier period is now lighted up, claimed, clothed on with the raiment of self-hood, by analogy with the subjective. The projective becomes *ejective;* that is, other people's bodies, says the child to himself, have experiences *in them* such as mine has. They are also *me's:* let them be assimilated to my *me*-copy. This is the third stage; the *ejective,* or ' social' self, is born.

" The *ego* and the *alter* are thus born together. Both are crude and unreflective, largely organic, an aggregate of sensations, prime among which are efforts, pushes, strains, physical pleasures and pains. And the two get purified and clarified together by this twofold reaction between project and subject, and between subject and eject. My sense of myself grows by imitation of you, and my sense of yourself grows in terms of my sense of myself. But *ego* and *alter*

[1] A similar view has also been reached by Professor Josiah Royce in various publications.

are thus essentially social; each is a *socius*, and each is an imitative creation. So for a long time the child's sense of self includes too much. The circumference of the notion is too wide. It includes the infant's mother, and little brother, and nurse, in a literal sense; for they are what he thinks of and aims to act like by imitation, when he thinks of himself. To be separated from his mother is to lose a part of himself, as much so as to be separated from a hand or foot. And he is dependent for his growth directly upon these suggestions which come in for imitation from his personal *milieu*."

§ 8. A further development of this with a view of determining something about the 'Genesis of Social Interests'[1] appears to bear out the conclusion that this so-called 'dialectic of personal growth,' whereby the child comes to a knowledge of himself, only by building up a sense of his social environment, may also be looked at from the side of social organization.

If we grant that the thought of self takes its rise as a gradual achievement on the part of the child by means of his constant experience of the personalities about him, and that he has not two different thoughts for himself and the other—the *ego* and the *alter*—but one thought common in the main for both[2]; then it becomes just as impossible to construe the social factor, the organized relationships between him and others, without taking account of his and their thoughts of self, as it is to construe the thought of self without taking account of the social relationships. The thought of self arises directly out of certain given social situations; indeed it is the form which these actual social relationships take on in the organization of a new personal experience. The ego of which he thinks at any time is not the isolated-and-in-his-body-alone-situated abstraction which our theories of personality usually lead us to believe. It is rather a sense of a network of relationships among you, me, and the others, in which certain necessities of pungent feeling, active life, and concrete thought require that I throw the emphasis on one pole sometimes, calling it me; and on the other pole sometimes, calling it you or him. But the social meaning of this state of things comes out when we look into its psychological presuppositions in the whole group. Let us then call the child's sense of the entire

[1] Art. in *The Monist*, Apl. 1897.
[2] This common or general part being, I think, a felt motor attitude (cf. my *Ment. Development*, p. 330).

personal situation in which he finds himself at any time in his thought, his *self-thought-situation.* [1]

Now, whatever is true of one individual's growth by imitative appropriation of personal material is true of all; and we have the giver turned into the taker and the taker into the giver everywhere. The growing sense of a ' self-thought-situation' in each is, *just to the extent that the social bonds are intimate and intrinsic, the same for all.* The possibility of coöperation—as, for example, the detailed coöperations of children's games— depends upon this essential sameness of the personal thoughts of the whole circle in each situation. My action depends upon my understanding of your thought and his, and your action depends upon your understanding of my thought and his, and so on.[2] Looked at objectively, we say that the children are in social relationship; looked at subjectively, the truth is that they are thinking the same thoughts of the personal-social situation, and this thought is just the ' self-thought' in the stage of development which it has reached in this little mind or that and brought out on this or that occasion. H understands E in terms of her own motives, desires, tendencies, likes and dislikes, and, acting on this understanding, finds that it works; so E treats her self-thought as true to H's thought, and it works; to find that either of these expectations did not work in the great run of cases of action would be to say objectively that the social relationship was dissolved. But this could not be without at the same time disintegrating, so far as the factors were intrinsic, the sense of personal self in each of the children, or taking it back toward the beginning of its development.

§ 9. The question of the material of social organization comes up here as soon as we ask what it is that the children pass about, give and take, in this inter-play with one another. And we find here just the distinction which occurred from the

---

[1] This phrase, which I use simply for shorthand, may be expanded *always* into: ' the social situation implicated in the thought of self.'

[2] In the nursery we may frequently see one child using this sameness of personal attitude for purposes of acute manipulation and childish intrigue. My child H (at 6 years) would put a high vocal value on something she did not want, and so lead E (4 years) to drop something else which H did want. H thus counted on the sameness of E's socially-induced desire and discounted it to her own private advantage.

consideration of the difference between human and animal organization. We find the child at first largely organic, instinctive, directly emotional under the influence of pleasures and pains. His sympathy is at first organic, and his antipathies likewise. But close observation shows that it is largely by the growing realization of personal distinctions, on the basis of which his thought of self develops, that he comes to have conscious imitations, original interpretations, hesitations, inhibitions, volitions. At first the relation is one of direct stimulation and direct response. If this state of things continued men would form ' companies,' not ' societies.' Direct suggestion, emotional reaction, as much coöperation as heredity might give consistently with the other features—that would be the state of things. But now let the child begin to think, and we find certain great features of social import springing up in his life. First, a distinction in the elements of his environment according as they are personal or not; second, a difference of attitude toward persons and toward different persons, according as the elements of personal suggestion which he gets will assimilate to this group of experiences or to that; third, the interpretation of the other persons in the same terms as himself, *i. e.*, as having attitudes like his in similar circumstances, and as thinking of him as he thinks of them. But all this is due to thought, involves knowledges, and the sorting of them out. The emotions now spring from thought experiences, and the attitudes, actions, responses now take on the character of means to a personal end, the end being the thought which issues in this or that attitude or action.

We may say then, as a first gain, from the consideration of the children, that what we call *objective social relationships are the objective manifestations to the onlooker of a common self-thought-situation in the different individuals, together with the movements of its growth in each as the immediate situation calls it out.*

§ 10. II. The next point offered in support of the position now outlined raises a question to which I attach so much importance from an historical point of view that I may take a little space to speak of the question itself before attempting its solution. In stating and criticising various theories above, there was intentionally omitted a class of thinkers whose doctrine, disregarding differences of detail, may be described as the 'ideal' theory of social life. This theory generally proceeds by deduction and reaches a view of society from the presuppositions of idealistic philosophy. For this reason, *i. e.*, that the doctrine is so purely deductive, it has little consideration from the more scientifically disposed thinkers in this field. And this is the more the case since it is with the name of Hegel, with the Neo-Hegelians, that this type of social theory is associated.

In its broadest outlines, this philosophy makes reality identical with thought; finds consciousness, and especially self-consciousness, the 'coming-to-itself' of reality; and sees in social organization the objectivation or universalizing of the self-consciousness which first 'comes-to-itself' in the individual. The general social positions of this school seem to be these : first, the essential character of reality, as thought, is not lost in the objectifying whereby the individual becomes universalized in society ; and second, the complete 'coming-to-itself' of reality, in society as in the individual, is in the form of a self. When we put these two positions together, we have the view that it is in the individual's formal thought of self that there is realized both the subjective form of reality and its objective form as actually existing in society.[1]

It is in this conclusion rather than in the metaphysics which lies back of it—and I wish to draw a sharp line between them— that our present interest lies. This statement regarding the *thought of self* it is which our detailed inductive investigation both of the child's development and of the movements of society seems to support. This will appear from the consideration of an aspect both of the thought of self and of real social organization which I may call *Publicity*. This it remains to bring out.

§ 11. We have already found so much justification for two positions: first, that the material of social organization must be considered as being thoughts which arise in individual minds and are then rethought by others, and so carried on through a social career; and second, that the child's social

---

[1] Hegel's distinction between 'subjective mind' and 'objective spirit.'

sense, that is his sense of all social situations, however meagre and contracted or however full and rich, arises and grows as a function of his thought of himself. In other words society to the child—society from the private subjective point of view—is a concrete situation involving related changes among the elements and attitudes which constitute his self-thought. The further question remains: given this objective social material—thought—and given also this subjective sense of society in the individual, *what is the objective character of social organization?* For, of course, the question of science is just this objective question; not only what does each individual think of the social situation when he thinks of it at all, but what must the observer think of it after he finds out scientifically all about it? His question then, in view of the two earlier determinations, is this: is the thought which constitutes the material of social organization any thought at random, thought X, thought Y, thought Z, these and others? Or must it be some particular sort of thought? And again, if the latter, must it be the sort of thought which the individual thinks when he reaches his sense of social situations as functions of his thought of himself? To come right to the conclusion, I think the last is true; and its truth appears again in what is called the *Publicity* of all social truth. What then is this Publicity? It may be gathered from this statement (which is illustrated and explained below) : *every social thought implies a public ' self-thought-situation' which is strictly analogous in its rise and progress to the ' self-thought-situation' of the individual member of society.*

We may take an illustration from the ordinary attitude which society takes toward human life, in contrast with the attitude which the individual might sometimes think himself justified in taking toward his own life. Let us say that there is a question in the mind of Mr. A., as to whether he shall put a barrier across his hay field to protect himself from injury at the point at which a railroad crosses the field. He says to himself "I have crossed that field many times; I have never been struck by a train; the chances are that I never shall be; it would be useless trouble and expense." So he takes the risk of his life, and is probably justified in doing so by the event. So the sanctions of a private kind, including that of his intelligence, would sustain him in this decision.

But now let us suppose that Mr. A is also a public official and has to consider the question of putting up barriers at railway crossings generally.   He is then told that at each place at which a railway crosses a road, a certain proportion of the pedestrians who go that way are killed each year.   He might say of each of these what he had before said of himself, that the chances were in favor of safety.   But now that he takes a *public* point of view this is no longer sanctioned in his thought. It is no longer the question of the continuance of the life of this one man or that.   It is now the question of the greatest possible safety to the collective or entire life of the community.   To put up barriers at all the crossings would undoubtedly prevent the loss of many citizens a year.   The social or public sanction, then, impels him in just the opposite direction; and he not only votes for the barriers, but bears a share of the taxation and *allows the barrier to be put up in his own hay field.*

If now we take this situation at its lowest terms and attempt to analyse it we find that it implies certain things:

1. A shifting of the individual's point of view, in such a way that the early private thought of self is held in check before a higher or ideal thought of self.   The self of the man acting in public is different; if he be true to it, he can no longer act out his private thought.   2. There is in his mind a sense of the *reciprocity of action of all the individuals* with reference to one another under this larger thought of self.

This sense of reciprocity follows from the doctrine which we have found it necessary to hold, of the *unity of the self-content,* in all its development.   We found that the *ego* and the *alter* were in great part identical, especially the part which constitutes them selves as opposed to mere bodies.   We found then that when I think of myself I *ipso facto* think of you, and that the sense or emotion which the thought arouses, and in view of which I take the active attitudes that I do, reflect that thought no matter which the real *ego* may be as determined by the external conditions.   But differences of attitudes arise in regular circumstances, according as this one self-thought is imitative, aggressive, etc. Having gone so far, the very necessity of making further use of society it is which leads the child on to the further step which I have called the growth of a general or ideal sense of self. This means the formation of a category of action which includes *the essential content of self as represented* by all his earlier partial thoughts. He thinks of self as independent of the private objective marks of individuality, bodies, locality, etc. To this thought all personal actions must conform; but the actual relationships of the two selves called *ego* and *alter* must still appear in the concrete situations into which this higher thought is brought. The higher thought of self is brought to judge the lower thoughts. But it is itself a function of the lower; it could not arise except for the unity of content which holds the two together. So the result of the assimilation, the actual attitude taken in any particulaɪ case toward one or other of the lower self-thoughts—the attitude which constitutes the sense of ethical well or ill-desert as well as social value—this is identically the same attitude toward each of the partial selves. I condemn the act of you as well as the same act of me; approve it, no matter whether it be objectively determined in a particular case as really mine or yours. And this reciprocal phase of the assimilation necessarily carries the judgment over upon all the possible other people whose *ego* the identical thought may stand for. This then brings in the ejective thought of *you as also reaching the same sense of approval or disapproval that I do.* Or, in other words, the thought that the judgment passed is *actually in the minds of all other men.*

This may be put in a different way. My thought of the ideal self is general; it must sustain relation to all the particular cases. Whatever mental movement it gives rise to—approval, disapproval—must be present in all the particular cases. I find it giving rise to a feeling of condemnation in my own case when a certain action is before me. It must give rise to the same condemnation of others by me and of me by each of them. But it is said, this is very different from saying that I must think that it is actually present to them. Certainly, but we must remember that I cannot think of myself with any self situation before me without in the act thinking ejectively on the same content; hence to think of myself, with this case before me, is to think of other men also with this case before them. To fall short of this is to think not in terms of the general thought of self, not with reference to the ideal, but in reference to some particular partial self to whose knowledge the case before me is confined.

If this is so then in the case in which I am conscious that no one but myself knows the act which I am committing, this consciousness contradicts a real element in the mental psychosis which arouses public and ethical sentiment; and as long as I fully assure myself of this, I cannot get a completely social or moral judgment. Of course it is impossible to maintain such a private state of mind in its purity; the drift toward the general statement of the case in social terms tends to establish the proper ethical sense, and imagination supplies the needed elements by whispering what my friends would say if they knew my conduct.

This means that when I think of this ideal, that is, when I bring a given action to the test of assimilation to it—for I cannot think of it in any circumstances which do not call for its application to a concrete case of action—a part of the content of my thought is necessarily the thought that the judgment is one of social generality, that others are making the same assimilation of this act to the same ideal. In case, then, I know that the action is quite private, quite secret, absolutely unknown to anybody else, then the full reinstatement of the conditions of a social and ethical judgment are *ipso facto* not present. My ideal category of action is not brought out; for to bring it out requires the very sense of reciprocity which my knowledge of privacy contradicts. If this be true to psychology, then it is no wonder that privacy destroys much of our ethical competence.

In brief we find that the 'ejective' self is incorporated in the very body of every concrete social thought since the 'self-thought situation' in the individual cannot be constituted without it. This is the essential truth in so-called 'publicity.'

3. It follows directly that it is only through the construction of a general thought of self that this publicity can be reached. For the public or reciprocal reference of the judgment in each

case arises only through the assimilation of the private and ejective self-thoughts in a larger whole of the same kind. The constituting of the larger self is just the evidence of the integrating of the more partial selves; and if the public reference is due to the common element in the different individuals' self-thoughts, then each individual must get the growth which the assimilation represents, and *all the individuals must construct somewhat the same ideal.* The former is secured in the normal growth of the self-thought-situation in each, and the latter *through their actual life in a common social tradition and heritage.*

Taking the point of view of society, further, in contrast with that of the individual, we find the state of things which social science is lead to recognize, *i. e.*, *an actual integration of individuals just through the identical higher self which their life together makes it possible for them to set up.* From this point of view, therefore, we may call this a public 'self-thought-situation,' (expanded: *a social situation implicated in a public self-thought*) and go on to enquire into the laws of progress and development which it shows, always with reference to the individuals of whose growth it is a function. It is interesting to note that in this public self thus understood, we have reached in some degree a genetic justification of a position taken up by Aristotle and so often reasserted in the history of ethical discussion: the position which finds itself obliged to fall back upon a hypothetical 'best man' or oracle, whose judgment would be correct if it could be had. In our development, however, this public self is the objective form of organization into which growing personalities normally fall.

§ 12. But it may be said, surely it is not necessary that all thoughts, inventions, schemes, ideas, reforms, etc., should have this quality which we have called 'publicity' in order to be available for the instruction or reforming of society. Yes, they should; and that is just the point which I wish most to urge. No knowledge, simply as knowledge, can be social knowledge or become the instrument of social advance until it be made over to the public self by becoming in the minds of the individuals who think it *a public thing*, in contradistinction to the private thoughts which they entertain simply as individuals. Whatever is thought, however great the invention, however pregnant the suggestion of reform, it is not of social value until, just by thinking it, I also attribute it to the ideal self whose entertainment of it gives it validity and general authority to all the other individuals of the group. I may, from my private judgment, discount this further development of my thought beforehand; that is, I may confidently expect that my invention will be ratified by the general thought and so come to have the requisite publicity; but I then only do so as I appeal just to that higher self already formed in my breast through social experience, and through it anticipate the fate of the thought which I thus value. But this is when the invention is looked at subjectively. As soon as we look at it objectively—that is from the point of view of the science of social organization—we have to say that no thought is social or socially available which is still in the mind of an individual awaiting that generalization by the public which will give it the character of publicity by reason of the essential attribution of it to a public self.

In other words, my private thought, in order to be social matter, must enter into that organization or integration of the public self-thought-situation which is reflected in every adult more or less adequately; it is thus thought also by that higher self in each which imposes law upon all. With this goes the thought by me that all men agree with me in thinking it, and that they will give the enforcement of it the same recognition (including its enforcement upon me) that I give it (including its enforcement upon them). The thought thus becomes involved in the growth of the personal self and just by this becomes public also. Without this connection it cannot be social. *The ultimate subjective criterion of social thought is the self-thought,* with all its wealth of implication as to the social situation. And *the ultimate objective criterion is the actual ratification of the thought by the individuals through common action upon the situation which they mutually recognize.* By this they show then common integration in a public 'self thought-situation.'

§ 13. We come therefore in closing in upon our question as last stated to see that the growing 'self-thought-situation' in the mind of the individual is, when viewed in its mutual interactions and correlations in the group, just the material of social organization itself; for nowhere else can we find the requisites for public availability fulfilled. Thus arises *ipso facto* a public ' self-thought-situation;' on no other view can we account for the response of individuals to the organization which society shows. So both from the side of the child's and man's growth, and from the side of society considered objectively, we are lead to identify the organization of the individual's personality directly with that of society, in respect both to its material and to its method of acting. This may be made a little clearer by a short criticism of two views which are on the surface similar in conclusion to this; I refer to that of Adam Smith on the one hand, and that of Hegel on the other hand.

§ 14. Adam Smith's wonderful treatment of the social bond under the term sympathy is familiar to all students of English ethics. The criticism which I wish to make upon it is that he assumes the ' publicity' requisite to social organization, and rests satisfied with that assumption. According to Adam Smith I sympathize with what I find 'suitable' in the affections of others since it would be what I myself should experience, and the sense of this agreement is moral approbation. Then transferred to myself, my judgment of myself is a reflex of my sense of your corresponding sympathy with me. But as soon as we come to a social situation as such, that is to a situation involving two persons, an aggressor and an aggressee, the question arises with which I shall sympathize. And the same question arises as soon as I come to ask about my own self-approbation or disapprobation, considered as a reflex of the sympathy of others with me. For I do not know whether the other will sympathize with, *i. e.*, approve of, me or the other whom my action affects. What then is the general element which will give publicity and constancy of value to a social action as such? This Adam Smith answers in a general way by saying that that action is approved which is most sympathized with, say as between the aggressor and aggressee. But this of course does not help matters; for how am I to know which of the two you sympathize with the more, except as I again ask myself which would call out the more sympathy in my own case. That is, the measure —strictly construing the doctrine—would after all be just what we started with, the individual's private sympathy. Adam Smith later on calls in the recognition of the judgment of a hypothetical best man to whom tacit appeal is made. But this seems to me to be simply an assumption to which he had no right; it certainly does not follow from the play of sympathies as he has depicted it.

The doctrine of Hegel on the other hand also makes the assumption of publicity. Metaphysically it makes this assumption from the start; finding just the coming of the individual to personal self-consciousness a manifestation of the universal self all the while implicit in nature. But in taking on individual form in the first stages of the realization of a self—genetically considered—it has temporarily lost this attribute; that it should get it again is to be expected; that social life is the essential stimulus to its getting it again, is *a priori* probable; and Hegel says that social life is in fact the realization of this expectation. Yet how? That is a question of fact.

Hegel's answer is, in its general character, allied to the view spoken of above as that of 'constraint.' To him the earliest fruitful social relation is that of subjection, master and slave. And its fruitfulness is, it seems, mainly for the slave, since he is domineered over, and so made to realize definite social situations. Thus certain regular self-limitations, mutual relationships, necessities of life and intercourse grow up which have the quality of general or public value when recognized by all.

This, I am aware, is a meagre enough statement of this development in Hegel's 'Phenomenology of Mind,' but Wallace's exposition may also be referred to as confirming its essential accuracy.[1] What is lacking is just the bridge from the private

---

[1] Professor Royce, who has kindly read this paper, thinks indeed that this statement regarding Hegel should be supplemented by reference to the functions of the family and state as described in Hegel's *Encyclopädie*. As Professor Royce agrees, however, that 'an express recognition of the imitative factor as such is what I miss in him' (Hegel), and that is my main point of criticism, I allow the passage to stand subject to later revision. I may acknowledge gratefully here other suggestions made by Professor Royce, which are to be more adequately recognized in my book.

thought to the public thought; this the imitative factor supplies. Given complex social situations, whence their validity for all the members equally, and whence the intrinsic element of public reference which is a necessity of social nature to us all? Hegel's metaphysics of course supplies this element; it is the nature of thought to recover or recognize itself as universal (*Anerkennung*) on this higher plane of social self-consciousness. But this, when scanned from the point of view of actual genetic growth, requires an empirical method of development both in the individual and in society.

§ 15. The evidence for the general conclusion now stated, drawn from the actual facts of social life, takes on many phases, and I have no space to develop it here. I may, however, note certain directions in which we may look for its confirmation.

1. Much of the matter accumulated by the great succession of English moralists to prove that sympathy in all its manifestations is a 'putting of oneself in another's shoes' is directly available. For we only have to substitute *imitative identity of the ego and the alter* for the artificial putting of one into the shoes of the other, and the results follow. This is to say that the old doctrine of sympathy is essentially correct as far as it goes, and it only needs supplementing by investigations into the genesis and nature of the class of phenomena covered by the term sympathy. This the view does which makes the self-thought a progressive imitative outcome with that play between the successive poles of its realization which is just the method of its growth. Thus a certain unity and lack of assumption is secured to the whole scheme. For example, one might take the fine catalogue of arguments given by Adam Smith at the beginning of his 'Moral Sentiments' and go over them one by one, finding that they all fall together on this view and support a derivation of publicity, where he could only assume it. For he assumes, first, that we sympathize with each other; this he makes his platform. And then he assumes that it is pleasant to both the parties when they are in a state of sympathy. Both positions are true as facts, and true also of animals. But the reason of the facts, lying in the identity of a progressive thought which just by its growth in each, integrates all in social

relationships, this is wanting. Both of these facts further are accounted for in man, by the view that from the first the gathering self-thought grows up by imitative suggestion. For on this view sympathy is a necessary motor attitude flowing from the identical thought of self; and the pleasure of mutual sympathy and coöperation is the pleasure of personal activity which is normally interwoven in a situation understood and appealed to by all the individuals.

2. We may cite the evidence which goes to show that each person does depend upon social stimulation in his personal growth, and does arrive at standards of social judgment and feeling which reflect in the main the standards current in his environment. Here the writings of Leslie Stephen, Höffding, S. Alexander, etc., may be utilized.

3. A farther interesting argument may be drawn from the statement of the same question in reference to ethical publicity, *i. e.*, the evidence which goes to show that genetically social suggestion and social beliefs are intrinsic to morality. This point is mentioned again below where the connection between ethical and social progress is indicated.

4. Finally, then is the evidence from the history of the social life of man, showing the constant ' give and take' between the individual and society which the position now taken would require.

The elaboration of any of these arguments is beyond the range of the present paper. The two last suggested lead us, however, to our final topic, *i. e.*, the consideration of the sort of doctrine of social progress we should have to hold if, as I have claimed, the matter of social organization is thought which has the attribute of publicity springing from its attribution in the mind of the social thinker to a common self, and that the method or type of function in social organization is all the while imitation.

§ 16. It has been intimated already that there are two opposed or contrasted functions in the progress of the thoughts which are socially available, seen respectively in the ' particularizing' done by the individual, and the 'generalizing' done by society. Both of these go on together, and give rise to the conditions which social life in all its complexity presents. We may call the individual then the *particularizing social force*; he invents, constructs, interprets, on the basis of the matter already current in society and administered to him through 'social heredity.' And society, as already organized, may be called the *generalizing social force*; it reduces, generalizes the inventions of the individual by integrating them in the public 'self-thought-situation' now described. The further question then arises: how and in what direction is social progress determined under the interplay of these two types of social force?

We are shut up, I think, to a very definite view of the determination of social progress as soon as we look into the implications of the positions already taken. The positions which immediately concern us now are three: 1. Individuals can particularize only on the basis of earlier generalizations of society. This gives an initial trend to the thought variations which are available for social use.[1] 2. Society in its new acquisitions is absolutely dependent upon the new thoughts, particularizations, of individuals, and it again generalizes them. It can get material from no other source. 3. Only when both these conditions are fulfilled—when old social matter is particularized by an individual and then again generalized by society—can new accretions be made to the social content and progress be secured to the organization as a whole. Looking at these requirements together, and attempting to discover what sort of a general movement will result we find what may be called the 'Dialectic of Social Growth,' an expression which is intended to suggest a contrast with the 'Dialectic of Personal Growth,' already described above.

§ 17. In the dialectic of personal growth we saw the development of self-consciousness proceeding by a two-fold relation of 'give and take' between the individual and his social fellows. Personal material, coming in the shape of suggestions from the environment, is first 'projective' as we called it; then it is taken over into the private circle of the inner life by imitation, and so becomes personal or 'subjective,' as belonging to the *ego;* and

[1] This has been developed in my article on 'The Genius and his Environ ment,' *Pop. Sci. Monthly,* July–August, 1896.

then again by a return movement between the same two poles, also imitative in its nature, the characters of the subject are ejected out into the *alter* personalities, so becoming 'ejective.'

The various stages into which consciousness grows—becoming social, ethical, etc.—by this one method of social give and take cannot be dwelt upon here; but it is interesting to see that this way of growing on the part of the individual consciousness m'ay be stated in terms which reproduce in a very precise analogy the three requirements which we now find it necessary to lay down as characteristic of the growth of society. We may say, (1) that the individual reaches new inventions, interpretations, particularizations, *in his own personal growth* only on the basis of what he already understands of personality; that is of what he has learned. Each step of his progress in understanding personality is a particularization of old material in his own thought, a personal interpretation, subjective in its character. And (2) only those particularizations, interpretations, inventions, thoughts of personality, are permanently available for his growth which he again ejects outward and finds to hold generally of others also; these are generalized as habits and stand as accretions to his growth. This last is also imitative, since only the imitable elements of his subjective thought are thus true and available in his treatment of others. (3) His self-thought-situation, grows only when both these phases are accomplished together.

Here then is personal growth quite accurately stated in the same terms as those which give the outcome of our detailed examination of social progress. I am not willing to leap to metaphysical or even logical conclusions on the basis of this analogy, striking as it seems to be. But we may · at least use it as an analogy, and see the further bearings of it in the matter of the determination of social progress.

Coming to make out the analogy in more detail, we see that society stands in a sense as a *quasi-personality* under a two-fold relation of give and take to the individuals who make up the social group. It is related to these individuals in two ways: first, as having become what it is by the absorption of the thoughts, struggles, sentiments, coöperations, etc., of individuals; and second, as itself finding its new lessons in personal (now social) growth in the new achievements of individuals. If we take any lesson which, society learns—any one thought which it adopts and makes a part of its organized content—we may trace the passage of this thought or element through the two poles of the dialectic of social growth, just as we can also trace the elements of personal suggestion in the case of the simpler dialectic of the individual's growth. The new thought is ' projective' to society as long as it exists in the individual's mind only; it becomes ' subjective' to society when society has generalized it and embodied it in some one of the institutions which are a part of her intimate organization; and then finally society makes it 'ejective' by requiring, by all her pedagogical, civil and religious sanctions, that each individual, class, or subordinate group which claims a share in her corporate life, shall realize it and live up to it.

Society, in other words, makes her peculiarizations, inventions, interpretations, through the individual man, just as the individual makes his through the *alter* individual who gives him his suggestion; and then society makes her generalizations by setting the results thus reached to work again for herself in the form of institutions, etc., just as the individual sets out for social confirmation and for conduct, the interpretations which he has reached. The growth of society is therefore a growth *in a sort of self-consciousness—an awareness of itself*—expressed in the general ways of action, feeling, etc., embodied in its institutions; and the individual gets his growth in self-consciousness in a way which shows by a sort of recapitulation this two-fold movement of society. So the method of growth in the two cases—what has been called the ' dialectic '—is the same.

§ 18. From these indications—which must in all cases be controled by an appeal to fact—we see the direction in which social progress must move. *The individual moves directly toward an ethical goal.* His intellectual sanctions tend, it is true, toward a personal and egoistic use of the forces of society; but that cannot go far, since, in its extreme, it runs counter to the coöperations on the basis of which the dialectic of his personal growth as such must proceed. So with social progress. The

use of intelligence for the private manipulation of social agencies does actually represent a level of social institutional life,
and in certain great departments of human intercourse—as especially the commercial—selfish ends, as seen in personal competition of wits, seems to be as high as society has yet gone.
But as with individual growth so here. As soon as the personal
use of the individual's wit brings him into conflict with either
of these two necessary movements by which society gradually
grows—or with the institutions which represent them—so soon
must the individual be restrained. And, further, the restraint is
no more an artificial thing, an external thing, in society than it
is in the individual. The very growth of intelligence in the individual is itself a generalizing process, and by this generalization, a measure of higher restraint is set on the elements which
enter into the generalization. The growth of intelligence must
itself issue in those ideal states of mind which are called social
and ethical and which set the direction of growth as a whole.
The ethical sanctions come to replace and limit the sphere of
application of the sanctions of desire and impulse; and so the
individual gets, in his private life, a bent toward social co-operation and ethical conduct.

The social or communal growth shows the same tendency
for the reason, altogether apart from analogy, that the actual
conditions in society are the same. Society is, as we have
seen, the generalizing force. It reduces the thoughts which
rise and claim recognition in its midst to forms of general acceptance, and to working shape. The very institution therefore, which embodies the new idea and enforces it upon the
individuals, is itself the work of the individuals, and represents
the restraint of their egoistic and personal sanctions in favor of
social and ethical coöperation.

Further, all the pedagogical sanctions of society, in the
family, the school, etc., are brought directly to bear for the production of those social forms of habit which confirm and en-
courage the development of toleration, forbearance and all the
virtues which are of social value.

There is, however, another and more profound reason that
the direction of social progress must be determined by ethical

and religious sanctions, and toward the goal represented by a state of ideal ethical coöperation. It is to be found in the fact of what was called above the 'publicity' of all ideal thought of personality. We saw that the individual can not be a wicked or a good individual in his own opinion—that is can not get a full ethical judgment on his own acts—without, at the same time, making his thought include the similar judgment passed by his fellow men. His private self-judgment is a judgment based on the sense of a prevalent public judgment. The sense of the opinion of the public is an ingredient or element in the very synthesis by which the ethical judgment is constituted. In so far, therefore, as the growth of his personality involves a general or ideal thought of self, so far is this self a public self whose thought is *ipso facto* the birth of a sanction of a public kind. The man says to himself: "I think thus of myself; other men think thus of me; I think thus of them when they are in my place; and all for the reason that what we each and all judge with reference to, is that ideal self which each of us only partially realizes. I partially realize it in my own way, and each of the others does in his own way; and it is by these partial realizations in concrete instances alone that this ideal gets its actuality."

Now, reflection shows that social growth proceeds by just this same development. Objectively, and in fact, it is seen in the actual publicity of social institutions and interests. But the same result comes out if we take the point of view which we may call subjective to society itself. If we went so far with the analogy from the individual's growth, as to speak of society as a quasi-personality, and asked what thought such a quasi-personality would have to think in order to grow and to go on developing by the method of personal dialectic seen in the individual—we should say that society would have to think in a manner which involves the publicity attaching to ideal and ethical personality. It would have to ask what institutions were good for its citizens as such, not what was good for this particular individual or that. Its thought of personality, all the way through, would be the form of general personality, which is realized in the individuals, of course, but which is not identical with any one of them. And with this thought of general personality, there would go the thought, also, that the thought that it did thus think was the outcome of all the partial personality thoughts which the individuals thought, of all the judgments which they passed on one another; otherwise the social quasi-personality would have no content out of which to constitute its general thought of itself.

All this is simply a realization in the community, in public opinion, of the ethical standards of judgment which the individual must have if he is to develop beyond the stage of concrete egoistic or altruistic intelligence or impulsive action. That the individual does go farther is a fact; and it is just the fact which we call his development. He has attained the form of general thinking about himself and others which carries with it sentiments of a social and ethical kind. This enables him to constitute society in a way which would be impossible if he had only reached the lower development of the animals, say with the sanctions for action which go with this lower development.

So when we come to ask what the direction of social progress must be, we find that it cannot be in a direction which violates the method and denies the meaning of those very states of mind—the ideal, social and ethical states—which have enabled the individual to come into his social relationships. The ethical sanction in the individual comes to control the other sanctions, since it generalizes and so transcends them. Society represents the embodiment of these generalizations. Its institutions both represent and further the individual's growth. Its trend forward, then, must be in the line in which the individual's higher growth also proceeds. This is the trend toward the complete regulation and use of the forces of the individual *by himself* in the interests of social and ethical unity and coöperation.

Two things are accordingly true of the determination of social progress. These two things are these: first, that social progress must be determined by the generalizing agency already remarked upon working upon the thoughts of individuals; and second, that this form of determination is necessarily in the direction of the realization of ethical standards and rules of conduct.

§ 19. Finally our outcome may be gathered up in a sentence of characterization of society as a whole. Society we may say is *the form of natural organization into which ethical personalities fall in their growth.* So also on the side of the individual, we may define ethical personality as *the form of natural development into which individuals grow who live in social relationship.* The true analogy then is not that which likens society to a physiological organism, but rather that which likens it to a *psychological organization;* and the sort of psychological organization to which it is analogous to that which is found in the individual in *ideal thinking.*

SHORTER CONTRIBUTIONS AND DISCUSSIONS.

LE DANTEC'S WORK ON BIOLOGICAL DETERMINISM AND CONSCIOUS PERSONALITY.[1]

The recent work of M. Le Dantec on biological determinism and conscious personality seems to me likely to perform a great service, since it expresses with remarkable precision, if I may say so, the confusion of ideas and words that has been tending to insert itself for some years into philosophical language; as a consequence this book may with advantage serve as occasion for a discussion which has really a more general range.

Let us say at the outset, to put ourselves in touch with M. Le Dantec, that this prolific author has published, within the last two or three years, a number of biological papers on the mechanism of digestion and on theories of life; he has, moreover, conceived a new theory of life, which I have already noticed in this REVIEW. His present volume is a continuation and development of the same ideas; the author endeavors to support two principal propositions: *first*, that the phenomena of consciousness have no sort of influence on material biological phenomena; and *second*, that the atoms and the molecules, not only of organic bodies, but also of inert substances, are endowed with consciousness. We shall not take up these two propositions directly, but shall discuss them as we trace the course of false ideas which the author has followed, in common with many of his contemporaries.

I wish to show, as briefly as possible, that five or six radically distinct notions have been completely confounded, and that this unfortunate confusion owes its origin to an inexact interpretation of the idea of freedom and of its contrary, determinism. Men have implicitly assumed—and that generally without being aware of the fact—that this notion of determinism is logically linked to certain other notions, and forms one with them. I shall endeavor to show the contrary, by defining anew the notions of determinism, mechanism, physiological functions, mental functions, spontaneity, and choice.

[1] Translated from the author's MS. by Professor H. C. Warren.

1. *Determinism.* — Determinism, in the very broad meaning which it received from Claude Bernard, expresses the law of universal causation; it means that there is no phenomenon without a cause, that the succession of phenomena is regular and determinate; in still other terms, it is the negative of freedom, contingency, and incoherence. Most scientists to-day admit the determinism of phenomena of the physical order; as to psychological determinism—the position opposed to that of free-will—it is accepted by some and rejected by others; the two chief arguments that are urged in opposition to it are that it compromises moral responsibility and contradicts the inner sense which every one possesses of his own free-will. I am not debating any theory now, consequently I need not take either side. To sum up, there exist two forms of determinism, *physical determinism* and *psychological determinism;* against the first is urged the doctrine of the *contingency* of the laws of nature, and against the second the doctrine of *free-will.*

2. *Mechanism.*—This is a concept radically distinct from the preceding; it is one of those which have been expressed in the greatest number of different terms, and which have consequently suffered most from equivocality. Let us, first of all, define the concept itself. In man the acts of thought, voluntary movements, etc., are of a twofold nature; they are at once physiological phenomena, occurring in the nervous system, and phenomena of consciousness. Many philosophers have supported the idea that the phenomenon of consciousness is an epiphenomenon—something superadded, which does not intervene in the series of physiological modifications, but whose rôle is that of a passive witness. Huxley was one of the most strenuous partisans of this theory, which he expressed in several striking figures; he compares consciousness to the shadow which follows the footsteps of the traveler without affecting his progress; or to light, which may illumine the wheels of a machine without exercising the slightest influence upon its functions. In France, Ribot for some time accepted this conception and popularized it; but he afterwards rejected it.

There are, indeed, some points of contact between determinism and mechanism; nevertheless these two concepts are quite distinct. One may be a determinist, for instance, without being a mechanist; one may admit that all phenomena are subject to the law of causation, and at the same time admit that the phenomena of consciousness play an active rôle, are influenced by physical phenomena, and influence them in turn; this is the *theory of the mutual influence of the physical and the moral,* a theory which is just the opposite of mechanism.

Some authors have been either unwilling or unable to make the distinction which we point out; confusing the two concepts together, they have maintained that consciousness is a useless attribute of living matter, because, if it were otherwise and consciousness could have any influence whatever on the succession of phenomena, this would be a denial of the law of causation. An example of this is met with in Le Dantec's book, when he maintains that " everything would come to pass just the same in the world if plastic substances possessed simply their physical and chemical properties, to the exclusion of the property of consciousness "—the mechanistic theory; he seems to have been led to this theory by the deterministic theory, which he expresses as follows: " Plastic substances, like all other inert substances, are subject to the law of inertia." We will not say that this author has confused these two concepts; but if he has distinguished them he has yet established between them a bond of solidarity which he supposes to hold of itself and which he does not justify in any other way.

One word more: the theory which we call *mechanism* has been most often designated by the name of automatism. I have not used this word, and indeed I am taking care to banish it from this article, since it is a word equivocal to the last degree. It has been given, as Morgan has recently shown, five or six entirely different meanings; men have called automatic an habitual act, a non-reflexive act, an act which is unaccompanied by consciousness, an act which is conscious but necessary and determined, etc. One can never be sure of himself in using it.

3. *Physiological function:* another notion which has become singularly obscure. Let us recall first some simple facts. We do not yet know the inner nature of the material phenomena which occur in a nerve center, in its cells and its nerves, when that center becomes active; it has nevertheless been held that many of the material modifications which occur there are chemical reactions; thus for a long time it has been maintained that vision has for its starting point a photo-chemical action in the retina, and quite recently Frey has gone so far as to suppose that the simple stimulation of the tactile papillæ is propagated by means of a chemical reaction which the contact sets up in the papilla or in the neighboring cells. However this may be, there still remains an essential difference between a chemical reaction set up in a test-tube and a physiological process properly so called; the latter is composed of a series, a chain of reactions, which mutually command and influence one another—which, in a word, are *organized*. Now this notion, so simple and natural, of the physiological

process, has been greatly obscured of late; some authors have rejected it, thinking that it involved a denial of physical determinism.

It is in connection with the life and relations of micro-organisms that this confusion has come about. Here is a little infusorian swimming in a drop of water under the microscope; it goes, comes, turns about, stops beside the nutritive particles suspended in the liquid, then starts off again, changes its direction, stops, etc. Men sought to explain the movements of this little creature; it was observed that these movements are, to a certain extent, under the voluntary control of the experimenter who watches them through the microscope; he is able, by means of appropriate stimuli, such as light, the electric current and certain chemical substances, to excite the same movements, known in advance and possible to foresee as a whole, in these micro-organisms. What do these ingenious experiments of Verworn, Pfeffer and others prove? Certainly that the movements of these creatures are *determined.* But it does not follow from this that they are simply chemical reactions. Men have wrongly believed that in order to express their determinateness it was necessary to assimilate them to chemical reactions; and then, under the pen of certain scientists, the strangest analogies have been evolved: Le Dantec (*Théorie nouvelle de la Vie,* p. 32) goes so far as to compare the infusorian in movement to a piece of potassium turning about in the water which it decomposes, and pushed mechanically by a stream of hydrogen and oxygen. This extraordinary comparison is only justified by the desire to prove that nothing is left to chance in the movement of these little creatures, and that all their movements are explicable by physical causes—the deterministic position. But the deterministic position in no wise implies the conclusion that the movements in question are not physiological reactions.

Another very curious example. We know that the living bacteria contained in a preparation mass themselves at the points where a release of oxygen is taking place; the same is true of the leucocytes in the blood. Some years ago, wishing to express the constancy and necessity of the movement of bacteria towards oxygen, an eminent physiologist explained these characteristics by a chemical attraction operating between the body of the bacteria and the molecules of oxygen. This was evidently nothing but a lapse into polemics!

4. *Spontaneity.*—The notion of spontaneity is very important both in psychology and in physiology. It is contrasted with that of a stimulated or a reflex act. A reflex act is one which follows directly upon external stimulation; it is the response, or echo to it; it would

not have been produced if this external stimulation had not taken place. A spontaneous act is one which does not directly respond to external irritation; it is produced by a memory, an act of reasoning, or an internal physiological cause, as for example the circulation of the blood. From every standpoint, not only from that of science, but also from that of practice and even of law, there is the greatest interest in distinguishing between spontaneous acts and stimulated acts; the former are in general more reflective; they are more personal to their author; they carry a greater juridical and moral responsibility. This is, therefore, a useful distinction and one which should be preserved. Many authors have sought to abolish it and to condemn the use of the term *spontaneity* as being unscientific. Why? It is easy to guess. These authors have misunderstood the meaning of the word *spontaneous*; they imagine that spontaneity means first cause, the absence of determination, and that it is a synonym for *freedom*.

5. *Choice.*—This word is probably the one that has occasioned the greatest amount of equivocation. It seemed as if the faculty of choosing implied free-will, and that if this faculty were accorded to any animalcule he was thereby removed from the influences of environment, and all determinism was suppressed. The responsibility for this confusion of ideas certainly rests upon the philosophers; it is they who, in the discussion of the free-will position, have represented choice as a demonstration of that position. A falling stone does not choose, it has been said, because its fall is determined by the laws of gravitation, whereas a thinking being can choose between several different courses; this is proof of his possessing a free|will. We need not enter into this discussion. Our aim is to show that apart from every theory, laying aside that of free-will and even admitting a determinism that is universal and without exception, it is possible to give a specific meaning to the word *choice.* We may again take an example from among the micro-organisms. It has been asked whether certain species of infusoria do not exercise choice in the matter of their nutrition. There are infusorian hunters, who traverse the waters of pools with their mouths open and their cilia always in motion, and who swallow all the particles suspended in the water, drawing them towards their mouth by the current which they produce with their peristome. These creatures, then, do not exercise choice at all; provided the particle be of a suitable size it is mechanically introduced into the mouth; it reaches the plasm of the body, and there it is either assimilated or rejected, according to its nature. The problem is to discover whether other infusoria do not choose their food before swallow-

ing, that is, whether the stimulation produced by the food does not, by a reflex route, excite a movement of prehension or rejection according to the nature of the food. Observation alone can give an answer to this problem. Whichever way it be resolved, it has at least been possible to propose it, and it has been proposed without any question of free-will; for choice, thus understood, is composed of a series of regular and rigorously determined reflexes.

6. *Psychic functions.* It is here that the greatest errors have accumulated—as it were, by choice! To a number of our contemporaries, little versed in psychology—which fact does not prevent them from constructing wretched psychology without knowing it—the phenomena of consciousness present a sort of phantasy, or phantasmagoria without cause and without law. We need not reply that a phenomenon of consciousness appears to us to be as rigorously determined, in its production, its quality and its minutest details, as the fall of a stone or the budding of a plant; but it is useless to stop over this point, since these are errors which it is only necessary to clearly set forth in order to refute with the same stroke. Let us follow out the effects of this preconceived idea on the interpretation of phenomena. The question comes up again in the interpretation of the movements and acts performed by micro-organisms. Some authors wishing to endow micro-organisms with psychic properties—a disputable point, be it understood, on which only hypothesis can be made—the principal objection raised against this interpretation consists in a naïve declaration that this would mean the suppression of fixed laws. " Here is a bacterium," says Le Dantec, "which starts off for a region of the infusion where he will find a substance which *pleases him*(!) I direct a ray of blue light upon him from another side, and he is compelled to change his route. But, it will be said, this is because he likes the light better than the food. Then I coax him in another direction by means of an attractive substance which is, however, noxious to him; he rushes up to it and dies from its effects; is this because I annoy him to such an extent that he commits suicide?"

This ironical method of reasoning is not peculiar to the author whom we cite; it may be considered as a very fair sample of the arguments of a certain number of physiologists. As regards M. Le Dantec himself, it is only necessary to notice this rather unexpected fact, that although he refuses to the infusorian, in the preceding passage, the faculty of being *pleased* with a substance, he, nevertheless, does not hesitate to accord consciousness to atoms of iron and chlorine. [1]

[1] *Vide* some savory lines on the *azotic consciousness* and the *atomic* consciousness, as opposed to the *molecular* consciousness, p. 84.

But there is no need of stopping over the question whether infusoria possess any rudiments of consciousness and sensibility; in the present article I do not propose to interpret observations or to fight for a theory. I limit myself to a criticism of ideas, and from this standpoint I find that the principal objection advanced against those who wish to allow psychical faculties to the protozoa is that such psychical faculties would be the expression of arbitrariness and phantasy, that they would be incompatible with the idea that "every operation performed by a protozoan depends solely on the conditions of environment and being under determinate conditions is itself determinate."

In a word, to place well in relief the matrix-idea of all the contradictions which have been noted, we may say that there exists, even among the best minds, a tendency to admit that determinism applies less vigorously to living matter than to inert matter, to the facts of consciousness than to the facts of physics, to complex phenomena than to simple phenomena.

ALFRED BINET.

SORBONNE, PARIS.

A NEW FACTOR IN WEBER'S LAW.

Does Weber's law depend upon the real or upon the apparent stimulus? It has always been assumed that it depends upon the so-called real physical stimulus. The measurements of some illusions[1] led me to question this and investigate whether it depends upon the apparent stimulus, and if so, according to what law.

To illustrate the theory I will state its application to the results of a series of experiments made for the purpose of testing this matter in the illusion of weight, which is due to the difference in size of bodies that have the same weight. (For details in regard to the measurements of this illusion, see article cited, pp. 1–29.) The apparatus consisted of three pairs of cylinders—A, B and C—each of the same weight, 80 g.; the same diameter, 37 mm.; and varying in height, A being 20 mm., B, 120 mm., and C, 50 mm. With these I measured (1) the threshold, or least perceptible difference, and (2) the amount of illusion in A and B respectively when measured by C as standard.

Representing the threshold value by Δ, the results are (1) $\Delta A = 2.8$ g., $\Delta B = 4.0$ g., $\Delta C = 3.3$ g.; and (2) the illusion in A as measured by C (K), is an overestimation of 15.8 g., and the illusion in

[1] *Stud. Yale Psych. Lab.*, 1895, III., 1–67.

B as measured by *C* (*K'*) is an underestimation of 12.1 g. These figures are averages of two complete measurements on each of twenty students of psychology who were aware of the facts and conditions of the illusion.

The constant multiples which would express Weber's law with reference to the standard, physical stimulus, 80 g., are here

$$\Delta A = \tfrac{1}{26}, \qquad\qquad \Delta B = \tfrac{1}{20}, \qquad\qquad \Delta C = \tfrac{1}{24}.$$

Now, all overestimation lowers the threshold and all underestimation raises it, and we notice, in the results, the following relations between the thresholds and the illusions:

$$\frac{\Delta A}{\Delta C} = \frac{C-K}{C}$$

$$\text{and } \frac{\Delta B}{\Delta C} = \frac{C+K'}{C}$$

The actual results are: for $\dfrac{\Delta A}{\Delta C}$, 0.85; for $\dfrac{C-K}{C}$, 0.80; for $\dfrac{\Delta B}{\Delta C}$, 1.21; for $\dfrac{C+K'}{C}$, 1.15. The errors involved by substituting the empirical values in the formulas are 5 % in the first and 6 % in the second. These lie well within the mean errors of observation which are: for ΔA, 43 %; for ΔB, 38 %; for ΔC, 48 %; for K, 30 %; and for K', 41 %. Therefore, within the limits here investigated, Weber's law depends upon the apparent weight and not upon the physical standard. And, since there appears to be a definite relation between the illusion and the threshold, if the one is given the other may be calculated; for, applying the same results to the following formulas:

$$\frac{\Delta A}{C-K} = \tfrac{1}{28};$$

$$\frac{\Delta B}{C+K'} = \tfrac{1}{28};$$

$$\text{and } \frac{\Delta C}{C} = \tfrac{1}{24};$$

we obtain a constant, in this case practically $\tfrac{1}{28}$. Hence we may state the principle for the dependence of Weber's law upon the apparent stimulus in estimation of weight, as

$$\frac{\Delta E}{S+K} = C$$

where ΔE is the threshold, S the standard weight, K the amount of the illusion (K will be plus or minus according as the illusion is an under or over estimation), and C a constant fraction. Hence the illusion may be used as an index to the threshold, and likewise the reverse.

Nearly all estimates of weight involve illusions, and it is probable that the above formula holds for all degrees of illusion of weight within the limits in which Weber's law is valid. It further follows from this theory that we shall find a more exact and more extensive validity for Weber's law when this fraction is taken into consideration, for most of the experiments on Weber's law have involved illusions like the one here discussed, but they have not been taken into account except by attempts to eliminate them. And, since Weber's law is a general law of all liminal sensations, we may assume, upon the basis of these experiments, that in whatever sense it has any validity it must be with reference to the apparent stimulus. A full account of these experiments will appear in *Stud. Yale Psych. Lab.*, Volume IV.

C. E. SEASHORE.

YALE UNIVERSITY.

NOTE ON THE RAPIDITY OF DREAMS.

Does association attain in dreams an altogether exceptional rapidity? Common opinion answers, yes, and appeals, for scientific support, to the records of such remarkable dreams as that of 'Maury guillotiné.' M. Victor Egger, however, in the *Revue Philosophique* for July, 1895 (40–46), subjects the evidence to searching criticism, and opposes the common opinion. He also hints at a method for investigating the question experimentally. Following this suggestion, though somewhat altering the method, I have obtained definite evidence for M. Egger's position and against the common belief.

The method is simply this: to time trains of association during normal waking conditions, count the number of scenes in such trains, and, when they are recollections, recall the time taken by the original experiences. The procedure is so simple as hardly to need description. The subject was told to begin at a signal and let his thoughts reel off as fast as they would. Sometimes he was stopped after 5 or 20 or 30 seconds, and sometimes allowed to keep on until he felt the thoughts come slowly. Immediately, he reviewed the images which had just passed through his mind, and made a mark, on a piece of paper, for each image. The 'images,' not always visual,

were required to have such a degree of separateness from the preceding and following as to be counted as separate stages of the associative
process. After making this count the subject generally went on to
record his reverie in detail.

The conditions of the experiment approximate closely to those of
a dream recalled on waking. The main difference is that in the
experiment the flow of imagination is less spontaneous, and probably,
therefore, somewhat slower than in either a dream or a perfectly spontaneous reverie.

For the purpose in hand there is no need of averages or of a large
number of experiments. It is sufficient to find, without looking far,
frequent instances of associations rapid enough to duplicate the
wonders of the famous dreams. Of the ten students on whom I experimented, one, a rather heavy, deliberate sort of man, required
about three seconds for an image. Few, however, required more
than half that time, and when the train of imagination was but five
seconds long the time required for an image sank as low as .6, .3 or
.25 seconds. Now Maury's dream, as recorded, contained not more
than 16 images, and these closely grouped into four scenes. So
much may easily be imagined by a man awake, in 3 or 4 seconds; and
Maury's dream may have taken as much time as that.

To the objection that in dreams we certainly do live over again
long series of events in a very short time, I would reply that, except
for the illusion of reality in dreams, the same thing occurs in waking
reveries. My slowest subject reviewed, in 110 seconds, a trip which
occupied 2½ days, recalling 35 distinct and complete scenes. Another
reviewed, in 37.5 seconds, a drive of three hours, recalling 19 images.
Another reviewed very thoroughly a two-weeks' canoe trip, in 82
seconds, by means of 72 images. Another reviewed, in 29.5 seconds,
two trips among the mountains, one occupying 4 hours, the other 20
hours. This last recollection was described as extremely full and
vivid, and as comprising, around each of the 45 images, "many others
of varying intensity which seem to be simultaneous." This same subject recalled, in 5 seconds, 20 images from an evening out. Still
another saw, in 5 seconds, a 9-scene panorama of a trip from Boston to
Detroit. Add to any of these the illusion present in a dream, and you
have all that is necessary for 'living over again,' in a few moments,
large segments of past experience.

I will transcribe the record of one of these experiments.

I started by looking at my table cover. Some round spots on this
made me think of flecks of foam on the sea; that called up a marine

painting which I had recently seen; next I had before me in rapid succession three scenes from a rowing trip taken last summer, five scenes from a bicycle ride on the adjacent shore, and three scenes from the railroad journey thence to Boston. That reminded me of a friend whom I met on the train; and next I saw myself leaving the Boston station, loaded down with baggage, and accompanied by my friend. Soon we separated, I taking one of his cards. I then thought of some visiting cards which I had ordered and expected by mail, then of a check I had just received, of going off and spending this money, of going to Europe, of climbing the Alps. Next I seemed to be swimming across the ocean; in the middle I met a good-sized codfish, which sported with me, and finally proceeded to swallow me. I passed right through the fish's body, coming out at the tip of his tail. Grabbing him by the tail, I swung him around in the air and slapped him against the water. Flames now rose around me, generating a gas which wafted me high into the sky; there I flopped over a few times and then, diving back into the water, penetrated deeper and deeper, straight through the earth, till I emerged in the Chinese sea. There on the grassy shore stood a row of gaily dressed Chinamen, who began a lively dance, but soon changed to a row of Chinese lanterns, bobbing in the wind.

At this point I consulted my watch, and found that the whole had taken 56 seconds. As there are but 39 images, the series is not nearly so rapid as some of those of my other subjects. Add the illusion of objective reality, and we have here the conditions of a dream of 'marvellous rapidity.' "Last night," the dreamer would report, "I had a dream in which, besides minor incidents, I took a four-hours' row, a three-hours' ride, a five-hours' journey by rail, a voyage abroad and tramp among the Alps, a swim half-way across the ocean, a flying trip to heaven and a diving trip in the other direction, ending on the shores of China." And all this in 56 seconds!

R. S. WOODWORTH.

HARVARD UNIVERSITY.

PSYCHOLOGICAL LITERATURE.

The Will to Believe and other Essays in Popular Philosophy.
WILLIAM JAMES. Longmans, Green & Co., 1897. Pp. xiv +
33².

In this volume Professor James has collected a number of discussions in 'popular philosophy,' which for the most part were first delivered as addresses before various associations and clubs, and then published in the Reviews. The title essay on 'The Will to Believe' and the second, 'Is Life Worth Living?' are the latest and, perhaps, the best known papers in the collection; but the reader will be grateful as well for the earlier pieces which are here included and will welcome the whole to a permanent place in his library.

Besides the two essays mentioned, the third on 'The Sentiment of Rationality,' and the fourth, 'Reflex Action and Theism,' are "largely concerned in defending the legitimacy of religious faith." The next four, 'The Dilemma of Determinism,' 'The Moral Philosopher and the Moral Life,' 'Great Men and their Environment' and 'The Influence of Individuals,' deal with questions of ethics and social progress. The ninth paper, 'On Some Hegelisms,' furnishes a sharp critique of certain of the Hegelian assumptions and certain features of the 'master's' method; while the last, 'What Psychical Research has Accomplished,' gives the author's well-known views on the subject in the hope of arousing interest in the field and aid for the work.

From the psychological standpoint the chief interest of these essays is to be found in the emphasis which is laid on the emotional and volitional elements in consciousness. It is probable that many readers will dissent from the conclusions reached concerning the legitimacy of the influence of the will on faith; but few will deny the accuracy of the psychological analysis, while it is time that all should recognize the deeper psychological principle involved, the principle of the interplay of the several phases of consciousness in the genesis of the various mental phenomena. How strange the 'psychologies' of the recent past, not to speak of contemporary works, will appear to the psychologists of the future! Not only the intellectualistic theories, but our analyses of consciousness as a class, will seem often to have

ignored the interconnections of the several kinds of conscious processes, or at best to have failed to supply an adequate account of them
though convinced of the truth of the principle of connection in general.

But the psychology of the question is merely incidental to the
purpose of the book under discussion. The author's philosophical
position is described in the preface (pp. VII ff.) as 'radical empiricism,' "'empiricism,' because it is contented to regard its most assured conclusions concerning matters of fact as hypotheses," and
"'radical,' because it treats the doctrine of monism itself as an hypothesis" and assumes in contrast the pluralistic view of the world.   On
this platform Professor James advocates as a general thesis that "our
passional nature not only lawfully may, but must, decide an option
between propositions, whenever it is a genuine option that can not by
its nature be decided on intellectual grounds; for to say, under such
circumstances, 'do not decide, but leave the question open,' is itself a
passional decision—just like the deciding yes or no—and is attended
with the same risk of losing the truth" (p. 11); and, in special,
argues the legitimacy of the religious and ethical view of the world,
that is to say, of the belief in a moral order, in the freedom and responsibility of man and in the existence of God.   Thus we get a
philosophy of belief which, though it guards against the vagaries of
unrestrained credulity (pp. x ff., 29 ff.), affirms at once the need of
faith and the legitimacy of its exercise, even when intellectual demonstration is unattained or unattainable.

In spite of the originality, one might almost say, the personality,
of Professor James's reasonings, the reader of recent apologetic literature will be reminded of a certain tendency toward similar conclusions
on the part of many thinkers, indeed of a certain similar tendency
noticeable in the spirit of the time.   And if he compare with the
present age those critical eras in the history of opinion with which it
is unquestionably to be classed, he will remember analogous developments in many periods when, received systems having been brought
into question or discarded, appeal has been taken from the impotent
conclusions of the reason to the deliverances of the heart and con-
science.   The issue, however, in recent times has become of broader
scope.   It is not merely the question of personal faith, momentous
though this be; or merely the legitimacy of the appeal to the heart
when the head has been brought into confusion, though, for one, the
reviewer is disposed to admit this, at least in part.   But modern philosophy, like modern psychology, despite its lapses from grace, has been

nearing the point at which overweening intellectualism begins to yield
before the perception of the truth, that practical principles as well as
theoretical are to be considered in the determination of fundamental
questions. The primacy of the practical reason, it is true, was succeeded by a tremendous assertion of the omnipotence of the abstract
reason. Nevertheless, it is becoming clear that we shall hardly escape from the chaos in which the downfall of the *a priori* systems
left us until some more inclusive synthesis than they shall be proposed,
the better to satisfy both intellectual and practical needs.

Thus the questions suggested by Professor James's work involve
more than a defense of faith. They lead into the heart of the problems immediately in the path of contemporary thought. In order to
meet them the philosophy of the near future will need to summon all
its forces. Thinkers acquainted with the present volume will eagerly
look for the more systematic treatise on empiricism of which the distinguished author gives us a partial promise (p. x.).

A. C. ARMSTRONG, JR.

WESLEYAN UNIVERSITY.

The Theory of Knowledge. L. T. HOBHOUSE. London, Methuen
& Co.; New York, The Macmillan Co., 1896. 8vo, pp. 626.

The division of the several sciences is a matter of convenience,
and one should, perhaps, not insist that an author must confine himself
in a given volume to one field and avoid all trespass upon those contiguous to it; but I cannot but think it is conducive to clearness to observe
certain limits with a good deal of care. Mr. Hobhouse describes his
book in a sub-title as a contribution to some problems of logic and
metaphysics, and in his pages the two disciplines do interpenetrate
one another. Three-fourths of his book is chiefly logical and the remaining fourth almost wholly metaphysical, or, as I should prefer to
call it, epistemological.

Logic, as the science of proof, can be successfully treated without
leaving the plain of the common understanding and entering into
those problems of reflective thought which we commonly regard as
strictly philosophical. Apprehension, construction and the processes
of inductive and deductive reasoning can be so treated (and Mr. Hobhouse often does so treat them) as to be clear to one who has not occupied himself with metaphysics, cares little to attack the question in
what sense the external world may be regarded as external, and never
raises at all the question of the validity of all knowledge or of the

nature of ultimate reality. To be sure, logical methods must obtain in treating all these problems, but they are problems which belong, I think, to a distinct and different science, to epistemology, as I should elect to use the term, and not to the science of logic. Had Mr. Hobhouse observed this distinction, I think he would have been in some places clearer than he is, and would have avoided a certain amount of polemic which appears to me not always immediately related to the matter chiefly at issue, though it is in itself interesting and acute. He would, moreover, possibly have been led to treat at greater length in a separate volume the subjects discussed at the end of this one, and such a treatise from his pen I should regard as valuable. However, he has, as it is, given us a very interesting and suggestive book, and we must not quarrel with him for rendering the meaning of the phrase ' Theory of Knowledge' so inclusive. He has sufficient precedent for extending the boundaries of the science of logic.

In his preface Mr. Hobhouse announces it as his intention to make an unprejudiced attempt to fuse what is true and valuable in the older English tradition with the newer doctrines which have become naturalized in England. One feels, however, that he is really much more in sympathy with Mill and Spencer than he is with Hegel, and one cannot help thinking that he owes most of his best work to an inspiration obtained from English sources. I regret that he has devoted so much attention to Mr. Bradley, who does not appear to me to be the most logical of writers on logic, and he has certainly not gotten his own careful and consistent habit of reasoning from this source. He cites Mr. Bradley, it is true, chiefly to disagree with him, but he still feels that he owes him much. It is clear that he differs from him widely in his conclusions.

The book is divided into three parts, as follows: (1) Data; including chapters on apprehension, memory, construction, ideas, resemblance and identity, and judgment and its validity. (2) Inference; containing a careful and detailed exposition of the methods of inductive and deductive reasoning, with an excellent chapter on explanation. (3) Knowledge; in which are discussed the nature of validity, the conception of external reality, substance, the notion of self, knowledge and reality, etc.

It is impossible in a brief review of so extended and comprehensive a work to point out in detail excellencies or to take exception to what appear defects. I should be inclined to find the latter not so much in the properly logical parts of the book as in the psychological and epistemological positions taken by the author; *e. g.*, in his view of our direct perception of space by sight and touch; in his putting the visual and the tangible object in the *same* place, with no further analysis of the significance of the phrase; in his distinction between consciousness as a mental activity and the content with which this activity concerns itself; in his argument to prove phenomena independent of perception and existent when not perceived—an argument which does not recognize the double sense of the word 'exist' touched upon by Berkeley and emphasized by Mill; and in his endeavor to prove, in his discussion of the conception of teleology, that a thing not yet existent but which will exist may be a determining cause of an action, whereas an action performed in view of an end which, for some reason, will not be attained cannot be regarded as determined by that end.

One of the chief excellencies of the book lies in the fact that the author is careful and consistent in his statements, a virtue not always found in philosophical writers. Evidently the work is the result of much conscientious labor, and its author has that most valuable possession, a clear mind. I feel well repaid for a careful perusal of the volume, which I shall read again with equal pleasure. In these days of much dogmatism regarding the *a priori* element in knowledge, it is a pleasure to meet with a thorough-going empiricist, who endeavors to keep his feet upon solid ground in all his reasonings, and who yet has a sympathetic comprehension of the works of those with whom he disagrees. Mr. Hobhouse refuses to accept the Neo-Kantian divorce of thought from sensation, with its subsequent illogical reconciliation, but finds, in the 'given' of apprehension, both form and content, maintaining that space, time and relations of various sorts are not the creation of thought, but are perceived by the mind, in the reality apprehended, as among its aspects or elements. Even the axioms of inference themselves he traces to a source in the 'given.' He finds them implicit in all good reasoning, and holds that they prove themselves valid in the only way in which they can conceivably be proved valid, *i. e.*, in satisfactorily reducing the whole mass of facts given to us in apprehension to a consistent and orderly system. They are proved valid, as all judgments are proved valid, by their harmony with the whole body of knowledge. One need not agree with the author in every detail, to have a strong sympathy with his general attitude upon this and other topics.

G. S. F.

Geschichte des Unendlichkeitsproblems im abendländischen Denken bis Kant. JONAS COHN. Leipzig, 1896. Pp. 261.

Dr. Cohn has given us a history of the problem of the infinite characterized by German thoroughness. From Anaximander to the Neo-Platonists, from Origen to the later scholastics, from Cusanus and Copernicus to Kant, the deliverances of the greater and of many of the lesser lights in the history of speculative thought are recorded and examined. The author has reserved for a later work a theoretic discussion of the problem, clearing the way in the present volume for such a discussion. It would, however, be impossible to make the history of any problem more than a dry catalogue of opinions, without analyzing and criticizing the various positions which have been taken with regard to it; and it is not difficult to guess from Dr. Cohn's criticisms what will be the general nature of his own discussion. He will stand as champion of the notion of the continuous; he will hold to the infinite divisibility of finite spaces and times, sympathizing, however, with the Aristotelian distinction between the infinitely divisible and the infinitely divided; and he will not believe that it is impossible for a point to move from one end to the other of a finite, infinitely divisible line, without coming to the end of an endless number of positions. In other words he will think that Aristotle has answered Zeno, and that Newton has better indicated the true nature of the infinitely little than has Leibnitz, at least in his popular utterances. What he will present will be in harmony with, I will not say the mathematical thought of our day, but rather the thought of the mathematician of our day, when he occupies himself with the discussion of this problem. His book will be interesting and suggestive, I am sure, for his knowledge of what others have written is wide, and his criticisms are acute.

Nevertheless, I cannot think that Dr. Cohn will give a clear and consistent solution of the problem under discussion unless he has—to use an American metaphor not wholly unintelligible to Europeans—some card up his sleeve better than those which appear to be in his hand. He will not be misled by mere verbal ambiguities into irrelevant discussions. He clearly recognizes in the present volume the several senses in which the word infinite has been used, and, to give an·example, he is not captivated by the glitter of timeless eternity. He sees clearly the true point at issue in any discussion of the infinite extent or of the infinite divisibility of space or time, but it does not appear to me that he is able satisfactorily to meet it. Let us consider for a moment the infinitely little.

The Zenonic argument to prove motion over a given finite distance impossible, on the supposition that the space to be moved through is infinitely divisible, cannot be refuted by bringing in the notion of the continuous. If a line is really infinitely divisible, a point moving along it must assume a really infinite number of positions, and must assume them successively. If the word 'infinite' really means 'endless,' the series of positions can really have no end. One faces here a flat contradiction, one which has been pointed out with much clearness by a number of thinkers quoted by Dr. Cohn, and one which has never yet been removed by those who wish to believe the line infinitely divisible.

It is no solution of the difficulty to say that the line contains potentially an infinite number of positions, but *in actu* it does not. The point actually has passed over the line, therefore, it actually has completed an endless series. Nor can we avoid the difficulty by distinguishing between what is actually true of the line itself, and what is true only of our thought about it; in other words, by saying that we may proceed in our division of a line as far as we please, and there are always new parts to distinguish, new positions to mark. For when we call a line infinitely divisible we mean, not merely that it is practically, but rather that it is theoretically, impossible to exhaust its divisions, *i. e.*, that its divisions are really infinite. It will not do to introduce without a previous examination of its content the conception of continuous motion, or if you assume all motion to be continuous, simply the conception of motion. This conception itself needs investigation. What is meant by the continuous? Have we merely cloaked our unwelcome contradiction by transferring it to this, or have we done away with it? Are we not guilty of a *petitio principii* in assuming motion to be (theoretically) possible, when this possibility is the very question at issue?

However the matter be viewed, the difficulty remains. Either the line is infinitely divisible or it is not. If it is not, continued division results (theoretically) in simple parts, and motion means a passage from part to part. If the line is infinitely divisible, a point in traversing it must take successively an endless series of positions. It must completely exhaust this series, which is, by hypothesis, inexhaustible. The moving point becomes a living contradiction, an intellectual monster.

The real solution of the problem lies, I think, in following out the suggestion of certain writers, of whose contributions to the literature of the subject Dr. Cohn speaks with some disparagement—Berkeley and Hume.   Far be it from me to defend all that these philosophers have said on the subject of mathematics.   But the suggestion that any finite line, though not infinitely divisible in itself, may be regarded as such in virtue of its proxies, appears to be fruitful.

I see a short line on the paper before me.   It is a certain distance from my eyes.   Division of it, carried to a certain point, results in the (apparently) non-extended.   If the paper be moved nearer to my eyes the (apparently) non-extended element is seen to be extended.   In other words, it is *replaced* by something which is evidently extended and divisible.   A similar substitution may be effected by the use of a microscope, and there appears to be no theoretical limit to the possibility of such substitutions.   Common usage justifies me in calling what I now see the *same* thing I saw before.   It is the same in one of the numerous senses in which the word is used.   I have substituted for a given experience another experience connected with it in a certain definite way in the order of nature, and I have abundant reason to believe that any system of mathematical relations legitimately derived from the latter may safely be carried over to all possible experiences connected with the former.   Such substitutions one makes instinctively, and a man may easily suppose he is still occupied with the apparently non-extended point with which he started, when he is dividing and subdividing its representative.   Provided his mode of procedure is good, it matters little whether he is clearly conscious of all the elements which enter into the process or not.   Similarly, it matters little whether the mathematician can tell us what he means by his infinitesimals or not, provided he uses his formulæ in such a way as to give fruitful results.

The above solution of the problem appears to me to make possible the acceptance of those things Dr. Cohn seems most anxious to retain —the notion of continuity and the idea of a potential infinite divisibility.   And it makes it possible to hold to them without falling into the Zenonic contradiction of a completed infinite.   It makes the mathematical point, line, and surface rather formulæ than individual things *sensualistisch genommen*.   I do not think that, properly worked out, it contains anything incompatible with a proper use of the infinitesimal calculus.

It is, of course, somewhat rash to guess, on the basis of one book, what the author will incorporate in a second.   Perhaps I have wrongly interpreted Dr. Cohn's position.   It would be wise for the reader to peruse for himself the ' History of the Problem of Infinity,' and I hope very much that my review may induce some to do so.

Most Americans are not so situated that they have access to many of the volumes from which our author gives citations. He has done us service in bringing this material together in convenient form.

G. S. F.

University of Pennsylvania.

The Logical Copula and Quantification of the Predicate. Edward Adamson. London, David Nutt, 1897. Pp. 51.

The author of this brief essay draws attention to the fact that the Copula must be regarded in compliance with the law of identity as indicating the identical existence of subject and predicate, and that in comprehension, the copula signifies internal existence reflectively, subjective existence, identical existence with *all* the attributes implied in the predicate. In extension, on the other hand, the copula signifies objective existence, distributive existence in several individuals united together and reduced to unity by the possession of one or more identical concepts or attributes, consequently it also signifies identical existence with a *part* only of the attributes implied in the predicate. This distinction the author makes as the ground for the difference in quantification according as the view is shifted from comprehension to that of extension. The essay is suggestive, but would be more satisfactory were the discussion somewhat fuller.

John Grier Hibben.

Princeton University.

Proceedings of the Society for Psychical Research, March, 1897. Appendix to Part XXXI., Vol. XII. Address by the President, William Crookes.

The address of Mr. Crookes contains much of interest. It is an attempt to disprove the *a priori* improbability of telepathic and kindred phenomena. He shows by analogy the possibility of there existing certain occult forces which may account for all such mysterious manifestations; for instance, he imagines a homunculus living in a corner of our world, indefinitely small, and endowed with microscopic vision; to such an one the laws of gravitation and other physical laws would seem to be violated again and again. So also, to a person of gigantic frame and organism, other laws and other conceptions of matter would necessarily obtain. And again, should we be capable of receiving sensations with increased or decreased rapidity, then, too, the time sense would be altered and a new world would have to be constructed. His conclusion is that we live in a world, only a part of whose forces we know, and to a part only do our sense-organs respond. And these forces, of which we are not at present cognizant, may involve nothing supernatural whatsoever, and yet they may account for the alleged facts of the occult phenomena of psychical research. Mr. Crookes offers a tentative hypothesis, as follows: That ether waves of far more rapid vibrations than those of the Roentgen rays may directly affect certain brain centers sensitive to them, without the intervention of the ordinary channels of the senses, and that such rays moreover may be freed from the limitations of space, as for instance the law of inverse squares. Thought may therefore be communicated at a great distance and without the physical connections and sequences which we deem indispensable to all communication between man and man. Mr. Crookes's speculations can not rank, however, as an hypothesis. At best he establishes merely the possibility of his speculation, for he presents no facts to indicate its probability or to save it from being relegated to the sphere of bare conjecture.

JOHN GRIER HIBBEN.

PRINCETON UNIVERSITY.

A Study in Apperception. WALTER B. PILLSBURY. Am. Jour. Psychology, VIII., pp. 315–393. April, 1897.

In this paper Dr. Pillsbury is engaged in the praiseworthy but difficult task of throwing light upon the problem of apperception versus association. He does this in a way that is extremely suggestive; namely, by analyzing the elements involved in the reading of a word. This, of course, involves both subjective and objective factors. The former may be analyzed into six or seven factors: the association between the letters of the word; the word as a whole; the preceding word; the events of the preceding day and hour, etc. The objective factors came from the letters themselves. The general scheme of the investigation was "to determine the amount of change which might be made in an object ordinarily perceived or assimilated in a certain way without change in the character of the resultant perception or assimilation." The object to be changed is a type-written word photographed and printed on a lantern slide. This was projected upon a ground-glass screen in front of the subject. After two-tenths of a second it was cut off, and the subject recorded what he 'saw.' Comparison of this record with the word exposed furnished means of determining the value of the various objective and subjective factors in the perception of the word. The influence of the objective factors was altered by omitting a letter or by substituting another letter or by printing an 'x' over the letter and so blurring it. The subjective factors were varied largely by Professor Münsterberg's method of calling a word, associated with the one to be shown, immediately before this one was given. The other subjective factors were the accidental variations which were noted in connection with the various experiments. The nature of all these experiments is such that the results do not admit of any complete tabulation. The tables given are merely so many examples of individual experiments, and it would be impossible to draw any conclusion from them alone. They do, however, show the comparative value of the various alterations in the conditions of subject or object. The omitted letter is most often noticed, the changed letter next often, and the blurred letter is more easily overlooked. Any change in the beginning of a word is more often noticed than if the change came later in the word. The experiments made with and without an association show that the percentage of misprints overlooked is greatly increased under the influence of the association.

The general conclusions of this study should be said to follow from the experiments, not to rest upon them. The author has taken Wundt's treatment of the theory of apperception and its relation to other mental states as a standard, and he begins his paper by a very good résumé of Wundt's theory. In the statement of the general theoretical results of his experiments, Dr. Pillsbury brings his own formulation of the process of perception into sharp contrast with Wundt's theory. " Wundt reduces the process to an associative part-process of *identity* between the parts seen and letters of the correct word, and an associative part-process of *contiguity* between these letters of the correct word and those usually combined with them to form the entire word. Apperception is present only in the passive form in which the objective or mechanical factors are alone determinant. We, on the contrary, have reduced association to a very subordinate place, and find active apperception to be the truly controlling factor." The scheme of psychology here advanced is: (1) *Sensation*, the element of all cognative states. (2) The *idea*—a complex of sensation. (3) *Association* connecting ideas. (4) *Apperception* connecting this idea with general experience. These processes are all abstractions. The first concrete conscious process is (5) *Assimilation*, or *perception*. " This includes Wundt's association synthesis, assimilation and complication, *i. e.*, all of his associative connections, as well as the apperceptive connections of apperceptive synthesis, the concept, the greater part of which is known as judgments, and probably agglutinations also." (6) Succession associations and (7) the highest stage of all, the true judgment; the general conclusion of the paper being "that conscious processes and their connections are not so simple as is usually supposed," and "and that what are ordinarily known as the 'higher' and 'lower' processes are not different in psychological structure and mode of composition."

J. E. Lough.

HARVARD UNIVERSITY.

Comparative Observations on the Involuntary Movements of Adults and Children. M. A. TUCKER. Am. Jour. Psychology, VIII., pp. 394–404.

These observations were made upon 18–36 adults and 13–38 children, by means of a Jastrow's automatograph. The experiments are considered in connection with the investigations of Stricker, Lehmann, Féré, and Jastrow. On the whole, the results of Féré and Lehmann are substantiated.

The results of the experiments are shown in a number of tables and cuts. As a final summary we find:

" 1. There is physiological tendency for the hands and arms resting in front of the body to move inward toward the median plane of the body.

" 2. There is no certainty that when we see an object we tend to move toward it. We may think of it simply as an object at rest, and the idea of motion is necessary to cause movement in that direction.

" 3. Involuntary muscular movements may be controlled by the influence of the sight or visual remembrance of moving objects, and the imitation of the direction of the moving stimuli is the result.

" 4. Children are governed by and subject to the same laws as adults, but to a less extent.

" 5. There is no sex or age difference in children, either in involuntary or controlled muscular movements."

J. E. Lough.

HARVARD UNIVERSITY.

Psicologia per le Scuole. GIUSEPPE SERGI. 2d edition. Milan, Fratelli Dumolard, 1895. Pp. vii + 227.

This little book, designed for the use of high schools, has, as a textbook, the merit of clearness, directness and consistency of method. The first part is purely physiological, and the physiological point of view is maintained throughout. Psychology is, for the author, a part of biology, namely, the study of the functions of the organism in so far as they are protective. Consciousness is only a quality which, for some reason not hinted at, some of these protective processes come to have. Consciousness is not, he tells us, a mode of being or a separate phenomenon. We might at this point like to be informed what a phenomenon means, and whether the utility for self-preservation which distinguishes those physiological functions which the author calls ' psychical' depends on their conscious quality or only on their physical complication. No theoretical question, however, is sharply faced or plainly dealt with, so that the work, in spite of its superficial clearness and dogmatism, will be far from leaving a clear impression of its doctrine upon anyone who reflects. It would have been better, perhaps, to have limited the subject to physiology proper. The author would then have remained upon ground congenial to himself and the student would not have been deceived by the idea that he had traversed the subject of psychology, when he is in fact left in well-nigh total ignorance of its historical problems and essential conceptions.

G. SANTAYANA.

HARVARD UNIVERSITY.

VISION.

On Reciprocal Action in the Retina as studied by means of some Rotating Discs. C. S. SHERRINGTON. Jour. of Physiology, XXI., 1897, 33-34.

Luminosity and Photometry. J. B. HAYCRAFT. Jour. of Phys., XXL, 1897, 126-146.

Ueber den Einfluss des Maculapigments auf Farbengleichungen. DR. BREUER. Ztsch. f. Psych., XIII., 464-473, 1897.

The object of Sherrington's experiment is to show that contrast is a real physiological occurrence, and not simply an illusion of the judgment, by showing that it produces an effect upon the speed of alternation necessary to extinguish flicker, even under circumstances such that it is not present at all as a conscious phenomenon. A circular disc is divided up into a number of semi-circular ring-bands, 12 mm. in width, which are painted blue, black and yellow, in such a fashion that, upon rotation, there will be (1) an inner and (2) an outer blue and black half ring-band, which will fuse in each case into a steely grayish blue, but with this difference: in (1) the blue and the black

ring-bands are neither of them accentuated by contrast, because they
have surfaces of the same brightness on either side of them, while in
(2) the black is blacker than it should be on account of being against
a bright yellow background, and the blue is brighter on account of
being bordered on either side by black. The difference in brightness
between the two ring-pairs is distinctly visible before rotation; and
upon rotation the effect is found to obtain which was predicted, viz:
a rapidity of rotation which gave 44 alternations of blue and black
per second was sufficient to cause complete vision in the inner ring-
band, while the outer one continued to flicker until the number of
alternations per second was sixty-eight, and this in spite of the fact
that the background *during rotation* was the same for both rings—
the blackish yellow of the fused yellow and black borders. The
grayish blue rings were also now indistinguishable in appearance. The
experiment is therefore conclusive as showing that a *consciousness* of
difference of background, far from being the sole cause of the contrast effect, is not essential to its production, and hence as showing
that contrast is something which takes place below the region of conscious judgments; if there were any individuals who were not convinced of this fact before, they will doubtless be brought over by this
ingenious arrangement. It will be noticed that Sherrington's result
is in contradiction with that of Baader, mentioned in the last number
of this REVIEW. He gives, in addition, a number of good experiments
to show the effect of successive contrast on flickering.

Haycraft points out that it is a pity to use the same word photometry for two things which are so intrinsically different as are isochro-
matic photometry and heterochromatic photometry. In the one case
we are measuring—by sensation, it is true, in the last instance—something which is at the same time a physical quantity (viz., the intensity
of the objective light which causes the sensation); in the other
we are measuring a sensation which has no counterpart in the objective world. But this is, of course, only a particular instance of the
lamentable fact that language has not yet provided us with any easy
means for distinguishing, in general, between objective *light* and subjective *light-sensation*, and it is another argument for making the
latter compound word more common than it is now. He uses himself the word *luminosity*, by which, however, he proposes to mean,
not exactly ' amount of visual sensation, ' because black is a *sensation*
as much as white is—namely, the sensation which is attached to the
resting state of the visual apparatus—but rather the ' amount of sensory deviation from black.' This he would take as being measured

by the number of intermediate steps which can be perceived to be such between black and a given gray, for instance. This measurement he has not yet carried out for the different spectral colors, but he has determined once more the relative objective intensity of the different parts of the spectrum at the threshold of color-perception both for the dark-adapted and for the light-adapted eye, his results agreeing with those of former observers. He also applied the flicker method to determine the relative luminosity along the spectrum. No great degree of precaution against errors seems to have been taken; " having made several such observations * * * the curve was drawn."

Dr. Breuer made a direct examination of the amount of spectral light of different colors absorbed by the macula, by comparing color-equations at or near the center with those taken in a field at from three to six degrees distant. His results confirm very closely those of Sachs made upon the extracted retina. He reaches the general conclusion that, since the total amount of absorption by the yellow pigment is so very small, individual differences in this amount cannot be of very great consequence. This fact has an important bearing, of course; it follows from it that something more is necessary to the explanation of the difference between the two types of red-green blindness.

C. L. Franklin.

Baltimore.

A Note on the Phenomena of Mescal Intoxication. Havelock Ellis. Lancet, June 5, 1897.

Mr Havelock Ellis has re-examined the wonderful vision-producing properties of mescal, which were first brought to notice by Prentiss, Morgan and Weir Mitchell. Mescal buttons are the fruit of *Anhalonium Lewinii;* they are eaten by the Kiowa and other Indians of New Mexico in connection with religious ceremonial. Three of the buttons were taken in three doses at intervals of an hour; an immediate effect was experienced in the relief of a headache, which had been rather serious at the beginning of the experiment, and in a consciousness of unusual energy and intellectual power. After two hours the expected visual phenomena began with a pale violet shadow floating over the pages of an open book. Objects seen peripherally were enlarged and heightened in color, and after-images were marked and persistent. Green shadows next appeared; soon afterwards vague, confused masses of color, of kaleidoscopic character, were seen with closed eyes, which presently became distinct and brilliant, while at the same time the air was filled with perfume. Later, when muscular incoördination had reached such a stage that writing was difficult, a golden tone lay over the paper, the pencil wrote in bright gold, and the hand seen in indirect vision was red. Dr. Weir Mitchell's visions were apparently much more brilliant than these, but he could see them only with closed eyes, while Mr. Ellis found it perfectly easy to see them with open eyes in a dark room, though they were less brilliant than when the eyes were closed. Insomnia persisted during the greater part of the following night, but it seemed to be less connected with the constantly shifting visions, which were always beautiful and agreeable, than with the vague alarm which was caused by a considerable degree of thoracic oppression and of auditory hyperæsthesia. The skin was hot and dry, and the knee-jerk was much exaggerated. A gas flame seemed to burn with great brilliancy and to send out waves of light which extended and contracted rhythmically in an enormously exaggerated manner. What was chiefly impressive, however, was the shadows, which came in all directions, heightened by flashes of red, green and especially violet. "The violet shadows especially reminded me of Monet's paintings, and as I gazed at them it occurred to me that mescal doubtless reproduces the same conditions of visual hyperæsthesia, or rather exhaustion, which is certainly produced in the artist by prolonged visual attention (although this point has as yet received no attention from psychologists)." These violet shadows may be conditioned by the dilatation of the pupils which always occurs in mescal intoxication, for Dobrowolsky has maintained that the erythropsia which is common after eye operations is due to the dilatation of the pupils produced by the atropine previously administered, "so that the color vision is really of the nature of an after-image due to bright light; Dobrowolsky's explanation seems to fit in accurately with my experiences under mescal." Mr. Ellis seems not to have noticed an important paper on Erythropsia by Dr. Ernst Fuchs in a late number of the *Archiv. für Ophthalmologie* (noticed in an earlier issue of this Journal). In this it is shown, with a great degree of probability, that erythropsia is in reality entoptic rod-pigment vision; after exposure to blinding snow-light, or to the excessive amount of light admitted by a widened pupil, the rod-pigment, which is usually overlooked on account of its constant presence, becomes rapidly reconstructed and hence produces for a few moments its proper color effect. In defects of nutrition it has been often noticed, first by Parinaud, that the rod-pigment is a substance which is among the earliest to suffer; hence, even without the dilatation of the pupil, an erythropsia due to this cause might be readily expected to occur in this case.

The phenomena of mescal intoxication are, according to Mr. Ellis, mainly a saturation of the specific senses, and chiefly an orgy of vision. He is convinced that all the senses are effected; there were vague dermal sensations, and a marked casual stimulation of the skin produced other sensory phenomena a heightening of the visions or an impression of sound—a fact which may throw an interesting light on the synæsthesiæ or ' secondary sensations .' The immediate cause of the sensory phenomena seems to have been a great and general disintegration or exhaustion of the sensory apparatus; in a slighter degree the same phenomena, even the color vision, are found in neurasthenia. The drug, it appears, is expected to have a great future as a specific in cases of neurasthenia; the homeopathists will therefore find their account in the fact that it produces, when taken in large doses, the very symptoms which it is most powerful to cure.

C. LADD FRANKLIN.

BALTIMORE, MD.

Sight, an Exposition of the Principles of Monocular and Binocular Vision. JOSEPH LE CONTE. 2d edition. New York, Appleton, 1897. Pp. 318. $1.50.

" In this second edition I have found little to *correct*; the changes are mainly in the form of *additions.*" Of these additions probably the most important is that on astigmatism; the portions of the book on the nature of space perception and of the laws of direction and on color have been amplified.

The conspicuous merits of the first edition are retained—the ingenuity of the illustrations, the clearness of the statements and the fascinating character of the experiments described. One characteristic still remains, namely, a misunderstanding of the psychological principles involved in monocular vision; the view is essentially a physiological one, whereas most of the facts are mental ones.

At the time the first edition was written there was no special science of psychology which was recognized by the other sciences. Introspective psychology was, for various reasons, regarded by the scientists as one stage of senile dementia. Here is an illustrative quotation from Le Conte (p. 69) concerning the theories of erect vision: " First, there have been metaphysical theories characteristic of this class of thinkers. According to these, erect and inverted are purely relative terms. If all things are inverted, then nothing is inverted. There is no up and down to the soul, etc. * * * The first we put aside as being non-scientific." Of course, this caricature resembles the original about as much as some of the American flags that float over Swiss hotels, with 5½ stripes and seven stars. The introspective method of psychological investigation has received complete vindication, through experimental psychology, as being the only possible one. The very theory dismissed by Professor Le Conte, *i. e.*, that there is no up or down in our visual field except through association with bodily space, is that of Helmholtz (Physiol. Optik, 2 ed., p. 680) and is based on a treatment of visual experiences from the standpoint of introspective psychology. It is impossible here to discuss fully Professor Le Conte's projection of impressions back along the ray line into space. The trouble arises from treating our own mental experiences as located in another person's brain. Professor Le Conte's view of erect vision is not wrong, but incomplete. The connection of the visual field (which is somewhat improperly termed the retinal field, the two being quite different affairs) with bodily space, together with certain visual experiences, gives us our ideas of the positions of objects; we know directly what up and down mean and we know nothing of our retinas or of outward projection.

The same difference of view characterizes the section on color-perception; this, in connection with physical methods of thinking about colors, leads to curious errors. 'Unplagued by any physical considerations there are seen' to be four primary colors: red, yellow, green and blue; this omits violet, which is to the eye as different from blue as yellow from red. 'In purple we see blue and red,' which is true only of those persons who have seen purple produced by mixtures of blue or violet and red. The very same persons who 'see' red and yellow in orange also 'see' yellow and blue in green (which contains neither when pure). This whole 'seeing' of primary and secondary colors and their relations is a matter of education; it is absolutely lacking in children, to whom orange is as much a primary color as red is. It was at least different in Newton, who 'saw' seven primary colors.

Another error is that concerning the fundamental colors. The psychological view of the color system as the resultant of the mixture of three *sensations*—so clearly stated by Helmholtz and König—finds no mention, although it is merely a statement of facts and empirical laws. On the other hand, the various hypotheses concerning the functions of the retina in regard to color are extensively discussed, although they are of no interest to the psychologist and are mainly speculations of rather doubtful nature.

These same objections apply, however, to nearly all physiologies and to most psychologies; they result, as I have tried to indicate, from a departure from the introspective standpoint. Concerning the physiology of the retina we know very little; concerning the physiology of the brain we know almost nothing; whereas our *direct* knowledge of color and space is highly developed and systematized. To attempt to systematize our psychological knowledge by deductions from the physiology of the eye is only one degree less unjustified than the attempt to produce a science of psychology by speculation on the actions of brain molecules.

When Professor Le Conte comes to binocular vision his physiology leaves him and he becomes a psychologist, experimenting and explaining directly what he sees. The clearness and completeness of his explanation leave nothing to be desired. The introduction of diagrams ready for use with the stereoscope makes this section highly interesting and practical. Amid the wealth of facts stated in the briefest and clearest manner, we find a large number of the cleverest illustrations probably ever introduced into a psychological book. In fact, the whole book, in spite of objections to its point of view, is by far the best elementary exposition of the psychology and physiology of vision with which I am acquainted, which seems an odd thing to acknowledge, when we consider that the author is a professor of geology and natural history. Professor Le Conte, indeed, is one of those leaders of science who can at any time step into a new field and get more out of it than even its own specialist.

The biologist is evident not only in rich chapters in the comparative physiology of vision and on the evolution of the eye, but also in characteristic explanations of various phenomena from the evolutionary point of view. For example, speaking of the indistinctness of vision outside of the point of sharpest vision, the author says: "Now, what is the use of this arrangement? Why would it not be much better to see equally distinctly over all portions of the field of view? I believe that the existence of the central spot is necessary to fixed, *thoughtful attention*, and this again in its turn is necessary for the development of the higher faculties of the mind. In passing down the animal scale the central spot is quickly lost. It exists only in man and the higher monkeys. In the lower animals it is necessary for safety that they should see well over a very wide field. In man, on the contrary, it is much more necessary that he should be able to fix undivided attention on the thing looked at" (p. 78).

E. W. SCRIPTURE.

YALE UNIVERSITY.

Pseudoptics: The Science of Optical Illusions. A series of psychological experiments for the classroom and home. Milton Bradley Co., Springfield, Mass. $5.00.

This series of charts and apparatus for experiments on visual illusions is especially intended to interest the general public in mental phenomena. For this purpose it is most valuable, and should be sold in many editions. The series will also be of much interest to teachers of psychology in schools, colleges and universities. We must all spend—I might say waste—a great deal of time in preparing illustrative material which it ought to be possible to buy. Much time and energy might be saved if the simpler instruments, devices and illustrative material devised by each could be used by all. It would not be amiss for the American Psychological Association to appoint a committee instructed to draw up a list of such material and the place where it could be secured. In such a list these *Pseudoptics* would stand at or near the head.

The material is placed in three boxes, each containing several portfolios. The first box illustrates illusions of length, direction, form, size and mövement, including 25 experiments in all. The charts are perhaps on the average 20 cm. square, sufficiently large for demonstration in a lecture, and the illusions in most cases appear better than in the illustrations given in text-books and articles. In nearly all cases the parts are movable, and simple devices are given for rotation, etc. We have thus not only illustrations, but a series of experiments which the student can himself carry out. The second box illustrates afterimages, color-mixture, contrast, indirect vision and the blind-spot— the term illusion being used in a sense wide enough to include all cases where, through the functions of the eye, nervous system or mind, we see things otherwise than as they 'really are.' The third box illustrates especially perspective and binocular vision.

The series is accompanied by an introduction explaining the objects and advantages of the experiments; the method for making each experiment is described in sufficient detail, and there are given explanations of the phenomena. These latter are of necessity brief, and in some cases may prove misleading, as they may cause the student to imagine that the phenomena are more simple and better understood than is in fact the case. The classification adopted may also in several cases prove misleading. Thus, for example, under 'multiple vision' are included phenomena so diverse as are binocular double vision and the doubling of the image in Schreiner's experiment. The apparent similarity and real diversity in such cases may easily confuse the student.

The author of *Pseudoptics* wished originally that his name might not be associated with it. But it has been announced by a firm of instrument makers, and there is now no reason why we should not give honor where honor is due, and thank Professor Münsterberg for his valuable service to education and to psychology.

J. McKEEN CATTELL.

Ueber die Bedeutung der Convergenz- und Accomodationsbewegungen für die Tiefenwahrnehmung. MAXIMILIAN ARRER. Philos. Studien, XIII. 1. 116–161. 2. 222–304.

The author investigates the problem of the perception of depth from the standpoint of the part played in such perception by the sensations of convergence and accommodation. In a dozen pages he reviews in concise statements the experiments and discussions on the subject in the past in so far as they involve these sensations. Chapter I. communicates the author's experiments on the perception of differences in depth by comparison of successive stimuli. It is believed that this problem, which was long ago investigated by Wundt, will bear a fresh investigation now, because of the objections which have been raised to Wundt on the grounds that his experiments are not numerous enough (this is admitted by Wundt) ; that the subject upon whom his experiments were carried out did not possess average capacity in the perception of depth owing to a defect in the mechanism of the eye, and that the theoretic constructions which Wundt gives to his results are not warranted. Chapter II. is an attempt at an explanation of the monocular and binocular experiments of chapter I. Chapter III. further attempts a negative confirmation of the theory of the former chapter.

The apparatus used in the first set of experiments, viz., in those on the monocular and binocular perception of differences of depth, was as follows: the subject looks through an inwardly blackened tube, which passes through a screen of black cardboard, upon a gray field. In the interval between the tube and the gray background two black threads are kept stretched perpendicularly by weights. The distances between the threads are varied by moving one of them nearer to or farther away from the other, which in turn remains unmoved during each series of experiments. After showing one thread until the subject has a clear image of its absolute distance from him, a screen is placed before the tube, the one thread is lifted up, the other is left to hang in its place in the field of vision, and the screen is removed, the problem being to say whether the second thread is at the same distance, nearer or farther away than the first one. The author's results agree, in the main, with those of Wundt. They differ in that they show smaller values for the recognition of differences of depth, but the author writes that he withholds further communications for another place. The author's explanations, however, differ quite essentially from those of Wundt. According to the latter, differences of depth in the direction of the eye of the observer are recognized through the sensations accompanying the movements of accommodation to the increased nearness of the object. Differences of greater distance away from the eye, on the other hand, are recognized by differences in the thickness and clearness of the thread, the theory being that the accommodations to increased distance are brought about by simple relaxations of the accommodation-muscles, corresponding to which there are no peculiar movement sensations. The author finds that the apparent differences in the thickness and in the distinctness of the thread are far too slight to serve as the grounds of the perceptions of difference which the tables show, and he accepts changes of sensation corresponding to the accommodations to greater distances. The results of the discussion of the binocular and monocular experiments are gathered together as follows: "(1) The sensible factors in localization in depth, relative and absolute, are sensations of convergence and accommodation. (2) The estimation of depth takes place, neither through an immediate perception of the degree of effort of convergence nor through an association between these sensations and the object to be located, but simply through the fact that these sensations are the particular elements in the space-representation (Raum-Vorstellung), which for our consciousness condition and bring to expression the relation of depth." The perception of depth is, according to the author, an assimilation process pure and simple. The most important moment in the monocular perception of depth is the sensations of accommodation; the most important in the binocular perception of depth is the convergence sensations.

The discussion represents a very large number of experiments and a careful study of the literature of the subject. Occasionally the discussion seems to be unnecessarily lengthened, whereas the views of other writers are sometimes somewhat too briefly given. From the writings of Descartes and De la Hire down to the recent discussions of Stumpf, Lipps, Dixon and others nothing seems to have escaped the notice of the author. Yet no mention is made in the entire thesis of the theory of James and Ward, and the author simply assumes the sensations of accommodation and convergence. In his discussion of the views of Wundt and Hering, one has the feeling that all has not been said which might be said. Those interested in the subject will in the future no doubt have to take this study into account.

G. A. TAWNEY.

BELOIT COLLEGE, Wisconsin.

SLEEP AND DREAMS.

Expérience sur les rêves. J. MOURLY VOLD. Édition privée. (Repr. fr. Rev. de l'Hypnotisme, January, 1896.) Christiana, Actie-Bogtrykkeriet, 1896. Pp. 16.

Einige Experimente über Gesichtsbilder im Traum. J. MOURLY VOLD. Zeitsch. f. Psychologie, 1896, XIII., 66–74. (Repr. sep.)

Die physiologischen Beziehungen der Traumvorgänge. CARL MAX GIESSLER. Halle, Niemeyer, 1896. Pp. 45.

Professor Vold's two papers describe some experiments upon the muscular and optical elements entering into dreams and the conclusions to which they lead. The experiments were performed upon the author and some forty others, of both sexes and for the most part adults, who volunteered their assistance.

The first paper reports the experiments upon muscular stimulation. The author met the subjects beforehand and explained to them in detail the nature of the experiments, but without a hint as to the expected outcome. The experiments were not to be begun until the day following the interview, in order to avoid any direct influence of the latter upon them, and the subjects were requested to refrain from all exertion on the evenings of the tests. Immediately on waking in the morning after each test the subjects were to answer. in writing a number of questions concerning the dreams of the past night. With most of the subjects a considerable number of tests were made. The conditions of the experiment consisted simply in confining certain sets of muscles with a glove, ribbon or string. The two hands and the tibiotarsal region were the parts especially used. The disturbing influence of the preparations for the experiment was obviated by duplicating them, in one case putting the glove on and then removing it before sleeping, the next evening keeping it on through the night. To distinguish between actual movements and sensations of movement due to the artificial muscular stimulation, the subject was asked to note carefully each time whether there were signs of his having moved just before waking. Experiments were made alternately with the right and left sides, and sometimes with both sides together, in order to determine the relative influence of these different conditions.

Among the more important results of these experiments, the author finds that we generally tend to notice the position of a flexed limb, whose sensations enter into our dreams and form an integral part of them; we rarely dream of being in a horizontal position. The influence of the bodily position on dreams is as follows: The part which is flexed or whose muscles are confined may be represented *statically*, as being in the position in which it actually is. Or the whole body may be represented as performing a *movement* of such a character that the part in question plays a prominent rôle in the activity. Again, this same movement may be dreamed of as opposed or prevented. At other times the dream represents another person or an animal as being in the position or performing the movement. Finally, in some cases where the fingers are confined, a dream occurs in which the subject is occupied with a number which corresponds to the number of fingers affected. In this last case the connection seems rather forced, and the author must give more detailed results before his position can be accepted.

Professor Vold supposes these different effects to be due to differences in the degree of fatigue of the interested centers. When fatigue is greatest the peripheral sensation may barely reach the threshold of consciousness, giving a general notion of the number in question, without any distinct idea of its peripheral origin or of its belonging to the subject himself. When fatigue is less the notion of the limb may be more distinct, but still without a tendency to associate it with his own person. In more superficial sleep, where fatigue is slight, the subject is at length able to associate the sensation with his own body. The author considers that the active interpretation of these sensations as movements is due to a greater degree of fatigue than the static, since the latter involves a clearer consciousness of the actual condition of the limb. We cannot but think that he lays too much weight on one hypothesis, which he uses as counterpoise for his experiments, viz., that we never remember dreams in which actual movements occur.

Professor Vold's second paper, read at the Psychological Congress last year, deals with the visual elements in dreams. The subjects were each provided with a parcel containing a number of small objects or figures cut from cardboard; this parcel they opened in bed and, placing the objects upon a black or white background, observed them fixedly for a certain length of time, generally from 2 to 10 minutes, but occasionally, with intervals of rest, for half an hour; they then extinguished the light without looking at the flame. The same method of reporting the results was used as in the muscular experiments. The success of the experiment seemed to depend upon a number of factors: the general disposition (Anlage) of the subject, the quiet and normal passing of the preceding evening, his health, the absence of undue fatigue, and the exact and systematic carrying out of the experimental conditions.

The results themselves, as reported, seem somewhat general and vague in character; the author limits himself to a few striking examples, and does not attempt to tabulate the experiments at all. The paper as a whole is, therefore, rather unsatisfactory to the exact scientist. The test-object, says Professor Vold, rarely enters into the dream unaltered. Its form and size may reappear with change of color, or *vice versa*, or one or more of these elements may appear transformed or become so in the course of the dream. White and black in the test-objects had the most marked influence; these would often appear in the dream under the form of simultaneous or successive contrast-effects. The test-object occasionally reappeared in the given color or its complementary, or another object would be seen in the color of the given test-object. With colors other than black and white, the given color was sometimes exactly reproduced, but oftener appeared changed as to saturation, brightness or color-tone; in some instances the complementary color appeared. Unfortunately nothing is said as to the relative frequency of these different cases, nor of the proportion of successful reproductions to the whole number of trials.

From these results the author deduces the conclusion that the visual apparatus immediately before waking reproduces to a certain extent the condition present at the beginning of sleep. The brain cells, however, work independently in sleep, and the syntheses of form, size, color and abstract representation constructed by day or in the evening are broken up; in place of these new syntheses are built up between the outlines and abstract representations of daily life, on the one hand, and the outlines and more especially the colors of objects which affect the visual apparatus just before the beginning of sleep.

In contrast with these two papers, which emphasize the psychological side, Dr. Giessler's is a contribution to the physiology of the dream processes. The author assumes at the outset that the distribution of nervous energy, which in waking life is directed into certain channels by the voluntary working of the attention, is in dreams, through the inhibition of the higher centers, mainly passive, uncoördinated and directed without effect to various points of the nervous system.

Dream illusions are due to several causes: 1. To peripheral stimuli which fail to reach the threshold; here the stimulus may either be transformed immediately into an illusion, without any sensation of the stimulated part coming into consciousness; or it may be transformed through a mediate association. 2. To stimuli which reach the threshold discontinuously; in this case the vague sensation of the part stimulated gives rise directly to an illusion. 3. To reflexes, which do not as such come into consciousness. 4. To sensations which reach consciousness, but are subjected either to changes of quality and localization or to an increase of intensity. 5. To feelings, which in connection with the intellectual elements bring about a heightening of the emotional side. The author proposes an explanation of the underlying physiological processes in each case. In the first case, *i. e.*, where the stimuli themselves do not reach consciousness directly, he supposes that certain stimuli at some period attain a high degree of intensity; a number of such stimuli are brought into association by a subcortical process, and the coördinated product is transmitted to the appropriate cortical center; there it stimulates the traces of former similar coördinations; between these an association is brought about, which appears as the memory image of a presentation that has previously accompanied a similar bodily condition. The physiology of the other cases is similarly explained. The author illustrates each case with the example of an actual dream. In the case cited he describes a dream in which he appeared to be standing before a booth at a fair, surrounded by a crowd of laughing acquaintances; he ascribes the situation to a peculiar posture in sleep which suggested standing; the laughter was suggested by the difficulty of breathing occasioned by his posture and by other bodily feelings which he noted on awakening.

Dr. Giessler next takes up dreams of hallucinatory character; these are due, as he explains, to an *idea* of some sort, rather than direct peripheral stimulation. Thus the strong notion of something to be avoided may give rise in dreams to the experience of its actual occurrence. The physiological process here consists, first, in the concentration of nervous energy along certain already formed paths, whose mental products are capable of giving a suitable turn to the dream; and second, in the prevention of its outflow to other centers which would produce unfavorable changes in the images; the assistance of the visual center is usually needed in such dreams as a support for the other centers. Hallucinatory dreams are divided into: (1) affective dreams; (2) those involving the higher mental functions; (3) the reproduction of common presentation-series.

The author discusses at considerable length the processes involved in three special cases: visual space-localization, speech and writing. The space relations are distorted in dreams in two ways. Since the muscles which raise the eye-ball offer greater resistance than those which depress it, the nervous energy which is transmitted to them gives rise to a lesser movement; the dreamer, therefore, estimates the upward movements as less in proportion than the downward, since they give rise to the feeling of a lesser outcome. As regards depth, the original position is usually estimated correctly; but when the eye moves to another point the innervation feeling of the accommodation center remains practically unchanged, and hence in dreams the distance from the eye of any two points fixated in turn is the same, or the difference seems much less than it really is in waking life. The estimate of lateral distances is not subjected to any distortion.

Dr. Giessler formulates six laws governing the production of dreams, two of which apply to the phases we have especially noticed. 1. There is a tendency in dreams to refer conditions which are caused by stimuli below the threshold of perception or above the threshold of apperception to a substratum outside of the dreamer's body, while those conditions caused by stimuli lying between these two thresholds are referred to the dreamer's own body. 2. The nervous energy sent out to a system of organs (*e. g.*, those which regulate space perception) stimulates the different parts of this system more quickly, more intensely and more definitely in proportion as they belong to an earlier epoch in the historic development of that system.

A very complete classification of dreams is given at the end of the paper, based on the nature of the mental functions involved.

HOWARD C. WARREN.

PRINCETON.

A Contribution to the Physiology of Sleep, based upon Plethysmographic Experiments. W. H. HOWELL. Journal of Experimental Medicine. Vol. II., No. 3, 1897.

Some twenty experiments were performed, but of this number only four or five gave entire satisfaction. Each experiment covered about four and a half hours of normal sleep. The volume changes in the hand and the lower part of the fore-arm were measured by means of a water plethysmograph, due precautions being taken to keep the enclosed parts immovable and to secure a comfortable position. The record was inscribed upon a drum revolving once in twelve hours, and was supplemented by the notes of a watcher. Neither pulse nor respiration was registered.

An examination of two curves obtained in successful experiments shows dilatation of the arm at the beginning of sleep, the maximum being reached at one to one and a half hours and maintained for an hour or two, when constriction appears, bringing the arm, first gradually, then more rapidly, to its normal volume at awaking. Within this general course of the curve there are waves of an hourly period and sharper oscillations that are much briefer. The larger variations indicate a lowering of the peripheral resistance in the skin area with diminution of arterial pressure and of the blood flow through the brain. The periodical wave-like oscillations point to rhythmic changes in the vaso-motor center, and the shorter oscillations are due to external stimuli, deep respiration or bodily movements.

A comparison of this plethysmographic curve and the intensity curves published by other investigators or obtained by the author himself, shows a resemblance during the first period only; the deepest sleep seems to correspond with the minimal flow of blood through the brain. Beyond this period, the parallelism ceases, the irritability of the cortex returning rapidly to the normal while the anæmic condition of the brain persists for some time.

Sleep, according to the theory advanced by Professor Howell, results from the combination of three factors: " A diminution of irritability, caused by fatigue, of large portions of the cortical area; voluntary withdrawal of sensory and mental stimuli involved in the preparations for sleep; a diminished blood supply to the brain, owing to a relaxation of tone in the vaso-motor center and the fall of general arterial pressure thereby produced. The last factor is the immediate cause of sleep and explains its comparatively sudden and nearly simultaneous occurrence over the entire cortex."

As to the possible play of psychical processes no distinct information is afforded by this paper, since the sleeper did not, in any of the experiments, have a conscious recollection of dreaming. It is noteworthy, however, that in some cases there was partial awakening without permanent constriction of the arm and consequently without permanent increase of the blood-flow to the brain. In explanation, the author suggests that the metabolic processes within the cortical cells might be increased by either internal or external causes other than changes in blood supply, and might thus rise above the threshold of consciousness. The conscious processes might then outlast the corresponding vaso-motor changes.

It may be permissible here to observe that in the much shorter sleep record published by Shields (Jour. Exp. Med., Vol. I., No. 1), odor stimulation did not affect the general direction of the curve showing increase of arm volume in the first period. Not all the odors employed were accompanied by the same change in direction or extent; nor was the action of any one odor uniform. While it would be difficult to draw satisfactory conclusions from these peculiarities, and while, as Shields has pointed out, these changes give no clear evidence of sensory reaction, it is conceivable that the effect of any stimulation is determined in some way by the condition of the vaso-motor center at the moment the stimulus is applied. As this center, according to Howell, is the seat of rhythmic changes which account for the large periodical variations in the plethysmographic curve, it would at least be interesting to observe the effects produced by stimulation in various phases of the rhythm.

E. A. PACE.

CATHOLIC UNIVERSITY, WASHINGTON.

GENETIC.

First 500 Days of a Child's Life. MRS. WINFIELD S. HALL. Child Study Monthly, November to March, 1896-7.

In five papers appearing under the above title Mrs. Hall has outlined the history of the first five hundred days of the life of her child. While less critical and less exhaustive than Miss Shinn's, where the two writers whose work can be so favorably compared have entered the same field, Mrs. Hall's observations are more completely classified, and she has not hesitated to point out a number of conclusions. Her observations have undoubtedly been carefully carried out, and this will render her history not only interesting in itself, but useful for purposes of correlation with the results of other observers. For the introductory chapter on growth we are indebted to Dr. Hall, the father of the child; but as the results of his measurements do not appear again in connection with the features of development which Mrs. Hall describes, we may pass this chapter over and go at once to the consideration of her own papers.

In the introductory outline of the classification according to which the observations are arranged, we find two main divisions of development, physical and psychical. Under physical development are subsumed muscular movements and coördinations; while included with senses and intellect under psychical development are emotions. If the motor element is as significant in consciousness as we are coming to believe, and if visceral sensations and emotional expressions constitute the differentiæ of the emotions in consciousness, this division is an unfortunate one, inasmuch as it separates these phenomena by such barriers as the terms physical and psychical would tend to produce.

In the second paper we regret to find among muscular movements records of so few inherent reactions, for without these a history of the development of muscular movements must be incomplete. For example, under ' grasping' no mention is made of a reflex, though it is recorded of the 57th day that " for the first time he seemed to know that he had something, and his fingers tightened upon it." The history of the development of grasping and of sucking the thumb is given on the whole as a history of voluntary movements, *i. e.*, attempted conscious adaptations, rather than as a history of muscular movements proper.

On page 395 Mrs. Hall describes the chance discovery of a useful movement, showing that the child, in common with young animals, may develop through the wider application of instinctive movement. There are many observations which suggest questions of interest. For example, the thumb was constantly enclosed in the fist till the 70th day. In the case of my own child the thumb was rarely enclosed in the fist. What, if any, is the significance of such differences in hand attitudes, and have they a bearing upon the subsequent development of hand movements? And we are impressed by the fact that many movements were taught to the child. Was this done in conformity to a prevalent belief that the various forms of habitual actions must be learned from another? Or was it proved experimentally in this case that the child would not or did not acquire these habits without instruction? If the last be true then there is one case to be cited in support of a popular belief. It is of importance to know whether these habitual movements can be acquired altogether without instruction or by imitation, or whether these are necessary or of assistance. Nearly all the movements described by Mrs. Hall are repeated or imitated movements, either repetitions of copies set for the child in terms of movement, or of those seen and translated by him from visual to motor terms. We should like to know whether he could reproduce a movement from a copy held in its own terms more easily, or at an earlier date, than he could reproduce one from a copy held first in the terms of another sense.

It is well to indicate the value of observing the development of coördinations, and Mrs. Hall's remarks upon this are extremely suggestive. But we feel the need of a more comprehensive history than she gives us. Here again we should know more of the inherent coördinations, and of how far imitation was influential in impressing combinations of movements upon the organism, and of how far experiment and the accidental results of chance movements tended, if at all, to modify a recognized order of development of coördinations.

The definition of coördination is open to criticism; for by the use therein of the word graceful, a number of skilled adjustments would be excluded from the list of coördinations. Many highly dextrous artisans are not graceful, and many exquisite adaptations required by the use of tools render grace of movement impossible. Later (p. 406), there is a second definition of coördination which is designed to fit a conception rather than the phenomena as they are seen to occur; for such movements as the symmetrical ones of the arms in early infancy are to be viewed as primitive coördinations, yet not as adjustments in time or of force, but rather as the preliminary steps by which data for the knowledge necessary to such adjustments are acquired.

The history of psychical development opens with observations on the senses. Among the records of vision there is little to note, but we cannot pass by the conclusions without pausing over the fourth one (p. 468). Here Mrs. Hall writes: "The time when visual perception becomes relatively clear precedes the following of moving objects by the eyes because: (a) this act is a voluntary one; and (b) the child cannot will to follow the motions of an object which it does not perceive." There is not, I believe, as yet enough evidence to establish a claim of priority for either fixation or following. Miss Shinn is of the impression that following may occur very early, and my own record shows that it may precede fixation. Nor can following be classed among voluntary movements, the evidence at hand going rather to show that its place is among the inherent ones. Under conclusion 9 the suggestive fact is noted that "attention is held much more closely when two senses are affected than when only one is affected." Among sensations we miss observations upon touch, taste and smell. When we come to the emotions and the intellect, however, we find fuller records, and this is especially true of the subdivision of intellect which treats of language. Over all of these we should like to linger, for the observations will well repay a careful analysis, and the conclusions are worthy of consideration.

One impression grows within us as we reach the conclusion of the fifth chapter: it is that every advance is in some sense a repetition of experience. There is not a case on record in which the child took an initiative, or launched on a wholly independent line of action. When something strikingly unusual was performed, such as is recorded on page 534, or of the occasion upon which he alternately struck two objects to produce different tones, he was accidentally led into these performances by the discovery of qualities in the objects. Such a collection of records gives a natural history of the development of conscious continuity. And we must mark it as a distinct advance that Mrs. Hall has contributed a history of mental development rather than a mere record of dates.

K. C. MOORE.

WAYNE, PA.

MENTAL FATIGUE.

Ueber die Beeinflussung einfacher psychischer Vorgänge durch körperliche und geistige Arbeit. S. BETTMANN. Psychol. Arbeiten I. Pp. 152–208.

Ueber den Einfluss von Arbeitspausen auf die geistige Leistungsfähigkeit. E. AMBERG. Psychol. Arbeiten I. Pp. 300–377.

Ueber Ermüdung und Erholung. W. H. R. RIVERS and E. KRAEPELIN. Psychol. Arbeiten I. Pp. 627–678.

On Mental Fatigue and Recovery. W. H. R. RIVERS. Journ. Ment. Sci. XLII. Pp. 525–528.

Studies of Fatigue. J. M. MOORE. Stud. Yale Psychol. Laboratory III. Pp. 68–95.

Untersuchungen über die Einflüsse der Arbeitsdauer und der Arbeitspausen auf die geistige Leistungsfähigkeit der Schulkinder. J. FRIEDRICH. Ztsch. f. Psychol. XIII. Pp. 1–53.

The influence of fatigue on mental performance is the subject of these six articles. Herr Bettmann has investigated the effects of fatigue, incident to both mental and physical work, on the time of certain mental processes; Amberg has experimented upon the influence of rest periods on mental ability; Dr. Rivers and Professor Kraepelin take the general problem of recovery from fatigue; Dr. Moore has investigated the effect of fatigue upon certain voluntary movements, while Herr Friedrich has given his work a practical turn, and found the effect of the fatigue of the school day upon children's ability to do some ordinary school tasks.

1. Bettmann's article gives the results of the influence of two hours' rapid walking or of one hour's adding figures upon choice re-actions, word reactions, memorizing figures, adding, and rapid read-ing. For the first of these processes he finds that the fatiguing mental work increased the time; average normal time 293σ, after adding 384σ. The reactions taken after the walking show a decrease in time, 257σ. This is explained by the number of false reactions apparently included here, the percentage of these under the different conditions being as follows: normal 2.6, after mental activity 1, after bodily work, 29. The bodily work as well as the mental increases the time for word re-actions. Memorizing was found more difficult after the fatigue of adding, the decrease being slightly greater after the bodily work, al-though during all the experiments there was a 'practice' advantage for the latter. The average number of figures learned in one-half hour was: normally, 661, mental work influencing, 476, bodily work influencing, 454. The influence of the two kinds of work shows itself clearly also in the average number of figures added during one-half hour: normal, 1793; after mental work, 1572; after bodily work, 1571. The average number of syllables read normally in one-half hour was 8798; after the mental work only 7660, and after the bodily only 8380 were read.

From these results the author concludes that *Turnstunden* and *Spazieren* should not be used as means of recreation before mental work. One must remember, however, that when we walk or swim or play tennis we do not do them *in recht raschem Tempo*, and that also in our recreations there is a decided interest which must have been lacking in the two hours' march. On the whole the work is well done, and the results are fully collated, but only one observer was tested. In common with the other two *Arbeiten* articles, and with Friedrich's article in the *Zeitschrift*, the material would have made more interesting reading if it were not spread over four times the space required.

2. In this research the author attempted to determine the effects of different periods of rest, of the difference in the kind and duration of work, and of personal differences. Adding and memorizing were the mental processes used in the investigation. A rest of five minutes between two half hours of adding showed a 6 per cent. increase in the amount done over that when no pause was made. When there was a continual change, five minutes work, five minutes rest, scarcely any increase was noted. For two observers, fifteen minute rests between two half hours' work showed no effects; when the work was two

hours long and the fifteen minute rest was taken between the hours
there was noted a slight increase in the amount of work done.   For
the author a fifteen minute rest between two half hours' memorizing
gave a 6½ per cent. decrease in amount accomplished; another observer, however, under like conditions showed an increase of 13 per
cent.   These rather conflicting results show the need of further and
more extended work in this direction.

3. Professor Kraepelin's and Dr. Rivers' paper is a partial answer
to the question: What period of rest is necessary for the recovery of
mental freshness?   Between the different half hours' adding of single
figures a rest of a half or of a full hour was taken.   The results show
that for a normal man a rest of the same duration or of that of double
the period of work is sufficient to restore the mental freshness once,
after which there is a rapid decrease in the capabilities which cannot be
balanced by a simple rest.   During the work many temporary personal
influences showed themselves.   How far the results of the latter two
researches can be extended to daily life, to all kinds of mental conditions, it is difficult to say; in all probability, the question of interest
would be one of the great influences in daily work, and to draw conclusions from uninteresting, not to say wearisome, experiments as to
what would happen under ordinary conditions, would be extremely
hazardous.

4. Dr. Rivers' second paper only gives the method and general results of the preceding research.

5. In Dr. Moore's studies, two observers were tested as to the
effect of fatigue on binocular estimate of depth and from the first to
the last experiment there is a gradual increase in error of estimate.
Three observers gave practically the same result in monocular estimation of depth.   The time of monocular accommodation increased for one
observer from .35 s. to .87 s. (296 experiments), for another observer,
first series, .36 s. to .46 s. (391 experiments), second series, .30 s. to
61 s. (261 experiments).   Taps were made as rapidly as possible
with an electric contact key.   Evidences of fatigue showed themselves
at about the 70th tap.   Fatigue lengthened the time of making each
tap, the average for the first ten being 200σ, and for the last ten (470th
to 480th) 359σ.   In most of the experiments a rhythm, similar to that
found by Lombard for finger contractions, was noted.   In general the
author finds that fatigue tends to make work less rapid, less accurate,
and highly irregular.

6. Herr Friedrich made his tests upon his class of children, their
average age being 10 years.   Accuracy of adding and of copying from

dictation was determined under the following conditions: *a*, before the first school hour; *b*, after the first hour; *c*, after the second hour with a rest of eight minutes between the two hours; *d*, after the second hour, no rest; *e*, after the third hour, rests of fifteen minutes between the hours; *f*, after the third hour, one rest of fifteen minutes between the second and third; *g*, after the third hour, no rests; *h*, before first afternoon hour; *j*, after first hour; *k*, after second hour with fifteen minutes between first and second; *l*, after second hour, no rest. The rests were filled with breathing exercises, etc. The results show an increase of errors from *a* to *g* and from *h* to *l*; for dictation experiments this amounted to 370% and 380%, respectively; for the adding series there was, respectively, 103% and 27% increase. It should be noted that only one test under each condition was made; conclusions from the work will consequently only be valid when confirmed by others. The article is important, however, as showing what elementary and secondary school teachers could do for the cause of scientific psychology.

These five studies are an advance beyond ordinary observation. It is slight to be sure, but enough to show the importance, practical and theoretical, of the problem, and to indicate what may be done and what should be done.

SHEPHERD IVORY FRANZ.

COLUMBIA UNIVERSITY.

CUTANEOUS SENSATION.

Localization of Cutaneous Impressions by Arm Movement without Pressure on the Skin. C. T. PARRISH. The American Journal of Psychology, VIII., 250–267.

Miss Parrish's experiments had a double purpose: first, to test the accuracy with which an observer can indicate, by a pencil held just off the skin, a point previously touched by the experimenter; and, second, to note the effect of trying to emphasize or to exclude visual images in performing this act of localization. Her work is thus closely connected with experiments already reported by Dr. Pillsbury and Miss Washburn.

The results show that in the absence of sensations of contact from the observer's pencil the error in localization is greater than when exploration of the skin is permitted. In those series where especial emphasis was laid on visualization, two of the four observers made smaller errors than when left to their own native freedom. The error in the case of all four observers reached its maximum, on the other hand, when they were charged to shut out, as far as possible, all visual images. The most accurate localizations were obtained by allowing the observers to see the stimulated point whose position they had subsequently to point out.

As to the *direction* of the error in localization, three of the observers inclined to indicate points too far to the left on both right and left arms; for which the author tentatively suggests the asymmetry of function of the two arms as the explanation. A more constant and striking error in direction, however, was that the point indicated by the observer usually lay nearer the wrist than the point actually stimulated; and the error kept this constant direction both when the arm with which the localization was indicated moved from an extended position and when it started from a position of flexion. The author, in substantial agreement with Dr. Pillsbury, explains this 'peripheral displacement' by a tendency to overestimate the extent of the flexion movements of the indicating arm, and to underestimate that of its extension movements. This is perhaps the true explanation. And yet, since the region of skin experimented on, both here and in Dr. Pillsbury's work, was just above the wrist, the constant direction of error may have been due to the direction of the nearest important basis of longitudinal orientation (that is, the wrist, or, less immediately, the fingers) and not primarily to a false estimate of the movements of the opposite arm. If it can be shown that the direction of error is quite independent of this matter of orientation, brought out so prominently in M. Henri's experiments, the explanation given in the paper will seem much more conclusive. But a passing doubt like this must not be allowed to conceal in the least the value and interest of the results Professor Parrish has given us.

Ueber die Wahrnehmung zweier Punkte mittelst des Tastsinnes, mit Rücksicht auf die Frage der Uebung und die Entstehung der Vexirfehler. GUY A. TAWNEY. Philosophische Studien, XIII., 163–221. Also in Princeton Contributions to Psychology, II., 1, April, 1897.

It has been known that practice usually brings a marked reduction in the threshold distance at which two points on the skin are felt as two; but it has never been quite clear whether repeated experiment on some single selected spot of skin causes a decrease in the threshold all over the body, or whether the decrease is only for the selected spot and for the one corresponding to it on the opposite side of the body. Volkmann, for instance, believed he had experimental evidence that in repeated determinations of the threshold for some one region of skin the threshold was reduced only over so much of the body as was supplied from closely connected sensory fibres, including the corresponding region on the opposite side. Professor Tawney, on the contrary, has here shown by extended experiments that practice in such a case not merely has a local effect, but lowers the threshold irregularly over the whole body. The changes which we designate as the result of ' practice ' are therefore central and psychical.

His farther contribution is in making clearer the exact nature of such practice as is really effective. The practice which causes the threshold to decline is not the mere *repetition* of the discriminative act; for, as Professor Tawney here shows, there may be indefinite repetition of the act, without any reduction of the threshold whatever. If the observer preserves, as far as possible, a calmly receptive attitude toward the stimulus, and allows his judgment to be formed spontaneously as a ready characterization of the external fact, then the threshold remains fairly constant, however often the experiment be repeated. The threshold seems to be reduced by practice only when the observer expects and strains for greater and greater nicety of discrimination as the experiment proceeds. In other words, some form of *suggestion* is the main factor in producing in this field the results hitherto vaguely ascribed to practice. Where suggestion was most carefully excluded, practice had little or no influence on the results. At the same time, the author warns us not to suppose that suggestion is absent merely because the observer has been kept in the dark as to the purpose or method of the experiment. Autosuggestion is at least as pervasive and disturbing an influence as is any other form of suggestion.

Another important feature of the experiments here reported is the intimate connection they seem to reveal between the reduction of the threshold and the puzzling phenomenon of illusory double contact (*Vexirfehler*), so exasperating to workers in this field. The observers were comparatively free from this illusion until practice had considerably reduced the threshold. And in those series where no reduction normally took place, the introduction, at the close of the series, of the suggestion which had been operative in the other cases was the signal both for a sudden drop in the threshold-value and for the appearance of *Vexirfehler*. Dr. Tawney's explanation is that the observer, in his effort to make the finest discrimination between one and two points, changes the mode of forming his judgment. The observer no longer, as at first, directs his attention to that visual image of the stimulating object which arises in strongest association with the dermal sensation; but now gives his main attention to the dermal sensation itself. The subject's analytic examination of the sensation either accentuates qualitative differences in it, or else produces them outright. And once having definitely before him a distinction within the sensation, it is easy to pass on to the judgment and even to the clear perception of two spatially separate points of contact. But if the observer could rid himself of the preconception that no more than two points were being used, he could often (and one of the subjects actually did) have the illusion of four or five contacts quite as well as of two. By variations in the direction of the suggestion, its influence was brought to light in various ways. However, for these and other interesting details the original paper must be consulted.

Dr. Tawney's account shows that his experiments were carefully arranged and carried out, and his paper is certainly a distinct and important gain for the special field indicated by the title of the article. But, besides this, the principles he touches, in showing the importance of suggestion, have their ramifications in all laboratory work. His admirable article, therefore, can hardly fail to be of assistance in avoiding pitfalls in many lines of psychological experiment other than that to which the author here confined himself.

George M. Stratton.

University of California.

Untersuchungen über die Sinnesfunctionen der menschlichen Haut. Erste Abhandlung ; Druckempfindung und Schmerz. Max von Frey. No. III., xxiii B. d. Abhand. d. math. phys. Classe d. König. Sächs. Gesell. d. Wissenschaften. Leipzig, S. Hirzel. 1896.

In this monograph Frey gives an account of experiments on the relations of pressure sensations and their stimuli. His problem was the physiological conditions of pressure stimulation, his method the determination of the threshold relations of time, place, area and intensity.

The first experiments described corroborate the familiar fact that pressure stimuli of a moderate intensity are perceived only a short time after application. Frey concludes that only stimuli near the threshold cause a temporary sensory effect, but in his experiments weights of 100 to 200 g. applied for 1 min. on 100 mm.², failed to cause continuous sensations. The removal of the weight was at times perceived as pressure. This is said by Frey to be due to pressure after-images, but heterogeneous stimuli of low intensity are easily confused. The rapid fading away of the pressure sensation is not necessarily due, as the author assumes, to the fatigue effect of constant stimuli. If the stimulus is not pressure, but the work done on the skin, the stimulus as well as the sensation is but momentary. This is practically admitted by Frey, for in another place he states that deformation of the skin is necessary for the production of pressure sensations.

More important are the experiments on the relations of the threshold to the area, place and rate of application of the stimulus. The apparatus consisted essentially of a lever connected with a balance to which weights were applied and clock work to regulate the rate of increase of the stimulus. Experiments on one observer showed that for him at least the threshold increased at first slowly and then rapidly from .2 to 2 g., as the rate decreased from 6.2 to .7 g. per sec. The data are very meagre, but the results corroborate those which I myself obtained by a less accurate method. It is evident that they support the movement theory of pressure stimulation. The experiments on the area made on two observers seem to show that for low rates of application, 1.2 to 4.3 g. per sec., the threshold increases faster than the area, but for rates of 6 to 11 g. per sec., the relation seemed more a direct proportion. Here, also, the number of experiments is inadequate. More than two constants should be used if even an approximately quantitative relation is to be obtained, especially when the results vary. Frey's conclusion that the intensity of stimulation per unit area varies inversely as the entire area—which he calls the law of ' hydrostatic pressure '—not only contradicts the results of experiments by me, according to which the threshold increases much more slowly than the area, but is also based upon very scant evidence. Curiously enough Frey misuses the term hydrostatic pressure, for liquid pressure increases with the area of application. The experiments on the place of stimulation were made on but one observer. The marked variation in the results for contiguous areas is ascribed to the varying distribution of pressure spots.

The experiments on the threshold made with hairs of known cross-section are of much interest. The law of ' hydrostatic pressure' was found not to hold for areas less than $\frac{1}{4}$ mm². The stimuli seemed to be equal when the pressure increased approximately in proportion not to the superficial, but to the linear magnitude. This proves, according to the author, that the organs of pressure sensation are not on the surface, and that they are in all probability the corpuscles of Meissner. This interpretation of the experiments was justified by an experiment on a physical model, which showed that under conditions somewhat similar to those of pressure stimulation the pressure exerted on the surface was not fully transmitted below the surface. With these hairs Frey made maps of the pressure points on the calf of the leg and the wrist. The threshold values run from ½ to 4 g. per mm. The average values were the same for these places as for the ball of the thumb and finger tips.

Experiments on the pain threshold were also made with hairs or cactus needles, one of which was affixed to a spring, the whole form-ing a delicate algometer. The values found for three observers vary from 25 to 50 g. per mm². The ' hydrostatic ' law of pressure and area of stimulation was found to hold for all the areas investigated, less than 12 mm². Hence, Frey concludes, the organs of pain are superficial. Their high threshold is explained by the rigidity of the epidermis. The topography of the pain spots was also studied, but apparently the reagent himself applied the stimulus. In these, as in other experiments, especially those on the topography of pressure spots, the author seems to have devoted his attention to physical and physiological rather than to psychological sources of error.

HAROLD GRIFFING.

NEW YORK.

NEW BOOKS.

Man's Place in the Cosmos and Other Essays. ANDREW SETH. New York, Scribners. 1897. Pp. viii+308. $2.

The Chances of Death and Other Studies in Evolution. KARL PEARSON. With illustrations. Two vols. London and New York, Ed. Arnold. 1897. Pp. ix+388 and 460. $8.

Émile Zola: enquête médico-psychologique. I. Introduction Gén-érale. ED. TOULOUSE. Paris, Société d'Éditions Scientifiques. 1896. Pp. xiv+285. Fr. 3.50.

Fourteenth and Fifteenth Annual Reports of the Bureau of Eth-nology (1892–3, and 1893–4). J. W. POWELL. Washington, Gov. Print. Office. 1896 and 1897. Two vols, pp. lxi+1136; and one vol. pp. cxxi+366.

Congrès international d'Anthropologie criminelle : Comptes Rendus de la IVe Session (Genève, 1896). Genève, George & Co. 1897. Pp. xxix+396.

La Structure du Protoplasma et les Théories sur l'Hérédité et les grands Problèms de la Biologie générale. YVES DELAGE. Paris, Reinwald & Cie. 1895. Pp. xiv+878. Fr. 24.

L'Année Biologique: Comptes Rendues annuels des travaux de Biologie générale (Première Année, 1895). YVES DELAGE. Paris, Reinwald & Cie. 1897. Pp. xlv+732.

Collezionismo e impulsi collezionistici. S. DE SANCTIS. Roma, Tip. Innocenzo Ortero. 1897. Pp. 30.

Sulla dignità morfologica dei segni detti ' Degenerativi.' V. GIUFFRIDA-RUGGERI. Roma, Loescher & Co. 1897. Pp. 117.

Appearance and Reality. F. H. BRADLEY. Second edition (revised), with an Appendix. London, Sonnenschein; New York, Macmillans. 1897. Pp. xxiv+628. $2.75.

NOTES.

IT is with regret that we record the death of Professor W. Preyer, the distinguished psychologist and physiologist, at Wiesbaden, on July 15th; and also that of Daniel Greenleaf Thompson, author of ' A System of Psychology,' etc., in New York, on June 10th.

MR. MUIR, now of Halifax University, has been appointed to the chair of psychology, and Miss Ethel Muir, Ph. D. (Cornell), assistant in philosophy in Mount Holyoke College.

IT is expected that the laboratory for Experimental Psychology in University College. London, will be opened in October under the direction of Dr. W. H. R. Rivers, of Cambridge.

A UNIVERSITY Lectureship in Experimental Psychology has now been voted by the Senate of Cambridge University, England.

MR. C. L. HERRICK, lately professor of biology at Denison University, has been elected President of the Territorial University at Albuquerque, New Mexico.

MR. H. P. HYLAN has been appointed instructor in psychology in the University of Illinois.

DR. A. R. HILL has been appointed professor of psychology and ethics in the University of Nebraska, and Dr. E. L. Hinman has been promoted to an adjunct professorship of philosophy in the same University.

F. D. SHERMAN, Ph.D. (Leipzig), has been given the position in psychology and pedagogy in the Oshkosh (Wis.) Normal School vacant by the removal of Dr. Hill to the University of Nebraska.

DR. SIDNEY E. MEZES has ,been promoted from adjunct to associate professor of philosophy at the University of Texas.

A *Rivista quindicinale di Psicologia, Psichiatria, Neuropatologia* has been inaugurated under the ' Direction' of Professor E. Sciamanna and Professor G. Sergi, with a board of editors of whom Dr. Santo De Sanctis is editor-in-chief, Via Penitenzieri, 13, Rome.

AN *American Journal of Physiology* will be published after the first of January next under the auspices of the American Physiological Society. And a semi-monthly organ of *Zoölogie, Botanique, Physiologie et Psychologie*, called *L'Intermédiaire des Biologistes*, is to be issued by Schleicher Frères, Paris, with M. Alf. Binet as director-in-chief.

NEW volumes in the Contemporary Science Series, edited by Mr. Havelock Ellis and published in England by Walter Scott and in America by Charles Scribner's Sons, will include ' The New Psychology,' by Dr. E. W. Scripture; ' Psychology of the Emotions,' by Professor Th. Ribot; and ' Hallucinations and Illusions,' by Mr. E. Parrish.

VOL. IV.   No. 6.   NOVEMBER, 1897.

THE PSYCHOLOGICAL REVIEW.

STUDIES FROM THE PRINCETON PSYCHOLOGI-
CAL LABORATORY, VI–VII.

VI. THE REACTION TIME OF COUNTING.

BY PROFESSOR H. C. WARREN.

Princeton University.

I. INTRODUCTION.

The problem underlying this study was the question as to how we determine the number of things in a group. The mental process concerned in this determination is evidently not the same as the function technically known to experimental psychologists as *discrimination*. The latter consists in distinguishing between two or more different things; an object is ascertained, by means of certain marks or characteristics, to be the thing sought for and not something else; or the absence of these characteristics is noted and it is thus known not to be the thing sought for. It is also a mental process distinct from *recognition*; we speak (technically) of recognizing an object or objects when we recall their former presence in consciousness by means of certain marks and are thereby able to class them or give them a name. The *knowledge of the number of things in a group*, on the other hand, is independent of marks or differences. Number depends solely on the *distinctness* or *separateness* of the objects; it has nothing to do with their complexion. The word discrimination might readily be applied to the numbering process, and so might the word recognition; but if this were done it could only be through a change from their techni-

cal connotation; 'numbering' is very different from the processes to which these two words are applied by experimenta-
lists; the mark of 'five-ness,' if we may use such a term, is
simply the spatial or temporal distinctness of the objects in the
group—any or all of the objects can be exchanged for any
others, however different, and the 'five-ness' remains unaltered;
this does not hold true in the case of ordinary recognition or
discrimination.

It is not necessary here to enter into any discussion of the
origin of the concepts 'one,' 'two,' 'three,' etc. This is
an entirely separate question, which has already received considerable attention from psychologists and mathematicians.[1]
In the present study we were concerned solely with the proper
application of these terms to given groups of objects. That is,
we were to investigate the concrete process of *numbering*,
rather than the process of acquiring the abstract *number
concepts.*

Whatever the nature of this numbering process, and whatever different kinds of numbering there may be, it is proper
enough to denote the function by the term *counting*, as we shall
do throughout this paper. But we must distinguish at the outset
between several varieties of counting. The most important distinction is that between counting proper and inferential counting.
In the former, objects are added up, so to speak, by a sort of
mental 'one-two-three-ing;' in the latter, some clue is given
by the form of the group, the amount of space it occupies, the
amount of time required to survey it, etc.; thus, the familiar
quincunx form (∵) is taken in as a whole—the form of the
figure is associated with the number-name, by a mass of former
experiences, as firmly as is the symbol '5.' The present study
was concerned primarily with the former process; the latter is
a species of association or inference (as the case may be),
whose investigation involves a different problem; indeed, its
chief rôle in our study was that of an enemy to be thwarted at
all hazards.

---

[1] On this point see 'The Number Concept,' by L. L. Conant, New York,
Macmillans, 1896, and 'The Number System of Algebra,' by H. B. Fine, Boston, Leach, Shewell & Sanborn, 1897.

A further distinction is to be noted, within the process of counting proper, between that which is practically instantaneous and that which involves the expenditure of time. If it takes no more time to count Three[1] than to count Two or One, it is evident that the apprehension of each separate object does not involve time ; if the reaction time of these numbers be practically the same, then their counting proceeds by an apprehension of the group as a whole, rather than by successive apprehension of its members. Whereas, if the reaction time of Four (say) is longer, the increment is time consumed in apprehending the extra unit. We may call these two processes *perceptive* and *progressive* counting, respectively ; add to this the process already noted, *inferential* counting, and we have three distinct methods of counting. I give this classification here without discussing its practical bearing (which will appear later), in order to make clear the nature of the problem and the precautions which had to be taken in the investigation to avoid confusion between the various distinct processes.

On the basis of this division two problems appeared which it was the object of this study to investigate. These were : (1) What is the largest number that can be counted by a single act of apprehension—on the one hand, without expenditure of extra time in taking in each additional object; on the other, without the assistance of association or inference? This is the problem of the limit of perceptive counting. (2) What is the part played by association and inference in our habitual acts of counting?

A third problem might have been added, viz., as to the law by which the time of progressive counting increases with the increase of number—in other words, the rate of progressive counting. This last inquiry was not followed up on account of its great complexity : it would have required a large amount of time to carry out the experiments, and the problem itself presented difficulties, on account of certain disturbing factors entering in, *e. g.*, the eye movements necessary to take in any extensive group of objects. As between the other two problems, the present investigation was more particularly concerned with the first.

[1] To avoid confusion the number-names will be printed with a capital.

II. HISTORICAL.

I may point out, first of all, the close relation that exists between this problem and that of the so-called *area of consciousness*. The area of consciousness (Umfang des Bewusstseins), as understood by the Leipzig investigators, is the sum total of impressions that can be held in consciousness at one time. The classic experiments of Dietze[1] on this topic aimed to determine this sum for a single case (the simplest) by means of groups of successive sounds. The subject was forbidden to count the sounds—he was to determine the difference between two groups after both had been given, by the mere fact of retaining all the members of each group in consciousness at once. The groups were compared as equal, greater or smaller, the hypothesis being that as long as this could be done correctly the subject must have had a simultaneous impression of each entire group. Dietze's subjects were able to distinguish differences correctly up to Sixteen when the sounds were uniform, and up to as many as Forty when each group was divided into subgroups of Eight by rhythmic accentuation. The highest numbers in each case were reached only when the rate of succession of the sounds was most favorable; thus these numbers, if the hypothesis be correct, represent the very maximum area of consciousness. The area of consciousness in the case of counting is a somewhat different thing. In Dietze's problem no mental act was involved *during the experiment* but the retention of the sounds in consciousness as distinct; in counting an active effort is required to bring the units together under the form of a number-concept. Still, I am of the opinion that the two problems really belong to the same category, the difference consisting chiefly in the presence of an act of apperception in counting, while Dietze's experiments involved merely perception. My subjects were not able to *gather in* at once numbers nearly so large as Dietze's could *hold together;* this was to be expected to some extent; but the wide difference between the two results, which will appear later, leads me to question whether Dietze's subjects succeeded altogether in avoiding counting *(i. e.*, progressive counting), and still more whether they

[1] Philos. Stud., 1885, II., 362 ff.

did not rely somewhat upon the length of time, and *infer* the size of the group from this—a tendency which (in another form) I found exceedingly difficult to prevent among my own subjects. In view of the importance and fundamental character of this problem, it seems strange that no one has ever undertaken to repeat Dietze's experiments.

Another problem somewhat analogous to the present one is the number of objects, letters, etc., that can be recognized at the same time. An investigation of this subject was made by Cattell[1] at Leipzig, in connection with his reaction time experiments, by a method of combined simultaneous and successive exposure. The objects were passed across a slit in a screen, the slit being varied in size so that any desired number of the objects could be seen simultaneously. He found that three, four or five letters could be recognized when passing at once—the maximum differing within these limits for different subjects; this was apart from the grouping of the letters into words, which, of course, involves association and is a very different process from the one under investigation.

The problem of counting was taken up by Cattell in a later investigation,[2] where he places it under the head of area of consciousness. Cattell's experiments consisted in exposing to view simultaneously and for a very short period (10σ) a number of lines drawn on cardboard; the subject was required to determine the number of lines on the card; the apparatus employed was a falling screen. In these experiments the method of right and wrong cases was used. The largest number for which the right answers exceeded the wrong varied between Five and Eleven, according to the subject. The higher numbers, however, were only correctly counted by those who had made many trials; this leads to the suggestion that the subject may have become familiar with the number of lines on each card in the course of his practice, and that he may have afterwards judged the number from the width of space occupied by the lines on the card—an inferential process again. On this account Cattell's results seem open to question,

[1] Philos. Stud., 1885, II., 635 ff.
[2] Philos. Stud., 1886, III., 121 ff.

and it was important that they be repeated with such changes in method as would avoid this possible criticism.   This was one object in the present investigation.

In connection with these experiments Cattell investigated the number of figures, letters and words, *recognizable* after a very brief exposure.   The same apparatus was used.   The results are as follows : Figures, 3 to 6; letters, 2 to 5 ; words, 1 to 4 ; the subjects almost without exception recognized one figure more than they could letters, and one letter more than they could words.   This agrees with his previous results, noticed above, by another method.   The problem, however, is different from that of counting, and I need not stop to discuss the results in detail.

Numerous other investigations have been made on the recognition time of colors, words, etc., which have only an indirect bearing on the present problem and need not be mentioned here.

III. PRELIMINARY EXPERIMENTS; HAND REACTIONS.

The problem of counting may be investigated, as we have seen, by the method of right and wrong cases ; given a short exposure (10σ) of a group of things, how large a group can be apprehended in that time so that the number is known?   This treatment of the problem can only be applied to simultaneous, or perceptive counting.   It can give no help in the discussion of successive, or progressive counting, and but little in the investigation of inferential counting.   A more effective method is that of reaction time.   The subject reacts on the number, and the reaction times of the different numbers are compared.   This avoids, for one thing, the possibility of counting from the after image.   The exposure need not be so short—it should be long enough to ensure the taking in of every member of the group, and is only shortened at all in order to stimulate attention to immediate activity.   In the present study the reaction method was adopted as principal; but the method of right and wrong cases served as check upon the results.   The times were thrown out whenever the count was wrong ; and further, if the wrong answers for a certain number equalled the right, the determination was set down as a guess rather than a count, unless the right reactions were perceptibly longer than the wrong.

Two separate investigations were made by the writer, both upon visual stimuli, but with somewhat different apparatus. The first series, carried out during the winter of 1895–6, developed a number of practical defects, which were remedied in the second series, made in the winter of 1896–7.

In the earlier series, the apparatus consisted of a large screen, with a slit 6 cm. wide and 16 cm. high, behind which swung a pendulum with a small screen attached; when the pendulum was up (and held in place by an electro-magnet) the small screen covered the slit in the larger one. The slit was on a level with the eyes of the subject, who was seated at a distance of 3 m. Behind the slit and the pendulum was fixed a holder, in which were placed, one at a time, the cards used in the experiment; this holder was of course concealed from view by the small screen when the pendulum was raised. The objects to be counted consisted of small white squares, of 5 mm.; these were pasted in a vertical line at distances of 5 mm. on the cards, which were black. In some cases the distances of the spots and their size were varied. The experimenter sat near the apparatus and was concealed (as well as the chronoscope) from the subject by another screen; he released the pendulum by means of a key. A contact was made at the point where the white spots first became visible to the subject, and the latter thereupon reacted on the number with a Morse key, at the same time calling out the number. The exposure was not limited, the pendulum being held back by a catch so that the spots remained full in view until after the reaction. By watching the (Hipp) chronoscope hands, the experimenter could tell whether the reaction preceded the speech; anticipatory reactions on the mere light stimulus were thus prevented.

Four subjects took part in these experiments, from only two of whom, however (C and G), were any large series obtained. A third (H) was unable to avoid anticipations; many of his results had to be discarded on this account, and he finally abandoned the work. The writer, who was the fourth subject (W), acted as experimenter most of the time, in order that the other subjects might not become too familiar with the appearance of the cards. The experiments were conducted in the daylight. On ordinarily bright days the spots were easily distinguishable by the subjects, and were yet close enough together to come within the range of clear vision, so that no eye-movements were necessary to distinguish them.

The method was open to the following criticisms: (1) On cloudy days the spots were less easily discernible than on bright days; it was impossible to measure the illumination or determine the effect of its variations upon the reaction time. (2) There was found to be a tendency on the part of the subjects, after a certain amount of practice, to *judge* the number of spots by the amount of space they covered on the card, *i. e.*, the length of the broken white line which they formed. (3) While it was possible for the experimenter to distinguish anticipatory *light* reactions, in the manner above mentioned, slight anticipations could not be detected; furthermore, (4), the attention being divided between the hand and the voice, the reactions themselves might not be reliably uniform. While this last objection did not appear to the writer to be borne out by the actual results, it was obviated in the second series by the use of a mouth key for the reactions; the third objection was met by this same change. The second objection was partly met in the earlier experiments by varying the size of the spots and their distance apart; but the conditions of the apparatus prevented this from being available—or at least effective—for numbers greater than Five; with larger numbers there was no room in the slit for greater distances, and with distances less than the normal the spots were difficult to distinguish; if larger or smaller spots were used, the new cards soon came to be recognized and judged as well as the original. In spite of the defects of this method, the results obtained are of service to compare with the later ones. They are also of value in themselves in several particulars.

There were in all 40 sittings in this series, of which 19 were made by C and 9 by G; in each case two sittings were set apart for preliminary practice in simple reaction; the results of these are not included in the tables. At the beginning of each regular sitting, before the counting reactions were begun, a series of 10 sensory reactions was taken on a card with four spots; a motor series was sometimes taken also. The subject C was of a distinctly sensory type, as these results show (Table I.) and as was proved by repeated tests elsewhere.

TABLE I.—SIMPLE REACTIONS; VISUAL, HAND, IN LIGHT.

	S	MV	No.	SER.	M'R	MV	No.	SER.
C	291.9	52.9	94	10	324.3	58.4	91	9
G	351.9	74.4	60	6	285.9	69.7	39	4
H	244.3	33.	40	4	222.2	28.3	30	3
W	235.6	58.9	43	4	179.3	40.4	21	2
C st.	192.1	34.8	50	3	247.8	58.6	30	2
C st. at.	185.9	26.9	10	1	——	——	—	—

S = sensory; M'r = motor; MV = mean variation; No. = number of reactions; Ser. = series of reactions; st. = reaction on strip of white paper; at. = reaction with great attention. The times are given in σ = .001 sec.

G and W were of the ordinary motor type; H was slightly motor. In Table I., C's first few series are omitted, as it was found that he frequently anticipated on account of a slight sound made by the pendulum in starting; this defect was remedied in all the later sittings. To determine the relation between these results and ordinary light reactions, four series were taken with a long white strip as stimulus in place of the spots; the results are given in the last two lines of the table; in one of these series (st. at.) the subject concentrated his attention to the utmost.

The reaction times on numbers are given in Table II., the sensory time for each subject being given first for the sake of comparison. The counting time for One is seen to be in every case over 100σ longer than the sensory time. As regards the relation between the times for the different numbers, I will delay comment until the later experiments have been presented.

TABLE II.

COUNTING REACTIONS; HAND, IN LIGHT.

	C			G			H			W		
	M	MV	No.	M	MV	No.	M	MV	No.	M	MV	No.
S	291.9	52.9	94	351.9	74.4	60	244.3	33.0	40	235.6	58.9	43
I	407.4	56.1	70	523.6	96.4	30	429.4	62.2	19	497.2	112.0	9
II	415.4	60.5	77	532.9	85.6	38	419.7	74.7	30	416.3	(50.0)	6
III	481.4	77.9	89	575.6	118.0	33	466.1	77.1	23	514.7	106.6	9
IV	620.8	94.4	74	652.7	108.5	41	600.2	118.9	16	613.8	(157.0)	5
V	934.8	195.9	53	853.5	231.6	35	828.8	(426.2)	5	638.8	(138.8)	8
VI	1274.7	311.9	47	1127.9	364.2	20	1167.7	(54.7)	4	(841.3)	(402.6)	3
VII	1783.0	448.5	26	1892.4	(206.1)	8	—	—	—	(1635.0)	—	1
VIII	1901.0	(172.0)	5	2369.2	(278.7)	4	—	—	—	(1782.5)	—	2

Roman numerals signify number of spots reacted on; S = sensory reaction; M = mean reaction time.

(Table III.)   Table III. shows the number and percentage of errors to the entire number of reactions; in no case (except with H) was the number of errors so great as to suggest that any other process but actual counting was used.

TABLE III.—ERRORS IN COUNTING; LONG EXPOSURE.

	C(19)			G(9)			H(6)			W(6)	
	No.	E	%E	No.	E	%E	No.	E	%E	No.	E
I	70	o	oo.	30	o	oo.	19	o	oo.	9	o
II	77	o	oo.	38	o	oo.	30	o	oo.	6	o
III	94	5	05.3	33	o	oo.	23	o	oo.	9	o
IV	81	7	08.6	41	o	oo.	22	6	27.2	7	2
V	65	12	18.8	36	1	02.8	7	2	28.6	9	1
VI	49	2	04.1	22	2	09.	7	3	42.8	3	o
VII	29	3	10.3	11	3	27.2	—	—	——	1	o
VIII	7	2	28.6	4	o	oo.	—	—	——	2	o

The numbers in brackets represent the series taken.

IV. EXPERIMENTS IN COUNTING, WITH MOUTH REACTION.

In the second series artificial illumination was used. A lamp giving practically uniform light was placed in a large enclosed space, within which the pendulum swung; the room was darkened. In the front side of the enclosure was an opening 12 cm. square, but a pyramidal tube extending out 35 cm. reduced the aperture through which the light could pass to 6 cm. square, and prevented its diffusion. Attached to the pendulum was a screen large enough to cover the aperture throughout the entire pendulum-swing; in this screen was a slit 25 mm. wide. The card holder was placed in front of the opening at a distance of 1.5 m., and was illuminated during 131σ when the pendulum swung; as the pendulum was held on the farther side by a catch there was but one illumination of the card before each reaction. The subject sat near the enclosure, and at a distance of 2 m. from the card; the latter was turned at such an angle (ca. 10°) as to prevent any sheen disturbance.

The cards used in these experiments were 16.5 cm. square; the spots were (in every case) circles of 14 mm. diameter, and were placed (in the main series) at uniform distances along the circumference of an imaginary circle, so that the center of every spot was exactly 6 cm. from the center of the card. As the spots were not in line, and the distances between them varied in different cards, and as each card could be used in four different positions, the tendency to use any ' inferential' aid in determining the number was believed to be avoided; the results and the testimony of the subjects themselves confirmed this. The spots were 18, 22 and 26 mm. apart, from edge to edge, in different cards; the same card was rarely used twice in succession, and every card was turned a quarter or half way around before using again; the end spots in the row were never on the vertical or horizontal diameters of the circle; these precautions effectually prevented inferential counting. To enable the subject to fixate the card before the experiment, a very dim gas flame was usually placed near and behind it; with one subject the slight illumination of the room was sufficient to show the outline of the card, without giving any indications as to the spots. The Hipp chronoscope was used in these experiments also, but was placed in another room, thus avoiding possible distraction from the sound. The writer, who generally attended to the cards and the pendulum, gave a preliminary signal, by shouting: 'Ready;' the subject then fixed his eyes on the card, and the Hipp was started by the person in charge. The subject reacted by means of a mouth key;[1] in the counting reactions he simply spoke the name of the number into the funnel of the key. There was thus no danger of anticipation, and no division of the attention, such as occurred when the hand key was used.

At the beginning of every sitting a series of from 10 to 20 sensory reactions was taken; the remainder of the hour was occupied with the counting reactions. The principal subjects were two in number, of whom one, C, had taken part in the

---

[1] The mouth key used in these experiments will be described and figured in a study by Professor Baldwin, entitled ' Type Variations in Reaction Times,' which will shortly appear in this REVIEW.

former series and in many other reaction experiments. The other, T, had never before reacted on visual stimuli. The writer acted as subject in a number of sittings, and his results are included in the tables also; some reactions were made by a fourth subject, Ta, who was called away, however, before the experiments had advanced far; his results are not included.[1]

There were 40 sittings in all, of which 18 were given by T and 12 by C; 10 of each included counting reactions with the mouth key. In the first six sittings with T, the hand key was used; the counting reactions made in this way are not included in the tables, but the sensory reactions are given in Table IV.,

TABLE IV.—COMPARISON OF MOUTH AND HAND REACTIONS.

		S	MV	No.	SER.	M'R	MV	No.	SER.
C	m. d.	298.3	44.7	130	10	476.8	48.7	20	1
	h. l.	291.9	52.9	94	10	324.3	58.4	91	9
	st. h. l.	192.1	34.8	50	3	247.8	58.6	30	2
W	m. d.	378.	55.4	81	5	288.1	22.8	30	2
	h. l.	235.6	58.9	43	4	179.3	40.4	21	2
T	m. d.	362.8	48.3	153	10	343.1	29.7	18	1
	h. d.	260.	23.2	75	4	250.2	31.4	59	3

All are simple visual reactions; m = mouth, h = hand reaction; d = in dark; l = in light; st = reaction on bright stimulus; cf. Table I.

for the sake of comparison; the simple reactions of C and W in the earlier series are also set down in this table along with their speech-key reactions. Of the reactions given in Table IV., only T's included mouth and hand reactions under uniform conditions of illumination; here the difference is close to 100σ, for both sensory and motor, in favor of the hand. In the cases of C and W, the hand reactions (as was observed above) include series in which the light stimulus differed greatly;

[1] The writer wishes to express his thanks to all who took part in the experiments; as well as to Professor Baldwin, for many valuable suggestions on both the practical and the theoretical sides of this investigation.

hence the wide variation in the results—for C a difference of 152.5σ in the motor and of only 6.4σ in the sensory.

In Table V. the simple reactions with the mouth key are brought together; as before, the first two (practice) series of

TABLE V.—SIMPLE REACTIONS; VISUAL, MOUTH, IN DARK.

	S	MV	No.	SER.	M'R	MV	No.	SER.
T	362.8	48.3	153	10	343.1	29.7	18	1
C	298.3	44.7	130	10	476.8	48.7	20	1
W	378.0	55.4	81	5	288.1	22.8	30	2

Symbols same as in Table I.

each subject are omitted.　T appears to be of a slightly motor type, while the earlier results with C and W are confirmed—they belong to distinctly sensory and motor types, respectively.

The two following tables give the counting reactions.　In Table VI. the mean reaction time (M) and mean variation

TABLE VI.—COUNTING REACTIONS; MOUTH IN DARK.

	T			C			W		
	M	MV	No.	M	MV	No.	M	MV	No.
S	362.8	48.3	153	298.3	44.7	130	37.8	55.4	81
I	567.1	83.8	23	553.1	62.6	19	573.3	75.	6
II	621.1	93.8	21	545.5	45.9	23	597.	(132.0)	3
III	655.	86.8	18	683.7	125.4	19	572.5	68.7	9
IV	683.8	123.1	42	740.4	91.2	35	588.8	(107.4)	5
V	812.3	155.8	34	1090.1	316.3	27	655.7	141.7	8
VI	938.1	154.6	17	1411.2	313.2	17	675.	53.6	6
VII	1265.	(26)	3	1352.3	362.3	6	786.8	(168.2)	5
VIII	—	—	0	(2828)	——	1	(689.3)	—	3
Zero	939.	(292)	3	831.5	(136.5)	4	717.3	—	3
Infinity	1007.7	434.	16	1128.	—	1	671.7	—	3

Symbols as in Table II.; *Zero* = reaction on blank card; Infinity = reaction on number too great to count.

(MV) are given for numbers from One up to Seven. The number of (successful) reactions for each number (No.) appears in a separate column. For the sake of comparison the corresponding data of the sensory reactions (S) are added also. As the mean variation is considerable, the reactions can be better compared by means of the upper and lower limits of their variation; these are given in Table VII., together with the

TABLE VII.—LIMITS OF MEAN VARIATION.

	T		C		W	
	Lower.	Upper.	Lower.	Upper.	Lower.	Upper.
S	314.5	411.1	253.6	343.	322.6	433.4
I	483.3	650.9	490.5	615.7	498.3	648.3
II	527.3	714.9	499.6	591.4	465.	729.
III	568.2	741.8	558.3	809.1	503.8	641.2
IV	560.7	806.9	649.2	831.6	481.4	696.2
V	656.5	968.1	773.8	1406.4	514.	797.4
VI	783.5	1092.7	1098.	1724.4	621.4	728.6
VII	1239.	1291.	990.	1714.6	618.2	955.

limits of the sensory reactions. From this table it appears that the counting reactions, even for One and Two, are very much longer than the simple reactions, while the difference between the times for successive numbers in every case (except T for Seven) falls within the limits of mean variation of the next. These results may be expressed under the two following propositions: (1) The shortest counting times are longer than the shortest sensory reactions by about 200σ; and (2) For successive numbers the counting time is approximately the same. Several remarks should be made on each of these statements.

As to the first: the question of the relation between counting and recognition times comes up at once. All the published experiments on recognition time having been made with the hand key, which gives decidedly shorter times than the mouth key here used (cf. Table IV.), it is impossible to compare them directly with these results.   They do admit of comparison, however, with our earlier series.   Comparing the latter with Titchener's results reported in the Philosophische Studien[1], we find the following: Titchener gives the sensory time on light stimulus, for three subjects, as 260, 266 and 279σ; and the reaction time on the recognition of a word as 319.3, 317 and 302.8σ for the same subjects.   My hand reaction experiments give the sensory times of C, G, H and W, respectively, as 291.9, 351.9, 244.3 and 235.6σ (cf., Table II.) ; and their counting reactions on One as 407.4, 523.6, 429.4 and 497.2σ. The counting time is thus seen to be somewhat longer than the recognition time, if different subjects can be compared ; as it happens, the writer (W) was the first-named subject in Titchener's experiments, which furnishes one case of direct comparison.

Returning to our second proposition, the following interpretation may be given : taking the mean time of counting One for standard, the subject is usually able to count Two, often Three, and occasionally Four and Five in the same time, *i. e.*, by the same kind of simple mental act.   With Four or more this seems to be due to a special effort of the attention, or (occasionally) to an expectation of that particular number ; in the earlier series there was some assistance from the judgment (inference), but this was carefully guarded against in the present series.   In general, then, *it seems to require a longer time, and hence a more complex mental act, to count numbers greater than Three.*   For Six and Seven the difference is so marked as nearly to double the length of the reaction time.   With these higher numbers, too, other elements come in, as will be seen when we examine Tables VIII. and X., so that the results represent something very different from simple perceptive counting.

In Table VIII. are shown the errors (E) committed in counting each number, and the percentage of errors (%E) to total reactions.[2]   In the two last columns for each subject the errors are clas-

---

[1] VIII., 138–144.

[2] A few reactions are included in this table, from which, through the fault of the apparatus or its operators, no reaction times were obtained, but which are available for the present purpose ; this will explain the discrepancy between the figures given in Tables VI. and VIII.

TABLE VIII.—ERRORS IN COUNTING. EXPOSURE OF 131σ.

	T					C					W			
No.	E	%E	+(∞)	—	No	E	%E	+(∞)	—	No.	E	%E	+(∞)	—
I	31	0	∞.	—	—	30	0	∞.	—	—	8	0	∞	—	—
II	34	0	∞.	—	—	30	1	03.4	1	0	8	0	∞	—	—
III	35	2	05.7	1	1	30	5	16.7	5	0	12	1	08.3	0	1
IV	58	7	12.1	6	1	50	4	08.	4	0	9	0	∞	0	0
V	53	12	22.6	5(1)	6	50	17	34.	8	9	19	4	21.	1(1)	2
VI	51	33	64.7	17(9)	7	50	30	60.	10(1)	19	16	6	37.5	0	6
VII	21	15	71.4	3(11)	1	10	4	40.	2	2	14	4	28.5	3	1
VIII	10	10	100	1(9)	0	5	4	80.	0	4	24	18	75.	(6)	12

sified according as the answers given were too great ($+$) or too small ($-$); in some cases, it will be noticed, the subject reacted on discovering that the number was too great to count (∞); these are given in brackets in the *plus* column. It will be seen that the percentage of errors increased steadily (with slight exceptions) in the two principal subjects from Three upwards, until at Eight it reached practically 100. This explains why no reaction times are given for Eight in Table VI.[1] No cards with more than eight spots were used, owing to this fact, but the subjects did not know of this till near the end of the series; it will be noticed that T gave one Nine-reaction and nine 'Infinity'-reactions on Eight.

The conclusion to be drawn at once from a comparison of these tables is that the upper limit of counting without inference and without eye-movements is Seven or less. In T's case the number of wrong answers begins to exceed the right at Six: In C's case it exceeds it at Six but not at Seven (where only ten trials were made). Moreover, if we take into account the 'doubtful cases,' 'guesses' and 'judgments or inferences' (cf. Table X.), *the limit for progressive counting without eye-movement falls in both cases to Five.*

The two subjects differed somewhat in their method of procedure, as shown by the differences in the number of errors,

[1] The bracketed numbers given there were of 'doubtful' reactions; cf. Table X.

guesses, inferences and 'Infinity '-reactions,[1] but their results
agree substantially in the limits for the various kinds of counting. Although these results cannot be generalized without
corroboration from other subjects, they are of great value as
coming from subjects of two distinct mental types, the sensory and the motor. The distinctions which the subjects made
between the different counting processes, simple perception
of number, inference or judgment, guessing and progressive counting agreed substantially also; these distinctions will
be explained and discussed later, in connection with the final
series of experiments on inferential counting. The reactions
of W are too few in number to be of much service; they present a substantial agreement with the others for the lower numbers; for the higher numbers the times are shorter and the proportion of errors far smaller; this is probably due to the writer
being familiar with the individual cards from having made them
and handled them in most of the experiments.

Before leaving the present question we may compare briefly
the results of the mouth-key experiments with the hand-key
experiments of the former series. It appears that the hand reactions are generally shorter; in the case of C, who acted as
subject in both series, the difference is very uniform except for
the higher numbers. In the hand reactions, it will be remembered, the number remained in view until after the subject had
reacted; there was thus an opportunity for 'progressive counting,' which was taken advantage of; so that instead of guessing or inferring the number (as was sometimes necessary in the
mouth reactions), the subject would take more time and 'count
up' the spots. The smaller percentage of errors and the longer
time required to count larger numbers, are indications of this
tendency.

V. EXPERIMENTS ON INFERENTIAL COUNTING.

When the main series with the mouth key were practically
completed, the subjects T and C were tested with a set of geometrical figures; for example, three spots in the form of a
triangle, four in the form of a square, five in a quincunx, etc.

---

[1] See Table X.; cf. also Table IX., especially the results for Eight.

Of the forms used, some were regular and others irregular. The apparatus and general procedure were the same as in the main series. As the figures had to be frequently changed to avoid mere recognition reaction, there were a great many different ones used, and it is impracticable to tabulate them all. A number of typical examples are given, however, in Table IX., showing the effects of various arrangements. The num-

TABLE IX.—COUNTING BY INFERENCE.

FIGURES.		T			C			
	N	M	N'	E	N	M	N'	E
III .˙.	2	784.	2	0	3	595.3	4	0
V :·:	4	836.2	8	0	4	810.	4	0
VI :::	6	1181.8		1	6	1546.6	7	1
VII :·:	8	1051.1	9	0	9	1452.2	9	0
VIII :::	0	—	4	4	3	3234.3	3	0
IX :::	2	1108.5	2	0	3	1603.	3	0
XII :·˙·:	2	1631.5	2	0	1	2108.	1	0

ber of successful reactions and mean reaction times are given in the columns headed N and M. The columns headed N' and E represent the whole number of attempted reactions and errors, respectively, as in Table VIII. It was found that for the higher numbers a regular arrangement facilitated the count, especially where the figure was compact; in the case of a straight line and a polygon of six sides or more the regularity rather impeded it; the count was still more impeded where the arrangement was irregular.

The fact that numbers as high as Twelve were correctly counted after so short an exposure shows at once that the process employed was different from that employed in the regular experiments. This is confirmed by the after-judgments of the subjects, who described the procedure as ' inference,' ' counting,' and ' guessing.' When these terms were explained they were found to indicate radically different processes. *Inference* was the term used when the number was judged from the shape, etc., or inferred from the memory of the same figure as seen before. *Counting* was applied to the progressive or 'one, two, three,' counting. *Guessing* was a combination of progressive counting for part of a group, with a guess or judgment of the remainder; it is really a species of inferential counting. The counting of some numbers, such as Nine and Twelve in the table, was performed by a kind of multiplication; the subject called this process inference (or judgment), explaining at the end of the test that he included multiplication under this head.

TABLE X.—CHARACTER OF REACTION AND COUNT.

		II	III	IV	V	VI	VII	VIII
T	Whole number of reactions	34	36	59	53	55	27	12
	Errors	0	2	7	11	24	4	1
	Reactions on light	0	1	1	0	2	2	0
	Too large; no reaction	0	0	0	0	2	4	2
	Too large; reaction (∞)	0	0	0	1	9	11	9
	Inferences	0	0	0	0	3	1	0
	Guesses	0	0	0	6	8	2	0
	Counts	0	0	0	0	3	1	0
	Unspecified	34	33	51	35	4	2	0
	Doubtful	0	1	1	4	1	3	0
C	Whole number of reactions	30	30	50	50	51	10	5
	Errors	1	5	4	17	29	4	4
	Reactions on light	0	0	0	0	1	0	0
	Too large; no reaction	0	0	0	0	0	0	0
	Too large reaction (∞)	0	0	0	0	1	0	0
	Inferences	0	0	0	1	2	0	1
	Guesses	0	0	2	8	4	3	0
	Counts	0	0	0	4	8	0	0
	Unspecified	29	25	44	20	6	3	0
	Doubtful	0	0	1	3	7	2	1
W	Whole number of reactions	8	12	10	20	16	14	25
	Errors	0	1	0	3	6	4	12
	Reactions on light	0	0	1	1	0	0	0
	Too large; no reaction	0	0	0	0	0	0	1
	Too large; reaction (∞)	0	0	0	1	0	0	6
	Inferences	0	0	0	0	0	1	0
	Guesses	0	0	0	0	0	1	0
	Counts	0	0	0	0	0	0	0
	Unspecified	8	11	9	15	10	8	6
	Doubtful	0	0	1	2	4	1	4

In Table X. are shown the processes used in the main series of counting experiments (cf. Tables VI. and VIII.), as described after each reaction by the subject; inferences and guesses were always reported; a large proportion of the successful reactions on numbers higher than Four, which are not expressly ascribed to one or other of these processes (those in the row labeled 'unspecified'), are undoubtedly cases of progressive counting ('counts').[1] No attempt was made in the present study to distinguish between inference and association; in the table both processes are included under the term inference. The word judgment, which was sometimes used by the subjects in place of inference, has been generally avoided in the discussion as being too broad and indefinite. Since 'guessing,' as here used, is a complex process whose chief characteristic is an inference, this leaves but three distinct processes by which the subjects gained their knowledge of the numbers, according to their own statements, viz., the processes which we have called perceptive, progressive and inferential counting.

VI. CONCLUSIONS.

Referring back to the questions proposed at the outset, we find that definite, if not complete, answers can be given to both as a result of the present investigation.

1. *The Limit of Perceptive Counting*—The limit of perceptive counting, with two adult subjects (T and C) one of motor and one of sensory type, both intellectually bright, but with no special talent for numbers, was found to lie at Four; this number was occasionally grasped and reacted on in the same time as One, but only of Three and Two could this be said generally. Investigations of other subjects (G, H and W, as well as C again) with hand reactions served to confirm this view. We conclude, therefore, that, *except under special stress of attention, or with subjects especially apt in this direction, the function of perceptive counting is limited to the numbers One, Two and Three.*

[1] In Table X. the rows are mutually exclusive, except the first and last; the 'whole number of reactions' equals the sum of the other rows, leaving out the row of 'doubtful' answers.

2. *The Rôle of Inference.*—To apprehend numbers greater than Four, then, some other function must come into play. The process by which this knowledge is first attained is what we have termed ' progressive counting.' It consists in establishing what mathematicians call a ' one-to-one' relation between the objects in the given group and the series of natural numbers; when the group is exhausted the last number reached in the count is known to be the number of objects in the group. But this process is comparatively slow, and in practice it is often shortened by one or another device. Thus we know by frequent experience (*e. g.*, with playing-cards or dominos) that the figure called a quincunx is a group of five things; when, therefore, we see such a figure, instead of counting the spots progressively, we *associate the number-name* (Five) with the group; and so of other figures which have become known by repeated experience. Or, again: given three rows of three spots each, although this particular figure may not be familiar to us, still we know from the multiplication table (which *is* familiar enough) that ' three times three is nine,' and upon perceiving the three spots on each side we immediately associate the number Nine with the group. A third case, not touched on in any of our experiments, is where the group is divided into sub-groups of various sizes; here we may count the sub-groups separately— by the perceptive or progressive processes—and reach the sum total at once through our knowledge of the addition table; this is another instance of inference based on association. Now it appears from our final series of experiments (Table IX.) that for the higher numbers the use of this inferential process shortens the reaction time, but that for the lower ones it does not—in fact, it tends rather to lengthen it. In other words, *inference tends to shorten progressive counting and to lengthen perceptive counting*, when it takes their place wholly or in part.

It would be useless to attempt to measure the *amount* of shortening produced by influence, since the time of the latter process itself varies within wide limits. In cases where we are very familiar with a certain grouping it may reduce the time enormously; in others, the inferential process is so complex that it is of little use in expediting the count. The chief result of the present experiments, as regards the higher numbers, is to show that progressive counting is a comparatively long process, and that we must resort habitually to some kind of inference in counting large groups. Familiar figures are rare, and are practically confined to groups of less than a dozen; but addition and multiplication, combined with perceptive or progressive counting are common resources. As a matter of fact, we do not often have occasion to count very large groups; when we do, we usually fall back upon one or other of these inferential processes.

VII. Some Experiments on the Successive Double-Point Threshold.

BY PROFESSOR G. A. TAWNEY, AND PROFESSOR C. W. HODGE.

Beloit College.   *Lafayette College.*

Nearly all of the experiments on the tactual double-point threshold have been carried on by the method of least changes, the original of which was first conceived and applied by that father of experimental methods, E. H. Weber. Of the very large number of discussions in this field, which have appeared since the original discussion of Weber, only one [1] investigates the double-point threshold with successive stimuli. At the same time, it has been well known by every experimentor in this field that the threshold for the perception of successive points must be much shorter than that for the perception of simultaneous stimuli on the same spot; for the effect of any slight failure to set the two points upon the skin simultaneously is always the perception of the two points before the ordinary threshold has been reached. The following is the report of some experiments which, if not sufficiently numerous to entitle them to the claim of completeness, may nevertheless be helpful as preparatory to a more protracted study.

The object of the experiments was to determine the thresh-

[1] Judd, Ueber Raumwahrnehmung im Gebiete des Tastsinnes, Phil. Stud., Bd. XII., 409–463.

old for the perception of spatial difference, and that for the direction of the difference (in eight different directions from the same spot of skin) with different intervals of time between the stimulations. Among the problems which were expected to appear in the course of the experiments were the following: (1) is the threshold for the perception of spatial difference, with successive stimuli, the same as that for direction, or is it different? (2) are they the same for all directions from the same spot of skin? (3) do they vary for different lengths of time-interval between the stimuli, and if so, according to what law? (4) is any light to be gained from these results upon simultaneous stimuli, and upon the general question as to the nature of tactual space-perception?

The subjects of these experiments were four, Professor H. C. Warren (W), Mr. J. F. Crawford (C), Dr. C. W. Hodge (H), Dr. G. A. Tawney (T). Excepting the latter none of these had any practice in the performance of such experiments. (T. had taken part in an extended series of experiments on the tactual double-point threshold for simultaneous stimuli.)

The arm of the subject rested upon the table, a screen concealing it and the apparatus from him. A piece of wood was so placed that the subject could grasp it, and thus preserve the same position of the arm during each hour. The spot investigated was also secured by marking the point on the skin which was first touched in each experiment. The temperature of the room was kept approximately constant, and the general conditions of the experiments, such as mental preoccupation, the mood and the health of the subject, the time of day, etc., were carefully noted before each hour.

The instrument used was a Verdin æsthesiometer. In order to facilitate the experiments, the instrument was suspended by a cord which passed over a pulley to a swinging weight. A difficulty arose in the determination of the distance on the arm of the second point stimulated from the first. We wished to use both points of the instrument in order to take advantage of the millimeter scale of the æsthesiometer, but the points could not rest upon the arm at the same time. One of the points was accordingly elevated by inserting a piece of wood beneath the indicator, the other point remaining extended to the full length of the spring. A card containing a small hole and fastened to a piece of wood was so placed that by passing the points of the æsthesiometer through the hole successively, the same spot on the skin could be touched by the extended point and then pointed to by the elevated point. In this way the distance of the second stimulation from the first could be read from the æsthesiometer scale without touching the arm with both points. The hole in the card was suspended over the same spot on the skin from day to day. The experiments were conducted in the following manner: The extended point was first passed through the hole in the card with a pressure against the skin of about 50 g. The æsthesiometer was then raised and the elevated or shortened point was made to pass through the hole and point to the spot just touched by the other point, while the other point pressed the skin at a distance measured by the horizontal graduated bar of the instrument. This second pressure was also about 50 g. The points were of bone suitably rounded off so as not to cause pain.

To regulate the duration of the stimulations, a metronome was made to vibrate at the desired rate in an instrument case across the room. The duration of the stimulation, as well as that of the interval between the stimulations, was regulated by counting the beats of the metronome. Another precaution was found necessary with reference to the pressure of the points. By the conditions of the experiments the first of each pair of stimulations occurred at the same spot on the arm throughout the series. But the repeated stimulation of this spot gave rise, in some cases, to a qualitative difference between the sensations, which soon came to be recognized by the subject as pain. Thus the second point might be recognized as different from the first without any perception of spatial difference. This, it is true, is an inference wherever it occurs, whereas the answers of the subject ought to be direct perceptions; but he very easily, as experience proved, mistakes his inference in this case for an act of perception, and even though he should not do so, it is very probable that the inferred knowledge that the points are in fact not the same would have a pronounced effect upon his answers.

To avoid this result, we simply lessened the pressure upon the first point as the hour proceeded, asking the reagent to inform us whenever any qualitative or quantitative differences appeared between the two sensations. It has been asserted that one of the conditions of these and similar experiments is that the two sensations be subjectively the same in intensity, and it is usually assumed that this is to be secured by the same objective pressure. But one finds in fact that two points on the skin are very seldom equally sensitive to the same objective pressure. The only adequate method of securing like subjective intensities is the empirical one of testing the two spots until we have ascertained their relative sensibility.

The object of the first series of experiments was to determine the threshold for the perception of spatial difference in two successive stimulations, and also that for the perception of the direction of the second stimulation from the first. The interval between the two stimulations was a constant one of three seconds in this series of experiments. Eight directions were chosen in all, viz. up (toward the shoulder), down (toward the hand), in (toward the little finger side of the arm), out (toward the thumb side of the arm), up-out (half way between up and out), and similarly down-out, down-in, up-in. According to the method of least changes, the series in any one direction should be reversed and the average drawn from the two thresholds thus obtained. As the direction of the second point from the first is known in the reverse series of these experiments, it seemed best to separate the two series and not to follow the usual custom of taking the average between the two. The question also arose whether the thresholds for the diagonals might not be different from those for the axes, owing to the direction, and it was decided to take the thresholds for the four axes first, then proceed to the thresholds for the diagonals, and lastly to take the eight directions together. In the latter case, the eight directions could not be taken without readjusting the apparatus and, rather than do this (which would notify the subject of the direction), one of the directions, viz. up, was omitted. The experiments on H were performed by T, and those on T by H. Tables I. II. and III. show the results of the di-

TABLE I.

Showing thresholds of difference and thresholds of direction on the axes from the originally stimulated point; also middle threshold and middle variation.

HODGE.

IN.		DOWN.		OUT.		UP.		Each Day.	Aver. Thresh.
Differ-ence.	Direc-tion.	Differ-ence.	Direc-tion.	Differ-ence.	Direc-tion.	Differ-ence.	Direc-tion.		
o	6	2	2	o	6	2	4	1.0	4.5
1	14	1	6	2	2	2	2	1.5	6.0
1	9	2	3	o	2	1	8	1.0	5.7
3	3	4	4	1	7	2	6	2.5	5.0
3	20+	1	20+	3	4	3	3	2.5	3.5
2	32	3	5	3	5	5	5	3.3	11.
20+	5	3	7	3	5	4	4	3.3	5.0
4.3	12.7	2.3	6.7	1.7	4.4	2.7	4.5	M. Thresh.	
4.5	8.1	.9	4.1	1.2	1.5	1.1	1.6	M. Var.	

TAWNEY.

IN.		DOWN.		OUT.		UP.		Each Day.	Aver. Thresh.
2	6	2	4	o	6	2	3	1.5	4.7
1	2	1	3	2	4	1	1	1.2	2.5
1	2	1	2	2	2	3	3	1.7	2.2
1	8	3	3	2	5	2	2	2.0	4.5
o	5	3	5	2	3	1	3	1.5	4.0
2	2	1	3	4	4	3	3	2.5	3.0
1.2	4.1	1.8	3	2	6	2	3.7	M. Thresh.	
	2.1		.6		2		1.2	M. Var.	

WARREN.

IN.		DOWN.		OUT.		UP.		Each Day.	Aver. Thresh.
1	14	1	12	1	12	20+	20+	1.0	12.5
3	10	2	9	2	11	1	20+	2.0	10.0
5	12	2	8	1	8	2	4	2.5	8.0
3	12	1.6	9.6	1.3	10.3	7.6	14.6	M. Thresh.	
1.3	1.3	0.4	1.5	0.4	1.5	8.2	7.1	M. Var.	

TABLE II.

Showing thresholds of difference and thresholds of direction on the four diagonals from the point originally stimulated, the middle variation and the middle threshold.

HODGE.

DOWN-IN.		DOWN-OUT.		UP-IN.		UP-OUT.		Each Day.	Aver. Thresh.
Difference.	Direction.	Difference.	Direction.	Difference.	Direction.	Difference.	Direction.		
5	6	1	5	1	11	4	4	2.7	6.5
3	6	4	4	2	5	2	3	2.7	4.5
2	7	3	5	3	3	3	3	2.7	4.5
1	5	4	5	2	5	5	5	3.0	5.0
4	5	3	3	2	6	4	4	3.2	4.5
3	5	1	2	4	12	1	1	2.2	5.0
4	6	3	3	3	6	1	6	2.7	4.2
3	5.7	3	3.8	2.5	6.8	3	3.7	M. Thresh.	
.9	.6	.9	1.2	.8	2.3	1.3	1.1	M. Var.	

TAWNEY.

2	6	3	5	2	2	1	3	2	4
3	3	3	3	1	1	5	6	3	3.2
1	2	0	1	2	2	1	1	1	1.5
0	3	2	7	2	2	1	8	1.2	5.0
1	2	2	3	1	2	1	2	1.2	2.2
1	2	2	6	1	5	1	3	1.2	4.0
1	3	1	2	1	2	1	5	1	3.0
1.3	3	2	3.8	1.4	4	1.6	4	M. Thresh.	
.7	.8	.7	1.8	.5	2	1	2	M. Var.	

WARREN.

1	10	1	10	1	6	1	2	1	7
1	7	1	7	2	2	1	1	1.2	4.2
1	8.5	1	8.5	1.5	4	1	1.5	M. Thresh.	
0	1.5	0	1.5	.5	2	0	.5	M. Var.	

different directions from the point originally stimulated, also the middle thresholds and middle variations.

	IN Differ-ence	IN Direc-tion	DOWN Differ-ence	DOWN Direc-tion	OUT Differ-ence	OUT Direc-tion	IN-UP Differ-ence	IN-UP Direc-tion	IN-DOWN Differ-ence	IN-DOWN Direc-tion	OUT-DOWN Differ-ence	OUT-DOWN Direc-tion	OUT UP Differ-ence	OUT UP Direc-tion	Each Day	Aver. Thresh.
	3	14	3	3	2	2	2	11	2	2	2	5	20+	20+	2.3	6.1
	2	14	3	3	3	5	4	8	3	7	3	3	2	12	3.0	7.2
	0	11	3	3	1	8	1	4	5	7	1	5	3	3	2.0	5.4
	4	11	4	4	3	3	3	7	3	6	3	3	3	3	3.3	4.8
	3	20+	2	20+	20+	10	0	20+	4	4	20+	5	20+	20+	2.2	2.7
M. Thresh.	2.4	14	3	6.6	5.9	5.6	2	10	3.4	5.2	5.9	4.2	9.6	11.6	M. Thresh.	
M. Var.	1.1	2.4	.4	5.3	5.7	2.7	1.2	4.4	.9	1.7	5.7	.96	8.3	6.9	M. Var.	
HODGE.																
	0	1	20+	20+	20+	6	20+	1	20+	2	0	1	1	2	1	2.1
	1	4	1	2	1	7	0	1	1	5	1	2	1	8	1	4.1
	1	3	1	1	0	7	0	1	1	2	1	5	1	5	.7	3.4
	2	5	1	4	2	9	1	1	1	3	3	3	3	4	2.	4.1
	3	2	2	2	0	3	2	4	2	2	2	3	1	2	1.6	2.5
M. Thresh.	1.2	3	5	5.9	4.6	6.4	4.6	1.6	5	2.8	1.4	2.8	1.4	4.2	M. Thresh.	
M. Var.	.4	1.2	6	5.7	6.1	1.5	6.1	0.9	6	0.9	.9	1.04	.64	1.8	M. Var.	
TAWNEY.																
	2	20+	20+	20+	1	20+	20+	20+	1	13	1	13	1	5	1.5	10.3
	1	3	1	6	1	5	1	1	1	5	2	2	2	2	1.3	3.14
	1	6	1	3	1	3	1	4	1	15	1	3	1	2	1	12.
M. Thresh.	1.3	9.6	7.3	9.6	1	9.3	7.3	8.3	1	11	1.3	6	1.3	3	M. Thresh.	
M. Var.	.4	6.8	8.4	6.8	0	7.1	8.4	7.7	0	4	.4	3.6	.4	1.3	M. Var.	
WARREN.																

rect series of experiments on the axis, on the diagonals, and on the axis and diagonals combined, the thresholds for difference and direction being given side by side. The number 20 indicates cases where a wrong suggestion prevailed to such an extent that a correct answer was never reached.

What impresses us first on looking over the tables is the difference between the two thresholds, *i. e.*, between that for spatial difference between the two stimulated points on the arm, and that for the direction of the second point from the first. This difference has lead the writer already referred to to the conclusion that the threshold for the tactual perception of spatial difference is shorter than that for the tactual perception of spatial direction under the conditions of these experiments. But when we consider that the idea of direction is inseparable in thought from the idea of spatial difference, it seems improbable that there should be a perception of spatial difference without a perception of the direction of one point from the other. In other words it seems difficult to sense spatial difference without direction. And yet we are told that this is the real nature of all those cases where the threshold for the perception of difference is shorter than that for the perception of direction. This means that space is after all not the form of tactual perception; at least, that space in three dimensions is not.

But again, the most of the cases, upon which this inference rests, do not pretend to be perceptions of spatial difference without any direction. A direction is usually given by the subject, but it happens to be false, and the inference is drawn by the operator that a difference is perceptible, but not the direction of the difference. Is it not possible that a difference is perceived which is not spatial at all, and that the subject comes to give it the worth of real space-perception by illusion? It should be remembered that we possess an objective standard for determining the direction-threshold, such as we do not possess for the difference-threshold. In the case of difference alone, the answer is usually correct, because a difference is, as a rule, actually present; but in the matter of direction we take the correctness of the answer as a criterion of a real perception of direction. Is it not possible that there may exist an illusion as to difference as well as to direction? After the discovery which has recently been made of the enormous part played by suggestion in the perception of two simultaneous points,[1] it is at least possible, not to say probable, that the same law works here also. Of this we can speak more advantageously later. What we are concerned here with is, first, that we have no right to apply an objective criterion of true perception in the case of direction unless we can apply the same standard in the case of difference; we should refrain from generalizing until the facts of the case have been more thoroughly looked into; secondly, this generalization, that the difference threshold is the smaller, would in no case be acceptable if it were possible to account for the observed facts by such a well established law as one which has been included under the general term, the association of ideas, but which we prefer to call suggestion. The direction given by the subject may be wrong, as it often is; but this merely constitutes a mistake of perception which, where persistent in any one direction, we call illusion.

Assuming that the apparent perceptions of difference without direction are not bona fide instances of perception in all respects, what explanation can be given for the errors in the judgments of direction? It seems as though a very natural explanation is to be found in experiences with which we are made familiar every day and hour. The perception-act in these experiments differs from that of ordinary experience in the fact that the subject is not allowed to see the spot stimulated and the instrument stimulating, at the same time he feels the touch. That constant practice of testing our tactual sensations by the sensations of a much more highly developed organ is therefore not possible here; and, consequently, the assimilation of the present impressions goes on by means of visual and motor images, as every one can easily persuade himself by trying the experiments on himself. Just as in reading we pass over typographical errors without being in the least conscious of their presence, because the actual visual images are assimilated to a correct visual image of the arrangement of the words and letters; so in these experi-

[1] Tawney, Ueber die Wahrnehmung zweier Punkte, etc., Phil. Stud., Bd. XIII., S. 163 ff.

ments, one assimilates the actual tactual impressions to a revival copy of similar experiences in the past, but to a copy which is actually not in accordance with the facts because the association bond between the tactual stimulus and the visual or motor image is not sufficiently close to be accurate. The local sign of the tactual sensation is, as has been said before, no simple quality of the sensation itself, but just this associational bond between the sensation and the visual or motor image to which it is assimilated. The question of most interest is, what determines the visual or motor image to be of this or that sort. One finds that both difference and direction are sometimes given when the same point has been stimulated twice in succession, that the direction given, even when the points are actually different, is often wrong, and that the error in the direction judgment seems to lie persistently in the direction of the judgments in the last series of experiments, in a direction suggested by the operator himself, or in a direction which the subject gets by autosuggestion. In some cases it is probable that more than one of these causes are present to determine the subject's answer.

Taking up the answers in which an actual difference is present between the two stimulations, but in which the direction given is wrong, they may be divided into three groups. Some follow some external suggestion, *i. e.*, they are influenced either by a previous judgment, or by the combined influence of the previous judgment and the stimulus. An illustration of the former sort would be as follows : Supposing that an up series has just been taken, and that the present series is one in which the distance increases downward, the subject gives the answer 'up.' The following would be an illustration of the latter : Supposing that an in series has just been taken, and that the present series is progressing downward, the subject answers 'down-in.' Out of 11 such wrong answers made by H during these experiments, 3 fell under the first head and 8 under the second. In the case of W, out of 13 wrong answers of this kind 9 belong to the first class and 4 to the second. T made only one wrong answer of this sort, belonging to the first class.

A second group of cases in which wrong answers were given admit of explanation as instances of autosuggestion.

From an objective point of view they seem to be accidental. The subjective process involved seems to be somewhat as follows : The subject feels the first and then the second stimulus, different in time, and at once strives to assimilate the two impressions to his past experiences. He represents the second impression in this or that direction from the first, in order to see whether the actual impression seems any different from the mental image of past experience. The tactual impression being very vague in space quality, he receives no correction, *i. e.*, the image and the impression seem the same and at once fuse into one perception. All perception seems to involve some such process as this. Every presentation is composed partly of elements of the present stimulation and partly of elements of past experience. The present sensation gives to the whole the vivid character which it itself possesses. Illusion always arises whenever the representation elements of the experience dominate over the whole so as to give it a meaning which the actual sensation elements do not possess. Of course this does not explain the cases at hand; it merely suggests a possible way in which the erroneous judgments of direction come to be given below the threshold for the perception of two points.

Another group of answers seem to be due, in one case, to autosuggestion combined with a stimulus element, and, in another case, to autosuggestion combined with the influence of the previous judgment. Of the former sort one finds in the answers of H 25 instances, and of the latter, 1 ; in the case of T, 37 of the former, and 3 of the latter; in the answers of W, 46 of the former kind and 16 of the latter.

Granting the hypothesis of suggestion to start with, it seems that all of these instances of wrong answers as to direction illustrate one form or another of the same process.

This conclusion seems the more probable when we consider the group of answers in which difference and direction are both given, while the same point on the skin is stimulated twice. This occurs much oftener in descending series than in ascending series, because in the former the actual direction of the second point from the first is distinctly felt in the first experiment of the series, and this knowledge operates as a suggestion after the difference between the points has disappeared. In the similar experiments of Dr. C. H. Judd,[1] the smallest threshold for the perception of spatial *difference* in descending series is o, as given in his table. All such instances are obviously due to some sort of suggestion. They correspond to the Vexirfehler in experiments with two simultaneous stimuli. In the case of ascending series the suggestion may be automatic, in descending, external, *i. e.*, from a previous judgment. In the ascending series, however, it may also be due, as above, to the influence of a previous series of judgments or of experiments. A test of this hypothesis, which seemed to be crucial, occurred in the often repeated answer of H, ' spatial difference without direction ;' but upon reflecting upon the subjective process involved, he believes these judgments to be at bottom inferences, based upon slight qualitative differences in the two stimulations. No direction can be given, simply because they are inferences ; were they perceptions they would be perceptions of direction, though erroneous. In the answers of W, two instances of this phenomenon are to be found. When questioned as to the subjective process involved, he replied, in the first instance, that he had not paid close attention to the first stimulus, and felt, when the second came, that it must be different because of the previous answers which he had made in the series, but that he had no idea whether the direction was the same as in previous instances or not. In the second instance he observed that a certain direction was present in his visual image of the point stimulated, but that he simply was not sure as to the correctness of the representation. Such cases did not occur with T.

A modification of this class of cases is seen in answers which indicate partial location, as, *e. g.*, where the answer is ' up or up-in,' ' out, up-out, or up.' Here the uncertainty as to the correctness of the mental representation is limited to a few alternatives. Where this occurs with H, who is a poor visualizer, the answer seems to be the result of self-questioning as to the probable direction in which the series is progressing. In the case of W, who is a good visualizer, it seems to express

---

[1] Loc. cit., pp. 420, 421.

uncertainty as to the correctness of the visual image, which, **as** he says, is usually present in these experiments. These **cases** also never occur with T.

TABLE IV.—SUGGESTIVE PROGRESSIONS.

*Showing the number of series in which the influence of sugges-
tion is obvious; the total number of series; the lower and upper limits of thresholds found, together with their mean; the
number of single wrong answers; and the ratio of wrong answers which seemed due to suggestion to the total number of
wrong answers.*

	H.	W.	T.
Number of Progressions	57	21	65
Number of Series	92	21	90
Threshold { Limits	1–32	1–15	1–9
Threshold { Mean	16.5	8	5
Number of wrong answers	442	134	199
Ratio of suggestions to wrong answers . . .	66 :442	87 :134	61 :199

A comprehensive view of the results of these experiments is offered in Table IV. In the upper line the total number of series of experiments in which suggestive influences are apparent, is given for each of the three subjects, H, W and T. Suggestions of different kinds sometimes appear within the same series, as (*e. g.*) when, after an up-series, the subject answers, when the same point is stimulated twice, ' up,' and continues this answer until the second stimulation has reached a distance of 5 mm, in the direction downward from the first; here he answers ' up-in,' and, as the series progresses and the distance becomes greater, ' in,' ' down-in,' and finally ' down.' Here we have the influence of a previous series of experiments and judgments at first dominating, then a combination of the influence of the actual stimulus with that of the previous judgments, and finally the influence of the stimulus alone; illustrating what is called in the table a suggestive progression.

In the second line the total number of series of experiments is given for comparison with the number in which suggestive influences appear. This line shows, in the case of H, W and T, respectively, that $\frac{51}{92}$, all, and $\frac{13}{18}$ of all the series were influenced in this way.

In the third line the lower and upper limits of threshold-variations, together with the mean of those two, are given to show the result of varying suggestive influences under similar external conditions. It must be remembered, however, that differences of direction are not taken into consideration in this line, and it is true that the threshold for some directions is lower than for others; other factors than suggestion, such as direction, thus come in to vary the threshold, but all other factors combined are not sufficient to account for the wide divergence apparent in these figures.

In the fourth and fifth lines are reported (1) the total number of single wrong answers occurring throughout the experiments, and (2) the ratio of those answers in which suggestive influences are apparent to the total number of wrong answers. A word should be said with reference to the wrong answers which are not referrable to the influence of suggestion. These were mostly the answer 'same,' meaning that the two stimulations seem to be on the same spot. This is the answer which one expects in response to all distances which lie below the threshold. Such answers sometimes occur, however, when the distance is above the threshold, and it is possible that suggestion has played some part in these. We are not in a position to say, however, that it does so, or to what extent it enters in, owing to the absence of objective criteria. Another group of answers were simple expressions of uncertainty and suspense, and are not to be counted among the wrong answers at all. The answer, 'same,' is often given at the beginning of series, *i. e.*, when the two stimulations are really the same, and the answer is then right. The difference between the wrong answers due to suggestion and those in which suggestive influences are not apparent seems to be chiefly this, that in the former class some element of mental content suddenly makes its appearance in consciousness and influences the judgment, while in the latter class nothing arises to modify the usual reaction of the attention to the stimulus; and this difference is what is meant by suggestion.

II.

Another group of experiments was begun in which the series were all descending. In the experiments the direction was necessarily known to the subject, the object of the experiments being to determine where difference and direction cease to be perceived. Table V. shows the results. Wherever no threshold is given, the subject continued to give a difference and a direction at the end of the series when the same point was stimulated twice.

The influence of suggestion is obvious throughout this table in the fact that the thresholds, where they appear at all, are much lower than those of the ascending series. All of the subjects continued to give a difference and a direction when the same point was stimulated twice. In the answers of T, 11 are of this kind; in those of H, 23; and in those of W, 22. These answers are due, we take it, to the same influence which produces the low thresholds.

III.

The following experiments were carried out by Dr. Hodge in the Princeton Laboratory for the purpose of determining what influence, if any, the length of the interval between the two stimulations has upon the threshold for the perception of spatial difference between the two stimulations. But before going on to describe the experiments, we will notice a few facts as to the subjective processes involved, which are closely connected with the foregoing. Professor W. is a good visualizer; he always closed his eyes during the experiments, and gave close attention to the arm and the spots stimulated as they appeared in the visual copy. Both subjects were given to making a judgment of difference or of direction, or of both, at the beginning of series where the same point was stimulated twice in succession. Such errors (corresponding to the Vexirfehler in experiments with simultaneous stimuli) could, in some cases, as above, in the experiments already reported, be accounted for by the influence of the preceding series, or that of a previous judgment, but the two subjects differ very decidedly in this respect. In the case of C such judgments could, as a rule, be traced to such influences,

TABLE V. REVERSED SERIES ON AXES, ON DIAGONALS, AND ON AXES AND DIAGONALS, WITH H, W AND T.

	D-OUT.	D-IN.	UP-IN.	UP-O.	OUT.	DOWN.	IN.		D-OUT.	UP-OUT.	UP-IN.	D-I.	OUT.	UP.	IN.	DOWN.
H	1 —	— 2	— 2	1 —	2 —	1 —	1 1		— 1	— —	1 —	1 —	— 1 —	2 2 1	2 1 —	1 2 —
W	2 1	1 —	1 —	— 2	— 1	— 1	1 —		— —	— 1	— 1	1 —	1 —	1 —	— 2	2 —
T	2 3	1 2	1 3	2 6	2 3	2 3	3 1		1 3	3 4	2 —	— 1	5 5 2	2 1 —	1 2 1	1 2 2

whereas, in the case of W they seemed, as a rule, to follow no law; they seemed to be purely accidental, so far as the outward conditions of the judgments were concerned. This difference corresponds to another which appears in the observations of W, that to him it seemed unnatural to pay attention to sensations of touch alone. He finds that it requires an especial effort to keep the tactual stimulus before the attention, while distraction from slight causes is easy and frequent. W finds it difficult to keep the first stimulus before the attention for the entire period between the first and the second, when this is 15 seconds.

All of these facts would seem to indicate that the perception of two points with W depends chiefly upon the presence of visual associations. It agrees with this that in some series his replies seem at the start to be determined partly by the stimulus and partly by autosuggestion, but as the series progresses it is not the stimulus which triumphs, as we expect, but the suggestion, and no continuance of the series will suffice to correct the persistent operation of the suggestion. Again, in some series, the presence of more than one suggestion is apparent, neither of which seems to be in any way connected with the stimulus. The visual image of the first point stimulated in each of the experiments of a given series seems to grow more and more distinct as the series progresses, showing that the difficulty in judging correctly lies, not in the absence of definite visual representations, but in the absence of the proper association links between the tactual excitations and the corresponding visual images. W seems to rely, as a matter of habit, far more on visual than upon tactual images for his knowledge of the objects with which he comes into contact. The series in which he knew nothing as to the nature of the series, whether it was along the axes or along the diagonals, were much longer than those in which he had some knowledge as to their nature from the start; showing the comparatively weak significance of the stimuli when experienced alone, it requiring much longer to recognize the direction.

With C tactual and motor images predominate; but the association between these images and the sensations is much closer than is the case with W.

C quite frequently remembers the first stimulus by the aid
of a motor image of himself stimulating the point with his left
hand. One notices in C also a greater tendency to use whatever data he may be able to acquire for *inferring* what the nature of the stimulus may be. He has a habit of assigning first
one direction to the second stimulus from the first, and then another until he finds one which brings the series to an end; and
no amount of instruction as to how the answers should be made
suffices to divert this tendency. He as a rule infers that his answer is not correct whenever the series is continued for more
than two or three experiments further. This is for him a constant suggestion, wherever it occurs. It was for W also in
some cases, although not so habitually as with C. The latter
also gets information as to the direction which probably is being
taken in the experiments by remembering the directions which
have already been tried. Sometimes he has the suggestion
that the direction pursued is one of two or three, and proceeds
by a method of elimination to go from one to another until he
reaches one which brings the series to an end. Occasionally
he forms an hypothesis as to the direction and answers accordingly until the sensations either confirm or contradict it, the process by which he forms the hypothesis being in some cases a
purely inferential one and in other cases an associative one. In
some cases, as he observes, he has no notion, prior to the stimulus, as to the direction in question, and answers according to the
tactual or motor images suggested by the second stimulus. For
C the tactual perception for spatial difference is always a result based upon certain qualitative differences between the sensations involved. When asked to describe the qualitative differences referred to, he speaks in terms which to us seem most
vague and indefinite, and which characterize nothing, so far as
we can determine, which enters into our own experience. To
him, however, they have a clear and definite character. It is,
moreover, significant that he observes the presence of certain
tactual and motor images as an assimilating factor in every perception; how the assimilation takes place he would not undertake to say, although this is probably the same process for tactual and motor images as W describes for visual. No doubt

C's answers were quite often inferences as much as assimilations; but it seems clear that his usual method of answering is one of assimilating his present sensations to tactual or motor images of previous experiences in the perception of two points.

Going on to the experiments conducted by Dr. Hodge to determine the relation between the length of interval between the two stimuli and the threshold for the perception of two points, the following were the results: The interval was determined as before by a metronome which was placed across the room in an instrument case. The intervals chosen were 2 sec., 5 sec., 10 sec., and 15 sec. It was impossible to make the interval shorter than two seconds and preserve the conditions constant, owing to the nature of the apparatus. A longer interval than 15 sec. could not be chosen because of the difficulty involved in retaining the first sensation in memory until the second should follow. The experiments were made in three groups as follows: first, those in which the directions were straight up, down, in, or out (the axes); those in which the diagonal directions were chosen, and those in which the eight directions were all taken within the same hour. One determination was made for each of the four intervals within each hour in order to have the conditions as near the same as possible for experiments which were to be compared. The number 20+ in the following tables indicate the series in which, because of some false suggestion, the subject never succeeded in making correct answers. The o's indicate the series in which, as a result of chance coincidence, the direction hit upon by the subject when, at the beginning of the series, the same point was stimulated twice, happened to be the correct one for that series. In such series it is of course impossible to determine what the real threshold is. The direction thresholds for the perception of two simultaneous points applied in the same regions as the following experiments were as follows: For C, across, 10 mm., up and down, 15 mm., diagonal toward the thumb, 14 mm., and diagonal toward the little finger, 14 mm. For W the same thresholds were: across, 8 mm., up and down, 13 mm., diagonal toward the thumb, 8 mm., and diagonal toward the little finger, 7 mm. None but the direction thresholds are given in the tables which follow, along with the average thresholds for each day in all the directions. Table IV. gives the experiments with C.

TABLE VI.

Showing the thresholds for the perception of two successive points at intervals of 2 sec., 5 sec., 10 secs., and 15 sec. on left forearm, volar side of C.

2 SECONDS.

AXES.				DIAGONALS.				EIGHT DIRECTIONS.								
in.	up.	d.	out.	u-i.	d-i.	u-o.	d-o.	in.	up.	d.	out.	u-i.	d-i.	u-o.	d-o.	
8	6	0	10	3	9	3	7	3	3	0	9	8	2	6	6	
4	4	9	1	4	2	7	2	5	1	3	13	3	5	5	5	
4	2	2	4	5	5	1	1	5	7	4	7	3	4	3	15	
2	4	3	3	1	7	3	0	4	4	3	8	5	6	3	3	
4.5	4	4.2	4.5	3.3	5.7	3.5	3.3	4.2	3.7	3.3	9.2	4.7	4.2	4.2	7.2	M.T.

5 SECONDS.

8	3	7	6	4	6	3	5	4	6	0	3	2	8	2	8	
9	3	5	3	5	6	4	1	6	10	3	9	13	10	13	3	
5	1	1	3	2	3	0	1	4	6	8	3	3	3	4	1	
2	1	5	1	3	4	3	4	5	10	3	2	3	6	6	1	
6	2	4.5	3.2	3 5	4.7	3.3	3.6	4.7	8	3.5	4.2	5.2	7	6.2	3.2	M.T.

10 SECONDS.

4	1	5	7	1	4	4	5	7	6	16	1	10	7	11	3	
4	5	11	4	6	3	6	3	10	2	5	3	4	3	1	1	
4	5	1	3	6	3	6	0	4	3	8	15	10	3	9	5	
6	1	3	5	4	3	5	1	5	2	5	6	4	4	13	5	
4.5	3	5	4.7	4.2	3.3	5.2	3	6.5	3.2	8.5	6.2	7	4.2	8.5	3.5	M.T.

15 SECONDS.

0	3	1	2	3	3	2	5	2	1	4	4	0	5	5	2	
6	5	1	1	5	4	5	0	10	6	3	2	8	3	12	2	
1	0	3	2	3	3	7	6	16	5	7	3	7	10	4	3	
4	2	4	1	5	3	5	1	5	0	3	7	4	4	4	4	
3.6	3.3	2.2	1.5	4	3.2	4.5	4	8.2	4	4.2	4	4.7	5.5	6.2	2.7	M.T.

In the column headings d stands for down; u-i for up and in; d-i for down and in; u-o for up and out; d-o for down and out. What one first notices in the table of C's experiments is the difference between the thresholds for successive stimuli 2 seconds apart and the corresponding simultaneous thresholds. For 'across' the latter was 10 mm., while the succession threshold for 'in' is 4.5 mm., and that for 'out' 4.5 mm.; the simultaneous threshold for 'up and down' is 15 mm., while that for 'up' in successive stimuli is 4 mm., and that for 'down' 4.2 mm.; the diagonal simultaneous threshold toward the little finger is 14 mm., while the two corresponding succession thresholds are 5.7 mm. and 3.5 mm.; the simultaneous diagonal toward the thumb also is 14 mm., while the two corresponding succession thresholds are 3.3 mm. and 3.3 mm. In other words, the succession thresholds are much lower than the simultaneous ones nearest corresponding to them. But if we expect that the succession thresholds will shorten in proportion to the inverse length of the interval between the stimuli, we shall find little to confirm the suspicion. The average of all the thresholds for the interval 2 seconds with C is about 4.6 mm.; that for 5 seconds about 4.55 mm.; that for 10 seconds about 5.03 mm., and that for 15 seconds about 4.1 mm., showing a slight decrease of 0.5 mm. between the thresholds for 2 seconds and those for 15 seconds, while that for 10 seconds is considerably longer than that for either 2 seconds or 5 seconds. This is not a sufficiently definite indication to generalize upon.

Going on to Table VII., showing the results of the experiments with W, similar conclusions are to be drawn. That the succession thresholds are shorter by a very appreciable amount (½ to ⅓) than the corresponding simultaneous is obvious. As to the question whether the threshold decreases as the interval increases, however, these experiments unite in indicating an opposite effect of lengthening the time-interval. The difficulty of retaining the first stimulus clearly in mind during the longer intervals, so marked in the case of W, may have had something to do with this result; and, on the other hand, the tendency of C to infer was no doubt assisted by the increase in the length of the interval, as it gave him somewhat more time.

TABLE VII.

Thresholds on the left forearm, volar side, of W., at intervals of 2 sec., 5 sec., 10 sec., and 15 sec.

2 SECONDS.

AXES.				DIAGONALS.				EIGHT DIRECTIONS.							
in.	up.	d.	out.	u-i.	u-o.	d-i.	d-o.	in.	up.	d.	out.	u-i.	u-o.	d-i.	d-o.
20+	12	3	5	6	3	4	1	6	5	13	6	9	0	10	14
17	6	6	0	3	8	3	4	5	0	3	8	1	8	8	2
5	2	2	6	20+	4	3	20+	7	2	0	7	7	3	7	4
3	10	3	3	4	6	7	2	14	5	3	11	3	3	11	10
1.2	7.5	3.5	4.5	8.2	5.2	4.2	6.7	8	3	4.7	8	5	4.5	9	7.5

5 SECONDS.

20+	5	4	11	8	1	7	2	8	2	10	4	4	8	9	5
8	5	5	5	20+	3	5	2	3	12	4	7	6	6	5	7
7	3	8.	8	0	7	2	10	10	4	2	20+	5	3	3	5
4	1	2	6	6	5	5	3	4	7	2	11	2	4	0	10
9.7	3.5	4.7	7.5	8.5	4	4.7	4.2	6.2	6.2	4.5	10.5	4.2	5.2	5.6	7

10 SECONDS.

20+	13	0	15	4	3	4	3	15	18	2	8	3	4	5	20+
5	6	2	6	10	6	3	5	18	0	5	7	3	1	2	7
8	6	3	5	8	3	2	4	6	20+	1	9	4	8	4	3
20+	3	4	6	20+	3	2	8	6	4	10	4	9	0	6	6
13.2	7	3	8	10.5	3.7	2.7	5	11	10.5	4.5	7	4.7	4.3	4.2	9

15 SECONDS.

3	9	0	5	6	4	9	5	8	0	7	8	6	8	7	18
5	4	10	13	7	4	9	16	2	20+	7	20+	7	11	10	6
9	8	4	11	10	4	2	8	10	6	6	13	8	3	7	20+
3	3	9	4	7	12	1	3	8	4	5	3	13	6	10	1
5	6	5.7	8.2	7.5	6	5.2	8	7	7.5	6.2	11	8.5	7	8.5	11.2

So far as these two sets of experiments go, therefore, we may conclude that the threshold for successive stimuli is much shorter than that for simultaneous, but that increasing the length of the interval between the successive stimuli does not further shorten it. This may have the contrary effect. Throughout these experiments it was observed that the same questions as to the relation of the difference to the direction threshold arose, as in the former series of experiments. The answer 'different without direction' was, however, somewhat more frequent in the experiments with successive stimuli, than in those with simultaneous stimuli; a result due, no doubt, to the suggestive effect of the succession.

Table VIII., corresponding to Table IV., offers a summary view of the part played by suggestion in this entire group of experiments. It will not be necessary to add to what has been said concerning the previous table of the same kind.

TABLE VIII. SUGGESTIVE PROGRESSIONS.

Showing the number of series in which the influence of suggestion is obvious; the total number of series; the lower and upper limits of thresholds found, together with their mean; the number of single wrong answers; and the ratio of wrong answers which seemed due to suggestion to the total number of wrong answers.

	W	C
Numbers of Progressions, ...	251	226
Numbers of Series, ...	255	255
Threshold { Limits, ...	1-18	1-16
Threshold { Mean, ...	9.5	8.5
Number of Wrong Answers, ...	1509	952
Ratio of Suggestions to Wrong Answers, . .	1380 : 1509˙	783 : 952

There seem to be no facts in connection with these experiments with successive stimuli which do not readily harmonize with the conclusion as to the nature of our tactual perception of two points arrived at two years ago as a result of a series of experiments[1] with simultaneous stimuli in Wundt's institute, viz., that the tactual perception of two points is an assimilation process, based on association, in which visual or motor images are the assimilating, and tactual sensations the assimilated factors. We may repeat again what has been already said, that the local sign is no simple quality of tactual sensations, but rather a relation of association between the different factors, visual, motor

[1] See article in Phil. Stud. referred to above.

and tactual, which enter into the perception image. It is gratifying to find that Solomons[1] has recently come to similar conclusions in regard to the nature of the process involved. Aside from his statement that the process of reducing the threshold by practice, " as well as its general bearing on the origin of cutaneons perceptions, has been considered only speculatively" (which is not literally true), his results, so far as they go, accord for the most part with our own.

The phenomenon which, more than any other, argues against this view seems to be the answer which is sometimes given by the subject, ' different without direction.' But we have found reason for believing that this answer is either an inference from data other than tactual or a sort of illusion which arises in one or other of the following ways: either some nonspatial qualitative difference between the sensations calls up visual or motor images in which this difference appears as spatial, or some suggestion foreign to the immediate experience brings into consciousness such images, and the tactual sensations are wrongly assimilated to them.

[1] Solomons ' Discrimination in Cutaneous Sensations,' PSYCHOLOGICAL REVIEW, Vol. IV., pp. 246-250, especially p. 248.

STUDIES FROM THE HARVARD PSYCHOLOGICAL LABORATORY, IX.

COMMUNICATED BY PROFESSOR E. B. DELABARRE.

THE FORCE AND RAPIDITY OF REACTION MOVEMENTS.

By E. B. Delabarre, Robert R. Logan and Alfred Z. Reed.

INTRODUCTORY NOTE.

It has long seemed desirable to measure, in the taking of reactions, not only the reaction-time itself, but also the degree of pressure used by the subject in reacting and the rapidity with which he contracts his reacting muscles. Reflection on the possible bearing of such measurements upon the matter of individual temperament, and the opportunity afforded by my recent connection with the Harvard Laboratory, led me to devise the apparatus and initiate the experiments herein described. The number of persons on whom measurements were taken is not large, and the number of records taken in the case of each is much smaller than would have been desirable. Yet the time at our disposal has not admitted of greater accomplishment. I publish our results as a beginning of research into this problem, and because they establish the value and suggestiveness of this inquiry, and the facts that a particular average and a particular range of force and of rapidity in reacting are peculiar to each individual. They may possibly prove so typical as to furnish an index to the individual's fundamental characteristics as a whole—a possibility which I plan to discuss in a separate paper on the Study of Temperament.

I cannot refrain from expressing my deep obligation to my two collaborators in this research, who have conducted the experiments with great care and accuracy, and have devoted to the research an amount of time and patience far in excess of what was demanded by their duty to the laboratory. They have jointly contributed the following account of the details of the experiments. E. B. D.

I. APPARATUS AND METHOD OF RESEARCH.

The apparatus used in these experiments consisted of a revolving drum, on which were recorded a time line indicating hundredths of a second, and parallel to it a signal line, whose deviations indicated the time of reaction and the duration of the reacting movement; a signal key, arranged to break a circuit on giving the signal for reaction; and a special apparatus designed to record the pressure exerted by the subject in reacting, and to close an electric circuit throughout the period during which his muscles are contracting.

The latter piece of apparatus is constructed as follows: A pair of metal jaws project horizontally from a vertical wooden support. They are of such size, and at such a distance apart, as to be conveniently grasped in the hand, or between the thumb and forefinger. The lower one is hinged to its support, so that it can be moved upward by the force of the grasp. The upper one furnishes a firm support for the hand. It is attached, not directly to the wooden support, but to a heavy metal rim, which latter is bolted to the wood. This rim surrounds and supports the upper part of a mercury well, whose flexible leather bottom rests on the lower jaw, and is raised and lowered by its movement. A glass tube projects vertically above the well, and the column of mercury within it stands at a fixed zero point when the lower jaw is in its normal resting position, to which it can be adjusted by a screw. When the hand contracts and the movable jaw is raised, the mercury column is forced upward in the tube to a height varying with the amount of pressure exerted, and with the particular point on the jaw to which the pressure is applied. This point of application of force is different when the jaws are grasped by the whole hand from what it is when their ends are held between thumb and forefinger. Two scales are therefore provided alongside the tube, indicating in kilograms the pressure exerted in either case. An indicator, made of felt, rises with the mercury column, but fits too tightly in the tube to fall back with it. It is pushed back to the zero point, after each experiment, by the weight of a thin rod which, when not in use for this purpose, hangs suspended with its end just within the top of the tube.

This arrangement works with great ease, responding delicately to the slightest movement of reaction. The kilogram divisions are so far apart (for the most part about an inch) that tenths can be easily estimated. Various conditions introduce an error by affecting the normal mercury level, but this error probably does not exceed one or two tenths of a kilogram.

The duration of the reacting movement is recorded on the drum by means of an electric contact made at the instant the movable jaw begins to rise and maintained throughout its upward movement. For this purpose a thin steel lever is provided, turning upon a pivot tight enough to prevent it from falling by its own weight. By means of a screw, its height can be so adjusted, that when at rest its movable end will almost, but not quite, be in contact with the movable end of the lower jaw. The moment the latter begins to move upward, contact is made; the moment it begins to drop back again, contact is broken. In practice it was found that the adjusting screw was unnecessary; for when the lever was pressed directly down upon the jaw its slight recoil due to the friction at its pivot, was sufficient to just raise it from actual contact.

Electrical connections were made as follows: From the batteries to the recording pen, thence to a brake for starting and stopping the drum; from the metal frame of the latter to the signal key and from the signal key to the batteries; thus completing the circuit, closed when the signal key is in normal position, open when the signal is given. The attachment to the brake of the drum is merely a switch to keep the circuit open when the drum is not being used; when the brake is taken off the governor, it is pushed over toward the metal framework; thus closing the circuit at the same time that the drum is made to revolve. Another circuit is made by connections from the signal key to the contact lever of the reaction apparatus, and from the batteries to its movable jaw, in such a way that the circuit, which is interrupted by the giving of the signal, is closed again by the reaction.

The experiments were conducted as follows:

The subject is seated in a chair beside the table upon which the reaction apparatus is placed, with his right elbow resting upon a cushion; it is important that the subject's position should be as comfortable as possible, in order to avoid fatigue. The subject is then directed to take hold of the jaws with the thumb and forefinger of the right hand, the thumb resting upon the upper one about an inch from the end and the forefinger lightly touching the under part of the lower one at a like distance from the end. It is well, in fact almost necessary, to have two experimenters or operators, one to start and stop the drum and give the signal, the other to record the pressure as indicated by the mercury column, to push the indicator back to zero, to adjust the connection between lever and jaw and to see that the subject keeps his fingers in the same position upon the jaws. The subject being told to what signal he is to react (the sound made by the striking of the signal key) and instructed to think only of making a quick re-action, allowing the force of the reaction to take care of itself, the first operator starts the drum, thus closing the circuit and bring-ing the recording pen slightly over to the right. When the drum has reacted its normal speed the operator strikes down the signal key, and keeps it pressed down, thus breaking the circuit and throwing the recording pen back to its original po-sitiou. The subject, upon hearing the signal, reacts by bring-ing together his thumb and finger, thus forcing the mercury up into the tube and making the circuit by the connection between lever and jaw, which brings the recording pen once more to the right and marks the time required for the reaction. So long as the subject continues his pressure the circuit remains closed, but the moment he ceases, the jaw drops away from the lever, the cir-cuit is broken and the recording pen goes back to the left, thus marking the duration of the reactioning movement. The first operator then stops the drum and releases the key, while the second records the pressure and readjusts the contact lever and the pressure indicator. It is better that the subject keep his eyes closed during each experiment, that his next reaction may not be influenced by seeing what pressure he has exerted. He should also be warned not to grasp the jaws tightly while wait-ing for the signal, for the slightest raising of the lower jaw brings it into contact with the lever. At the end of the experiment the first operator moves the drum along horizontally, so that the pens will have fresh surface to mark on, and is then ready for the next experiment. It was found that space on the cylinder was saved by moving the drum along after each experiment rather than arranging it to move automatically to one side at the same time that it revolves. From thirteen to sixteen records could be taken on a single roll of smoked paper.

The object of these experiments being to determine the individual peculiarities of the subject's manner of reacting, it was desirable to turn away his attention as much as possible from the reacting movement itself, in order that attention to it might not interfere with its being carried out unconsciously and naturally. In the above described simple reaction experiments this aim was largely secured, since the subject was fully occupied with the endeavor to react as quickly as he could. Besides the simple reactions, however, another series was taken of associative reactions, in the hope that the greater degree of concentration required in the search for an association would withdraw the attention still more fully from the reaction movement. The time of association itself was recorded. But since its duration was not the prime object of investigation, the operators contented themselves with the accuracy obtainable by the endeavor on the part of signal giver and reactor to speak their words as simultaneously as they could with the pressing of their keys; and used no special apparatus to make this simultaneity absolute.

II. EXPLANATION OF TABLES.

The subjects were fifteen in number. They are designated at the head of the tables by letters of the alphabet. On each subject two series of experiments were performed. Series I. deals with simple reactions, Series II. with association reactions. In each series the results are set down, in the order in which the experiments were performed, in three columns. Column R gives the reaction time (simple or associated) expressed in thousandths of a second (σ). Column D gives the 'duration time;' the period, that is to say, during which the pressure of the reacting muscles increases in intensity, and is expressed also in thousandths of a second. Column P gives the maximum pressure expressed in tenths of a kilogram. In all three columns alike, the last digit of the tabulated quantity was estimated by the eye, the remaining digits being recorded by mechanical means.

In addition to these three columns of figures, which represent the direct results of experimentation, the pressure index of each experiment has been divided by the corresponding duration time, and the quotient expressed accurately to two places of decimals. Since P is expressed in tenths of a kilogram and D in thousandths of a second, this quotient shows the average number of hectograms (or, considered not as a fraction but as a whole number, the average number of grams) of pressure exerted by the contracting muscles during each σ of their contraction. It is therefore an index to the rapidity with which the movement of contraction is executed.

Finally the average and the average variation of columns R, P and $\dfrac{P}{D}$, have been worked out.

An asterisk (*) in the first three columns indicates that owing to imperfections in the mechanical records the numerical result is missing; or, when figures are given, that they are not absolutely trustworthy. The asterisk has been inserted whenever there was the slightest question as to the exact figures. In every other case the operators feel confident of the entire accuracy of their results, except in so far as the final digits are subject to errors in assessment.

The letter A placed before any quantity signifies that that quantity has not been reckoned in making up the average and average variation of the column; and the letter A placed outside, on the left of the columns of figures, signifies that none of the quantities, on the line on which it stands, have been reckoued in making up these averages. The A is usually added in case of possible inaccuracy marked by the asterisk; and is also employed when one quantity or set of quantities shows a striking and unexplained divergence from the other quantities in that series.

It will also be observed that when the asterisk shows possible inaccuracy in a duration time or pressure index, the corresponding $\dfrac{P}{D}$ relation has not, as a rule, been worked out.

A.

	Series I.				Series II.			
	R	D	P	$\frac{P}{D}$	R	D	P	$\frac{P}{D}$
	A331	332	63	0.19	534	792	37	0.05
	260	350	69	0.19	769	419	68	0.16
	275	490	79	0.16	761	453	62	0.14
	234	302	50	0.17	730	524	57	0.11
	173	482	97	0.20	886	505	70	0.14
	231	331	61	0.18	690	554	75	0.14
	225	339	68	0.20	940	519	63	0.12
	180	373	43	0.11	827	450	59	0.13
	221	404	59	0.15	900	572	71	0.12
	A371	340	67	0.20	753	590	70	0.12
	224	312	64	0.21	636	671	77	0.11
	220	345	63	0.18	614	543	88	0.16
	264	336	64	0.19	726	484	82	0.17
A	187	*371	68					
Average . . .	228		65	0.18	751	544	68	0.13
Av. Var. . . .	22		8	0.02	89	78	9	0.02

B.

	Series I.				Series II.			
	R	D	P	$\frac{P}{D}$	R	D	P	$\frac{P}{D}$
	225	276	54	0.20	802	321	66	0.21
	251	*287	63	0.22	*	*	66	
	226	258	55	0.21	*	*	59	
	219	337	74	0.22	726	250	52	0.21
	209	346	85	0.25	675	285	54	0.19
	175	238	51	0.21	775	294	58	0.20
	207	165	37	0.23	669	297	54	0.18
	202	229	47	0.21	683	218	48	0.22
	290	200	46	0.23	1086	274	45	0.16
	A393	232	52	0.22	840	399	70	0.18
	181	247	53	0.21	998	325	52	0.16
	185	196	45	0.23	740	292	58	0.20
	216	196	42	0.21	508	222	51	0.23
	236	201	47	0.23				
	225	*189	44	0.23				
Average . . .	218		53	0.22	773		56	0.19
Av. Var. . . .	21		9	0.01	116		6	0.02

C.

	SERIES I.				SERIES II.			
	R	D	P	$\frac{P}{D}$	R	D	P	$\frac{P}{D}$
	146	263	105	A0.40	510	525	A+110*	
	220	366	88	0.22	430	667	113	0.17
	152	474	A+120*		280	448	111	0.25
	207	370	115	0.31	360	440	110	0.25
	201	307	83	0.27	437	445	105	0.24
	268	294	86	0.29	335	445	91	0.20
	154	320	88	0.27	285	455	84	0.18
	146	298	87	0.29	A145	670	107	0.16
	225	312	86	0.28	500	575	100	0.18
	134	273	75	0.27	410	715	95	0.13
	170	500	*120	0.24	705	440	98	0.22
	97	486	101	0.21	457	350	70	0.20
					390	410	85	0.21
Average .	177		94	0.27	425		95	0.20
Av. Var. .	37		12	0.02	81		11	0.03

D.

	SERIES I.				SERIES II.			
	R	D	P	$\frac{P}{D}$	R	D	P	$\frac{P}{D}$
	115	124	*		1062	395	79	0.20
	A390	248	30	0.12	1524	410	67	0.16
	180	170	39	0.23	1167	412	73	0.18
	160	145	35	0.24	1435	360	62	0.17
	145	223	47	0.21	1760	340	65	0.19
	161	235	49	0.21	1174	350	60	0.17
	A220*	A240*	32		1080	320	64	0.20
	154	235	50	0.21	1376	327	69	0.21
	150	175	35	0.20	1610	308	67	0.21
	162	278	43	0.15	1090	350	74	0.21
	148	263	54	0.21	1667	324	68	0.21
	168	267	44	0.16	990	345	77	0.22
	166	300	58	0.19				
	167	315	60	0.19				
	145	298	52	0.17				
Average .	155		45	0.19	1328		69	0.19
Av. Var. .	12		8	0.03	234		5	0.02

E.

	Series I.				Series II.		
R	D	P	$\frac{P}{D}$	R	D	P	$\frac{P}{D}$
185	358	54	0.15	871	380	51	0.13
143	327	60	0.18	A987*	A456*	52	
159	278	49	0.18	A1588	371	55	0.15
155	287	50	0.17	915	279	36	0.13
150	224	46	0.21	737	350	50	0.14
178	178	40	0.22	955	409	42	0.10
140	175	A35*		694	A870	47	
147	219	42	0.19	706	297	54	0.18
190	215	40	0.19	570	282	50	0.18
191	191	41	0.21	664	283	52	0.18
167	194	41	0.21	654	253	46	0.18
190	191	37	0.19	*	*	45	
157	150	33	0.22	*	*	51	
				624	312	48	0.15
				A1293	484	66	0.14
Average . 166		44	0.19	739		50	0.15
Av. Var. . 17		6	0.02	104		4	0.02

F.

	Series I.				Series II.		
R	D	P	$\frac{P}{D}$	R	D	P	$\frac{P}{D}$
220	200	59	0.29	710	630	67	0.11
200	170	53	0.31	1110	340	54	0.16
200	295	58	0.20	1035	375	68	0.18
195	222	50	0.23	970	500	75	0.15
186	366	56	0.15	900	335	70	0.21
125	315	52	0.17	1150	337	67	0.20
180	320	70	0.22	830	361	69	0.19
140	320	61	0.19	981	328	63	0.20
115	260	69	0.27	1760	400	58	0.14
115	315	54	0.17	1712	340	61	0.18
165	280	56	0.20	880	365	76	0.21
160	265	54	0.20				
Average . 167		58	0.22	1094		66	0.18
Av. Var. . 30		5	0.04	246		5	0.02

G.

	SERIES I.				SERIES II.		
R	D	P	$\frac{P}{D}$	R	D	P	$\frac{P}{D}$
328	412	56	0.14	1460	481	83	0.17
252	473	54	0.11	1098	469	73	0.16
314	223	34	0.15	A1105*	A400*	50	
231	463	63	0.14	A1710*	A420*	50	
210	290	37	0.13	862	383	55	0.14
243	270	37	0.14	800	317	35	0.11
222	263	37	0.14	822	332	37	0.11
230	256	36	0.14	1073	328	37	0.11
207	467	63	0.13	780	549	34	0.06
216	367	57	0.16	599	834	32	0.04
264	350	51	0.15	828	489	35	0.07
220	202	34	0.17	848	547	36	0.07
360	234	33	0.14				
193	352	41	0.12				
Average . 249		45	0.14	917		46.5	0.10
Av. Var. . 39		10	0.01	176		13	0.04

H.

	SERIES I.				SERIES II.		
R	D	P	$\frac{P}{D}$	R	D	P	$\frac{P}{D}$
A300	435	70	0.16	*	*	62	
160	350	70	0.20	1100	556	98	0.18
126	300	61	0.20	1304	438	95	0.22
155	360	80	0.22	895	480	84	0.17
165	310	65	0.21	700	494	60	0.12
162	292	50	0.17	855	343	70	0.20
218	305	49	0.16	590	400	77	0.19
130	360	75	0.21	897	408	61	0.15
142	340	70	0.21	1333	355	45	0.13
122	400	82	0.20	790	618	90	0.15
144	493	88	0.18	1875	607	58	0.10
165	463	99	0.21				
170	400	84	0.21				
155	413	88	0.21				
Average . 155		74	0.20	1034		73	0.16
Av. Var. . 17		11	0.02	275		15	0.03

J.

	SERIES I.				SERIES II.			
	R	D	P	$\frac{P}{D}$	R	D	P	$\frac{P}{D}$
A	350	294	43		1203	621	88	0.14
	293	401	53	0.13	2271	577	67	0.12
	183	300	43	0.14	1300	542	67	0.12
	249	347	47	0.14	1423	573	68	0.12
	173	403	56	0.14	A556	A975	74	
	190	430	60	0.14	1222	724	77	0.11
	147	418	49	0.12	1190	561	83	0.15
	188	457	53	0.12	1594	586	62	0.11
	299	432	63	0.15	1490	514	59	0.11
	200	475	60	0.13	1097	A386*	67	
	180	487	57	0.12	1009	486	69	0.14
	172	470	54	0.12				
	194	481	61	0.13				
Average .	206		55	0.13	1380		71	0.12
Av. Var. .	37		5	0.01	252		7	0.01

K.

	SERIES I.				SERIES II.			
	R	D	P	$\frac{P}{D}$	R	D	P	$\frac{P}{D}$
	227	321	A38	A0.12	1391	331	71	0.21
	229	403	69	0.17	995	359	73	0.20
	158	355	69	0.19	984	372	72	0.19
	181	340	66	0.19	1731	320	64	0.20
	181	288	54	0.19	1818	348	73	0.21
	204	256	59	0.23	1131	354	61	0.17
	291	341	69	0.20	1217	408	75	0.18
	167	232	53	0.23	1152	326	69	0.21
	173	301	58	0.19	1337	363	77	0.21
	169	320	57	0.18	1494	291	63	0.22
	175	302	60	0.20	*	A510	65	
	165	266	53	0.20	1037	355	67	0.19
	180	267	58	0.22	1113	353	73	0.21
	174	207	46	0.22				
Average .	191		59	0.20	1283		69	0.20
Av. Var. .	27		6	0.01	226		4	0.01

L.

	SERIES I.				SERIES II.		
	R	D	P	$\frac{P}{D}$	R	D	P	$\frac{P}{D}$
	143	464	42	0.09	629	293	49	0.17
	127	238	32	0.14	384	219	38	0.17
	153	264	41	0.16	481	378	54	0.14
	188	134	20	0.15	415	292	40	0.14
	166	236	37	0.16	402	411	47	0.11
	153	244	40	0.16	602	336	47	0.14
	164	230	47	0.20	473	401	43	0.11
	173	156	35	0.22	540	290	41	0.14
	151	205	43	0.21	455	379	57	0.15
	110	177	37	0.21	703	307	42	0.14
	150	180	35	0.19	575	373	51	0.14
	163	217	41	0.19	952	260	44	0.17
	*	*	24		731	266	46	0.17
Average .	153		37	0.17	565		46	0.15
Av. Var. .	14		6	0.03	124		4	0.02

M.

	SERIES I.				SERIES II.			
	R	D	P	$\frac{P}{D}$	R	D	P	$\frac{P}{D}$
	176	437	87	0.20	1107	307	66	0.21 (1)
	180	294	60	0.20	1058	321	57	0.18 (1)
	250	205	40	0.20	881	944	59	0.06 (2)
	165	170	39	0.23	1110	755	57	0.08 (2)
	180	174	41	0.24	1200	795	52	0.07 (2)
	163	295	60	0.20	700	250	50	0.20 (1)
	190	162	43	0.27	*	*	54	
	175	123	33	0.27	1310	520	58	0.11 (2)
	215	226	47	0.21	*	*	45	
	170	154	40	0.26	1345	1007	63	0.06 (2)
	195	277	60	0.22	803	1165	45	0.04 (2)
	150	251	57	0.23	1120	420	56	0.13 (2)
	165	225	49	0.22				
	180	272	60	0.22				
Average .	182		51	0.23	1063		55	0.11
Av. Var. .	17		11	0.02	162		5	0.05
Average .								(1) (2)
								0.20 0.08
Av. Var. .								0.01 0.02

N.

	R	D	P	$\frac{P}{D}$	R	D	P	$\frac{P}{D}$
	Series I.				**Series II.**			
	205	320	47	0.15	907	830	71	0.09
	280	355	51	0.14	*	*	70	
	180	247	66	0.27	905	550	61	0.11
	280	216	65	0.30	805	530	75	0.14
	185	255	56	0.22	800	520	59	0.11
A	336	274	58	0.21	575	580	69	0.12
	222	232	63	0.27	565	545	66	0.12
	219	261	74	0.28	460	615	77	0.13
	205	141	56	0.39	535	617	65	0.11
	263	186	62	0.33	505	485	71	0.15
	256	202	61	0.30	700	660	80	0.12
	204	182	64	0.35	662	612	76	0.12
	209	170	57	0.34	625	675	70	0.10
					620	399	65	0.16
					690	360	52	0.14
Average .	226		60	0.28	668		68	0.12
Av. Var. .	30		6	0.06	114		6	0.01

O.

	R	D	P	$\frac{P}{D}$	R	D	P	$\frac{P}{D}$
	Series I.				**Series II.**			
	270	433	103	0.24	614	563	80	0.14
	380	338	61	0.18	700	360	69	0.19
	395	386	71	0.18	800	517	78	0.15
	170	360	74	0.21	685	*	81	
	175	370	83	0.22	817	466	78	0.17
	225	392	79	0.20	937	570	83	0.15
	179	440	85	0.19	760	430	62	0.14
	290	400	78	0.19	400	360	61	0.17
	210	335	71	0.21	265	521	79	0.15
	204	255	58	0.23	A1795	*	73	
	190	215	50	0.23	820	360	68	0.19
	230	165	50	0.30				
	205	200	58	0.29				
Average .	240		71	0.22	680		74	0.16
Av. Var. .	57		12	0.03	152		7	0.02

P.

	SERIES I.				SERIES II.			
	R	D	P	$\frac{P}{D}$	R	D	P	$\frac{P}{D}$
A	320	225	45	0.20	1240	506	40	A0.08
	237	180	31	0.17	1176	317	43	0.14
	207	270	34	0.13	1057	242	39	0.16
	200	187	32	0.17	1026	A1080	32	
	215	152	32	0.21	1195	234	33	0.14
	215	165	30	0.18	1491	255	*	
	275	333	36	0.11	1380	212	31	0.15
	265	175	*20+	0.14	990	196	35	0.18
	210	195	33	0.17	1796	350	43	0.12
	222	166	31	0.19	A2320	270	43	0.16
A	199	385	32	A0.08	1730	265	37	0.14
	213	206	32	0.16	870	345	45	0.13
	270	287	47	0.16				
	231	276	44	0.16				
Average .	230	216	34	0.16	1268		38	0.15
Av. Var. .	21	50	4	0.02	241		4	0.01

III. RESULTS.

The present operators have had but little time to devote to the interpretation of their results. But even so, several facts can be pointed out, which certainly do not prove laws, but which as certainly are suggestive and point the way to development by future workers in this fascinating research.

1. First, what perhaps we should have been led *a priori* to expect, is corroborated. Divide *P* by *D*, the pressure index by the duration time, and the resultant quotient, representing the rapidity of contraction of the reacting muscles, tends, for the same individual and the same series, to be constant. Look, for instance, examining the tables almost at random, at B I; where the pressure varies from 37.5 up to 85, the duration varies so uniformly in proportion, that the quotients $\frac{P}{D}$ are all found within a range of 0.05—from 0.20 to 0.25 ; where there was an average variation in the case of P. of 9, there is an average

Tabular Summary.

Subject and Series.	Pressure.					Rapidity.				
	Max.	Min.	Av.	Av. Var.	Med.*	Max.	Min.	Av.	Av. Var.	Med.*
A I	97	43	65	8	64	.21	.11	.18	.02	.19
II	88	37	68	9	70	.17	.05	.13	.02	.13
B I	85	37	53	9	51	.25	.20	.22	.01	.22
II	70	45	56	6	54	.23	.16	.19	·02	.20
C I	115	75	94	12	88	.31	.21	.27	.02	.27
II	113	70	95	11	100	.25	.13	.20	.03	.20
D I	60	30	45	8	45	.24	.12	.19	.03	.20
II	79	62	69	5	68	.22	.16	.19	.02	.20
E I	60	33	44	6	42	.22	.15	.19	.02	.19
II	66	36	50	4	51	.18	.10	.15	.02	.15
F I	70	50	58	5	55	.31	.15	.22	.04	.20
II	76	54	66	5	67	.21	.11	.18	.02	.18
G I	63	33	45	10	39	.17	.11	.14	.01	.14
II	83	32	46	13	37	.17	.04	.10	.04	.11
H I	99	49	74	11	70	.22	.16	.20	.02	.21
II	98	45	73	15	70	.22	.10	.16	.03	.16
J I	63	43	55	5	54	.15	.12	.13	.01	.13
II	88	59	71	7	68	.15	.11	.12	.01	.12
K I	69	46	59	6	58	.23	.17	.20	.01	.20
II	75	61	69	4	71	.22	.17	.20	.01	.20
L I	47	20	37	6	37	.22	.09	.17	.03	.17
II	57	38	46	4	46	.17	.11	.15	.02	.14
M I	87	33	51	11	48	.27	.20	.23	.02	.22
II	66	45	55	5	55	.21	.04	.11	.05	.09
N I	74	47	60	6	61	.39	.14	.28	.06	.28
II	80	52	68	6	70	.16	.09	.12	.01	.12
O I	103	50	71	12	71	.30	.18	.22	.03	.21
II	83	61	74	7	78	.19	.14	.16	.02	.15
P I	47	30	34	4	32	.21	.11	.16	.02	.16
II	45	31	38	4	39	.18	.12	.15	.01	.14

variation in the case of $\dfrac{P}{D}$ of only o.oi.

2. Secondly, there are well marked differences in rapidity between the different individuals, and between the two series of the same individual. These differences are of two kinds:

*In column ' Med.' is given the ' Median' as distinguished from the average.

First, absolute.   The average value of $\dfrac{P}{D}$ in Series I. for subject J is 0.13; for N it is 0.28.   J's maximum is 0.15; N's minimum is 0.14.   They then just overlap; but J's minimum is 0.12, and N's maximum 0.39.   The second way in which individuals differ is in this range of variation in value of $\dfrac{P}{D}$. Compare the comparative constancy of subjects J, H, B and M in Series I., with the extraordinary freedom from law and the trammels of consistency, which C, F and N display.

3. Thirdly, it is observable that although the two series overlap each other a great deal, yet in no case is the maximum value of $\dfrac{P}{D}$ in Series II. greater than in Series I.; and in no case is the average value in Series II. the greater.   How far this uniform lessening in rapidity in Series II. is due to untraced workings of consciousness, and in how far to the frequently observed tendency of the reagent in Series II. to increase his duration time by starting to react before he had really found his associated idea, is a question for subsequent investigation to determine.

4. Although the range of variation in pressure is larger than in rapidity, yet similar observations can be made for it also. The degree of pressure exerted and the range of its variation are characteristic of the individual.   Each has his own special tendencies and his own limits of variation, differing from those of the others.   Some exert little pressure in reacting, some much.   Some are fairly constant, while others range over varying pressures whose extremes are widely apart.   In the majority of cases a comparison of the two series shows for each individual a manner of reacting similar in both series, even though the absolute values of average and limits may differ in the two.   This correspondence of the two series, in spite of the small number of experiments entering into each, furnishes strong evidence that we here gain insight into fundamental characteristics of the individual.

5. If we compare Series I. with Series II., it will be noted that in every case but one the average pressure is greater in

Series II. ; whereas it has been seen that the rapidity is greater in Series I. Both facts might easily be due to the above mentioned increase in duration of the reacting movement.

Many further questions readily present themselves. What relations, if any, has R in either series to P or to D or to $\dfrac{P}{D}$? So far as this investigation can show, there would seem to be no fixed relation between them. Will further research confirm the hypothesis so strongly supported by the experiments here reported, namely, that everyone has his own personal and comparatively constant manner of reacting, his own usual degree of rapidity and of force in making movements when his attention is not occupied with the way in which he carries them out, and his own limits of possible variation from their average ? Under what circumstances does he vary in particular ways within these limits ? What is the cause of these individual tendencies and differences ? Are they affair of mood, or of temperament, or of other causes ? Are the values found in simple reactions, or in associative reactions, or in both together, or even in some other yet uninvestigated form, more characteristic of the individual ? These questions, and many more which easily arise, can be answered only by spending much time and labor in collecting more data along these lines ; and still more time and labor in digesting and interpreting the data so obtained.

AFTER–SENSATIONS OF TOUCH.

By FRANK N. SPINDLER.

The subject of investigation for this series of experiments has been what are generally called After-Images of Touch, but which should more properly be called After-Sensations of Touch. The word Image applies well to the case of aftereffects of sight, but would seem to have no particular application to the after-feeling of a sensation of touch.

We are all more or less familiar with after-sensations of all sorts, but the very fact that these after-sensations are so common and often undifferentiated, makes them very difficult to study with any accuracy. Most of us have never attended to an after-sensation of touch or pressure long enough to be certain of its quality or duration. These sensations are all merged into the general and common muscular and organic feelings and hence pass unnoticed.

An after-sensation of touch or pressure by no means implies any illusion as to the pressure still continuing. The experiment is often tried of blindfolding a person and then pressing a coin upon the forehead; on removing it the subject will not for some time notice that it is gone. We often feel a pen be-hind the ear even after it is no longer there, or think our hat is on when it is off. But in all these cases a little analysis would enable the subject to distinguish between the actual touch or pressure and the after-sensation. The latter is qualitatively, as well as quantitatively, distinct from the actual feeling of the stimulation.

The literature on the subject of after-sensations of touch is meagre. Many psychologists make no mention whatever of the subject, while others refer to it but briefly.

James, speaking in general of after-sensations of all kinds, says that the nervous matter has an inertia and elasticity, a certain time of stimulation is necessary to excite any kind of a sensation, a certain time then conversely might be expected to be necessary for the sensation to fade away. Sensations then outlast, for a little time, the objective stimuli which occasion them. They show that profound rearrangements and slow settlings into a new equilibrium are going on in the neural substance.

Baldwin, speaking of after-sensations in a general way, says likewise: " There is a vibratory persistence, in the nervous organism, of peripheral shocks, which tends to continue the central process and its accompanying mental state. And the same residum or after-effect is also probably a mental necessity, since time is needed for the shifting movements of attention in its transition to new experiences; during this period there is nothing to drive the former experience from consciousness and it persists a noticeable time."

If we turn to Külpe we find an attempt to give a more particular description of the actual mechanism of after-sensation. He fails, however, to distinguish between two completely distinct types of after-effect in the field of contact and pressure. A light, quick touch on some portions of the skin occasions not only an ordinary sensation of contact, but also, after a brief interval—a second or less—a second quick pulse of sensation. To observe this, the stimulating object must be immediately removed, else the secondary sensation will be drowned in the continuing primary sensation. This effect, however, is not at all analogous to the after-images, positive and negative, which occur in vision and in other senses, due to continuance of the excitation in the peripheral organ, or to a restoration of its equilibrium, after the stimulation has ceased. Yet the sense of touch presents after-sensations of this kind also, and these Külpe does not mention. His theoretical discussion as to whether the after-sensation is due to a double path of conduction through the spinal cord, or to the existence and coöperation of centrifugal with centripetal sensory fibers, applies only to the brief secondary sensation after brief stimulation—the first type of after-effect mentioned above. The present study, however, has been only of the after-sensations of the other type—the varying sensations which follow the cessation of a more or less prolonged stimulation of the skin by means of pressure.

To investigate these weights were used of from 25 up to 1,000 grams. These were placed upon a brass holder with a round base seven-eighths of an inch in diameter, covered on the bottom with paper, so as to prevent differences of temperature between the metal and the skin.

The weights were applied to the backs of the hands, these being the most convenient parts of the body to practice on and also the parts especially susceptible to pressure sensations. They were left in contact during lengths of time varying from five seconds to ten minutes. Record was then made of the different sensations following their removal.

These experiments, however, labor under the disadvantage of being entirely dependent upon introspection for results, and also of dealing with very vague, indefinite and irregular phenomena. It is difficult to judge accurately the presence and nature of these after-sensations; to distinguish them from the subjective sensations easily discoverable whenever attention is directed to the skin; to analyze them out from among the mass of organic feelings with which they so easily fuse; to determine the moment of their appearance or disappearance.

There is a marked difference in subjects as to their power to discriminate these after-sensations. Some are very sensitive to them and get all sorts of after-sensations, while others cannot get any whatever, although their failure is probably due to lack of practice in introspection.

The physical and mental condition of the subject has a marked effect. If the subject is tired or sick, or gloomy, the after-sensations are dull and shorter continued than when the subject is well and cheerful. In the writer's own introspection he found that when he was melancholy and in a state of general depression or exhaustion, with languid circulation and slow pulse beat, there would be hardly any after-sensations experienced at all, even after long stimulation, while in a more cheerful and active state of mind and body the after-sensations would be vivid and long continued even after brief stimulation. This difference is doubtless due, in part, to the fact that, when depressed, one is skeptical of any feeling or sensation of any kind. In view of these difficulties it is not surprising that the most striking characteristic of the results we have gained consists in their extreme irregularity and apparent inconsistency. It seems impossible to establish any definite and consistent relation between the time of stimulation and the duration of the after-sensation, or between the degree of pressure and the duration or vividness of the after-effect. Such indefinite formulation as is possible, however, will be attempted in the following account of our results.

I. SHORTEST DURATION OF STIMULATION NECESSARY FOR THE APPEARANCE OF AN AFTER-SENSATION.

It was found that 100 gms. for 5 seconds gave no perceptible after-sensation, but only a feeling of relief on removal of the weight; 25 gms. for 1 minute, gave a strong after-sensation lasting 3 minutes; 150 gms. for 5 seconds, however, gave a weak after-sensation in the shape of a feeling of warmth and contraction, lasting about ten seconds; 150 gms. for 5 seconds then was about the lowest threshold as to time of stimulation.

2. INTERVAL BETWEEN END OF STIMULATION AND APPEARANCE OF AFTER-SENSATION.

There occurs always a certain interval between the removal of the stimulus and the conscious beginning of the after-sensations. The average duration of all these intervals, in this series of experiments, was about 36½ seconds. Their length varies with the time of stimulation, as will be seen from the following table for different stimulations of from 10 seconds up to 10 minutes. Each interval here given is an average from several trials:

TIME OF STIMULATION.	INTERVAL.	DURATION OF AFTER-SENSATION.
10 seconds.	5 seconds.	30 seconds.
30 "	10 "	4½ minutes.
1 minute.	39 "	5 "
2 minutes.	47½ "	4½ "
3 "	1 minute, 22½ seconds.	5 " and 18 seconds.
5 "	44 seconds.	9 "
10 "	44½ "	10 "

There appears to be but little relation here, either between the duration of the stimulation and the length of the interval between end of stimulation and after-sensation, or between the length of the stimulation and the duration of the after-sensation itself. The intervals, however, seem to increase up to stimulations of 3 minutes' duration and then to drop again, being about the same for a 5 or a 10 minute stimulation as for a 2 or a 3 minute one.

3. DURATION OF THE AFTER-SENSATION.

The absence of any fixed dependence of the duration of the after-sensation upon the time of stimulation is also apparent from the above table. For any time of stimulation from 1 to 3 minutes the after-sensation seems to be about the same in duration, that is about 5 minutes; while for a 5 to 10 minute stimulation the average after-sensation lasts 10 minutes.

It is absolutely impossible to have these results exactly accurate, for the after-sensations of touch fade away so gradually, and it is so easy to call them back even an hour after first ceasing to notice them, that to say absolutely when they stop is not possible. Under the most careful attention, however, they seem not to last more than 10 minutes at most. Their later recurrence is apparently not actually a matter of direct after-effect, but rather a result of turning attention to the skin, which always easily arouses subjective sensations, without previous special stimulation.

The most that we can say is that there seems to be a tendency for a longer stimulation to produce a longer after-sensation, but not a relatively longer one. For example, stimulations of 1 minute produce after-sensations averaging 5 minutes in duration, while stimulations of 10 minutes average 10 minutes; those of 5 minutes produce after-sensations averaging 9 minutes, and those of 2 or 3 minutes produce after-sensations averaging 5 minutes.

There seems then to be a limit to the time the after-sensation can naturally continue, and a longer stimulation cannot produce a proportionately longer after-sensation. Indeed, there may be a tendency in a long continued touch or pressure to deaden the nervous sensibility, as there is no reason to suppose nerve substance to be capable of indefinite reaction without exhaustion and lethargy.

It might be supposed that there would be a more definite relation between the heaviness of the weights used and the duration and strength of the after-sensations. We might expect perhaps that the heavier the weight, the longer and more vivid the after-sensation would be. But here also the results are very irregular, as the following tables will show.

The weights of from 150 to 500 grams seem to produce the longest after-sensations, but even this is contradicted in the cases of stimulation of 5 minutes' duration, where 100 grams

Weight.	Time of Pressure.	Average Duration of After-Sensation.
100 gms. 150 " 200 " 500 " 1000 ".	1 minute. 1 " 1 " 1 1	4 minutes and 48 seconds. 3 " 8 " " 30 " 7 " " 12 " 6
100 gms. 150 " 200 " 500 ' 1000 ".	2 minutes. 2 " 2 " 2 2	4 minutes. 5 " and 6 seconds. 4 " " 36 " 7 5
100 gms. 500 " 1000 "	3 minutes. 3 " 3 "	5 minutes and 18 seconds. 10 " 7 " " 30 "
100 gms. 150 " 200 " 500 ' 1000 "	5 minutes. 5 " 5 " 5 5	10 minutes. 8 " 8 " and 18 seconds. 8 7 " " 30 "
100 gms. 150 " 200 " 1000 '	10 minutes. 10 " 10 " 10	7½ minutes. 10 " 10 " 7½

for 5 minutes gives a 10 minute after-sensation. These results may seem erratic, but, as has been said, the introspection necessary to distinguish the cessation of an after-sensation of touch is extremely difficult. The effect is one that fades gradually away and the exact moment when the sensation is dropped from consciousness is hard to decide.

It is noticeable, however, that 1,000 grams in every case produced a shorter after-sensation than did 500 grams, or even 150 or 200 grams, for the same time of pressure. This would agree with Bain's assertion that the papillæ touched lightly give a greater reaction than when a heavy weight is applied, for the latter seems to deaden the conductibility of the nerves and gives comparatively little sensation.

4. QUALITY AND VARIETY OF THE AFTER–SENSATIONS.

To the writer's own introspection an after-sensation of touch assumes simply a feeling of contraction as if the spot were painted with collodion or mucilage. This contracted feeling was generally strongest at from 2 to 3 minutes after the removal of the stimulus and then faded gradually away. But other subjects got more of a richness and variety of feeling out of their after-sensations than this. They got the feeling of contraction of the skin, but also temperature sensations, both warm and cold, external smarting sensations, and also a deeper dull ache. Let me give a subject's account of an after-sensation. 100 grams were applied for 5 minutes. After a negative interval of 40 seconds after removal of weight a touch sensation was felt. At 1 minute, warmth; 1 minute 20 seconds, very warm with touch sensations; 2 minutes, pain with heat; 3 minutes, touch again more prominent, and also a feeling of contraction in the spot, the pain and touch alternate; 5 minutes, principally pain; 7 minutes, pain, unpleasant; 8 minutes, pain in whole hand, contracted feeling in the spot brought out on bending the hand; 9 minutes, pain fades; 10 minutes, no sensation.

Here we have a fairly constant touch sensation together with alternating pain and temperature, and finally the pain alone persisting and then fading. This subject sometimes had sensations of cold as well as of heat.

Another experiment, on another subject, gave the following results: One hundred grams were applied to back of right hand for 1 minute; negative interval of 1 minute. After one minute, a slight cold feeling felt in spot; after 2 minutes, colder; after 2½ minutes, warmth; after 4 minutes, pain deep seated in hand; after seven minutes, vague discomfort; after 9 minutes, cold; after 9 minutes 20 seconds, no sensation.

In this subject then we see temperature sensation in waves, also a touch sensation as of contraction of the skin and also a deeper seated pain.

Another subject got even a more remarkable lot of feelings out of the after-sensations.

In one experiment, for example, 100 grams were applied for 5 minutes, negative interval of 50 seconds. After 1 minute, a drawing sensation; after 1 minute and 20 seconds, itching; after 1 minute and 50 seconds, deep, dull ache; after 2 minutes, warm, feverish sensation; after 2½ minutes, sharp pain, with waves of heat; after 3½ minutes, dull ache; after 4 minutes, sharp toothache pain; after 5 minutes, decided dull ache; after 6 minutes, decided dull ache; after 7 minutes, decided dull ache; after 8 minutes, intervals of no sensation; after 8½ minutes, heat; after 9 minutes, slight heat; after 10 minutes, no sensation. There are here two surface sensations—one of touch, the other of smarting; and also a deeper dull ache—besides the temperature sensations, which were pronounced sometimes cold and sometimes hot.

This subject had indeed a remarkable faculty of getting sensations. In several instances with him the weight was placed on one hand and then the attention was fixed upon a symmetrical spot on the other hand. The spot on the hand actually pressed would force itself upon the attention after an interval and give sensations of touch, heat, etc., but the hand where the spot was attended to without previous pressure would, after a few minutes, go through the same series of sensations as the actually stimulated spot, although not at first so intensely. But if this subject kept his attention turned to a spot on the hand its sensations become in time exceedingly disagreeable.

As for the writer's own introspection in regard to an actually stimulated spot on one hand and a symmetrical spot on the other hand simply attended to, the actually stimulated spot seemed to yield a stronger after-sensation than the sensation which arose in the spot merely attended to, and of a different quality of sensation, yet so similar that some might call it merely a difference of degree.

The very fact, however, that by turning our attention to a spot we can cause lasting and, indeed, even painful sensations, seemingly as strong as those given by actually stimulated spots, and to some subjects qualitatively the same, increases enormously the difficulty of investigating the actual after-effects of stimulation themselves. This difficulty we have kept in mind, and have eliminated, so far as possible, its influence in the records whose results are above tabulated.

We may sum up the results of this study very briefly, as follows:

The minimal time of stimulation which will yield an after-sensation of the kind under investigation is about 5 seconds, with a pressure of 150 grams.

The relation between the duration of stimulation and the length of the interval which elapses before the appearance of the after-sensation is very irregular. The intervals increase up to stimulations of about 3 minutes, and then again decrease.

The duration of the after-sensation increases with the duration of stimulation, though without any discoverable regularity. It is possible that there is a limit to this increase—a possibility which we have not subjected to full investigation.

The longest duration of after-sensations is given by pressures of from 150 to 500 grams. Above and below these limits of pressure the duration decreases.

In quality the after-sensations are very variable.

The writer could discover no waves in his own after-sensations, but only a steady persistent feeling of contraction. Other subjects, however, experienced waves of heat, of pain, etc.; but they also in most cases felt a steady persistent underlying touch or contraction sensation, lasting through the dull aches, the smarts, and the heat or cold.

DISCUSSION AND REPORTS.

THE COLOR–VISION OF APPROACHING SLEEP.

The experiment of Mr. Havelock Ellis on the color producing properties of mescal (noticed in the September number of this REVIEW), gives me occasion for describing an experience of my own which I have not seen referred to by others. It sometimes happens to me to fall asleep over a book, and upon such occasions I sometimes catch a play of various colors upon the printed page. The first time that this occurred I was very nearly sound asleep, although my eyes were still open. The colors were very brilliant, and they presented a rather regular wavy pattern in red and green, something like this:

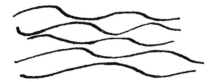

I should mention that I am rather more apt than most people to go to sleep piecemeal, if I may express it so. I have more than once continued reading aloud, so as to be understood, for a full sentence or two after I had absolutely lost consciousness of what I was doing. Upon the occasion I refer to I was certainly waked up suddenly from distinct slumber by the startlingly brilliant colors on the page before me. They were so interesting, as soon as I caught sight of them, that they caused me to become at once wide awake, and then they immediately disappeared. This experience of seeing very pure and brilliant colors I have had only half a dozen times in all,—the first case occurring about a year ago. But since I have become familiar with the phenomenon, I can see any evening, as soon as I begin to get sleepy, that the page before me is broken up into largish patches of violet and a complementary yellowish green, neither brilliant nor saturated. If the page is a newspaper, or other irregular surface, it is evident that the violet color covers its shadier portions.

The occasions when the phenomenon was distinctly different from this, of which I have notes made at the time, are the following : The page had rather even, smaller patches of brilliant green and blue; each letter, of a rather coarse print, had a brilliant border of green; no other color was seen at this time; the white spaces between the print-lines of a page of the *Archiv für Ophthalmologie* were of a bright green, not at all yellowish.

Once only there were three colors present, all very brilliant and of fundamental tone. The usual patches of red and green were separated from each other by a band of even width of intense blue.

As some irregularity of accommodation has seemed to me to be among the possible causes of the phenomenon, I have frequently prepared for a nap by arranging in my field of view a white surface with darker objects raised two millimetres above it, and by the side of it a dark surface with white elevations. But, upon all such occasions, if I have fallen asleep at all, it has been without catching the phenomenon. It is possible that mere fatigue—general fatigue, of course, not visual fatigue—is the sufficient explanation, as suggested by Mr. Havelock Ellis in cases of neurasthenia and of mescal intoxication. It is also possible that, in the colors which are of normal occurrence, the violet is due to some reconstruction of the visual purple, and that the green is the green of contrast. I am familiar with the color of the visual purple when seen subjectively, for I have no trouble in getting at any time the normal erythropsia described lately by Dr. Ernst Fuchs. (See this REVIEW, Vol. IV., p. 221.) Some years ago, after walking over a bright pavement in a glaring sunlight, with one eye covered, in preparation for an experiment, I found that I could get this effect very brilliantly, and that it lasted for a long time —much longer than four minutes. The fact that it was only in one eye, and that the sensation of the other eye served to prevent the rapid fading out which occurs when any sensation is widespread and continuous, made the circumstances peculiarly favorable.

I confirm Fuchs' observation that the color does not extend quite so far as the field of vision, and that it is wanting at the centre. The color-tone of this normal erythropsia is quite the same as that of the violet on going to sleep. The other colors have, of course, no connection with this, but they belong, I believe, to a much deeper degree of sleep. I have frequently experienced the green vision (as well as the erythropsia) upon the first instant of waking up in the morning. This was explained by its discoverer as being due to the green fibres awakening a little sooner than the other two kinds—those both awakening together, apparently! A recent writer in the *Wissenschaft-liche Rundschau* believes it to be the contrast effect of the red caused by the blood vessels of the eye, to which a sensitiveness persists for a few moments; but if this were the correct explanation it would seem that the red ought also to be perceived, which is not the case.

I should be interested to know if any one else gets these colors upon the on-coming of sleep.

C. L. FRANKLIN.

BALTIMORE.

PROFESSOR WUNDT'S 'UEBER NAIVEN UND KRIT-ISCHEN REALISMUS.'[1]

In this article Professor Wundt handles with marked critical insight and thoroughness, some of the crucial problems which arise in the so called Immanental Philosophy of such men as Schuppe, Schubert-Soldern and Rhemke.

The burden of his criticism is that the logic of the system brings it into immediate conflict with the basal principles of Natural and Psychological Science as well as with their accredited results.

I. In denying any transcendence of the object the Immanental Philosophy runs counter to the naïve consciousness as well as the scientific critical reconstruction of the same. Believing with all other theories of knowledge in touch with the realistic tone of the time, that we must retrace the steps of original naïve knowledge undisturbed by reflection, except in so far as needed to correct errors, the Immanental Philosophy sets about the task of correction. This is, however, nothing less than an attempt to sweep away the whole 'absurd' notion of a transcendental object. It is concluded that if a transcendence of all experience is inconceivable, it is likewise impossible to conceive of a transcendence of consciousness, and so all reality is reduced to conscious content, as immanent in the subject. This reconstruction of naïve thought, since it takes away its fundamental concept, is impossible either for it or for the scientific reconstruction of the same. Natural Science recognizes all elements as objective reality which, without contradictions among themselves, remain after all abstraction of subjective perception. She rests her whole claim to objectivity upon the possibility of abstracting from the subject, and goes out from the principles : "*Jeden Inhalt der naïven Erfahrung so*

[1] An abstract of Professor Wundt's article in *Philosophische Studien*, XII., XIII., 1896, 1897.

*lange als gegeben anzuerkennen als er nicht, durch nachweisbare
Widersprüche, zu denen dies führt, als ein blosser Schein nach-
gewiesen sei.*" Now the point that Professor Wundt makes, and very
properly too, is that this criterion of objectivity is part of the logic
of Natural Science, and, since scientific processes are but a refinement
of common naïve knowledge (with this advantage: that, by a long
development through experience and reflection subjective elements
have been eliminated, and a settled logic of scientific thought attained) scientific criteria of objectivity are final for any theory of
knowledge. The Immanental Philosophy, in denying the concept of
transcendent objectivity, in reducing all reality to conscious content, runs up against the logic of the sciences.

II. But the believer in the idea that *esse=percipi* has found in more
recent times a new criterion which may be substituted for the scientific. He argues that the latter, demanding merely a contradictionless
whole of experience, is in reality no criterion of the content of truth,
but is purely formal and negative, and leaves the problem of truth
unsettled except in so far as, by an endless series of experiments and
abstractions, a relatively contradictionless whole of experience is
attained. Therefore an *a priori* criterion is substituted—it is the test
of the 'gattungsmässige' of the social consciousness, of social categories. What is socially experienced is true as over against the subjective
opinions and errors of the individual. The problem is accordingly resolved into a conflict of criteria; and for the social criterion Wundt has
nothing but ridicule. How, he asks, is the logical argument that
the individual ego presupposes social consciousness a possibility without the very assumption of the existence of external objects in which
the other consciousness belongs? Otherwise it is a mere abstraction.
As for the empirical worth of the criteria of the common social
consciousness, the simplest optical illusion suffices to show its useless-
ness, and the entire history of scientific method, splendidly illustrated
in the Copernican System, shows that the real criterion of knowledge
is the perception of the individual object, corrected by experiment.

III. The real difficulty comes, however, in the application of this
criterion to the actual content of consciousness. What are the 'gat-
tungsmassige,' the common elements of the social consciousness, when
the individual ego is abstracted. First of all, *sensations* in space and
time. Since they are given immediately in the naïve consciousness,
and are common property of the *Socius*, they must be accepted as
objectively real, and the question of their origin is not a proper problem for a theory of knowledge. Whether all sensations, or simply

those of the higher sense of sight, are to be taken as objective, the Immanentalists have not yet settled among themselves. But this is immaterial for the principle and the suggestion of Schubert-Soldern, that all sensations may be reduced to one ground sensation, the differences being merely qualitative expressions of relations which Natural Science seeks to express by means of its transcendental atoms, is a thoroughly logical solution of this uncertainty.

To Professor Wundt's thinking such a doctrine means nothing less than a denial of centuries of accredited work on the part of science, and, secondly, an utter confusion of the boundaries between Natural Science and Psychology.

Since Galileo, the great presupposition of modern science has been the subjectivity of sensations—and on the ability to abstract from the same, and upon their reference to external moving bodies, as their source, rests modern mechanics and molecular physics. The doctrine which maintains the objectivity of sensation runs counter to all this and the suggestion that all sensations might be reducible to a fundamental one would have as its logical outcome a rejuvenation of the Aristotelian color theory, which reduced all light phenomena to two ground sensations, light and dark. With modern optics Wundt holds it is entirely incompatible.

But the difficulties to which it gives rise in the determination of the boundaries between Natural Science and Psychology are alone sufficient to show the untenability of the doctrine of the objectivity of sensation. If sensations are objective, then they are the data of objective Natural Science. On the other hand, Psychology can have to do only with the ' non-gattungsmässige,' or individual elements of consciousness, which leaves no basis for general laws. The philosophers of this school, accordingly find in the reproductive processes of memory and imagination the sphere of Psychology, or otherwise distinguish it as the object of individual introspection, while the objects of Natural Science are the primary sensations of the many. But the simple facts of Psychology make impossible such a distinction. Between sense perceptions and the reproductive processes there is no distinct line, as Hume conceived in his impossible theory of strong and weak impressions. A pure sensation is an abstraction, sensation is not known apart from the reproductive processes. Thus, if sensations be the data of Natural Science, the latter must logically be subsumed under Psychology. This is however equally distasteful to both sciences. Natural Science cannot allow of such a subjectification of its problem, nor can Psychology admit this formalistic metaphysical determination of her field of work. The abstract concept of the individual is powerless to give her material and, without the investigation of the rise of sensations, it is impossible for her to understand the reproductive processes based upon them. The whole difficulty lies in the false presupposition that the two sciences deal with different kinds of content, a deplorable modern putting of the Kantian distinction of ' inner' and ' outer' sense. In fact, both deal with the same content, for there is only one object, but each approaches it from a different standpoint. Natural Science has found it necessary to abstract from all subjective elements, *including sensation;* it is just this subjective side, however, that is the peculiar sphere of Psychology, the whole immediate, subjective side of reality. If the ideals and methods of the sciences are understood there is perfect harmony. It is only where these are ignored, and a *priori* theories of knowledge, developed by uncontrolable reflection upon naïve thought, are substituted, that conflict arises.

WILBUR M. URBAN.

PRINCETON UNIVERSITY.

PSYCHOLOGICAL LITERATURE.

Philosophy of Knowledge: An Inquiry Into the Nature, Limits and Validity of Human Cognitive Faculty. GEORGE TRUMBULL LADD. New York, Charles Scribner's Sons, 1897. Pp. xv +609.

The stately succession of Professor Ladd's treatises in philosophical science, consisting of 'The Elements of Physiological Psychology,' 'Psychology, Descriptive and Explanatory,' 'The Philosophy of Mind,' is now carried forward by 'The Philosophy of Knowledge,' upon which at least one further installment, A Philosophy of Being, is, we are told, to follow. The present volume contains an elaborate treatment of the chief problems of the theory of knowledge. Not at first sight nor in its arrangement, but after some slight scrutiny, the interdependent structure and fine convergence of the argument appear. It is independent, if not original; and it is presented in a style which, if diffuse, elusive and sometimes pedantic, is of a remarkable continuity, an almost consistent academic elegance and at times an outspoken vigor.

Dr. Ladd's philosophy of knowledge centres, one may say, in the thought of the self-conscious self. In the immediately revealed nature and the express deliverance of the self we have the key to the problems of perception, of judgment, of memory, of reasoning, of the nature of the cause, of the nature of the object, of the nature of the universe. The ontological doctrines are in the present work, of course, only adumbrated.

The theory of the self, which had previously been set forth in 'The Philosophy of Mind,' is of marked interest. There had been those who held to a 'thinking substance,' a substratum of mind, or an indefinable 'subject.' Transcendentalists (most of them) and cruder spiritualists agreed in maintaining that there is a single agent or principle (neither party would accept the terms of the other) which knows in all knowledge, feels in all feeling, and wills in all volition, but which is not itself of the content of consciousness nor appears in an act of objective cognition amongst the beings known. Consciousness 'inheres in it,' or 'implies it,' or 'involves it as a condition;' it is the eye which, well as it may be aware that its own existence is necessary

to seeing, is not amongst the objects of its own vision.   On the other
hand was the proposed psychological analysis of the self into elements
of the conscious content, the doctrine that it is no undecomposable
entity or ultimate 'principle,' but in one sense the total group of presentations, in another a distinguished part of that group.   The former
of these doctrines Dr. Ladd rejects with energy as adding to consciousness an unmeaning encumbrance, the latter he apparently passes
by as withholding from consciousness its most essential feature.   It is
a striking circumstance that his own theory takes elements in some
sense from both.   The self is, indeed, a fact known by and in consciousness, it is *the* fact so known, being the fact and entity of consciousness itself.   It is not a thinking substance 'beneath,' and hence
outside of consciousness, nor is it a complex group of the particular
facts of consciousness.   Rather is it a thinking substance within consciousness, known for what it is, a single and active being which exists
only in being conscious.   The view is not (or not merely) that ontological principles oblige us to assume a substance or unit-being for
mind, but that the mind directly announces itself such a unit-being.
We have here, in modern form and the explicitness that a sense of past
controversy gives, a view notably like that of Descartes.   The soul is
one substance, but its whole nature is *cogitatio.*   And, Dr. Ladd
further asserts, 'states of consciousness,' psychoses, are not existences,
but phases or acts of an existence.   Lastly, the continuity or personal
identity of a self in time consists in nothing else than its ability to
refer to its own past by the act of recognitive memory and to build up
in its successive states an orderly life.

   The self-knowledge of the self in a single moment is the perfect
type of complete knowledge; and the part the self plays in knowledge
of whatever kind is all-important.   Knowledge professes by its very
nature to be an affirmation of existence transcending itself.   The assertion that we only know phenomena is absurdly false to the facts of
cognition.   The object in order to be object is inevitably recognized
as 'not me,' as 'out of me,' as 'not my state of consciousness nor any
man's state of consciousness,' as 'extra-mental,' as 'transcendent;'
iteration could hardly go further as to the 'realistic' import of cognitive states.   But this is to say that the object is explicitly recognized
as not *self*, that it is set over against a recognized self; that self-consciousness is thus an indispensable condition of objective consciousness.   And there are also in every cognitive state ingredients of will
and feeling which involve further references to self.   The object is
felt as an alien *other* contrasted with *me*, and it opposes me as '*that-*

which-will-not always as *I will.'* More than this, when we come to ask what manner of existence the 'transcendent' thing is, we can, in the last resort, draw our predicates from but one source; from the only being we immediately know, from ourselves. The continuous identity of an object is somehow conceived in terms of the identity of the subject. The 'causality' or action of an object is conceived in terms of our own conscious action. Our ordinary explanations have their origin and their justification in " *the primal and universal experience of man with the self, as consciously acting and having its activity resisted, while at the same time observing the simultaneous and succeeding changes which go on in the appearance of things.*" And " *if the cognized facts are deeds done by a self, with a consciously recognized end in view, then it is possible to explain to its very centre the 'reason' for the facts.*" Again: " *The grounds on which all acts of reasoning repose, so far as they can possibly be explored by an analysis of knowledge itself, are laid bare when we behold the nature of the self rewarding itself in the pursuit of some conscious good.* This is the final answer to the question: 'Why ?'"

When at last we set ourselves to realize the nature of the entire universe, our means of conception bear the same stamp. Our postulates imply (1) some sort of unitary Being for this really existent, (2) that this Being is Will, (3) that the differentiation of the activity of this Will, and the connection of the differentiated 'momenta'—the separate beings of the world—is teleological and rational. That is, it must be thought of 'after the analogy of the life of a self.' And in the concluding words of the book, knowledge is described as "the establishment of a relation between the Revealer, the Absolute Self, and the Self to whom the revelation comes."

In sketching thus in scantiest outline some noteworthy aspects of Dr. Ladd's work one is obliged to neglect many important discussions; such as his argument as to 'The Teleology of Knowledge,' his trenchant treatment of the 'antinomies,' his comments on the conception of invariable law, and his special form of the argument for a cosmic mind.

The species of 'Ideal-Realism' before us has a height and breadth of build and a harmony of form that places it amongst the more imposing styles of speculative architecture. This world of wills is interesting. Meanwhile its conception and proof contain, of course, save in slight details, nothing novel. There is, by the bye, a curious passage in the preface in which the author says of his volume: "It asks and should receive the treatment due to a pioneer work." And again, remarking that his task would have been easier if he had had " more predecessors among modern writers on philosophy in English :" " So far as I am aware there are none from whom any help is to be derived." One does not know to just what species or degree of indulgence a pioneer-work in the nineteenth century upon some of the hoariest problems of philosophy lays claim; but one is, indeed, moved to make allowance for an author who has been unable to find stimulus or suggestion in the epistemological writing (for almost random example) of J. S. Mill, Mr. Bradley (a juxtaposition that only the former would have tolerated), Mr. Hodgson, Mr. Balfour (in his ' Philosophic Doubt,' for instance), or from any of twenty years' contributions to the periodical ' Mind.' The passage is mystifying, and one has a guilty sense of its being perhaps a needless touch of critical acerbity to refer to its existence. But whatever its exact meaning may be, the tendency is significant. The prime need of the day in our somewhat distracted science is to make discussion effective by bringing the opposing forces really to bear. As it is, two hostile theories will keep up their ceremonial duel for generations by simply firing into the air, which is thus filled with smoke and lurid flashes while their own vitals remain unharmed. A little marksmanship and economy of powder, and something may come out of the day; loud reports and beclouded fulgurations, pistol- or artillery-practice on whatever scale, are in themselves a dubious end. We shall do ill to forget that scientific labor will advance by growing genuinely social; that it demands a keen sense of what is already done and what needed. The spirit of lucid controversy is a fine effluence of civilization, and its effort to grasp extant ideas with delicate justice, and with precision of strength to break apart or rivet them closer, is almost the worthiest discipline of the intelligence. We can hardly look for a signal exhibition of it from one who stands in the thick-trodden market-place with the unshaken conviction that he is a pioneer.

And, in fact, on certain long-controverted topics, Dr. Ladd shows no such fine sense of his own or his adversaries' position as would enable him to carry us an inch nearer to ' a consensus of the competent.' This is markedly true of his theory of the realistic import of cognitive consciousness. The phenomenist might simply deny the alleged trans-subjective intention, the implication of the ' transcendent' in knowledge—as the present writer at all events does deny it— might declare that there is no such psychological fact; and Dr. Ladd could have nothing for it but asseverations. But not by the ' assertory method' on either side is inquiry furthered. Rather by something more analytic. And upon analysis it turns out that no such 'extramental reference' is psychologically possible. In order that our consciousness should affirm that something does not belong to it, it must have a generic conception of itself, an accurate universal idea of what 'belonging to consciousness' means. Now it is obvious that those familiar authorities, the child and the rustic, not to come nearer home, have no such idea. Such an accurate idea—and a testimony of consciousness based on inaccurate ideas of the situation would hardly be cited as evidence—is a complex product of philosophic analysis. Epistemological realists (notably Mr. Spencer and Professor A. Seth) have sometimes spoken as if idealists supposed that what we first know in perception is that we have a sensation, a mental phenomenon; a view which they very easily refute by showing that 'sensation' or 'mental phenomenon' is a later conception than object. But if they add (what they mean) 'extra-mental object,' if they declare that what we are first conscious of is that here is an object external to consciousness, they have confuted themselves in advance. To judge 'Extra-mental!' is to have a conception of the mental, which they have just pronounced at this stage impossible. The inference is that the first stage is to have a sense of the presence of an object—*to have an object*—without classifying it either as mental or as extra-mental. It is to the subsequent reflection of the metaphysician that grounds appear for terming it mental.

To this Dr. Ladd might, perchance, reply that no complex conception is needed but only the *perception* or immediate consciousness of self. To judge a thing in cognition as 'not-self' is to contrast it not with an abstractly conceived but a directly felt self. The answer is (even granting our author's theory of the *ego* and our knowledge of it) that such a concrete perception of self is not sufficient to yield the clear deliverance of consciousness on which he relies. It is not enough to deny that the object is the self; of course it is not the self. The question is whether it is not a content-fragment of the self's consciousness. And it is not enough to deny that it is *this* content-fragment or *that* content-fragment; of course there are content-fragments which it is not. The question is whether it is a content-fragment at all. To deny that is to employ the generic conception.

But, perhaps, Dr. Ladd means simply to reaffirm the old doctrine that a certain psychosis, namely, a cognition, concretely distinguishes its object from itself, pronouncing the former external to itself. In that case, forbearing remark on the logical atrocity here perpetrated, one might rest content with the old appeal to introspection. Perception is not thus double; we do not have in view an object *plus* a professed percept; we have in view only an object; and the whole psychological phenomenon is what we subsequently class as a percept. It may, however, further be said that distinction is a mental process involving two mental terms and that to say that one mental term is not another is true, but does not assert the existence of anything extra-mental. Is it suggested that the discrimination is between one term and the thing expressed by the other? The suggestion assumes all over again and without analysis the possibility of that ' expression of the transcendent,' that ' trans-subjective reference,' which is the very matter of dispute.

Lastly, if our author should maintain that the ' trans-subjective reference' is precisely an unanalyzable and ultimate fact, a mysterious ' meaning of the mind' or ' cognitive property of thoughts' which may be felt but not understood, one may reply in Mr. Meredith's words : " Many people are mystics until they have written out a fair copy of their meaning."

For not only does psychology find no terms in which such a ' reference' could be consummated, but logic exposes it as a self-contradiction. One existence, a thought (or if our author will, a thinking self) is to designate another existence, an extra-mental object. How is it to do so? It may resemble such an object (if the object be of a psychic nature the idealist need not deny that it may exist) or contain something resembling it. But no, it must also contain indications of the numerical identity of the object as different from its own. Now this is in the end unmeaning. One existence may resemble in quality another and thus to a person informed (as consistently with phenomenism one in some cases may be) that the former is to serve as a sign or representative of the latter, convey its character. But it cannot (so to speak) resemble another in its numerical identity and thus by its own being convey the existence of something else. One is familiar, of course, with the common mode of speech as to the manner of this conveyance; about a cognition containing the object ideally without containing its reality. It must be remembered, however, that ideas and cognitions are realities too and what we are discussing is the relation between two realities. An idea may actually operate so as to guide our conduct towards something not itself. But it cannot, without sharp self-contradiction, be said to contain what is non-identical with any or all of its parts. Until something is done to relieve this difficulty the theory of a trans-subjective reference stands discredited.

In the other great problem of epistemology, the ground of inductive generalization, and in further points of theory that cannot here be touched on, Dr. Ladd tries to improve the situation rather by firmer exposition than by deeper analysis. I cannot think that one who had fully mastered Hume's arguments as to cause and effect could imagine their force to be dissipated by interpreting the relation through ' the self's experience of its own action and suffering.' This is a door of escape that Hume expressly guarded. That form of sequence which we know as our own mental activity reveals virtue going out of the cause into the effect as little as any other sequence in experience; and it reveals the cause as sufficient condition of the effect no whit more than any other. To conceive material bodies acting as we feel ourselves to act—to conceive their action as a series of conscious states external to our own—is not to conceive them as extended masses at all. As such a philosophy is talking about something else than the plain man's matter, it cannot hope to have epitomized the plain man's notion of material cause. Cause cannot have meant to the multitude of men what such a philosophy means by it.

As already said, the root of Dr. Ladd's theory of knowledge lies in his theory of the nature of mind; and of that there is small room to speak here. If the unit-self is a fact of consciousness and exists only in consciousness and comprises the whole being of consciousness; then it simply *is* consciousness, called a unit-being: and whether justly so called depends upon the meaning of unit. Consciousness, as Dr. Ladd amply testifies, has multiplicity; it has unity, or rather (for that term, through varied usage, has lost the edge of its meaning) it has conjunction of elements into a group or whole, in that there is an ultimate relation of jointness between (for instance) my taste and my hearing at this moment, which does not subsist between my taste and your hearing; and in that there is a relation of continuous change (not ultimate, but analyzable in a complex formula) between the total present consciousness called mine, and any total past consciousness called mine. When, however, Dr. Ladd incidentally drops that a so-called ' state of consciousness '—the total consciousness of a moment —is not an existence, but the mere state or the mere act of an existence, he is led away by the scholastic terms he has used in rendering the deliverance of consciousness about itself into an ontological inference that flatly gives the lie to that deliverance. Consciousness in its totality at this moment—what is called in the old loose terms ' my present state of consciousness '—is identical with the unit-self at this moment in what ought in consistency to be Dr. Ladd's sense of the word.

In this fragmentary comment, which can pretend to no kind of complete justice to a work so comprehensive and mature, there has been much mere assertion. So far as this has failed to suggest the analyses which could not in full be here performed, it has been of course quite futile.

D. S. MILLER.

BRYN MAWR COLLEGE.

PSYCHICAL RESEARCH AND PATHOLOGY.

Involuntary Whispering Considered in Relation to Thought-Transference. HENRY SIDGWICK. Proceedings of S. P. R., XII., 298–318. December, 1896.

Messrs. Lehmann and Hansen, it will be remembered (PSYCH. REV. Vol. III., p. 98), sought to prove that a certain series of experiments in thought-transference, by Professor and Mrs. Sidgwick, were explicable because the agent's inward articulation of the numbers guessed was probably heard hyperæsthetically by the hynotized percipients. ˜Repeating the experiments so that the percipient could actually hear the agent's suppressed whispering, they found that not only the successes, but also the mistakes resembled those in the Sidgwick series, and from such like effects they think that we ought to infer like causes.

Their paper, the carefulness of which is a refreshing exception to most criticism of the Psychical Research Work, is reviewed by Professor Sidgwick, who concludes that their experiments do not show positive evidence for whispering as the source of the English results. Much of his reply is too minute for reproduction. The most telling point he makes is an empirical one. Happening to have the record of an old series of pure chance-guesses at numbers, made with the agent and percipient in separate closed rooms, he compares this with the guesses of the Danish series. Of course, the number of successes differ widely in the two series, but the errors run even more closely parallel than they do when the Danish whispering series and the English 'thought-transference' series are compared. As such an amount of similarity in error with the whispered series is obviously fortuitous in this case, so it may be fortuitous in the thought-tranference case. Professor Sidgwick would partly explain the degree of similarity found (which is but slight[1]) by an unconscious preference for

[1] The Danish authors made only 500 experiments, obviously too small a number for safe conclusions. The better to frame critical opinion, I

certain numbers in the guesses of both sets of percipients. If, for example, both tended frequently to guess ' five,' five as a frequent error would occur in both series, and make them in so far forth agree.[1]

Sidgwick, although admitting that whispering may possibly have been a cause of successful guessing when agent and percipient were in the same room, thus denies that Professor Lehmann has proved the point. And he absolutely denies Lehmann's explanation where the agent and successful percipient were separated by closed doors. Passing to a general discussion of the subject, especially so far as drawings were the things guessed, he gives a *resumé*, in brief, of the whole body of evidence which many readers will find a convenient summary to refer to.

I Fenomeni Telepatice e le Allucinazione Veridiche; Osservazione Critiche Sul Neomisticismo Psicologico. ENRICO MORSELLI. Firenze, Landi, 1897. Pp. 58.

A courteously written plea against accepting the recently published evidence for thought-transference and veridical hallucination. The

have myself collected a series of upwards of 1,000 guesses at bi-digital numbers whispered with closed lips by the agent. Following Lehmann's method, and comparing the four most frequent erroneous guesses at each digit of the numbers whispered with the four most frequent errors made in divining the same digits in the English thought-transference series, I find (taking the digits from 1 to 9) that 20 of the erroneous digits are common to the two series. But I find that if one compares the four *least* frequent erroneous guesses in my whispered series with the *most* frequent corresponding ones in the thought-transference series, one gets 15, no great difference. Taking the one most frequent error of substitution for each digit in my series, I find but 2 agreements with the thought-transference series, and 2 with the Sidgwick series of pure guesses. Plotting the frequency of the various errors in the several series as curves shows so great a discrepancy between my whispered series and the Danish one that it becomes obvious that the series are too short to serve as proper terms of comparison with the thought-transference series. Moreover, the curves of my series and those of the thought-transference series show at special points variations from each other so great, when compared with the absolute figures which they represent, that the same conclusion is again obvious. Both the agreements and the disagreements are thus probably accidental. I, myself, agree then entirely with Professor Sidgwick that Professor Lehmann has failed to prove his particular hypothesis of whispering as the cause of the ' thought-transference' results; and I am pleased to notice that Mr. Parish, in the work noticed below (Hallucinations and Illusions, p. 320, note), also considers Professor Sidgwick ' perfectly justified in his contention '

[1] In my own series, the tendency to run on favorite numbers in guessing was a well marked phenomenon, to eliminate the effects of which many thousands of guesses would be required.

familiar methodological generalities about what should constitute satisfactory scientific evidence for such phenomena are laid down at excessive length, but the author gets in some short-range work in criticizing the evidential defects of several narratives published as good
ones by the French, Italian and English psychical researchers. A curious prejudice runs through his pages that no evidence for supernormal
cognition can be drawn from cases of persons of neuropathic consti-
tutions, or from those in whom there have been multiple experiences
of the sort. He even thinks that he discredits veridical apparitions by
saying that the majority of them seem to have occurred in ' English
misses' at the change of life. Can he be so sure in advance that
neuropathic constitution, or even the ' menopause,' might not be predisposing conditions for telepathic susceptibility, if such a thing
should, in point of fact, exist? And, as for persons with multiple experiences, they would seem *a priori* to be just those from whom evidence might be best obtained. In point of fact they are so—one subject
of ' psychic temperament' being worth many with single experiences.
Professor Morselli, at the close of his pamphlet, gives a list of conditions
which be seems to regard as alternatives to telepathy—no case should
be counted as telepathic if it be possible to conceive it " under one or
another of the following psycho-physical explanations; simple suggestion, auto-suggestion, individual and collective credulity, psycho-
physical automatism, hypnoid or sub-conscious conditions, sensorial
illusion, psychical illusion, *e. g.*, from accidental coincidence, pro-
voked hallucination, especially with *point de repère*, unconscious perception, emotion or movement, involuntary expression of one's own
thought, doubling of personality, dream or hypnagogic hallucinations, illusions of memory, after-images or retarded sensations, sensations induced by imperceptible or unappreciated physical agents (heat,
electricity, magnetism, light), conditions of ecstacy (monoideism),
hysteria, epilepsy and epileptoid, cataleptic, or somnambulic states, with
loss or obscuration of consciousness, lucid forms of insanity, especially
with hallucinatory fixed ideas, psychic mimicry and imitative of psychosis, or collective hallucination, intense emotional conditions with
their effects, transient states of cerebral intoxication, whether endog-
enous or exogenous * * * ." Once more, one is tempted to ask
why must all these things be *alternatives* to supernormal cognition?
Why, if it exist at all, may it not co-exist with some of them? Why,
indeed, may not some of them be its most predisposing conditions?
Again, in point of fact, if there be supernormal cognition, it looks
as if this were the case with it.

It is a pleasure to turn from the generalities and abstractions of the learned Genoese professor to the criticism at closer quarters of the next author on our list.

Zur Kritik des telepathischen Beweismaterials. EDMUND PARISH. Leipzig, Barth, 1897. 8°. Pp. 48.
Hallucinations and Illusions, a Study of the Fallacies of Perception. EDMUND PARISH. London, Walter Scott; New York, Charles Scribner's Sons. 1897. 12°. Pp. 390.

The English version of Mr. Parish's book, already reviewed in its German shape in Vol. II., p. 65 of this REVIEW, is greatly improved and brought up to date. The author incorporates in it much of the criticism contained in the lecture ' *Zur Kritik*,' etc. He was collector for Germany of the Census of Hallucinations reviewed there and in the present lecture he criticizes the Sidgwick report. Although he gives the authors credit in the handsomest terms for the quality of their work, he nevertheless thinks that their conclusion—that apparitions on the day of death are far too frequent to be ascribed to chance—will not hold good. His chief reasons are as follows: First, they have believed the reported amount of coincidence between the apparition and the event to be greater than facts warrant. He gives cases to show how a figure, not recognized when seen, may be described, when news of a death is later received, as the figure of the person dead. This error, which he calls *Erinnerungs-adaptation*, he believes to be very frequent in the narratives. Secondly, he doubts whether most of the hallucinations which figure as veridical are *waking* hallucinations at all, believing them to be more probably dreams or hypnagogic visions. But if dreams are to slip in and get counted, the numerical statistical argument, he says, is entirely upset; for dreams are such frequent occurrences that coincidences between them and distant events must be frequent in proportion. And that the so-called waking hallucinations *were* mostly dreams, he proves in detail by analyzing the 26 cases which the English report prints as 'best accredited.' Most of them actually occurred at night, when the percipient was in bed or sitting up watching, or else in some other situation where a nap might naturally have occurred unawares.

This latter seems to me by far the strongest objection yet made to the Sidgwick report. In my own review of the Sidgwick report (*supra*, Vol. II., p. 74, note), I admitted this to be its weakest point.

But another objection of Herr Parish's, and the one which he himself considers his weightiest, seems to me to have very little weight indeed. He shows, by three examples, through what sub-conscious links of association, granting the hallucinatory tendency to be there, the ensuing hallucination may have its subject-matter deter-mined, and then says: Not till *the possibility of all such associative links is excluded*, are we entitled to invoke an hypothetic agency like 'telepathic impact' as the cause of the hallucinatory content. But one does not see how this should effect the statistical argument, unless associative links are in themselves more likely than unassigned organic or other causes to produce visions *coincidental with deaths.* If the mental associations of the percipient belong to a cycle of events disconnected with the cycle concerned in the distant person's death, it remains as improbable as ever that the several outcomes of the two cycles coincident in content should also coincide so often in *date.* That they actually do so shows, according to Mr. Parish, a methodical flaw in the Sidgwick report. Its authors accept as an em-pirical fact (with a slight correction for oblivion) the measure of fre-quency given by the Census for visions of recognized persons, and then proceed to cipher out the improbability that any one such vision will occur by accident on the day when its object dies. But they ought rather, says their German critic, to have ciphered out, from the number of *such coincidences* as an empirical fact *what the real frequency*, as distinguished from the recollected and reported fre-quency, of the visions must actually have been. This would give (as I apply his reasoning) the figure of 35 hallucinations at least, of the species immediately discussed, to each adult in the community, and 60 times that number, or over 2,000 miscellaneous hallucinations of all kinds to each head of population,[1] most of which we must sup-pose to be forgotten immediately, if the reasoning is to be seriously applied to facts. Mr. Parish, of course, would not so apply it, for the result is absurd and incredible. He only makes a logical nut of it for the other side to crack, disbelieving himself that the returns of the Census have any definite numerical value at all. In this contemp-tuons estimate I cannot possibly agree.   W. J.

[1] The computation is this: By the English figures 17,000 persons yielded 32 death-visions, each of which had only 1 pure chance in 19,000 of occurring when it did. To produce the 32 happy chances there must, therefore, have been 19,000 × 32 such visions in the whole 17,000 persons, or 19,000 × 32 ÷ 17,000 = 35.7 such visions in each one of the 17,000. But, since the 32 death-visions were extracted from 1,942 hallucinations of all kinds experienced by the 17,000 answers of the Census question, each answer must have had a number of hallucinations of all kinds as much greater than 35 as 1,942 is greater than 32, which would give him approximately 2,000 hallucinations, not one of which in 9 cases out of 10 he would have remembered, for roughly 9-tenths of those questioned in the Census replied 'No.'

Lo Studio Dell' Attenzione Conativa, Ricerche Sperimentali. SANCTE DE SANCTIS. Atti della Società Romana di Antropologia· Vol. IV., Fascicolo II. Pp. 19.

Experiments on the changes in the extent of the field of vision when the attention was distracted, first, by auditory appeals, or painful stimuli to the skin; second, by the task of counting the number of details in a circular diagram presented at the centre of the field. Two normal subjects (one more cultivated and intelligent than the other), one melancholic, and one ' hallucinated ' (paranoiac?) subject were tested by the perimeter. The results showed contraction of the field in all cases. The contraction was only moderate under the first kind of distraction. Under the second kind it was considerable; the paranoiac suffering in both cases the greater loss.

W. J.

Collezionismo e Impulsi Collezionistici. SANCTE DE SANCTIS. Bulletino Della Società Lancisiana Degli Ospedali di Roma, Anno XVII., fasc. I. Roma, Tipografia Innocenzo Artero, 1897.

A careful discussion of the definition of ' Collectomania ' or ' morbid collectionism,' on the basis of the case of a woman of 63, in poor health, with depression of spirits, who took to collecting and secreting pieces of bread, hair, bones, and refuse of all sorts. Wherever she saw any such object lying she was compelled to pick it up and add it to the collection. She complained of the symptoms as a sort of insanity, and said they were relieved when she drank wine; and this induced the doctors, suspecting alcoholism, to proscribe wine altogether, when the symptoms disappeared. When pressed for her motives, she at last reluctantly said that she thought the neighbors might use the objects in question for casting spells upon her.

De Sanctis finds the absence of consciousness of morbidness, and of reason for the acts, not essential to the definition of morbid collecting mania. The coercive impulse, he thinks, is primary, explanation secondary; and the sense of foolishness which may in any case exist on reflection between active fits, may be more or less actively or constantly present, according to the freshness of the case, or the intelligence of the subject.

W. J.

Sulle Cosidette Allucinazioni Antagonistiche. SANCTE DE SANC-TIS e MARIA MONTESSORI. Roma, Società Editrice Dante Al·ghieri, 1897. Pp. 17.

This article contains a detailed description of a number of clinical cases in the University of Rome which presented the phenomena of

antagonistic hallucination.   The various symptoms observed seemed
to admit of a classification somewhat as follows: 1. As to whether
the opposed hallucinations appeared as simultaneous or successive.
2. As to the manner in which the hallucination is received by the
sense organ, as in hearing whether the one hallucination is heard in
one ear and the opposed in the other, or whether the two are heard
promiscuously in both ears.   3. As to whether the hallucinations are
homonymous or heteronymous; that is, whether perceived in one and
the same sphere of sensation or in different; for instance, the two hallucinations may both be auditory, or one auditory and the other visual.
4. As to whether the antagonism observed manifests a logical contradiction and is therefore absolute, or whether the antagonism is one which
is rather personal and relative.   5. As to whether the hallucinations
are of a physical or psychical nature.   6. As to whether the hallucinations are episodical or accidental on the one hand, or on the other en-
during and systematic.

The explanation of the antagonistic hallucinations as given by the
authors of the pamphlet is that of a tendency to association by contrast which tendency in pathological cases is abnormally exaggerated,
giving rise to the opposed hallucinations as observed.

                                        JOHN GRIER HIBBEN.
PRINCETON UNIVERSITY.

SOCIAL PSYCHOLOGY.

The Principles of Sociology. FRANKLIN H. GIDDINGS.   New
York, The Macmillan Company.   1896.   Pp. xvi+476.   3d Edition.   1897.

The Theory of Socialization.   Same author and publishers.   1897.
Pp. xiv+47.

The Genesis of Social Interests.   J. MARK BALDWIN.   The Monist,
April, 1897.

The psychologist can scarcely read Professor Giddings' ' Sociology'
and its accompanying syllabus which puts into connected form the
theoretical principles and psychological presuppositions of the larger
work, without feeling convinced that the day of psychology has only
begun to dawn.   Unless all signs fail, the study of sociology is to take
its place not merely in the graduate schools of universities, but in the
under-graduate work of the colleges, side by side with economics and
politics.   Professor Giddings book, by its more rigorous effort to define
the province of the science, and to determine the fundamental unit of

explanation, will be the most potent instrument which has yet appeared in making possible such a recognition in educational curricula of the investigations which reflect the actual interests of our day. But if sociology, as in these works, is defined as a psychological science, or even as a branch of psychology, it is evident that this must mean a highly increased interest in psychology and a new demand upon the psychologist. Just as the eighteenth century's interest in the individual's moral life called out the psychology of its time, just as the nineteenth century's interest in natural science has created the experimental psychology of to-day, so the growing social interest promises to evoke a social psychology, which in my judgment has a broader field than any of its predecessors.

The delimination of sociology from psychology is to be effected, according to the author, "by restricting psychology to a study of the phenomena of the individual mind and by assigning to sociology the investigation of the more special and complex phenomena of minds in association with one another." " Psychology is the science of the association of ideas. Sociology is the science of the association of minds" (Princ. Soc., pp. 241). The impossibility of such a delimitation has been pointed out in previous notices of ' Social Psychology' in this REVIEW. Just as there are no individual ' ideas' which can be studied, in isolation, so there is no individual mind which can be studied and comprehended apart from its relations to others; and just as psychology has learned that no ' association' of such ideas could make up a mind, so sociology must learn that no association of individual minds—if they were really individuals which could be dealt with as such—can make a society. A true analysis of the social condition will not give an ' individual' as its unit for synthesis.

In the syllabus the formulation is somewhat different. The ' four great processes which make up the practical activities of life' are there stated to be: (1) ' Getting used to the world by attempting to obtain the utmost knowledge and feeling from external things,' which is the process of ' appreciation.' (2) ' Adapting the external world to ourselves,' ' utilization.' (3) ' Adapting ourselves to the external world,' ' characterization.' (4) ' Adapting ourselves to one another,' ' socialization.' These four processes are studied respectively, by psychology, economics, ethics and sociology. It is somewhat startling to be told that ethics deals rather with our relations to the external world than with our relations to each other, and the author himself states that psychology deals with more than the process of appreciation, so that it is to be feared that the fascinating symmetry of this latter scheme will not avail to make it practically workable. Moreover, to the psychologist the definition of his own subject as the 'science of the association of ideas' has an anachronistic sound, which prepares him to be suspicious of the presuppositions involved in a 'science of the association of minds.'

What these presuppositions are appears in the author's fundamental principle of 'consciousness of kind.' This is attained as follows: Socialization requires some degree of similarity, of which the important modes are three: (1) Kinship. (2) Mental and moral similarity. (3) Potential likeness or capacity for assimilation. "Consciousness of kind is a state of consciousness in which any being, whether low or high in the scale of life, recognizes another conscious being as of like kind with itself" (Pr. Soc., p. 17). This is analyzed in the syllabus into a combination of (a) perception of resemblance, (b) sympathy and liking, and (c) a desire for recognition. It is declared to be the simplest or elementary social state of mind, and the chief socializing force. It modifies appetites and desire, 'impression' (the mental power of one over another) and imitation so that the individual motives become socializing forces.

The first query which suggests itself is as to whether we are not liable to assume an altogether too highly developed consciousness if we make a consciousness of kind co-extensive with society. It is, of course, true that a bee or dog or horse reacts in a peculiar way toward what we call his kind, but this is far from implying that there is any trace of such a process in the animal consciousness as a recognition of likeness. It is well known that smell is the organ mainly depended on by many of the sociable animals, and it seems far more likely that there is no comparison of the odor from the other, with that from the animal's own body, but merely a direct reaction upon a grateful stimulus. Nor does the attachment of kinship seem to me to be the result of any such comparative process. So far as it is found in higher animals, or even in simpler human conditions, it seems to be in the case of parent for offspring, a direct instinct, selected in the struggle for existence; in the case of offspring for parent, it doesn't exist, i. e., any source of nourishment and entertainment is equally liked by the little animal or human infant, unless other circumstances, familiarity, etc., enter; in the case of brothers and sisters, it doesn't exist as the result of a perception of kinship or resemblance— any group of children brought up together from infancy develop as much affection as the average family of the same blood. In a word, the attachment is either a direct, not an indirect instinct in which there is no comparison prior to attachment, or it is the result of processes much more intricate than the perception of resemblance, which appear clearly in the case of clan feeling. The theory, as applied in such simpler cases, implies that there is a consciousness of self as a definite, distinct individual and that others are compared and found to agree or disagree. This is an assumption which the psychologist will be slow to admit.

Is the difficulty met by the point of view of the syllabus, which regards ' consciousness of kind ' not as a simple recognition that another is of like kind with the self, but as a complex state, involving the three elements named above, with the chief emphasis upon sympathy which is, indeed, often used as epitomizing the phrase? This will depend on what is understood by sympathy (Syllabus, 126). If it is conceived merely as ' imitation of emotions,' then, as Spinoza saw, it may mean emulation or conflict as well as compassion or sociability. If it is individualistic in its elements the combination will not be social. Sympathy, as a social force, must mean not a state in which A and B merely *have* like feelings, not merely a state in which B's feeling is caused by associations evoked by perceiving A's actions when under said feeling, but a state in which A and his feelings have really become a part of B's own interests, *i. e.*, of B's self, so that B is no longer a particular, exclusive self, who is B and B only, but is rather a self that includes A within it, in fact, a truly social self. Professor Giddings speaks of the case of two persons mentally giving and taking and thereby becoming alike. This is to stop just this side of insight into the essential factor in the social. The point is that they not merely become alike, but that the content of each personality is made to include something of the other; the self, while still individual, is not particular, but social.

This is, in fact, the fundamental inadequacy in Professor Gidding's psychology of the social self, that he treats it as the older psychology treated ideas, as ready-made, irreducible units, which could be associated, but not analyzed. If he had read and taken to heart James' chapter on the self, it could hardly have failed to suggest a different treatment, but Mr. Spencer seems to be the author's chief and almost sole authority in psychology.

It seems ungracious, however, to find fault with a sociologist for his psychology when one reflects how little psychologists have done in this field of the analysis of the social self since Adam Smith sketched the origin and growth of the moral sentiments. In fact, in view especially of recent French investigations, it might fairly be said that sociology is at present doing more for psychology than psychology is doing for sociology. A work like this of Professor Giddings, which brings together such a mass of material, and makes so strenuous an effort toward its explanation on psychological principles, comes to the psychologist as a distinct challenge to a more adequate analysis of the social consciousness.

Professor Baldwin's article is a successful attempt to meet the challenge, not necessarily of this special work, but of current social and political theories. The concept of person is shown to be a complex content, in which the 'myself' is always merely one pole of a shifting field of other selves, and so is always defined in terms of others, just as others are defined in terms of it. In the case of a child in a family, the other pole is sometimes the parent, in which case the 'me' of the child is imitative, feeling itself to be the inferior pole; or, again, the other pole is the younger brother or sister when the 'me' becomes aggressive and exploits its superior power. The point is that it is absurd to call the child altruistic in the one case and selfish in the other, since its attitude is in both cases alike, the result of the other pole. The other pole, the *socius* or *alter*, is then fundamentally essential to the content of the developing consciousness of self, for the child not only thinks of the other, the *alter*, as his *socius*, but he thinks of himself as the other's *socius*. ' In short, *the real self is the social self, the socius.*' A child's 'self' will then normally include as part of its content, the family or group, his 'interests' reflect the interest of the group, and this identity of personal and family interests ' is responsible for the rise of the family, considered from an evolution point of view.'

J. H. Tufts.

University of Chicago.

VISION.

I. *Weitere Beiträge zum Sehenlernen blindgeborenen und später mit Erfolg operierten Menschen, sowie zu dem gelegentlich vorkommenden Verlernen des Sehens bei jüngeren kindern, nebst psychologischen Bemerkungen bie totalen kongenitalen Amaurose.* W. Ubthoff. Zeitschr. f. psych. u. physiol. d. Sinn. XIV., 3, 197–241.

II. *Demonstration des Scheinerschen Versuches nebst Betrachtungen über das Zustandekommen von Raumvorstellungen.* Heine. Zeitschr. f. psych. u. physiol. d. Sinn. XIV., 4, 274–281.

Professor Uhthoff reports upon the development of visual ideas in three subjects. The first is an intelligent boy operated upon for congenital double cataract at the age of five. His mother declared that he had always been totally blind, but some tests seemed to indicate that he received vague sight impressions from large or moving objects, and that he could probably distinguish between large surfaces of red and green. The second (previously reported) is a feeble boy, operated upon at the age of seven for total, double congenital blindness, examined for some time then and again after a lapse of two and a half years. The third is a girl who became totally blind when four months old and received sight by operation at the age of three and a half years. The genetic theory of sight is upheld. The rate of development in vision differed surprisingly with the difference in the general intelligence of the subjects. The experience of the first subject in learning to recognize his own image in a mirror is specially valuable as a description of the struggle and fluctuation in the development of the consciousness of self. Colors were taught with difficulty. Color surfaces were at first only ' objects.' Indirect vision was much slower to develop than direct vision. In counting by sight the subjects moved their heads along the series instead of turning the eyes. The perception of form, size and distance was at first impossible and was learned through association with touch, as the author thinks.

The last section of the article is a report of interviews with a congenitally blind (microphthalmic) woman aged 32, with good power of introspection. She has no conception of light or darkness, but has marked preferences for colors. These are due entirely to associations, *e. g.*, she dislikes red because it is gaudy, something unbecoming to an unfortunate, and perhaps more so because as a child she was told that the flames of a certain fatal fire in the vicinity were intensely red. Her æsthetic conceptions are based rather upon intellectual and emotional grounds than upon sensory images. In remembering adults she constructs images on a large scale after the fashion of a child she has handled. She can form no conception of a picture. She commits to memory better when listening than when reading from the blind alphabet. She perceives the approach of large objects mainly by differences in ' air pressure.' She has medium power of estimating the distance of objects by sound and tactual space by movement. Tests with the æsthesiometer reveal no finer skin sensitiveness than the normal. This suggestive report upon observations reveals the need and possibility, and perhaps some method of experimental investigation on the subject.

Heine explains an excellent method of demonstrating Scheiner's experiment on a large scale. It is done by imitating the mechanism of the eye by arranging screens and refracting media so that all the conditions of the image are plainly set forth. By this means he demonstrates the condition of the emmetropic eye and reproduces the effects of myopia and hypermetropia. Using the same apparatus with two slits covered by differently colored glasses, he explains the physical and physiological conditions of the single image in binocular vision. '

C. E. SEASHORE.

UNIVERSITY OF IOWA.

PEDAGOGICAL.

Der Stundenplan. Ein Kapitel aus der Pàdagogischen Psychologie und Physiologie. H. SCHILLER. Heft. I., Abh. d. Paed. etc. Berlin, Reuther u. Reichard, 1897. Pp. 65.

Although no psycho-physiological topic has received so much attention of recent years as that of fatigue, yet there are a number of reasons why the results of the experiments usually employed in these investigations are of a doubtful pedagogical value: (1) The tests are of an *unusual* nature, such as memorizing meaningless syllables, etc. (2) They are to the last degree monotonous, and, therefore, awaken no interest in the persons experimented upon. (3) They are protracted over unusually long periods of time, with no intermission or change. In a word, the conditions of the experiments do not correspond to the actual conditions of the school-room. Professor Ebbinghaus, of Breslau, has attempted to avoid this difficulty by testing the faculty with which children solve simple mathematical problems during the first ten minutes of each recitation, and he has tried similar experiments for the special purpose of testing the pupil's memory during different hours of the day. Dr. Griesbach, of Mühlhaus, has suggested that there exists a close connection between fatigue and the sensitiveness of the skin as tested by one's ability to distinguish two slightly removed points of a compass. This method of determining the amount of fatigue has proved to be the most satisfactory of all. The question of fatigue lies at the basis of an intelligent school programme.

The only complete restorative from fatigue is sleep. According to Axel Key, children between six and eleven, may, without hesitation, be allowed from ten to twelve hours daily, and even more; while youths of seventeen or eighteen should be allowed not less than nine or ten hours. These figures should be borne in mind in fixing the hour for opening the school. The children should not be deprived of their sleep, nor, on the other hand, should the hour be fixed so late that they lose their freshness before school begins. No hour is suitable for all localities and under all circumstances, since the habits of the people vary. One can only say that in general residents of the large cities, except those of the manufacturing quarters, keep later hours than those of smaller towns and the country. With due allowance for local usages, Professor Schiller thinks the three lower classes should not assemble before nine o'clock, and he thinks there can be no doubt that seven o'clock, the usual hour in Germany during the summer semester, is too early.

More difficult is the question of a suitable closing hour and the distribution of pauses for. recreation. The usual morning session in Germany lasts five hours, with a short recess after each hour. The object of the recess is complete recovery, if possible, from the fatigue of the preceding exercise, so that the amounts accomplished during the various periods may be nearly equal. In spite of numerous experiments, it is still impossible to determine exactly the length of the recesses necessary to this purpose. In the gymnasium at Giessen there is a ten minutes' recess after each hour except the second, when there is fifteen minutes, and each successive hour is shortened by about five minutes, the figures varying somewhat for the upper and lower classes. This system gives far better results than the old practice of allowing only one recess of fifteen or twenty minutes in the middle of the forenoon.

Dr. Wagner, of Darmstadt, has employed the method of determining fatigue suggested by Dr. Giesbach, with the following results: Fatigue increases with the greatest rapidity during the first hour, after which it increases but slowly. Mathematics, Latin and written exercises are specially fatiguing. Exercise in the gymnasium brings no recuperation, but often, and in proportion to its intensity, increases the fatigue. In accordance with these results, Professor Schiller proposes that the first hour be devoted to the most difficult subject, either Latin, mathematics or those subjects which require written exercises, preferably the last. These are difficult because they are more or less abstract and awaken little interest in the mind of the average child. They should be followed by subjects of more general interest, such as History, Geography, Religion or Drawing. The second hour is followed by a somewhat longer recess, after which the child is prepared for another difficult subject, preferably mathematics

and the foreign languages. The last hour should be devoted to the
natural sciences, writing, singing, gymnastic drill, etc. When only
two hours a week are devoted to a subject, it gives much better results if the exercises come on consecutive days, or even on consecutive
hours.

GUERNSEY JONES.

UNIVERSITY OF NEBRASKA.

ÆSTHETICS.

1. *Gedanken zu einer Æsthetik auf entwickelungsgeschichtlicher
   Grundlage.* KONRAD LANGE. Zeitschrift für Psychologie und
   Physiologie der Sinnesorgane, XIV., 3. May, 1897.
2. *Kritische Studien zur Æsthetik der Gegenwart.* HUGO SPIT-
   ZER. Leipzig and Wien. 1897.

I. With Groos' book, 'Die Spiele der Thiere,' Lange conceives a
new epoch of æsthetic study begun, because finally it is to be based
securely upon the evolutionary hypothesis. The play instinct has been
shown to have an important place in Natural Selection, and by that
means the æsthetic consciousness has been brought directly into relation with the development of the species.

But, that the important relation of the play instinct to the æsthetic
consciousness be properly understood, it is necessary that the distinction of play phenomena from other activities be carefully drawn;
and, secondly, that the psychological nature of the play consciousness be clearly defined. Otherwise the theory of the importance of
play in development may rest upon a too inclusive concept of play
and our connection of the play consciousness with æsthetic upon insufficient psychological data.

As to the first, Lange criticizes the tendency of Groos to include too
much under the concept of play. For instance, in the consideration
of the plays of illusion, which is the kernel of the problem, the line
between 'play' and 'earnest' is not clearly enough drawn,[1] although
the importance of its distinction is recognized. Accordingly the
plays (so called by Groos) which are a direct and purposeful bringing
into activity of the parental and love instinct and all that leads to the
gratification of the same, are, according to Lange, really not plays.
Neither the acts of winning the other sex, nor the building acts that
prepare for the reception of offspring can be classed as play. Nor
can we call the torture of one animal by another, nor the fight for life

[1] Cf. Prof. Baldwin's criticism of Groos in *Science*, Feb. 26, 1897.

and death, illustrated in one case, by the play of a cat with the mouse, or, in the other, by the fight of two steers for a mate, play phenomena, as does Groos. All these phenomena can only be classed as play so long as they are of the nature of an imitation of the real, when the sense of simulation and illusion is present. As soon as illusion vanishes, earnest reality takes its place.

The temptation to confuse play and earnest has arisen out of the desire of bringing the concept of play under the rubric of the 'useful,' thus making it amenable to the operation of Natural Selection, entirely unnecessarily, as Lange thinks, if the real notion of illusion be kept in mind. For it is just in the fact that through conscious illusion instincts *are played with*, without leading to the practical results of the exercise of the instincts themselves, that the great value of play in the individual and the species may be seen. By means of play the instincts are brought into activity without going to the lengths of reality. Such instincts as are important for the promotion of the species are thus kept constantly in exercise, while, if used in reality, the exercise would be infrequent, owing to the weakness of the young and the dangers and natural opposition of the environment. " Die Thiere spielen nicht, weil sie jung sind, aber sie haben eine Jugend, weil sie spielen müssen "—in the words of Groos.

In this way Lange sees the doctrine of *bewusste Selbsttäuschung* brought under the concept of Natural Selection, and finds in it (agreeing with Gross?) ground for a modification of our idea of the struggle for existence. Through this illusion, play becomes the means of raising the simple reflex instinct to the first steps of intelligence, in that play is the first sense of new modifications of the instincts.

And now the problem of æsthetics. Can the same argument that gives to play such weight in the development of the animal, be equally cogent in giving the æsthetic consciousness a ruling place in the development of the human species. On the basis of the similarity of the play instincts with the æsthetic consciousness, which must be here assumed, though fully treated elsewhere by both authors, the conclusion of Lange, that æsthetic feelings play a large rôle in the development of the race, seems justified. As there are certain instincts whose exercise is necessary to the maintenance of an animal species, and for which the proper exercise can be obtained only through simulation in play, so there are social instincts, courage, patriotism, ambition, etc., necessary for the maintenance of society, whose strength and exercise is constantly kept up by outside simulations and representations of the same. Man needs art just as animals and children need play, to preserve alive the feelings which tend to the maintenance of the social organism.

II. Spitzer's collection of short critical essays upon books that have recently appeared in the æsthetic literature of Germany serves equally well the purposes of introduction to, or criticism upon the authors with whom they deal. The first, ' *Vom characteristisch Schönen?* and the fourth ' *Die Entwickelung von Schiller's Æsthetik,*' are of interest for the historical problems of æsthetics. The second essay deals with a recent book of A. Biese, ' *Die Philosophie des Metaphorischen,*' written in the spirit of Feuerbach's ' *Theogonie,*' and attempting to give an account of the metaphor in art, religion and philosophy. The criticism points out a failure common to most psychological attempts of this nature, and one which Feuerbach himself did not escape, a failure of definition, in which the boundaries of the metaphorical are drawn too widely and include much which, through the abstraction and criticism of centuries, has taken on an intellectual and technical cast. The criticism, in the third essay, of the æsthetical portion of Dessoir's ' *Geschichte der neueren deutschen Psychologie,*' deals with that radicalism of historical interpretation which many of its readers feel to be characteristic of the entire work. The last essay has for its subject a work of immediate interest in K. Lange's ' *Die bewusste Selbsttaüschung als Kern des aesthetischen Genusses.*' Spitzer considers the theory in no wise equal to the Hutcheson-Zimmermann doctrine of the characteristic as an explanatory æsthetical principle, and finds it subject to numerous psychological doubts.

The test case of the illusion theory is, however, its application to the non-imitative arts, architecture, lyric and music. Here, of course, there can be no illusion in the sense of comparison of image with the real object, and to fill up the break the idea of ' *Schein-Gefühle'* is introduced. Lange points out, especially for architecture, that there are certain static and dynamic feelings of pressure, strain, etc., which we put into the art object, but which in reality are not there. This idea of an illusion existing between the feelings and the object, Spitzer, as well as others, finds untenable. All feelings, then, are elements of reality, and the expression, ' *Schein-Gefühle,*' is a *contradictio in adjecto.* The objection is justified to this extent: that it is a fault of expression to say that feelings are an appearance, and therefore, can be the source of illusion. All feeling is immediately given as real. The illusion arises when from these feelings there develop *vague ideas* of forces which we read into the art object, but which in reality are not there. The apparent difficulty is solved when we consider that the feelings are part of the whole reality of the art object, the illusion is between this reality and the vague ideas we apply to it, between the ideas of external forces and our feelings.

The second difficulty which Spitzer finds in the idea of oscillation between semblance and reality, is the same which presents itself to Groos in 'Die Spiele der Thiere,' *i. e.*, that in many artistic intuitions the subject is entirely sunk in contemplation and no question of appearance and reality arises. From this fact Spitzer draws the conclusion that the illusion theory is itself faulty, while Groos simply directs the attention from the oscillating nature of the process. The truth seems to be that the degree of illusion, as well as the question whether it is continuous or an oscillation between appearance and reality, depends very much upon the nature of the arts under consideration—that is upon the relative freedom of the imagination and upon the number and character of the moments which tend to disturb the illusion. Music, with very few disturbing moments and a maximum of freedom, allows of long sinking of oneself in the illusion. On the other hand Painting, in which the critical faculty finds many moments to disturb, shows more of the process of passing to and fro between reality and illusion.

In conclusion it should be said that Spitzer finds in the illusion theory, as Lange also suggests, only one of several principles of explanation of æsthetic phenomena, and calls attention to the necessity of more accurate psychological research—especially in the spheres of natural beauty and the minor arts, to which the champions of the theory have not found it necessary to turn their attention.

WILBUR M. URBAN.

PRINCETON.

LOGICAL.

Über die Scheidung von grammatischem, logischem und psychologischem Subject resp. Prädicat. A. MARTY. Archiv für systematische Philosophe, 1897. 174–190 and 294–333.

The writer's purpose is to refute the generally received doctrine that there may be a fundamental discrepancy between the logical (or psychological) and grammatical elements of a judgment. By logical subject or predicate he means the elements of the thought itself, and by grammatical he means the expression of these in words. Two kinds of discrepancy, indeed, he admits at once: first, where the thought is not completely expressed, but where an element is indi-

cated by a gesture or left to be understood by the hearer; and, second, where there is in the proposition a *seeming* (scheinbares) subject or predicate, without any element in the thought corresponding
to it.   Under the latter class he includes existentials (put in the form
but not having the value of categoricals), and categoroids (negatives
like ' green is not red ' which have the value of negative existentials,
there is no red that is green).

The writer denies, however, that there are cases where the logical
and grammatical elements are all present, but do not correspond to
each other, the logical subject (or predicate) being expressed by a
word which fulfills in the sentence quite a different function.   In defense of this position he introduces a searching criticism of several
writers, chief of whom is Benno Erdmann.   Erdmann holds that the
logical subject and predicate have no reference to their syntactical expression, but are determined solely by the objective relation of the
ideas in the judgment, a relation he calls one of logical immanence.
This relation is that of substance and accident, or an extension of it
by analogy; it provides a rule for the distinction of logical subject
and predicate in the content of the judgment.   (' To the brave belongs the world;' logical subject, ' the brave.')   If this is true, of
course any judgment may have many forms of expression.

The writer, however, denies that Erdmann's rule is fundamental.
As the most fundamental distinction he makes the subject the better
known, the predicate, what is new.   But other distinctions, originally
or usually coinciding with this one, become established through custom, and often come finally to conflict with it.   Among such distinctions are those of whole and part, substance and accident, first and last,
and many more; and which one shall in any case prevail depends on
custom and circumstances.   The writer's point is that it is just these
varying conditions which are brought out in the grammatical structure
of the sentence, and that the syntactical functions of this structure do
correspond to the logical functions of the thought.

To the objection that the sentence actually chosen often fails to express the exact judgment of the speaker, or even awakens a judgment
different from itself in the mind of the hearer, the writer replies that
the judgment expressed is responsible neither for other judgments in the
mind of the speaker which he should but does not express, nor for
judgments which the hearer afterwards reaches by association or inference.   The sentence on the whole is an adequate expression of the
thought below it, and grammatical relations stand for logical ones.

While this conclusion is well made out, the writer introduces

Brentano's distinctive view of judgment without any bearing on his main theme, and it would seem without adequate support. He has an interesting section on the origin of the grammatical consciousness, a subject which has been passed over too lightly even by the newer logicians. The paper, on the whole, marks a forward step.

J. FORSYTH CRAWFORD.
CHICAGO.

BIOLOGICAL.

La Structure du Protoplasma et les Théories sur L'hérédité et les Grands Problèmes de la Biologie Générale. Y. DELAGE. Paris: Reinwald, 1895. Pp. xiv +878.

Thirty years ago this title would have suggested that the book was a hopeless hodge-podge. Now that we see more deeply into the relation of things we recognize that the author could hardly have dealt with less and treated it completely. For, on the one hand, it is clear that heredity depends upon the specific constitution of the protoplasm, has to do with the causes of ontogenesis, and, combined with variation, makes possible evolution. On the other hand, the structure of protoplasm has no meaning apart from heredity, individual development, and phylogeny, so that the modern text-book on the cell must consider its significance in development and inheritance. The cell, the individual, and the race are merely units of different order in the world of living substance.

In the book before us Professor Delage has preserved a very satisfactory balance between the facts concerning the cell, the individual, and the race (300 pages) and the theories which have been offered to group and explain them (500 pages). He has put himself into every page, so that the book is nowhere a mere compilation; but, more than that, his extensive review has enabled him to render valuable judgment upon theories and to offer a highly satisfactory explanation of the cause of phylogenetic differentiation.

A glance at the table of contents will best reveal the broad scope of the book. The cell: Its constitution; its physiology; its reproduction, including the relation of nucleus to cytoplasm. The individual: Regeneration; grafts; generation by fission and budding, sexual and asexual reproduction; ontogenesis; metamorphosis and the alternation of generations; sex and the secondary sexual characters; latent characters; teratogenesis; correlation; death, immortality and the germ-plasma. The race: Transmissibility of characters innate and acquired

I. ANIMISTS
1. Soul.
2. Nisus formativus.
3. Vital force.

Plato, Saint Augustin, Van Helmont.
Blumenbach, Needham.
Barthez, Bordeu, Lordat, old school of Montpelier.

II. EVOLUTIONISTS
1. Spermatists.
2. Ovists.

Erasistratus, Diogenes of Laërte.
Galen, Leuwenhoek, Andry, Dalempatius.
Harvey, Graaf, Swammerdam, Malpighi, Haller, C. Bonnet, Spallanzani, De Blainville

III. MICROMERISTS

1. Universal, immortal particles. { Organic molecules. Microzymas. }

Buffon. Béchamp.

A. All of the same nature; all exercise, with equal share, their influence in the deter. of all the parts. Active.

1. By their polarity.—*Physiological units: Polarigenesis.*
2. By their form and their molecular forces.—Gemmæ and Gemmaria.
   - *Annular atoms* ....
   - *Conservation of the Plastidules* ....
   - *Pangenesis of the Plastidules* ....
3. By their vibratory movements.
   - *Undulatory propagation of the organogenic excitation to the limits [of the germ.]*
   - *Kinetogenesis and Catagenesis.—Bathmism and Catagenesis.*
   - *Morphogenic action of habitual functioning* ....

Spencer. Haacke. Dolbear. Evisberg, Haeckel } PERIGENISTS
His. Cope.—Mantia. Orr.—Mantia. } PERIGENISTS AND ITS VARIANTS.

Hanstein. Berthold.

Chevreul, Geddes, Thompson, Gautier, Danilewsky.

Fol. Maggi. Altmann. Wiesner.

B. of different species and charged with diverse functions.

Non-Representative:
a. simple chemical molecules. Active:
   - a. By their physico-chemical properties ....
   - b. By their pure chemical properties ....
b. Aggregates of a higher order.
   - a. Electric apparatus.
   - b. Chemical apparatus.
   - c. Initial particles endowed with vital properties.

Representative:
a. Of Ancestral plasms.
   - *Gemmules* ....
   - *Germs, representative of organs* ....
   - *Filaments with appetence and molecules with propensities*
   - *Stirpes* ....
   - *Odoriferous gemmules* ....
   - *Female germs and male germs* ....
   - *Cytozoaires* ....
   - *Stereometric structure of protoplasm* ....

Weismann (in theory).

PANGENESIS.
Ch. Darwin, PANGENESIS, s. s.
Maupertuis
Erasmus Darwin. } PRECURSORS.
Galton, Jaeger, Brooks, Gawle, Platt-Ball, Hallez, } VARIANTS.

b. Of cells of the body.

c. Of elementary characters and properties of the organism. { *Micellis, Idioplasma* / *Nuclear idioplasm* / *Intracellular pangenesis* / *Idioblasts* } ....

Naegeli. Kölliker. De Vries. O. Hertwig.

d. At the same time of the parts of the body and the elementary characters.

Weismann (2d theory).

2. Particles which are destroyed after death.

IV. ORGANICISTS.

Descartes, von Baer, His, Bichat, Cl. Bernard, Roux (Driesch, O. Hertwig.)

and of transitory states in the parent; concerning telegony and xeny; heredity in asexual and sexual generation, in close unions, in hybridization, and in grafting; variation, its sorts and its causes; the facts concerning the origin of species. In the second part, a hundred pages are devoted to theories relating to the foregoing phenomena. In the third part, the general biological theories are explained and criticized. These have been classified by Delage as in the accompanying table.

The author's own 'theory of actual causes' is now brought forward. The course of ontogenesis depends not only upon the constitution of the germinative plasma, but also upon tropisms and tactisms, functional excitation and the various external conditions of development. The origin of adaptation in species is not due to the summation by selection of favorable individual variations for, as G. Pfeffer has pointed out, the killing off in selection generally occurs during immaturity so it can hardly determine the adaptation of the adult. Delage believes that sports only exceptionally form species, at least they cannot account for the adaptation so characteristic of species. The adaptive specific qualities which any theory of the origin of species must recognize and explain are produced as follows: Species are variations become fixed. Adaptive variations are brought about by self adaptation (or accommodation) of the individual under the influence of functional excitation. When the conditions under which development occurs change, the individual adapts itself to the new excitations it encounters. But how does this adaptation in the individual bring about an adaptation in the species? There is, strictly, no species adaptation but only individual adaptation. Let us assume a change from any cause in the germ plasm. This change is adaptive or non-adaptive. If adaptive so much the better for the individuals; if unadaptive the individuals will not all die off, but "the individual efforts will be more energetic and more sustained, the somatic adaptation will be perfected by a more energetic functional excitation, a certain number of individuals will, without doubt, succumb among the less plastic or the more delicate, and thus the auto-regulation of the mean number of individuals of the species will be effected, but the species will continue none the less to live. It is only when the variation is radically pernicious that it will succumb. Usually the variation which (through correlation) affects necessarily, although to very diverse degrees, all parts and all functions, will be injurious for some, advantageous for others, indifferent for most, and an (individual) compensation will be established which will make the injurious pass under the protection of the advantageous."

A word concerning the place of Delage's theory. It is confessedly a descendant of Roux's. It is also closely related to George Pfeffer's theory,[1] differing chiefly in that it lays less stress upon the selection of plasticity in the organism.

Enough has been said to indicate that Delage's book is valuable, not merely as an indispensible encyclopœdia of facts and bibliography, but as a substantial contribution to theoretical biology.

C. B. DAVENPORT.

HARVARD UNIVERSITY.

The Average Contribution of Each Several Ancestor to the Total Heritage of the Offspring. FRANCIS GALTON. Proceedings of the Royal Society. Vol. 61, 401-413. (Read June 3, 1897.)

In his work on 'Natural Inheritance' (1889) Dr. Galton stated tentatively, that the influence of each parent on its offspring would be one-fourth, of each grandparent one-sixteenth, etc. This result was deduced from a discussion of his data on human stature, and he announced at the time that for the purpose of testing it he had in progress experiments on moths. In the paper before us Dr. Galton states that the experiments on moths failed, but that he has found excellent

---

[1] Pfeffer's theory has such points of similarity to that recently proposed by Baldwin, that it may be worth while to translate here Pfeffer's own summary of his theory, which is to be found in the 'Verhandlungen des Naturwissenschaftlichen Vereins in Hamburg,' 1893, pages 44 to 87.

"The struggle for existence rejects all pernicious individuals and lets survive some individuals belonging to the average of their race; changes in the external conditions of life change the species, since they change the average of the surviving individuals, impress thus upon the mass of the species a different facies, and permit them to appear, alongside of their relatives, as a different race, variety or species. The remaining part of the Darwinian theory, namely, the gradual production of new races and species, seems, consequently, unnecessary; the pristine characteristic Darwinian principle of the survival of fitness suffices for the comprehension of the form-changes with which we are concerned."

I have translated by 'survival of fitness,' the phrase, 'Uberleben des Passenden.' It is possible that 'fittingness' or capacity for accommodation would have given the idea better. This conclusion would seem to be justified by the following words of Pfeffer on page 71 : "Von allen jungen Tieren gehen unbedingt diejenigen zu Grunde, deren körperliche Verhältnisse *nicht* zu einer praktischen Handhabung der erforderlichen Eigenschaften für das jeweilige Leben führen; der Kampf ums Dasein merzt die mangelnde Geschicklichkeit und damit die mangelhafte körperliche Grundlage und deren Besitzer aus. Also führt die Veränderung der äusseren Lebensbedingungen zu einer immer weiter fortschreitenden Ausbildung körperlicher Verhältnisse, welche eine geschicktere Bewegung des betreffenden Tieres unter den neuen Bedingungen ermöglichen."

material in the records of a pedigree stock of Basset hounds. These hounds have two, and only two, recognized varieties of color—transitional cases being very rare—which may be called T (tricolor) and N (non-tricolor). With 817 cases at his disposal, Dr. Galton could trace the ancestry of the hounds and determine the influence of the parents, of the grandparents, and (in 187 cases) of the great-grandparents, on the offspring. The results confirm his principle with surprising accuracy. Thus, for example, in the simplest case, where one parent and two grandparents were T, one-half the offspring (subject to a slight correction for an excess of T in the great-grandparents) should be T, and of 60 cases 36 were T. When all the parents and grandparents were T, of the 119 cases 108 should be T, and 106 were in fact T. The grand totals give in the cases where the grandparents were known 387 T, as compared with a theoretical 391, and in those cases where the great-grandparents were known, 181 T, as compared with a theoretical 180. In this special case the hypothesis is fully confirmed, and it may fairly be called a law of heredity. The law is stated: " The two parents contribute between them, on the average, one-half or (0.5) of the total heritage of the offspring; the four grandparents, one-quarter, or $(0.5)^2$; the eight great-grandparents one-eight, or $(0.5)^3$, and so on."

It should, however, be noted that in Dr. Galton's material we have a trait that must be present or absent, and is normally present in about one-half of all the cases. I am not sure that he is justified in extending the law generally to human, animal and plant heredity. If the Basset hounds were crossed with mongrels one-half of the offspring would not be T or N. Dr. Galton has himself argued that variations obtained by artificial selection tend to revert to the racial mean, even when maintained for a long series of generations, and individuals having such variations cannot influence the offspring as much as is required by this law. I should suppose that the greater the departure of the parent from the mean of the race, or the more rare the variation, the less, as a rule, would be its potency in heredity. It seems to me that the stability of variation must, in each case, be determined by observation or experiment, Dr. Galton's law being too simple to fit the complexity of nature.

J. McKeen Cattell.

Columbia University.

VOLITION AND GENERAL.

Voluntary Action. G. F. Stout. Mind, July, 1896. Pp. 354–366.

Types of Will. Alexander F. Shand. Mind, July, 1897. Pp. 289–325.

In an article in *Mind*, October, 1895, Mr. Shand maintained that will, though analyzable up to a certain point, had, in the last resort, a distinctive quality, incapable of further analysis or description. Mr. Stout here offers as an alternative the theory that will is desire qualified and defined by a certain sort of judgment, the judgment, namely, " that, so far as in us lies, we shall bring about the attainment of the desired end." The characteristic difference between indecision and decision is that in the former we do not yet know what we are going to do, while in the latter we do. Mr. Stout explains by means of this conception the distinction between voluntary and involuntary action which Mr. Shand made so much of. Thus, *e. g.*, the sneeze of a soldier marching to surprise a fortress is involuntary, because, although foreseen, it is not foreseen as something he desires to bring about; the indulgence of a morbid appetite may express the volition of the moment, but may be regarded as involuntary with reference to the man's general volition, etc.

In what is virtually a reply, but has the form of an independent essay, Mr. Shand endeavors to show that Stout's theory like all other general theories of the will, fails to take proper account of different types of volition. Urging the necessity of studying these before resting in any one general formula, he distinguishes and analyzes a number of volitional types and arrives, substantially, at the following conclusions: (I) *Simple volition.* We first seem to have will, as distinguished from inferior conations, when, along with the idea of a desired action, we have the judgment that, as far as in us lies, we are going to realize it. This agrees with Mr. Stout's formula. Simple volition is the state described without doubt or conflict of motives; complex volition is the state described preceded by such doubt or conflict. (II) *Will as negation.* The above definition includes only positive judgments. But there are volitions with the negative judgment, I am not going to do this. And this is a distinct type; for though logically the negative judgment implies the positive, this is not true psychologically. The psychological accompaniment of negative volition is not necessarily a contrary positive judgment, but a contrary positive conation. We must accordingly modify our definition and say that the distinguishing character of will is either a judgment that we are, or a judgment that we are not, going to do something, or it is a mixture of both judgments. (III) *Hypothetical and Disjunctive Will.* But beside volitions of the categorical type, there are hypothetical and disjunctive volitions; and the peculiarity of the former is that they do not affirm that we are going to do anything, while the latter affirm that we are going to do one thing or another. Thus volitional judgment may assume a variety of forms, categorical, hypothetical, disjunctive, positive and negative. But the characteristic of will is not in the form of the judgment, but in the content, namely, in the emphasis on the agency of the self (which is, however, not peculiar to will), and in the belief that, conditionally, or unconditionally, we shall try to do (or not do) something. (IV) *Fictitious Choice.* Complex volition, or choice, is so defined that the following types must be taken to represent not real, but fictitious choice. (1) A traveler already decided to take the shortest road, on learning that this is the shortest, decides to take this. Here the antecedent conflict is purely intellectual. (2) He had not previously decided on the shortest, but on learning which is the shortest, at once decides to take that. Here blind conation develops into will without any conflict of desire. (3) A youth in easy circumstances determines to choose the profession for which his inclination is strongest, but is in doubt as to which is his strongest inclination. Until the final decision, there is conflict of desires, but no conflict of motives; as in (1) the volition becomes definite, but is essentially unchanged. (4) A child is set to choose between two playthings. If we assume a blind conation, at the start, to choose ' the nicer,' then, here too, in spite of the conflict of desires and apparent motives, the final volition is only the development of the original conation. In all four types, there is no real conflict of motives, consequently no real choice. The judgment is made up and defines the conation; but volition may run counter to the judgment, choose the worse, etc. (V) *Involuntary Action.* The most interesting cases are ideo-motor actions. (1) Actions produced suddenly through fear. If we maintain Mr. Stout's definition of an involuntary action and require the simultaneous existence of a voluntary resolution, such actions will have to be regarded, not as involuntary, but only as non-voluntary. (2) Actions produced by fear, but preceded by a determination not to do them. (3) Types in which conflict of desire is present, *e. g.*, the soldier endangering his own life and the army's by coughing. This case shows plainly that the distinctive constituent of will cannot be the judgment that we are going to do something. (4) Possibly types involving choice; but an unambiguous case is hard to find.　(VI) *Will as Imperative.*　So far from it being true that volition is essentially determined by the judgment, I am going to do something, some volitions are expressed, not by a judgment at all, but by an imperative.　Such imperative volitions always have for their object the control of another's conduct, and though usually simple, they may, by sympathy, be complex and involve choice.　This type cannot be eliminated by assuming that imperatives are merely means for getting preformed volitions accomplished, for in some cases the conation issues in the imperative too suddenly.　Nor can it be resolved into any of the judgment types; it is a unique differentiation.　The judgment is either true or false, the imperative is neither true nor false.　Finally (VII) *Desire and Will* do not always have the relation ascribed to them by Mr. Stout.　Will is sometimes determined, not by desire, but by the less strong aversion.　Thus the condemned man allowed to choose the form of his execution, actually wills to do what he desires not to do, since he desires to escape death in every form.　There are in fact three types :　(1) desire is the motive;　(2) desire is effaced from the motive (*e. g.*, 'duty for duty's sake');　(3) desire is replaced by aversion.

Issue may fairly be taken with some of these contentions.　If, *e. g.*, the condemned man choose to be shot rather than hung, it seems incorrect to say that his will is contrary to his desire because he does not desire to be shot.　He does not will to be shot simply, but to be shot rather than hung.　He is averse to being hung, he is also averse to being shot; but he has, among other stronger desires, this desire also, to get through with the disagreeable necessity in the least obnoxious way possible under the circumstances, and he resolves accordingly.　In regard to 'imperative volition,' it may be doubted whether, *e. g.*, the command 'Do this' expresses more than a mere wish or desire apart from the implied consciousness, "I am determined that, as far as I can control your conduct, you shall."　Finally, as regards the interpretation of the soldier's involuntary cough or sneeze, it seems beside the mark to say that it proves that the fore-knowledge, I am about to do this, is not the essential character in will; for nobody, certainly not Mr. Stout, said that it was.

H. N. Gardiner.

Smith College.

Genesis of Number Forms.　D. E. Phillips.　Amer. Jour. of Psychol.　VIII., 4, p. 506.　July, 1897.

This study is noticeable for the fulness of its material, comprising returns from about two thousand persons.　Half of these (974) were from children of ten to sixteen years in the Worcester grammar schools, and one-sixth (332) were from students in a normal school. Most of the children were privately questioned and precautions were taken against their 'imagining forms for the occasion.' The writer of this notice, from her own experience, cordially endorses the conclusions of Mr. Phillips, from this verification, agreeing with him that "after giving the slightest explanation, a close observer will hardly fail to distinguish every one having distinct number forms. Those who have no form," the author adds, "have no idea of what you are speaking. * * * Those having a form show an entirely different attitude."

The most significant result of the paper is the conclusion of Mr. Phillips that the possession of mental forms is no sporadic aberration of a few individuals, but merely the pronounced manifestation of a very general characteristic. "There is no more reason," he says, "for isolating these mental activities from a much larger field, than there is for isolating exceptional cases of memory or imagination from these general powers of the mind." The statistics of the study do not at first sight lead to this result, for only sixteen per cent. of the subjects claimed a number form, when originally questioned. But the attention of Mr. Phillips was attracted by the experience of Dr. Story who "denied that he had a number form, but remarked that large numbers appeared far off." This led to a re-examination of 250 of the adults of the former investigation who had denied having a form, and to the discovery that 210 of these "have a feeling that numbers in some way recede from them."

This result, as Mr. Phillips suggests, not only shows that "nearly all persons possess some idea of extension of numbers, more or less indefinite," but it throws some light on the baffling subject of the psychology of numbers. The fact that the most primitive number-form seems to be a 'sensation of following in some particular direction' allies the numerical series with the tendency of motion. The number-form is thus an indication of the close connection between the motor and the spatial image, and between the arithmetical and the geometrical unit.

The universality and the thoroughly 'normal' nature of the number-form is indirectly suggested by other results of the study with which, in general, the statistics of similar investigations by the writer of this notice very definitely agree. In the first place, all those who remember the origin of these forms refer them to ordinary experiences in learning to count and to read (p. 514). Furthermore, inquiry fails to reveal a greater proportion of forms among the ' intellectually active,' or the ' imaginative,' which suggests that the form is not the adjunct of the riotous fancy merely. The permanence of forms is shown by the discovery of 14 per cent. among adults, as over against only 18 per cent. among children. Finally, the utility of forms points to their general occurrence, and 97 of the 212 who answered the questions of Mr. Phillips are sure that forms are helpful in the mental life, while only one counts them ' troublesome.'

The study of Mr. Phillips is valuable, therefore, because it tends to lure the number-form from the *terra* more or less *incognita* of the abnormal, into the familiar domain of the normal psychic life.

MARY WHITON CALKINS.

WELLESLEY COLLEGE.

Sull'Importanza delle Ricerche Relative alla Storia delle Scienze. GIOVANNI VAILATI. Torino, Roux Frassati e Co. 1897. Pp. 22.

This is a lecture introductory to a special course upon the history of mechanics. The author insists that an intimate knowledge of the historical development of a science is absolutely necessary to a thorough understanding and right appreciation of its present day methods and results. By many historical instances he shows how the men of one generation have been indebted to the labors of those of preceding generations, for methods of observation and experiment, for proved and established principles and laws, for working formulæ, and for a vast and ever increasing accumulation of classified facts, and arranged material. He illustrates this dependence upon the past by references especially to the history of mathematics naturally leading to a special disquisition upon the development of the science of mechanics, the latter being the author's objective end in view throughout this introductory lecture. He draws attention to the fact that in the European universities there is an increased number of courses offered this year in the history of the various sciences. This signifies the importance which is now attached to historical research as an aid in the present development of science. JOHN GRIER HIBBEN.

PRINCETON UNIVERSITY.

Die Assoziationsfestigkeit in ihrer Abhängigkeit von der Verteilung der Wiederholungen. ADOLF JOST. Zeitschrift für Psychologie u. Physiologie der Sinnesorgane, XIV., 6. pp. 436-472.

This paper gives an account of experiments carried on in the Göt-

tingen Psychological Institute with the view of investigating the relative value of distribution and summation of repetitions in the process
of memorizing series of nonsense syllables. The experiments were
made with series of 12 syllables constructed according to the method
employed by Müller and Schumann in their research on memory.

The first experiments were directed to the more exact investigation
of a point on which some experiments of Ebbinghaus had already
thrown light, viz., the advantage of distributing over several days the
total number of repetitions employed in learning. In one group of
experiments the series (*Cumulationsreihen*) were repeated 30 times
on one day, and learned by heart next day; in the other group the series
(*Vertheilungsreihen*) were repeated 10 times on each of 3 successive
days and then learned by heart on the fourth. The result was that
with both the subjects on whom the experiments were made the number of repetitions required for learning the series by heart was about
15% less in the second group than in the first. The next set of experiments was designed to show whether the lesser effectiveness of
the accumulated repetitions was due to fatigue or to some specific new
factor. The repetitions in this group (24 in number) were so
arranged that the fatigue incident to persistent repetition was distributed equally over the *Cumulations* and *Vertheilungsreihen*
which were read in the same hour. Here the advantage on the side
of distribution was not so great, but was still quite marked.

The next step consisted in testing the value of various forms of
distribution, three different forms being tried, viz., 2 repetitions on 12
days, 4 on 6 days and 8 on 3 days. Here the strength of association
was tested by a new method (*Treffermethode*). Six syllables from
each of the series which had been already memorized were presented
in succession to the subject, who was required to name the syllables which had followed these in the original series; the reaction time
for each reproduction was, at the same time, determined by means of
Hipp chronoscope and lip-key. It was found that the number of syllables rightly named increased progressively with the extent of the distribution, being greatest where the 24 repetitions were spread over 12
days. The reaction time was longest for the series spread over 3
days; the effect of distribution, however, seemed to be partly obscured
by the fact, which has been established in the Göttingen laboratory, that
older associations, though more correctly reproduced, have longer reaction times than those more recently formed. The attempt to measure the value of varying extent of repetitions by any known method
is declared by Jost to be impossible. In regard to the method em-

ployed by me in the research on ' The Place of Repetition in Memory,'[1] he remarks that any given number of repetitions has its effect not only in the reproduction of certain syllables, but in a certain ' *Hebung der Bereitschaft*,' of others which are not reproduced; this latter factor, however, we can ' *im einzelnen Falle garnicht beurtheilen.*' It is true that we cannot in any particular case measure this supposed *Hebung;* we cannot well do it in general, for it is something which remains below the threshold of consciousness. But this does not destroy the importance of the fact which the Münsterberg method has established, viz., that the number of syllables which are actually reproduced bears a definite relation to the number of prior repetitions.

The next experiments were devoted to proof of the proposition that if two associations are of equal strength, but of different ages, a new repetition has a greater effect on the older of the two associations. A number of series *(alte Reihen)* repeated 30 times on one day were compared next day by the *Treffermethode* with other series *(junge Reihen)* repeated four times during the hour in which the first series were being tested; the first series, it was found, gave fewer right syllables and took longer reaction times than the latter series. But it was found at the same time that with other series arranged in the same way, but tested by the number of repetitions required for learning by heart, the ' old' series required nearly 40% fewer repetitions than the ' young' series. The last question which was experimentally investigated was more practical : what is the most economical way of learning a series ? In one set of experiments the series were repeated 4 times each day, while in another set they were repeated twice, and this was continued with the series until each was learned. The result was not very decided, but, so far as it went, tended to show that the advantage lay with the wider distribution.

As may be seen from the foregoing report, the experiments furnish a valuable addition to the scientific knowledge of the laws of memory. Their value for educational science not merely in direct result, but in the promise of further development, is no less evident.

SMITH COLLEGE.   W. G. SMITH.

Beiträge zur speciellen Dispositionstheorie. STEPHAN WITASEK. Archiv für Systematische Philosophie, III., pp. 273–293.
Beiträge zur Psychologie der Komplexionen. STEPHAN WITASEK. Zeitschrift für Psychologie u. Physiologie der Sinnesorgane, XIV., 6, pp. 401–435.

---

[1]This REVIEW, III., p. 21.

In these two articles we have contributions to the development of various elements in the psychological theory of the school which has Meinong for its leading representative. In the first article Witasek discusses the classification of dispositions; in the second the chief subject is the formation of *Komplexionen höherer Ordnung*, of more complex synthetic ideas.

"The modern concept of disposition," says Witasek, "has for its content * * * the causal relation between a relatively persistent property of the active subject *(Dispositionsgrundlage)* as cause and its product *(Dispositionscorrelat)* as effect." It is not the disposition, but its basis, the property of the subject, which has reality. Modern physiology and psychology are recognizing the existence of dispositions; it is of great importance to attain to exact notions regarding the dispositions whose interplay is evident in our mental life. Psychology has long recognized that perceptions are the correlate of an *Empfindungsdisposition*, and that ideas or memory images are the correlate of a *Reproductionsdisposition*. There is also to be assumed a disposition corresponding to the new form of psychical content present in the *Komplexionen*, or complex ideas. But these complex ideas may arise in the mind either by way of direct construction—first, the constituent elements, then the new connecting element—or indirectly, in which case the relation is the primary object, the content which is related arising at the same time. Common examples of the latter fact are found in our recollection of complex related content. It can be seen in this case that, when once the relating synthetic activity has been operating, a disposition to the renewal of that activity will be formed. But analysis becomes more difficult when we consider the complex forms of combination involved in imaginative construction. It is not sufficient to adduce here as explanatory factors reproduction of unrelated content and subsequent relating activity; for, in that case, the characteristic feature would be neglected—the presence as a primary object of the form or ideal outline which becomes filled up by further activity. We must assume that in imagination or phantasy we find the operation of a new specific disposition.

Having thus given his grounds for assuming three dispositions in the domain of *Komplexionen*, viz., the dispositions implied in the relating activity itself, in the reproduction of complex ideas and in imaginative construction, Witasek proceeds to the further questions, whether the relating activity can be intensified and whether it can lose its effectiveness. The proof for an affirmative answer to the first question is taken chiefly from the sphere of music; the beginner may easily fail to understand a musical work in its connection and complete form, but with practice his power of understanding and appreciating may be greatly increased.   In many lines of mental activity our perception of relations is already so thoroughly trained, when we begin to attend to it, that an improvement can with difficulty be traced.   When a previously attained facility is lost we have to do in reality not with a loss of faculty but a loss of practice.   The operation of such factors as exhaustion and recovery cannot be easily demonstrated; their presence is, however, highly probable.

In the introduction to the second paper Witasek takes up the question of perception of change in connection with the discussion on this subject at the Psychological Congress in Munich.   In addition to indirect or ratiocinative perception of change Dr. Stern had seemed to distinguish two other forms, that in which all the factors of change are immediate contents of consciousness—direct or specific perception of change—and that which is completed in momentary perception. According to Witasek the last two forms are fundamentally similar, the essential fact in both being the presence, in addition to the changing sensational content and in inseparable union with it, of a new synthetic content which has no correlate in the series of physical stimuli, and which is in reality of the same character as the *fundierte Inhalte* for which Meinong and others contend.

The proper object of the paper is the investigation of two problems in regard to the *Komplexionen*.   The first problem is this: how are we to explain the fact that out of the unconnected manifold of sensations which we receive in experience certain elements are singled out and combined with others in quite definite complex ideas?   Take a complex musical work for example: the manifold of tones which is heard will be grouped and interpreted in various ways by different individuals.   The perceived content does not give the complete reason for the different groupings.   But if, on the other hand, we appeal to the activity of the subject for an explanation, we seem to be left in danger of subjective caprice.   Often. indeed, the forms and connections of what is perceived seem fixed apart from choice; on the other hand, in such processes as comparing, relating and imaginative construction the subject is evidently an active participant.   Where the subject apparently has no choice there are in the perceived content determining factors such as ' weight' of an idea and likeness among elements, which influence the attention and the relating activity. Where such moments in the complex of tones are weaker a certain effort is required to appreciate the music; here it is the function of a subjective synthetic activity to bring to completion the connections which are obscurely indicated. It is in this activity that Witasek finds the true ground for the more complex ideal formations. Analysis plays its part in preparing the material for the relating activity. But where, as in music, we have to resist the wrong combinations which press themselves on our attention and expend effort in realizing the true interpretation, there it is evident that a specific synthetic activity of the subject is in operation.

The second discussion is devoted to a comparison of discrimination, as it affects on the one hand the constituent elements of a complex idea and on the other the form, shape or relation in the idea itself. From a consideration of further examples in the domain of music Witasek concludes that in the comparison of two complex objects the difference between the parts may be evident, and yet the difference between the forms and total relations of the two objects may be below the threshold. In some cases we seem to be able to manipulate and determine the complex forms more readily and securely than the parts, yet if we examine more closely we shall see that in no case do we really have perceptible difference of forms where the parts cannot be discriminated; what is lacking to the parts is only attentive analysis. In cases where, while noticing the difference of the parts, we wrongly assert an identity of the forms, there we are again misled by lack of analysis and by too great attention to common elements. Language often fails to give needed help to analysis.

This brief account of Witasek's argument will show in what direction the ' new way of ideas' is tending. The main characteristic seems to be a tendency to assume a new psychical content or activity where there appears a well marked feature or grouping of content which does not include in its immediate context all the conditions of its realization. But whatever their ultimate worth may be, such developments are valuable in calling attention to that neglected chapter, the psychological analysis of the more complex processes of thought and ideal activity.

W. G. SMITH.

SMITH COLLEGE.

NEW BOOKS.

Hypnotism and Its Application to Practical Medicine. O. G. WETTERSTRAND. Translated by H. G. Peterson. With letters on Hypno-Suggestion, by the translator. New York and London, Putnams. 1897. Pp. xvii+166. $2.

The Psychology of the Emotions. TH. RIBOT. English translation in Contemp. Science Series. London, W. Scott; New York, Scribners. 1897. Pp. xix+455. $1.25.

Hallucinations and Illusions. E. PARISH. London. English translation in Contemp. Science Series. London, W. Scott; New York, Scribners. 1897. Pp. xiv+390. $1.25.

Magic, Stage Illusions and Scientific Diversions, Including Trick Photography. Compiled by A. A. HOPKINS. With Introduction by H. R. Evans, and four hundred illustrations. New York, Munn & Co. 1897. Pp. xii+556. $2.50.

The New Psychology. E. W. SCRIPTURE. Contemp. Science Series. London, W. Scott; New York, Scribners. 1897. Pp. xxiv+500. $1.25.

Ethische Principienlehre. H. HÖFFDING. Bonn, Siebert. 1897. Pp. 64. M. .60.

L'Anneé Philosophique; Septième Anneé. 1896. F. PILLON. Paris, Alcan. 1897. Pp. 316. Fr. 5.

L'Évolution des Idées Générales. TH. RIBOT. Paris, Alcan. 1897. Pp. 260. Fr. 5.

I Riflesse vascolari nelle Membra e nel Cervello dell'uomo. M. L. PATRIZI. Reggio Emilia, Calderini. 1897. Rep. from Riv. Sper. di Freniat. Pp. 85.

Zur Psychologie der logischen Grundthatsachen. H. GOMPERZ. Leipzig, Deuticke. 1897. Pp. 103. M. 2.

Introduction to Philosophy. O. KÜLPE. Trans. by W. B. PILLSBURY and E. B. TITCHENER. London, Sonnenschein; New York, Macmillans. 1897. Pp. x+245. $1.60.

The Conception of God. J. ROYCE, J. LE CONTE, G. H. HOWISON, S. E. MEGES. Publications Philosoph. Union Univ. of California. Vol. I. New York and London, Macmillans. 1897. Pp. xxxviii+354. $1.75.

Darwin and after Darwin. III. Isolation and Physiological Selection. G. J. ROMANES. Chicago, Open Court Co. 1897. Pp. vi+181. $1.

Raumæsthetik und geometrisch-optische Täuschungen. TH.
LIPPS. Schriften der gesell. f. psych. Forschung, heft 9-10 (II
Sammlung). Leipzig, Barth. 1897. Pp. viii+424. M. 12.

The Subconscious Self and its Relation to Education and Health.
L. WALDSTEIN. New York, Scribners. 1897. Pp. 171. $1.25.

Richerche psicofisiologiche sull'Attenzione. S. DE SANCTIS. Roma,
Tip, Innocenzo artero. 1897. Pp. 48.

Il Tempo di Reagione Semplice. M. L. PATRIZI. Reggio-Emilia,
Calderini. 1897. Pp. 15.

A Study of Puzzles. E. H. LINDLEY. Diss. for Doctorate, Clark
Univ. (Rep. from Amer. Journ. of Psych.), VIII, 4. 1897.

The Impersonal Judgment. S. F. MACLENNAN. Diss. for Doctorate, Chicago Univ., Chicago Univ. Press. 1897. Pp. 49.

*The Psychic Development of Young Animals. Cortical Cerebral
Localization. The Functional Development of the Cerebral
Cortex.* WESLEY MILLS. Three papers reprinted from Trans.
Roy. Soc., Canada. Vol. II., Sec. IV. 1896.

*Sixteenth Annual Report of the Bureau of Ethnology, 1894–
1895.* J. N. POWELL Director, Washington, Gov. Print. Office.
1897. Pp. cxix+326.

Sleep: its Physiology, Pathology, Hygiene and Psychology.
MARIE DE MADACÉINE. Contemp. Science Series. London,
W. Scott; New York, Scribners. 1897. Pp. vii+341. $1.25.

Social and Ethical Interpretations in Mental Development. A
Study in Social Psychology. J. MARK BALDWIN. New York
and London, Macmillans. 1897. Pp. xiv+574. $2.60.

NOTES.

A LABORATORY for experimental psychology has been opened in
the Illinois Eastern Hospital for the Insane, at Hospital, Ill., under
the direction of Dr. W. O. Krohn, who has given up his position in
the University of Illinois.

THE *Zeitschrift f. Psychologie u. Phys. der Sinnesorgane* is now
published by Barth, Leipzig. The same firm will also publish Helmholtz' *Vorlesungen über theoretische Physik*, and the series of
Abhandlungen zur Physiologie der Gesichtsempfindungen, edited
by v. Kries, of which the first number has already appeared (M. 5).

Francis Kennedy, Ph.D., Leipzig, has been appointed demonstrator in experimental psychology in Princeton University.

In the current number (Bd. III., Heft. 4) of the *Arch. f. Syst. Philosophie*, there is issued a *Bibliographie der gesamten philosophischen Literatur* for the year 1896, comprising 1831 titles.

All communications for the editors of The Psychological Review, together with books, reprints, etc., intended for review, should be sent, during the year beginning November 1, 1897, to Professor J. McK. Cattell, Garrison-on-Hudson, New York.

INDEX OF NAMES.

INDEX OF SUBJECTS.

Lightning Source UK Ltd.
Milton Keynes UK
UKHW020654211218
334381UK00011B/633/P